ASPEN CASEBOOK SERIES

Modern Consumer Law

Katherine Porter
Professor of Law
University of California, Irvine School of Law

Published by Wolters Kluwer in New York.

Wolters Kluwer Legal & Regulatory US serves customers worldwide with CCH, Aspen Publishers, and Kluwer Law International products. (www.WKLegaledu.com)

To contact Customer Service, e-mail customer.service@wolterskluwer.com, call 1-800-234-1660, fax 1-800-901-9075, or mail correspondence to:

Wolters Kluwer
Attn: Order Department
PO Box 990
Frederick, MD 21705

Printed in the United States of America.

2 3 4 5 6 7 8 9 0

ISBN 978-1-4548-2503-6

Library of Congress Cataloging-in-Publication Data

Names: Porter, Katherine (Katherine M.), author.
Title: Modern consumer law / Katherine Porter, Professor of Law, University of California, Irvine School of Law.
Description: New York : Wolters Kluwer, 2016. | Series: Aspen casebook series
Identifiers: LCCN 2016005507 | ISBN 9781454825036
Subjects: LCSH: Consumer protection — Law and legislation — United States. | LCGFT: Casebooks.
Classification: LCC KF1609 .P669 2016 | DDC 343.7307/1 — dc23
LC record available at http://lccn.loc.gov/2016005507

About Wolters Kluwer Legal & Regulatory US

Wolters Kluwer Legal & Regulatory US delivers expert content and solutions in the areas of law, corporate compliance, health compliance, reimbursement, and legal education. Its practical solutions help customers successfully navigate the demands of a changing environment to drive their daily activities, enhance decision quality and inspire confident outcomes.

Serving customers worldwide, its legal and regulatory portfolio includes products under the Aspen Publishers, CCH Incorporated, Kluwer Law International, ftwilliam.com and MediRegs names. They are regarded as exceptional and trusted resources for general legal and practice-specific knowledge, compliance and risk management, dynamic workflow solutions, and expert commentary.

To Betsy, Paul, and Luke,
who remind me that fairness is a matter of perspective.

— K.P.

Summary of Contents

Contents

Part Three
Doing the Deal: Terms and Financing   159

Preface

Consumer law is incredibly complex, despite its applicability to millions of people engaged in everyday transactions. The complexity is reflected both in the law itself and in the challenges of trying to teach and learn consumer law. Consumer law has porous boundaries and comes from multiple sources rather than a single lawmaker or an integrated statutory code. Because consumer law is diffuse, many lawyers may practice in this area but not explicitly identify as "consumer lawyers." Anyone who represents individual people in civil cases, however, will find many client problems that arise from consumer transactions, and the demand from consumers for legal help greatly overwhelms the supply of knowledgeable lawyers. From the other side, nearly any business that sells goods or services to individuals will face consumer law issues with compliance and litigation.

Consumer law is rapidly growing in importance. A 2013 poll of professors found that consumer law ranked first as the area of law deserving more attention in the legal academy, beating out hot topics such as immigration law, energy law, and alternative dispute resolution. See Brian Leiter's Law School Reports blog, Apr. 18, 2013 at http://tinyurl.com/k3d7p4a. While law schools need to ramp up offerings in consumer law, the legal system and economy are more concerned with consumer issues now than at any time since the 1970s. The Dodd-Frank Wall Street Reform and Consumer Protection Act of 2010 contained sweeping law reforms and rearranged the very structure of consumer regulation. It created a Consumer Financial Protection Bureau to administer most federal consumer laws governing credit. This change reflects the unprecedented levels of household borrowing in the last twenty years and the importance of consumer spending to the overall economy. Because consumer law governs these purchases and loans, it has grown in size and complexity in tandem with its economic importance.

This book tackles the challenges of consumer law with a three-prong approach. First, it situates consumer law within the business law curriculum. At first this may seem counterintuitive, and of course, many who represent consumers do so in roles as government lawyers, legal services lawyers, or poverty lawyers. But consumer transactions, by definition, also involve businesses. Indeed, it is this consumer-to-business nature of the transaction that gives rise to the impetus for most consumer law. When businesses purchase property, goods, or services from each other (for example, a retailer that buys inventory from a wholesaler), consumer laws do not apply. Consumer law governs, however, when that retailer goes to sell the inventory in the form of goods on a shelf to a consumer. From this perspective, consumer law can be understood as the legal system's effort to address the disparities in sophistication and power that typically exist between consumers and businesses.

This book is built around the fact that consumer law is big business — both for lawyers and for the economy in general. The book reflects this "consumer law as business law" philosophy in its content and its pedagogy. It spends time explaining the economics and business structure of many consumer transactions. It seeks to explore and explain the relevant market: How are these deals structured? Who makes money? Is the market competitive or constrained? How does information flow in the market? In its pedagogical approach, the book refrains from assuming the student shares the normative perspective of a consumer. The problems often ask students to advise businesses on the compliance issues or litigation risks created by consumer law, as well as advocate for a beleaguered consumer. This tactic recognizes that the world of consumer practice offers opportunities for lawyers to represent consumers (as government lawyers, policy advocates, and plaintiffs' attorneys) and to represent businesses (as in-house counsel, defense attorneys, and lobbyists).

Second, this book attempts to give consumer law a sharp theoretical framework by situating it at the intersection of contract and tort. Consumer law is more than a collection of laws with the word "consumer" in them. It is, as suggested above, the law's response to the failures of traditional law to achieve satisfactory outcomes in consumer-business transactions. The book repeatedly returns to the doctrines of fraud (from tort law) and unconscionability (from contract law) to see how the common law in these areas has been reshaped by statutes and regulations. Newer consumer laws typically provide more protection for consumers and impose more duties on businesses than the common law did. Consumer law is an ideal place to expand on the first-year law school curriculum, adding skills in statutory analysis, administrative law, and policymaking to the student's toolkit. The book also attempts to show the artificiality of a public law/private law divide. It highlights the way in which private transactions have public effects, and conversely how public goals find their way into laws that inhibit or limit private deals.

The third approach of the book is its commitment to a legal realist perspective on consumer law. In this regard, the book marshals empirical research on topics related to consumer law such as financial literacy, household finance, and the legal profession. It also points out where important knowledge is missing and asks how such data could be obtained. Law is neither practiced nor made in a vacuum; the book reflects the belief that well-equipped lawyers are comfortable with a broad range of social science including psychology, marketing, sociology, and economics. The legal realism approach repeatedly turns to the gap between the law as written and the law as experienced, asking questions about the value of a law that remains unused or underenforced and the ways in which lawyers and courts struggle to engage successfully with consumers who lack legal knowledge. Of course, such problems plague many other areas of law but are predominant in consumer law.

These three characteristics of this book lead to a "casebook" that is quite far from the traditional law text. In fact, the book contains relatively few cases as compared to the amount of expository text. The goal is to focus students on the statutes and regulations that are the heart of modern consumer law. It also mirrors the reality that case law often does not exist on a particular point or is of little importance to a business lawyer or consumer lawyer trying to design a litigation strategy sharply constrained by reputational risks (business) or financial limits on affording counsel (consumer). The book's cases illustrate the factual context of the transactions as much as they teach the dispositive law. The book also uses rules, legislative history, research studies, websites, videos, and even things like cartoons and newspaper stories to teach consumer law. Part of the justification for this is that consumers themselves are likely to learn about their rights from these sources, rather than from published case law. The text tries to be explanatory in tone. As stated in this preface's first sentence, consumer law is hard. This book outlines the basic law and provides opportunities for using the core legal competencies of reading and analyzing law to see how the law applies in context.

The book is designed to be taught using a strong form of the problem-method. Unlike the questions following cases in a traditional text, the problems are not to be skimmed and treated as rhetorical. The problems are to be read, analyzed, worked, and "solved" to the best of students' abilities before class. The problems take several typical forms. These include: 1) statute readers that highlight key points or ambiguities in the law itself; 2) transactional problems that pose questions of compliance, planning, and client counseling; 3) theoretical puzzlers that push on the persistent difficulties of consumer law as a legal subject; and 4) policy problems that require identifying the social, economic, and political issues at play in consumer lawmaking. The problems are fact-specific and contextual. This means that as in real life, some problems have clear answers and others are ambiguous. Some problems intentionally omit key facts because limited information is a real problem in lawyering. Other problems reflect that a half-victory or partial solution is often the only outcome, asking students to identify the barriers to a more comprehensive resolution.

This book's coverage is selective. It is organized around several major aspects of transactions: getting into a transaction, the substantive terms of the transactions, and enforcement if the transaction goes awry. It does not cover all the goods, services, or property that consumers buy or all the types of financial products used in these transactions. Instead it selects certain products as emblematic of different approaches to consumer law. The intuition is that consumers and businesses face similar information and power disparities across transactions. Once students see how consumer law grapples with these issues in a particular context, they can identify similar problems and solutions in other areas. This approach has particular merit in consumer law, where the scams and frauds of today are regulated or litigated out of existence tomorrow only to be replaced with new scams and frauds. Underneath activities ranging from advertising cold remedies to creating digital currency, the fundamental problems of consumer law remain. What is the appropriate amount of intervention in the market? How much should the law expect consumers to protect themselves? When is the burden on business so great that it creates economic hardships that outweigh the social benefits of regulations?

This book is organized into five major parts. It opens by asking some basic questions about the nature of consumer law. This part provides an opportunity to tackle the boundary problem of consumer law and to introduce students to the multiple origins of consumer law. The book gives heavy weight to federal consumer law but covers state law as applicable, doing so by focusing on a particular jurisdiction to illustrate a typical approach. Part 2 focuses on the initial contact between the consumer and business; it addresses issues related to advertising, marketing, and access to credit. Part 3 considers the terms of a consumer-business transaction in two ways. It begins with a study of substantive limits on the sale of products and the extension of credit, looking at issues like warranties, disclosure, and credit cost. Then, it offers one or more in-depth assignments on each of several major consumer products: homes, automobiles, credit cards, student loans, etc. Part 4 of the book studies the rights and remedies of consumers and businesses if the transaction does not go as planned. It considers how the law balances enforcement of the contracted-for bargain against protection of consumers. It also distinguishes between the enforcement mechanisms used in consumer law: private litigation, public action, and alternate dispute methods. The final section, Part 5, addresses consumer law policymaking by studying emerging topics for consumer law.

Consumer law is sometimes derided as the law of small problems. In my view, this characterization is inaccurate. Consumers may be "small" in their individual contexts, but their force in the economy and in society is formidable. Being a consumer is one of the key ways that people engage in the world. The laws that allow or curb how consumers and business transact with each other reflect core values about capitalism and democracy. Consumer law is a fertile ground for examining normative principles about our economy and our society. I have found studying and shaping consumer law to have many rewards and challenges. I hope this book inspires you to identify and engage as a lawyer, and as a citizen, with consumer law issues. Consumers and businesses will benefit from a new generation of people passionate about consumer law.

February 2016
Irvine, California

Katherine Porter

Acknowledgments

This section brings happy memories of bright and passionate people who share my interest in consumer law. From the students who endured not-quite-done book versions to the colleagues who patiently explained points of law or practice, I am grateful for the help. All errors are my own; the book has significantly fewer mistakes or misstatements because of the help of my students and the consumer law professors and lawyers that I know.

I owe particular debts to Cathy Lesser Mansfield and Tara Twomey. They introduced me to consumer law as a distinct area of law, and their deep knowledge continues to inspire me. Elizabeth Warren's pioneering textbooks that use the problem method to teach statutory areas of law are obviously a model for this book. She is an inspiring public servant, but for me, she will always be the best-ever professor.

Several amazing teachers of consumer law encouraged this project and contributed to my understanding through their scholarship and presentations. This group includes Tom Brown, Prentiss Cox, Melissa Jacoby, Dalie Jimenez, Lynn LoPucki, Ronald Mann, Bill Maurer, Natalie Martin, Ted Mermin, Lea Krikivas Shepard, Jeff Sovern, and Alan White. The late Jean Braucher was a special friend and mentor to me on all things consumer-oriented. I also benefited from conversations with many leading consumer law practitioners. I thank Ronald Ady, Tim Blood and his colleagues at Blood, Hurst & O'Reardon, Pete Carroll, Gary Klein, Suzanne Martindale, John Rao, and Noah Zinner. The former Executive Director of the National Consumer Law Center, Will Ogburn, equipped me with my very own set of NCLC's treatises. This book is infinitely more accurate and better sourced for that generosity.

My work on this book was interrupted by a few years of consumer law practice when I served as an expert to the California Attorney General's Office on mortgage servicing issues. In particular, I thank Charlie Carriere, Benjamin Diehl, Kamala Harris, Brian Nelson, Jennifer Song, and Michael Troncoso for their perspectives on consumer law issues, particularly pertaining to public and private enforcement. The State of California has a proud legacy of consumer protection, and I was honored to continue its work.

I have enjoyed research assistants who brought good cheer to hard projects. I thank the following: Gina Lavarda and Sandra Sears from the University of Iowa College of Law; Clare Selden from Harvard Law School, and Zachary Adams, Ryan Beall, and Amy Lieberman from the University of California, Irvine. As this project had some fits and starts (to understate the situation), I apologize deeply to any research assistants who toiled on projects that found their way into this book but whose contributions I cannot recall specifically. I am especially thankful to Amy Lieberman, who contributed substantive material on online transactions and crowdfunding, and to Carolyn Luong, who contributed to the book's content on digital gaming.

My editor, Darren Kelly, perhaps doubted if this book would come to fruition, but I will always be grateful that he never let that on to me. His loyalty and commitment to this project were invaluable in completing the book. I also thank Andrew Blevins at Froebe Group for his assistance. A special acknowledgment to Cameron Stuart, the copyeditor, who not only improved the manuscript, but took the time to send encouraging words about it.

No people were more important to this project than my administrative assistants in recent years: Faye DeLeon, Amanda Hudson, and Lynh Tran. From turning up "lost" assignments with Post-It notes proclaiming "one less thing to write," to fielding status inquiries on manuscript completion with discretion, to hiding my stash of emergency chocolate from me, they were true partners. In particular, Amanda Hudson was invaluable in organizing this project. She wrote a draft of the student loan assignment and advocated for the inclusion of the topic, and she edited and proofread the entire book. I am the luckiest law professor in the world to have a writer of her caliber to assist me. Finally, thank you to my mother who encouraged me to stay up late and to push harder, and to Julian Willis who encouraged me to go to bed and to be reasonable. Balance is a blessing.

Katherine Porter
Professor of Law
Irvine, California
February 2016

I also thank the following authors and copyright holders for permission to use their materials:

"*Consumer Protection Act,*" cartoon by BART. Copyright © 2008 Cartoon-Stock, www.cartoonstock.com.

Halpern, Jake, *Bad Paper* (2014). Copyright © 2014 by Jake Halpern. Excerpts from "The King of Crap" reprinted by permission of Farrar, Straus and Giroux, LLC.

Hasen, Rick, *Beware Buying Overseas Airline Tickets @Expedia: Not Seat Selection or Changes—And No Disclosure!* Election Law Blog (Nov. 22, 2015). Copyright © 2015 Election Law Blog. Used by permission of the author.

Hynes, Richard & Eric A. Posner, *The Law and Economics of Consumer Finance,* 4 Am. Law Econ. Rev. 197-198 (2002). Copyright © 2002 American Law and Economics Association. Republished from American Law and Economics Review with permission of Oxford University Press. Permission conveyed through Copyright Clearance Center.

Martin, Nathalie, *1,000% Interest—Good While Supplies Last: A Study of Payday Loan Practices and Solutions,* 52 Ariz. L. Rev. 563 (2010). Copyright © 2010 Nathalie Martin. Used with permission of the author.

Peterson, Christopher L., *Fannie Mae, Freddie Mac, and the Home Mortgage Foreclosure Crisis,* 10 Loyola J. of Public Interest L. 149, 156 (2009). Copyright © 2009 Christopher L. Peterson. Used with permission of the author.

Peterson, Christopher L., *Usury Law, Payday Loans, and Statutory Sleight of Hand: Salience Distortion in American Credit Pricing Limits,* 92 Minn. L. Rev.

Special Notice

The problems in this book are filled with consumers, lawyers, businesses, and others who are the product of my imagination. Any resemblance to any real person is purely coincidental and uninspired.

I have edited cases for smoother reading. Citations and footnotes have been deleted without indication. Footnotes that were not eliminated retain their original numbers.

Citations of federal statutes are to the United States Code, despite popular usage of public law section numbers for some laws. Citations to federal regulations are to the Federal Register; if more than one agency jointly has the authority to issue regulations, the citation is to the Consumer Financial Protection Bureau's regulations.

Part One.   Overview of Consumer Law

Assignment 1.   What Is Consumer Law?

Consumer law has great economic and social importance in the United States. It has a long history in the common law and today occupies thousands of pages of statutes. Literally millions of transactions each day are covered by its rules. The duties of consumer law apply to nearly every business, and all individuals enjoy the legal protections of consumer law.

Despite its wide reach, consumer law occupies a vague, gray space in the legal world. It has poorly defined boundaries, both in law school curricula and in legal practice. In some ways, the porous nature of consumer law is an attribute. Lawyers who practice in this area often get to work on a wide variety of issues, and the umbrella of advocates who can be drawn into consumer issues is large.

For the student and teacher, however, the amorphous nature of consumer law presents challenges. To be coherent, and to be teachable in a single course, consumer law cannot merely be every law that contains the word "consumer" or that deals with an individual person. U.S. Senator Elizabeth Warren, a former consumer law scholar, explains this as the purple socks problem. Many laws govern purple socks—the safety of the dye, the wages paid to the laborers, the warranty given upon sale—but nobody teaches a course called Purple Socks Law. Consumer law exists as a legal field because it is defined by a common set of actors, transactions, and issues. As a one-sentence definition, consider this: Consumer laws provide rights to individuals and duties on businesses when these parties engage in a transaction for money or value. This definition is both under- and over-inclusive, and some would take an entirely different approach in defining consumer law.

Your first task in learning consumer law is to ask yourself what you think consumer law is, and to consider its history, current developments, and similar laws in working through your own answer to that question. With new consumer laws popping up as the marketplace and social norms evolve, identifying the shared features and purposes of consumer law is an essential foundation.

A.   Origins of Consumer Law

The problems of consumer law are ancient. *See* William H. Hamilton, *The Ancient Maxim Caveat Emptor*, 40 YALE L.J. 1133, 1136 (1931). Many of its legal protections directly reflect the limits of human cognition, including our emotional capacities for optimism and trust, and our later feelings of regret and anger. For thousands of years, when consumers were treated unfairly, they sought non-legal remedies (a club to the head of the wrongdoer?). Or consumers simply moved on—usually poorer and wiser for the unsatisfactory transaction.

Modern consumer law intervenes to prevent, or failing that, to remedy, the harms of some consumer transactions. The rise of consumer law is traceable to the development of capitalism and to the growth of a robust market for goods and services. When a government or a feudal lord was responsible for providing food, shelter, and other necessities, the most pressing failures and injustices were problems related to citizenship and rights of personhood. These problems remain at the fore in developing countries. But countries with advanced market economies face an additional set of concerns related to how consumers and households get goods and services. Along with free markets came market failures. When those failures occur, consumer law intervenes to set parameters and provide remedies.

The legal system developed in tandem with economic markets. The ability to contract, the right to own property, and the rise of monetary and banking systems were all necessary legal precursors for the consumer marketplace. When people could make — and break — contracts, a system of law developed to help resolve such disputes. The common law of contracts is foundational to consumer law. At its heart, the question is whether an enforceable promise was made between a consumer and a business and whether the business should be held accountable when a consumer regrets the deal. Should consumers know that some products are too good to be true?

Carlill v. The Carbolic Smoke Ball Co.

Queen's Bench, 1892
2 Q.B. 484, aff'd, 2Q.B. 256 (Court of Appeals, 1983)

. . . The defendants, who are the proprietors and vendors of a medical preparation called "the Carbolic Smoke Ball," inserted in the *Pall Mall Gazette* of November 13, 1891, the following advertisement:

Figure 2

. . . The plaintiff, a lady, having read that advertisement, on the faith of it bought one of the defendants' carbolic smoke balls, and used it as directed three times a day, from November 20 till January 17, 1892, when she was attacked by influenza. She thereupon brought this action against the defendants to cover the £100 promised in their advertisement.

The defendants pleaded that there was no contract between the plaintiff and the defendants that the defendants should pay £100 in the event which happened; and that if there was such a contract it was void, either under eight & nine Vict. C. 109, as being a contract by way of wagering, or under 14 Geo. 3, c. 48, s. 2, as being a contract of insurance not made in accordance with the provisions of that section, or as being contrary to public policy. The action came on for trial before Hawkins, J., and a jury; but the facts not being in dispute, the learned judge reserved the case for further consideration on the points of law raised in the defence. . . .

Four questions require consideration in determining this case.

1st. Was there a contract of any kind between the parties to this action?

2nd. Was such contract, if any, wholly or partly in writing so as to require a stamp?

3rd. Was the contract a wagering contract?

4th. Was it a contract of insurance affected by statute, 14 Geo. 3, c. 48, s. 2.?

As regards the first question, I am of opinion that the offer or proposal in the advertisement, coupled with the performance by the plaintiff of the condition, created a contract on the part of the defendants to pay the £100 upon the happening of the event mentioned in the proposal. It seems to me that the contract may be thus described. In consideration that the plaintiff would use the carbolic smoke ball three times daily for two weeks according to printed directions supplied with the ball, the defendants would pay to her £100 if after having so used the ball she contracted the epidemic known as influenza.

The advertisement inserted in the *Pall Mall Gazette* in large type was undoubtedly so inserted in the hope that it would be read by all who read that journal, and the announcement that £1000 had been deposited with the Alliance Bank could only have been inserted with the object of leading those who read it to believe that the defendants were serious in their proposal, and would fulfill their promise in the event mentioned; their words, "*showing our sincerity* in the matter," state as much. It may be that, of the many readers of the advertisement, very few of the sensible ones would have entertained expectations that in the event of the smoke ball failing to act as a preventive against the disease, the defendants had any intention to fulfill their attractive and alluring promise; but it must be remembered that such advertisements do not appeal so much to the wise and thoughtful as to the credulous and weak portions of the community; and if the vendor of an article, whether it be medicine smoke or anything else, with a view to increase its sale or use, thinks fit publicly to promise to all who buy or use it that, to those who shall not find it as surely efficacious as it is represented by him to be he will pay a substantial sum of money, he must not be surprised if occasionally he is held to his promise. . . .

The third question is whether the contract I have found to exist is a contract by way of gaming or wagering within the meaning of statute eight & nine Vict. C. 109,

s. 18, which renders such contracts null and void, and, therefore, not enforceable by action. I think it is not. It is not easy to define with precision what amounts to a wagering contract, nor the narrow line of demarcation which separates a wagering from an ordinary contract; but, according to my view, a wagering contract is one by which two persons, professing to hold opposite views touching the issue of a future uncertain event, mutually agree that, dependent upon the determination of that event, one shall win from the other, and that other shall pay or hand over to him, a sum of money or other stake; neither of the contracting parties having any other interest in that contract than the sum or stake he will so win or lose, there being no other real consideration for the making of such contract by either of the parties. It is essential to a wagering contract that each party may under it either win or lose, whether he will win or lose being dependent on the issue of the event, and, therefore, remaining uncertain until that issue is known. If either of the parties may win but cannot lose, or may lose but cannot win, it is not a wagering contract. . . .

In the present case an essential element of a wagering contract is absent. The event upon which the defendants promised to pay the £100 depended upon the plaintiff's contracting the epidemic influenza after using the ball; but, on the happening of that event, the plaintiff alone could derive benefit. On the other hand, if that event did not happen, the defendants could gain nothing, for there was no promise on the plaintiff's part to pay or do anything if the ball had the desired effect. When the contract first of all came into existence (i.e., when the plaintiff had performed the consideration for the defendants' promise), in no event could the plaintiff lose anything, nor could the defendants win anything. At the trial it was not even suggested that any evidence could be offered to alter the character of the contract or the facts as deposed to by the plaintiff. I am clearly of opinion that, if those facts established a contract, as I think they did, it was not of a wagering character. . . .

In the pleadings I find a further defence that the contract was contrary to public policy; but the learned counsel for the defendants was unable to point out to me any grounds for such a contention other than those I have already discussed.

It follows from what I have said that, in my opinion, the plaintiff is entitled to recover the £100. I therefore direct a verdict to be entered for the plaintiff for £100, and judgment accordingly with costs.

Judgment for the plaintiff.

Carbolic Smoke Ball is a classic. It is frequently used in contract classes to illustrate doctrines of contract formation. Yet, it holds important lessons for consumer law too. It illustrates that consumers, if they manage to recover from illness and file a lawsuit, can hold businesses accountable for the statements in their advertisements. Note that defendants did not raise the efficacy of the smokeball as a defense, relying instead on doctrinal distinctions between a wagering or insurance contract and an ordinary contract. In today's world of technology and information, complete with services like Yelp and Google, consumers should be much better equipped to spotting scams like a cure for cold or flu.

Federal Trade Commission v. Airborne Health, Inc.

(CV08-05300 C.D.C.A.)

STIPULATED FINAL JUDGMENT AND ORDER FOR INJUNCTIVE AND OTHER EQUITABLE RELIEF

Plaintiff, the Federal Trade Commission ("Commission" or "FTC"), filed a Complaint for Injunctive and Other Equitable Relief against Defendants Airborne Health, Inc., . . . pursuant to Section 13(b) of the Federal Trade Commission Act ("FTC Act"), 15 U.S.C. §53(b), alleging deceptive acts or practices and false advertisements in violation of Sections 5(a) and 12 of the FTC Act, 15 U.S.C. §§45(a) and 52.

The Commission and Defendants . . . without Defendants admitting or denying liability for any of the conduct alleged in the Complaint, have stipulated to entry of the following agreement for permanent injunction and settlement of claims for monetary relief in settlement of the Commission's allegations against Defendants.

The Court, having been presented with this Stipulated Final Judgment and Order for Injunctive and other Equitable Relief ("Order"), finds as follows:

FINDINGS

1. This Court has jurisdiction over the subject matter of this case and jurisdiction over all parties. Venue in the Central District of California is proper.

2. The acts and practices of Defendants are in or affecting commerce, as defined in Section 4 of the FTC Act, 15 U.S.C. §44.

3. The Complaint states a claim upon which relief can be granted under Sections 5(a) and 12 of the FTC Act, 15 U.S.C. §§45(a) and 52, and the Commission has the authority to seek the relief it has requested.

. . .

10. The commission's action against Defendants is an exercise of the Commission's police or regulatory power as a governmental unit.

11. The paragraphs of this Order shall be read as the necessary requirements for compliance and not as alternatives for compliance, and no paragraph served so modify another paragraph unless expressly so stated.

12. Each party shall bear its own costs and attorneys' fees.

13. Entry of this Order is in the public interest.

14. The Plaintiff and Defendants, by and through their counsel, have agreed that entry of this Order resolves all matters in dispute between them arising from the facts and circumstances alleged in the Complaint in this action, up to the date of entry of this Order.

. . .

I. PROHIBITED REPRESENTATIONS REGARDING COVERED PRODUCTS

IT IS HEREBY ORDERED that Defendants, directly or through any corporation, partnership, subsidiary, division, trade name, or other device, and their officers, agents, servants, employees, and all persons or entities in active concert or participation with them who receive actual notice of this Order, by personal service or otherwise, in connection with the manufacturing, labeling, advertising, promotion, offering for sale, sale, or distribution of any Covered Product, in or affecting commerce, are hereby permanently restrained and enjoined from making, or assisting others in making, directly or by implication, including through the use of a product name, endorsement, depiction or illustration, any representation:

A. That such product:

1. Reduces the risk of or prevents colds, sickness, or infection;
2. Protects against or helps fight germs;
3. Reduces the severity or duration of colds; or
4. Protects against colds, sickness, or infection in crowded places such as airplanes, offices, or schools;

unless the representation is true, not misleading, and, at the time it is made, Defendants possess and rely upon competent and reliable scientific evidence that substantiates the representation.

B. About the efficacy or health-related benefits of any Covered Product, unless the representation is true, not misleading, and, at the time it is made, Defendants possess and rely upon competent and reliable scientific evidence that substantiates the representation.

Provided however, that Defendant Airborne Health may continue to deplete its existing inventory of Airborne Products plastic tube packaging. *Provided further,* that Airborne Health may continue to deplete its existing inventory of Airborne Products paper cartons and display trays specified in Attachments A1 and A2, for a period of 90 days after the entry of this Order, or until October 31, 2008, whichever is sooner. Airborne Health may not ship any existing inventory of Airborne Products packaging not specified in this Part after the date of entry of this Order.

II. PROHIBITED REPRESENTATIONS REGARDING TESTS OR STUDIES

IT IS FURTHER ORDERED that the Individual Defendants, directly or through any corporation, partnership, subsidiary, division, trade name, or other device, and their officers, agents, servants, employees, and all persons or entities in active concert or participation with them who receive actual notice of this Order, by personal service or otherwise, in connection with manufacturing, labeling, advertising, promotion, offering for sale, sale, or distribution of any Covered Product, in or affecting commerce, are hereby permanently restrained and enjoined from misrepresenting, in any manner, expressly or by implication, including through the use of any product name or endorsement, the existence, contents, validity, results, conclusions, or interpretations of any test, study, or research.

. . .

IV. MONETARY JUDGMENT AND CONSUMER REDRESS

JUDGMENT IS HEREBY ENTERED in favor of the Commission and against Defendants, jointly and severally, the amount of thirty million dollars ($30,000,000).

EXHIBIT A, *FTC v. AIRBORNE* COMPLAINT RADIO ADVERTISEMENT

(Sneezing.)

Female Announcer: Are these hideous sounds familiar to you, dear friend? Then why haven't you tried Airborne, the amazing new product created by a school teacher who was sick of catching colds in class. First came the wheel, then canned food and the Internet. Now, Airborne. Do you get a sore throat every time you turn around, catch colds at the office or on airplanes? Well, then your ship's come in, baby. Just listen to our fan mail. "Airborne got rid of my cold in one hour," writes David Mars. "A miracle cold buster," says Tommy Greico *(ph)*. So, next time you feel a cold coming on, take Airborne. Yeah!

Victoria Knight-McDowell: Hi, this is Victoria Knight-McDowell. I'm a second grade teacher and I developed the dietary supplement, Airborne, because I was sick of catching colds in class. When you feel that first cold symptom, won't you please give Airborne a try? Thank you.

More than one hundred years later, consumers have much more knowledge of the science of illness, as well as ready resources to investigate assertions in advertisements (e.g., Google). Yet, the common cold still is fodder for scams. The exploitation of trust for profit endures because consumers make mistakes and imperfect choices. Jean Braucher & Barak Orbach, *Scamming: The Misunderstood Confidence Man*, 27 Yale J.L. & Human. 249 (2015).

What has evolved significantly is the approach of consumer law to address the problem. In the place of a common law action for contract, as seen in *Carbolic Smokeball*, are a variety of statutes that require disclosures, define how terms or statements can be used in advertisements, and impose warranties on the sales of goods. These developments can be seen as a response to the shortcomings of contract law. The common law ideas of a promise and of a meeting of the minds rest on an idealized transaction in which the party and counterparty have equal bargaining power and complete information.

Consumer law also has origins in tort law, in particular the common law actions of deceit or fraud. Such actions are difficult to prove, or even to plead, and the common law eventually embraced a set of less stringent actions such as negligent misrepresentation or fraud by omission. Proving the elements of tort can remain difficult for consumers because damages are often minimal or because there is no duty in a given circumstance from business to consumer. Statutes that ban unfair or deceptive acts or practices, which was the basis for the FTC's action against Airborne, are a partial response of modern consumer law to the limitations of tort.

The twin foundations of consumer law in contract and tort highlight that consumer law is fundamentally private law. The two key actors in a transaction governed by consumer law are private parties: a consumer and a business. Also, the typical injury is economic, another common feature of private law actions. The evolution in consumer law from common law to statutory law, however, has increased the role of government in the consumer law system. Legislatures make the bulk of consumer law in the public sphere, rather than courts in response to private activity. Enforcement of consumer statutes is often by public officials, such as states' attorneys general, rather than private litigants.

The evolution from *Carbolic Smokeball* to *FTC v. Airborne* shows the developments in the theory of such a case and illustrates the reliance on public enforcement. These changes in lawmaking make it difficult to characterize consumer law as solely a matter of private concern. Today, consumer law bridges the public law and private law divide; it is as often shaped by public law such as administrative law and by private law such as tort suits.

B. Consumer Law in the Modern Marketplace

A central debate in consumer law is whether a particular market is sufficiently broken to justify legal intervention. Efficient marketplaces require that parties be able to acquire relevant information in a timely fashion, to communicate successfully with each other, and to have the power to enter into a deal or look elsewhere for a better one. Classic economics often assumes the existence of such features in the marketplace. A growing body of research and probably your own experiences suggest that such assumptions are often not met in the real world. Behavioral economics, psychology, marketing, and other disciplines study the ways in which consumers deviate from perfectly rational behavior, have cognitive barriers to decision-making, or are susceptible to having their actions shaped by businesses. Back in 1936, famed economist John Maynard Keynes acknowledged the role of emotions in influencing human behavior in the marketplace. He observed that "most, probably, of our decisions to do something positive, the full consequences of which will be drawn out over many days to come, can only be taken as the result of animal spirits — a spontaneous urge to action rather than inaction, and not as the outcome of a weighted average of quantitative benefits multiplied by quantitative probabilities." *See* The General Theory of Employment, Interest, and Money 161-162 (1936). Consumer laws are written on this backdrop of human psychology. Depending on the situation, the law intervenes to protect people from their own behavior and decisions, or leaves them unfettered to act and enjoy or suffer the consequences.

A primary defensive tool of consumer law is the provision of information. Many consumer laws require the business to make disclosures, either before or at the time of a transaction. The idea is to compensate for a failure of consumers to seek out information or for the ability of businesses to shroud key information from consumers. The theory goes that with better information, the marketplace is repaired so consumers can then be held to the bargains they made because they did so with full knowledge of the deal and its consequences.

Consumer law may fall short of these goals in its disclosure-based provisions. The problem is that both parties to the transaction may not give the disclosure the due intended by the law. Businesses may ignore requirements to provide disclosures or consumers may fail to read the disclosures. One study of clickwrap agreements, the online contracts in which a button is clicked to indicate assent, found that only one out of one thousand consumers reads such agreements. *See* Yannis Bakos, Florencia Marotta-Wurgler, & David Trossen, *Does Anyone Read the Fine Print? Testing a Law and Economics Approach to Standard Form Contracts* 43 J. LEGAL STUD. 1-35 (2014). Even if they are given the disclosures and are willing to spend the time to review them, consumers may be unable to understand mandatory disclosures. Credit card contracts, for example, are written at a reading level that exceeds the comprehension ability of 80 percent of Americans. *See* Connie Prater, U.S. Credit Card Agreements Unreadable to four out of five adults, http://www.creditcards.com/credit-card-news/credit-card-agreement-readability-1282.php. Another problem is language itself; about 20 percent of people living in the United States do not read in English. Disclosures also impose costs on businesses. The trade publication of nearly every industry contains laments about the costs of compliance related to disclosure.

Scholars have begun to identify harms of disclosure that go beyond the dollars and cents that businesses spend and the time that consumers use. Law professors Omri Ben-Shahar and Carl Schneider argue that it is often difficult to cabin the amount of information disclosed, such that useful information is crowded out, and that disclosure as a remedy can undermine other consumer laws. As an example of the latter problem, they note that the common law defense of unconscionability often rests on a consumer showing that a particular term was hidden and thus the deal was unfair. By burying extensive terms in mandated disclosures, businesses may shield themselves from unconscionability litigation for only a fraction of a penny per transaction in compliance costs. *See* Omri Ben-Shahar & Carl Schneider, *The Failure of Mandated Disclosure*, 159 U. PA. L. REV. 704-706 (2011). Despite such concerns, disclosure remains a bulwark of consumer protection law, perhaps because it seems wrongheaded to argue against information. For free market advocates, information permits the freedom of choice. From the other side, information is a tool to deliver much needed protection from the market.

Consumer law also imposes substantive limits on transactions. These laws typically arise from an intuition that market failure is driven by unequal bargaining power rather than a lack of information. That is, consumers may know, or at least fear, that they are being ripped off but may lack the ability to negotiate for a better deal. Examples of this approach are rules that prohibit lenders from taking household goods such as baby cribs as collateral for certain loans and limits on mandatory arbitration clauses in some contracts. In the former case, the concern is that lenders are taking the collateral only for its hostage value and not because it is economically meaningfully protection for their interests. In the latter case, policymakers might worry that contracts of adhesion and a small number of market actors may effectively prohibit consumers from choosing a contract that allows them to litigate disputes. Substantive limits place a heavier check on people's and businesses' freedom than disclosure laws. Such remedies are often reserved for high-stakes transactions or when mandatory information disclosure has failed to eliminate the troubling transactions or conduct.

In addition to disclosure laws and substantive regulation, consumer laws may be motivated by a desire to enhance the remedies available to wronged consumers. For example, while a suitable cause of action under the common law may exist for a particular transaction, it may be extraordinarily difficult to prove damages given the facts. Alternatively, the damages for that transaction may be easy to prove but be paltry in dollar amount. The outcome of either situation is to curb sharply the practical ability and interest of consumers (and their lawyers — who want to earn a living) in bringing such actions. Consumer statutes sometimes address these problems by permitting class actions or by providing for statutory or exemplary damages. These laws can be seen as addressing a different broken market: consumers seeking legal services. Enhanced remedies try to incentivize lawyers to represent consumers and thereby police the market. These are interventions in the market for legal services and in the court system, rather than duties or rights that change the substantive law of how consumers and businesses may transact.

Regardless of form, consumer laws are subject to a fundamental debate. Are such laws designed to enhance the marketplace or weaken it? The first stone thrown by most critics of consumer laws is paternalism. Why should government protect those who can and should protect themselves? To be valid, a contract must be agreed upon by a consumer. Is this mindset of protecting people from their own choices consistent with democracy and capitalism? The debate over this question goes to the heart of the kind of economy and society that a country wants. Proponents of consumer laws may accuse their adversaries of callousness to human suffering or of being willing to accept injustice as an irremediable consequence of markets, an assumption that they sharply challenge. More moderately, they may point to human biases that inhere to all consumers as errors that reduce the efficacy of a market-based system.

The concepts of "consumer rights" and "economic justice" illustrate the concerns behind such debates. These concepts are more prevalent in developing nations and Europe than in the United States. They draw on a human rights framework, which sees consumer law as a necessary tool for allowing people to realize their human capabilities and to accumulate adequate resources for health, safety, and political participation. The United Nations has promulgated Guidelines for Consumer Protection that give a good flavor of these ideas. In the United States, the relatively recent activism by labor unions and race membership groups on consumer credit issues seems motivated by similar concerns. In this view, consumers should be able to rely on government to keep them safe, including from the harms that can occur when buying goods or services or borrowing money. The battle for adequate wages produces little benefit to welfare if consumers are swindled out of their pay.

C.   Consumer Law Compared to Consumer Protection

Consumer law is not a synonym for consumer protection — at least not in this book. Such a distinction is not merely semantic. It goes to the issue of whether consumer law is about intervention in a marketplace for the benefit of all, or protecting the vulnerable from wrongdoers. This book is titled "Consumer Law" to reflect its focus on the former. (Note that your course may be called "Consumer Protection," which itself is worth pondering as the course continues.) The core theory of this book is that markets require intervention on behalf of consumers, at least some of the time and in certain ways, to be robust and reliable. Better markets do not only benefit consumers but also improve the nature of competition as a whole. Corrections to markets can help competing businesses have a level playing field and make transactions more efficient. Both outcomes help keep the economy humming along at optimal levels. An illustration of this point is that the Federal Reserve has a Division of Consumer Affairs and Community Development. Even at the macro level of the central bank, consumer transactions matter.

Protection for the most vulnerable members of society, on the other hand, is sometimes characterized as being about helping the "few" instead of improving the lot of the "many." Such ideas may be incorrect, but consumer protection as a term bears a mantle of social activism that the label of consumer law does not. In the 1970s when consumer law entered the law school curricula, classes nearly always focused on the perspective of the consumer. The attorney was the champion of the downtrodden, and the goal of consumer law was to empower the consumer. Concerns about discrimination and economic disparities, coming out of the civil rights movement, were twined with ideas about consumer protection. This was the early Ralph Nader era and harkened back to the progressive era battles between workers and capitalists.

In the last thirty years, however, consumer law has morphed. The role of law and economics in the legal academy and the deregulation movement in policymaking have pushed and pulled consumer law away from its consumer protection origins and toward market concerns. In *The Law and Economics of Consumer Finance*, Richard Hynes and Eric Posner give a flavor of today's debate about credit, a major area of consumer law.

> Regulation of the market for consumer credit provides a number of benefits to consumers. It gives them information about the terms and consequences of the credit transaction, it provides them insurance against shocks, and it protects them from discrimination. But a proper defense of consumer credit regulation must explain why the market would not supply these benefits if consumers are willing to pay for them. The availability of credit insurance, the many ways in which typical credit transactions trade off between interest rate and risk, and the existence of information intermediaries all suggest that the market does respond to some degree to consumer demand for credit protections.
>
> Models that incorporate information asymmetry and market power have ambiguous implications for consumer credit regulation. Information problems do prevent markets from achieving the first best, and laws regulating the credit market can in theory increase social welfare. But it is difficult to determine whether the premises of the models are met in reality. Complicating the analysis, it is not clear how sensitive consumers and creditors are to the law, whether because of irrationality or "rational ignorance." And it is not clear how much the law would influence the behavior of even a rational, well-informed consumer, given the many loopholes, the limited penalty structures, and the many ways in which creditors can evade the law and creditors and debtors can contract around it.

Richard Hynes & Eric A. Posner, *The Law and Economics of Consumer Finance*, 4 Am. Law Econ. Rev. 197-198 (2002).

The cautious tone of this excerpt about the value of law is a far cry from the heyday of consumer protection. The authors frame the debate in terms of markets. The vulnerable consumer makes no appearance in the analysis, largely replaced by an idealized, rational consumer who can be inserted into economic models.

Today, consumer law may be trending back toward consumer protection. The global financial crisis that began in 2008 has sparked a new level of activism about the appropriate balance of power between businesses and consumers. Laws are rapidly changing, and the debate is moving at the margin. The market perspective will likely remain powerful in the United States, however, with undercurrents of consumer protection existing in an ocean of broadly-oriented consumer law.

D.   Fields Related to Consumer Law

The preceding sections give an introduction to the key themes of consumer law. These themes help circumscribe the areas of study for a consumer law course. A consumer law is one that applies to consumer-to-business transactions for the purchase of goods, services, or property, and the financing of such purchases. Consumer law statutes are built on the common law foundations of tort, contract, and occasionally, property law. The statutory protections and remedies are typically cumulative of common law actions, a point often lost on litigants who struggle to fit their situation into the twists and turns of a statute but fail to plead a simple breach of contract or fraud action.

Contract law and tort law, in both their common law and statutory forms, are part of the body of consumer law. In particular, the Uniform Commercial Code (U.C.C.) is an important supplement to other consumer statutes. It provides the substantive law on sales, secured lending, and payment systems. Despite its name, the U.C.C. generally applies to consumer-to-business transactions. It also contains some specialized provisions that provide additional rules when one party is a consumer. Consumer law focuses on these rules, and asks why exceptions are made to the law that applies in business-to-business deals. The generally applicable rules of the Uniform Commercial Code are taught in one or more courses on commercial law, including secured transactions or payment systems.

Laws that touch on concerns about information asymmetry, unequal bargaining power, economic empowerment, and the like as they relate to purchasing or borrowing are nearly always put under the umbrella of "consumer law." Other consumer-to-business interactions, such as employment relationships, may reflect similar concerns but are excluded from the body of consumer law. Examining why some subjects are typically outside the realm of consumer law helps reveal the common concerns of consumer law.

Because consumer law regulates the purchase of goods, the law of products liability is implicated in many transactions. Unlike products liability, consumer law rarely imposes strict liability. Consumer transactions are framed as contracts, with the legal twists often being the imposition of additional duties, such as mandatory disclosure of information, as part of the contract. An example may help illustrate the point. The Magnuson-Moss Warranty Act is a staple of consumer law. It does not substantively create liability for defective goods, as does products liability law. Instead, the Magnuson-Moss Act regulates the language and meaning of warranty terms in consumer contracts. Magnuson-Moss does not impose warranty obligations but defines how such terms can be used. Products liability provides an important layer of protection for consumers harmed or shortchanged by defective goods, but its frame is different from the contractual approach of consumer law.

Banking law is a natural cousin of consumer law. Consumers must pay for the goods and services that they purchase, and this nearly always involves their use of payment systems such as cash, credit or debit cards, or checks. Financial institutions are the intermediaries in consumer-to-business transactions in processing these payments. Particularly in recent decades, many consumer purchases are financed by borrowing. This can occur through traditional loans, such as mortgages, or through products that blur the line between payment and borrowing such as credit cards. Banks and financial institutions bear the risks of such lending. The regulation of these entities can have a powerful effect on consumer purchasing and borrowing. This nexus between banking law and consumer law was hotly debated in 2010 by Congress when it created the Consumer Financial Protection Bureau in the aftermath of the global financial crisis. Part of the justification for a separate agency focused on consumers was that the traditional concerns of banking regulators on the safety and soundness of banks led such regulators, at best, to overlook consumer protection issues, or at worst, to permit practices that were deleterious to consumers. Practices that are highly profitable for financial institutions — and thus enhance the safety and soundness of the bank (in at least the short term) — may be so profitable precisely because consumers do not understand or benefit from such practices. This tension means that banking lawyers and consumer lawyers often see themselves as members of unrelated — if not warring — tribes. The key difference between banking law and consumer law may be one of perspective about whose economic health — families or financial institutions — is paramount.

Antitrust is another relative of consumer law. Like consumer law, it attempts to intervene in broken markets. The focus is on restraints to competition between businesses, however, rather than on the interaction of consumers and businesses. Antitrust seeks to protect the larger economy from anticompetitive practices, which helps businesses grow. Antitrust law does have some concern with consumers' well-being. Consumer injury, for example, is an aspect of claims under the Sherman Antitrust Act. The consequences of uncompetitive markets certainly reach down to the consumer level, in the form of limited product selection and higher prices, for example. Consumers do not usually rely on antitrust laws. The typical antitrust action is brought by a competitor or would-be competitor who alleges that remedying the anticompetitive activity would help consumers but who is usually motivated to file suit by a desire to increase its market share or profits.

Consumer transactions involve risk to the parties. The business often has continuing obligations on warranties or compliance with consumer law, and continuing concerns about whether a consumer will pay up for the good or service. Consumers have the inverse issues. Will this product or service be as promised? Can I repay the loan? Two areas of law address financial risk:

insurance law and bankruptcy law. Insurance is precautionary. It helps parties guard against financial loss from risks. Bankruptcy is reactionary. When risk management was insufficient or foresight impossible, bankruptcy provides a way to limit the harms of financial failure. Both areas of law exist as separate fields from consumer law. One main reason is that each system also has a complex set of rules for non-consumer transactions. Bankruptcy law deals with the problem of overwhelming consumer credit, but it also provides mechanisms for multinational corporations dealing with overwhelming debenture obligations. Insurance law has provisions to aid consumers in understanding their insurance contracts and ensuring that they are paid on claims, but it also regulates the solvency of insurers and other squarely commercial issues in the industry.

Because most of consumer law is statutory, consumer law also examines how lawmakers craft statutes and how courts interpret them. Consumer law is also administrative law. Consumer statutes frequently require government bodies to promulgate regulations, provide services to consumers, or regulate businesses in their dealing with consumers. Understanding the boundaries of government actors, and the overlapping roles of different levels of government, is an important aspect of consumer law.

Unlike many law school courses that largely focus on understanding whether a plaintiff or defendant is entitled to judgment on a set of facts, consumer law takes a keen interest in the ability of plaintiffs to bring an action in the first place and to receive meaningful relief. Conversely, consumer law also is about the tools available to defendants to defeat plaintiffs even when they have substantive law on their side. The study of consumer law is necessarily a study of civil procedure and remedies, including alternate dispute resolution.

Consumer law inevitably bleeds into other areas of law. The main feature of consumer law is a concern with the disparities between consumers and businesses in purchase and credit transactions. The primary goals of consumer law are to keep markets for goods and services functioning well and to protect consumers from harm when market mechanisms fall short.

Problem Set 1

1.1. Make a list of five consumer laws that have affected your life in the last 24 hours. Don't do any research but simply think about your interactions with businesses. Do not worry about the names of the laws; just describe the transaction and what you think the law adds to your role as a consumer in the transaction. For each law, note whether you think it is aimed at correcting a broad marketplace gap or protecting a vulnerable consumer. Be prepared to share your list.

1.2. Your clients are frightened out of their wits—and their home. Upon retirement, the couple purchased a large Victorian home in the country. On moving day, their neighbors commended them for their bravery in being willing to occupy a house possessed by poltergeists, filling them in on the national publicity the house had received for its apparitions. The couple wants to rescind the sale. They've had to purchase another place to live, and two mortgages are straining their fixed income in retirement to the breaking point. What areas of law are implicated in this transaction and the litigation that your clients want to pursue? Is this a problem for consumer law? (Or for the Ghostbusters?)

1.3. What is the perspective of the cartoonist on consumer law? From your experience, identify an actual disclosure that seems unnecessary. Be prepared to discuss your example, to explain why you think it was put into place, and to argue why such a disclosure should be eliminated.

1.4. In 2007, future U.S. Senator (then law professor) Elizabeth Warren made the case for a separate federal government agency to protect consumers when they engage in financial transactions. The article carried a byline of, "If it's good enough for microwaves, it's good enough for mortgages. Why we need a Financial Product Safety Commission." She wrote:

> It is impossible to buy a toaster that has a one-in-five chance of bursting into flames and burning down your house. But it is possible to refinance an existing home with a mortgage that has the same one-in-five chance of putting the family out on the street — and the mortgage won't even carry a disclosure of that fact to the homeowner. Similarly, it's impossible to change the price on a toaster once it has been purchased. But long after the papers have been signed, it is possible to triple the price of the credit used to finance the purchase of that appliance, even if the customer meets all the credit terms, in full and on time. Why are consumers safe when they purchase tangible consumer products with

cash, but when they sign up for routine financial products like mortgages and credit cards they are left at the mercy of their creditors? . . .

Consumers can enter the market to buy physical products confident that they won't be tricked into buying exploding toasters and other unreasonably dangerous products. They can concentrate their shopping efforts in other directions, helping to drive a competitive market that keeps costs low and encourages innovation in convenience, durability, and style. Consumers entering the market to buy financial products should enjoy the same protection. Just as the Consumer Product Safety Commission (CPSC) protects buyers of goods and supports a competitive market, we need the same for consumers of financial products–a new regulatory regime, and even a new regulatory body, to protect consumers who use credit cards, home mortgages, car loans, and a host of other products. The time has come to put scaremongering to rest and to recognize that regulation can often support and advance efficient and more dynamic markets.

Elizabeth Warren, *Unsafe at Any Rate*, 5 Democracy 8 (2007), at http://www .democracyjournal.org/5/6528.php.

Are you persuaded by the analogy? How are financial products, and consumer credit specifically, different from physical products? What are the advantages and disadvantages to her comparison to the Consumer Product Safety Commission, which regulates things like baby cribs and lawn mowers?

Assignment 2.   Who Is a Consumer?

To say that consumer law is about consumers is painfully unsatisfying. First, there is the definitional problem. Everyone engages as a consumer at some moments, but we also take on a variety of other roles that are separately defined by the legal system — for example, as parents, as employees, as taxpayers. The law needs to define the types of people and transactions that come within the purview of consumer law. Often, the key task is distinguishing consumers from businesses. The law may further define consumer in its substantive content when it describes when a consumer is engaged in conduct that is covered by the particular law. Second, the law must consider whether to design consumer law around the "typical" consumer or a more narrow class of persons. This Assignment looks at a number of differing approaches to defining a consumer.

A.   Definitions of Consumer

No less venerable an American than U.S. President John F. Kennedy grappled with explaining how to think about who was covered by consumer law. In a 1962 speech introducing a Consumer Bill of Rights (which was not enacted), he explained:

> Consumers, by definition, include us all. They are the largest economic group in the economy, affecting and affected by almost every public and private economic decision. Two-thirds of all spending in the economy is by consumers. But they are the only group in the economy who are not effectively organized, whose views are often not heard.

President Kennedy went for the big grab in his definition. In his conception, consumers become synonymous with citizens, which is a neat political trick. Businesses tend to resist such broad definitions, despite the clarity of including everyone and excluding no one.

Definitions of consumers appear in most, but not all, consumer law statutes. It is overwhelming and probably unnecessary to study all the definitions. This assignment focuses on a few of the most important definitions; they are important in part because they have often served as a model for later laws that adopt the same approach.

The Truth in Lending Act (TILA) is a federal statute that regulates the disclosure of the cost of consumer credit and related issues. Enacted in 1968, TILA remains a cornerstone of the federal consumer law regime. Its definition of consumer, or slight variations of it, is typical of most statutes. It offers a good starting point for considering who is a consumer for purposes of the law.

On its face, TILA makes short work of the definitional task. It states that a "consumer" is a "natural person." 15 U.S.C. §1602(h); 12 C.F.R. §1026.2(a)(11). What, you might wonder, is an unnatural person—an alien? Crazy cousin Hubert? The language is designed to differ from other statutes that use the word "person" to indicate all entities. *Cf.* 11 U.S.C. §101(41) (Bankruptcy Code definition of person includes corporations, partnerships, etc.). Section 1603 of TILA specifically exempts from its purview credit granted to "organizations." Case law has affirmed that regardless of their purposes, corporations and organizations are not consumers under most provisions of TILA. *See e.g., Prifti v. PNC Bank,* 2001 WL 1198653 (E.D. Pa. Oct. 9, 2011). An exception is that certain rules on credit cards, including those on unauthorized use, unsolicited issuance, and criminal misuse, do apply to organizations. This is accomplished by defining "cardholder" as a subcategory of the general consumer definition. *See* 12 C.F.R. §1026.2(a)(8).

A slightly different approach to defining consumer is used in the Fair Credit Reporting Act (FCRA), which defines consumers only as "an individual." 15 U.S.C. §1681a(c). In its official commentary on the statute, the Federal Trade Commission has clarified that "individual" means "natural persons." Despite the different language in TILA and FCRA, the end result is the same. The Consumer Financial Protection Bureau also defines a consumer to be an "individual," but broadens this to include "an agent, trustee, or representative acting on behalf of an individual." Dodd-Frank Wall Street Reform and Consumer Protection Act, 12 U.S.C. §5481 (Dodd-Frank Act). The intent here was to sweep in situations when a consumer may be represented by a guardian or similar entity, perhaps because of mental incapacity or death. The case law interpreting TILA and FCRA also have been interpreted to cover such agents and the like.

This examination of definitions of consumer illustrates a structural point about statutes. Despite being enacted at one moment in time, they endure. In the case of FCRA, the implementing agency has explained the statute in such a way to make it match the definition in TILA, despite Congress' choice to use different words in FCRA than it had used in TILA. In the case of the Consumer Financial Protection Bureau, the Dodd-Frank Act was written decades later and reflects an effort to incorporate issues flushed out by case law into an improved (and more detailed) statute that gives more clarification than its predecessors. These evolutionary processes in statutes can be difficult to track. Unlike in case law, there is no quick look at appellate review. Often the legislative history provides little guidance of where its drafters looked for inspiration in wording.

Some statutes that are part of the canon of consumer law do not make any effort to limit their scopes and apply equally to consumers and businesses. For example, the Equal Credit Opportunity Act, 15 U.S.C. §1691 et seq. applies to business credit, albeit to a slightly lesser extent than to consumer credit. Another important instance of broad applicability is the federal unfair and deceptive acts or practices law, 15 U.S.C. §45, which states that "unfair methods of competition in or affecting commerce, and unfair or deceptive acts or practices in or affecting commerce, are hereby declared unlawful." There is no mention of consumers, despite this being a foundation of the consumer law framework. Every state has a similar statute banning unfair practices. Most of these are limited to consumers, however, picking up the TILA definition that transactions governed by the statute must involve a consumer as a person who uses the good or service at issue for personal, family, or household use. The Texas Deceptive Trade Practices Act uses a broader definition, as the below case illustrates.

Houston Livestock Show and Rodeo, Inc. v. Hamrick

125 S.W.3d 555 (Tex. App. 2003)

YEAKEL, Appellate Judge.

Appellant Houston Livestock Show and Rodeo, Inc. (Livestock Show) appeals from a judgment awarding appellees Leslie Hamrick and her parents, T.L. Hamrick and Connie Hamrick, Jimmy Barton and his parents, Craig Barton and Jacque Barton, and Kevin Copeland, damages. . . . Appellees sued the Livestock Show and the Texas Veterinary Medical Diagnostic Laboratory (Lab) alleging breach of contract, conversion, negligence, gross negligence, defamation, intentional or reckless infliction of emotional distress, and [for violations under] the Texas Deceptive Trade practices Act (DTPA), Tex. Bus. & Com. Code §§17.41-.63.

The jury returned a favorable verdict for appellees against the Livestock Show for the DTPA violations and defamation, as well as negligence and gross negligence against the Lab. . . . The Livestock Show brings this appeal . . . challenging the . . . consumer status of the parents. . . . We will reform the district-court judgment and, as reformed, affirm.

FACTUAL AND PROCEDURAL BACKGROUND

In 1991 Leslie Hamrick, Jimmy Barton, and Kevin Copeland, all high-school students, entered farm animals they had raised in the Junior Livestock Show competition at the Livestock Show. They vied with other competitors in various animal classes for a chance at winning the contest and auction proceeds from the sale of their animals. As prescribed by Livestock Show rules, the Exhibitors were members of their schools' FFA or 4-H programs, operating under the guidance of the Texas Education Agency. Their FFA and 4-H programs, and to a certain extent their parents, supervised the Exhibitors' raising of their animals. Hamrick and Barton entered lambs, and Copeland entered a steer in the Junior Livestock Show. Each won their respective class, entitling them to participate in the Livestock Show's junior auction. The competition's rules required the animals to undergo drug testing for illegal substances, commonly used to improve an animal's appearance. The drug tests revealed illegal substances in all three animals, and the Livestock Show disqualified the Exhibitors. This action arises from the drug testing procedures and the Livestock Show's actions toward appellees.

Junior Livestock Show rule 16 states that "unethically fitted livestock" are prohibited, and exhibitors showing such animals would be disqualified and "barred from future competition" at the Livestock Show. The Livestock Show instituted animal drug testing to "teach and reward 4-H and FFA students for good animal husbandry," while "endeavor[ing] to protect the public from consuming tainted meat." Moreover, the rule warned exhibitors that the Livestock Show's drug test results were final and without recourse.

Livestock Show applications and entry fees submitted by Agricultural Science Teachers and County Extension Agents included the signature of both instructor and exhibitor. The reverse side of each application included a waiver of liability and a statement notifying the signatories that the Livestock Show had the right to test the animals for medication or drugs. Below this statement, the application contained lines on which the exhibitor and the exhibitor's parent or guardian signed. The exhibitors and their parents or guardians also signed and returned a notarized form stating that they would abide by the rules, and that no unauthorized substances had been given to the animals. In the event an animal required testing, the exhibitor and his or her parent or guardian would witness the collection of a urine specimen from the animal and sign another form acknowledging that they were present for the collection. Pending a successful drug test, the prizes and auction proceeds, less the Livestock Show's commission, would be disbursed.

Appellees paid the appropriate entry fees and submitted their applications. Each won ribbons in their respective class, entitling them to participate in the auction. At auction, Hamrick's lamb brought $12,020, Barton's lamb brought $1520, and Copeland's steer brought $5060. Pursuant to its drug testing rules, the Livestock Show obtained a urine sample from Barton's lamb on February 27. The next day, the Livestock Show collected urine samples from Hamrick's lamb and Copeland's steer. The Livestock Show split the samples into two parts, with the Lab [at Texas A&M University] testing one half, while the Livestock Show retained and froze the remainder. The Lab tested the specimens following the auction, and the Livestock Show retained the auction proceeds pending review of the results.

. . . [T]he Lab reported to the Livestock Show that Hamrick's lamb had tested positive. Nine days later, the Lab reported that Barton's lamb and Copeland's steer had both tested positive as well. Thereafter, the Livestock Show notified the Exhibitors and their schools that they had been disqualified because of the positive drug tests. Additionally, the Livestock Show informed appellees that they were barred from participating in Houston Livestock Shows for the remainder of their lives. . . .

The procedural history of the case spans more than ten years and the record is extensive. [But ultimately, a] jury found the following in favor of appellees: 1) $300,000 in mental anguish damages; 2) $115,000 in injury-to-reputation damages; 3) $12,020 for Leslie Hamrick's loss of prize money; 4) $190,000 in attorney's fees for trial and appeal; and 5) $630,000 in additional DTPA damages. [Defendants appealed]

THE PARENTS AS CONSUMERS UNDER THE DTPA

[T]he Livestock Show argues that the appellee parents are not consumers for purposes of the DTPA and that there is no evidence or factually insufficient evidence to support their status as consumers. The Livestock Show contends that "[t]he basis of [appellee parents'] complaint is the drug testing performed by the Diagnostic Lab, [and] [t]hat is not a valid basis for a claim against the [Livestock Show] under the DTPA." The Livestock Show argues that the parents sought, acquired, or purchased nothing from the Livestock Show that could form the basis of the complaint and that they were not exhibitors in the show. . . .

The DTPA mandates liberal construction to promote the underlying purpose of the act. Tex. Bus. & Com. Code §17.44 (2011). A "consumer" under the DTPA is defined as "an individual, partnership, corporation, this state, or a subdivision or agency of this state who seeks or acquires, by purchase or lease, any goods or services." Id. §17.45(4). To qualify as a consumer, the plaintiff must meet two requirements: (1) the person must seek or acquire goods or services by purchase or lease and (2) the goods or services purchased or leased must form the basis of the complaint. Sherman Simon Enters., Inc. v. Lorac Serv. Corp., 724 S.W.2d 13, 14 (Tex. 1987); see also Tex. Bus.& Com. Code §17.45(2) (2011) ("Services' means work, labor, or service purchased or leased for use. . . ."). The word "purchase," in the context of the DTPA, has been defined as the actual transmission of services from one person to another by voluntary act or agreement, founded on valuable consideration. Hall v. Bean, 582 S.W.2d 263, 265 (Tex. Civ. App. 1979). A plaintiff's standing as a consumer is established by its relationship to the transaction, not by a contractual relationship with the defendant. Flenniken v. Longview Bank & Trust Co., 661 S.W.2d 705, 707 (Tex. 1983). Whether a plaintiff is a consumer under the DTPA is a question of law for the trial court).

The district court determined as a matter of law that the parents were consumers, and the evidence adduced at trial supports such holding. The parents were involved in the entire animal-showing process. The parents signed waivers of liability, which approved the Livestock Show's right to test the animals for unauthorized drugs. They also signed a notarized form stating that they would abide by the Livestock Show rules and that no illegal substances had been administered to the animals.

Additionally, when an Exhibitor's animal was subjected to drug testing, an Exhibitor's parent witnessed the taking of the sample, after which the parent signed another form acknowledging that the parents witnessed the event. The parents, as well as the Exhibitors, were subject to the threat of a lifetime banishment from future shows in the event of a disqualification resulting from illegal drug use. The myriad of services that the Livestock Show provided to the Exhibitors and their parents included the use of the facilities for their children, animal judging, drug testing, and the auction. Simply stated, the Exhibitors could not have entered the competition without their parents' express joinder and participation.

We hold that the district court was correct in concluding the parties were consumers because (1) the parents did seek or acquire the services of the Livestock Show, indicated by their authorization, participation, and potential exclusion from all future shows; and (2) the services provided by the Livestock Show form the basis of the complaint.

Showing livestock may seem far from the mainstream definition of being a consumer, but consumer protection laws are designed to be remedial and sweep broadly. Checking each law's definition of "consumer," or noting the absence of such a definition, is a critical first step in analyzing any consumer law problem.

B.   Defining a Consumer Transaction

Beyond consumers meaning individuals and not entities, definitions typically contain limitations designed to separate out individuals acting as business people and individuals acting as consumers. These limitations come in a couple of different forms. Sometimes certain transactions are excluded from the applicable law, even if they are made by consumers acting as consumers. Usually this is because the size or nature of the transaction is much more common by business people than by consumers or because the transaction is of such a size or importance that the law expects consumers to be sufficiently engaged to protect their own interests. The other common limit is to examine the purpose of the transaction and ask whether its purpose was business in nature. This section considers these approaches in turn, but many statutes use both approaches in combination. The result is a patchwork of coverage for individuals that is less comprehensive than it may initially appear.

Laws that exempt certain transactions, even when made by individuals acting for their own benefit, can use different kinds of triggers for exclusion. TILA contains a major exemption from its scope based on a dollar threshold, exempting credit transactions of over $50,000 in amount. 15 U.S.C. §1603(3); 12 C.F.R. §1026.3(b). (As part of the Dodd-Frank Act, the $50,000 limit is adjusted for inflation. In 2015, it stood at $54,600.) This change was designed to sweep more ordinary consumer purchases, like cars, under the scope of TILA, which with its 1968 original $25,000 limit would have covered nearly all car purchases but failed to do so today. The intuition behind the dollar-figure exemption could be that when the stakes get high enough consumers will, or should, make specialized detailed inquiries about the deal, and therefore do not need mandatory disclosures. Alternatively, the dollar limit may reflect a belief that transactions of this size are rarely for personal, family, or household use and that to require TILA disclosure in such situations would overburden companies that primarily engage in business deals.

There is an important "exception to the exemption" (try saying that phrase five times quickly) of the dollar-limit threshold. Any extension of credit secured by real property, or secured by personal property used or expected to be used as the principal residence of a consumer, is covered by TILA. 15 U.S.C. §1603(3). Regardless of the value of the loan, when a house is the collateral, TILA applies to the transaction. The theory here is the inverse of the general dollar-limit idea: home mortgages have such high stakes, they always warrant disclosures.

TILA contains another type of exemption, which is the categorical exclusion of certain transactions from its scope. Student loans guaranteed by the United States or a state guaranty agency, such as Stafford loans, are exempt from TILA. 15 U.S.C. §1603(7). The Higher Education Act, 20 U.S.C. §1083 et seq., mandates alternate disclosures of credit cost for student loans and so presumably the TILA exemption prevents duplicative disclosures. TILA also exempts layaway plans, tax liens, borrowing against a pension account, letters of credit, and a few other items. *See* Official Staff Commentary, §226(a)(14)-1. These exemptions likely emanate from a varied set of justifications, including that the transaction is not an extension of credit.

Again, TILA provides the leading definition of a consumer transaction. A consumer credit transaction is one in which the "money, property, or services which are the subject of the transaction are primarily for personal, family, or household purposes." 15 U.S.C. §1602(h); 12 C.F.R. §1026.2(a)(12). The limitation to personal, family, or household purposes is strengthened in TILA by an exemption from coverage for "transactions involving extensions of credit primarily for business, commercial, or agricultural purposes." 15 U.S.C. §1603. The personal, family, or household purpose" definition has been widely adopted in other consumer statutes. *See* 12 U.S.C. §5481 (defining "consumer financial product or service" subject to the Bureau as "any financial product or service that" . . . "is offered or provided for use by consumers primarily for personal, family, or household purposes.") and the Fair Credit Reporting Act, 15 U.S.C. §1691(a)(d)(1)(A) (defining a "consumer report" as one used or collected for "credit or insurance to be used primarily for personal, family, or household purposes.").

A large body of case law exists on whether a particular transaction is for personal, family, or household use. In some instances, the answer may differ depending on the exact statute at issue—even if its wording is identical to another statute—because courts look to the overarching purpose of the statute as part of their consideration. In deciding whether something meets the personal, family, or household use criteria, the key issue is the reason for the transaction. The identity of the creditor or the type of collateral does not shield something from being for personal, family, or household purposes.

The most challenging cases are those involving mixed uses, in which the good or service is used both for personal and for business use. In these cases, courts look to the "primary" purpose. Determining the primary purpose is a factual determination, requiring evidence about how often and how extensively the good is used. Most courts say that to be primary, a use does not have to be exclusive. *See* Palmer v. Statewide Group, U.S. App. Lexis 1497 (9th Cir. 1998) (interpreting TILA). If more than half of the use is for personal, family, or household purposes, this is usually sufficient evidence. Occasional consumer use is insufficient to defeat characterization as a business purpose. Once the primary purpose is identified, a court must decide the legal issue of whether that purpose is consumer or business in nature. The relevant timing for the determination is what occurred prior to and at the closing of the transaction, not later changes in use.

Gallegos v. Stokes
593 F.2d 372 (10th Cir. 1979)

Logan, Circuit Judge.

This is an appeal from a trial court judgment in favor of plaintiff-appellee Inez Gallegos against Mel Stokes.

The issues on appeal only concern Truth-In-Lending Act (TIL) violations: whether the trial court properly entertained the defense by Stokes that the transaction with

Gallegos was commercial and not subject to the disclosure requirements of TIL; whether this is a consumer credit transaction covered by TIL, or an exempted commercial transaction; and whether Stokes can avoid liability because the disclosure errors were made unintentionally and in good faith. For the reasons stated below, we affirm the judgment of the trial court.

On August 15, 1975, Gallegos purchased a 1969 Dodge pickup truck from Stokes, who was manager of Hopper Auto Sales in Albuquerque. (It is stipulated that Stokes, who later purchased the business, is the proper defendant.) The total cash price was $1,395. Gallegos traded in her 1965 Chevrolet station wagon and some jewelry, valued at $150 and $200 respectively, reducing the total due to $1,045. A $45 fee for license, certificate of title and registration was not included in the cash price.

Stokes prepared a security agreement and the other papers necessary to complete the transaction. The agreement provided for 24 monthly installments of $59.46 each, to begin on September 5, 1975. The annual percentage interest rate was stated as 27.40% and the total finance charge as $321.56. Gallegos failed to make the first payment and Hopper Motors repossessed the truck. None of her down payment was returned, and no deficiency judgment was sought by Hopper Motors.

We accept the findings of the trial court that the total finance charge should have been stated as $292.60, based on N.M. Stat. Ann. §50-15-8 which permits a 14% annual percentage rate calculated without regard to whether the sale provides for installment payments. The monthly payments would have been $55.73 and the annual percentage rate as 24.93%. The disclosure provisions were violated by overstating the finance charge, §1605 and 12 C.F.R. §226.4, the annual percentage rate, §1606 and 12 C.F.R. §226.5(b), and the monthly payment, §1638(a)(8) and 12 C.F.R. §226.8(b)(3). In addition, Stokes violated 12 C.F.R. §226.4(b)(4) because he neither included the finance charge nor itemized and separately disclosed the license, certificate of title, and registration fees. . . .

II

We turn next to whether the trial court was clearly erroneous in deciding that Gallegos' purchase was not within the commercial use exception to TIL. This is a factual issue to be resolved by the trier of fact. Redhouse v. Quality Ford Sales, Inc., 511 F.2d 230 (10th Cir.), op. on rehearing en banc, 523 F.2d 1 (10th Cir. 1975). We find sufficient evidence in the record to support the trial judge's finding that the truck was primarily for personal use. Mrs. Gallegos traded in her only automobile, and the truck became her sole means of transportation. Stokes accepted her jewelry as part of the down payment. Her testimony at trial indicated she bought a truck because she moved often, and it would help transport her family and possessions. The defense also elicited testimony that she intended to use the truck to sell fresh produce, obtained from the Estancia Valley, as a means of making money. But Stokes made an attempt to comply with the TIL disclosures requirements, evidently assuming this was a consumer credit transaction. Had he believed then that the sale was not "primarily for personal, family, household, or agricultural purposes" he would not have attempted to comply.

Cases considering whether a transaction is primarily consumer or commercial in nature look to the transaction as a whole and the purpose for which credit was extended. Many involve mortgaging real property or property purchased for rental use. Gerasta v. Hibernia Nat'l Bank, 411 F. Supp. 176, 185 (E.D. La. 1975) (second mortgage on future residence is consumer transaction); Adema v. Great N. Dev. Co., 374 F. Supp. 318, 319 (N.D. Ga.1973) (lots purchased for investment reasons do not make buyer a consumer); Puckett v. Georgia Homes, Inc., 369 F. Supp. 614, 619 (D.S.C. 1974) (purchase of mobile home to be used as rental unit is not a consumer credit transaction); Sapenter v. Dreyco, Inc., 326 F. Supp. 871, 873 (E.D. La.) (cash from second mortgage on residence to meet payments on investment property is not consumer transaction).

In a case where a truck was purchased for personal as well as business use, the TIL disclosures were required to be made. Allen v. City Dodge, Inc., 5 Cons. Cred. Guide (CCH) ¶ 98,428 (N.D. Ga. Sept. 8, 1975). The situation here presents an even stronger case for requiring disclosure, since it is more likely she would use it primarily for personal, family and household purposes.

The purpose of TIL is to provide consumers with meaningful disclosures of credit terms and conditions, and encourage the informed use of credit. 15 U.S.C. §1601(a). Theoretically TIL permits a consumer to "shop for credit" and thus compensate for a weaker bargaining position compared with business and commercial borrowers. Mrs. Gallegos did not have an ongoing business when she purchased the truck, nor the prospect of establishing one. She was a widow with a fifth grade education, who traded her only car and personal jewelry in on this purchase. Even if we take her testimony in the light most favorable to Stokes, she was a person engaged in a consumer credit transaction of the type intended to be protected by the required TIL disclosures.

We therefore affirm the trial court award of damages, costs and attorney's fees. Mrs. Gallegos is also entitled to attorney's fees for the successful defense of this appeal. See Thomas v. Myers-Dickson Furniture Co., 479 F.2d 740 (5th Cir. 1973). We grant an additional $300 for attorney's fees for the appeal.

––––––––––––

The line between personal, household, and family versus business use may be blurred more frequently in today's economy. As more people work from home or are employed as freelance consultants, there may be more overlap in their activities as consumers and businesses. Michael Troncoso, *The Sharing Economy's Next Phase: The Active Venue Firm*, (June 30, 2015), http://www.law360.com/articles/673249/the-sharing-economy-s-next-phase-the-active-venue-firm.

The increasing number of independent contractors and sole proprietorships also raises questions about whether consumer law's assumption that consumers need protection but businesses can protect themselves is useful. Do people really become more sophisticated or rational, or turn into better negotiators, when they lose their jobs and start performing the same work for a fee rather than for wages? If small business is the key to the American economy, shouldn't they enjoy the same protections from larger businesses as consumers?

The European Union has struggled with this issue. While its law does not apply to legal persons, even if they have a non-business character, such as a non-profit association, many of the E.U. member states have a broader reach. *See* Ewoud Hondius, *The Notion of Consumer: European Union versus Member States*, 28 SYDNEY L. REV. 89 (2006). The justification is that some types of legal entities are just fictions for an individual person making a decision, such as with sole proprietorships.

C. Who Is Consumer Law Trying to Protect?

Even if it distinguishes between people acting as consumers and people acting as business people, consumer law must grapple with another issue of identity. Who is "the consumer" that the law is trying to protect? The legal solution to a perceived problem will depend on who is being harmed. In consumer law, this issue often squarely raises a debate about the degree to which the law should expect consumers to protect themselves. This abstract problem in conceptualizing the consumer has crucial implications for policy. It also can powerfully affect the enforcement of consumer laws because regardless of the written law, the resources might only be expended for a lawsuit if it is perceived that consumers are being taken advantage of.

People, even narrowed to those living in America, have a wide variety of characteristics that bear on how they engage in consumer transactions. Demographic qualities such as educational attainment, age, and race may shape how consumers make purchases or choose financial products. Other factors related to a consumer's life experience, including fluency in English, or whether the consumer has a special status under the law, such as being a veteran or receiving government benefits, may also suggest that a different set of protections is appropriate. The challenge for policymakers is identifying the qualities that might be relevant to the appropriate scope of the law and to balance the need to protect some consumers with the law against the desire to give freedom to other consumers from the law.

Consumer law takes its cue on constructing the consumer from the common law of tort and contract. At the simplest level, the issue is similar to that of the infamous "eggshell plaintiff" and the tort doctrine that you take your defendant as you find him. *See* MARC A. FRANKLIN, ROBERT L. RABIN & MICHAEL D. GREEN, TORT LAW AND ALTERNATIVES CASES AND MATERIALS 394 (9th ed. 2011). Some consumers have the equivalent of eggshell skulls when it comes to their financial transactions. They may have little education or experience, or merely may be particularly gullible or susceptible to sales pressure. What level of sophistication should a business be able to assume of its consumers? Are businesses required to assess a consumer's understanding of a deal or risk being unable to enforce it later?

In contracts, this discussion usually centers on unconscionability, a justification for a court's refusal to enforce a bargain. Nearly every contracts law book presents *Williams v. Walker-Thomas Furniture Co.* to illustrate the doctrine. 350 F.2d 445 (D.C. Cir. 1965). Its key elements are an absence of meaningful choice, often created by gross inequality of bargaining power, and contract terms that are unreasonably favorable to the other party. Inequality of bargaining power often corresponds to demographic and economic characteristics, most obviously low incomes. Recall that Ms. Williams was a welfare recipient when she engaged in the purchases at issue in that case. The implication of the case is that those in poverty or who suffer other disadvantages that create bargaining inequities should be given special protection by the law. They are one type of "eggshell" consumer and perhaps consumer laws should be designed to protect the most vulnerable, rather than the typical or average consumer. The consequence is restricted freedom of contract for the most sophisticated. This debate is being played out in the wake of the mortgage crisis over the desirability of products like complex adjustable-rate mortgages. These products may be appropriate for a small subset of consumers with particular financial circumstances and the acumen to understand their risks and consequence. The typical American may be better suited to a traditional long-term fixed-rate mortgage. The debate continues on whether regulations to ban the complex products are appropriate on the basis that a majority (or even vast majority) of consumers would be better served by simpler products.

This discussion about the ideal consumer implicates racial discrimination and other forms of economic oppression. The stereotypical consumer in the minds of lawmakers may have an income, education, and credit market access that are more common among white Americans. For example, the laws protecting certain assets of debtors may mirror the typical wealth accumulation of white families, who are more likely to be homeowners than non-white families of similar means, and thus to benefit from homestead protections. *See* A. Mechele Dickerson, *Race Matters in Bankruptcy*, 61 WASH. & LEE L. REV. 1725 (2004). Similar issues arise in assessing the value of mandating disclosures in a consumer's primary language. If one thinks non-English speakers are a small fraction of the population, the costs of such disclosures may seem unduly onerous to business. The cost-benefit analysis is different if one knows that the fraction of non-English speakers is sizeable. In the U.S. Census, 2011 American Community Survey, 20.8 percent — about 60.6 million people — do not speak English. About two-thirds of these people speak Spanish.

These discussions about race, gender, class, and other issues are often difficult. One's instinct, regardless of one's substantive views, may be to allow the issue to be latent, an undercurrent to discussions about consumer "sophistication" that remains unspoken. The subject has now been raised by your casebook, hopefully encouraging you and your classmates to explore these issues as they present themselves in the remainder of the course. Later in this book, the separate laws that prohibit discrimination toward racial minorities, women, immigrants, and others in purchasing goods and obtaining credit are studied in detail.

D. Special Categories of Consumers

Contract law restricts the enforceability of contracts entered into by minors. It also refuses to enforce contracts when one party lacks mental capacity.

The focus of both restrictions is to limit contracting activity to people who are able to understand the deal and appreciate its effects. These rules continue to apply in contracts for consumer goods and services and are supplemented by special rules for particular groups of consumers. One example is the restriction on the issuance of a credit card to any person under the age of 21, unless they have an adult co-signer or can establish proof that they have the means to repay their likely debts. 15 U.S.C. §1637(c)(8). This rule may reflect the perceptions about the complexity of credit cards; they are just too complicated in their terms for people between the age of 18 (the typical age of majority for contract) and 21. Some parents supported the rule on different grounds. They noted that if their children became overindebted, the parents as a practical matter would pay off such debts. It made sense, the argument went, to require a co-signer and avoid parental surprise. Interestingly, there is no similar limitation on higher dollar amounts of credit, such as car loans and mortgages, which are legally available to those 18 years and older.

At the other end of the age spectrum from students are older Americans. This group of consumers also raises concerns about financial sophistication and mental capacity. One in five people aged 80 years or more has dementia but the condition is often undiagnosed or does not result in a loss of legal capacity to contract (although it may latter be raised as a defense to the contract). Older Americans may also have fewer contacts with government, workplaces, and social centers where they may learn about new financial products or may be less likely to use the power of the Internet to identify scams. They may also have different attitudes about being able to trust financial institutions or intermediaries. *See generally* Deborah Thorne, *The (Interconnected) Reasons that Elder Americans File Consumer Bankruptcy*, 22 J. AGING & SOC. POL'Y 188 (2010); Priscilla Vargas Wrosch, *What More Can Congress Do About the Elder Abuse Epidemic? A Proposal for National Movement*, 23 TEMP. POL. & CIV. RTS. L. REV. 1 (2013). As a result of these and similar issues, many elder law practitioners spend a significant amount of their client representation working on consumer law problems.

Reverse mortgages are a financial product designed for older Americans, who have often built up substantial equity in their homes. The loans can provide funds either in a fixed amount or as a line of credit (or a combination of both) and do not require repayment until the house is sold (likely to be when the person dies or moves to housing for seniors). The government requires an information session from a specially-trained reverse-mortgage counselor as a condition of its reverse mortgage program. While some of this is due to the complexity of the product, similar counseling was never required for other "exotic" mortgages such as 2-28 teaser ARMs (see, even the name is mystifying!). The counseling probably reflects normative desires to protect older Americans from disastrous financial mistakes and a belief that as an empirical matter older Americans are less able to protect themselves in financial transactions than their younger counterparts. Another example of additional protection for older American is a North Dakota statute that generally gives consumers three days to change their minds and cancel a door-to-door sale, but extends that period to fifteen days for consumers over 65 years of age. N.D. Cent. Code §51-18-02.

Another group of people subject to special consumer rules are members of the armed forces. The "Talent Amendment" to the defense appropriations bill of 2007 imposed limitations on and requirements for certain kinds of consumer credit extended to active duty military and their spouses and dependents. Pub. L. 109-364, §670 (codified at 10 U.S.C. §987). Its most controversial provision is the creation of a price restriction on consumer credit; the "military annual percentage rate" cannot exceed 36 percent. Depending on interest rates at the time, this figure may not seem unduly restrictive. One might observe that most credit cards, car loans, and other transactions carry lower rates. The Talent Amendment, however, regulates high-cost, short-term credit: payday loans, motor vehicle title loans, and tax refund anticipation loans. These transactions often carry annual percentage rates above 100 percent and sometime as high as 500 percent. Given the hostility of modern consumer law to price regulation, the Talent Amendment is an important enactment.

The justifications for intervention in the credit markets available to service members illustrate some concerns beyond the typical fears about vulnerable citizens. After all, if you are brave enough to serve on active duty, surely you can protect yourself from a piece of paper and a pushy loan officer? The evidence suggested the fallacy of this assumption. A study by Steven Graves and Christopher Peterson on the geography of payday loans showed that military counties and zip codes have very high densities of payday lenders compared to non-military areas. Stephen M. Graves & Christopher Peterson, *Predatory Lending and the Military: The Law and Geography of "Payday" Loans*, 66 Ohio St. L.J. 653 (2005). Their findings suggest that payday lenders target service members because they are a highly profitable demographic. Numerous military leaders testified about the effects of unmanageable debts on troop morale and on the quality of life for service members. Bad credit could undermine military readiness, either because troops were distracted by debt problems facing their household or because debt problems were grounds for losing security clearance. Another point was that high-cost credit strained the ability of military families to make ends meet. Salaries come out of the tax coffers, and so perhaps the government should have a greater say in the degree to which service members commit themselves to paying off hundreds of dollars of interest each month.

One interesting debate was over the assertion that service members needed protection because of their financial naivety. Service members frequently are young and they may have limited experience with financial transactions. Countering this argument was the military's required program of financial literacy. Unlike typical Americans, most of whom are never required to take a financial education class, service members attend mandatory sessions where the basics of credit math are taught. The Talent Amendment may reflect a conclusion that such education cannot fully substitute for substantive regulation, a point considered more fully in Assignment 26.

Problem Set 2

2.1. After trying the practice of law for a year, Janis Wallace decided she was better suited to life as a law professor. She is on the tenure track at Hogg University in Iowa and under pressure to produce a fascinating article on her area of specialty, consumer law, before the end of the academic year. Her personal charm and notoriously short reading assignments have made her a very popular teacher, however, and when she is in her office, she struggles to write her article because of student interruptions. She has taken to working each morning at her local branch of a national coffee shop. She has learned to sip a $1.65 cup of tea for four hours, while enjoying a clean table, comfy chair, and complimentary Wi-Fi for research.

Yesterday, while doing some research on Wikipedia, a virus attacked Professor Wallace's computer, decimating all of its memory and all of her work on her tenure article. The virus attack occurred when the store Wi-Fi was hijacked and involuntarily redirected her to a hacker site that infected the computer. After the attack, Professor Wallace burst into tears for a good hour, like a fragile academic, and then reverted to her lawyer roots by threatening to sue the coffee shop for its defective Wi-Fi. The manager admitted that the store provided no firewall or made any other effort to secure its Wi-Fi against intruders, but refused to provide her with any compensation (not even a free tea!), announcing that "you get what you pay for."

Professor Wallace has realized that she will not get tenure and instead has thrown herself into her lawsuit against the coffee shop. You are its in-house counsel, and the complaint is on your desk. What are your best arguments and tactics to defeat Professor Wallace's action under the unfair or deceptive acts and practices law? Iowa Code §714.16(1) and (2).

2.2. Your law school classmate, Ricardo Levin, chose the big firm route, spending the last six years working on discovery in a single case; you established a solo practice doing a bit of everything. Ricardo posted to Facebook yesterday that he needed a "real" lawyer to represent him. Intrigued, you called Ricardo and learned that his big firm went big-time bankrupt. Ricardo has been receiving letters from Barristers Bank, relating to a credit card that his firm gave him to use for entertaining clients, his extensive travel to client locations, and other purposes. When his firm was short on cash and changed its reimbursement policy, Ricardo continued to use the card to pay for meals and taxis when he worked late out of habit.

In the firm's bankruptcy, Barristers Bank was paid only ten cents for each dollar it was owed. It is now threatening to sue Ricardo for the rest of the debt. Ricardo has looked at the credit card agreement he was given. It clearly states that he is personally obligated on the debt if his firm fails to pay. Ricardo wonders if perhaps he can settle this matter, or even make it go away, by finding Barristers Bank liable for some mistake in the credit card transaction.

You ask Ricardo to send you all the paperwork he was given when the card was issued and note that no Truth-in-Lending disclosure was provided. What do you need to know to figure out whether a TILA disclosure should have been given? How will you get such information? 15 U.S.C. §§1602(i) and 1603; 12 C.F.R. §1026, Supplement I — Official Staff Interpretation 1026.3(a).

2.3. You are the senior aide to the Chair of the House Committee on Government Oversight. A constituent has recently expressed concern that the Consumer Financial Protection Bureau (CFPB) may target her business of making loans to students in the weeks before school starts when they are waiting for their financial aid checks to arrive. You remind the constituent that section 1013 of the Dodd-Frank Act requires the CFPB to have two units focused on certain kinds of consumers and point out that students are not mentioned. The constituent suggests that you "review the organizational chart on CFPB's website (www.consumerfinance.gov/the-bureau) and get back to her when you've figured out how to reign in this overreaching government." What does your investigation reveal? What should the Committee do in response, if anything, about this situation? The committee members will want to know their legal options as well as the policy and political concerns.

Assignment 3.   Who Makes Consumer Law?

Consumer law comes from a number of sources. First, there are the kinds of law (e.g., the source of that doctrine is statutory). Statutes and regulations are the most voluminous, and therefore probably onerous source of consumer law. The common law of contract and tort continue to be important, however, and increasingly consumer law is even popping up in other places such as trade treaties. All of these laws are interpreted and applied by courts or take on practical meaning from consensual settlements. Second, there are the kinds of lawmakers (e.g., the source of that doctrine is federal). Consumer laws exist at the international, federal, state, and local levels. Preemption is a major issue in consumer law, as actors battle for the right to make law. This Assignment provides a directory of the players in making consumer law and describes cooperation or conflict that characterizes their interactions.

A.   Types of Law

1. Statutes

Most consumer law is statutory. It is difficult to conclude whether federal or state statutes are more important. For some issues, one lawmaker is dominant, while for others there is a balance of power. Federal legislation obviously is more sweeping in scope, while the impact of state legislation is more modest. That is primarily a function of the number of consumers in any given state's population, although some states have an outsized effect because many institutions are chartered there. The prevalence of credit card companies in South Dakota is a good example. On the other hand, the states are often more aggressive in their lawmaking, acting before there is awareness or consensus at the federal level that a law is needed. The National Mortgage Settlement between the five largest mortgage servicers and 49 states' attorneys general illustrates this dynamic. The deal was reached in February 2012, and its standards were nearly entirely swept into the CFPB's mortgage servicing regulations, but were not effective until January 2014.

When a bill is passed by both parts of Congress and signed by the President, it becomes a public law. It receives a public law number to uniquely identify it that begins with the session of Congress in which the bill was passed. It also has a common name, as specified in the bill text. For example, the Dodd-Frank Wall Street Reform and Consumer Protection Act is Public Law 111-203. These laws are published quickly in the Statutes-At-Large by the government printing office. The Dodd-Frank Act begins at 124 Stat. 1376.

Most consumer law, because it is permanent and substantive (as opposed to something like an appropriation budget that is specific to one year), is then "codified." This means that it inserted into the United States Code at a particular location. The U.S. Code is broken down into titles, each of which cover large areas of substantive law. For instance, Title 12 is called "Banks and Banking." This book uses the U.S. Code to identify statutes whenever possible for consistency purposes and for ease of research. Be warned though that some of the most important consumer laws are still commonly referenced in the practice world by the section numbers contained in their public laws. A good example of this is the 1994 Home Ownership and Equity Protection Act (HOEPA), which is codified in TILA, of the Consumer Credit Protection Act, at 15 U.S.C. §1639. Nonetheless, people talk about "HOEPA loans" rather than referring to these generally under TILA.

The most complete codification of federal consumer law is in the Consumer Credit Protection Act. The seven subchapters studied in this course, along with their common names and acronyms, are:

I.	Consumer Credit Cost Disclosure (Truth in Lending Act, TILA or TIL)	15 U.S.C. §§1601-1677
III.	Restrictions on Garnishment	15 U.S.C. §§1671-1677
IV.	Credit Repair Organizations Act (CROA)	15 U.S.C. §§1679-1679j
VI.	Fair Credit Reporting Act (Fair Credit Reporting Act, FCRA)	15 U.S.C. §§1681-1681x
VII.	Equal Credit Opportunity Act (ECOA)	15 U.S.C. §§1691-1691f
VIII.	Fair Debt Collection Practices Act (FDCPA)	15 U.S.C. §§1692-1692p
IX.	Electronic Fund Transfer Act (EFT)	15 U.S.C. §§1693-1693r

These laws were not all passed at the same time, but rather were brought together in the codification process. Some have been aggressively amended since enactment, such as TILA, while others remain largely in their original form, such as the FDCPA. In practice you are particularly likely to see the credit reporting, equal credit, and fair debt laws referenced by the section numbers from the public law, rather than the U.S. Code. This is partially because when these laws were put into the U.S. Code, numbers were in short supply. To avoid ticking up to §1700, entire acts were stuffed into one section number. The result, for the Fair Credit Reporting Act, is a numbering scheme of §1681, §1681a, §1681b, etc. Inside each of these sections are the usual subparts. Take a look at §1681c-1(a)(1)(A) for an example of how *not* to make an easy-to-reference law.

If this alphabet soup has your head swimming, take an aspirin before you continue reading. It gets worse (or more fun, for the few of you who love this kind of detail). The other federal consumer laws are scattered in the U.S. Code. The most important of these is the Federal Trade Commission Act, 15 U.S.C. §41 et seq., which makes unfair and deceptive practices unlawful. This law was the basis of the *Airborne* settlement featured in Assignment 1. Beyond this, people might differ on what federal consumer laws are most worthy of study. This book will examine several, including the Real Estate Settlement Procedures Act (RESPA), the Telemarketing and Consumer Fraud and Abuse Prevention Act, the Gramm-Leach-Bliley Act, the Magnuson-Moss Warranty Act, and the

Federal Arbitration Act. These are codified in different titles in the U.S. Code — in part, a reflection of the difficulty of conceptualizing consumer law.

Most statutes delegate additional authority to specific government agencies. In consumer law, the main activities are rulemaking and enforcement. The decisions of these agencies are constrained by administrative law. Its doctrines legitimate and limit the actions of agencies. Questions often arise about whether the agency's action is within its powers or within the boundaries of the statute. As a substantive matter, the primary constraint is the statute itself pursuant to which the agency is taking action. The Administrative Procedure Act, 5 U.S.C. §551 et seq., sets out the procedural requirements for federal agency activities. This includes notification and timing processes for making rules to implement statutes. Because consumer law is complex, regulations are many. The result is that administrative law serves as an important backdrop to all federal consumer law statutes. Agencies are also restricted in part by their structure, funding, and political pressures. Many lawyers earn a living helping clients influence rulemakings and comply with enacted rules.

States also are an important source of common law. In the interests of brevity, and perhaps a hope that you can retain some of this Assignment, these are not listed. Generally, these are covered in each assignment simultaneous to any applicable federal law. For example, Assignment 14 covers both federal law on mortgages as well as state laws that provide additional rules.

A general distinction in state statutes is between uniform state laws and non-uniform state laws. The best example here is the Uniform Commercial Code, which is identical or nearly identical in each state, as you might gather from its name. It is promulgated by non-government bodies, in this case the American Law Institute and the Uniform Law Commission, a project of the National Conference of Commissioners on Uniform State Laws (NCCUSL, pronounced "na-CUE-zal", similar to recusal). The uniform act is then enacted by all or many state legislatures, essentially unchanged. Because the law is then the same in all 50 states, these laws have broad applicability.

By contrast, other state laws may be one-of-a-kind or may sharply differ from state to state. A good illustration here is usury laws, which restrict the amount of interest that may be charged. Some states have no restrictions at all; other states have usury caps but these vary a great deal in the rate restriction and the transactions to which they apply. Another example is state laws that ban unfair and deceptive practices. These are not strictly uniform, but they do tend to follow certain patterns, as some states were influenced by their predecessors in drafting their own laws. These disparate state laws apply more narrowly than federal law or uniform state law; it is impossible to study them all. Instead, this book selects certain state laws to provide examples of representative state approaches. Problem 2.1 illustrated this approach by asking you to apply Iowa's unfair and deceptive acts and practices statute.

2. Regulations

Most federal consumer statutes empower one or more federal agencies to pass substantive rules (sometimes called legislative rules). These have the force and effect of law and must be rooted in the grant of power from Congress in the statute under which the rule is made. These rules effectively expand the statute by filling in details. Rules may provide factors to be considered in determining a violation of a law or define frequently used terms.

Most consumer law rules are made by informal or "notice and comment" rulemaking. This process has three major steps. First, the agency will give notice, usually by publication in the Federal Register. The notice should include either the terms or substance of the proposed rules and a description of the rules (called a "preamble"). Sometimes the agency will give an earlier form of notice, called an Advance Notice of Proposed Rulemaking, which provides less detail and invites participation at a more generic level. Second, time must elapse after notice to allow all interested persons the opportunity to submit comments on the proposed rules. The agency has a duty to consider the public comments. When it promulgates its final rule, it will normally address the nature of the received comments and the agency's reaction to those comments. Third, final rules are published in the Federal Register and codified in the Code of Federal Regulations (CFR). For the Consumer Credit Protection Act, these regulations have letters that identify the statute to which they correspond (Reg. Z, for example, accompanies TILA). This book will cite to the CFR, in parallel to its citation to the U.S. Code for statutes. Note that in similar fashion to statutes, the common text names such as Reg. Z or Reg. B are widely used rather than the CFR. Below is a quick guide to some of the key regulations.

Regulation Z	12 C.F.R. §1026: Truth in Lending
Regulation M	12 C.F.R. §1013: Consumer Leasing
Regulation B	12 C.F.R. §1002: Equal Credit Opportunity
Regulation E	12 C.F.R. §1005: Electronic Fund Transfers
Regulation V	12 C.F.R. §1022: FCRA Regulations
Military Lending Act	32 C.F.R. §232: Limitations on Terms of Consumer Credit Extended to Service Members and Dependents

3. Guidance/Commentary

In addition to rulemaking, agencies sometimes issue guidance documents. These lack the binding force of law and need only be published in the Federal Register for the agency to be able to rely upon them in taking action. The purpose of such guidance is to inform the public of the agency's interpretations and to promote consistency among agency personnel on how to apply ambiguous laws or to address new situations. Depending on the agency, these can take different forms, including bulletins, manuals, interpretive guidelines, official staff commentary, etc. This less formal lawmaking is widely used by some agencies but eschewed by others.

4. Case Law

The prominence of statutes in consumer law does not make cases irrelevant. Courts interpret ambiguous statutes, apply them to unique factual situations, and sometimes overturn either statutes or rules. The prevalence of case law depends a great deal on the statute and the level of litigation it generates. There are hundreds of cases on certain issues and virtually no cases on other issues. The number of cases does not reflect the frequency with which the issue arises or its social importance. Rather, litigation — and published opinions in particular — mirror the ability of consumers to file complaints and litigate through the courts. If damages are small or an area of law is complex, fewer consumers may file suit.

B.   Federal Government

The two main federal agencies in today's consumer law landscape are the Federal Trade Commission (FTC) and the Consumer Financial Protection Bureau (CFPB). They have different responsibilities, structures, funding, and oversight. The balance of power between the CFPB and the FTC is evolving as the CFPB was created in July 2010 and had its effective "transfer date" of authority from the FTC and other agencies in July 2011.

1.   Federal Trade Commission

administrator p.roce
injuction only

The Federal Trade Commission has authority to regulate unfair practices "in or affecting interstate commerce." 15 U.S.C. §45 et seq. In the decades since that law was enacted in 1938, the FTC has promulgated regulations on hundreds of industries, ranging from fur products to funeral homes. The FTC regulations are codified in title 16 of the Code of Federal Regulations. These have the force of law. The FTC also has issued guidance documents on several statutes, including the Magnuson-Moss Warranty Act. These are not regulations but provide insight about how the FTC might react to a particular practice in deciding whether to bring an action.

The FTC has a narrower swath of responsibility in the financial services area than before the creation of the CFPB, but it is still a significant player. It shares authority with the CFPB on some issues. For non-financial industries or laws other than "federal consumer law" as defined in Dodd-Frank (see Assignment 2), the FTC is the primary consumer regulator. The FTC also retains exclusive federal authority over dealers of automobiles, boats, motor homes, and the like, even when these dealers engage in consumer lending that would otherwise subject them to CFPB oversight. 12 U.S.C. §5519.

The FTC is a five-member commission. Its key powers, in addition to rule-making, are an ability to obtain information and the ability to litigate. Section 6(b) of the FTC Act empowers the commission to require the filing of "annual or special . . . reports or answers in writing to specific questions" for the purpose of obtaining information about "the organization, business, conduct, practices, management, and relation to other corporations, partnerships, and individuals" of the entities to whom the inquiry is addressed. This enables it to conduct wide-ranging economic studies that do not have a specific law enforcement purpose. For example, the FTC has studied debt collection. *See* Repairing a Broken System: Protecting Consumers in Debt Collection Litigation (July 2010), http://www.ftc.gov/os/2010/07/debtcollectionreport.pdf), and children using the Internet. *See* Virtual Worlds and Kids: Mapping the Risks: A Federal Trade Commission Report to Congress (December 2009), http://www.ftc.gov/os/2009/12/oecd-vwrpt.pdf. The commission can also investigate possible unfair or deceptive acts or practices by making a "civil investigative demand." 15 U.S.C. §57b-1. An amendment in 1980 eliminated the ability of the FTC to use traditional subpoenas for its consumer protection work, although that power remains for its antitrust activities. The civil investigative demand lets the FTC obtain existing documents and oral testimony, require the filing of written reports or answers to questions, and require the production of tangible things. Businesses that fail to comply with a civil investigative demand could face suit in federal court and penalties for noncompliance.

The FTC enforces consumer protection law through both judicial and administrative processes. The FTC can seek preliminary and permanent injunctions to remedy "any provision of law enforced by the Federal Trade Commission." 15 U.S.C. §53(b). Courts have held that the statutory reference to "permanent injunction" entitles the FTC to obtain an order not only permanently barring deceptive practices, but also imposing various kinds of monetary equitable relief (*i.e.*, restitution and rescission of contracts) to remedy past violations. *See FTC v. Ross*, 743 F.3d 866, 891 (2013). The FTC also has successfully argued that to preserve the possibility of ultimate monetary equitable relief, it can obtain a freeze of assets and imposition of temporary receivers in appropriate cases.

In the administrative process, the FTC makes the initial determination that a practice violates the law in either an adjudicative or rulemaking proceeding. To issue a complaint, the FTC must have reason to believe that a law violation has occurred. If the party elects to settle the charges, it may sign a consent agreement (without admitting liability), consent to entry of a final order, and waive all right to judicial review. These agreements are placed in the public record for comment before the FTC decides to make the orders final. If a party elects to contest the charges, the complaint is adjudicated before an administrative law judge in a trial-type proceeding. If the administrative law judge determines a practice is unfair or deceptive, the FTC must still seek the aid of a court to obtain civil penalties or consumer redress for violations of its orders to cease and desist or trade regulation rules. For this reason, a judicial suit is preferable to the adjudicatory process. Nearly all consumer protection enforcement by the FTC occurs outside the administrative adjudication process.

2. Consumer Financial Protection Bureau

In July 2010, Congress created a Consumer Financial Protection Bureau as part of its sweeping financial overhaul in the Dodd-Frank Wall Street Reform and Consumer Protection Act, 12 U.S.C. §5481. Its enumerated purpose is to "seek to implement and, where applicable, enforce Federal consumer financial law consistently for the purpose of ensuring that all consumers have access to markets for consumer financial products and services and that markets for consumer financial products and services are fair, transparent, and competitive." 12 U.S.C. §5511. The statute set forth six specific functions of the CFPB:

(1) conducting financial education programs;

(2) collecting, investigating, and responding to consumer complaints;

(3) collecting, researching, monitoring, and publishing information relevant to the functioning of markets for consumer financial products and services to identify risks to consumers and the proper functioning of such markets;

(4) supervising covered persons for compliance with Federal consumer financial law, and taking appropriate enforcement action to address violations of Federal consumer financial law;

(5) issuing rules, orders, and guidance implementing Federal consumer financial law; and

(6) performing such support activities as may be necessary or useful to facilitate the other functions of the Bureau.

12 U.S.C. §5511. The federal consumer law that is the CFPB's province is defined to include 17 federal statutes. The CFPB consolidated regulatory authority over banks and non-banks in one location. Previously, depending on the charter, a financial institution could face different rules and enforcement activity. National banks were regulated by the Office of Comptroller of the Currency (OCC), while other state-chartered banks had the Federal Deposit Insurance Corporation (FDIC) and the Federal Reserve Board as regulators. The model of the CFPB is regulation by product type, rather than by provider type. Now, all entities that issue credit cards will be governed by the CFPB and its single set of rules. In its rulemaking activities, the CFPB is subject to the normal strictures of the Administrative Procedures Act.

The CFPB is structurally part of the Federal Reserve Board but has several measures of independence. 12 U.S.C. §5491. Its Director is appointed by the President and confirmed by the Senate, with a five-year term that can be terminated only for cause. The statute prohibits the Federal Reserve from intervening in any matter or delaying or preventing the issuance of any CFPB rule or order. Congress has directed the CFPB to coordinate with other banking regulators and the FTC to "promote consistent regulatory treatment of consumer financial and investment products and services." 12 U.S.C. §5495. The budget for the CFPB is not subject to typical appropriations but rather is to be "an amount determined by the Director to be reasonably necessary" up to a maximum of 12 percent of the Federal Reserve's operating budget. 12 U.S.C. §5497.

In addition to being charged with "carry[ing] out the purposes and objectives of the Federal consumer financial laws, and to prevent evasions thereof," 12 U.S.C. §5511, the CFPB has also a separate generic charge that is reminiscent of the FTC Act. Its powers include the ability to "take any action . . . to prevent a covered person or service provider from committing or engaging in an unfair, deceptive, or abusive act or practice under Federal law in connection with any transaction with a consumer for a consumer financial product or service, or the offering of a consumer financial product or service." 12 U.S.C. §5531. The financial services industry has latched on to the word "abusive" as a major addition to the FTC Act's reference to "unfair or deceptive"; the term seems to have produced sleepless nights among bank attorneys and their outside counsel. Perhaps in response to this industry anxiety, the CFPB waited years after its creation — until 2014 — to assert that a practice was abusive. The substantive definitions of unfair, deceptive, and abusive are the subject of Part II of this book.

In enforcing federal consumer law or preventing unfair, deceptive, or abusive practices, the CFPB has an array of enforcement powers. These tools include the power to issue subpoenas, conduct hearings, issue cease and desist orders, and file actions in federal district court or state court for "all appropriate legal and equitable relief including a permanent or temporary injunction as permitted by law." 12 U.S.C. §5563. The CFPB can also file suit to result in the rescission of contracts, refunds of money, disgorgement for unjust enrichment, damages, and civil penalties. 12 U.S.C. §5565.

3. Other Regulators

Before 2011, the list of other federal regulators of consumer law would have been lengthy and included the Federal Reserve Board, the Office of the Comptroller of the Currency, the Federal Deposit Insurance Corporation, the National Credit Union Administration, and the Office of Thrift Supervision (now defunct), among others. For consumer financial services, enforcement now resides with the CFPB. Some agencies still have enforcement powers on some types of consumer statutes — if that term is broadly defined — but had a significant amount of their powers transferred to the CFPB. The Department of Housing and Urban Development (HUD) retains full authority over the Fair Housing Act, for example, but its powers related to the Real Estate Settlement Procedures Act were transferred to the CFPB. Most of these regulations still exist but focus on the safety and soundness of the financial institutions, not compliance with consumer law.

C. State and Local Government as Lawmakers

1. Attorneys General

Attorneys general are the chief law enforcement officer for the states. They have myriad responsibilities, including defending the state in lawsuits. Some attorneys general place relatively more emphasis on consumer protection than others, and this often changes with the elected person's priorities. In recent years, attorneys general are working more frequently together on "multistate" actions; their combined power is formidable as the tobacco settlement revealed.

Attorneys general are able to enforce their state's unfair and deceptive practices act. The attorneys general may also have responsibility under other state laws that are on limited substantive topics. Attorneys general receive and try to resolve consumer complaints, produce consumer education materials, publicize frauds or scams, and conduct investigations into companies' business practices. The attorneys general also file lawsuits when they believe a business is violating a consumer protection law. Usually, such action is reserved for situations in which there have been a large number of complaints, a pattern or practice of fraud, or an important question of law is at issue. When litigating, the attorney general represents the public good and not individual complainants. Depending on the relief obtained, however, consumers may receive restitution as a result of litigation.

2. State Banking Regulators

Each state has a person in charge of state-chartered banks (as opposed to banks that have a federal charter) issued by an organization such as the Office of the Comptroller of the Currency or the National Credit Union Administration. Nearly all very large banks have federal charters. These "Banking Commissioners," or "Superintendents of Banking," regulate the financial institutions through examinations. Some state banking authorities are very active in consumer protection, such as Colorado's Department of Banking declaring that it "embraces [its] mission of consumer protection and works to protect public interest and preserve public trust in the Colorado banking industry." Others do very little consumer protection enforcement. Because banks have a choice between a state or a federal charter, concern arose about a "race to the bottom" among regulators to attract financial institutions seeking reduced consumer protection burdens. The consolidation of federal authority in the CFPB addressed competition between federal regulators but not between state agencies and federal agencies.

3.   City Government

During the last decade, a few city governments have taken an active interest in consumer law. New York City has mandated calorie and nutritional labeling on menus for most restaurants, and San Francisco launched a major investigation of the practices of a credit card issuer. Cities' recent activism largely has been motivated by the harms of the foreclosure crisis that began in 2007. Vacant properties after foreclosure can lead to delinquent tax bills, higher crime, and public nuisance problems, such as abandoned swimming pools or overgrown yards. The city of Baltimore filed three separate lawsuits, beginning in 2008, against Wells Fargo Bank, alleging that it violated the Fair Housing Act by targeting minority neighborhoods with unaffordable loans. The city claimed tens of millions in damages, and the U.S. Department of Justice got involved. After a brief but vigorous defense, Wells Fargo settled with the federal government for $175 million, about $10 million of which went to Baltimore and its residents.

D. Preemption

While consumer law was traditionally the province of the States, in the post-New Deal era, Congress promulgated more federal consumer law. As a result, federal regulators grew in size and power. The result was an increasing number of conflicts about whether a given federal law preempted a state law. In the banking context, the Supreme Court issued a number of decisions favorable to federal regulators, beginning with *Marquette National Bank of Minneapolis v. First of Omaha Service Corp.* 439 U.S. 299 (1978).

The Dodd-Frank Act reshaped the preemption landscape, tilting back toward more equal authority between state and federal actors. First, Congress made clear that Dodd-Frank itself was not designed to enlarge federal power at the expense of the states. If a state's statute, regulation, order, or interpretation provides greater protection than Dodd-Frank, it is not "inconsistent" with the provisions of 12 U.S.C. §5551. Second, Dodd-Frank reversed *Watters v. Wachovia Bank, N.A.*, 550 U.S. 1 (2007); bank operating subsidiaries are now subject to state law. Third, the standard for preemption for consumer financial laws was changed.

> State consumer financial laws are preempted, only if [1] "application of a State consumer financial law would have a discriminatory effect on national banks, in comparison with the effect of the law on a bank chartered by that State, and [2] in accordance with the legal standard for preemption in [*Barnett Bank v. Nelson*], the State consumer financial law prevents or significantly interferes with the exercise by the national bank of its powers; or by regulation or order of the Comptroller of the Currency on a case-by-case basis, in accordance with applicable law.

12 U.S.C. §25. The effect of this statutory language is unclear. The first step in untangling the morass is to study the *Barnett* decision.

Barnett Bank of Marion County, N.A. v. Bill Nelson, Florida Insurance Commissioner, et al.
517 U.S. 25 (1996)

BREYER, Justice.

In 1916 Congress enacted a federal statute that says that certain national banks "may" sell insurance in small towns. It provides in relevant part:

> "In addition to the powers now vested by law in national [banks] organized under the laws of the United States *any such [bank]* located and doing business in any place [with a population] . . . [of not more than] five thousand . . . *may*, under such rules and regulations as may be prescribed by the Comptroller of the Currency, *act as the agent for any fire, life, or other insurance company* authorized by the authorities of the

State . . . to do business [there], . . . by soliciting and selling insurance . . . Provided, however, That no such bank shall . . . guarantee the payment of any premium . . . And provided further, That the bank shall not guarantee the truth of any statement made by an assured [when applying] . . . for insurance." Act of Sept. 7, 1916 (Federal Statute), 39 Stat. 753, 12 U.S.C. §92 (emphases changed).

In 1974 Florida enacted a statute that prohibits certain banks from selling most kinds of insurance. It says:

"No [Florida licensed] insurance agent . . . who is associated with, . . . owned or controlled by . . . a financial institution shall engage in insurance agency activities. . . ." Fla. Stat. Ann. §626.988(2) (Supp. 1996) (State Statute).

The term "financial institution" includes

"any bank . . . [except for a] bank which is not a subsidiary or affiliate of a bank holding company and is located in a city having a population of less than 5,000. . . ." §626.988(1)(a).

Thus, the State Statute says, in essence, that banks cannot sell insurance in Florida — except that an *unaffiliated* small town bank (*i.e.,* a bank that is not affiliated with a bank holding company) may sell insurance in a small town. Ibid.

In October 1993 petitioner Barnett Bank, an "affiliate[d]" national bank which does business through a branch in a small Florida town, bought a Florida licensed insurance agency. The Florida State Insurance Commissioner, pointing to the State Statute, (and noting that the unaffiliated small town bank exception did not apply), ordered Barnett's insurance agency to stop selling the prohibited forms of insurance. Barnett, claiming that the Federal Statute pre-empted the State Statute, then filed this action for declaratory and injunctive relief in federal court. . . .

We granted certiorari due to uncertainty among lower courts about the pre-emptive effect of this Federal Statute. We now reverse the Eleventh Circuit.

We shall . . . begin by asking whether, in the absence of that rule, we should construe the Federal Statute to pre-empt the State Statute. This question is basically one of congressional intent. Did Congress, in enacting the Federal Statute, intend to exercise its constitutionally delegated authority to set aside the laws of a State? If so, the Supremacy Clause requires courts to follow federal, not state, law. U.S. Const., Art. VI, cl. 2.

Sometimes courts, when facing the pre-emption question, find language in the federal statute that reveals an explicit congressional intent to pre-empt state law. More often, explicit pre-emption language does not appear, or does not directly answer the question. In that event, courts must consider whether the federal statute's "structure and purpose," or nonspecific statutory language, nonetheless reveal a clear, but implicit, pre-emptive intent. A federal statute, for example, may create a scheme of federal regulation "so pervasive as to make reasonable the inference that Congress left no room for the States to supplement it." Rice v. Santa Fe Elevator Corp., 331 U.S. 218, 230 (1947). Alternatively, federal law may be in "irreconcilable conflict" with state law. Rice v. Norman Williams Co., 458 U.S. 654, 659 (1982). Compliance with both statutes, for example, may be a "physical impossibility," Florida Lime & Avocado Growers, Inc. v. Paul, 373 U.S. 132, 142-143

(1963); or, the state law may "stan[d] as an obstacle to the accomplishment and execution of the full purposes and objectives of Congress." Hines v. Davidowitz, 312 U.S. 52, 67 (1941).

In this case we must ask whether or not the Federal and State Statutes are in "irreconcilable conflict." The two statutes do not impose directly conflicting duties on national banks — as they would, for example, if the federal law said, "you must sell insurance," while the state law said, "you may not." Nonetheless, the Federal Statute authorizes national banks to engage in activities that the State Statute expressly forbids. Thus, the State's prohibition of those activities would seem to "stan[d] as an obstacle to the accomplishment" of one of the Federal Statute's purposes — unless, of course, that federal purpose is to grant the bank only a very *limited* permission, that is, permission to sell insurance *to the extent that state law also grants permission to do so.*

That is what the State of Florida and its supporting *amici* argue. They say that the Federal Statute grants national banks a permission that is limited to circumstances where state law is not to the contrary. In their view, the Federal Statute removes only federal legal obstacles, not state legal obstacles, to the sale of insurance by national banks. But we do not find this, or the State's related, ordinary pre-emption arguments convincing.

For one thing, the Federal Statute's language suggests a broad, not a limited, permission. That language says, without relevant qualification, that national banks "may . . . act as the agent" for insurance sales. 12 U.S.C. §92. It specifically refers to "rules and regulations" that will govern such sales, while citing as their source not state law, but the federal Comptroller of the Currency. Ibid. It also specifically refers to state regulation, while limiting that reference to licensing — not of banks or insurance agents, but of the insurance companies whose policies the bank, as insurance agent, will sell. Ibid.

For another thing, the Federal Statute says that its grant of authority to sell insurance is an "addition to the *powers* now vested by law in national [banks]." Ibid. (emphasis added). In using the word "powers," the statute chooses a legal concept that, in the context of national bank legislation, has a history. That history is one of interpreting grants of both enumerated and incidental "powers" to national banks as grants of authority not normally limited by, but rather ordinarily pre-empting, contrary state law. Thus, this Court, in a case quite similar to this one, held that a federal statute permitting, but not requiring, national banks to receive savings deposits, pre-empts a state statute prohibiting certain state and national banks from using the word "savings" in their advertising. Franklin Nat. Bank v. New York, 347 U.S. 373, 375-379 (1954) (Federal Reserve Act provision that national banks "may continue . . . to receive . . . savings deposits" read as "declaratory of the right of a national bank to enter into or remain in that type of business").

In defining the pre-emptive scope of statutes and regulations granting a power to national banks, these cases take the view that normally Congress would not want States to forbid, or to impair significantly, the exercise of a power that Congress explicitly granted. To say this is not to deprive States of the power to regulate national banks, where (unlike here) doing so does not prevent or significantly interfere with the national bank's exercise of its powers. See, e.g., Anderson Nat. Bank v. Luckett, 321 U.S. 233, 247-252 (1944) (state statute administering abandoned deposit accounts did not "unlawful[ly] encroac[h] on the rights and privileges of national banks"); McClellan v. Chipman, 164 U.S. 347, 358 (1896) (application to national banks of state statute forbidding certain real estate transfers by insolvent transferees would not "destro[y] or hampe[r]" national banks' functions); National Bank v. Commonwealth, 9 Wall. 353, 362 (1870) (national banks subject to state law that does not "interfere with, or impair [national banks'] efficiency in performing the functions by which they are designed to serve [the Federal] Government"). . . .

The Federal Statute before us, as in *Franklin Nat. Bank*, explicitly grants a national bank an authorization, permission, or power. And, as in *Franklin Nat. Bank*, it contains no "indication" that Congress intended to subject that power to local restriction. Thus, the Court's discussion in *Franklin Nat. Bank*, the holding of that case, and the other precedent we have cited above, strongly argue for a similar interpretation here — a broad interpretation of the word "may" that does not condition federal permission upon that of the State. . . .

In light of these considerations, we conclude that the Federal Statute means to grant small town national banks authority to sell insurance, whether or not a State grants its own state banks or national banks similar approval. Were we to apply ordinary legal principles of pre-emption, the federal law would pre-empt that of the State.

The Court reversed the judgment of the Court of Appeals. The result was to invalidate a state law that prohibited a national bank from engaging in an activity that federal law authorized. The question is how to apply this standard in narrower situations of preemption. Most advocates read the Dodd-Frank Act to weaken the federal government's ability to assert preemption. One regulator, the Office of Comptroller of the Currency (OCC), claimed that its broad preemption regulations were consistent with the *Barnett* standard. On July 21, 2011, the OCC issued a final rule that "clarified" its preemption standards.

> [T]he OCC concludes that the Dodd-Frank Act does not create a new, standalone "prevents or significantly interferes" preemption standard, but rather, incorporates the conflict preemption legal standard and the reasoning that supports it in the Supreme Court's *Barnett* decision. . . . The "legal standard for preemption" employed in the Court's decision is conflict preemption, applied in the context of powers granted national banks under Federal law. "Prevent or significantly interfere" is not "the legal standard for preemption in the decision"; it is part of the Court's discussion of its reasoning; an observation made describing other Supreme Court precedent that is cited in the Court's decision. . . . Accordingly, because we conclude that the Dodd-Frank Act preserves the *Barnett* conflict preemption standard, precedents consistent with that analysis — which may include regulations adopted consistent with such a conflict preemption justification — are also preserved. . . .
>
> Some commenters asserted that the "obstruct, impair, or condition" phrasing in the 2004 preemption rules was not only inconsistent with *Barnett* but also inconsistent with the new, narrower "prevents or significantly interferes" standard that they assert is imposed by the Dodd-Frank Act. As discussed above, we conclude that the Dodd-Frank Act *Barnett* standard is the conflict preemption standard employed in the Court's decision, not a new test. The

question remains, however, of the relationship between that standard and the "obstruct, impair or condition" formulation. . . . [T]he words "obstruct, impair or condition" as used in the 2004 preemption rules were intended to reflect the precedents cited in *Barnett*, not to create a new preemption standard. Nevertheless, we acknowledge that the phrase created confusion and misunderstanding well before enactment of the Dodd-Frank Act. We also recognize that inclusion of the "prevents or significantly interfere" conflict preemption formulation in the *Barnett* standard preemption provision may have been intended to change the OCC's approach by shifting the basis of preemption back to the decision itself, rather than placing reliance on the OCC's effort to distill the *Barnett* principles in this manner. . . . For these reasons, the OCC is deleting the phrase in the final rule.

OCC Final Rule, pertaining to 12 CFR Parts 4, 5, 7, 8, 28, and 34 (July 21, 2011), http://www.occ.gov/news-issuances/news-releases/2011/nr-occ-2011-95a.pdf.

The OCC's rule modifies the language of its preemption regulation but that, in its view, does not change any positions that the OCC has taken to date on preemption. This is certainly different than reverting to the preemption doctrine as existed at the time that *Barnett* was decided. These issues will almost certainly be raised in court challenges. An early decision, *Baptista v. JPMorgan Chase Bank, N.A.*, 640 F.3d 1194, 1197 (11th Cir. 2011), seems to side with the OCC, stating that "the proper preemption test asks whether there is a significant conflict between the state and federal statutes — that is, the test for conflict preemption." The standard for judicial review for OCC preemption regulations was clarified under Dodd-Frank. Rather than the deferential *Chevron* standard, the OCC's preemption regulations will require satisfying a court that substantial evidence supported the OCC's determination. Dodd-Frank also says that the OCC should make preemption decisions on a case-by-case basis and shall first consult with the CFPB, taking its views into account. 12 U.S.C. §25b. These additional requirements, plus the murky issues of interpretation around *Barnett*, suggest that preemption will remain an important battleground between businesses and consumers in the upcoming years.

Problem Set 3

3.1. You are a mid-level associate at a law firm, excited to have the help of a summer associate for the first time in your career. You recently were given a new project concerning a client whose credit card bill seems to be completely wrong. You asked the summer associate, Gloria Ho, to get you the "law" on this and warned her that "there is undoubtedly a statute or something; I don't want to see a bill for ten hours of searching in the case law database for this." Gloria just emailed you the files below with a note that said "Off to the firm hula hoop party (you should see my awesome costume!) but wanted to send your way the law on credit billing. See ya!" Professionalism concerns aside, what do you make of the files below? Which is the "law?" Why did she send them both to you?

15 U.S.C. §1666. Correction of Billing Errors

(b) Billing error

For the purpose of this section, a "billing error" consists of any of the following:

(1) A reflection on a statement of an extension of credit which was not in the amount reflected on such statement.

(2) A reflection on a statement of an extension of credit for which the obligor requests additional clarification including documentary evidence thereof.

(3) A reflection on a statement of goods or services not accepted.

(4) The creditor's failure to reflect properly on a statement a payment made by the obligor or a credit issued to the obligor.

(5) A computation error or similar error of an accounting nature of the creditor on a statement.

(6) Failure to transmit the statement required under section 1637(b) of this title to the last address of the obligor which has been disclosed to the creditor, unless that address was furnished less than twenty days before the end of the billing cycle for which the statement is required.

(7) Any other error described in regulations of the Board.

12 C.F.R. §1026.13. Billing Error Resolution

(a) Definition of a billing error. For purposes of this section, the term billing error means:

(1) A reflection on or with a periodic statement of an extension of credit that is not made to the consumer or to a person who has actual, implied, or apparent authority to use the consumer's credit card or open-end credit plan.

(2) A reflection on or with a periodic statement of an extension of credit that is not identified in accordance with the requirements of §§1026.7(b) and 1026.8.

(3) A reflection on or with a periodic statement of an extension of credit for property or services not accepted by the consumer or the consumer's designee, or not delivered to the consumer or the consumer's designee as agreed.

(4) A reflection on a periodic statement of the creditor's failure to credit properly a payment or other credit issued to the consumer's account.

(5) A reflection on a periodic statement of a computational or similar error of an accounting nature that is made by the creditor.

(6) A reflection on a periodic statement of an extension of credit for which the consumer requests additional clarification, including documentary evidence.

(7) The creditor's failure to mail or deliver a periodic statement to the consumer's last known address if that address was received by the creditor, in writing, at least 20 days before the end of the billing cycle for which the statement was required.

3.2. You represent a federally-chartered bank that primarily serves immigrant communities, offering them access to banking products at a pricing scheme that is pitched to the bank's shareholders as "aggressive" in its potential for profits. While you regularly get complaints sent over from the Attorney General's Office in your state, so far your response system of adding those to a file folder seems adequate. Yesterday, however, you learned that the CFPB has issued a rule declaring the practice of failing to give disclosures in a native language to a person "that the financial institution knows, or reasonably should know does not speak English" is an unfair and abusive practice. As outside counsel, you try to limit just how much you know about what really happens in the bank's branches, but you have a bad feeling about this new rule. The compliance or liability costs could cripple the bank's profits and send it straight out of business. What responses are available to your client? Can you intervene to alter the CFPB's position? If not, who might take enforcement action against the bank? *See* 12 U.S.C. §§25b, 513, 5552, 5563, 5565.

3.3. Senator Stamm is looking to make a splash in the Senate before his first reelection campaign. He is a moderate but thinks that that the zeitgeist of the day in America is anti-government. He has asked for advice on a bill that passed the House, H.R. 1315, "The Consumer Financial Protection Safety and Soundness Act." He wonders if he should lead the charge in the Senate to pass this bill. He would like you, his legislative director, to advise him on whether the CFPB should be run by a Commission, as described in section 104 of the bill, rather than by a Director. What are the benefits of such a change? What are the best counter-arguments to the bill to expect from the CFPB's defenders? As he told you, "I want to make a splash; I don't want to drown out there."

Part Two.   Consumer Meets Business: Getting Into the Deal

Assignment 4.   Solicitations

In a marketplace, consumers sometimes go looking for businesses, searching for the best provider or for a particular product. Other times, businesses seek out consumers. A company may try to make a consumer aware of its superiority to competitors or to establish in consumers' minds that their lives would be better if they had a good or service. Three distinct processes, listed from most general to most specific, are part of getting consumers to make a purchase. Marketing is the umbrella term for the processes that businesses use to identify customers and to deploy strategies about how to connect with consumers and sell goods or services to them. Advertisements are designed to have a broad appeal to potential customers and be displayed in a public forum (billboards, radio ads, etc.). Solicitations are targeted approaches to potential customers. They may occur in a variety of settings, such as door-to-door or by email, and often reflect a certain amount of personalized knowledge about the consumer.

Consumer law contains several limits on solicitations and advertising. There are at least three broad approaches. First, restrictions try to prevent consumers from being subjected to undue pressure from solicitations or simply overwhelmed by the sheer number of solicitations. In this category are innovations like cooling-off periods after in-home sales and the do-not-call list. Second, laws can mandate statements on advertising or product materials, such as certain kinds of labels or the addition of specified language to advertisements. This is a type of forced speech that alters the businesses advertisements or solicitations in response to legal requirements. Third, laws try to curb unfair or deceptive practices in solicitations or advertising, for example, by forbidding statements that mislead consumers or are untrue. The FTC's action against *Airborne*, in Assignment 1, was an example of this issue.

A.   In-Home Solicitations

The oldest form of selling is face-to-face. When this occurs outside of a business establishment, consumers may feel constrained from leaving. Sales presentations that involve a day-long tour of condos, complete with bus transportation to the property so that a consumer cannot drive off, is an example. The pressure to buy to escape the sales pitch is a particular problem when a salesperson comes to a consumer's home. Consumers may feel trapped or intimidated in their homes and be willing to make purchases merely to rid themselves of the intruding seller.

The FTC has promulgated a regulation under the Unfair and Deceptive Practices Act that regulates door-to-door sales. The rule extends to all sales in which the seller "personally solicits the sale, including those in response to or following an invitation by the buyer, and the buyer's agreement or offer to purchase is made at a place other than the place of business of the seller." 16 C.F.R. §429.0(a). Of course, there are exceptions. Three merit particular mention: 1) tent sales, provided that the seller has a permanent place of business, and art fairs, 16 C.F.R. §429.3; 2) sales "actually consummated" in a consumer's home, if they follow prior negotiations at the seller's place of business, Statement of Basis and Purpose, 37 Fed. Reg. 22946 (Oct. 26, 1972); and 3) sales for less than $25. 16 C.F.R. §429.0(a). The exceptions reflect situations in which the consumer is more likely to feel free to exercise free will in deciding whether to purchase.

The federal rule is often called the "cooling-off" law. Its primary substantive provision is that door-to-door transactions must contain a provision giving the buyer the right to cancel the transaction for three business days from the date on which the contract was signed. Failure to put the required language in the contract is an unfair and deceptive act or practice under 15 U.S.C. §45. The federal home sales law also requires that the contract be in the language used to conduct the oral sales presentation. 16 C.F.R. §429.1(a), and that the buyer must be informed orally of the right to cancel. 16 C.F.R. §429.1(e). These are difficult to prove in litigation because they essentially come down to the consumer's testimony against the seller's testimony — and if the seller had a good general business lawyer, a written handbook with policies requiring compliance with these regulations.

Every state also has a law regulating door-to-door sales. *See* National Consumer Law Center, Federal Deception Law, §2.5, n. 220 (2012). State laws that are not "directly inconsistent" with the federal rule are not preempted. 16 C.F.R. §429.2(b). While the state and federal rules may seem straightforward enough, compliance seems to be difficult in practice.

Pinnacle Energy, L.L.C. v. Price
2001 Del. C.P. LEXIS 28 (March 21, 2001)

SMALLS, Chief Judge.

Pinnacle Energy, L.L.C. (hereinafter "Pinnacle") brings this action to recover against Catherine Price and Otis Price for breach of contract. Pinnacle claims $3,950 for items refused, $1,000 in liquidated damages, pre- and post-judgment interest of 24%, costs and attorney's fees. This is the Court's decision after trial on February 12, 2001 and written submissions.

Pinnacle is in the business of selling custom fit windows and doors. Pinnacle employs high school and college age students to "canvass" various areas and schedule sales appointments. Once an appointment is scheduled, a Pinnacle salesman makes sales calls to the potential customer. Pinnacle testified it is their normal business practice to telephone twice, first to confirm an appointment the day before, and secondly, to ensure someone is home the day of the appointment.

In these proceedings Carlo Pinto, co-owner and president of Pinnacle, testified an appointment was scheduled through the Prices' grandson. Pinto stated he called to confirm the sales appointment twice before he went to the Prices' house. The Prices, however, testified their first contact with Pinto occurred when he appeared at their house on the morning of April 17, 1999. They concede they were in the market for new windows and doors, and after negotiations agreed to purchase five new windows and three new doors, to be installed by agents of Pinnacle. A contract was signed between the Prices and Pinnacle, which provided for the purchase and installation of the windows and doors.

Pinto testified their manufacturer, Mid South, went to the Prices' house on April 22, 1999, re-measured the windows, and they were ordered May 3, 1999. The installation was scheduled for June 4, 1999. The installation of the windows and doors was not completed due to the refusal of the Prices on the date of delivery. The Prices testified that no one from Mid South came to measure the windows and the next contact they had with Pinnacle was when they appeared to install the windows and doors. The Prices also testified they made numerous attempts to contact Pinto at Pinnacle to inform him of their desire to cancel the agreement. Pinto claims he never received notice of their efforts to cancel the contract until the day of delivery. Further, Pinnacle relies upon a clause at the bottom of the contract in bold print which purports to give the right to cancel required by the statute.

At the close of the Plaintiff's case-in-chief, Defendants moved for a directed verdict. Defendants argue the contract failed to comply with the Home Solicitation and Sales Act (hereinafter "the Act") 6 Del. C. §§4401-4405. After argument, the Court concluded the contract failed to comply with §4404(1) of the "Home Solicitation Sales Act" which provides the language of how a buyer may cancel the contract be "printed in an ink of conspicuous color other than that used for the rest of the contract and/or receipt." Additionally, the Court now concludes plaintiff failed to prove by a preponderance that the "Notice of Cancellation" form required under §4404(2) and (3) was attached to the contract. While Plaintiff produced a blank copy of the form notice to cancel, there was no signed notice and Plaintiff explained this was merely missing from its file. I find this justification has little merit. I also find unpersuasive Pinnacle's argument that it had numerous contacts with the Prices after the initial contract was signed and the date of delivery.

Pinnacle correctly notes the language of the statute does not provide a specific remedy for failure to comply with notice requirements. The Act merely gives the buyer "remedies . . . at law or in equity." 6 Del. C. §4407. Therefore, following the Court's decision on the statutory violation, testimony was heard on the timeliness of the Defendant's notice and appropriate remedy. . . . These issues herein have not been addressed in Delaware, but they have been considered by the states of New Jersey and Maryland. The New Jersey case of Swiss v. Williams, 445 A.2d 486, 489-490 (1982) held the consumer has a "continuing right to rescind until such time as the home repair contractor complies with the statutory requirements by providing [the buyer] with receipt complying with the form set forth in the act." The Maryland Court has taken a slightly different view. In *Crystal v. West & Callahan, Inc.*, 614 A.2d 560, 571. it was held where the seller fails to comply with the statutory notice, the buyer has a right to cancel for a reasonable amount of time after the contract date.

The Prices argue the Maryland statute is indistinguishable from Delaware's in that, Maryland's statute provides non-compliance is "an unfair or deceptive trade practice," where Delaware makes such non-compliance an unlawful practice. The Prices further argue that even if the court does not adopt the New Jersey view of actual compliance, under these facts they meet the Maryland "reasonableness" analysis. I note that one of the factors which influenced the Maryland decision was the trial court's finding that the defendants had accepted the work and did not complain of the quality. Further, defendants waited one and one-half years to raise the "notice" defense.

In these proceedings, when concluding at trial that Pinnacle did not comply with the act, the court noted the Delaware statute was remedial. In its declaration of purpose it provides in §4401, that: "This chapter shall be interpreted and administered so as to give the greatest effect to the public policy of this State, which declares that it is a basic right of every Delaware citizen to be free of, and protected from, high-pressure door-to-door sales tactics and the resultant inequities to the consumer found in certain ambiguous or misleading contracts, poor quality merchandise and the quick discounting of evidence of indebtedness."

It is clear that the purpose of the statute is to afford the consumer the greatest protection available. Therefore, I find that the analysis found under Swiss case is more consistent with the Delaware statutory language than that of Crystal. However, I need not go as far as the court in *Swiss* because I conclude the Prices gave notice of cancellation within a reasonable period of time.

During their case-in-chief, both Mr. and Mrs. Price testified that they called Pinnacle and Mr. Pinto to cancel the sale. Further, it is undisputed that on the date Pinnacle scheduled for delivery, the Prices refused delivery and cancelled the contract. Pinnacle alleged, but has not produced an acknowledged copy of the notice of right to cancel, as required by the statute. It is clear that one may not accept products under the contract where there are no complaints regarding quality, and later refuses to pay the cost thereof on the basis of the statute. However, that is not the case in these proceedings. Here, there is evidence of the buyers' efforts to cancel prior to delivery. Therefore, based upon the facts herein and the language set forth in the statute, I hereby find the Prices gave notice of cancellation within a reasonable period, and Pinnacle may not collect under the terms of the contract.

Accordingly, I find for the defendants, with the costs to be paid by the respective parties.

Reading the regulation suggests a three-day window. The case reveals that the right to cancel can actually run for many months or even years after the transaction. The key question is whether the consumer can persuade the factfinder that there was no compliance at the time of the deal. The premise of this extended liability is a theme that will recur in consumer law — people cannot exercise rights that they do not know that they have. The case also illustrates that areas of statutory law require more research. It is not enough to find the statute. One must also find the regulations and the case law interpreting the statute and regulations.

B.   Telephone Solicitations

Telemarketing is a routine strategy to solicit customers in certain industries. The calls are often placed from a call center, which is less charitably described as a "boiler room," a rented space with hundreds of operators calling continuously. "Robo-calling" eliminates the human operator from the process, replacing her with computer-generated dialing or even a prerecorded message that is broadcast to consumers or their answering machines. Telemarketing often involves more than one call or efforts to extend the length of the call, both of which presumably motivate customers to make purchases. While many consumers find the calls are a nuisance and never or rarely purchase, telemarketing continues to be widely used. The reason is that the technology of calling has driven down the costs of solicitation so low that even a small response rate can generate profits. (This is same reason that a decade later, spam emails asking for money wires to Nigeria continue to arrive in your inbox.)

Telemarketing is legal within two boundaries. The first limit, discussed here, is that telemarketers cannot engage in fraud or deceptive practices. The second limit, discussed in the next section, is that there are restrictions on when and how often consumers may be contacted.

1.   Telemarketing Fraud

The primary laws regulating telemarketing fraud are the Telemarketing and Consumer Fraud and Abuse Prevention Act, 15 U.S.C. §6101 et seq., and the FTC's Telemarketing Sales Rule, 16 C.F.R. §310.4.

The FTC defines telemarketing as "a plan, program, or campaign which is conducted to induce purchases of goods or services, or a charitable contribution, donation, or gift of money or any other thing of value, by use of one or more telephones and which involves more than one interstate telephone call. The term does not include the solicitation of sales through the mailing of a catalog [under certain limitations, including only receiving calls initiated by customers in response to the catalog]." 16 C.F.R. §310.2(dd). Seller-initiated calls are the main focus. For some industries, consumer-initiated calls are covered, such as calls in response to advertisements or mailings for services such as credit repair or prize promotions. 16 C.F.R. §310.6(b)(5). Calls for these and some other services are subject to additional consumer protection restrictions, many of which are motivated by concern that telemarketers do not deliver the promised services.

The Telemarketing Sales Rule requires disclosures for any covered calls. Most fundamentally, the telemarketer must reveal that the purpose of the call is to sell goods or services and the nature of the goods or services. 16 C.F.R. §310.4(d)(2). Telemarketers must also reveal the total costs, any restrictions or conditions on purchase, and all material terms and conditions of a refund policy, including, if applicable, the lack of any right to a refund. In complying with these disclosure requirements, telemarketers cannot make deceptive statements, for example by misrepresenting the goods or services being sold.

The following case provides an example of the kinds of behavior that violate the Telemarketing Sales Rule.

Federal Trade Commission v. Bay Area Business Council Inc.

423 F.3d 627 (7th Cir. 2005)

ROVNER, Circuit Judge

In 2002 the Federal Trade Commission ("FTC") initiated an action for injunctive and other equitable relief against several Florida corporations and their officers and directors. The FTC alleged that the following interrelated corporations, run by Peter Porcelli, Bonnie Harris, and Christopher Tomasulo, engaged in deceptive trade practices in violation of section 5(a) of the Federal Trade Commission Act ("FTC Act"), 15 U.S.C. §45(a), and the Telemarketing Sales Rule ("TSR"), 16 C.F.R. §310.1-10.9. Bay Area Business Council, Inc. ("BABC"); Bay Area Business Council Customer Service Corp. ("BABC Customer Service"); American Leisure Card Corp. ("American Leisure"); Bay Memberships, Inc.; Bay Vacations, Inc.; and Sr. Marketing Consultants, Inc. In particular, the FTC alleged that the defendants misled consumers into believing that they would receive a credit card in exchange for a hefty "one-time" fee. The district court granted the FTC's motion for summary judgment against all of the corporate defendants and Porcelli and Harris. The defendants appeal, and we affirm.

I.

The FTC based its action on an alleged telemarketing scheme run primarily out of Largo, Florida. Managing BABC and later American Leisure, Porcelli contracted with a telemarketing company in Utah to call consumers throughout the United States who had recently applied for and been denied consumer credit. Referring to those credit applications, telemarketers opened by saying, "Our records indicate that within the past 12 months, you filed an application for a credit card and you are now eligible to receive your MasterCard." After answering a few short "verification" questions, consumers were told that they were "guaranteed to receive a MasterCard that does not require a security deposit with an initial pay as you go limit of $2,000."

In addition to the "MasterCard," consumers were promised a "fabulous" Florida vacation and a free 30-day trial "BABC membership." These offers, however, did not figure prominently in the script, which focused on the "MasterCard." The card was offered as a way to boost flagging credit ratings, as demonstrated by the following scripted promise: "[N]othing [customer name] looks better on your Equifax credit report than a MasterCard."

This supposed opportunity, however, came at a cost. Telemarketers explained that "like most cards there is a one time processing [fee] of $174.95 plus shipping and handling, which covers the cost of processing the MasterCard order and getting the vacation package delivered to you on a priority basis." In order to pay the fee, consumers were required to provide personal account information. After obtaining an account number and securing agreement from the consumer, tele-marketers played an automated "disclosure" concluding with, "you agree to every-thing we spoke about over the phone today, Correct?" Within days of the call, BABC and American Leisure debited customer accounts for anywhere from $199 (includ-ing "shipping and handling") to $499.

Some time later, customers received the "MasterCard" and accompanying package from BABC or American Leisure. Instead of a credit card, the package contained an "acceptance form" for a "ChexCard TM MasterCard®." The card stated "Bay Area Business Council" prominently across the top and contained a copy of the MasterCard logo in the lower right-hand corner. The back contained a meaningless painted-on black stripe in place of the customary magnetic strip on credit and debit cards. The explanatory material revealed that the card was a "stored value card" that the customer could receive only after mailing in a $15 activation fee. After the actual card arrived (four to six weeks later), it could only be used if a customer pre-loaded his or her own funds onto it.

In addition to the inoperable "ChexCard," customers received information on redeeming their free vacation (a time share presentation) and on their BABC "mem-bership." The "membership" supposedly entitled consumers to take advantage of numerous "free" goods and services, such as gasoline, nationwide long distance, internet access, voice mail, and film developing. Although this was not mentioned in the materials, the privilege of BABC membership cost the consumer $10 a month. The only notice of the fee was contained in the automated "disclosure" played in the initial sales call, where it was revealed that the $10 would be taken directly from the consumer's account each month.

Not surprisingly, BABC received a host of complaints from customers who thought they had been going to receive a credit card. Incorporated separately but doing business under the name Bay Area Business Council, BABC Customer Service handled customer's complaints and requests for refunds. Special Tech-nologies, Inc. essentially succeeded BABC Customer Service in July 2002. Both operated from a suite in Largo next to the offices of Porcelli and Harris. That suite received all calls placed to the toll free numbers for BABC, American Lei-sure, Sr. Marketing Consultants, and Bay Memberships, Inc. In addition to calls from disgruntled consumers, corporate records reveal that between November 2001 and July 2002, BABC received over 900 written consumer complaints for-warded from the Better Business Bureau, state attorney generals' offices, and private lawyers.

The remaining corporate defendants also worked in conjunction with BABC. Like BABC Customer Service, Sr. Marketing Consultants, Inc. did business under BABC's name. Sr. Marketing Consultants, however, had only four employees, three of whom were related to Porcelli. They operated from Porcelli's mother-in-law's home in Dunedin, Florida. Sr. Marketing Consultants charged BABC and American Leisure for the "ChexCards," and then, through a series of transactions, gave the proceeds to Harris, who handled most of BABC's finances. At the end of July 2002, Porcelli created Bay Memberships, Inc. as a way to ensure that banks, which had begun refusing to process payments to BABC and American Leisure, would con-tinue to charge customers. In the three weeks that Bay Memberships, Inc. operated, it processed approximately $200,000 in debits from customer accounts. Although it is not entirely clear from the record, Bay Vacations, Inc. was apparently another shell corporation doing business for BABC. . . .

On that record, the court granted the FTC's motion for summary judgment. The court concluded that the undisputed facts established that the defendants had violated section 5 of the FTC Act by misleading reasonable consumers into believing they would receive a credit card. See 15 U.S.C. §45(a) (forbidding deceptive practices affecting commerce). This deception, the court concluded, also violated 16 C.F.R. §310.3(a)(2)(iii) (prohibiting misrepresentations about any material aspect of a sales offer) and §310.3(a)(4) (forbidding misleading statements to induce payment for goods). And the court determined that the defendants violated 16 C.F.R. §310.3(a)(1)(i) by failing to tell consumers about the extra $15 fee required to obtain the "ChexCard," id. (requiring clear and conspicuous disclosure of all costs associated with goods offered for sale). Finally, the district court concluded that Porcelli and Harris were individually liable for the corporate defendants' deceptive practices because both had authority to control the corporate defendants and knew about their deceptive practices. The court then entered an order permanently enjoining the defendants from telemarketing, promoting or selling credit-related products, making misleading statements to consumers, failing to comply with the TSR, or disclosing any information about customers except to the FTC. The court also held the corporate defendants, Harris, and Porcelli jointly and severally liable for $12.5 million in consumer redress. See 15 U.S.C. §57b(b) (giving court jurisdiction to authorize consumer redress for a corporation's deceptive trade practices).

• • •

Accordingly, in our de novo review of the court's grant of summary judgment, we consider only those facts in the FTC's Rule 56.1 statement, which is amply supported by citations to the relevant record evidence. Although we accept as true the facts in the FTC's Rule 56.1 statement, we still view them in the light most favorable to the defendants in determining whether there exist disputed issues of material fact. See Fed.R.Civ.P. 56(c); Anderson v. Liberty Lobby Inc., 477 U.S. 242, 255 (1986); Laborers' Pension Fund v. RES Env't Servs. Inc., 377 F.3d 735, 737 (7th Cir. 2004). Although the defendants aver generally that there are disputed issues of fact that make summary judgment improper, nothing they point to undercuts the FTC's undisputed evidence that they engaged in unfair trade practices, see 15 U.S.C. §45(a), and violated multiple provisions of the TSR, see 16 C.F.R. §310.1-10.9.

Section 5 of the FTC Act prohibits "unfair or deceptive acts or practices in or affecting commerce." 15 U.S.C. §45(a)(1). The FTC is empowered to initiate federal court actions to enforce violations of section 5 and seek appropriate equitable relief. Id. §§53(a)-(b), 57b. The FTC may establish corporate liability under section 5 with evidence that a corporation made material representations likely to mislead a reasonable consumer. See FTC v. Tashman, 318 F.3d 1273, 1277 (11th Cir. 2003); FTC v. World Travel Vacation Brokers, Inc., 861 F.2d 1020, 1029 (7th Cir. 1988). The FTC is not, however, required to prove intent to deceive. FTC v. Freecom Communications, Inc., 401 F.3d 1192, 1202 (10th Cir. 2005); FTC v. Amy Travel Serv., Inc., 875 F.2d 564, 573 (7th Cir. 1989); World Travel, 861 F.2d at 1029. Additionally, the omission of a material fact, without an affirmative misrepresentation, may give rise to an FTC Act violation. Amy Travel, 875 F.2d at 573; World Travel, 861 F.2d at 1029. The corporate defendants do not dispute the district court's conclusion that they operated as a "common enterprise" such that they are jointly and severally liable for the injuries caused by their violations of the FTC Act and the TSR. We thus consider them collectively when analyzing corporate liability.

Throughout their brief, the defendants maintain that they never sold a credit card. They characterize this issue as a material fact in dispute. The FTC, however, does not dispute that the defendants did not actually sell credit cards. Indeed, their failure to provide a "credit card" lies at the heart of this case. We take the defendants at their word that they never sold a credit card. Unfortunately, they misled consumers into believing that was exactly what they were doing. See Freecom Communications, 401 F.3d at 1202 (in analyzing whether act or practice is deceptive, principal inquiry is the practice's likely effect on mind of ordinary consumer).

One look at the scripts used by telemarketers for BABC and American Leisure confirms that the corporate defendants misled reasonable consumers into believing they would receive a credit card. The script opens by referring to the consumer's recent application for "a credit card." The potential customer is then told, "you are now eligible to receive your MasterCard." It is hard to imagine what consumer would not construe this as an offer for a credit card. Indeed, the entire script is tailored to giving consumers that impression. From calling the card a "MasterCard" to promising that nothing would look better on an Equifax credit report, telemarketers gave consumers the impression that they were going to receive a credit card in the mail. Instead, they received a useless card with a MasterCard logo. From that, a consumer could mail additional funds to receive a functional "ChexCard," which could only be used when the consumer pre-loaded it with her or her own funds. We think it safe to say that no reasonable consumer would pay close to $200 for the opportunity to order this "ChexCard." Any doubt that consumers were misled is dispelled by the number of consumer complaints. BABC Customer Service records reveal that in the two-month window from June to August 2002, over 200 consumers called to complain that they thought they would be getting a credit card. Accordingly, the corporate defendants violated section 5 of the FTC Act. See FTC v. World Media Brokers, 415 F.3d 758 (7th Cir. 2005).

The evidence also establishes multiple violations of the TSR, 16 C.F.R. §310.1-10.9, the FTC's Trade Regulation promulgated to implement the Telemarketing and Consumer Fraud and Abuse Prevention Act, 15 U.S.C. §6101-6108. The FTC alleged that the defendants violated three provisions of the TSR, which we consider in turn.

Section 310.3(a)(1)(i) requires telemarketers to clearly and conspicuously disclose "[t]he total costs to purchase, receive, or use . . . any goods and services" offered for sale. 16 C.F.R. §310.3(a)(1)(i). Although telemarketers assured consumers that the "MasterCard" had a "one time" fee of $174.95 plus shipping and handling, that was not the case. After a consumer's checking account was debited anywhere from $199 up to $399, he or she received the BABC "membership" materials in the mail. Those materials contained the useless "ChexCard TM MasterCard®" with an accompanying form explaining that it was not a credit card. In order to use the "stored value card" consumers then had to mail an additional, previously undisclosed $15 in certified funds to "SMC Bank Card Offer" (presumably Sr. Marketing Consultants, the four-employee operation run from Porcelli's mother-in-law's home). By failing to provide advance warning of the additional $15 fee, the corporate defendants violated §310.3(a)(1)(i).

Likewise, the defendants violated §310.3(a)(2)(iii), which prohibits telemarketers from misrepresenting any material aspect of the performance of the goods or services offered for sale. As our discussion regarding section 5 of the FTC Act makes clear, the corporate defendants misled consumers into believing that they would receive a credit card. We need not linger on the obvious point that the lack of any available credit on the "MasterCard" qualifies as a material aspect of its performance subject to disclosure. Cf. World Media, 415 F.3d 758 (defendants' failure to disclose illegality of sales offer violated related provision of TSR requiring disclosure of all material restrictions on goods or services).

Finally, the defendants violated §310.3(a)(4) by leading consumers to believe that the substantial fee charged would be used to secure a credit card on their behalf. Subsection (a)(4) forbids telemarketers from making a false or misleading statement to induce payment for goods or services. 16 C.F.R. §310.3(a)(4); see also World Media, 415 F.3d 758. In addition to suggesting that consumers would receive a credit card, the telemarketers falsely assured consumers that the card would boost their credit ratings. Despite the promise that "nothing" looked better on an "Equifax credit report than a MasterCard," use of the pay-as-you go "Mastercard" was not reported to credit reporting bureaus like Equifax. No doubt this false promise induced consumers, targeted for their poor credit histories, into paying for the supposed "MasterCard."

· · ·

For the foregoing reasons, we affirm the district court's grant of summary judgment in favor of the FTC.

In the case, the FTC relied on its authority to stop practices that involve deception in commerce as well as violations of specific rules. The Telemarketing and Consumer Fraud Abuse Prevention Act does not have separate remedy provisions for the FTC, which is instead directed to sue under the general FTC Act. The Telemarketing statute does, however, empower state Attorneys General to enforce the federal law, 15 U.S.C. §6103, and when the amount in controversy is greater than $50,000, even permits a private person to sue. 15 U.S.C. §6102. This overlapping enforcement scheme illustrates the point of Assignment 3; there are a lot of cooks in the consumer protection kitchen, which can lead to conflict or to inaction, as one regulator defers enforcement in the belief that another entity is the better party to act.

In addition to federal telemarketing regulations, telemarketers must also adhere to separate state regulations. Many states require telemarketers to register with a state regulator and have separate rules covering things like whether calls may be recorded, whether the telemarketer must obtain a consumer's consent to continue with a call, and whether a written contract is required to be sent to make the sale effective.

2.   Do-not-call List

The Telephone Consumer Protection Act of 1991 (TCPA), 47 U.S.C. §227, places limits on telemarketing activity, including limits on robo-calling and unsolicited faxes. This law also contains limits on telemarketing that are designed to regulate solicitations, with some duplication with the Telemarketing and Consumer Fraud and Abuse Prevention Act. One important difference is that the TCPA is enforced by the Federal Communications Commission (FCC), rather than the FTC.

The focus of the TCPA is somewhat more on the use of the technology than the FTC's rule. For example, its regulations address both faxes and telephone calls. 47 C.F.R. §64.1200. While the law was passed in 1991, in part to address fax spam, it has evolved with technology. The regulation prohibits uninitiated calling of pagers and cellular telephones, and treats text messages as calls for purposes of regulation. 47 C.F.R. §64.1200(a)(1)(iii). This is a protection for everyone, reflecting one approach to the scope of consumer law. The TCPA also gives extra protection to vulnerable consumers. It bans calls to landlines of consumers who reside in "any guest room or patient room of a hospital, health care facility, elderly home, or similar establishment." 47 C.F.R. §64.1200(a)(1)(ii).

The centerpiece of such efforts is the National Do-Not-Call Registry. In 2003, the FTC and the FCC established a national do-not-call rule. The registry met with immediate challenges, first to the FTC's authority, which was immediately resolved by Congress. *See* An Act to Ratify the Authority of the Federal Trade Commission to Establish a Do-Not-Call Registry, Pub. L. No. 108-82, 117 Stat. 1006 (2003). Then came the constitutional attack.

Mainstream Marketing Services, Inc. v. Federal Trade Commission

358 F.3d 1228 (10th Cir. 2004)

EBEL, Circuit Judge.

I. BACKGROUND

In 2003, two federal agencies the Federal Trade Commission (FTC) and the Federal Communications Commission (FCC) promulgated rules that together created the national do-not-call registry. *See* 16 C.F.R. §310.4(b)(1)(iii)(B) (FTC rule); 47 C.F.R. §64.1200(c)(2) (FCC rule). The national do-not-call registry is a list containing the personal telephone numbers of telephone subscribers who have voluntarily indicated that they do not wish to receive unsolicited calls from commercial telemarketers. Commercial telemarketers are generally prohibited from calling phone numbers that have been placed on the do-not-call registry, and they must pay an annual fee to access the numbers on the registry so that they can delete those numbers from their telephone solicitation lists. So far, consumers have registered more than 50 million phone numbers on the national do-not-call registry.

The national do-not-call registry's restrictions apply only to telemarketing calls made by or on behalf of sellers of goods or services, and not to charitable or political fundraising calls. 16 C.F.R. §§310.4(b)(1)(iii)(B), 310.6(a); 47 C.F.R. 64.1200(c)(2), 64.1200(f)(9). Additionally, a seller may call consumers who have signed up for the national registry if it has an established business relationship with the consumer or if the consumer has given that seller express written permission to call. 16 C.F.R. §310.4(b)(1)(iii)(B)(i-ii); 47 C.F.R. §64.1200(f)(9)(i-ii). Telemarketers generally have three months from the date on which a consumer signs up for the registry to remove the consumer's phone number from their call lists. 16 C.F.R. §310.4(b)(3)(iv); 47 C.F.R. §64.1200(c)(2)(i)(D).

. . .

III. FIRST AMENDMENT ANALYSIS

The national do-not-call registry's telemarketing restrictions apply only to commercial speech. Like most commercial speech regulations, the do-not-call rules draw a line between commercial and non-commercial speech on the basis of content. See Metromedia, Inc. v. City of San Diego, 453 U.S. 490, 504 n.11 (1981) ("If commercial speech is to be distinguished, it must be distinguished by its content."); Bates v. State Bar of Ariz., 433 U.S. 350, 363 (1977) (same). In reviewing commercial speech regulations, we apply the *Central Hudson* test. Central Hudson Gas & Elec. Corp. v. Pub. Serv. Comm'n of N.Y., 447 U.S. 557, 566 (1980). *Central Hudson* established a three-part test governing First Amendment challenges to regulations restricting non-misleading commercial speech that relates to lawful activity. First, the government must assert a substantial interest to be achieved by the regulation. Central Hudson, 447 U.S. at 564. Second, the regulation must directly advance that governmental interest, meaning that it must do more than provide "only ineffective or remote support for the government's purpose." Id. Third, although the regulation need not be the least restrictive measure available, it must be narrowly tailored not to restrict more speech than necessary. See id.; Board of Trs. of the State Univ. of N.Y. v. Fox, 492 U.S. 469, 480 (1989). Together, these final two factors require that there be a reasonable fit between the government's objectives and the means it chooses to accomplish those ends.

The government bears the burden of asserting one or more substantial governmental interests and demonstrating a reasonable fit between those interests and the challenged regulation. The government is not limited in the evidence it may use to meet its burden. For example, a commercial speech regulation may be justified by anecdotes, history, consensus, or simple common sense. Yet we may not take it upon ourselves to supplant the interests put forward by the state with our own ideas of what goals the challenged laws might serve.

A. Governmental Interests

The government asserts that the do-not-call regulations are justified by its interests in 1) protecting the privacy of individuals in their homes, and 2) protecting consumers against the risk of fraudulent and abusive solicitation. See 68 Fed. Reg. 44144; 68 Fed. Reg. at 4635. Both of these justifications are undisputedly substantial governmental interests.

In *Rowan v. United States Post Office Dep't*, the Supreme Court upheld the right of a homeowner to restrict material that could be mailed to his or her house. 397 U.S. 728 (1970). The Court emphasized the importance of individual privacy, particularly in the context of the home, stating that "the ancient concept that 'a man's home is his castle' into which 'not even the king may enter' has lost none of its vitality." Id. at 737. In *Frisby v. Schultz*, the Court again stressed the unique nature of the home and recognized that "the State's interest in protecting the well-being, tranquility, and privacy of the home is certainly of the highest order in a free and civilized society." 487 U.S. 474, 484 (1988) (quoting Carey v. Brown, 447 U.S. 455, 471 (1980)). As the Court held in *Frisby*:

> One important aspect of residential privacy is protection of the unwilling listener. . . . [A] special benefit of the privacy all citizens enjoy within their own walls, which the State may legislate to protect, is an ability to avoid intrusions. Thus, we have repeatedly held that individuals are not required to welcome unwanted speech into their own homes and that the government may protect this freedom.

Id. at 484-85 (citations omitted). Likewise, in *Hill v. Colorado*, the Court called the unwilling listener's interest in avoiding unwanted communication part of the broader right to be let alone that Justice Brandeis described as "the right most valued by civilized men." 530 U.S. 703, 716-17 (2000) (quoting Olmstead v. United States, 277 U.S. 438, 478 (1928) (Brandeis, J., dissenting)). The Court added that the right to avoid unwanted speech has special force in the context of the home. Id. . . .

In other words, the national do-not-call registry is valid if it is designed to provide effective support for the government's purposes and if the government did not suppress an excessive amount of speech when substantially narrower restrictions would have worked just as well. See Central Hudson, 447 U.S. at 564-65. These criteria are plainly established in this case. The do-not-call registry directly advances the government's interests by effectively blocking a significant number of the calls that cause the problems the government sought to redress. It is narrowly tailored because its opt-in character ensures that it does not inhibit any speech directed at the home of a willing listener.

1. Effectiveness

The telemarketers assert that the do-not-call registry is unconstitutionally underinclusive because it does not apply to charitable and political callers. First Amendment challenges based on underinclusiveness face an uphill battle in the commercial speech context. As a general rule, the First Amendment does not require that the government regulate all aspects of a problem before it can make progress on any front. United States v. Edge Broad. Co., 509 U.S. 418, 434 (1993). "Within the bounds of the general protection provided by the Constitution to commercial speech, we allow room for legislative judgments." Id. The underinclusiveness of a commercial speech regulation is relevant only if it renders the regulatory framework so irrational that it fails materially to advance the aims that it was purportedly designed to further. See Rubin v. Coors Brewing Co., 514 U.S. 476, 489 (1995).

In *Rubin*, for example, the Supreme Court struck down a law prohibiting brewers from putting the alcohol content of their product on beer labels, purportedly in an effort to discourage "strength wars." 514 U.S. at 478. However, the law allowed advertisements disclosing the alcohol content of beers, allowed sellers of wines and spirits to disclose alcohol content on labels (and even required such disclosure for certain wines), and allowed brewers to signal high alcohol content by using the term "malt liquor." Id. at 488-89. Under these circumstances, the Court concluded that there was little chance that the beer label rule would materially deter strength wars in light of the "irrationality of this unique and puzzling regulatory framework." Id. at 489. . . .

As discussed above, the national do-not-call registry is designed to reduce intrusions into personal privacy and the risk of telemarketing fraud and abuse that accompany unwanted telephone solicitation. The registry directly advances those goals. So far, more than 50 million telephone numbers have been registered on the do-not-call list, and the do-not-call regulations protect these households from receiving most unwanted telemarketing calls. According to the telemarketers' own estimate, 2.64 telemarketing calls per week or more than 137 calls annually were directed at an average consumer before the do-not-call list came into effect. Cf. 68 Fed. Reg. at 44152 (discussing the five-fold increase in the total number of telemarketing calls between 1991 and 2003). Accordingly, absent the do-not-call registry, telemarketers would call those consumers who have already signed up for the registry an estimated total of 6.85 billion times each year.

To be sure, the do-not-call list will not block all of these calls. Nevertheless, it will prohibit a substantial number of them, making it difficult to fathom how the registry could be called an "ineffective" means of stopping invasive or abusive calls, or a regulation that "furnish[es] only speculative or marginal support" for the government's interests. See also id. (noting the effectiveness of state do-not-call lists in reducing unwanted telemarketing calls). . . .

The telemarketers asserted before the FTC that they might have to lay off up to 50 percent of their employees if the national do-not-call registry came into effect. See 68 Fed. Reg. at 4631. It is reasonable to conclude that the telemarketers' planned reduction in force corresponds to a decrease in the amount of calls they will make. Significantly, the percentage of unwanted calls that will be prohibited will be even higher than the percentage of all unsolicited calls blocked by the list. The individuals on the do-not-call list have declared that they do not wish to receive unsolicited commercial telemarketing calls, whereas those who do want to continue receiving such calls will not register. Cf. 68 Fed. Reg. at 4632 (under the national do-not-call regulations, "telemarketers would reduce time spent calling consumers who do not want to receive telemarketing calls and would be able to focus their calls only on those who do not object").

Finally, the type of unsolicited calls that the do-not-call list does prohibit, commercial sales calls, is the type that Congress, the FTC and the FCC have all determined to be most to blame for the problems the government is seeking to redress. According to the legislative history accompanying the TCPA, "[c]omplaint statistics show that unwanted commercial calls are a far bigger problem than unsolicited calls from political or charitable organizations." H.R. Rep. No. 102-317, at 16 (1991) (noting that non-commercial calls were less intrusive to consumers' privacy because they are more expected and because there is a lower volume of such calls);

see also 68 Fed. Reg. at 44153. Similarly, the FCC determined that calls from solicitors with an established business relationship with the recipient are less problematic than other commercial calls. 68 Fed. Reg. at 44154 ("Consumers are more likely to anticipate contacts from companies with whom they have an existing relationship and the volume of such calls will most likely be lower."). . . .

In sum, the do-not-call list directly advances the government's interests, reducing intrusions upon consumer privacy and the risk of fraud or abuse by restricting a substantial number (and also a substantial percentage) of the calls that cause these problems. Unlike the regulations struck down in Rubin and Discovery Network, the do-not-call list is not so underinclusive that it fails materially to advance the government's goals.

2. Narrow Tailoring

Although the least restrictive means test is not the test to be used in the commercial speech context, commercial speech regulations do at least have to be "narrowly tailored" and provide a "reasonable fit" between the problem and the solution. Whether or not there are "numerous and obvious less-burdensome alternatives" is a relevant consideration in our narrow tailoring analysis. Went For It, 515 U.S. at 632. A law is narrowly tailored if it "promotes a substantial government interest that would be achieved less effectively absent the regulation." Ward v. Rock Against Racism, 491 U.S. 781, 799 (1989). Accordingly, we consider whether there are numerous and obvious alternatives that would restrict less speech and would serve the government's interest as effectively as the challenged law. See Central Hudson, 447 U.S. at 565; Edge Broad., 509 U.S. at 430.

We hold that the national do-not-call registry is narrowly tailored because it does not over-regulate protected speech; rather, it restricts only calls that are targeted at unwilling recipients. Cf. Frisby v. Schultz, 487 U.S. 474, 485 (1988) ("There simply is no right to force speech into the home of an unwilling listener."); Rowan v. United States Post Office Dep't, 397 U.S. 728, 738 (1970) ("We therefore categorically reject the argument that a vendor has a right under the Constitution or otherwise to send unwanted material into the home of another."). The do-not-call registry prohibits only telemarketing calls aimed at consumers who have affirmatively indicated that they do not want to receive such calls and for whom such calls would constitute an invasion of privacy. See Hill v. Colorado, 530 U.S. 703, 716-17 (2000) (the right of privacy includes an unwilling listener's interest in avoiding unwanted communication). . . .

Like the do-not-mail regulation approved in *Rowan*, the national do-not-call registry does not itself prohibit any speech. Instead, it merely "permits a citizen to erect a wall . . . that no advertiser may penetrate without his acquiescence." See Rowan, 397 U.S. at 738. Almost by definition, the do-not-call regulations only block calls that would constitute unwanted intrusions into the privacy of consumers who have signed up for the list. Moreover, it allows consumers who feel susceptible to telephone fraud or abuse to ensure that most commercial callers will not have an opportunity to victimize them. Under the circumstances we address in this case, we conclude that the do-not-call registry's opt-in feature renders it a narrowly tailored commercial speech regulation.

The do-not-call registry's narrow tailoring is further demonstrated by the fact that it presents both sellers and consumers with a number of options to make and receive sales offers. From the seller's perspective, the do-not-call registry restricts only one avenue by which solicitors can communicate with consumers who have registered for the list. In particular, the do-not-call regulations do not prevent businesses from corresponding with potential customers by mail or by means of advertising through other media.

From the consumer's perspective, the do-not-call rules provide a number of different options allowing consumers to dictate what telemarketing calls they wish to receive and what calls they wish to avoid. Consumers who would like to receive some commercial sales calls but not others can sign up for the national do-not-call registry but give written permission to call to those businesses from whom they wish to receive offers. See 16 C.F.R. 310.4(b)(1)(iii)(B)(i); 47 C.F.R. 64.1200(f)(9)(i). Alternatively, they may decline to sign up on the national registry but make company-specific do-not-call requests with those particular businesses from whom they do not wish to receive calls. See 16 C.F.R. 310.4(b)(1)(iii)(A); 47 C.F.R. 64.1200(d)(3). Therefore, under the current regulations, consumers choose between two default rules either that telemarketers may call or that they may not. Then, consumers may make company-specific modifications to either of these default rules as they see fit, either granting particular sellers permission to call or blocking calls from certain sellers.

. . .

For the reasons discussed above, the government has asserted substantial interests to be served by the do-not-call registry (privacy and consumer protection), the do-not-call registry will directly advance those interests by banning a substantial amount of unwanted telemarketing calls, and the regulation is narrowly tailored because its opt-in feature ensures that it does not restrict any speech directed at a willing listener. In other words, the do-not-call registry bears a reasonable fit with the purposes the government sought to advance. Therefore, it is consistent with the limits the First Amendment imposes on laws restricting commercial speech.

The national do-not-call registry does not apply to telemarketers who solicit charitable donations. 16 C.F.R. §310.6(a). Like commercial telemarketers, however, non-profit callers must maintain a do-not-call list for their organization. The Telemarketing Sales Rule prohibits consumers who have previously asked to be on such a list from being contacted again. The constitutionality of this rule was challenged by non-profit organizations and held to be constitutional. *See Natl'l Federation of the Blind v. Fed. Trade Comm'n*, 420 F.3d 331, 341-42 (4th Cir. 2005).

Although the initial regulations would have required consumers to recommit their number to the registry every five years, the FTC changed this policy near the expiration of the first five-year period and numbers put on the list do not expire. FCC regulations also prohibit telemarketers from using automated dialers to call cell phone numbers. As more people only have mobile phones, it may be getting harder for telemarketers to distinguish cell and landline numbers, making a quick trip to www.ftc.gov/donotcall for cell phones probably worthwhile. (The registry does accept cell phone numbers and has since its inception.)

A related issue with mobile phones is that people take their phones with them. This is true both for short trips and for longer relocations, such as for years after a cross-country move. Telemarketers must call between 8:00 a.m. and 9:00 p.m. per federal law, 16 C.F.R. §310.4(c), and some state laws impose even shorter hours for operation. With mobile numbers, the telemarketer does not know the consumer's time zone. Query if it would be permissible for a company to use the area code to make an assumption about the consumer's time zone, even in light of the company having an address for the consumer putting them in a different time zone.

Even for those who wish to receive calls and have not put themselves on the registry, consumers find some forms of contact particularly annoying. The laws often regulate such types of contact. For example, federal laws try to limit the incidence of abandoned calls, which occur when a consumer rushes to answer the phone only to find nobody on the line. The FTC Telemarketing Sales Rule requires that each call ring for at least fifteen seconds or four complete rings before disconnecting and places a limit of 3 percent on the permissible incidence of abandoned calls. 16 C.F.R. §310.4(b)(v)(B)(i). The FTC regulations ban robo-calls, which are prerecorded telemarketing calls, unless the telemarketers have obtained "prior express written consent" from the consumer that they wish to receive such calls. 16 C.F.R. §310.4(b)(1)(v). Purely informational calls, such as flight cancellations, school notices, and appointment reminders, are not covered by the ban.

C. Email Solicitations

Federal law attempts to prevent unsolicited emails (a.k.a. "spam"). The title of the law gives you some sense of Congress' view on commercial email solicitations. *See* Controlling the Assault of Non-Solicited Pornography and Marketing Act of 2003 (CAN-SPAM), 15 U.S.C. §7701 et seq. The CAN-SPAM Act states that unsolicited commercial email makes up over half of all electronic email traffic, §7701(a)(2). Consensus seems to be that spam continues to grow, and that any perceptions that it is dwindling come from improved filtering and management techniques rather than from diminished sender activity.

The CAN-SPAM Act contains limitations on the content of messages and on the procurement of addresses. At the most basic level, the message must specify that it is a solicitation, and the message headers and subject headings must not be deceptive. 15 U.S.C. §7704(a)(1), (2) and (4). Such messages must inform consumers that they have the right not to receive further messages and must facilitate consumers' opting out from those messages. To do so, senders must provide a valid physical postal address (presumably so the consumer has another way to contact the company besides relying on email) and a link or return email address that operates for thirty days from the date of transmission that can be used to opt out. 15 U.S.C. §7704(a)(4) and (6). Email addresses should generally be obtained the old-fashioned way, by purchase of such lists, rather than through automated procedures that take best guesses at valid addresses using dictionaries and lists of names.

Liability under the CAN-SPAM Act is not limited to those who physically cause spam to be transmitted, such as the actual sender, but also extends to those who "procure the origination" of spam, which could include a company that hires a spammer to act on its behalf. 15 U.S.C. §7702(9). The effect seems to have been to deter large and legitimate companies, including exclusively online sellers, from sending unsolicited commercial email; companies who are hard to track down, have few resources and need not fear being sued, or are fly-by-night operations seem to still heavily use spam. Of course, these are the companies that consumers may least want to hear from, leading some to question whether the CAN-SPAM Act is deterring desirable messages without eliminating undesirable ones.

D.   Referral Schemes and Other Solicitation Techniques

Word of mouth is great advertising. Referral or pyramid schemes take this one step farther. A person buys goods or services and is promised either a discount on additional purchases or cash income from obtaining other customers for the seller. This entire method of solicitation is illegal in some states. For example, Iowa's UDAP statute declares as an unlawful practice the "sale, lease, or rental of any merchandise at a price or with a rebate or payment or other consideration to the purchaser which is contingent upon the procurement of prospective customers provided by the purchaser, or the procurement of sales, leases, or rentals to persons suggested by the purchaser." Iowa Code §714.16(2)(b). In other states, a plaintiff may rely on case law interpreting the state UDAP statute in ways that limit referral sales schemes. At a federal level, the FTC pursues referral schemes using the UDAP statute, 15 U.S.C. §45.

Federal Trade Commission v. Skybiz.Com, Inc.
No: 01-CV-396 (N.D. Okl. Aug. 31, 2001)

KERN, Chief Judge.

FINDINGS OF FACT AND CONCLUSIONS OF LAW AND ORDER
FOR PRELIMINARY INJUNCTION

On May 30, 2001, Plaintiff filed suit against SkyBiz.com, Inc., World Service Corporation (WSC), WorldWide Service Corporation (WWSC), Nanci Corporation International, James S. Brown, Stephen D. McCullough, Elias F. Masso, Nanci Masso, Kier F. Masso, and Ronald E. Blanton alleging that Defendants: 1) made false and misleading earnings claims to consumers; 2) provided others with the means and instrumentalities to make the same deceptive claims; 3) failed to disclose to consumers that SkyBiz's pyramid structure would not allow many of SkyBiz's participants to achieve the benefits promised by Defendants; and 4) were operating a pyramid scheme, all in violation of Section 5 of the FTC Act. [ED. NOTE — This is codified at 15 U.S.C. §45.] After issuing an Order requiring the Defendants to show cause why a preliminary injunction should not issue, the Court held a hearing. Now having considered the complaint, the evidence presented, the exhibits, the proposed Findings of Fact and Conclusions of Law submitted by the parties, and the applicable law, the Court renders the following Findings of Fact and Conclusions of Law with respect to SkyBiz.com, Inc., WSC, and WWSC.

. . .

I. FINDINGS OF FACT

. . .

E. DEFENDANTS' BUSINESS STRATEGY

21. Since its inception in 1998, all of the Defendants have been involved in some way with "The SkyBiz Program."

22. The SkyBiz Program is a MLM [multi-level marketing] scheme which involves the sale of an Internet product called a Web Pak. The program is promoted as a work-from-home business opportunity whereby interested individuals ("Associates") can sell the Web Pak product and achieve unlimited success if they put forth a reasonable amount of diligence. If an individual does not wish to purchase a Web Pak, he may become a "Compensation Only" Associate and simply receive compensation for participating in the program.

23. The Web Pak is a personal computer-related package which allegedly consists of the tools to create a 35 megabyte Internet website, various tutorials for beginner computer users, and an electronic mail account.

24. SkyBiz sells the Web Pak for $100.00 per year, plus a one-time processing charge of $25.00.

25. Associates buy the Web Pak which entitles them to participate in the SkyBiz Program. In order to earn income, they must recruit new Associates who purchase the SkyBiz Program from Defendants and who, in turn, recruit new Associates who purchase the SkyBiz Program from Defendants, and so on. Once an Associate sells two Web Paks, he is eligible to receive commissions. In this way, each Associate creates a "downline" consisting of all the people sponsored directly or indirectly by that Associate. Once an associate has personally sold nine (9) Web Paks, or has sold nine (9) indirectly through those in his "downline," that Associate receives a commission check from SkyBiz. As long as the Associate's downlines recruit new members, the Associate can earn commissions. A total of twenty-seven (27) sales must be made in an Associate's downline before his initial $125.00 is recouped. (Twenty-seven sales actually amounts to $140.00.)

26. Many new Associates are encouraged to buy more than one Web Pak at the outset because there is greater earning potential. . . . Some people were even

convinced to buy more than three. (Ken Klein testimony) (purchased five Web Paks); (Declaration of George Brackenrich) (purchased six Web Paks—two "3PAKs"; later persuaded to buy eight "7PAKs," plus one more Web Pak for a total of sixty-three Web Paks at a total cost of over $7,000.00).

27. The SkyBiz Program is promoted both directly by the Defendants and through their network of recruited Associates. Defendants urge Associates to use word-of-mouth referrals to get potential recruits to attend in-person sales presentations given by SkyBiz officers, corporate-sponsored presenters and more senior Associates.

28. In addition, Defendants sponsor conference calls and prerecorded calls to pitch the SkyBiz Program to prospective Associates. To assist their Associates in recruiting new participants in the SkyBiz Program, Defendants sell CD-ROMs, computer disks, videos, and books promoting the SkyBiz Program, and they provide a PowerPoint presentation that Associates may download.

29. In their live presentations, telephone calls, marketing materials and on their websites, defendants represent that participants are likely to receive substantial income by participating in the SkyBiz Program.

30. In their marketing materials and at seminars, Defendants have also featured "testimonials" from participants in the SkyBiz Program. In these testimonials, the individuals describe how successful they have become through participation in the SkyBiz Program.

31. Under SkyBiz's structure, approximately 87% of SkyBiz participants at any given time will not be able to qualify for commissions. This same structure also ensures that approximately 94% of SkyBiz's members at any given time will not recoup their investment. These facts are concealed when the SkyBiz program is pitched.

32. SkyBiz Associates and others affiliated with SkyBiz (including at least some of its principals) who market its product made numerous representations to consumers—potential Associates—that by participating in the SkyBiz program, they could earn substantial amounts of money. These representations have come in various forms: verbal representations in-person at live seminars and in visits to individual homes; verbal representations over the phone and in conference calls; and written representations on some Associates' websites. The promotional efforts of SkyBiz are designed to recruit new Associates by promising them the opportunity to achieve fabulous wealth with little or no effort through the recruitment of new Associates.

33. Although SkyBiz claims that its main function is to market the product, the emphasis of the seminars and Associate testimonials is on the earning potential one can realize if they become a SkyBiz Associate. Thus, the emphasis is placed on recruiting more Associates and not on selling the Web Pak.

34. The Receiver [Ed. Note—The FTC had a court-appointed receiver put in place when it filed suit] estimates that there are over 1.9 million Associates enrolled in the SkyBiz program.

35. The Receiver found that, out of all Web Pak sales, there have been only 428 sales of Web Paks to individuals who did not want to participate in the Compensation Plan.

36. In a study prepared in connection with the prosecution of criminal charges against SkyBiz Associates in Canada, the Royal Canadian Mounted Police found that 85% of the assigned websites were never developed. The defense's expert in that

same proceeding, whose expenses were paid by SkyBiz, testified that 87% of all assigned websites were not developed. Defendants' real product is the right to recruit new members.

37. There is little, if any, evidence that the Web Pak alone is a sought-after product. The parties have a difficult time convincingly demonstrating that there are consumers who have bought the Web Pak without any intention of participating in the MLM scheme. Furthermore, Defendants have presented no evidence that a significant number of purchasers of Web Paks use, maintain or renew their websites. This information is solely within the control or knowledge of Defendants. This notable absence of information clarifies to the Court that the interest in SkyBiz appears to lie in the opportunity to make money, which comes only with the recruitment of more members.

38. There is sufficient evidence to conclude that the SkyBiz Program is a deceptive marketing scheme.

39. There is sufficient evidence to conclude that individuals associated with the SkyBiz Program made misrepresentations and misleading claims to consumers about the potential for effortlessly earning great amounts of money.

II. CONCLUSIONS OF LAW

. . .

56. The misrepresentations made by Defendants and their Associates led consumers to believe that if they took part in the SkyBiz Program, they could earn substantial amounts of money. It is reasonable to expect that consumers could rely on the express claims of the representatives of the SkyBiz Program. See Five-Star Auto Club, 97 F. Supp. 2d at 528. SkyBiz representatives are aware that consumers will rely on these representations and, it is hoped, become participants.

57. Illegal pyramid schemes "are characterized by the payment by participants of money to the company in return for which they receive (1) the right to sell a product and (2) the right to receive in return for recruiting other participants into the program rewards which are unrelated to sale of the product to ultimate users." In re Koscot Interplanetary, Inc., 86 F.T.C. 1106 (1975). Several courts have adopted the *Koscot* test for pyramid schemes. See, e.g., US. v. Gold Unlimited, Inc., 177 F. 3d 472, 480 (6th Cir. 1999); Webster v. Omnitrition Intern., Inc., 79 F.3d 776, 781-82 (9th Cir. 1996).[3]

58. A lawful multi-level marketing program is distinguishable from an illegal pyramid scheme in the sense that the "primary purpose" of the enterprise and its associated individuals is to sell or market an end-product with end-consumers, and not to reward associated individuals for the recruitment of more marketers or "associates." See Gold Unlimited, 177 F.3d at 483-84 (suggesting that based on a

---

3. To date, the Tenth Circuit has not defined, nor has it adopted a definition for, a pyramid scheme. However, the Tenth Circuit defines a "Ponzi Scheme," which is a different sort of fraudulent enterprise than the one at bar, as: an investment scheme in which returns to investors are not financed through the success of the underlying business venture, but are taken from principal sums of newly attracted investments. Typically, investors are promised large returns for their investments. Initial investors are actually paid the promised returns, which attract additional investors. In re Hedged Investments Associates, Inc., 48 F.3d 470, 471 n.2 (10th Cir. 1995).

statutory survey of state criminal laws against pyramid schemes, this is a difference). See also Ger-Ro-Mar, Inc. v. FTC, 518 F.2d 33, 36 (2d Cir. 1975) (explaining that the distributors profited by earning commissions from their own sales and those of their recruits); In re Amway Corp., 93 F.T.C. 618, 716 (1979) (sponsors do not make money from their recruits' efforts until a newly recruited distributor begins to make wholesale purchases from his sponsor and sales to consumers).

59. Another distinction is that an unlawful pyramid scheme will saturate the market of potential participants to the point where it is unrealistic to expect that such a large number of individuals will become involved and the pyramid must therefore eventually collapse. A legitimate MLM does not have such a propensity for saturation. See Five-Star Auto Club, 97 F. Supp. 2d at 518 (S.D.N.Y. 2000) ("[i]f . . . each Five Star participant recruited only three new members, Five Star would have 387,000,000 members . . . exceed[ing] the populations of the United States and Canada"); Gold Unlimited, 177 F.3d at 481; Ger-Ro-Mar, 518 F.2d at 36-38 (if even a small number of individuals are recruited each month by each member, after a year the number of members would exceed the population of the United States); Amway, 93 F.T.C. at 716-17.

60. While the Web Pak product marketed and sold by SkyBiz appears to have some value to customers interested in purchasing it, the Court is not convinced that the primary purpose of SkyBiz is to sell Web Paks and to have its Associates sell Web Paks. Instead, the primary purpose of SkyBiz appears to be recruitment of Associates and to reward its members for that recruitment. In addition, whether SkyBiz's product has inherent value is of little consequence. While the product value could affect the quantum of harm suffered by the consumer, the issue of consumer harm is irrelevant to the Court's inquiry when the FTC brings an enforcement action such as this. See Miller, *supra* at ¶ 48. Furthermore, simply because a MLM's product has value does not render an unlawful pyramid scheme lawful. The other elements of a legal MLM program must also be present. See Gold Unlimited, Ger-Ro-Mar, and In re Amway, supra, at ¶ 58.

61. In addition, as pointed out by the FTC's expert, the structure of SkyBiz will ultimately result in the company's collapse. Because SkyBiz does not concentrate its business on sales of its single product, but instead on recruitment of members, the exponential growth which would be required to sustain the incomes anticipated by successful recruiters is impossible to attain and spells eventual collapse, or saturation, of the business.

62. There is good cause to believe that, under the more lenient standard, the FTC will ultimately prevail on the merits of this case and establish that Defendants have violated §5(a) of the FTC Act. The Court is convinced that without the entry of preliminary relief, Defendants will continue to violate §5(a) by making false or misleading representations about the SkyBiz program and its marketing plan which emphasizes potential for success for Associates who take part in the scheme. . . .

The court issued a preliminary injunction designed to not just to eliminate the sale of the Web Pak product but to restrain all defendants, including the individuals, from operating any pyramid marketing scheme. This remedy takes aim at the problem of individuals beginning a new referral sales company, with a different name and product but the same practices.

At the other end of the spectrum from referral schemes, which rely on consumers being social beings, are unsolicited goods, which just arrive at one's doorstep without any contact with the company or its representatives. The statutes regulating U.S. mail prohibit sending unordered goods, with the exception of free gifts, which must both be truly free and bear a notice telling consumers they are free. 39 U.S.C. §3009. Violations of this law are per se violations of the FTC Act, and quite often scams that use unordered goods and other deceptive practices, such as enclosing documents that suggest a consumer placed an order for the merchandise or is obligated to pay for return shipping.

Problem Set 4

4.1. Lucy Ling founded an interior decoration company, Lovely Living. She goes directly to people's homes, either having called in advance or without notice, and sells decorating plans. Ronald James has really let his house go since his wife's death two decades ago and was persuaded by Lucy's pitch that she could "bring the house back to life" with simple decorating plans that Ronald could execute "with a couple of trips to big-box retailer House, Home, and Hearth." To design the plan, Lucy followed her usual practices of taking digital photos and asking for a few small items of personal property to make pleasing color matches. Ronald gave her a pillow cushion and signed the contract. The plan's total cost is $500, with $300 payable up-front, which Ronald paid with a personal check. Lucy gave Ronald a copy of the signed contract, with all the blanks filled in neatly. The contract contained a prominent disclosure of right to cancel for three days. On the back of the contract were printed two copies of a lengthy term labeled "NOTICE OF CANCELLATION." Lucy's neighbor, a retired lawyer, wrote that language for her, telling her "it is the exact FTC-required language from the Internet." As fate would have it, Ronald fell instantly in love at a bingo tournament just one week later. His new special lady is herself an interior decorator and is excited about the opportunity to bring her unique touch to Ronald's home. Can Ronald cancel the contract with Lovely Living? *See* 16 C.F.R. §429.1.

4.2. Phijheeta Agrawal works for a telemarketing company, Beaches or Bust, that calls consumers to sell them vacation packages. When she makes her calls, Phijheeta identifies herself as an employee of Beaches or Bust, and states that the purpose of the call is to sell vacation packages that include hotel stays, ground transfers, and tours. She enjoys most aspects of her job, including describing the exotic locations and getting to talk to customers from all over the country. Phijheeta sometimes encounters a hostile caller, including some who demand her name, social security number, employee ID number, date of birth, or other details. In those instances, she usually just gives her name as Ann Smith or Jane Wood, in part because people mispronounce her name making it rhyme with "fajita." She politely refuses to give the other information and reminds the consumer that they may end the call at any time. Is Phijheeta violating the FTC's telemarketing sales rule? *See* 16 C.F.R. §§310.3, 310.4, and 310.5.

4.3. Hunt Hudson is the newly elected governor in a state whose populace is purple on the political spectrum (a perfect blend of "red" (Republicans) and "blue" (Democratic) citizens). Like all politicians, he needs initiatives that will be offensive to few and be loved by many. Inspired by his own difficulty in managing the flow of email on his iPhone, he has asked what you think of creating a state-wide "do-not-email" registry that would provide parallel protection to the do-not-call registry for unsolicited phone calls. Could a state enact such a law? What exceptions, if any, might Governor Hudson want to include in his proposed registry for certain kinds of emails? *See* 15 U.S.C. §§7707(b); 7702(2)(A); 7702(17).

4.4. Bethany Smith has a tough job as a receptionist at a law firm. She works long hours and to unwind she finds nothing beats a good massage. A new business called Massage Mates opened on the first floor of the skyscraper where she works. Bethany stopped in and learned that it is a members-only club. The initiation fee is $100 but that can be reduced by $10 for every friend that Bethany brings with her at the time that she joins. The monthly membership fee is $50 and includes one massage per month. Additional massages per month cost $40. The contract lasts for one year. Bethany can bring non-member friends for a one-time massage at a cost of $60. If they join within one month of receiving the massage, Bethany gets $10 off the next month's membership fee. Bethany had a bad experience a few years ago getting out of a gym contract after paying a hefty joining fee. She asks you, the most junior associate at the firm, whether she should join Massage Mates. In answering, consider the following statute:

> With respect to a consumer sale of goods or services, the seller may not give or offer to give a rebate or discount or otherwise pay or offer to pay value to the consumer as an inducement for a sale for the consumer giving the seller the names of prospective buyers, or otherwise aiding the seller in making a sale to another person, IF earning the rebate, discount, or other value is contingent upon the occurrence of an event AFTER the time the consumer agrees to buy.

Assignment 5.   Advertising

Advertising can help both consumers and businesses. Consumers benefit from awareness of and information about goods and services, and businesses benefit from new customers and increased product demand. Consumer law curbs advertising when it harms consumers by giving them false information. The usual legal maneuver is to prohibit certain statements on the grounds that they are deceptive. In some situations, however, consumer law affirmatively compels businesses to give information through labeling or other disclosures to counter problems with misinformation in a market.

Legally, advertising is a form of commercial speech. It is entitled to some constitutional protection from government regulation but significantly less than non-commercial speech. *See* Robert C. Post, *The Constitutional Status of Commercial Speech*, 48 U.C.L.A. L. REV. 1 (2010). This assignment touches the constitutional aspects lightly, focusing instead on the way in which accurate advertising improves markets and aids consumers.

A.   Unfair and Deceptive Advertising

1.   False Advertising

Advertisements that are untrue can be attacked under several legal theories. The common law of fraud or misrepresentation is one such tool, as is rescission of a contract on the ground that it was induced by fraud. These actions often focus on when advertising crosses the line from harmless puffery to false advertising. *See* David Hoffman, *The Best Puffery Article Ever*, 91 IOWA L. REV. 1395 (2006). At both the federal and state level, false advertising may be attacked as a deceptive practice banned under a UDAP statute or may violate a more specific law that targets false advertising. As the following case discusses, the statutes use a lower standard than the common law.

———————

State of Iowa ex rel. Miller, Attorney General of Iowa v. Pace
677 N.W.2d 761 (Iowa 2004)

TERNUS, Justice.

The defendant, Edwin Pace, appeals a district court judgment finding he had violated various state laws in his marketing and sale of payphones, awarding monetary remedies and penalties, and granting injunctive relief. . . . Pace also asserts the State failed to prove he committed unlawful practices under Iowa's consumer fraud law. . . .

I. BACKGROUND FACTS AND PROCEEDINGS.

. . . Beginning in 1997, but primarily in 1999 and continuing through June of 2000, the defendant sold payphones, known as customer-owned, coin-operated telephones (COCOTS), in Iowa. . . . [T]he investor entered into an agreement to purchase a payphone and then simultaneously leased the payphone to a management company. The payphone was then delivered directly to the management company for placement and operation. During the three- to five-year term of the lease, the investor had no involvement in the day-to-day operation of the payphone; all management rights rested in the management company in exchange for a monthly payment of $75-$82 to the investor. . . . [The] investors were only interested in the sale/leaseback plan because they had no expertise in operating or ability to manage a payphone. Thus, . . . the only COCOTS actually sold by the defendant were under the sale/leaseback plan.

Pace worked with a number of marketing companies, including Tri-Financial Group, Bee Communications, and ATC, Inc. Each company selling payphones was associated or affiliated with a particular management company. Although Pace claimed only to sell payphones and to have no relationship with the management companies, he would forward a request for lease information directly to the management company upon an investor's decision to go with the sale/leaseback option. Each payphone was sold for $5000 to $7000, and Pace earned a commission of between 10-12% on each sale. . . .

On September 17, 2001, the State filed a petition charging Pace with violations of the Iowa Uniform Security Act, Iowa Code chapter 502, the Iowa Business Opportunity Act, Iowa Code chapter 523B, and the Iowa Consumer Fraud Act, Iowa Code §714.16. At trial, the facts previously reviewed were brought out. In addition, several investors testified about the information given to them by Pace. They said Pace told them they would own the payphones; they could cancel the lease at any time and receive a refund of all or some portion of the purchase price; the management companies were financially strong; there was little risk in this investment and the investors would receive a return of 13-14%; and that COCOTS were legal in Iowa. One witness testified that Pace even told an elderly investor that COCOTS were fully insured by Lloyds of London.

The State also called a financial expert who had reviewed the financial statements of ETS. He testified that it was "obvious" the phone program could not be maintained without the continuous sale of payphones because the only way the lease payments could be made was through proceeds from future payphone sales.

In its subsequent decision, the district court made factual findings consistent with our review of the pertinent facts. The court found that even though material was available to Pace indicating significant legal issues with COCOTS across the country, he continued to represent to prospective purchasers that there were no concerns with selling the product in Iowa. He also repeatedly represented to potential investors that they would realize immediate and significant income from the ownership of a COCOT, that the COCOT was a liquid and safe investment, and that the COCOT was recession proof. . . .

Based on the same representations and omissions, the trial court concluded Pace's conduct constituted an "unfair practice" and "deception" under the consumer fraud provision of chapter 714. See id. §714.16. Because the court found Pace's violations were committed against "older persons," the court held the additional civil penalties of §714.16A applied.

The district court ordered Pace to pay restitution in the amount of $302,000. See id. §§502.501(1) (providing for restitution by person found in violation of chapter 502), 502.604(2)(d) (allowing commissioner of insurance to obtain court order for restitution). It also ordered him to disgorge to the State of Iowa all commissions received from the sale of COCOTS. See id. §502.604(2)(d) (allowing commissioner to obtain order providing for disgorgement by person found in violation of chapter 502). In addition, Pace was enjoined from violating chapters 502 and 523B, as well as §714.16, and from selling unregistered securities and business opportunities in Iowa. The court imposed a civil penalty of $4000 ($1000 for each commission of an unlawful practice), and a civil penalty of $1000 ($250 for each commission of consumer fraud against the elderly). See id. §§714.16(7) (providing for civil penalty of up to $40,000 per violation of §714.16), 714.16A(1) (providing for civil penalty of up to $5000 for each violation of §714.16 committed against an older person). Pace was made responsible for court costs, costs of investigation, and reasonable attorney fees. See id. §714.16(11) (permitting recovery of court costs, investigative costs, and attorney fees).

Pace appealed the trial court's decision. He asserts several grounds for reversal [including] . . . the State failed to prove the representations made by Pace were untrue; [and] the State failed to prove consumer fraud.

. . .

V. DID PACE COMMIT AN UNLAWFUL PRACTICE PROHIBITED
BY THE CONSUMER FRAUD LAW IN HIS SALE OF COCOTS?

The trial court held that Pace violated Iowa Code §714.16, which provides in relevant part:

> The act, use or employment by a person of an unfair practice, deception, fraud, false pretense, false promise, or misrepresentation, or the concealment, suppression, or omission of a material fact with intent that others rely upon the concealment, suppression, or omission, in connection with the lease, sale, or advertisement of any merchandise . . . , whether or not a person has in fact been misled, deceived, or damaged, is an unlawful practice.

This statute is not a codification of common law fraud principles. See State ex rel. Miller v. Hydro Mag, Ltd., 436 N.W.2d 617, 622 (Iowa 1989). It permits relief upon a lesser showing that the defendant made a misrepresentation or omitted a material fact "with the intent that others rely upon the . . . omission." Iowa Code §714.16(2)(a).

In the present case, the trial court found that Pace made the following false, deceptive and misleading representations to consumers in selling

COCOTS: (1) "an investment in COCOTS was guaranteed and was as safe or safer than bank certificates of deposit, annuity products, and insurance products"; (2) "the COCOTS program he offered was properly registered for sale in Iowa"; (3) the investors "would receive a 14% annual return on their COCOT investment and . . . they would receive a return of . . . 114% on their money"; (4) the investors "would own an asset in the form of a payphone"; and (5) "the payphone companies were financially strong." In addition, the court found that Pace "failed to share facts [that] would have been material [to investors] in making a decision to invest money in COCOTS." The material, undisclosed facts included: (1) the investment was high risk; (2) the high returns promised by the management companies could not realistically be expected; (3) the program was a Ponzi scheme; (4) the offers were not registered as a security or a business opportunity; (5) Pace was not registered as a securities agent in Iowa; and (6) Pace received significant commissions for each sale and he was required to return his commission should an investor liquidate his or her investment. See generally Goettsch, 561 N.W.2d at 378 (defining a Ponzi scheme).

The court also held these misrepresentations and material omissions constituted securities fraud under §502.401(2). Because the standard of proof is higher under §714.16, we consider Pace's challenge to the court's findings of misrepresentation and material omission only under the consumer fraud provisions of chapter 714.

Pace challenges the trial court's finding of consumer fraud on three bases. He denies making the statements attributed to him by the trial court and contends that even if he did make these representations, they were not shown to be false. He also claims that he acted innocently because he simply passed along the information he received from the marketing companies and had no idea this information was false.

Addressing the last argument first, we point out that it is not necessary for the State to prove that the violator acted with an intent to deceive, as is required for common law fraud. See Miller v. William Chevrolet/GEO, Inc., 326 Ill. App. 3d 642, 762 N.E.2d 1, 12, 260 Ill. Dec. 735 (Ill. App. Ct. 2001) (interpreting identical statutory language and stating, "Nor need the defendant have intended to deceive the [investor]."); Gennari v. Weichert Co. Realtors, 148 N.J. 582, 691 A.2d 350, 365 (N.J. 1997) (interpreting nearly identical statutory language and stating, "an intent to deceive is not a prerequisite to the imposition of liability"). As we noted above, the only intent required by the statute is that the defendant act "with the intent *that others rely*" upon his omissions. Iowa Code §714.16(2)(a) (emphasis added). In addition, there is no requirement under the statute that a violator have knowledge of the falsity of his or her representations. See Gennari, 691 A.2d at 365 ("One who makes an affirmative misrepresentation is liable even in the absence of knowledge of the falsity of the misrepresentation, negligence, or the intent to deceive."). Similarly, the Iowa statute does not require knowledge with respect to the omission or concealment of a material fact. See Miller, 762 N.E.2d at 12 (holding "innocent misrepresentations or material omissions" are actionable under consumer fraud law that included "the concealment, suppression or omission of any material fact" within definition of unlawful practice); *cf.* Gennari, 691 A.2d at 365 (holding "for liability to attach to an omission or failure to disclose, . . . the plaintiff must show that the defendant acted with knowledge" under statutory definition of unlawful practice that included "*knowing* concealment, suppression, or omission of any material fact" (emphasis added)). Thus, the defendant's contention that he was misled by the payphone companies just like his client is immaterial. Our consumer fraud statute places the consequences of being uninformed on the agent, not the investor. . . .

AFFIRMED.

Under federal law, an advertisement is false if it is "misleading in a material respect." 15 U.S.C. §55(a)(1). The definition includes not only representations but also the "extent to which the advertisement fails to reveal facts material in the light of such representations or material with respect to consequences which may result from the use of commodity. . . ." *Id.* The misrepresentation can be found anywhere, including on the product itself or in a separate advertisement.

Kraft, Inc. v. Federal Trade Commission

970 F.2d 311 (7th Cir. 1992)

FLAUM, Circuit Judge.

Kraft, Inc. ("Kraft") asks us to review an order of the Federal Trade Commission ("FTC" or "Commission") finding that it violated the Federal Trade Commission Act ("Act"), 15 U.S.C. §§45, 52. The FTC determined that Kraft, in an advertising campaign, had misrepresented information regarding the amount of calcium contained in Kraft Singles American Pasteurized Process Cheese Food ("Singles") relative to the calcium content in five ounces of milk and in imitation cheese slices. The FTC ordered Kraft to cease and desist from making these misrepresentations and Kraft filed this petition for review. We enforce the Commission's order. . . .

Process cheese food slices, also known as "dairy slices," must contain at least 51% natural cheese by federal regulation. 21 C.F.R. §133.173(a)(5). Imitation cheese slices, by contrast, contain little or no natural cheese and consist primarily of water, vegetable oil, flavoring agents, and fortifying agents. While imitation slices are as healthy as process cheese food slices in some nutrient categories, they are as a whole considered "nutritionally inferior" and must carry the label "imitation." Id. at §101.3(e). . . .

Kraft Singles are process cheese food slices. In the early 1980s, Kraft began losing market share to an increasing number of imitation slices that were advertised as both less expense and equally nutritious as dairy slices like Singles. Kraft responded with a series of advertisements, collectively known as the "Five Ounces of Milk" campaign, designed to inform consumers that Kraft Singles cost more than imitation slices because they are made from five ounces of milk rather than less expensive ingredients. The ads also focused on the calcium content of Kraft Singles in an effort to capitalize on growing consumer interest in adequate calcium consumption.

The FTC filed a complaint against Kraft charging that this advertising campaign materially misrepresented the calcium content and relative calcium benefit of Kraft

Singles. The FTC Act makes it unlawful to engage in unfair or deceptive commercial practices, 15 U.S.C. §45, or to induce consumers to purchase certain products through advertising that is misleading in a material respect. Id. at §§52, 55. Thus, an advertisement is deceptive under the Act if it is likely to mislead consumers, acting reasonably under the circumstances, in a material respect. In implementing this standard, the Commission examines the overall net impression of an ad and engages in a three-part inquiry: (1) what claims are conveyed in the ad; (2) are those claims false or misleading; and (3) are those claims material to prospective consumers.

Two facts are critical to understanding the allegations against Kraft. First, although Kraft does use five ounces of milk in making each Kraft Single, roughly 30% of the calcium contained in the milk is lost during processing. Second, the vast majority of imitation slices sold in the United States contain 15% of the U.S. Recommended Daily Allowance (RDA) of calcium per ounce, roughly the same amount contained in Kraft Singles. Specifically then, the FTC complaint alleged that the challenged advertisements made two implied claims, neither of which was true: (1) that a slice of Kraft Singles contains the same amount of calcium as five ounces of milk (the "milk equivalency" claim); and (2) that Kraft Singles contain more calcium than do most imitation cheese slices (the "imitation superiority" claim).

The two sets of ads at issue in this case, referred to as the "Skimp" ads and the "Class Picture" ads, ran nationally in print and broadcast media between 1985 and 1987. The Skimp ads were designed to communicate the nutritional benefit of Kraft Singles by referring expressly to their milk and calcium content. The broadcast version of this ad on which the FTC focused contained the following audio copy:

> Lady (voice over): I admit it. I thought of skimping. Could you look into those big blue eyes and skimp on her? So I buy Kraft Singles. Imitation slices use hardly any milk. But Kraft has five ounces per slice. Five ounces. So her little bones get calcium they need to grow. No, she doesn't know what that big Kraft means. Good thing I do.
>
> Singers: Kraft Singles. More milk makes 'em . . . more milk makes 'em good.
> Lady (voice over): Skimp on her? No way.

The visual image corresponding to this copy shows, among other things, milk pouring into a glass until it reaches a mark on the glass denoted "five ounces." The commercial also shows milk pouring into a glass which bears the phrase "5 oz. milk slice" and which gradually becomes part of the label on a package of Singles. In January 1986, Kraft revised this ad, changing "Kraft has five ounces per slice" to "Kraft is made from five ounces per slice," and in March 1987, Kraft added the disclosure, "one 3/4 ounce slice has 70% of the calcium of five ounces of milk" as a subscript in the television commercial and as a footnote in the print ads.

The Class Picture ads also emphasized the milk and calcium content of Kraft Singles but, unlike the Skimp ads, did not make an express comparison to imitation slices. The version of this ad examined by the FTC depicts a group of school children having their class picture taken, and contains the following audio copy:

> Announcer (voice over): Can you see what's missing in this picture?
>
> Well, a government study says that half the school kids in America don't get all the calcium recommended for growing kids. That's why Kraft Singles are important. Kraft

is made from five ounces of milk per slice. So they're concentrated with calcium. Calcium the government recommends for strong bones and healthy teeth!

Photographer: Say Cheese!

Kids: Cheese!

Announcer (voice over): Say Kraft Singles. 'Cause kids love Kraft Singles, right down to their bones.

. . .

As to the Skimp ads, the Commission found that four elements conveyed the milk equivalency claim: (1) the use of the word "has" in the phrase "Kraft has five ounces per slice"; (2) repetition of the precise amount of milk in a Kraft Single (five ounces); (3) the use of the word "so" to link the reference to milk with the reference to calcium; and (4) the visual image of milk being poured into a glass up to a five-ounce mark, and the superimposition of that image onto a package of Singles. It also found two additional elements that conveyed the imitation superiority claim: (1) the express reference to imitation slices combined with the use of comparative language ("hardly any," "but"); and (2) the image of a glass containing very little milk during the reference to imitation slices, followed by the image of a glass being filled to the five-ounce mark during the reference to Kraft Singles. The Commission based all of these findings on its own impression of the advertisements and found it unnecessary to resort to extrinsic evidence; it did note, however, that the available extrinsic evidence was consistent with its determinations.

The Commission then examined the Class Picture ads—once again, without resorting to extrinsic evidence—and found that they contained copy substantially similar to the copy in the Skimp ads that conveyed the impression of milk equivalency.

. . .

Kraft makes numerous arguments on appeal, but its principal claim is that the FTC erred as a matter of law in not requiring extrinsic evidence of consumer deception. Without such evidence, Kraft claims (1) that the FTC had no objective basis for determining if its ads actually contained the implied claims alleged, and (2) that the FTC's order chills constitutionally protected commercial speech. Alternatively, Kraft contends that substantial evidence does not support the FTC's finding that the Class Picture ads contain the milk equivalency claim. Finally, Kraft maintains that even if it did make the alleged milk equivalency and imitation superiority claims, substantial evidence does not support the FTC's finding that these claims were material to consumers. We address each contention in turn.

In determining what claims are conveyed by a challenged advertisement, the Commission relies on two sources of information: its own viewing of the ad and extrinsic evidence. Its practice is to view the ad first and, if it is unable on its own to determine with confidence what claims are conveyed in a challenged ad, to turn to extrinsic evidence. Thompson Medical, 104 F.T.C. at 788-89; Cliffdale Assocs., 103 F.T.C. 110, 164-66 (1984); FTC Policy Statement, 103 F.T.C. at 176. The most convincing extrinsic evidence is a survey "of what consumers thought upon reading the advertisement in question," Thompson Medical, 104 F.T.C. at 788-89, but the Commission also relies on other forms of extrinsic evidence including consumer testimony, expert opinion, and copy tests of ads. FTC Policy Statement, 103 F.T.C. at 176 n. 8.

Kraft has no quarrel with this approach when it comes to determining whether an ad conveys express claims, but contends that the FTC should be required, as a matter of law, to rely on extrinsic evidence rather than its own subjective analysis in all cases involving allegedly implied claims. The basis for this argument is that implied claims, by definition, are not self-evident from the face of an ad. This, combined with the fact that consumer perceptions are shaped by a host of external variables — including their social and educational backgrounds, the environment in which they view the ad, and prior experiences with the product advertised, see Richard Craswell, *Interpreting Deceptive Advertising*, 65 B.U. L. Rev. 658, 672-74, 717 (1985); Richard Pollay, *Deceptive Advertising and Consumer Behavior: A Case for Legislative and Judicial Reform*, 17 U. Kan. L. Rev. 625, 629-31 (1969) — makes review of implied claims by a five-member commission inherently unreliable. The Commissioners, Kraft argues, are simply incapable of determining what implicit messages consumers are likely to perceive in an ad. Making matters worse, Kraft asserts that the Commissioners are predisposed to find implied claims because the claims have been identified in the complaint, rendering it virtually impossible for them to reflect the perceptions of unbiased consumers. . . .

While Kraft's arguments may have some force as a matter of policy, they are unavailing as a matter of law. Courts, including the Supreme Court, have uniformly rejected imposing such a requirement on the FTC, see Colgate-Palmolive, 380 U.S. at 391-92, 85 S. Ct. at 1046 (FTC not required to conduct consumer surveys before determining that a commercial has a tendency to mislead); and we decline to do so as well. We hold that the Commission may rely on its own reasoned analysis to determine what claims, including implied ones, are conveyed in a challenged advertisement, so long as those claims are reasonably clear from the face of the advertisement.

Kraft's case for a per se rule . . . rests on the faulty premise that implied claims are inescapably subjective and unpredictable. In fact, implied claims fall on a continuum, ranging from the obvious to the barely discernible. The Commission does not have license to go on a fishing expedition to pin liability on advertisers for barely imaginable claims falling at the end of this spectrum. However, when confronted with claims that are implied, yet conspicuous, extrinsic evidence is unnecessary because common sense and administrative experience provide the Commission with adequate tools to makes its findings. The implied claims Kraft made are reasonably clear from the face of the advertisements, and hence the Commission was not required to utilize consumer surveys in reaching its decision.

. . .

Alternatively, Kraft argues that substantial evidence does not support the FTC's finding that the Class Picture ads convey a milk equivalency claim. Kraft claims that the Commission merely extrapolated its analysis from the Skimp ads to the Class Picture ads without considering significant differences between the two. The Commission stated, for example, that the Class Picture ads "contain copy elements substantially similar to the 'Skimp' ad elements that convey the impression of milk equivalency." In re Kraft, Inc., FTC No. 9208, slip op. at 22. Kraft points out that the Class Picture ads contain only one of the four elements of the Skimp ads — the reference to five ounces of milk juxtaposed with a reference to calcium content — that contributed to the FTC's milk equivalence finding. And Kraft adds that the reference to five ounces of milk per slice and to calcium merely states that each slice has a large amount of calcium because of its milk content, a completely true inference. The ads do not state or imply that each slice actually contains five ounces of milk or its calcium equivalent. Indeed, Kraft asserts that no reasonable consumer could think that a 3/4 ounce of slice of cheese contains five ounces of milk.

We find substantial evidence in the record to support the FTC's finding. Although Kraft downplays the nexus in the ads between milk and calcium, the ads emphasize visually and verbally that five ounces of milk go into a slice of Kraft Singles; this image is linked to calcium content, strongly implying that the consumer gets the calcium found in five ounces of milk. The fact that the Commission listed four elements in finding an implied claim in the Skimp ads does not mean that those same elements must all be present in the Class Picture ad to reach that same conclusion. Furthermore, the Class Picture ads contained one other element reinforcing the milk equivalency claim, the phrase "5 oz. milk slice" inside the image of a glass superimposed on the Singles package, and it was reasonable for the Commission to conclude that there were important similarities between these two ads. Finally, to support its own interpretation of the ads, the Commission examined available extrinsic evidence and this evidence, in the Commission's view, bolstered its findings.

Kraft asserts that the literal truth of the Class Picture ads — they are made from five ounces of milk and they do have a high concentration of calcium — makes it illogical to render a finding of consumer deception. The difficulty with this argument is that even literally true statements can have misleading implications. Here, the average consumer is not likely to know that much of the calcium in five ounces of milk (30%) is lost in processing, which leaves consumers with a misleading impression about calcium content. The critical fact is not that reasonable consumers might believe that a 3/4 ounce slice of cheese actually contains five ounces of milk, but that reasonable consumers might believe that a 3/4 ounce slice actually contains the calcium in five ounces of milk. . . .

Kraft next asserts that the milk equivalency and imitation superiority claims, even if made, are not material to consumers. A claim is considered material if it "involves information that is important to consumers and, hence, likely to affect their choice of, or conduct regarding a product." Cliffdale Assocs., 103 F.T.C. at 165; FTC Policy Statement, 103 F.T.C. at 175, 182. The Commission is entitled to apply, within reason, a presumption of materiality, Colgate-Palmolive, 380 U.S. at 392, and it does so with three types of claims: (1) express claims; (2) implied claims where there is evidence that the seller intended to make the claim; and (3) claims that significantly involve health, safety, or other areas with which reasonable consumers would be concerned. Thompson Medical, 104 F.T.C. at 816-17; FTC Policy Statement, 103 F.T.C. at 182-83. Absent one of these situations, the Commission examines the record and makes a finding of materiality or immateriality. Id. . . .

In determining that the milk equivalency claim was material to consumers, the FTC cited Kraft surveys showing that 71% of respondents rated calcium content an extremely or very important factor in their decision to buy Kraft Singles, and that 52% of female, and 40% of all respondents, reported significant personal concerns about adequate calcium consumption. The FTC further noted that the ads were targeted to female homemakers with children and that the 60 milligram difference between the calcium contained in five ounces of milk and that contained in a Kraft Single would make up for most of the RDA calcium deficiency shown in girls aged 9-11. Finally, the FTC found evidence in the record that Kraft designed the ads with the intent to capitalize on consumer calcium deficiency concerns.

Significantly, the FTC found further evidence of materiality in Kraft's conduct: despite repeated warnings, Kraft persisted in running the challenged ads. Before the ads even ran, ABC television raised a red flag when it asked Kraft to substantiate the milk and calcium claims in the ads. Kraft's ad agency also warned Kraft in a legal memorandum to substantiate the claims before running the ads. Moreover, in October 1985, a consumer group warned Kraft that it believed the Skimp ads were potentially deceptive. Nonetheless, a high-level Kraft executive recommended that the ad copy remain unaltered because the "Singles business is growing for the first time in four years due in large part to the copy." Finally, the FTC and the California Attorney General's Office independently notified the company in early 1986 that investigations had been initiated to determine whether the ads conveyed the milk equivalency claims. Notwithstanding these warnings, Kraft continued to run the ads and even rejected proposed alternatives that would have allayed concerns over their deceptive nature. From this, the FTC inferred — we believe, reasonably — that Kraft thought the challenged milk equivalency claim induced consumers to purchase Singles and hence that the claim was material to consumers. *See* Cliffdale Associates, 103 F.T.C. at 165; FTC Policy Statement, 103 F.T.C. at 175, 182.

With regard to the imitation superiority claim, the Commission applied a presumption of materiality after finding evidence that Kraft intended the challenged ads to convey this message. (Recall that intent to convey a claim is one of three categories qualifying for a presumption of materiality. See, e.g., Thompson Medical, 104 F.T.C. at 816-17.) It found this presumption buttressed by the fact that the challenged ad copy led to increased sales of Singles, even though they cost 40% more than imitation slices. Finally, the FTC determined that Kraft's consumer surveys were insufficient to rebut this inference and in particular criticized Kraft's survey methodology because it offered limited response options to consumers.

Kraft asserts that neither materiality finding is supported by substantial evidence. It contends that the survey evidence on which the Commission relied shows only that calcium, not milk equivalency, is important to consumers. Materiality, Kraft maintains, turns on whether the claim itself, rather than the subject matter of the claim, affects consumer decision-making; accordingly, the Commission had to show that consumers would have acted differently with knowledge that Singles contain 70% rather than 100% of the calcium in five ounces of milk. *See* FTC Policy Statement, 103 F.T.C. at 175 (claim is material if it is "likely to affect the consumer's conduct or decision with regard to a product"). With the inquiry defined in this manner, the only relevant evidence on point — a Kraft consumer survey showing that 1.7% of respondents would stop buying Singles if informed of the effect of processing on calcium content — definitively disproves materiality. With regard to its conduct, Kraft argues it persisted in running the ads because it thought the ads as a whole, not the milk equivalency claim per se, contributed to increased sales and that, in any event, it responded to warnings by making a good faith attempt to modify the ads. . . .

Kraft's arguments lack merit. The FTC found solid evidence that consumers placed great importance on calcium consumption and from this reasonably inferred that a claim quantifying the calcium in Kraft Singles would be material to consumers. It rationally concluded that a 30% exaggeration of calcium content was a nutritionally significant claim that would affect consumer purchasing decisions. This finding was supported by expert witnesses who agreed that consumers would prefer a slice of cheese with 100% of the calcium in five ounces of milk over one with only 70%. Likewise, the materiality presumption applied to the imitation superiority claim was supported by substantial evidence. This finding rested on internal company documents showing that Kraft designed the ads to deliver an imitation superiority message. *See* CX 32B, 120, 122A, 4S. Although Kraft produced a study refuting this finding, the Commission discounted that study after finding its methodology flawed. Kraft concedes that the Skimp ads increased sales of Singles, but contends that the Commission cannot carry its burden of demonstrating a linkage between the ads and the imitation superiority claim per se. However, this increase in sales corresponded directly with the ad campaign and indisputably reversed that sagging sales and market share of Kraft Singles that had been attributed to competition from imitation slices. Moreover, Kraft's increase in market share came at a time when Singles were priced roughly 40% higher than imitation slices. Thus, the Commission reasonably inferred that the imitation superiority message, as a central theme in the ads, contributed to increased sales and market share.

. . .

For the foregoing reasons, Kraft's petition to set-aside the order is DENIED and the Commission's order is ENFORCED.

The reasonableness standard for consumers means that survey evidence can be important in asserting or defending a claim of deceptive advertising. It is uncertain, however, how many consumers must have a particular impression from an advertisement to make it likely to mislead. For example, the New Balance company has relied on an FTC survey showing that two-thirds of consumers said that a "made in the USA" label was appropriate if at least 70 percent of a good was made in the United States to label its shoes. The FTC's guide, however, takes a stronger stance, requiring that a product labeled "Made in USA" must be "all or virtually all" made in the U.S. and defining "all or virtually all" to mean that the good contain no — or negligible — foreign content. FTC, Complying with the Made in the USA Standard (Dec. 1998).

In addition to cease and desist orders, like the one obtained in the *Kraft* case, the FTC sometimes pursues corrective advertising as a remedy. *See Novartis Corp. v. FTC*, 223 F.3d 783 (D.C. Cir. 2000). At issue in these situations is the duration and scope of the corrective advertising campaign, and whether the advertisement should reference the prior ads, for example, with statements such as "Contrary to prior advertising" or "The FTC wants us to correct some points in our advertisements."

2.   Bait and Switch

One of the oldest advertising scams is called "bait and switch." The basic scheme is to offer something desirable in an advertisement but then sell the consumer something of lesser quality, quantity, or price. The FTC issued a Guide Against Bait Advertising, 16 C.F.R. §§238.0-238.4. It requires that any offer to sell a product should be "bona fide"; the primary aim must be to sell the advertised product and not to switch consumers to a different product. Sometimes this is done by disparaging the original product or by informing consumers that it is unavailable. The FTC guide takes into consideration whether the merchant had a sufficient quantity of the advertised product to meet demand in determining whether a bait and switch scheme is being used.

A set of tactics to bait and switch are advertising practices that lure consumers into stores (and into making purchases) with statements that may be deceptive. Among the regulated practices are "going out of business sales," advertising "factory prices," and comparisons with artificially inflated "retail values." Many states have specific statutes on these practices; the federal government also has provided guidance to retailers on how to avoid deceptive pricing. *See* FTC Guide Against Deceptive Pricing, 16 C.F.R. §§233.1-233.5. The thrust of the guidance is to require that statements about the nature of prices or sales be factually true. For example, an advertisement touting a "complete liquidation sale" at "bankrupt prices" is misleading unless there is actually a court-supervised bankruptcy sale occurring. Similarly, companies must limit the length of a going-out-of-business or liquidation sale under many states' laws. To advertise such a sale as a near perpetual situation is to lure in customers who will believe they are getting a special sale opportunity rather than the businesses' usual prices.

B.   Commercial Speech

1.   Constitutional Standard

Since the mid-1970s, the Supreme Court has recognized that commercial speech is entitled to some constitutional protection, albeit to a lesser degree than noncommercial speech. *See Virginia State Board of Pharmacy v. Virginia Citizens Consumer Council, Inc.*, 425 U.S. 748 (1976). The primary justification for striking down speech restrictions as unconstitutional was the public's interest in the free flow of information to help it make decisions as market actors. In *Central Hudson Gas & Electric Corp. v. Public Service Comm'n of New York*, the Court set forth its test for commercial speech.

> In commercial speech cases, then, a four-part analysis has developed. At the outset, we must determine whether the expression is protected by the First Amendment. For commercial speech to come within that provision, it at least must concern lawful activity and not be misleading. Next we ask whether the asserted governmental interest is substantial. If both inquiries yield positive answers, we must determine whether the regulation directly advances the governmental interest asserted, and whether it is not more extensive than is necessary to serve that interest.

447 U.S. 557, 566 (1980). The court has applied this test in several factual contexts to hold that advertising restrictions were impermissible. For example, in

44 Liquormart, Inc. v. Rhode Island, 517 U.S. 484 (1996), the Court overturned a state law ban on advertising the price of alcoholic beverages, and in *Lorillard Tobacco Co. v. Reilly*, 533 U.S. 525 (2001), the Court struck down a near-ban on outdoor advertisements of cigarettes.

Despite its move to greater protection of commercial speech, the Court has consistently affirmed the ability to states to regulate advertisements that are deceptive or misleading. Assignment 4 provided an example of this with the failed constitutional challenges to the do-not-call registry. The main issues tend to be whether the conduct of the business is, in fact, commercial or non-commercial speech, *see Kasky v. Nike, Inc.*, 45 P.3d 243 (2002), and whether the government action is narrowly limited to only the misleading aspects of the advertisements, *see Zauderer v. Office of Disciplinary Counsel*, 471 U.S. 626 (1985).

2. Forced Speech

Sometimes the government forces companies to engage in speech for the sake of protecting consumers. Mandatory labels are one prominent example; the credit disclosures covered in Part Three of this book are another. The FTC generally distinguishes between labels and advertising, specifically referencing in its false advertising definition that an advertisement "is not labeling." 15 U.S.C. §55(a)(1). Labels are often regulated by industry-specific regulators, such as the Food and Drug Administration or the Environmental Protection Agency.

Labeling or disclosure requirements are treated differently under the law than voluntary advertising. Rather than the test in *Central Hudson* described above, the Supreme Court uses a more deferential standard that upholds mandatory factual disclosures if the requirements are "reasonably related to the state's interest" and are not "unjustified or unduly burdensome." *Zauderer v. Office of Disciplinary Counsel*, 471 U.S. 626, 651 (1985). In another case involving attorney advertising (like *Zauderer*), the Court affirmed that mandatory factual disclosures are entitled to only "minimal" constitutional protection, if any. *Milavetz, Gallop, & Milavetz, P.A. v. U.S.*, 559 U.S. 229, 130 S. Ct. 1324, 1340 (2010) (upholding disclosures to consumers required in the federal bankruptcy law). The Court noted that the statute required the disclosure only of accurate information and did not limit the ability of the business to provide additional information. *Id.* at 1340. In a challenge to New York City's menu-labeling law requiring the disclosure of calorie information, the Second Circuit explained the rationale for treating disclosure differently than other forms of commercial speech.

> Commercial disclosure requirements are treated differently from restrictions on commercial speech because mandated disclosure of accurate, factual, commercial information does not offend the core First Amendment values of promoting efficient exchange of information or protecting individual liberty interests. Such disclosure furthers, rather than hinders, the First Amendment goal of the discovery of truth and contributes to the efficiency of the "marketplace of ideas." Protection of the robust and free flow of accurate information is the principal First Amendment justification for protecting commercial speech, and requiring disclosure of truthful information promotes that goal.

N.Y. State Restaurant Ass'n v. NYC Bd. of Health, 556 F.3d. 114, 132 (2d Cir. 2009) (quoting *Nat'l Elec. Mfrs. Ass'n v. Sorrell*, 272 F.3d 104, 113-114 (2d Cir. 2001)).

As the government relies more on labeling and disclosure, however, companies are pushing back with challenges. Recently, several large tobacco companies filed a lawsuit arguing that new regulations requiring graphic warnings about the harms of smoking on cigarettes compel them to speak as advocates against their own product, and therefore violate the First Amendment of the U.S. Constitution.

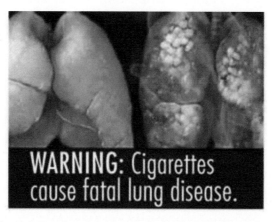

Health warnings for U.S. Food and Drug Administration proposed regulation "Required Warnings for Cigarette Packages and Advertisements"

See Complaint, *R.J. Reynolds Tobacco Co. et al. v. Food and Drug Administration, et al.,* Case 1:11-cv-01482 (Dist. D.C. Aug. 16, 2011). The Court of Appeals determined that photographs and written warnings required by the FDA were not meant to address any deceptive claims, and accordingly, applied a higher standard of review and invalidated the labels. *R.J. Reynolds Tobacco Co. v. Food & Drug Admin.,* 696 F.3d 1205, 1216-1218 (2012). A later case clarified that the government may mandate commercial speech, even in the absence of deception. *American Meat Institute v. USDA,* 760 F.3d 18 (D.C. Cir. 2014) (upholding a disclosure that required country-of-origin labeling on grounds that this information would be useful to a consumer). The restrictions on misleading advertising, and the ability to require factual labeling work in tandem. The former limits the inaccurate information put in front of consumers, while the latter adds accurate information to consumers' knowledge.

C.   Credit Advertising

Advertisements for credit present double compliance challenges. First, such ads should not be false or deceptive. Generally, credit advertising is subject to the rules applicable to other goods and services discussed above. Second, advertisements for credit are separately regulated by the Truth in Lending

Act. *See* 15 U.S.C. §§1661-1665b. The main approach of credit advertising rules is to focus on "trigger terms." If creditors engage in advertising using certain specified words, additional disclosures are mandated. This approach to advertisements is used for both open-end credit (revolving credit, such as credit cards) and closed-end credit (one-time deals, such as an auto loan), although the exact nature of the disclosures are different for the two types of credit. For example, if a creditor states a rate of interest, that rate must be expressed as an annual percentage rate. 15 U.S.C. §1664(d). Credit disclosures, which include both advertisements and the information to be given at the consummation of the transaction, are examined in Part Three of this book.

Problem Set 5

5.1. Amazing Amazonia specializes in bringing the secrets of the rain forest to suburban Americans. Its field explorers identified an edible berry that is consumed during festivals by a group of indigenous South Americans. Upon consuming the berry, the explorers noted feelings of euphoria. They nicknamed the product the Bliss Berry and brought it to the lab at Amazing Amazonia. The product development team has made it into a delicious tasting drink, which Amazing Amazonia now markets as Bliss Beer. The company's advertisements extol the virtues of Bliss Beer, claiming that it "fights depression" and "promotes sound mental health." The FTC has filed a complaint against Amazing Amazonia, alleging that it has engaged in false advertising and unfair and deceptive practices. Phoebe Max, the CEO of Amazing Amazonia, denounced the lawsuit as "wasting taxpayer dollars to persecute the Bliss Berry." She has retained your firm and is coming to an initial client meeting. She is bringing to the meeting the Bliss Berry portable file cabinet, which she says contains "all the secrets of the Bliss Berry and its powers." What are your strategies to defend the lawsuit? What documents will you want to look for to mount a vigorous defense? *See* the FTC Policy Statement on Advertising Substantiation.

5.2. Melissa Blechman's cosmetic empire, Masculine Masks, is flourishing, in part because of her sales strategy. Because her customers are men, Melissa dispensed with the usual promotions and glossy ads. Instead, the advertisements ask "What do you think you are worth?" and states that "prices reflect customer's needs, and may include introductory pricing, gifts, and bonus offers." After a product demonstration, salespeople directly negotiate prices with individual customers. Melissa has trained her staff to offer the first item at a low price, and then escalate the price for later items. When the customer balks, he is then offered a three-item bonus package (the mini-mask sampler) if he accepts the last price offered for all the merchandise under consideration. The executives that Masculine Masks targets as its customers seem to enjoy this competitive pricing activity, but a recent sales pitch to a lawyer left Melissa nervous, especially his parting line "I hope my skin is glowing when I see you in court." Do Masculine Masks' advertising and pricing tactics violate the law? *See* 16 C.F.R. §251.1.

5.3. Bruce Holtry has gotten into bad credit trouble over the years. He recently filed bankruptcy and is committed to improving his credit. His newfound frugality is largely the result of his girlfriend Sharon, whose father is a banker and who absolutely will not consent to Bruce and Sharon getting married until Bruce has a credit report "so clean that I'd eat off it." Bruce's bankruptcy attorney told him that the law entitles him to a free credit report and that he should monitor his report periodically. Bruce typed "free credit report" into a search engine and went to the top link: www.freecreditreport .com. Visit that site. Should Bruce order his credit report there? *See* 16 C.F.R. §610.4.

5.4. Jaime Rodriguez is a 22-year-old senior in college and is eager to obtain his first credit card. Walking across the street from campus, he saw a tent for College Bank and was lured in by the free handout of great iPhone cases in school colors, marred only by a very discrete College Bank logo on one side. The College Bank representative, Trixie, gave Jaime a big hello hug, handed him a credit card application that could be mailed in to College Bank if Jaime decided to apply, and hooked him up with two iPhone cases because he seemed so enthusiastic about getting a card. Inside the tent, Jaime noted the big banner stating "College Bank Card: Fixed 6% APR for college students."

Jaime thought College Bank and its card sounded like a perfect fit for him and was filling out his application during class when his professor, Chester Arnold, noticed Jaime was not paying attention. Professor Arnold snatched the application out of his hands and probed Jaime about how he acquired the application. He then spun on his heel and announced that class was dismissed immediately so he could go speak to the college's president about this "College Bank situation." While some students in Jaime's class think Professor Arnold just wants to get an iPhone case for himself before supplies run out, Jaime is worried that Trixie and her employer will get in trouble with the university administration. Did College Bank violate any laws? *See* 12 C.F.R. §1026.16(b) and (f); 12 C.F.R. §1026.57; 12 C.F.R. §1026.51(b).

Assignment 6.   Consumer Privacy and Identity Theft

In their dealings with consumers, businesses learn a great deal about consumers' identities and preferences. Consumers give such information as part of their contact with the business, but may not want the business that collected the data to use it for additional purposes, or to sell it to other companies. Technology has expanded the potential for businesses to harness consumer information in cost-effective ways, and a market for consumer data is flourishing. Consumer information is a valuable commodity for businesses. At the same time, the growth in data volume and the growth in sophisticated analytics have both increased consumers' sensitivities about disclosure. The risks and consequences of identity theft have grown as face-to-face transactions have declined. This assignment looks at when and how the law should impose restrictions or duties on business in the name of consumer privacy.

A.   The General Approach to Consumer Privacy

In the United States, businesses generally are free to gather and use consumers' information. Most U.S. privacy laws restrict information dissemination, rather than information collection or information processing. That is, businesses can gather and sort a vast amount of information with few legal restrictions. Any rules tend to be imposed when the data are shared or used. A primary concern is that dissemination would increase risks of intolerable invasions by businesses into consumers' ongoing activities. *See* Daniel J. Solove, *A Taxonomy of Privacy*, 154 U. Pa. L. Rev. 477 (2006).

The basic approach to consumer privacy in the United States is "notice and choice." The FTC has reaffirmed its commitment to that model. Federal Trade Commission, *Protecting Consumer Privacy in an Era of Rapid Change* (Dec. 2010). The report urged companies to promote "privacy by design" by paying more attention to privacy issues at every stage of the development of their products and services. The FTC acknowledged that consumers often lacked an understanding of privacy policies but sought to remedy that by urging improvements to consumer choice mechanisms. They focused on the standardization, readability, and timing of disclosures.

The European Union takes a markedly different approach to consumer privacy: comprehensive privacy legislation. The general rule is that personal data should not be processed at all, except when the consumer has been informed and has consented, and only for specified legitimate purposes. E.U. Data

Protection Directive, 95/46/EC. The U.S. Department of Commerce has developed a "Safe Harbor" framework that U.S. businesses can adopt that the European Union has agreed meets the "adequacy" standard for privacy protection under the Directive. Among other things, the Safe Harbor Privacy Principles require that consumers be given notice of the purposes for collecting and using information and that consumers have the opportunity to opt out (or for sensitive information to be shared with third parties, to opt in to disclosure). Individuals also must have access to personal information about them, including an opportunity to correct, amend, or delete that information. While many large international corporations have chosen to comply with the Safe Harbor framework, privacy of most consumer information in the United States remains largely unregulated.

The U.S. law that does govern online privacy is fairly limited and dated. For example, the 1998 Children's Online Privacy Protection Act mandates the existence and disclosure of a privacy policy for sites that 1) target children, 2) have actual knowledge of children's use of the site, or 3) have a children's section of a general site. 15 U.S.C. §6501. Notably, the privacy policy does not have to be presented in a way that children could read and understand, despite the statute's concern with children, a special category of consumers with limited literacy.

Electronic means of gathering and storing data has revolutionized the use of consumer information, as discussed further in this assignment. The case below remains good law. Query if a jury might assess the facts or interpret the question of damages differently today. Privacy may be a malleable concept that adjusts to the perceived risks and the baseline practices of most businesses.

In re JetBlue Airways Corp. Privacy Litigation

379 F. Supp. 2d 299 (E.D.N.Y. 2005)

AMON, District Judge.

INTRODUCTION

A nationwide class of plaintiffs brings this action against JetBlue Airways Corporation ("JetBlue"), Torch Concepts, Inc. ("Torch"), Acxiom Corporation ("Acxiom"), and SRS Technologies ("SRS") for alleged violations of the Electronic Communications Privacy Act of 1986 ("ECPA"), 18 U.S.C. §2701, et seq. (1986), and violations of state and common law. Plaintiffs claim that defendants violated their privacy rights by unlawfully transferring their personal information to Torch for use in a federally-funded study on military base security. Plaintiffs seek a minimum of $1,000 in damages per class member, or injunctive relief to the extent that damages are unavailable, as well as a declaratory judgment. Defendants have moved to dismiss the Amended Complaint pursuant to Rule 12(b)(6) of the Federal

Rules of Civil Procedure on the grounds that plaintiffs have failed to state a federal cause of action under the ECPA, that plaintiffs' state law claims are federally preempted, and that plaintiffs have failed to state any claim under state law.

STATEMENT OF FACTS

Unless otherwise indicated, the following facts set forth in plaintiffs' Amended Complaint are presumed to be true for purposes of defendants' motions to dismiss. JetBlue has a practice of compiling and maintaining personal information, known in the airline industry as Passenger Name Records ("PNRs"), on each of its adult and minor passengers. Information contained in PNRs includes, for example, passenger names, addresses, phone numbers, and travel itineraries. The PNRs are maintained, or temporarily stored, on JetBlue's computer servers, and passengers are able to modify their stored information. Acxiom, a world leader in customer and information management solutions, maintains personally-identifiable information on almost eighty percent of the U.S. population, including many JetBlue passengers, which it uses to assist companies such as JetBlue in customer and information management solutions.

The personal information that forms the basis of JetBlue's PNRs is obtained from its passengers over the telephone and through its Internet website during the selection and purchase of travel arrangements. In order to encourage the provision of personal information in this manner, JetBlue created a privacy policy which provided that the company would use computer IP addresses only to help diagnose server problems, cookies to save consumers' names, e-mail addresses to alleviate consumers from having to re-enter such data on future occasions, and optional passenger contact information to send the user updates and offers from JetBlue. The JetBlue privacy policy specifically represented that any financial and personal information collected by JetBlue would not be shared with third parties and would be protected by secure servers. JetBlue also purported to have security measures in place to guard against the loss, misuse, or alteration of consumer information under its control.

In the wake of September 11, 2001, Torch, a data mining company similar to Acxiom, presented the Department of Defense ("DOD") with a data pattern analysis proposal geared toward improving the security of military installations in the United States and possibly abroad. Torch suggested that a rigorous analysis of personal characteristics of persons who sought access to military installations might be used to predict which individuals pose a risk to the security of those installations. DOD showed interest in Torch's proposal and added Torch as a subcontractor to an existing contract with SRS so that Torch could carry out a limited initial test of its proposed study. The SRS contract was amended to include airline PNRs as a possible data source in connection with Torch's study. Because Torch needed access to a large national-level database of personal information and because no federal agencies approached by Torch would grant access to their own governmental databases, Torch independently contacted a number of airlines in search of private databases that might contain adequate information to serve its requirements. These airlines declined to share their passengers' personal information unless the Department of Transportation ("DOT") and/or the Transportation Security Administration ("TSA") were involved and approved of such data sharing.

Unable to obtain the data through its own devices, Torch asked members of Congress to intervene on its behalf with the airlines or federal agencies. Torch also contacted the DOT directly. Following a series of meetings, the DOT and the TSA agreed to assist Torch in obtaining consent from a national airline to share its passenger information. On July 30, 2002, the TSA sent JetBlue a written request to supply its data to the DOD, and JetBlue agreed to cooperate. In September 2002, JetBlue and Acxiom collectively transferred approximately five million electronically-stored PNRs to Torch in connection with the SRS/DOD contract. Then, in October 2002, Torch separately purchased additional data from Acxiom for use in connection with the SRS contract. This data was merged with the September 2002 data to create a single database of JetBlue passenger information including each passenger's name, address, gender, home ownership or rental status, economic status, social security number, occupation, and the number of adults and children in the passenger's family as well as the number of vehicles owned or leased. Using this data, Torch began its data analysis and created a customer profiling scheme designed to identify high-risk passengers among those traveling on JetBlue.

In or about September 2003, government disclosures and ensuing public investigations concerning the data transfer to Torch prompted JetBlue Chief Executive Officer David Neelman to acknowledge that the transfer had been a violation of JetBlue's privacy policy. A class of plaintiffs whose personal information was among that transferred now brings this action against JetBlue, Torch, Acxiom, and SRS, seeking monetary damages, including punitive damages, and injunctive relief. Plaintiffs assert five causes of action against all defendants: (1) violation of the ECPA, 18 U.S.C. §2701, et seq., (2) violation of the New York General Business Law and other similar state consumer protection statutes, (3) trespass to property, (4) unjust enrichment, and (5) declaratory judgment. In addition, plaintiffs bring a sixth claim for breach of contract against JetBlue. . . .

ELECTRONIC COMMUNICATIONS PRIVACY ACT

Plaintiffs allege that all defendants violated §2702 of the ECPA, by divulging stored passenger communications without the passengers' authorization or consent. Section 2702 provides, in pertinent part, that:

> (1) a person or entity providing an electronic communication service to the public shall not knowingly divulge to any person or entity the contents of a communication while in electronic storage by that service. . . .

> (2) a person or entity providing remote computing service to the public shall not knowingly divulge to any person or entity the contents of any communication which is carried or maintained on that service. . . .

18 U.S.C. §2702(a). The statute defines "electronic communication service" as "any service which provides to users the ability to send or receive wire or electronic communications." 18 U.S.C. §2510(15). The term "electronic communication" includes "any transfer of signs, signals, writing, images, sounds, data, or intelligence of any nature transmitted in whole or in part by wire, radio, electronic, photoelectronic or photoptical system that affects interstate or foreign commerce." 18 U.S.C. §2510(12). "[R]emote computing service" refers to "the provision to the public of computer storage or processing services by means of an electronic communication system." 18 U.S.C. §2711(2). . . .

The term "electronic communication service," as defined, refers to a service that provides users with capacity to transmit electronic communications. Although Jet-Blue operates a website that receives and transmits data to and from its customers, it is undisputed that it is not the provider of the electronic communication service that allows such data to be transmitted over the Internet. Rather, JetBlue is more appropriately characterized as a provider of air travel services and a consumer of electronic communication services. The website that it operates, like a telephone, enables the company to communicate with its customers in the regular course of business. Mere operation of the website, however, does not transform JetBlue into a provider of internet access, just as the use of a telephone to accept telephone reservations does not transform the company into a provider of telephone service. Thus, a company such as JetBlue does not become an "electronic communication service" provider simply because it maintains a website that allows for the transmission of electronic communications between itself and its customers.

This reading of the statute finds substantial support in the case law. Although the Second Circuit has not yet had occasion to construe the term "electronic communication service," a number of courts in this and other circuits have done so, some in cases factually similar to this case. The weight of this persuasive authority holds that companies that provide traditional products and services over the Internet, as opposed to Internet access itself, are not "electronic communication service" providers within the meaning of the ECPA. . . .

Relying on these authorities, a number of courts have specifically addressed the applicability of the term "electronic communication service" to national airlines that operate on-line reservations systems similar to that maintained by JetBlue. Almost without exception, those courts have concluded that the term does not encompass companies that sell air travel over the Internet but are not in the business of selling Internet access itself. See Dyer v. Northwest Airlines Corporations, 334 F. Supp. 2d 1196, 1199 (D.N.D. 2004) ("[B]usinesses offering their traditional products and services online through a website are not providing an 'electronic communication service.'"); In re Northwest Airlines Privacy Litigation, 2004 WL 1278459, at *2 (D. Minn. June 6, 2004) ("Defining electronic communication service to include online merchants or service providers like Northwest stretches the ECPA too far.") The facts underlying those cases are indistinguishable from those present here.

. . .

Plaintiffs have also failed to establish that JetBlue is a remote computing service. . . . Although plaintiffs allege that JetBlue operates a website and computer servers, no facts alleged indicate that JetBlue provides either computer processing services or computer storage to the public. As such, under the plain meaning of the statute, JetBlue is not a remote computing service.

For the foregoing reasons, JetBlue as a matter of law is not liable under §2702 of the ECPA.

. . .

FAILURE TO STATE A CLAIM UNDER STATE OR COMMON LAW

In addition to arguing that plaintiffs' state and common law claims are preempted, defendants argue that plaintiffs have failed to state a cause of action for any claim under state law. . . .

A. Breach of Contract

JetBlue is the only defendant charged with breach of contract in this case. Plaintiffs allege that they made reservations to fly with JetBlue in reliance on express promises made by JetBlue in the company's privacy policy. The substance of the contract alleged is therefore a promise by JetBlue not to disclose passengers' personal information to third parties. Plaintiffs allege that JetBlue breached that promise, thereby causing injury.

An action for breach of contract under New York law requires proof of four elements: (1) the existence of a contract, (2) performance of the contract by one party, (3) breach by the other party, and (4) damages. Rexnord Holdings, Inc. v. Bidermann, 21 F.3d 522, 525 (2d Cir. 1994). JetBlue contends that plaintiffs have failed to plead facts sufficient to establish the existence of a contract or that they suffered damages.

With regard to the existence of a contract, plaintiffs contend that JetBlue undertook a "self-imposed contractual obligation by and between [itself] and the consumers with whom it transacted business" by publishing privacy policies on its website or otherwise disclosing such policies to its consumers. . . . [Plaintiffs argue] that a stand-alone contract was formed at the moment they made flight reservations in reliance on express promises contained in JetBlue's privacy policy. JetBlue posits no persuasive argument why this alternative formulation does not form the basis of a contract.

[ED. NOTE—The court held that an allegation of reliance to encompass an allegation that some putative members of the class read or viewed the privacy policy and that the issue of who actually read and relied on the policy would be better addressed at class certification.]

JetBlue also argues that plaintiffs have failed to meet their pleading requirement with respect to damages, citing an absence of any facts in the Amended Complaint to support this element of the claim. Plaintiffs' sole allegation on the element of contract damages consists of the statement that JetBlue's breach of the company privacy policy injured plaintiffs and members of the class and that JetBlue is therefore liable for "actual damages in an amount to be determined at trial." In response to JetBlue's opposition on this point, plaintiffs contend that the Amended Complaint is "replete" with facts demonstrating how plaintiffs were damaged but cite to nothing more than the boilerplate allegation referenced above and another allegation in the Amended Complaint that they were "injured." At oral argument, when pressed to identify the "injuries" or damages referred to in the Amended Complaint, counsel for plaintiffs stated that the "contract damage could be the loss of privacy" acknowledging that loss of privacy "may" be a contract damage. The support for this proposition was counsel's proffer that he had never seen a case that indicates that loss of privacy cannot as a matter of law be a contract damage. In response to the Court's inquiry as to whether a further specification of damages could be set forth in a second amended complaint, counsel suggested only that perhaps it could be alleged or argued that plaintiffs were deprived of the "economic value" of their information. Despite being offered the opportunity to expand their claim for damages, plaintiffs failed to proffer any other element or form of damages that they would seek if given the opportunity to amend the complaint. . . .

It is apparent based on the briefing and oral argument held in this case that the sparseness of the damages allegations is a direct result of plaintiffs' inability to plead or prove any actual contract damages. As plaintiffs' counsel concedes, the only damage that can be read into the present complaint is a loss of privacy. At least one recent case has specifically held that this is not a damage available in a breach of contract action. See Trikas v. Universal Card Services Corp., 351 F. Supp. 2d 37, 46 (E.D.N.Y. 2005). This holding naturally follows from the well-settled principle that "recovery in contract, unlike recovery in tort, allows only for economic losses flowing directly from the breach." Young v. U.S. Dep't of Justice, 882 F.2d 633, 641 (2d Cir. 1989) (citations omitted); see Katz v. Dime Savings Bank, FSB, 992 F. Supp. 250, 255 (W.D.N.Y. 1997) (non-economic loss is not compensable in a contract action).

Plaintiffs allege that in a second amended complaint, they could assert as a contract damage the loss of the economic value of their information, but while that claim sounds in economic loss, the argument ignores the nature of the contract asserted. . . . A similarly basic principle of contract law is that the "purpose of contract damages is to put a plaintiff in the same economic position he or she would have occupied had the contract been fully performed." Katz, 992 F. Supp. at 255. Plaintiffs may well have expected that in return for providing their personal information to JetBlue and paying the purchase price, they would obtain a ticket for air travel and the promise that their personal information would be safeguarded consistent with the terms of the privacy policy. They had no reason to expect that they would be compensated for the "value" of their personal information. In addition, there is absolutely no support for the proposition that the personal information of an individual JetBlue passenger had any value for which that passenger could have expected to be compensated. It strains credulity to believe that, had JetBlue not provided the PNR data en masse to Torch, Torch would have gone to each individual JetBlue passenger and compensated him or her for access to his or her personal information. There is likewise no support for the proposition that an individual passenger's personal information has or had any compensable value in the economy at large.

Accordingly, plaintiffs having claimed no other form of damages apart from those discussed herein and having sought no other form of relief in connection with the breach of contract claim, JetBlue's motion to dismiss the claim is granted.

B. Trespass to Property

Plaintiffs allege that defendants committed trespass to property by participating in the transfer of data containing their personal and private information. Because their claim concerns an alleged trespass to something other than real property, it is most accurately treated as a claim for trespass to chattels. . . .

Under New York law, liability only obtains on this cause of action if a defendant causes harm to "the [owner's] materially valuable interest in the physical condition, quality, or value of the chattel, or if the [owner] is deprived of the use of the chattel for a substantial time." Kuprewicz, 771 N.Y.S.2d at 807-08 (quoting Restatement (Second) of Torts §218, com. e (1965)). . . . [Plaintiffs do not] allege that the quality or value of their personal information was in any way diminished as a result of defendants' actions, nor do they allege any facts that could sustain such a showing. The only type of harm plaintiffs allege anywhere in the Amended Complaint is harm to their privacy interests, and even if their privacy interests were indeed infringed by the data transfer, such a harm does not amount to a diminishment of the quality or value of a materially valuable interest in their personal information. Plaintiffs also have not been deprived of the use of their personal information at any point, let alone for a substantial period of time. See Kuprewicz, 771 N.Y.S.2d at 807-08. Thus, plaintiffs have not established that they suffered the type of harm that may be redressed through a claim for trespass to chattels.

Other courts have refused to recognize the disclosure or unauthorized use of personal information as a compensable harm. In *Dwyer v. American Express Co.*, 652 N.E.2d 1351 (Ill. 1995), the court held that unwanted solicitations do not constitute an actionable harm because consumers suffered no damage.

Jet Blue illustrates the relevance of state law in privacy disputes. In an omitted part of the opinion, the court rejected the defendants' preemption claims. The limited approach to preemption is somewhat surprising in the realm of privacy because the nature of the issue means that the geographic location of the consumer or transaction is often difficult to discern. One effect is to increase the relevance of any state laws that do exist. Businesses cannot easily discern when consumers reside in California, so the privacy policy tends to comply with the most consumer-friendly state rules. In California, privacy enjoys constitutional status. Pursuing and obtaining privacy is an inalienable right. Cal. Const. Art 1, §1. Some states have statutes that provide privacy rights. The California Online Privacy Protection Act, Cal. Bus. & Prof. Code §§22575-22579, requires that commercial websites or online services conspicuously post their privacy policies.

Despite this trend toward greater privacy protection from the law, the best strategy for consumers is to avoid doing business with companies that collect or share information. Discovering these companies requires finding and reading each one's privacy policy (assuming a company has such a policy). To reduce the burden on consumers, some have urged privacy disclosures be broken down and delivered "in-context" and "just-in-time." For example, when a consumer registers as a user or signs up for a mailing list, the business may collect and share more personal information than when the consumer was browsing. A special notice or link to privacy controls, delivered as part of the sign-up process, may be more likely to be read by a consumer than a link to a long, generic privacy policy somewhere on the site.

B.   Big Data

The vast majority of U.S. consumers have Internet access. In addition to large amounts of data stored on computers and transmitted over the Internet, mobile devices track additional information such as geographic location. This is an example of device-generated data, which can then be added to user-generated data such as visiting a webpage or downloading an app. Cameras and videos add observational data, and social media has multiplied the amount and frequency of self-reported data. This increased connectivity creates a data environment termed "always-on, always-on-us," in which millions of people generate data actively and passively every minute. A 2013 estimate stated that that an astonishing 90 percent of the world's data was generated in the two preceding years. The output of data is doubling every two years. Chairwoman Edith Ramirez, *Welcoming and Opening Remarks*, FTC Conference, Big Data: A Tool for Inclusion or Exclusion Workshop (Sept. 15, 2014).

Meanwhile, the costs of collecting, storing, and processing information is plummeting. An entire industry called data brokering has developed to facilitate trade in consumer information. Businesses can now accumulate and store virtually unlimited amounts of data, and then use increasingly sophisticated tools to analyze it. "Big data" is the catch phrase to describe these phenomena. Big data is commonly explained in terms of three v's: 1) the volume of data is exploding, 2) the velocity at which data is accumulated is increasing, and 3) the variety of formats of data is proliferating. Industry is the main beneficiary of big data, in part because government is subject to constitutional checks on invasions of privacy.

The few available stories of what companies are doing with big data are provocative. For example, Eric Horvitz, a researcher at Microsoft, was able to predict with a high probability whether an individual was going to be hospitalized within the next 48 hours. His tools were Bing search engine data and algorithms to look for patterns therein. FTC conference, Big Data: A Tool for Inclusion or Exclusion Workshop (Sept. 15, 2014) (transcript at 54). While big data may already be well developed and powerful, the law surrounding its use is nascent.

The benefits of big data are its potential to permit businesses to do more personalization and its segmentation of consumers. Put more bluntly, big data discriminates. Its very nature is to analyze vast amounts of information to differentiate quickly among people based on predictive models. Advocates herald the arrival of targeted medical treatments, responsive education, and time or energy-saving innovations, such as a home thermostat that kicks on when your mobile device nears your home. Big data tailors the advertisements that you see based on its inferences about your ethnicity, income, religion, age, and taste preferences.

The segmentation and personalization of big data are only possible because statistical models can position one consumer in relation to a whole variety of other individuals. In doing so, it relies on relationships and networks that were not intentionally designed to exist or fit together. For example, Bing was assuredly not designed as a preventative health tool, yet that is clearly its potential. Big data can reward loyal customers with shorter wait times, but it can also differ prices based on predictions about willingness or ability to pay. At a FTC conference, a researcher showed how something as mundane as the price of a stapler varied from online retailers based on geo-location data derived from the user's cellular or wireless connection—and even the type of device or operating system. Ashkan Soltani, *Emerging Trends in Online Pricing*, FTC Spring Privacy Series: Alternative Scoring Products Conference (Mar. 19, 2014) (transcript at 67-68). Detractors of big data call such practices digital redlining, a reference to lenders who used red pen to mark "no-loan zones" on maps in neighborhoods with high concentrations of minorities.

A softer term is "discrimination by algorithm," which emphasizes the limited role of intent — and human decision-making — in big data processes.

The concern is big data will be used in ways that exacerbate existing disparities. Any decision that uses the past as a basis for inferring future likelihoods is potentially reproducing historic outcomes or behaviors. Big data's segmentation function could prevent some consumers from obtaining services and cause some consumers to even pay more for goods, or even change one's job prospects. A web search of names popular in the black community was more likely to produce display ads about how to expunge criminal records than a search of names popular among non-black people. If a job recruiter searched a candidate's name on the Internet, the advertisement might suggest (often wrongly) that the person had a criminal record. While many people claim to ignore such advertisements when they are online, impressions are more malleable and subconscious than most of us understand. The risk of big data is that it assesses the characteristics of particular populations, albeit with more sophistication and information than in the past, rather than returning verified information about a person at an individual level. Yet it is assuredly an individual person who experiences the benefits or burdens of the algorithmic inference.

The law has yet to catch up to big data technology. Other than sometimes requiring disclosure of privacy policies, the law largely does not reach how data can be used. The main exception is with respect to credit, where models and scoring have decades of use and a tainted legacy. While the next assignments cover credit laws in more detail, a few points are relevant now. Generally, credit laws apply at the individual level. Their application is less clear when the action is being taken based on predictions that one is a member of a certain group. The Equal Credit Opportunity Act, which explicitly limits using certain protected categories in credit decisions, requires that use of a factor that correlates to protected status have a demonstrably and statistically sound relationship with creditworthiness. 12 C.F.R. §1002.2(p). But the very beauty — and threat — of big data is its ability to surface relationships that were not intuitively obvious in first place. That makes explaining such relationships to consumers or regulators very difficult or even impossible. Most consumers may be skeptical that their network of Facebook friends is a valid predictor of their creditworthiness, but at least some lenders assert such a relationship. CNN Money, *Facebook Friends Could Change Your Credit Score*, Aug. 26, 2013, http://money.cnn.com/2013/08/26/technology/social/facebook-credit-score.

Some have suggested that the path forward with regard to big data is to harness its techniques to detect and combat discrimination. The difficulty is that it is unclear that businesses can profit from countering discrimination.

C. Consumer Privacy with Financial Institutions

The most onerous (or beneficial, depending on your perspective as either a business or consumer, respectively) of privacy laws take aim at a specific industry. A familiar example, reinforced by any doctor or dentist visit, is the treatment of health care information. The Health Insurance Portability and Accountability Act of 1996 (HIPAA), codified at 42 U.S.C. §17935, requires that medical providers give a disclosure to each patient regarding health care records. HIPAA killed a legion of trees with its paperwork and produced a lot of work for compliance lawyers. It also raised the awareness of consumers about medical records and provoked debate among the medical profession about what confidentiality means in a multi-player health system that includes insurance companies, outside labs, and multiple care providers.

Financial institutions, including banks, insurance companies, financial advisors, and investment companies, also have specific statutory duties that limit how they can use consumer information. The Gramm-Leach-Bliley Act (GLB), 15 U.S.C. §6801 et seq., has three main rules. First, it requires financial institutions to develop privacy policies. Those policies address the security and confidentiality of customer records and protect against unauthorized access or breaches that could harm consumers. The second requirement is that financial institutions give customers a copy of their privacy policies (which means such institutions must, in turn, make such policies). Third, GLB gives consumers the right to "opt-out" of financial institutions being able to share their nonpublic personal information with unaffiliated third parties. An example of conduct that motivated the enactment of GLB was a bank's sale in 1997 of millions of credit card numbers to an adult website company, which then fraudulently billed customers for charges to access porn sites.

A financial institution's privacy policy should detail the categories of non-public personal information that the financial institution collects and discloses. The treatment of information may vary. Institutions may disclose names and contact information to be used by companies who wish to send solicitations, but not disclose additional information on the customer's use of the financial product. (Some types of information should almost never be disclosed, such as account numbers.) Additional disclosures are required if the financial institution discloses nonpublic personal information to nonaffiliated third parties. As seems inevitable with mandatory disclosures, the statute requires that the disclosures be "clear and conspicuous."

GLB disclosures must be given at the "time of establishing a customer relationship" and "not less than annually" during the continuation of the relationship. 15 U.S.C. §6803(a). Upon the law's 2001 effective date, consumers were inundated with disclosures. The evidence suggests that about two-thirds of consumers remember one or more notices, and maybe as many as half even read them, but that consumers do not exercise their right to opt-out of disclosure regardless of the notices. *See* Fred H. Cate, et al., *Financial Privacy, Consumer Prosperity, and the Public Good: Maintaining the Balance*, http://www.ftc.gov/bcp/workshops/infoflows/statements/cate01.pdf (reporting that less than 5 percent of consumers opted-out per GLB provisions). The opt-out notice must provide a "reasonable means by which the consumer may exercise the right to opt out." 16 C.F.R. §313.7. Examples of such means are check-off boxes in a form that can be returned or a toll-free number to call. The notices can be delivered by mail, or if the consumer agrees, by electronic means; it is insufficient to post a sign or publish an advertisement. 16 C.F.R. §313.9.

D.   Identity Theft

Identity theft is the appropriation of someone else's identity. Victims of identity theft often do not discover the nefarious activity for months or years, by which time significant activity has occurred without their knowledge or consent. Identity theft is a federal crime. 18 U.S.C. §1028(a)(7). The U.S. Department of Justice, the U.S. Postal Inspection Service, and the Federal Bureau of Investigation investigate identity theft. Local police regularly take identity theft reports, which are then passed along by consumers to credit reporting agencies, but virtually never investigate unless the identity theft was part of another crime or on a large scale. Despite multiple levels of law enforcement on the job, prosecutions are rare compared with the incidence of theft. In 2010, over 250,000 Americans reported an identity theft to the FTC, making it the leading reason for complaint. Underreporting—or reporting to other agencies—makes counting identity theft difficult. The FTC itself has estimated that as many as 9 million Americans may have their identities misused each year.

Identity thieves often obtain credit in the victim's name and then default on those obligations. Much of the legislative response to the problem of identity theft has focused on credit harms and on the remediation of credit reports as a response. Thieves may make other uses of the victim's identity, including purchasing firearms, obtaining medical care, receiving government benefits, or seeking employment. One survey found that 15 percent of victims had false criminal records because of crimes committed by identity thieves. Jeff Sovern, *The Jewel of Their Souls: Preventing Identity Theft Through Loss Allocation Rules*, 64 U. Pitt. L. Rev. 343, 345 (2003).

The Fair and Accurate Credit Transactions Act (FACTA) added tools to credit reporting laws to help identity theft victims prevent credit harms. The credit reporting agencies must have a "one-call" procedure for consumers to verify their identities and request a fraud alert be put on the consumer's file for 90 days. If the consumer provides a police report, an extended alert, good for a period of several years, can be activated. The credit reporting agencies must provide these fraud alerts to creditors or other credit report users when they provide the consumer's report. 15 U.S.C §1681c-1.

Another set of provisions is designed to help identity theft victims repair damage to their credit reports. If a consumer can show appropriate proof of identity and a copy of an identity theft report, the consumer can request that a credit reporting agency block any information in the consumer's file that the consumer states was the result of an identity theft. Upon the consumer making such a request, the credit reporting agency also must promptly notify the furnisher of the information that it may be the result of identity theft. 15 U.S.C. §1681c-2. By putting the duty to inform on the credit reporting agency, the law tries to eliminate some of the heavy burden on consumers to contact all the parties with whom the thief had dealings. The furnisher is not required to take any specific action, however, and could continue to try to collect from the victim. This means that while a lender may have strong evidence that a debt was incurred fraudulently by an identity thief, it can still make collection calls to the consumer.

Because identity theft is often enabled by business' collection of consumer information, it is intertwined with consumer privacy protections. The more information businesses have and the fewer burdens they have to keep it secure and confidential, the greater the opportunity for identity theft. Given the difficulty in prosecutions and remediation, the prevention of identity theft may be the best tactic. How much of a burden should businesses have in verifying someone's identity?

Andrews v. TRW

225 F.3d 1063 (9th Cir. 2000) (rev'd on other grounds, 534 U.S. 19 (2001))

NOONAN, Circuit Judge.

Adelaide Andrews (Andrews) appeals the judgment by the district court in her suit against TRW, Inc. The case involves the rights under the Fair Credit Reporting Act, 15 U.S.C. §§1681-1681u (1994 & Supp. II) (FCRA), and Cal. Bus. & Prof. Code §17200 et. seq. (1996), of a person claiming to be damaged by the disclosure of inaccurate credit information by a consumer credit reporting agency such as TRW. . . .

In June 1993, Andrea Andrews (hereafter the Imposter) obtained the social security number and California driver's license number of Adelaide Andrews (hereafter the Plaintiff). The Imposter did so simply by misusing her position as a doctor's receptionist and copying the information that the Plaintiff, as a patient in that office, supplied to the doctor.

In 1994-1995 the Imposter applied for credit to four companies subscribing to TRW's credit reports. For example, on July 25, 1994, to First Consumers National Bank (FCNB), the Imposter applied as Andrea A. Andrews, 3993-1/2 Harvard Blvd., Los Angeles, CA, 90062, phone 213-312-0605, employed at Spensor-Robbyns Products, Los Angeles. The Imposter gave the birth date and social security number of the Plaintiff.

In this application the only misinformation was the Imposter's use of the Plaintiff's social security number and date of birth. On October 28, 1994 to Express Department Stores the Imposter made a comparable credit application, using her own identity except for the Plaintiff's social security number. Again, in January 1995, to Commercial Credit the Imposter applied for credit, using her own identity, except for Plaintiff's social security number and a clumsy misspelling of her first name as "Adeliade."

TRW responded to the credit inquiries of the three companies by treating the applications as made by the Plaintiff. TRW furnished the information in its file on the Plaintiff and added the three inquiries to the Plaintiff's file.

Each of the credit applications applied for by the Imposter was turned down by the company getting the TRW report. In addition, the Imposter applied for cable service to a public utility, Prime Cable of Las Vegas, which was required by law to provide cable services but nonetheless asked for a TRW report. The Imposter applied as Andrea Andrews, 4201 S. Decatur #2202, Las Vegas, NV, 89103, Phone 248-6352. The Imposter used the social security number of the Plaintiff, which was the only stolen item of identity provided. This account became delinquent and was referred to a collection agency.

The Plaintiff, however, became aware of the Imposter only on May 31, 1995, when she sought to refinance the mortgage on her home. The bank from which the financing was sought received a report from Chase Credit Research, not a party to this case, whose report combined information from TRW and two other credit reporting agencies. Now aware of the fraud, Andrews contacted TRW and requested deletion from her file of all reference to the Imposter's fraudulent activities. TRW complied.

On October 21, 1996, the Plaintiff filed this suit in the district court. In her first claim she alleged that TRW had furnished credit reports without "reasonable grounds for believing" that she was the consumer whom the credit applications involved, contrary to 15 U.S.C. §§1681b and 1681e(a), and that as a consequence she had suffered damages including an expenditure of time and money and "commercial impairment, inconvenience, embarrassment, humiliation, and emotional distress including physical manifestations." In her second claim, she alleged that TRW had violated §1681e by not maintaining the "reasonable procedures" required by that statute in order "to assure maximum possible accuracy of the information concerning the individual about whom the report relates." 15 U.S.C. §1681e(b). She alleged the same damages. She asserted that both violations were willful and that both also violated Cal. Bus. & Prof. Code §17200 et. seq. [ED. NOTE — California's version of UDAP statute.] She sought actual and punitive damages and an injunction requiring TRW to comply with the Fair Credit Reporting Act by "requiring a sufficient number of corresponding points of reference" before disseminating an individual's credit history or attributing information to an individual's credit file.

[ED. NOTE — The district court ruled that the disclosures to Express and Commercial were made for a purpose permissible under §1681b(a)(3)(A), because the Plaintiff, even against her will, was "involved" in the credit transaction initiated by the Imposter. Any other rule, the court said, would place "too heavy a burden on credit reporting agencies." The court also held that TRW had used "reasonable procedures" as required by §1681e(a) to limit disclosures. For these several reasons, the court granted summary judgment to TRW on the Plaintiff's first claim. The other claims went to a jury, which returned a verdict in favor of TRW.]

. . .

Disclosure Without Reasonable Belief. Under §1681b TRW could only furnish a report on a consumer to a customer which it had "reason to believe" intended to use the information in connection with "a credit transaction involving the consumer on whom the information is to be furnished." 15 U.S.C. §1681b(a)(3). Did TRW have a reasonable belief that the Plaintiff was the consumer involved in the credit transactions as to which the four companies sought a report from TRW? As the district court observed, there are 250,000,000 persons in the United States (not all of them having Social Security numbers) and 1,000,000,000 possibilities as to what any one Social Security number may be. The random chance of anyone matching a name to a number is very small. If TRW could assume that only such chance matching would occur, it was reasonable as a matter of law in releasing the Plaintiff's file when an application matched her last name and the number. But we do not live in a world in which such matches are made only by chance.

We take judicial notice that in many ways persons are required to make their social security numbers available so that they are no longer private or confidential but open to scrutiny and copying. Not least of these ways is on applications for credit, as TRW had reason to know. In a world where names are disseminated with the numbers attached and dishonest persons exist, the matching of a name to a number is not a random matter. It is quintessentially a job for a jury to decide whether identity theft has been common enough for it to be reasonable for a credit reporting agency to disclose credit information merely because a last name matches a social security number on file.

In making that determination the jury would be helped by expert opinion on the prevalence of identity theft, as the district court would have been helped if it had given consideration to the Plaintiff's witnesses on this point before giving summary judgment.

The reasonableness of TRW's responses should also have been assessed by a jury with reference to the information TRW had indicating that the Imposter was not the Plaintiff. TRW argues that people do use nicknames and change addresses. But how many people misspell their first name? How many people mistake their date of birth? No rule of law answers these questions. A jury will have to say how reasonable a belief is that let a social security number trump all evidence of dissimilarity between the Plaintiff and the Imposter.

The district court held that the Plaintiff was involved in the transaction because her number was used. The statutory phrase is "a credit transaction involving the consumer." 15 U.S.C. §1681b(a)(3)(A). "Involve" has two dictionary meanings that are relevant: (1) "to draw in as a participant" or (2) "to oblige to become associated." The district court understood the word in the second sense. We are reluctant to conclude that Congress meant to harness any consumer to any transaction where any crook chose to use his or her number. The first meaning of the statutory term must be preferred here. In that sense the Plaintiff was not involved.

Another consideration for the district court was that a different rule would impose too heavy a cost on TRW. The statute, however, has already made the determination as to what is a bearable cost for a credit reporting agency. The cost is what it takes to have a reasonable belief. In this case that belief needed determination by a jury not a judge.

We reinstate the Plaintiff's first claim together with her request for punitive damages based upon it.

Under federal law, creditors do not need consumers' consent to obtain reports. In California, and several other states, consumers can request that their credit reports remain confidential unless the requesting party has obtained the consumer's express authorization. Cal. Civ. Code §1785.11.2. This "security freeze" must be affirmatively requested in writing by the consumer and contains several exceptions, including for law enforcement, tax collection and child support actions. The initial statute was ruled unconstitutional because the security freeze allowed a consumer to prevent the collection and distribution of information in the public record, such as evictions or bankruptcies. An amendment cured that defect, Cal. Civ. Code §1785.11.2(m), but most Californians remain unaware of this right or have not exercised it. While the security freeze concept was promoted as a way for consumers to take control of their personal information, the low uptake suggests an enduring consumer law problem — getting consumers to do the work involved in exercising a legal right.

Another strategy, adopted in California, is to forbid a certain type of user — retail sellers — from furnishing information unless it can provide several pieces of information about the consumer that match information the credit bureau has on file. Cal. Civ. Code §1785.14(a)(1). The weakness of this rule is that in a serious identity theft situation, the thief may well know things such as the consumer's birth date, sex, and social security number. More stringent requirements to verify identity might be imposed in the future, including fingerprints or other forms of biometric identification.

Problem Set 6

6.1. Streams Co. operates a successful online video and e-book business in which consumers pay a fixed $1 fee to watch videos via online streaming or to download e-books. Streams has entered into a partnership with Bellow, a recommender website where people review products and services and can sign up to receive new reviews from people they know. Streams and Bellow will match all their data, creating a merged data set. As part of the partnership, Bellow will display personalized solicitations for each user that will be based on the videos or books that Bellow users' online contacts had seen or read from Streams. For example, on Mother's Day, Bellow plans an advertisement that says "Get to Know Mom: Watch Her Favorite Movie with Her" and will list titles that Streams' data shows that a Bellow user's mother has watched. Does this use of consumer information by Streams and Bellow violate the law? *See* 18 U.S.C. §2710.

6.2. Foreclosure Facts is a start-up trying to capitalize on the real estate downturn. It pays banks for bulk data, which it then reformulates into a searchable database and a foreclosure auction map, which are available to subscribers for $5 per month. Foreclosure Facts' customers are potential buyers at foreclosure sales and journalists who feature homeowners in stories on the foreclosure crisis. The banks sell the following data for each customer's house that is in foreclosure to Foreclosure Facts: the property address, the amount of the mortgage, the tax assessment of the property's value, and the stage of foreclosure process. The banks provide privacy notices as mandated by Gramm-Leach-Bliley, which state, "We do not disclose any nonpublic personal information about our customers or former customers to anyone, except as permitted by law." Are the financial institutions violating Gramm-Leach-Bliley? *See* 15 U.S.C. §6809(4); 16 C.F.R. §§313.3(n-p); 313.10(a)(1).

6.3. Twenty-five years ago, your mother gave you a nice simple name: Mark Zuckerberg. In childhood, you were just one of several million people enjoying the sunshine in California. In the last several years, your name has been causing you considerable headaches. Two weeks ago, your Facebook account was shut down. The notification from Facebook gave no reason at all. You contacted customer service and were told that the reason was "false identity." Your Facebook page used a picture of Mark Zuckerberg, Facebook founder, as a joke. You also chose to "friend" people who may have thought you were Facebook founder, Mark Zuckerberg, responding to the requests with a

"Be sure to see my *Social Network* movie!" line. Otherwise, your Facebook page made no reference to the "other" Mark Zuckerberg and had photos and posts of you. In creating and maintaining the account, did you violate California law? *See* Cal. Penal Code §528.5. What rights or remedies do you have to get your Facebook account restored?

6.4. You are an intern for a leading consumer rights organization. Tired of fighting about financial regulation and Dodd-Frank, it is turning its attention to advertising and privacy issues. It has asked you to conduct research and make a recommendation about whether it should issue a consumer education bulletin about the site www.AboutTheData.com. Unfortunately, that is all the instruction you have and everyone is away at a conference. Your first step should be visiting the site and poking around. What are your steps in investigating the site? What is your tentative recommendation? Should consumers be encouraged to register at the site? Or warned against it?

Assignment 7. Credit Reporting

Lenders are avid gathers and users of data about consumers. The primary mechanism for disseminating such information is credit reports that are generated by "consumer reporting agencies" (sometimes called bureaus). Creditors, known in this context as "furnishers" because they supply information, contribute data to the agencies. Creditors also are "users" of credit reports when they access reports to collect names for solicitations or to evaluate applicants' creditworthiness. The triangulation between reporting agencies, furnishers, and users creates layers of responsibility for legal compliance. It also produces a tangled statutory framework.

The Fair Credit Reporting Act (FCRA) is the foundation of Title VI of the Consumer Credit Protection Act. 15 U.S.C. §1681 et seq. FCRA was enacted in 1970 when less technology was used in credit reporting and underwriting. Congress has repeatedly amended the law, with substantial amendments in 2003, the Fair and Accurate Credit Transactions Act (FACTA). Most states also have laws governing credit reporting. These are little used because some statutes largely mirror federal law, and several aspects of credit reporting are preempted by FCRA. The law on preemption in this area is a thicket, even by the intimidating standards for consumer law. As a matter of practice, the wisest course for a plaintiff is often to plead violations under FCRA and state law. Correspondingly, savvy defendants will make use of preemption arguments in responding to suits.

Because credit reporting laws are part of "federal consumer law" as identified by the Dodd-Frank Act, the CPFB is now the rule maker and enforcer for FCRA and FACTA. The CFPB also has exercised supervisory authority, including examination power, over the main reporting agencies under the "larger participant" rule. 12 U.S.C. §5514. This assignment has some references to the FTC as a matter of historical record, and because the FTC retains jurisdiction over the use of consumer reports for purposes other than consumer financial products or services (such as landlords or insurance companies). The FTC withdrew its Official Commentary on credit reporting when the CFPB gained responsibility, creating some uncertainty about how the CFPB will apply the law.

A. Content of Consumer Reports

1. Types of Reports

"Credit report," while common parlance, does not accurately describe the content and use of the reports. The law actually uses the more appropriate term "consumer report," 15 U.S.C. §1681a(d)(1), because the reports include communications about character, reputation, personal characteristics, and residence, as well as credit data. This definition is so broad that you might think every update or comment on a social network site is a consumer report. However, the law requires that a consumer report be "used or expected to be used or collected in whole or in part for the purpose of serving as a factor in establishing the consumer's eligibility" for credit or insurance, employment, or any other purpose authorized in FCRA. 15 U.S.C. §1681a(d)(1). It is the purpose of the report that contributes to the "credit report" moniker at least as much as its content.

The law distinguishes between ordinary consumer reports and "investigative" consumer reports. The latter are a subset of consumer reports in which information is "obtained through personal interviews with neighbors, friends, or associates" of the consumer, rather than "specific factual information" obtained from a creditor. 15 U.S.C. §1681a(e). Because of their more invasive process, consumers must be notified in writing within three days of a request for an investigative report. 15 U.S.C. §1681d.

Investigative reports are much less common than the more familiar consumer reports, generated most frequently by three credit reporting agencies: Equifax, Experian, and TransUnion. Over 200 million American adults have a file with these agencies.

2. Data Collected

A consumer report is "any written, oral, or other communication of any information by a consumer reporting agency bearing on a consumer's credit worthiness, credit standing, credit capacity, character, general reputation, personal characteristics, or mode of living which is used or expected to be used or collected in whole or in part for the purpose of serving as a factor in establishing the consumer's eligibility for (A) credit or insurance to be used primarily for personal family, or household purposes, (B) employment purposes; or (C) any other purposes authorized under section 1681b of this title." 15 U.S.C. §1681a(d). The statute only applies to consumer reporting agencies, and only when such communications are for making certain decisions or for specified purposes. Without these restrictions, a consumer report would be the gossipy conversation around the holiday table about Great Uncle Jeb or Todd or Elmer and their latest shenanigans.

In general, a consumer report may contain any information that is complete, accurate, and not obsolete. When preparing reports, agencies are to follow procedures to assure "maximum possible accuracy." 15 U.S.C. §1681e(b). Furnishers also are required to have reasonable written procedures on the accuracy and integrity of data that they transmit to a consumer reporting agency. 12 C.F.R. §1022.40.

The typical consumer report contains several major categories of information. Most obviously, it includes personal identifiers such as name, current and former addresses, employer, date of birth, and social security number. This information is critical to making sure that information provided by furnishers is inserted into the file of the correct consumer and in providing users with the correct file for the requested person.

The bulk of a report consists of account-level data for current and past creditors. Mortgages, credit cards, auto loans, student loans and bank lines-of-credit nearly always appear on credit reports. Other routine payments made by households such as rental or utility payments rarely appear, although this is changing as newer market entrants challenge the large actors to use a wider swath of information. The report will flag adverse accounts on which there have been late payments or other types of delinquencies.

Below is an excerpt of the account information from a TransUnion report, with the account numbers blacked out. The "x" marks indicate that information was not provided in certain months, often because there was no account balance or activity in those months. This report was obtained in late 2011; note the dates of some account information. Credit reports have a very long shelf life.

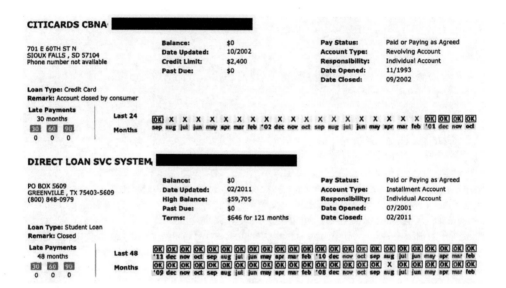

Credit reporting agencies also collect information that appears in public records. Examples here include lawsuits, tax liens, bankruptcies, and delinquent child support. If you have no public record section on your report, then that is a good sign as such information is always negative.

Reports also contain data on user inquiries and consumer statements. User inquiries are typically divided into two types. Regular inquiries are those created by a consumer, usually as a result of a consumer applying for loans or employment. Promotional or account review inquiries are initiated by a creditor without consumer consent. They are used to make decisions about whether to extend credit or change credit terms. Consumer statements are items such as fraud alerts, discussed in Assignment 6 in relationship to identity theft, or other statements that the law permits consumers to require agencies to include in reports, as discussed in the next section.

The credit report system is refreshed on a near-constant basis. Each month the consumer reporting agencies add an estimated 4.5 billion pieces of information to their databases. Some of the information in a credit report is used to calculate credit scores, a numerical estimate of a consumer's credit risk. While there is one dominant player in the business of designing score algorithms, the Fair Isaac Co., and people speak of a FICO score to refer to that company, each of the big three credit reporting agencies use slightly different calculations for their scores. Creditors often have in-house algorithms as well, some of which are designed for a particular loan product, or are for more specialized purposes such as Experian and VISA's "BankruptcyPredict" score.

For FICO scores, the Fair Isaac Company says that five categories of information make the following relative contributions to a score: 1) payment history: 35 percent, 2) amounts owed: 30 percent, 3) length of credit history: 15 percent, 4) new credit: 10 percent, and 5) types of credit in use: 10 percent. For any given person and any particularized score, however, the weighting can be different. These different weightings, and many other details, are part of the proprietary "black box" of credit scoring. While companies often urge consumers to monitor their credit scores and aim for a high score, consumer advocates typically focus on the credit report because consumers can only indirectly affect the scores by changing the content of reports.

B. Uses of Credit Reports

The major motivation behind the enactment of FCRA was consumer privacy. To that end, FCRA limits the situations under which an agency may furnish a report. 15 U.S.C. §1681b. The simplest rule is that reports can be furnished "[i]n accordance with the written instructions of the consumer to whom it relates." 15 U.S.C. §1681b(a)(2). In most instances, there is tiny print somewhere in an application that a consumer signs that gives such permission. As with any standard form contract, this generally suffices as consent. Reports also can be obtained for use in several kinds of legal processes, including by grand jury subpoena, court order, or for use in child support enforcement. For the other categories of uses, the agency needs to possess "reason to believe" that a user has a permissible purpose. Users are forbidden from using reports provided by agencies unless the users have a permissible purpose, which is defined by reference back to the permissible purposes for agencies. 15 U.S.C. §1681b(f)(1). The most common purposes are discussed in detail below.

1. Credit

Consumer reports may be furnished and used "in connection with a credit transaction involving the consumer . . . involving the extension of credit to, or review or collection of an account of, the consumer." 15 U.S.C. §1681b(a)(3)(A). Credit is defined broadly. Other financial transactions are arguably not credit but get swept in under other permissible purposes. One example is a potential investor or insurer who wants to assess and value an existing credit obligation. That is, there is already a loan but the company is trying to sell the obligation, buy insurance against its default, or perhaps use it as collateral. These purposes require valuing the loan, which is driven by the borrower's creditworthiness, in part.

Several cases have looked at whether check verification services and merchants' uses of such services are covered by FCRA. In its commentary, the FTC had opined that "bad check lists" were consumer reports, and courts had followed that guidance. *Greenway v. Information Dynamics, Ltd.*, 399 F. Supp. 1092 (D. Ariz. 1974) (holding that lists with check cashing history of potential customers is a consumer report under the FCRA); *Peasley v. Telecheck of Kan., Inc.*, 6 Kan. App. 2d 990, 637 P.2d 437 (1981) (holding that check approval system is a consumer report under Kansas statute that is modeled after the FCRA). Courts had also grappled with whether checks are "extensions of credit" because checks are supposed to be good when written — the money should be in the bank. Some courts got around the issue by finding that payees had a "legitimate business need" to obtain a consumer report to decide whether to accept or reject a check in payment. *Estiverne v. Sak's Fifth Ave.*, 9 F.3d 1171 (5th Cir. 1993).

Once a creditor has made a loan, it can obtain consumer reports to monitor the account and reassess credit risk. After a review of the report, the creditor could change the rate, close the account, or extend additional credit, if such actions are permitted by the loan agreement.

Creditors can also use consumer reports to help them collect from delinquent consumers. In this process, called "skip tracing," the creditor primarily wants the debtor's address information, rather than data on creditworthiness (after all, the consumer is already delinquent — that's some powerful data right there). Some obligations did not begin as credit but fall into that category after a lawsuit is filed and a judgment against the consumer is obtained. At that point, a credit relationship exists, and the business can use a credit report to find the consumer.

2. Insurance

Credit reports may be obtained by users who "intend to use the information in connection with the underwriting of insurance involving the consumer." 15 U.S.C. §1681b(a)(3)(C). Consumer reports are used initially for underwriting but also on an ongoing basis for deciding whether to cancel a policy or adjust terms.

While insurance companies always have had access to credit reports, the practice of calculating and using scores for underwriting is controversial. In 2003, Congress directed the FTC to study the use of credit-based insurance scores and to report on how those scores were calculated and used, particularly their impact on low-income or minority consumers. In July 2007, the FTC issued a 250-page report, Credit-Based Insurance Scores: Impacts on Consumers of Automobile Insurance, focusing solely on auto insurance.

The FTC's analysis demonstrates that credit-based insurance scores are effective predictors of risk under automobile insurance policies. Using scores is likely to make the price of insurance conform more closely to the risk of loss that consumers pose, resulting, on average, in higher-risk consumers paying higher premiums and lower-risk consumers paying lower premiums. It has not been clearly established why scores are predictive of risk.

Credit-based insurance scores may benefit consumers overall. Scores may permit insurance companies to evaluate risk with greater accuracy, which may make them more willing to offer insurance to higher-risk consumers. Scores also may make the process of granting and pricing insurance quicker and cheaper, cost savings that may be passed on to consumers in the form of lower premiums. However, little hard data was submitted or available to the FTC to quantify the magnitude of these potential benefits to consumers. Credit-based insurance scores are distributed differently among racial and ethnic groups. The FTC's analysis revealed that the use of scores for consumers whose information was included in the FTC's database caused the average predicted risk for African Americans and Hispanics to increase by 10% and 4.2%, respectively, while it caused the average predicted risk for non-Hispanic whites and Asians to decrease by 1.6% and 4.9%, respectively. These changes in predicted risk are likely to have an effect on the insurance premiums that these groups on average pay.

Credit-based insurance scores predict risk within racial, ethnic, and income groups. Scores have only a small effect as a 'proxy' for membership in racial and ethnic groups in estimating of insurance risk, remaining strong predictors of risk when controls for race, ethnicity and income are included in risk models.

The FTC report drew sharp criticism, including a dissent from one commissioner. One major critique of the report was its reliance on limited industry-supplied data, and its failure to explain why it did not detect racial effects found in studies of consumers with insurance in Texas and Missouri. *See* Dissenting Statement of Commissioner Pamela Jones Harbour (July 2007), at www.ftc.gov/os/2007/07/P044804_facta_dissenting_harbour.pdf. In response to a class-action lawsuit that challenged the permissibility of credit-based scores for homeowner and auto insurance, the Texas Supreme Court upheld the Texas statute that permitted insurers to use scores that were race-neutral (in that they did not include race as a factor), even if the scores had a disparate racial impact on insurance pricing. *See Ojo, et al. v. Farmers Group et al.,* 256 S.W.3d 421 (Tex. 2011).

3.   *Employment*

The Fair Credit Reporting Act says that employment is a permissible purpose for obtaining a consumer report. 15 U.S.C. §1681b(a)(3)(B). Employment purpose is defined to include both evaluations of applicants and of current employees for purposes of promotion, reassignment, or retention. For employment, the user should not procure the report unless it has made a "clear and conspicuous disclosure" to the consumer and obtained written authorization. 15 U.S.C. §1681b(b)(2)(A).

Kelchner v. Sycamore Manor Health Center

135 Fed. Appx. 499 (3d Cir. 2005) (not precedential)

FUENTES, Circuit Judge.

Petitioner Lisa Kelchner appeals the District Court's order of partial summary judgment dismissing her claims under the Fair Credit Reporting Act, 15 U.S.C. §1681 et seq. ("FCRA" or "the Act"). The District Court held that Kelchner's employer, Sycamore Manor Health Center ("Sycamore"), did not violate the FCRA by requiring Kelchner to sign a blanket authorization entitling Sycamore to obtain Kelchner's credit report in the future. Because such blanket authorizations are not inconsistent with the requirements of the FCRA, we will affirm.

I.

As we write only for the parties, we recite only the essential facts. Kelchner had been employed at Sycamore for about nineteen years when, in February 2001, she and other employees of Sycamore's parent, Presbyterian Homes, Inc. (PHI), were asked to sign an "Annual Statement of Personnel Policy Understanding."[1] When Kelchner refused to sign the Annual Statement she was informed that execution of the Statement was a condition of continued employment and that if she failed to sign the Statement by March 21, 2000, she would be taken off the active schedule. Because she refused to sign, Kelchner's work hours were reduced to zero on March 21, 2001. Kelchner remained on the payroll, however, and on June 12, 2001, PHI sent her a second, revised Annual Statement to be signed by June 19, 2001. The revised Statement sought authorization to obtain "consumer reports" containing information relating to employees' "credit standing, character, general reputation, personal characteristics, or mode of living" for the purposes of investigating "theft from residents, coworkers, or PHI property; potential fraud in insurance claims; or other forms of dishonesty." Kelchner was warned that if she did not sign the revised Statement, PHI would deem her employment "abandoned." Kelchner again refused to sign and her employment at PHI ended on June 30, 2001.

Kelchner claimed that she was wrongfully terminated, and that a class of plaintiffs employed by PHI and its subsidiary Sycamore signed the authorization forms under duress due to threat of termination. The District Court held that blanket authorization forms such as those required by PHI are permissible under the FCRA and certified the issue for interlocutory appeal. Although it had earlier conditionally certified a plaintiffs class of all persons employed by PHI from whom PHI sought authorization to procure consumer reports, the District Court decertified the class when it granted partial summary judgment to the defendants on Kelchner's FCRA claims.

---

1. The Annual Statement would authorize PHI to obtain "investigative consumer reports" that "may involve personal interviews with sources such as neighbors, friends, or associates" for "employment related purposes only."

II.

Kelchner claims that (1) PHI had no valid employment purpose for which it sought her credit report authorization; (2) PHI could not require Kelchner and other employees to sign a blanket, advance authorization form; and (3) that it was improper for PHI to constructively terminate Kelchner upon her refusal to sign the authorization form.[2] . . .

A.

The Fair Credit Reporting Act provides that, if certain conditions are met, credit reports may be issued to employers for "employment purposes." 15 U.S.C. §1681b(a)(3)(B). The FCRA defines "employment purposes" as those relating to "[evaluation of] a consumer for employment, promotion, reassignment or retention as an employee." 15 U.S.C. §1681a(h). Kelchner's first contention is that, because her retention as an employee was not in question, PHI had no valid employment purpose for procuring her credit report.

Kelchner is right that Congress implicitly recognized employees' privacy interest in avoiding procurement of their credit reports for invalid purposes. But PHI maintains that it needs access to employee credit reports in order to investigate theft, fraud and other dishonesty if and when it arises.[3] PHI claims that it newly imposed the requirement that its employees sign the credit report authorization forms in response to the allegedly broad scope of its protective and investigative duties as an employer, as well as new constraints on its access to information about employees under the FCRA. PHI is persuasive that its ability effectively to investigate allegations pertaining to an employee would be substantially impaired if it had to wait until the investigation was underway before it could obtain authorization from her.

It is important to note that PHI did not actually obtain a credit report on Kelchner. It sought authorization to do so in the future, if and when the need arose. While we do not foreclose the possibility that under certain circumstances an employer may have a valid employment purpose for which to obtain a credit report even before an employee is the subject of internal investigation, here, PHI sought only authorization to procure a report if and when the need arose, and the potential needs it identified clearly qualify as valid employment purposes.

---

2. Kelchner initially asserted claims under the Employment Retirement Income Security Act of 1874 ("ERISA"), 29 U.S.C. §§1001-1461, as amended by the Consolidated Omnibus Reconciliation Act of 1985 ("COBRA"), 29 U.S.C. §1161, et seq., in addition to her Pennsylvania state law claim of wrongful termination.

We address the issues raised under the FCRA only insofar as they are relevant to determining whether PHI and Sycamore Manor are liable for wrongful termination. See Highhouse v. Avery Transportation, 660 A.2d 1374, 1377 (Pa. Super. 1995) ("An employer's liability for wrongful discharge rests on whether a 'well-recognized facet of public policy is at stake'" and "courts have consistently held that employers violate the public policy of this Commonwealth by discharging employees for exercising legal rights"); see also Nazar v. Clark Distribution Sys. Inc., 46 Pa. D. & C. 4th 28 (Pa. Com. Pl. 2000) (finding discharge violated public policy expressed in federal law). Therefore, our resolution of this case does not rest on any implication that there would be a private right of action to bring a claim for equitable relief directly under the FCRA. . . .

3. PHI's revised disclosure and authorization form also indicated that PHI would obtain driving records for employees assigned regular driving duties. Although those reports would also serve a clear employment purpose, that provision is not applicable to Kelchner.

B.

Kelchner's second contention is that PHI was prohibited from procuring credit reports regarding its employees based on blanket, one-time authorization forms. Under the FCRA, an employer may obtain a credit report for employment purposes if "a clear and conspicuous disclosure has been made in writing to the consumer *at any time before the report is procured* or caused to be procured, in a document that consists solely of the disclosure, that a consumer report may be obtained for employment purposes; and the consumer has authorized in writing . . . the procurement of the report by that person." 15 U.S.C. §1681b(b)(2)(A)(i) (emphasis added). The consumer-employee must authorize disclosure in writing. See 15 U.S.C. §1681b(b)(2)(A)(ii).

The requirement that an employer obtain authorization "at any time before the report is procured" is unambiguous. The plain language of the statute authorizes the employer to obtain an employee's written authorization at "any time" during the employment relationship. See 15 U.S.C. §1681b(b)(2)(A)(i); see also Valansi v. Ashcroft, 278 F.3d 203, 209 (3d Cir. 2002) ("When the statutory language has a clear meaning, we need not look further.").

C.

We turn to Kelchner's final contention. Kelchner claims that employee authorization under 15 U.S.C. §1681b(b) must be voluntary in that it cannot be compelled as a condition of employment. However, we see nothing in the statute that implies such a limit on an employer's ability to obtain blanket authorization from an employee, at least in the context of an at-will employment relationship. But even if we were to view the statute as ambiguous on this point, we are persuaded by a 1999 advisory opinion letter issued by the FTC, which opined that the FCRA "does not prohibit an employer from taking adverse action against an employee or applicant who refuses to authorize the employer to procure a consumer report." Oct. 1, 1999, FTC Opinion Letter. See also Christensen v. Harris County, 529 U.S. 576, 587 (2000) (holding that an opinion letter by the administering agency is entitled to respect under Skidmore v. Swift & Co., 323 U.S. 134, 140 (1944)). In sum, we agree that an employer is not prohibited from terminating an employee if she refuses to authorize her employer to obtain her consumer credit report.

III.

For all the foregoing reasons, the District Court was clearly correct in its interpretation of the Act and the defendants were entitled to summary judgment on Kelchner's claims under the FCRA. We will affirm.

More employers in recent years are using credit reports and scores, although there remains no clear relationship between these data and employment behavior. In the last decade or so, several states have enacted laws that restrict the use of consumer reports for employment. As of late 2015, the states with restrictions on employer's access to or use of credit information were: California, Colorado, Connecticut, Hawaii, Illinois, Maryland, Nevada, Oregon, Vermont, and Washington. Bills are currently pending in about two dozen other states' legislatures. In the fall of 2015, New York City passed a strong local ordinance against employers' use of consumer reports.

> Except as provided in this subdivision, it shall be an unlawful discriminatory practice for an employer, labor organization, employment agency, or agent thereof to request or to use for employment purposes the consumer credit history of an applicant for employment or employee, or otherwise discriminate against an applicant or employee with regard to hiring, compensation, or the terms, conditions or privileges of employment based on the consumer credit history of the applicant or employee.

New York City Local Law Int. §261-A. The law has relatively few exceptions compared to the similar state bills. Momentum is gathering to prohibit credit checks on employees.

C. Decisions Based on Reports

1. Adverse Action Defined

"Adverse action" is a term of art under FCRA. It describes a decision that is deemed to be unfavorable to the consumer. It is defined separately for insurance, employment, and credit purposes. 15 U.S.C. §1681a(k)(1)(B)(i)-(iv). A denial later always constitutes adverse action, but the term is significantly broader than that, and includes an increase in cost or an otherwise unfavorable change in terms. That is not to suggest that every decision that differentiates among consumers is an adverse action. For example, being excluded from a marketing list constructed from consumer report data may not be an adverse action. After all, how many of us would view it as adverse to get less unsolicited marketing mail?

A vexing issue in the adverse action context has been the treatment of risk-based pricing, which includes granting credit or insurance on terms "materially less favorable than the most favorable terms available to a substantial proportion of consumers." 15 U.S.C. §1681m(h) (requiring notice to be given to a consumer for credit decisions meeting this standard). The Supreme Court recently assessed what constitutes an adverse action in the insurance context.

———————

Safeco Insurance Co. of America et al. v. Burr et al.

551 U.S. 47 (2007)

SOUTER, Justice.

The Fair Credit Reporting Act (FCRA or Act) requires notice to any consumer subjected to "adverse action . . . based in whole or in part on any information contained in a consumer [credit] report." 15 U.S.C. §1681m(a). Anyone who "willfully fails" to provide notice is civilly liable to the consumer. §1681n(a). The questions in these consolidated cases are whether willful failure covers a violation committed in reckless disregard of the notice obligation, and, if so, whether petitioners Safeco and GEICO committed reckless violations. We hold that reckless action is covered, that GEICO did not violate the statute, and that while Safeco might have, it did not act recklessly.

I.

A.

Congress enacted FCRA in 1970 to ensure fair and accurate credit reporting, promote efficiency in the banking system, and protect consumer privacy. See 84 Stat. 1128, 15 U.S.C. §1681; TRW Inc. v. Andrews, 534 U.S. 19, 23 (2001). The Act requires, among other things, that "any person [who] takes any adverse action with respect to any consumer that is based in whole or in part on any information contained in a consumer report" must notify the affected consumer. 15 U.S.C. §1681m(a). The notice must point out the adverse action, explain how to reach the agency that reported on the consumer's credit, and tell the consumer that he can get a free copy of the report and dispute its accuracy with the agency. Ibid. As it applies to an insurance company, "adverse action" is "a denial or cancellation of, an increase in any charge for, or a reduction or other adverse or unfavorable change in the terms of coverage or amount of, any insurance, existing or applied for." §1681a(k)(1)(B)(i).

FCRA provides a private right of action against businesses that use consumer reports but fail to comply. If a violation is negligent, the affected consumer is entitled to actual damages. If willful, however, the consumer may have actual damages, or statutory damages ranging from $100 to $1,000, and even punitive damages. §1681n(a).

B.

Petitioner GEICO writes auto insurance through four subsidiaries: GEICO General, which sells "preferred" policies at low rates to low-risk customers; Government Employees, which also sells "preferred" policies, but only to government employees; GEICO Indemnity, which sells standard policies to moderate-risk customers; and GEICO Casualty, which sells nonstandard policies at higher rates to high-risk customers. Potential customers call a toll-free number answered by an agent of the four affiliates, who takes information and, with permission, gets the applicant's credit score. This information goes into GEICO's computer system, which selects any appropriate company and the particular rate at which a policy may be issued.

For some time after FCRA went into effect, GEICO sent adverse action notices to all applicants who were not offered "preferred" policies from GEICO General or Government Employees. GEICO changed its practice, however, after a method to "neutralize" an applicant's credit score was devised: the applicant's company and tier placement is compared with the company and tier placement he would have been assigned with a "neutral" credit score, that is, one calculated without reliance on credit history.[4] Under this new scheme, it is only if using a neutral credit score would have put the applicant in a lower priced tier or company that GEICO sends an adverse action notice; the applicant is not otherwise told if he would have gotten better terms with a better credit score.

Respondent Ajene Edo applied for auto insurance with GEICO. After obtaining Edo's credit score, GEICO offered him a standard policy with GEICO Indemnity (at rates higher than the most favorable), which he accepted. Because Edo's company and tier placement would have been the same with a neutral score, GEICO did not give Edo an adverse action notice. Edo later filed this proposed class action against GEICO, alleging willful failure to give notice in violation of §1681m(a); he claimed no actual harm, but sought statutory and punitive damages under §1681n(a). The District Court granted summary judgment for GEICO, finding there was no adverse action when "the premium charged to [Edo] . . . would have been the same even if GEICO Indemnity did not consider information in [his] consumer credit history." Edo v. GEICO Casualty Co., 2004 U.S. Dist. LEXIS 28522, *12 (D. Ore., Feb. 23, 2004).

Like GEICO, petitioner Safeco relies on credit reports to set initial insurance premiums, as it did for respondents Charles Burr and Shannon Massey, who were offered higher rates than the best rates possible. Safeco sent them no adverse action notices, and they later joined a proposed class action against the company, alleging willful violation of §1681m(a) and seeking statutory and punitive damages under §1681n(a). The District Court ordered summary judgment for Safeco, on the understanding that offering a single, initial rate for insurance cannot be "adverse action."

The Court of Appeals for the Ninth Circuit reversed both judgments. In GEICO's case, it held that whenever a consumer "would have received a lower rate for his insurance had the information in his consumer report been more favorable, an adverse action has been taken against him." Reynolds v. Hartford Financial Servs. Group, Inc., 435 F.3d 1081, 1093 (2006). Since a better credit score would have placed Edo with GEICO General, not GEICO Indemnity, the appeals court held that GEICO's failure to give notice was an adverse action.

The Ninth Circuit also held that an insurer "willfully" fails to comply with FCRA if it acts with "reckless disregard" of a consumer's rights under the Act. Id., at 1099. It explained that a company would not be acting recklessly if it "diligently and in good faith attempted to fulfill its statutory obligations" and came to a "tenable, albeit

---

4. A number of States permit the use of such "neutral" credit scores to ensure that consumers with thin or unidentifiable credit histories are not treated disadvantageously. See, e.g., N.Y. Ins. Law Ann. §§2802(e), (e)(1) (West 2006) (generally prohibiting an insurer from "consider[ing] an absence of credit information," but allowing it to do so if it "treats the consumer as if the applicant or insured had neutral credit information, as defined by the insurer").

erroneous, interpretation of the statute." Ibid. The court went on to say that "a deliberate failure to determine the extent of its obligations" would not ordinarily escape liability under §1681n, any more than "reliance on creative lawyering that provides indefensible answers." Ibid. Because the court believed that the enquiry into GEICO's reckless disregard might turn on undisclosed circumstances surrounding GEICO's revision of its notification policy, the Court of Appeals remanded the company's case for further proceedings.

In the action against Safeco, the Court of Appeals rejected the District Court's position, relying on its reasoning in GEICO's case (where it had held that the notice requirement applies to a single statement of an initial charge for a new policy). Spano v. Safeco Corp., 140 Fed. Appx. 746 (2005). The Court of Appeals also rejected Safeco's argument that its conduct was not willful, again citing the GEICO case, and remanded for further proceedings.

We consolidated the two matters and granted certiorari to resolve a conflict in the Circuits as to whether §1681n(a) reaches reckless disregard of FCRA's obligations, and to clarify the notice requirement in §1681m(a). We now reverse in both cases.

II.

GEICO and Safeco argue that liability under §1681n(a) for "willfully fail[ing] to comply" with FCRA goes only to acts known to violate the Act, not to reckless disregard of statutory duty, but we think they are wrong. We have said before that "willfully" is a "word of many meanings whose construction is often dependent on the context in which it appears," Bryan v. United States, 524 U.S. 184, 191 (1998) (internal quotation marks omitted); and where willfulness is a statutory condition of civil liability, we have generally taken it to cover not only knowing violations of a standard, but reckless ones as well, see McLaughlin v. Richland Shoe Co., 486 U.S. 128, 132–133 (1988) ("willful," as used in a limitation provision for actions under the Fair Labor Standards Act, covers claims of reckless violation) . . . The standard civil usage thus counsels reading the phrase "willfully fails to comply" in §1681n(a) as reaching reckless FCRA violations, and this is so both on the interpretive assumption that Congress knows how we construe statutes and expects us to run true to form, see Commissioner v. Keystone Consol. Industries, Inc., 508 U.S. 152, 159 (1993), and under the general rule that a common law term in a statute comes with a common law meaning, absent anything pointing another way, Beck v. Prupis, 529 U.S. 494, 500–501 (2000).

. . .

III.

A.

Before getting to the claims that the companies acted recklessly, we have the antecedent question whether either company violated the adverse action notice requirement at all. In both cases, respondent-plaintiffs' claims are premised on initial rates charged for new insurance policies, which are not "adverse" actions unless quoting or charging a first-time premium is "an increase in any charge for . . . any insurance, existing or applied for." 15 U.S.C. §1681a(k)(1)(B)(i).

In Safeco's case, the District Court held that the initial rate for a new insurance policy cannot be an "increase" because there is no prior dealing. The phrase "increase in any charge for . . . insurance" is readily understood to mean a change in treatment for an insured, which assumes a previous charge for comparison. See Webster's New International Dictionary 1260 (2d ed. 1957) (defining "increase" as "[a]ddition or enlargement in size, extent, quantity, number, intensity, value, substance, etc.; augmentation; growth; multiplication"). Since the District Court understood "increase" to speak of change just as much as of comparative size or quantity, it reasoned that the statute's "increase" never touches the initial rate offer, where there is no change.

The Government takes the part of the Court of Appeals in construing "increase" to reach a first-time rate. It says that regular usage of the term is not as narrow as the District Court thought: the point from which to measure difference can just as easily be understood without referring to prior individual dealing. The Government gives the example of a gas station owner who charges more than the posted price for gas to customers he doesn't like; it makes sense to say that the owner increases the price and that the driver pays an increased price, even if he never pulled in there for gas before. See Brief for United States as Amicus Curiae 26. The Government implies, then, that reading "increase" requires a choice, and the chosen reading should be the broad one in order to conform to what Congress had in mind.

We think the Government's reading has the better fit with the ambitious objective set out in the Act's statement of purpose, which uses expansive terms to describe the adverse effects of unfair and inaccurate credit reporting and the responsibilities of consumer reporting agencies. See §1681(a) (inaccurate reports "directly impair the efficiency of the banking system"; unfair reporting methods undermine public confidence "essential to the continued functioning of the banking system"; need to "insure" that reporting agencies "exercise their grave responsibilities" fairly, impartially, and with respect for privacy). The descriptions of systemic problem and systemic need as Congress saw them do nothing to suggest that remedies for consumers placed at a disadvantage by unsound credit ratings should be denied to first-time victims, and the legislative histories of FCRA's original enactment and of the 1996 amendment reveal no reason to confine attention to customers and businesses with prior dealings. Quite the contrary. Finally, there is nothing about insurance contracts to suggest that Congress might have meant to differentiate applicants from existing customers when it set the notice requirement; the newly insured who gets charged more owing to an erroneous report is in the same boat with the renewal applicant.[12] We therefore hold that the "increase" required for "adverse action," 15 U.S.C. §1681a(k)(1)(B)(i), speaks to a disadvantageous rate even with no prior dealing; the term reaches initial rates for new applicants.

---

12. In fact, notice in the context of an initially offered rate may be of greater significance than notice in the context of a renewal rate; if, for instance, insurance is offered on the basis of a single, long-term guaranteed rate, a consumer who is not given notice during the initial application process may never have an opportunity to learn of any adverse treatment.

B.

Although offering the initial rate for new insurance can be an "adverse action," respondent-plaintiffs have another hurdle to clear, for §1681m(a) calls for notice only when the adverse action is "based in whole or in part on" a credit report. GEICO argues that in order to have adverse action "based on" a credit report, consideration of the report must be a necessary condition for the increased rate. The Government and respondent-plaintiffs do not explicitly take a position on this point.

To the extent there is any disagreement on the issue, we accept GEICO's reading. In common talk, the phrase "based on" indicates a but-for causal relationship and thus a necessary logical condition. Under this most natural reading of §1681m(a), then, an increased rate is not "based in whole or in part on" the credit report unless the report was a necessary condition of the increase.

As before, there are textual arguments pointing another way. The statute speaks in terms of basing the action "in part" as well as wholly on the credit report, and this phrasing could mean that adverse action is "based on" a credit report whenever the report was considered in the rate-setting process, even without being a necessary condition for the rate increase. But there are good reasons to think Congress preferred GEICO's necessary-condition reading.

If the statute has any claim to lucidity, not all "adverse actions" require notice, only those "based . . . on" information in a credit report. Since the statute does not explicitly call for notice when a business acts adversely merely after consulting a report, conditioning the requirement on action "based . . . on" a report suggests that the duty to report arises from some practical consequence of reading the report, not merely some subsequent adverse occurrence that would have happened anyway. If the credit report has no identifiable effect on the rate, the consumer has no immediately practical reason to worry about it (unless he has the power to change every other fact that stands between himself and the best possible deal); both the company and the consumer are just where they would have been if the company had never seen the report.[13] And if examining reports that make no difference was supposed to trigger a reporting requirement, it would be hard to find any practical point in imposing the "based . . . on" restriction. So it makes more sense to suspect that Congress meant to require notice and prompt a challenge by the consumer only when the consumer would gain something if the challenge succeeded.

C.

To sum up, the difference required for an increase can be understood without reference to prior dealing (allowing a first-time applicant to sue), and considering the credit report must be a necessary condition for the difference. The remaining step in determining a duty to notify in cases like these is identifying the benchmark for determining whether a first-time rate is a disadvantageous increase. And in dealing with this issue, the pragmatic reading of "based . . . on" as a condition necessary to make a practical difference carries a helpful suggestion.

---

13. For instance, if a consumer's driving record is so poor that no insurer would give him anything but the highest possible rate regardless of his credit report, whether or not an insurer happened to look at his credit report should have no bearing on whether the consumer must receive notice, since he has not been treated differently as a result of it.

The Government and respondent-plaintiffs argue that the baseline should be the rate that the applicant would have received with the best possible credit score, while GEICO contends it is what the applicant would have had if the company had not taken his credit score into account (the "neutral score" rate GEICO used in Edo's case). We think GEICO has the better position, primarily because its "increase" baseline is more comfortable with the understanding of causation just discussed, which requires notice under §1681m(a) only when the effect of the credit report on the initial rate offered is necessary to put the consumer in a worse position than other relevant facts would have decreed anyway. If Congress was this concerned with practical consequences when it adopted a "based . . . on" causation standard, it presumably thought in equally practical terms when it spoke of an "increase" that must be defined by a baseline to measure from. Congress was therefore more likely concerned with the practical question whether the consumer's rate actually suffered when the company took his credit report into account than the theoretical question whether the consumer would have gotten a better rate with perfect credit.

The Government objects that this reading leaves a loophole, since it keeps first-time applicants who actually deserve better-than-neutral credit scores from getting notice, even when errors in credit reports saddle them with unfair rates. This is true; the neutral-score baseline will leave some consumers without a notice that might lead to discovering errors. But we do not know how often these cases will occur, whereas we see a more demonstrable and serious disadvantage inhering in the Government's position.

Since the best rates (the Government's preferred baseline) presumably go only to a minority of consumers, adopting the Government's view would require insurers to send slews of adverse action notices; every young applicant who had yet to establish a gilt-edged credit report, for example, would get a notice that his charge had been "increased" based on his credit report. We think that the consequence of sending out notices on this scale would undercut the obvious policy behind the notice requirement, for notices as common as these would take on the character of formalities, and formalities tend to be ignored. It would get around that new insurance usually comes with an adverse action notice, owing to some legal quirk, and instead of piquing an applicant's interest about the accuracy of his credit record, the commonplace notices would mean just about nothing and go the way of junk mail. Assuming that Congress meant a notice of adverse action to get some attention, we think the cost of closing the loophole would be too high. . . .

IV.

A.

In GEICO's case, the initial rate offered to Edo was the one he would have received if his credit score had not been taken into account, and GEICO owed him no adverse action notice under §1681m(a).

B.

Safeco did not give Burr and Massey any notice because it thought §1681m(a) did not apply to initial applications, a mistake that left the company in violation of the statute if Burr and Massey received higher rates "based in whole or in part" on their credit reports; if they did, Safeco would be liable to them on a showing of reckless conduct (or worse). The first issue we can forget, however, for although the record does not reliably indicate what rates they would have obtained if their credit reports had not been considered, it is clear enough that if Safeco did violate the statute, the company was not reckless in falling down in its duty. . . . Here, there is no need to pinpoint the negligence/recklessness line, for Safeco's reading of the statute, albeit erroneous, was not objectively unreasonable. As we said, §1681a(k)(1)(B)(i) is silent on the point from which to measure "increase." On the rationale that "increase" presupposes prior dealing, Safeco took the definition as excluding initial rate offers for new insurance, and so sent no adverse action notices to Burr and Massey. While we disagree with Safeco's analysis, we recognize that its reading has a foundation in the statutory text, and a sufficiently convincing justification to have persuaded the District Court to adopt it and rule in Safeco's favor.

This is not a case in which the business subject to the Act had the benefit of guidance from the courts of appeals or the Federal Trade Commission (FTC) that might have warned it away from the view it took. Before these cases, no court of appeals had spoken on the issue, and no authoritative guidance has yet come from the FTC . . . Given this dearth of guidance and the less-than-pellucid statutory text, Safeco's reading was not objectively unreasonable, and so falls well short of raising the "unjustifiably high risk" of violating the statute necessary for reckless liability.

. . .

The Court of Appeals correctly held that reckless disregard of a requirement of FCRA would qualify as a willful violation within the meaning of §1681n(a). But there was no need for that court to remand the cases for factual development. GEICO's decision to issue no adverse action notice to Edo was not a violation of §1681m(a), and Safeco's misreading of the statute was not reckless. The judgments of the Court of Appeals are therefore reversed in both cases, which are remanded for further proceedings consistent with this opinion.

Justice Stevens, with whom Justice Ginsburg joins, concurring in part and concurring in the judgment.

While I join the Court's judgment and Parts I, II, III-A, and IV-B of the Court's opinion, I disagree with the reasoning in Parts III-B and III-C, as well as with Part IV-A, which relies on that reasoning.

An adverse action taken after reviewing a credit report "is based in whole or in part on" that report within the meaning of 15 U.S.C. §1681m(a). That is true even if the company would have made the same decision without looking at the report, because what the company actually did is more relevant than what it might have done. I find nothing in the statute making the examination of a credit report a "necessary condition" of any resulting increase. The more natural reading is that reviewing a report is only a sufficient condition.

The Court's contrary position leads to a serious anomaly. As a matter of federal law, companies are free to adopt whatever "neutral" credit scores they want. That score need not (and probably will not) reflect the median consumer credit score. More likely, it will reflect a company's assessment of the creditworthiness of a run-of-the-mill applicant who lacks a credit report. Because those who have yet to develop a credit history are unlikely to be good credit risks, "neutral" credit scores will in many cases be quite low. Yet under the Court's reasoning, only those consumers with credit scores even lower than what may already be a very low "neutral" score will ever receive adverse action notices.

While the Court acknowledges that "the neutral-score baseline will leave some consumers without a notice that might lead to discovering errors," it finds this unobjectionable because Congress was likely uninterested in "the theoretical question of whether the consumer would have gotten a better rate with perfect credit." The Court's decision, however, disserves not only those consumers with "gilt-edged credit report[s]," but also the much larger category of consumers with better-than-"neutral" scores. I find it difficult to believe that Congress could have intended for a company's unrestrained adoption of a "neutral" score to keep many (if not most) consumers from ever hearing that their credit reports are costing them money. In my view, the statute's text is amenable to a more sensible interpretation.

---

2. Duties if Adverse Action Is Taken

Taking adverse action triggers duties for a user. The user must inform the consumer of the adverse action and provide the contact information for the agency that the user relied upon. 15 U.S.C. §1681m(a). The user also must tell the consumer that she has a right to obtain a free copy of the consumer report used in making the decision to take adverse action and that the consumer has a right to dispute the accuracy or completeness of any information in a consumer report furnished by the agency. These disclosures can be made orally, written, or by electronic means. These rules apply to adverse actions taken for all permissible purposes, including insurance, employment, and credit.

For credit transactions for personal, family, or household use, if the creditor relied on information other than from a consumer reporting agency, additional disclosures are required. 15 U.S.C. §1681m(b). The most important of these is that the consumer has a right to request the reason for the adverse action. The consumer has 60 days to make such a request. Upon its receipt, the user must provide the reasons within a reasonable time.

If a user of a report takes an adverse action or makes a risk-based pricing decision, the user must notify the consumer of the actual credit score used in making the decision. 15 U.S.C. §1681m(a)(2) and (h)(5)(E).

D. Accuracy in Credit Reporting

1. Detecting Errors

Given their widespread use and potential consequences, inaccuracies in consumer reports are a serious concern. As one advocate told Congress, "a poor credit history is the 'Scarlet Letter' of 20th century America." Fair Credit Reporting Act: How It Functions for Consumers and the Economy: Hearing Before the Subcomm. on Fin. Inst. and Consumer Credit of the H. Comm. On Fin. Servs., 108th Cong. (2003) (statement of Anthony Rodriguez, Staff Attorney, National Consumer Law Center.)

Amendments to FCRA frequently have been motivated by concern about accuracy but empirical estimates of the degree and nature of the problem vary. In 2012, the FTC had 1,000 consumers review their reports from one or more consumer reporting agencies. It found that one in four consumers identified errors on their credit reports that might affect their credit scores. When consumers disputed the information, 80 percent had some modification to their credit reports. Most of these errors did not change consumers' credit scores. However, about one in ten consumers saw a change in their credit score after the disputed information was changed. Most changes were small, but 5 percent of consumers had a score change of more than 25 points. FTC Report to Congress under §310 of the Fair and Accurate Credit Transactions Act of 2002 (2012), https://www.ftc.gov/sites/default/files/documents/reports/section-319-fair-and-accurate-credit-transactions-act-2003-fifth-interim-federal-trade-commission/130211factareport.pdf. Other estimates or errors have been much higher, although these studies are dated. A 2004 study of over 150 consumer files found errors in 79 percent of reports; 25 percent of those were significant enough to cause a potential denial of credit. *See* Alison Cassidy, and Edmund Mierzwinski, *Mistakes Do Happen: A Look at Errors in Consumer Credit Reports*, U.S. PIRG (June 2004). Errors can go in either direction, with the missing or incorrect information either being positive or negative about consumers' past actions. Errors of omission are a particular concern for consumers trying to improve a score. One study found that 78 percent of files were missing a revolving account that was in good standing, and 31 percent of files were missing a mortgage account that had never been delinquent. *See* Consumer Federation of America & National Credit Reporting Ass'n, *Credit Score Accuracy and Implications for Consumers* (Dec., 17, 2002) at http://www.consumerfed.org/pdfs/121702CFA_NCRA_Credit_Score_Report_Final.pdf.

The disparate results of the studies are likely the result of differences in defining what constitutes an inaccuracy, how serious of an inaccuracy is a cause for concern, and improvements in accuracy over time. Even with relatively low percentages of errors, however, the numbers become meaningful. Just a 1 percent error rate would still mean 2 million affected consumers, a large scale problem for law and policy to address.

Several types of errors are of concern. One is that information is added to a report that does not belong to the identified consumer. While this can indicate identity theft, it also results from similar or identical names. A related problem is an agency sending a user a report that may be correct in all its contents, but it is the report of a different person than the person of interest to the user. The major problem is inaccurate information, a category that includes information that is incorrect, information that is incomplete, and information that is missing.

In a follow-up study by the FTC to its 2012 report, the consumers who had completed the FCRA dispute process were provided with new credit reports and credit scores in 2014. The new credit reports were then compared to the old reports to assess whether the consumer reporting agencies had modified the reports in response to the disputes. The FTC looked at the "reinsertion rate," meaning the frequency with which previously removed negative information reappeared on a credit report. It found that 70 percent of consumers believed that at least one piece of previously disputed information remained inaccurate. FTC Report to Congress under Section 310 of the Fair and Accurate Credit Transactions Act of 2002 (2015), https://www.ftc.gov/system/files/documents/reports/section-319-fair-accurate-credit-transactions-act-2003-sixth-interim-final-report-federal-trade/150121factareport.pdf.

A key step to improving accuracy is getting consumers to review their reports and to detect errors. To do so, consumers first must obtain their reports. In addition to the disclosure of reports in adverse actions discussed above, FCRA requires "nationwide" agencies to provide consumers with a free copy of their reports one time each year, upon the consumers' requests. This rule effectively means that consumers could make an inquiry every four months, rotating the three major agencies, allowing them to keep fairly close tabs on their reports. The law requires a centralized process for making this request, and the big three agencies operate a website, www.annualcreditreport.com, and a toll-free telephone number for so doing. The free annual credit report does not include the consumer's credit score, giving rise to a thriving trade in selling credit scores and credit monitoring products to consumers. Visit www.freecreditreport.com for an example of such a business.

The second step in improving accuracy is reviewing the included information. The law constrains what may be in the report. 15 U.S.C. §1681c. Even if the information is permissible, it may be inaccurate. Before 1996 when Congress amended FCRA, there were no legal obligations on businesses who furnished information to consumer reporting agencies. A furnisher now has a legal obligation to avoid furnishing any information that it "knows or has reasonable cause to believe is inaccurate." 15 U.S.C. §1681s-2(a)(1). One way a furnisher may learn such information is inaccurate is if a consumer provides it with notice at the furnisher's specified address. However, a furnisher does not have reasonable cause to believe the information is inaccurate solely because of a consumer's allegations. A furnisher who receives notice that a consumer disputes information must pass along the existence of a dispute when it furnishes further information to the consumer reporting agency.

While there is no obligation for any particular business to supply a credit reporting agency with information, once a company does so, it takes on additional obligations under FCRA. Those who "regularly and in the ordinary course of business furnishes information to one or more consumer reporting agencies . . . and determine [such information] is not complete or accurate, shall promptly notify the consumer reporting agency of that determination and provide to the agency any corrections to that information. . . ." 15 U.S.C. §1681s-2(a)(2). Furnishers who regularly provide data also must notify credit reporting agencies of the voluntary closure of an account by a consumer. Consumers often rely on their credit reports to verify that a business has closed their account and may be concerned that a failure to report an account as closed lowers a credit score by suggesting access to credit that does not exist. Furnishers that are financial institutions have an additional duty. They must notify consumers in writing if they supply negative information to an agency. 15 U.S.C. §1681s-2(a)(7).

Agencies also have a duty to use reasonable procedures to ensure "maximum possible accuracy." 15 U.S.C. §1681e(b). The most commonly used measure of reasonableness that courts have used is a balancing test that weighs "the potential that the information will create a misleading impression against the availability of more accurate information and the burden of providing such information." *Wilson v. Rental Research Serv., Inc.*, 165 F.3d 642 (8th Cir. 1999).

These legal obligations have little meaning unless they are enforced. Under current law, errors do not result in liability. In 2014, the CFPB began to require that major consumer reporting agencies provide "regular accuracy" reports that identify furnishers with the largest number of consumer disputes. This will provide insight into which furnishers, or type of industries that furnish data, are more likely to contribute inaccurate or disputed data.

2. Disputing Information

When consumers believe inaccurate information is in their consumer reports, they can take two actions. First, they can initiate a dispute with the consumer reporting agency that keeps the report. Upon notification of a dispute, the law mandates that the agency "shall, free of charge, conduct a reasonable reinvestigation to determine whether the disputed information is inaccurate and record the current status of the disputed information, or delete the item." The agency has 30 days from receipt of the notice of dispute to conduct its reinvestigation. 15 U.S.C. §1681i(a)(1)(A). (By the way, it is a mystery why it is called a "reinvestigation" because this can be the first investigation of the matter; perhaps the idea is that the consumer has already asked the data furnisher to take action, although the law does not require this.) The agency has five business days from receipt of the consumer's notice to inform the furnisher of the dispute. The agency should pass along all relevant information it received from the consumer about the nature of the dispute. 15 U.S.C. §1681i(a)(2)(A).

Upon review of the dispute notice, the agency may determine that the dispute is "frivolous or irrelevant" and refuse to conduct a reinvestigation. 15 U.S.C. §1681i(a)(3). If it does so, it must tell the consumer of its determination within five business days. The agency also has the option of simply deleting the disputed information; this choice also lets it avoid conducting a reinvestigation. 15 U.S.C. §1681i(a)(1)(A). Note though that deletion of incorrect information may be less helpful to a consumer than correcting information and leaving it in the report. This is particularly true for those with a "thin" file with little information.

If the agency does reinvestigate, it must provide written notice to the consumer of the results. The communication should be sent within 5 business days of completing the reinvestigation and contain the following information:

(i) a statement that the reinvestigation is completed;

(ii) a consumer report that is based upon the consumer's file as that file is revised as a result of the reinvestigation;

(iii) a notice that, if requested by the consumer, a description of the procedure used to determine the accuracy and completeness of the information shall be provided to the consumer by the agency, including the business name and address of any furnisher of information contacted in connection with such information and the telephone number of such furnisher, if reasonably available;

(iv) a notice that the consumer has the right to add a statement to the consumer's file disputing the accuracy or completeness of the information; and

(v) a notice that the consumer has the right to request under subsection (d) that the consumer reporting agency furnish notifications under that subsection.

15 U.S.C. §1681i(a)(6). If its reinvestigation leads the agency to conclude that the information is inaccurate, incomplete, or unverifiable, it must promptly delete or modify that information as appropriate and notify the furnisher of the disputed information of its actions. 15 U.S.C. §1681i(a)(5). Agencies must have procedures to prevent the reappearance of the inaccurate information on the report. For example, the agency must have a certification from the furnisher that the information is complete and accurate before it can reinsert deleted disputed data. 15 U.S.C. §1681i(a)(5)(B). To prevent the problem from appearing with another consumer reporting agency, the furnisher also has to update the information with all other consumer reporting agencies to which the person furnished the information.

A second avenue for a consumer concerned about inaccurate information is to dispute the information directly with the furnisher, rather than with the agency. To do so, the consumer needs to contact the furnisher at a specified address, explain the basis for the dispute, and include all supporting documentation "required by the furnisher to substantiate the basis of the dispute." 15 U.S.C. §1681s-2(a)(8). This last requirement can be difficult because the consumer may feel that the furnisher is the party in possession of the information to disprove the accuracy of the information. FCRA provides that furnishers can essentially ignore a dispute if it "reasonably determines that the dispute is frivolous or irrelevant" and that failure to provide sufficient information can be the basis for such a determination. 15 U.S.C. §1681s-2(a)(8)(F)(i).

Upon receipt of a dispute, a furnisher has an obligation to conduct an investigation that includes a review of all relevant information provided by the consumer. This investigation must be completed within 30 days and its results reported to the consumer. If the furnisher found an inaccuracy, it must provide the credit reporting agency with information to correct the data. Crucially, there is not a private right of action against a furnisher for failure to comply with the dispute provisions.

The CFPB can bring enforcement actions, however, and has taken some initiatives in this area. For example, the CFPB urged credit card companies to provide free credit scores on monthly bills. It also issued a prominent report showing that half of delinquent/collection items on credit reports are medical debts. In response, the New York Attorney General reached an agreement with the three major consumer reporting agencies to change how they record and update medical debt. NPR, *Credit Agencies Agree to Wait Before Adding Medical Debt to Ratings* (March 3, 2015).

3.   Credit Repair

The growth in the credit reporting industry has been paralleled by the rise of businesses that claim to help consumers improve their credit. The vast majority of these companies provide little benefit, beyond instructing the consumer how to dispute inaccurate information. In most instances, the only "cure" for bad credit is time.

   To address abuses, the Credit Repair Organizations Act, 15 U.S.C. §1679-1679j, regulates credit repair businesses. It gives consumers three days to rescind a contract for credit repair and mandates a notice of this right to cancel. The statute also prohibits credit repair businesses from false or misleading practices, which presumably were already prohibited by the federal and state unfair and deceptive acts. The law does provide for the greater of actual damages or the amount paid to the business, as well as punitive damages. Few suits seem to be filed, however, despite the fact that a quick search of the Internet reveals dozens of companies offering dubious services, many starting at just $49 per month for the first year.

E.   Enforcement for FCRA Violations

In addition to dispute provisions, other types of FCRA violations can give rise to both public and private actions. If a violation of FCRA constituted an unfair, deceptive, or abusive practice under a Consumer Financial Protection Bureau rule or an unfair or deceptive practice under state law, the Consumer Financial Protection Bureau or the state attorneys general could bring enforcement proceedings. Public enforcement is crucial in the context of FCRA because private liability actions face some obstacles. First, as discussed above in *Safeco Insurance v. Burr*, there are two recovery provisions: willful noncompliance (§1681n) and negligent noncompliance (§1681o). With willful noncompliance, recovery includes actual damages of not less than $100 and not more than $1,000, punitive damages, court costs, and reasonable attorney's fees. Negligent noncompliance differs in that liability is for "actual damages" without reference to a dollar cap and that punitive damages are unavailable. The problem is that the statutory damages are low (for willful noncompliance) and actual damages can be nonexistent or hard to prove (for negligent noncompliance). Second, it can be difficult to show negligence in any given case. Because several of the substantive provisions of FCRA require parties to have "reasonable procedures," the mere failure to comply with the statute can be overcome by showing procedures were in place that reasonably should have resulted in compliance. Third, FCRA preempted common law actions that were used before its enactment, including defamation, invasion of privacy, and negligence. 15 U.S.C. §1681h(e). These are specific concerns to FCRA, in addition to the general issues with private enforcement of consumer law that are the subject of Assignment 24, *infra*.

Problem Set 7

7.1. Harold Weckerly has been feeling old lately, perhaps because he just celebrated his 92nd birthday. His relatives fuss over him constantly and give him unsolicited advice. One of his grandchildren, Marcus, recently "helped" Harold obtain his credit report and is trying to get Harold worked up about its contents. Along with Harold's one active account, a credit card that another grandchild insisted that he needed, the report shows the following: 1) a bankruptcy dated eight years ago; 2) a foreclosure dated seven years ago; 3) a mortgage account that was closed seven years ago while in delinquent status; 4) a revolving account with Sears that was opened in 1971 and closed in 1982, shown paid up in full and closed by consumer; and 5) a criminal conviction for disturbing the peace from 1942 just before Harold entered the Army. Harold has told Marcus that these entries are all accurate, saying that the entries are explained, respectively, by a gambling problem he had a few years ago that led to him telling his relatives that he "sold" his vacation home, his desire for new kitchen appliances in avocado green in the 1970s, and his being a bit of a wild one in his younger years before he got straightened out by World War II. Marcus continues to insist that Harold's character is being unfairly impugned by the consumer reporting agency. Harold has no intention of initiating a dispute. He wonders though if Marcus could be kept occupied by researching the situation, giving him the satisfaction of providing more unwanted "help." Should Harold's report contain the five items listed above? *See* 15 U.S.C. §1681c.

7.2. AutoBarn is a used car dealer specializing in high-mileage hybrid vehicles. It prides itself on its service, promising customers they can complete a car purchase in one hour from when they walk onto the lot. To expedite the process, AutoBarn has a consumer complete a short data form asking for name, address, date of birth, and last four digits of social security number, before it will allow a consumer to take a car out for a test drive. The form also asks the consumer to rate, at that time, the consumer's level of interest from five (very interested) to one (not interested) in closing a sale using Autobarn's "One Hour to Hybrid Happiness" process and contains a place for the consumer's signature. If a consumer indicates a four or five for interest level and signs the form, an employee starts filling out the purchase and financing paperwork, including requesting a credit report and score from a consumer reporting agency, while the consumer is doing the test drive. When the consumer returns, the employee asks the consumer if they wish to purchase the car, and if so, presents them with the partially-complete paperwork, including a finance package for consideration. Does AutoBarn violate FCRA in its practices? *See* 15 U.S.C. §1681b; 1681e(d); 1681m.

7.3. InsureAll is a new entrant to the consumer reporting business. It collects similar data from similar furnishers as do the other large consumer reporting agencies but its business exclusively serves insurance companies as users. InsureAll provides a free copy of their reports to consumers who make a request via a website and toll-free number.

InsureAll recently received a request from a consumer, Kristine Leung, for a copy of her credit score. InsureAll wrote back it would provide Kristine with her score if she submitted $25. Kristine did so, and received back a short message, stating: "As of the date of this response, the InsureAll RiskScore of Kristine Leung is JJ." Kristine has emailed you, the lawyer who handled her divorce, to ask for your help in understanding this score. What do you tell her? *See* 15 U.S.C. §1681g(c); 15 U.S.C. §1681g(f).

7.4. You are a policy analyst for a presidential candidate. A congressperson has introduced the following bill:

Employment for All Act

(1) GENERAL PROHIBITION—Except as provided in paragraph (3), a person, including a prospective employer or current employer, may not use a consumer report or investigative consumer report, or cause a consumer report or investigative consumer report to be procured, with respect to any consumer where any information contained in the report bears on the consumer's creditworthiness, credit standing, or credit capacity for employment purposes.

(2) SOURCE OF CONSUMER REPORT IRRELEVANT—The prohibition described in paragraph (1) shall apply even if the consumer consents or otherwise authorizes the procurement or use of a consumer report for employment purposes.

(3) EXCEPTIONS—Notwithstanding the prohibitions set forth in this subsection, an employer may use a consumer report with respect to a consumer in the following situations:
   (A) When the consumer applies for, or currently holds, employment that requires national security or FDIC clearance.
   (B) When the consumer applies for, or currently holds, employment with a State or local government agency which otherwise requires use of a consumer report.
   (C) When the consumer applies for, or currently holds, a supervisory, managerial, professional, or executive position at a financial institution.
   (D) When otherwise required by law.

You anticipate your boss will be asked on the campaign trail if she supports this bill. Give her some talking points to explain the issue to potential voters and advise her on the best position for her to take. Be sure to identify how the position she takes may relate to her commitment to job growth and limiting regulations on business.

Assignment 8.   Credit Discrimination

Credit is a major vehicle for economic and social mobility in the United States. Families borrow to buy homes, pay for education, and meet unexpected expenses. Access to loans can help people improve their quality of life and avoid hardships. Because of its roles as a safety net and mechanism for upward opportunity, discrimination in credit can hold back individuals and hurt their life chances.

Consumer laws prohibit discrimination in the credit process based on a statutorily prescribed list of characteristics. While discrimination in other contexts (such as employment or education) is not considered "consumer" law, those laws influence the enforcement and interpretation of credit discrimination laws.

A. History of Credit Discrimination

For much of its history, credit opportunity did not exist in the United States for large swaths of the population. African Americans simply were not served at many financial institutions, single women were denied credit because they lacked husbands that lenders believed were necessary for financial stability, and immigrants were marginalized to specialized lenders.

The government was complicit in credit discrimination. In the 1930s, a federal agency charged with preventing foreclosure, the Home Owners Loan Corporation, created maps to indicate the risks of lending that used race as a negative factor. High-concentration areas of African Americans were outlined in red. Today, the term "redlining" is used to generally describe discriminatory lending practices.

In the wake of the Civil Rights movement, several laws were enacted to prohibit discrimination in credit markets. Borrowing opportunities increased to racial minorities, women, and other groups, such as older Americans and disabled Americans, who may have income from government support. During the 1970s and 1980s, other policy efforts included the expansion of community banks, education to consumers about their rights to be given fair consideration for credit, and the examination of the lending practices of financial institutions for discrimination.

In the late 1990s, the concerns about discrimination morphed from unfair denials of credit to aggressive extensions of high-cost, unfavorable credit terms to minorities and other groups. Advocates and policymakers began to worry about "reverse redlining," a term that encompassed the practices of inundating certain neighborhoods or certain individuals with offers for exploitative loans.

These loans often featured expensive fees, above-market rates, and unfavorable terms. As a net result, these credit "opportunities" actually harmed, rather than improved, a person's financial situation. Such predatory loans were disproportionately offered to racial minorities and other groups traditionally limited in opportunities for credit, such as non-English speakers or older Americans. The City of Baltimore sued Wells Fargo in 2008 alleging that unfair credit terms in mortgage loans produced a high foreclosure rate that cost the city millions in lost property taxes and public investment. The city's analysis found that in 2006, high-rate loans went to 65 percent of black Baltimore borrowers and 15 percent of white Baltimore borrowers. Wells Fargo contested the charges on the grounds that its loan pricing was based on credit risk. *Mayor of Baltimore v. Wells Fargo Bank*, 631 F. Supp. 2d 702 (D. Md. 2009) (denying bank's motion to dismiss). The Department of Justice took over as plaintiff to resolve questions about the city's standing as a plaintiff; ultimately Wells Fargo settled for $175 million without admitting any wrongdoing.

In the wake of the 2010 Dodd-Frank Act, the pendulum has swung back to worry about a lack of borrowing opportunity. Credit retrenchment can limit opportunities for individuals to build wealth, access education, or start a small business. With a higher rate of denials and more conservative underwriting comes more concern about discrimination in those decisions. Today, the talk is about "expanding the credit box," and in particular to considering how data analytics and credit scoring may disproportionately harm people in protected groups. As the market responds with specialized products for those excluded from mainstream credit by tighter standards, the cycle likely will repeat itself. Both aggressive credit-markups and credit denials—if either reflects discrimination—are potential acts that limit social and economic mobility in troubling ways.

B.   Prohibited Bases of Discrimination

The Equal Credit Opportunity Act (ECOA), 15 U.S.C. §1691 et seq., is the most sweeping of the federal laws pertaining to credit discrimination. Several other laws supplement its coverage, either by prohibiting credit decisions on additional bases not covered by ECOA or by providing different remedies. These laws include the Fair Housing Act, the Americans with Disabilities Act, the Federal Civil Rights Act, and a host of equivalent state laws. A related law is the Community Reinvestment Act, 12 U.S.C. §2903 et seq., which requires regulators to monitor the level of service that banks provide to low- and moderate-income communities. It is most frequently used to challenge mergers or sales of financial institutions that might result in the closing of less profitable branches in low-income neighborhoods. Because the Community Reinvestment Act does not give protections to individual consumers, it is not considered further in this Assignment. Its viability as a tool to ensure access to financial services may be weakened by the growth in online and mobile lending, and the corresponding reduction in physical bank branches.

   The general approach of credit discrimination laws is to prohibit any consideration of certain factors in credit applications and decisions. It is not a defense that the factor might bear a statistically provable correlation with credit risk; the creditor's reasonableness is irrelevant. If the factor or an obvious proxy for the factor is considered, discrimination has occurred.

1. Sex or Gender

ECOA was enacted in 1974, in the midst of the struggle to pass an Equal Rights Amendment, the widespread adoption of no-fault divorce laws, and rapid growth in women's college enrollment and professional workforce participation. ECOA itself prohibits discrimination based on "sex." Regulation B, which implements ECOA, prohibits creditors from requesting information about an applicant's birth control practices, intention or capacity to bear children, or intention to rear children. 12 C.F.R. §1002.5(b)(2). These were frequent proxies for determining if an applicant was a woman and sometimes were bases for discrimination themselves (on the theory, for example, that a woman would quit working after becoming a mother).
   Marital status and familial status are closely related to sex discrimination because historically women were required to be married and to rely on their husbands' incomes to obtain loans. Regulation B sharply limits when marital or familial status may be considered in the credit process. The idea is that a consumer should have control of whether she or he wants the financial institution to rely on assets or income that are tied to the marriage. For example, if joint property is being offered as collateral, a creditor can require both spouses to complete a credit application. 12 C.F.R. §1002.7(d)(1). The general rule is that married women have the right to seek credit independent of their spouses or fathers and to be evaluated as individuals based on the woman's creditworthiness. The following case is dated but offers a lucid explanation of the concerns with regard to sex and marital status that undergirded ECOA.

Markham v. Colonial Mortgage Serv. Co.

605 F.2d 566 (D.C. Cir. 1979)

Swygert, Circuit Judge.
   The Equal Credit Opportunity Act, 15 U.S.C. §§1691, et seq., prohibits creditors from discriminating against applicants on the basis of sex or marital status. We are asked to decide whether this prohibition prevents creditors from refusing to aggregate the incomes of two unmarried joint mortgage applicants when determining their creditworthiness in a situation where the incomes of two similarly situated married joint applicants would have been aggregated. The plaintiffs in this action, Jerry and Marcia Markham, appeal the judgment of the district court granting

defendant Illinois Federal Service Savings and Loan Association's motion for summary judgment. We reverse. . . .

In November 1976, plaintiffs Marcia J. Harris and Jerry Markham announced their engagement and began looking for a residence in the Capitol Hill section of Washington, D.C. One of the real estate firms which they contacted, defendant B.W. Real Estate, Inc., found suitable property for them, and in December 1976, Markham and Harris signed a contract of sale for the property.

Upon the recommendation of B.W. Real Estate, plaintiffs agreed to have defendant Colonial Mortgage Service Co. Associates, Inc. conduct a credit check. Plaintiffs subsequently submitted a joint mortgage application to Colonial Mortgage . . . [which was eventually submitted] to Illinois Federal.

Plaintiffs and B.W. Real Estate had decided that February 4, 1977 would be an appropriate closing date for the purchase of the Capitol Hill residence. Accordingly, plaintiffs arranged to terminate their current leases, change mailing addresses, and begin utility service at the new property. On February 1, the loan committee of Illinois Federal rejected the plaintiffs' application. On February 3, the eve of the settlement date, plaintiffs were informed through a B.W. Real Estate agent that their loan application had been denied because they were not married. They were advised that their application would be resubmitted to the "investor" who was not identified on February 8, but that approval would be contingent upon the submission of a marriage certificate.

On February 8, the Illinois Federal loan committee reconsidered the plaintiffs' application, but again denied it. A letter was sent that date from Illinois Federal . . . that the application had been rejected with the statement: "Separate income not sufficient for loan and job tenure."

On February 9, 1977 plaintiffs filed this suit, alleging violation of the Equal Credit Opportunity Act. After the district court separately granted the motions of Illinois Federal and the other defendants for summary judgment on May 25, 1978, plaintiffs brought this appeal.

II.

A.

We address first the appeal from the district court's summary judgment entered in favor of Illinois Federal. The district court concluded as a matter of law that plaintiffs could not state a claim under the Equal Credit Opportunity Act even if they showed that Illinois Federal's refusal to aggregate their incomes resulted, in whole or in part, in the denial of their loan application. This conclusion was based on the premise that creditors need not ignore the "special legal ties created between two people by the marital bond." It was the court's conclusion that under Illinois law the mere fact of marriage provides creditors with greater rights and remedies against married applicants than are available against unmarried applicants. Presumably the district court believed that this excused Illinois Federal under 15 U.S.C. §1691d(b), which allows a creditor to take "(s)tate property laws directly or indirectly affecting creditworthiness" into consideration in making credit decisions.

We fail to see the relevance of any special legal ties created by marriage with respect to the legal obligations of joint debtors. This was not an instance where a single person is applying for credit individually and claiming income from a third party for purposes of determining creditworthiness. In such an instance, the absence of a legal obligation requiring continuance of the income claimed by the applicant from the third party would reflect on the credit applicant's creditworthiness. Inasmuch as the Markhams applied for their mortgage jointly, they would have been jointly and severally liable on the debt. Each joint debtor would be bound to pay the full amount of the debt; he would then have a right to contribution from his joint debtor. See 4 A. Corbin, Contracts §§924, 928 (1951). See also Clayman v. Goodman Properties, Inc., 518 F.2d 1026 (1973). While it may be true that judicially-enforceable rights such as support and maintenance are legal consequences of married status, they are irrelevancies as far as the creditworthiness of joint applicants is concerned. Illinois Federal would have had no greater rights against the Markhams had they been married, nor would the Markhams have had greater rights against each other on this particular obligation. Thus, inasmuch as the state laws attaching in the event of marriage would not affect the creditworthiness of these joint applicants, section 1691d(b) may not be used to justify the refusal to aggregate the plaintiffs' incomes on the basis of marital status.

B.

We turn to a consideration of whether the Equal Credit Opportunity Act's prohibition of discrimination on the basis of sex or marital status makes illegal Illinois Federal's refusal to aggregate plaintiffs' income when determining their creditworthiness. Illinois Federal contends that neither the purpose nor the language of the Act requires it to combine the incomes of unmarried joint applicants when making that determination.

We start, as we must, with the language of the statute itself. March v. United States, 506 F.2d 1306, 1313 (1974). 15 U.S.C. §1691(a) provides:

> It shall be unlawful for any creditor to discriminate against any applicant, with respect to any aspect of a credit transaction
> (1) on the basis of . . . sex or marital status

This language is simple, and its meaning is not difficult to comprehend. Illinois Federal itself has correctly phrased the standard in its brief: The Act forbids discrimination "on the basis of a person's marital status, that is, to treat persons differently, all other facts being the same, because of their marital status. . . ." Brief for Defendant Illinois Federal at 18. Illinois Federal does not contend that they would not have aggregated plaintiffs' income had they been married at the time. Indeed, Illinois Federal concedes that the law would have required it to do so.[4] Thus, it is plain that Illinois Federal treated plaintiffs differently that is, refused to aggregate their incomes solely because of their marital status, which is precisely the sort of discrimination prohibited by section 1691(a)(1) on its face.

Despite the section's clarity of language, Illinois Federal seeks to avoid a finding of prohibited discrimination by arguing that it was not the Congressional purpose

---

4. 12 U.S.C. §1735f-5 requires that "every person engaged in making mortgage loans secured by residential real property consider without prejudice the combined income of both husband and wife for the purpose of extending mortgage credit . . . to a married couple or either member thereof."

to require such an aggregation of the incomes of non-married applicants. It can be assumed, *arguendo*, that one, perhaps even the main, purpose of the act was to eradicate credit discrimination waged against women, especially married women whom creditors traditionally refused to consider apart from their husbands as individually worthy of credit. But granting such an assumption does not negate the clear language of the Act itself that discrimination against *any* applicant, with respect to *any* aspect of a credit transaction, which is based on marital status is outlawed. When the plain meaning of a statute appears on its face, we need not concern ourselves with legislative history, see Caminetti v. United States, 242 U.S. 470 (1917), especially when evidence of the legislation's history as has been presented to us does not argue persuasively for a narrower meaning than that which is apparent from the statutory language. See Boston Sand & Gravel Co. v. United States, 278 U.S. 41, 48 (1928). We believe that the meaning of the words chosen by Congress is readily apparent.

Illinois Federal expresses the fear that a holding such as we reach today will require it to aggregate the incomes of all persons who apply for credit as a group. Lest it be misinterpreted, we note that our holding is not itself that far-reaching. It does no more than require Illinois Federal to treat plaintiffs — a couple jointly applying for credit — the same as they would be treated if married. We have not been asked to decide what the effect of the Act would have been had plaintiffs not applied for credit jointly. Nor do we have before us a question of whether the Act's marital status provision in any way applies to a situation where more than two people jointly request credit. We hold only that, under the Act Illinois Federal should have treated plaintiffs an unmarried couple applying for credit jointly the same as it would have treated them had they been married at the time.

C.

Illinois Federal also contends that, regardless of this court's decision on the issue of income aggregation, the judgment of the district court should be affirmed. The premise of this contention is that, even had the incomes of plaintiffs' been combined, Illinois Federal would still not have extended the loan because of lack of sufficient job tenure or credit history. Due to the district court's basis for decision and the state of the record, we are not in position to pass on the validity of this separate issue. . . .

Although Illinois Federal contends that plaintiffs would remain ineligible regardless of aggregation, plaintiffs assert that they were told the loan would be forthcoming if they produced a marriage certificate. Because we remand the case to the district court, we deem it sufficient to note the appearance of a genuine issue of material fact on this state of the record. . . .

_____

The interpretation in this case limited the ability of creditors to discriminate against same-sex couples applying for credit. And in the wake of *United States v. Windsor*, 133 S. Ct. 2675 (2013), the CFPB clarified that it would treat same-sex married couples identically to opposite-sex married couples. CFPB, *Memorandum on Ensuring Equal Treatment for Same-Sex Married Couples* (June 25, 2014).

As with other areas of discrimination, however, the law often lags behavior and social norms. Passed over 40 years ago, ECOA does not use the term "gender." It arguably does cover discrimination against transgender persons or gender expression, *see Rosa v. Park West Bank & Trust Co.,* 214 F.3d 213 (1st Cir. 2000), but some states have amended their laws to provide protection, *see* Cal. Civ. Code §51 (defining sex for civil rights laws to include "gender identity" and "gender expression").

2.   Race and Color

Race and color are prohibited bases under nearly all laws applying to credit discrimination, including ECOA and the Fair Housing Act. ECOA also protects whites, who either may claim direct discrimination, *see Moore v. U.S. Dep't of Agriculture,* 993 F.2d 1222 (5th Cir. 1993), or because the creditor associates them with a protected group. An example of the latter situation is a denial of credit to a white applicant who lives in a heavily minority neighborhood, *see Cherry v. Amoco Oil Co.,* 481 F. Supp. 727 (N.D. Ga. 1979) (denying defendant's motion for summary judgment because plaintiff stated a claim under ECOA based on creditor using plaintiff's zip code as negative credit factor, given segregated housing pattern). These arguments may fail in their application, however, given the difficulty of proving discrimination. *See Cherry v. Amoco Oil Co.,* 490 F. Supp. 1026, 1031 (1980) (ruling for defendant creditor).

   In addition to mortgage lending, where ideas about residential segregation are at play, studies have found a relationship between being African-American and paying more for a car loan. Ian Ayres, *Fair Driving: Gender and Race Discrimination in Retail Car Negotiations,* 104 Harvard L. Rev. 817 (1991); Ian Ayres, *Further Evidence of Discrimination in New Car Negotiations and Estimates of Its Cause,* 94 Mich. L. Rev. 109 (1995) (replicating and expanding the initial study). In 2014 and 2015, the CFPB has reached settlements with a number of banks or auto finance companies over allegations of racial discrimination. *See* Jonelle Marte, *Fifth Third Bank Fined for Discriminating Against Minorities Seeking Auto Loans,* Wash. Post (Sept. 28, 2015); Devlin Barrett, *Honda Finance Arm to Pay $25 Million to Settle Discriminatory Lending Allegations,* Wall St. J. (July 14, 2014).

3.   National Origin

National origin differs from race or color discrimination in that it focuses on ancestry and life history. This includes discouragement or discrimination based on individuals' surnames being associated with certain places of origin or based on individuals' countries of birth. Discrimination on the basis of immigration status is permitted; for example, creditors may distinguish between people with permanent resident status and student visas, and inquire about the immigration situation of an applicant who seeks credit. 12 C.F.R. §1002.5(e).

   Prohibiting discrimination based on national origin can provide some protection from discrimination against non-English speakers, as language preference/ability and national origin are often correlated. Regulation B explicitly permits lenders to provide credit contracts and disclosures in languages other than English, 12 C.F.R. §1002.4(e), provided that the disclosures are identical in content to English-language versions. The federal government has taken some enforcement actions against creditors who reject applicants based on English-language ability. For example, the U.S. Department of Justice condemned as "blatant discrimination" the practice of a financial institution of intentionally avoiding marketing credit products to any customer who had indicated a Spanish-language preference or who resided in Puerto Rico. Elizabeth Olsen, *GE Consumer Finance Units Reach Settlement*, N.Y. Times (June 19, 2014). States have enacted laws that require loan documents to be translated or that regulate the use of oral translators in loan negotiations. *See, e.g.,* Tex. Fin. Code §341.502(a); Cal. Civ. Code §1632(a).

4. Other Bases

Other characteristics that are prohibited bases of credit discrimination under ECOA are religion, age, receipt of income from a public assistance program, or the applicant's exercise of rights under the entire Consumer Credit Protection Act (which includes ECOA). 15 U.S.C. §1691(a). A number of state and municipal laws ban discrimination based on sexual orientation, *see, e.g.,* Cal. Gov't. Code §12955, and less commonly on other characteristics such as military service or political affiliation. Disabled or handicapped people, those with a physical or mental impairment that substantially limits one or more major life activities, may fall under the protection of the anti-discrimination protections in the Americans with Disabilities Act or the Fair Housing Act.

The Fair Housing Act also prohibits discriminating against people who have children under 18 years old in their households. Even if the landlord has an honest belief that children will not be safe in the building, it is illegal to deny the housing on that basis. Some landlords try to steer families to more distant parts of the building (the back or the basement) or impose low-occupancy limits. The latter are set by the Housing and Urban Development department based on square footage to remove landlord discretion. The complaint in *United States v. Twin Oaks Mobile Home Park, Inc.* (14-CV-710, W.D. Wis. Oct. 17, 2014), illustrates conduct that will be challenged as housing discrimination. The Department of Justice alleged that the owner and managers of a 230-unit mobile home community enforced explicit policies making sections of the community unavailable to families with children and prevented the sale of a mobile home to a single mother with a two-year-old child.

The lengthier discussion of certain characteristics in this section reflects the historical importance of these factors in enacting ECOA, with its roots in the civil rights movement and women's movement; it is not a reflection of the scope or harm of such discrimination or the desirability of legal protection. Discrimination is rooted in history and culture, and the protected factors and enforcement activity continue to evolve.

C.   Credit Process

Discrimination can occur at various stages of the credit process. Each of the laws that can be used to combat discrimination has a slightly different scope. Perhaps the most broadly applicable are the federal Civil Rights Acts, which apply to making and enforcing contracts and transactions involving real property. 42 U.S.C. §§1681; 1682. The Fair Housing Act prohibits discriminatory conduct in the rental, sale, or financing of a home. 42 U.S.C. §3604(a). It applies to property owners as well as municipalities.

The Equal Credit Opportunity Act also applies to several stages of a credit transaction. The application and evaluation processes are each considered below.

1.   Applications

ECOA liability may exist for creditors' determinations in pre-application stages. Regulation B forbids creditors from discouraging prospective consumers on a prohibited basis. 12 C.F.R. §1002.4(b). In the race context, marketing discrimination may be alleged if advertisements feature only white people, if advertising occurs only in media serving non-minority areas, or if words or symbols are used in advertising or on applications that imply a discriminatory preference.

At the application stage, discrimination can arise from seeking information from protected class applicants that should be irrelevant to credit evaluation or from making protected class applicants provide additional information. 12 C.F.R. §1002.5(b). For example, creditors should not seek to identify the sex or marital status of an applicant by requiring them to indicate a prefix like Mr., Mrs. or Ms. Requests for such information must be marked optional on credit applications. 12 C.F.R. §1002.5(b)(2). The exception to inquiries about race, color, religion, and other protected bases is if the lender is conducting a self-test to monitor its own compliance with ECOA. 12 C.F.R. §1002.5(b)(1).

Discrimination can also occur if a lender provides different levels of support and guidance in the application process based on a prohibited characteristic. This might occur by offering suggestions to white applicants on how to improve their applications without offering similar advice to minority applicants. In 2015, the CFPB and the DOJ reached a settlement with a lender under ECOA that was premised in part on the lender refusing to accept mortgage applications at branches in minority-dominated neighborhoods but accepting them in predominately white neighborhoods.

2.   Evaluations

Creditors violate ECOA if they rely on a prohibited basis in "any system of evaluating the creditworthiness of applicants." 12 C.F.R. §1002.6(b). This means that lenders cannot have different underwriting standards based on factors such as race, sex, national origin, etc. The same rule applies whether the lender uses a credit scoring model based on data or exercises individualized judgment in assessing applications. Informational barriers make it difficult to prove discrimination in either context. In the wake of ECOA, lenders revised procedures and trained employees to avoid blatant discrimination. Reducing or eliminating subtle or unconscious bias is much more difficult.

The evaluation of applicants consists of not just the denial of credit but also on variation in price and term. Historically, most studies of mortgage lending, where the data availability is greatest, focus on credit denials. In a recent study, however, researchers limited the sample to approved applicants for home loans. Their results suggest that black applicants pay about 29 basis points (1 basis point is 1/100th of a percent), which is more than comparable with white borrowers. Ping Cheng et al., *Racial Discrepancy in Mortgage Interest Rates*, 51 J. Real Estate Fin. & Econ. 1 (2015). Studies also are beginning to explore whether the theory of intersectionality applies in credit discrimination. The above study finds that discrimination is more likely when creditors may believe that a person fits into multiple protected categories. The researchers concluded that while blacks paid higher rates than comparable whites across the credit spectrum, black women at the lower end of creditworthiness suffered the most from higher credit costs.

3. Data Collection

Regulation B imposes record keeping requirements on creditors. Section 1002.12(b) requires the retention of application forms, other information used in evaluating the applicant, written notification of the credit decision, written notification of the specific reasons for adverse action, and any statement submitted by an applicant alleging an ECOA violation. Such records should be kept for 25 months from the notification of the applicant. The time period was justified by the two-year statute of limitations for bringing an ECOA action but Dodd-Frank lengthened to five years the period in which a plaintiff may sue under ECOA. 15 U.S.C. §1691e(f). Creditors also must keep information on how they select customers for pre-screened solicitations and copies of those solicitations. During regulatory exams, creditors are reviewed for fair lending compliance. This typically includes ensuring that a lender has proper policies and procedures and also an audit of selected individual loan-level files.

If the credit is being sought for the purchase or refinance of a home, additional data collection is required. The justification for more records is both the historical problems with discriminatory mortgage lending and also the importance of home purchases to allowing consumers to build wealth, access quality public schools, and have safe, high-quality housing. The Home Mortgage Disclosure Act (HMDA), 12 U.S.C. §2801, requires creditors accepting a mortgage loan application to request information on applicants' ethnicity (using specified categories), sex, marital status, and age. Creditors must also note the geographic location of the home sought to be purchased. The applicant must be told that he or she is not required to provide the information but that the data is being requested by the federal government for the purpose of monitoring credit discrimination. If an applicant does not provide the information, creditors are required to note that fact and "to the extent possible" document the ethnicity, race, and sex of the applicant "on the basis of visual observation or surname." 12 C.F.R. §1002.13. HMDA is a major departure from ECOA's approach to discrimination. Recall that creditors are explicitly banned from asking for characteristics such as race, age, and sex.

Another major innovation of HMDA is that institutions are required to disclose loan-level data to the public. 12 U.S.C. §2803. Only large lenders are required to comply with HMDA but they cover a large share of the market. The 2012 data include information on 15.3 million home loan applications (of which nearly 9.8 million resulted in loan originations) and 3.2 million loan purchases, for a total of nearly 18.5 million actions. The usefulness of HMDA data to detect discrimination is expected to improve in future years because the Dodd-Frank Act passed in 2010 requires the collection and disclosure of additional information about applicants' creditworthiness that can be used as a control in statistical models to identify disparate treatment. As of 2015, the CFPB was still in the process of issuing rules under Regulation C to implement the Dodd-Frank provisions.

D. Proving Liability

Case law defining the contours of prohibited application procedures or impermissible evaluation of applicants is very sparse. Aside from a spate of cases in the late 1970s following ECOA's enactment that alleged direct discrimination, litigation is rare. A lack of data and expense are the main barriers in indirect discrimination cases. The problem is particularly acute outside the mortgage context because of the lack of a comparable law to HMDA for non-mortgage lending. *See* Winnie Taylor, *Proving Racial Discrimination and Monitoring Fair Lending Compliance: The Missing Data Problem in Nonmortgage Credit*, 31 Rev. of Banking & Fin. Law 199 (2011). The National Consumer Law Center, which served as co-counsel, described the $1 million expenditure for discovery, computer analysis, and expert review, necessary in its successful trial against an auto lender for ECOA violations, *Borlay v. Primus Automotive Financial Services*, CV 02-0382. Filed in 1998, the cases ended seven years later in a bench ruling that plaintiffs had proved their case. Without sufficient evidence at the start, but unable to front the costs for discovery, plaintiffs may settle or lose on a motion to dismiss for failure to state a claim.

Defendants also have incentives to prevent ECOA claims from going to trial, even if their deeper pockets would permit litigation on the merits. One reason is that if an ECOA violation is established, punitive damages are available under nearly all credit discrimination laws, and may be mandatory under ECOA. 15 U.S.C. §1691e(b). Perhaps equally, or more important, are the reputational effects of being named a plaintiff in a discrimination lawsuit. Public enforcement is much more common than private litigation in credit discrimination cases. Problems of proof make it easier for regulators to obtain, analyze, and assemble a prima facie case, although even they face challenges in their efforts to establish facts showing discrimination.

1. Disparate Treatment

Disparate treatment requires a showing of discriminatory motive or intent. The evidence can be direct, showing a specific link between the discriminatory intent and the challenged act. For example, a company policy of giving those with Latino surnames a lower credit limit would be an explicit and unambiguous statement of the lender's intent to treat adversely people protected by ECOA. Such overt discrimination is rare.

A prima facie case alleging an ECOA violation requires proof that a lender rejected or acted unfavorably to a creditworthy applicant in an ECOA-protected group and that the lender approved or acted more favorably to those outside the group. The key is comparative evidence showing that applicants with one protected characteristic were treated better, despite similar creditworthiness. The actions must be intentional, but the evidence of discriminatory intent can be indirect. The plaintiffs can then invoke the burden-shifting framework set forth in the employment discrimination case of *McDonnell Douglas Corp. v. Green*, 411 U.S. 792 (1973), and the lender must present a non-discriminatory justification for its different treatment.

2. Disparate Impact

Disparate impact reduces the plaintiff's evidentiary burden even more than disparate treatment. Even if a plaintiff cannot show a creditor is treating applicants differently, discrimination can be established if there is a discriminatory effect of the creditors' neutral practices. Put another way, a lender engaged in a neutral act without intent could nonetheless be harming a protected group. The focus is on the harm, not the motive. As with disparate treatment, the analysis borrows heavily from the framework used in employment cases. And as with employment discrimination, the legal theory of disparate impact is hotly contested. The case below interprets the Fair Housing Act but likely also will be cited with regard to the availability of disparate impact claims under ECOA.

Tex. Dep't of Housing and Community Affairs, et al. v. The Inclusive Communities Project, Inc., et al.

135 S. Ct. 2507 (2015)

KENNEDY, Justice.

The underlying dispute in this case concerns where housing for low-income persons should be constructed in Dallas, Texas — that is, whether the housing should be built in the inner city or in the suburbs. This dispute comes to the Court on a disparate-impact theory of liability. In contrast to a disparate-treatment case, where a "plaintiff must establish that the defendant had a discriminatory intent or motive," a plaintiff bringing a disparate-impact claim challenges practices that have a "disproportionately adverse effect on minorities" and are otherwise unjustified by a legitimate rationale. Ricci v. DeSteffano, 557 U.S. 557, 577 (2009). The question presented for the Court's determination is whether disparate-impact claims are cognizable under the Fair Housing Act (or FHA), 42 U.S.C. §3601 et seq.

I.

Before turning to the question presented, it is necessary to discuss a different federal statute that gives rise to this dispute. The Federal Government provides low-income housing tax credits that are distributed to developers through designated state agencies. 26 U.S.C. §42. Congress has directed States to develop plans identifying selection criteria for distributing the credits. §42(m)(1). Those plans must include certain criteria, such as public housing waiting lists, §42(m)(1)(C), as well as certain preferences, including that low-income housing units "contribut[e] to a concerted community revitalization plan" and be built in census tracts populated predominantly by low-income residents. §§42(m)(1)(B)(ii)(III), 42(d)(5)(ii)(I). Federal law thus favors the distribution of these tax credits for the development of housing units in low-income areas.

In the State of Texas these federal credits are distributed by the Texas Department of Housing and Community Affairs (Department). Under Texas law, a developer's application for the tax credits is scored under a point system that gives priority to statutory criteria, such as the financial feasibility of the development project and the income level of tenants. Tex. Govt. Code Ann. §2306.6710(a)-(b) (West 2008). The Texas Attorney General has interpreted state law to permit the consideration of additional criteria, such as whether the housing units will be built in a neighborhood with good schools. Those criteria cannot be awarded more points than statutorily mandated criteria. Tex. Op. Atty. Gen. No. GA-0208, pp. 2-6 (2004), 2004 WL 1434796, *4-*6.

The Inclusive Communities Project, Inc. (ICP), is a Texas-based nonprofit corporation that assists low-income families in obtaining affordable housing. In 2008, the ICP brought this suit against the Department and its officers in the United States District Court for the Northern District of Texas. As relevant here, it brought a disparate-impact claim under §§804(a) and 805(a) of the FHA. The ICP alleged the Department has caused continued segregated housing patterns by its disproportionate allocation of the tax credits, granting too many credits for housing in predominantly black inner-city areas and too few in predominantly white suburban neighborhoods. The ICP contended that the Department must modify its selection criteria in order to encourage the construction of low-income housing in suburban communities.

The District Court concluded that the ICP had established a prima facie case of disparate impact. It relied on two pieces of statistical evidence. First, it found "from 1999-2008, [the Department] approved tax credits for 49.7% of proposed non-elderly units in 0% to 9.9% Caucasian areas, but only approved 37.4% of proposed non-elderly units in 90% to 100% Caucasian areas." 749 F. Supp. 2d 486, 499 (ND

Tex. 2010) (footnote omitted). Second, it found "92.29% of [low-income housing tax credit] units in the city of Dallas were located in census tracts with less than 50% Caucasian residents." Ibid.

The District Court then placed the burden on the Department to rebut the ICP's prima facie showing of disparate impact. 860 F. Supp. 2d 312, 322-323 (2012). After assuming the Department's proffered interests were legitimate, id., at 326, the District Court held that a defendant—here the Department—must prove "that there are no other less discriminatory alternatives to advancing their proffered interests," ibid. Because, in its view, the Department "failed to meet [its] burden of proving that there are no less discriminatory alternatives," the District Court ruled for the ICP. Id., at 331.

. . .

II.

The issue here is whether, under a proper interpretation of the FHA, housing decisions with a disparate impact are prohibited. Before turning to the FHA, however, it is necessary to consider two other antidiscrimination statutes that preceded it.

The first relevant statute is §703(a) of Title VII of the Civil Rights Act of 1964, 78 Stat. 255. The Court addressed the concept of disparate impact under this statute in *Griggs v. Duke Power Co.,* 401 U.S. 424 (1971).

. . .

In interpreting §703(a)(2), the Court reasoned that disparate-impact liability furthered the purpose and design of the statute. The Court explained that, in §703(a)(2), Congress "proscribe[d] not only overt discrimination but also practices that are fair in form, but discriminatory in operation." Id., at 431. For that reason, as the Court noted, "Congress directed the thrust of [§703(a)(2)] to the consequences of employment practices, not simply the motivation." Id., at 432. In light of the statute's goal of achieving "equality of employment opportunities and remov[ing] barriers that have operated in the past" to favor some races over others, the Court held §703(a)(2) of Title VII must be interpreted to allow disparate-impact claims. Id., at 429-430.

The Court put important limits on its holding: namely, not all employment practices causing a disparate impact impose liability under §703(a)(2). In this respect, the Court held that "business necessity" constitutes a defense to disparate-impact claims. Id., at 431. . . .

The second relevant statute that bears on the proper interpretation of the FHA is the Age Discrimination in Employment Act of 1967 (ADEA). . . . The Court first addressed whether [section 4 of the ADEA] allows disparate-impact claims in *Smith v. City of Jackson,* 544 U.S. 228 (2005). There, a group of older employees challenged their employer's decision to give proportionately greater raises to employees with less than five years of experience.

Explaining that *Griggs* "represented the better reading of [Title VII's] statutory text," 544 U.S., at 235, a plurality of the Court concluded that the same reasoning pertained to §4(a)(2) of the ADEA. The *Smith* plurality emphasized that both §703(a)(2) of Title VII and §4(a)(2) of the ADEA contain language "prohibit[ing] such actions that 'deprive any individual of employment opportunities or otherwise adversely affect his status as an employee, because of such individual's' race or age." 544 U.S., at 235. As the plurality observed, the text of these provisions "focuses on the effects of the action on the employee rather than the motivation for the action of the employer" and therefore compels recognition of disparate-impact liability. Id., at 236. . . .

Together, *Griggs* holds and the plurality in *Smith* instructs that antidiscrimination laws must be construed to encompass disparate-impact claims when their text refers to the consequences of actions and not just to the mindset of actors, and where that interpretation is consistent with statutory purpose. These cases also teach that disparate-impact liability must be limited so employers and other regulated entities are able to make the practical business choices and profit-related decisions that sustain a vibrant and dynamic free-enterprise system. And before rejecting a business justification — or, in the case of a governmental entity, an analogous public interest — a court must determine that a plaintiff has shown that there is "an available alternative . . . practice that has less disparate impact and serves the [entity's] legitimate needs." Ricci, supra, at 578. The cases interpreting Title VII and the ADEA provide essential background and instruction in the case now before the Court.

Turning to the FHA, the ICP relies on two provisions. Section 804(a) provides that it shall be unlawful:

> "To refuse to sell or rent after the making of a bona fide offer, or to refuse to negotiate for the sale or rental of, or otherwise make unavailable or deny, a dwelling to any person because of race, color, religion, sex, familial status, or national origin." 42 U.S.C. §3604(a).

Here, the phrase "otherwise make unavailable" is of central importance to the analysis that follows.

Section 805(a), in turn, provides:

> "It shall be unlawful for any person or other entity whose business includes engaging in real estate-related transactions to discriminate against any person in making available such a transaction, or in the terms or conditions of such a transaction, because of race, color, religion, sex, handicap, familial status, or national origin." §3605(a).

Applied here, the logic of *Griggs* and *Smith* provides strong support for the conclusion that the FHA encompasses disparate-impact claims. Congress' use of the phrase "otherwise make unavailable" refers to the consequences of an action rather than the actor's intent. See United States v. Giles, 300 U.S. 41, 48 (1937) (explaining that the "word 'make' has many meanings, among them '[t]o cause to exist, appear or occur'" (quoting Webster's New International Dictionary 1485 (2d ed. 1934))). This results-oriented language counsels in favor of recognizing disparate-impact liability. See Smith, supra, at 236. The Court has construed statutory language similar to §805(a) to include disparate-impact liability. See, e.g., Board of Ed. of City School Dist. of New York v. Harris, 444 U.S. 130, 140-141 (1979) (holding the term "discriminat[e]" encompassed disparate-impact liability in the context of a statute's text, history, purpose, and structure).

. . .

A comparison to the antidiscrimination statutes examined in *Griggs* and *Smith* is useful. Title VII's and the ADEA's "otherwise adversely affect" language is equivalent in function and purpose to the FHA's "otherwise make unavailable" language. In these three statutes the operative text looks to results. The relevant statutory phrases, moreover, play an identical role in the structure common to all three statutes: Located at the end of lengthy sentences that begin with prohibitions on disparate treatment, they serve as catchall phrases looking to consequences, not intent. And all three statutes use the word "otherwise" to introduce the results-oriented phrase. "Otherwise" means "in a different way or manner," thus signaling a shift in emphasis from an actor's intent to the consequences of his actions. Webster's Third New International Dictionary 1598 (1971). This similarity in text and structure is all the more compelling given that Congress passed the FHA in 1968—only four years after passing Title VII and only four months after enacting the ADEA.

Further and convincing confirmation of Congress' understanding that disparate-impact liability exists under the FHA is revealed by the substance of the 1988 amendments. The amendments included three exemptions from liability that assume the existence of disparate-impact claims. The most logical conclusion is that the three amendments were deemed necessary because Congress presupposed disparate impact under the FHA as it had been enacted in 1968.

The relevant 1988 amendments were as follows. First, Congress added a clarifying provision: "Nothing in [the FHA] prohibits a person engaged in the business of furnishing appraisals of real property to take into consideration factors other than race, color, religion, national origin, sex, handicap, or familial status." 42 U.S.C. §3605(c). Second, Congress provided: "Nothing in [the FHA] prohibits conduct against a person because such person has been convicted by any court of competent jurisdiction of the illegal manufacture or distribution of a controlled substance." §3607(b)(4). And finally, Congress specified: "Nothing in [the FHA] limits the applicability of any reasonable . . . restrictions regarding the maximum number of occupants permitted to occupy a dwelling." §3607(b)(1).

The exemptions embodied in these amendments would be superfluous if Congress had assumed that disparate-impact liability did not exist under the FHA. Indeed, none of these amendments would make sense if the FHA encompassed only disparate-treatment claims. If that were the sole ground for liability, the amendments merely restate black-letter law. If an actor makes a decision based on reasons other than a protected category, there is no disparate-treatment liability. See, e.g., Texas Dept. of Community Affairs v. Burdine, 450 U.S. 248, 254 (1981). But the amendments do constrain disparate-impact liability. For instance, certain criminal convictions are correlated with sex and race. See, e.g., Kimbrough v. United States, 552 U.S. 85, 98 (2007) (discussing the racial disparity in convictions for crack cocaine offenses). By adding an exemption from liability for exclusionary practices aimed at individuals with drug convictions, Congress ensured disparate-impact liability would not lie if a landlord excluded tenants with such convictions. The same is true of the provision allowing for reasonable restrictions on occupancy. And the exemption from liability for real-estate appraisers is in the same section as §805(a)'s prohibition of discriminatory practices in real-estate transactions, thus indicating Congress' recognition that disparate-impact liability arose under §805(a). In short, the 1988 amendments signal that Congress ratified disparate-impact liability.

. . .

Recognition of disparate-impact claims is consistent with the FHA's central purpose. The FHA, like Title VII and the ADEA, was enacted to eradicate discriminatory practices within a sector of our Nation's economy. See 42 U.S.C. §3601 ("It is the policy of the United States to provide, within constitutional limitations, for fair housing throughout the United States"); H.R. Rep., at 15 (explaining the FHA "provides a clear national policy against discrimination in housing").

These unlawful practices include zoning laws and other housing restrictions that function unfairly to exclude minorities from certain neighborhoods without any sufficient justification. Suits targeting such practices reside at the heartland of disparate-impact liability. See, e.g., Huntington, 488 U.S., at 16-18 (invalidating zoning law preventing construction of multifamily rental units); Black Jack, 508 F.2d, at 1182-1188 (invalidating ordinance prohibiting construction of new multifamily dwellings); Greater New Orleans Fair Housing Action Center v. St. Bernard Parish, 641 F. Supp. 2d 563, 569, 577-578 (E.D. La. 2009) (invalidating post-Hurricane Katrina ordinance restricting the rental of housing units to only "'blood relative[s]'" in an area of the city that was 88.3% white and 7.6% black). . . . Recognition of disparate-impact liability under the FHA also plays a role in uncovering discriminatory intent: It permits plaintiffs to counteract unconscious prejudices and disguised animus that escape easy classification as disparate treatment. In this way disparate-impact liability may prevent segregated housing patterns that might otherwise result from covert and illicit stereotyping.

. . .

An important and appropriate means of ensuring that disparate-impact liability is properly limited is to give housing authorities and private developers leeway to state and explain the valid interest served by their policies. This step of the analysis is analogous to the business necessity standard under Title VII and provides a defense against disparate-impact liability. See 78 Fed. Reg. 11470 (explaining that HUD did not use the phrase "business necessity" because that "phrase may not be easily understood to cover the full scope of practices covered by the Fair Housing Act, which applies to individuals, businesses, nonprofit organizations, and public entities"). As the Court explained in *Ricci*, an entity "could be liable for disparate-impact discrimination only if the [challenged practices] were not job related and consistent with business necessity." 557 U.S., at 587. Just as an employer may maintain a workplace requirement that causes a disparate impact if that requirement is a "reasonable measure[ment] of job performance," Griggs, supra, at 436, so too must housing authorities and private developers be allowed to maintain a policy if they can prove it is necessary to achieve a valid interest. To be sure, the Title VII framework may not transfer exactly to the fair-housing context, but the comparison suffices for present purposes.

It would be paradoxical to construe the FHA to impose onerous costs on actors who encourage revitalizing dilapidated housing in our Nation's cities merely because some other priority might seem preferable. Entrepreneurs must be given latitude to consider market factors. Zoning officials, moreover, must often make decisions based on a mix of factors, both objective (such as cost and traffic patterns) and, at least to some extent, subjective (such as preserving historic architecture). These factors contribute to a community's quality of life and are legitimate concerns for housing authorities. The FHA does not decree a particular vision of urban development; and it does not put housing authorities and private developers in a double bind of liability, subject to suit whether they choose to rejuvenate a city core or to promote new low-income housing in suburban communities. As HUD itself recognized in its recent rulemaking, disparate-impact liability "does not mandate that affordable housing be located in neighborhoods with any particular characteristic." 78 Fed. Reg. 11476.

In a similar vein, a disparate-impact claim that relies on a statistical disparity must fail if the plaintiff cannot point to a defendant's policy or policies causing that disparity. A robust causality requirement ensures that "[r]acial imbalance . . . does not, without more, establish a prima facie case of disparate impact" and thus protects defendants from being held liable for racial disparities they did not create.

· · ·

Courts must therefore examine with care whether a plaintiff has made out a prima facie case of disparate impact and prompt resolution of these cases is important. A plaintiff who fails to allege facts at the pleading stage or produce statistical evidence demonstrating a causal connection cannot make out a prima facie case of disparate impact. For instance, a plaintiff challenging the decision of a private developer to construct a new building in one location rather than another will not easily be able to show this is a policy causing a disparate impact because such a one-time decision may not be a policy at all. It may also be difficult to establish causation because of the multiple factors that go into investment decisions about where to construct or renovate housing units. And as Judge Jones observed below, if the ICP cannot show a causal connection between the Department's policy and a disparate impact — for instance, because federal law substantially limits the Department's discretion — that should result in dismissal of this case. 747 F. 3d, at 283-284 (specially concurring opinion).

· · ·

The Court holds that disparate-impact claims are cognizable under the Fair Housing Act upon considering its results-oriented language, the Court's interpretation of similar language in Title VII and the ADEA, Congress' ratification of disparate-impact claims in 1988 against the backdrop of the unanimous view of nine Courts of Appeals, and the statutory purpose.

· · ·

Justice ALITO, with whom THE CHIEF JUSTICE, Justice SCALIA, and Justice THOMAS join, dissenting.

No one wants to live in a rat's nest. Yet in *Gallagher v. Magner*, 619 F.3d 823 (2010), a case that we agreed to review several terms ago, the Eighth Circuit held that the Fair Housing Act (or FHA), 42 U.S.C. §3601 et seq., could be used to attack St. Paul, Minnesota's efforts to combat "rodent infestation" and other violations of the city's housing code. 619 F.3d, at 830. The court agreed that there was no basis to "infer discriminatory intent" on the part of St. Paul. Id., at 833. Even so, it concluded that the city's "aggressive enforcement of the Housing Code" was actionable because making landlords respond to "rodent infestation, missing dead-bolt locks, inadequate sanitation facilities, inadequate heat, inoperable smoke detectors, broken or missing doors," and the like increased the price of rent. Id., at 830, 835. Since minorities were statistically more likely fall into "the bottom bracket for household adjusted median family income," they were disproportionately affected by those rent increases, i.e., there was a "disparate impact." Id., at 834. The upshot was that even St. Paul's good-faith attempt to ensure minimally acceptable housing for its poorest residents could not ward off a disparate-impact lawsuit.

Today, the Court embraces the same theory that drove the decision in *Magner*. This is a serious mistake. The Fair Housing Act does not create disparate-impact liability, nor do this Court's precedents. And today's decision will have unfortunate consequences for local government, private enterprise, and those living in poverty. Something has gone badly awry when a city can't even make slumlords kill rats without fear of a lawsuit. Because Congress did not authorize any of this, I respectfully dissent.

I.

Everyone agrees that the FHA punishes intentional discrimination. Treating someone "less favorably than others because of a protected trait" is "'the most easily understood type of discrimination.'" Ricci v. DeStefano, 557 U.S. 557, 577 (2009) (quoting Teamsters v. United States, 431 U.S. 324, 335, n.15 (1977). Indeed, this classic form of discrimination—called disparate treatment—is the only one prohibited by the Constitution itself. See, e.g., Arlington Heights v. Metropolitan Housing Development Corp., 429 U.S. 252, 264-265 (1977). It is obvious that Congress intended the FHA to cover disparate treatment.

The question presented here, however, is whether the FHA also punishes "practices that are not intended to discriminate but in fact have a disproportionately adverse effect on minorities." Ricci, supra, at 577. The answer is equally clear. The FHA does not authorize disparate-impact claims. No such liability was created when the law was enacted in 1968. And nothing has happened since then to change the law's meaning.

I begin with the text. Section 804(a) of the FHA makes it unlawful "[t]o refuse to sell or rent after the making of a bona fide offer, or to refuse to negotiate for the sale or rental of, or otherwise make unavailable or deny, a dwelling to any person because of race, color, religion, sex, familial status, or national origin." 42 U.S.C. §3604(a) (emphasis added). Similarly, §805(a) prohibits any party "whose business includes engaging in residential real estate-related transactions" from "discriminat[ing]" against any person in making available such a transaction, or in the terms or conditions of such a transaction, because of race, color, religion, sex, handicap, familial status, or national origin." §3605(a) (emphasis added).

In both sections, the key phrase is "because of." These provisions list covered actions ("refus[ing] to sell or rent . . . a dwelling," "refus[ing] to negotiate for the sale or rental of . . . a dwelling," "discriminat[ing]" in a residential real estate transaction, etc.) and protected characteristics ("race," "religion," etc.). The link between the actions and the protected characteristics is "because of."

. . .

Without torturing the English language, the meaning of these provisions of the FHA cannot be denied. They make it unlawful to engage in any of the covered actions "because of"—meaning "by reason of" or "on account of," *Nassar*, supra, at _____—race, religion, etc. Put another way, "the terms [after] the 'because of' clauses in the FHA supply the prohibited motivations for the intentional acts . . . that the Act makes unlawful." American Ins. Assn. v. Department of

Housing and Urban Development, 74 F. Supp. 3d 30, 41, n. 20 (D.C. 2014). Congress accordingly outlawed the covered actions only when they are motivated by race or one of the other protected characteristics.

It follows that the FHA does not authorize disparate-impact suits. Under a statute like the FHA that prohibits actions taken "because of" protected characteristics, intent makes all the difference.

. . .

V.

Not only is the decision of the Court inconsistent with what the FHA says and our precedents, it will have unfortunate consequences. Disparate-impact liability has very different implications in housing and employment cases.

Disparate impact puts housing authorities in a very difficult position because programs that are designed and implemented to help the poor can provide the grounds for a disparate-impact claim. As *Magner* shows, when disparate impact is on the table, even a city's good-faith attempt to remedy deplorable housing conditions can be branded "discriminatory." 619 F.3d, at 834. Disparate-impact claims thus threaten "a whole range of tax, welfare, public service, regulatory, and licensing statutes." Washington v. Davis, 426 U.S. 229, 248 (1976).

This case illustrates the point. The Texas Department of Housing and Community Affairs (the Department) has only so many tax credits to distribute. If it gives credits for housing in lower income areas, many families — including many minority families — will obtain better housing. That is a good thing. But if the Department gives credits for housing in higher income areas, some of those families will be able to afford to move into more desirable neighborhoods. That is also a good thing. Either path, however, might trigger a disparate-impact suit.

This is not mere speculation. Here, one respondent has sued the Department for not allocating enough credits to higher income areas. See Brief for Respondent Inclusive Communities Project, Inc., 23. But another respondent argues that giving credits to wealthy neighborhoods violates "the moral imperative to improve the substandard and inadequate affordable housing in many of our inner cities." Reply Brief for Respondent Frazier Revitalization Inc. 1. This latter argument has special force because a city can build more housing where property is least expensive, thus benefiting more people. In fact, federal law often favors projects that revitalize low-income communities. See ante, at 2.

No matter what the Department decides, one of these respondents will be able to bring a disparate-impact case. And if the Department opts to compromise by dividing the credits, both respondents might be able to sue. Congress surely did not mean to put local governments in such a position.

The Solicitor General's answer to such problems is that HUD will come to the rescue. In particular, HUD regulations provide a defense against disparate-impact liability if a defendant can show that its actions serve "substantial, legitimate, nondiscriminatory interests" that "necessar[ily]" cannot be met by "another practice that has a less discriminatory effect." 24 C.F.R. §100.500(b) (2014). (There is, of course, no hint of anything like this defense in the text of the FHA. But then, there is no hint of disparate-impact liability in the text of the FHA either.)

The effect of these regulations, not surprisingly, is to confer enormous discretion on HUD — without actually solving the problem. What is a "substantial" interest? Is there a difference between a "legitimate" interest and a "nondiscriminatory" interest? To what degree must an interest be met for a practice to be "necessary"? How are parties and courts to measure "discriminatory effect"?

These questions are not answered by the Court's assurance that the FHA's disparate-impact "analysis 'is analogous to the Title VII requirement that an employer's interest in an employment practice with a disparate impact be job related.'" Ante, at 4 (quoting 78 Fed. Reg. 11470). See also ante, at 18 (likening the defense to "the business necessity standard"). The business-necessity defense is complicated enough in employment cases; what it means when plopped into the housing context is anybody's guess. What is the FHA analogue of "job related"? Is it "housing related"? But a vast array of municipal decisions affect property values and thus relate (at least indirectly) to housing. And what is the FHA analogue of "business necessity"? "Housing-policy necessity"? What does that mean?

Compounding the problem, the Court proclaims that "governmental entities . . . must not be prevented from achieving legitimate objectives, such as ensuring compliance with health and safety codes." Ante, at 21. But what does the Court mean by a "legitimate" objective? And does the Court mean to say that there can be no disparate-impact lawsuit if the objective is "legitimate"? That is certainly not the view of the Government, which takes the position that a disparate-impact claim may be brought to challenge actions taken with such worthy objectives as improving housing in poor neighborhoods and making financially sound lending decisions. See Brief for United States as Amicus Curiae 30, n. 7.

Because HUD's regulations and the Court's pronouncements are so "hazy," Central Bank, 511 U.S., at 188-189, courts — lacking expertise in the field of housing policy — may inadvertently harm the very people that the FHA is meant to help. Local governments make countless decisions that may have some disparate impact related to housing. See ante, at 19-20. Certainly Congress did not intend to "engage the federal courts in an endless exercise of second-guessing" local programs. Canton v. Harris, 489 U.S. 378, 392 (1989).

. . .

I would interpret the Fair Housing Act as written and so would reverse the judgment of the Court of Appeals.

E.   Adverse Action and Data Collection

1.   General Notices

ECOA requires that creditors provide a response to all applicants. 15 U.S.C. §1691(d). The purpose of this rule is to prevent creditors from skirting liability by never taking action on applications from individuals with certain characteristics. The problem that ECOA sought to solve was not just explicit denials but also a failure to make any decision at all. Both rejection and endless delay have the same harmful effect of reducing access to credit or increasing the cost of credit. If an individual never received a decision from a mainstream lender, the individual then might seek credit from a higher-cost lender or give up entirely.

Regulation B, §1002.9, prescribes the timeframe for making decisions on applications. For a completed application, a creditor has 30 days to respond. For an incomplete application, the same 30-day window applies if the creditor is taking adverse action (discussed in the next section). Alternatively, creditors may respond to an incomplete application by notifying applicants of the information needed and informing them that a failure to respond will result in no further consideration of the application. Creditors may also respond to a credit application by making a counteroffer with credit on different terms that originally sought. The creditor has up to 90 days after extending the counteroffer to provide a withdrawal notice to applicants who have not responded by accepting or using the credit.

2.   Adverse Action Notices

ECOA, like FCRA, uses the term "adverse action" to describe unfavorable outcomes from credit determinations. ECOA defines adverse action broadly to include not just a denial or revocation of credit, but also "a change in the terms of an existing credit arrangement, or a refusal to grant credit in substantially the amount or on substantially the terms requested." 12 C.F.R. §1002.2(c)(1). The law has two important exclusions. It is not an "adverse action" to refuse to exceed a firm credit limit (such as a maximum on a credit card or home equity line of credit) that was previously set. Creditors also do not engage in adverse action under ECOA when they do not extend additional credit under an existing credit arrangement to a consumer who is delinquent or in default. Consumers will certainly perceive these decisions as adverse to them, a reminder that the law's technical definitions make it difficult to educate consumers about their rights.

If the creditor is taking adverse action, there are special requirements for notification. First, the notice of adverse action must be in writing. This rule actually helps protect lenders. ECOA compliance has pushed lenders to use form letters to deliver credit decisions, rather than making oral statements that could give rise to perceptions of discrimination and that allow for more variance. Second, the notice must inform the consumer that the ECOA prohibits credit discrimination on the basis of race, color, religion, national origin, sex, marital status, age (provided the applicant has the capacity to enter into a binding contract); because all or part of the applicant's income derives from any public assistance program; or because the applicant has in good faith exercised any right under the Consumer Credit Protection Act. The actual notice given to consumers basically parrots 15 U.S.C. §1691(a), with no effort to explain what the Consumer Credit Protection Act is to consumers. The notice also must provide the applicant with the federal agency that administers compliance, which is the Consumer Financial Protection Bureau.

Third, creditors must give in writing the "specific reasons" for their having taken adverse action or at least a written disclosure of the applicant's right to obtain a statement of specific reasons by making a request within 30 days of the notice. 15 U.S.C. §1691(d)(2). It will not surprise you that lenders do not list a discriminatory purpose as a specific reason. In fact, they may not provide much helpful information at all.

Williams v. MBNA America Bank, N.A.

538 F. Supp. 2d 1015 (E.D. Mich. 2008)

ROSEN, District Judge.

Plaintiff Kim Williams filed her one-count Equal Credit Opportunity Act ("ECOA") complaint in this action alleging that Defendant MBNA America Bank's letter notifying her of its rejection of her credit card application did not comply with the ECOA's notice requirements. Defendant MBNA now moves to dismiss Plaintiff's Complaint pursuant to Fed. R. Civ. P. 12(b)(6) for failure to state a claim upon which relief can be granted. . . .

The relevant facts are not complex and are not disputed. Plaintiff Kim Williams applied for an MBNA American Express credit card via telephone on May 2, 2006. Plaintiff first spoke with a telemarketer who input identifying and credit information she provided and, by computer, interfaced with Experian Information Services to obtain Plaintiff's credit history. Plaintiff's application was then transferred by the MBNA computer system to a human MBNA credit analyst who personally spoke with Plaintiff.

From Plaintiff and Experian, MBNA was provided with the following information: (i) Plaintiff had a total revolving credit from a variety of sources in the amount of $26,596; (ii) of this amount, she had balances due on such revolving credit in the amount of $13,285; and (iii) although Plaintiff's household had a gross income of $70,000, Plaintiff herself had no income of her own (she was a student). Thus, as of May 2, 2006, Plaintiff had a total amount of unused credit available to her in the amount of $13,311.

MBNA's credit analyst denied Plaintiff's application and informed Plaintiff of the denial during the May, 2, 2006 telephone conversation with her. The credit analyst then assigned two "reason codes" (codes which specified the principal reasons credit was being denied) — 1010 and 1020 — to Plaintiff's application, and input them into the MBNA system. The reason codes were assigned respectively to the following two reasons (i) "You have sufficient balances on your revolving credit lines;" and (ii) "You have sufficient credit available considering your income." The credit analyst explained these reason codes to Plaintiff during the May 2, 2006 telephone conversation, as well.

The MBNA system then automatically incorporated the text corresponding to the reason codes into a form letter to be sent to Plaintiff denying her application for credit and specifying that these were the principal reasons her credit application was being denied. The letter was dated May 2, 2006 and was mailed to Plaintiff the same day or shortly thereafter. Plaintiff does not deny receiving this letter. In fact, the letter is at the heart of Plaintiff's Complaint.

The first page of the May 2, 2006 letter stated as follows:

> After careful review, we are unable to approve your request because you have sufficient balances on your revolving credit lines and you have sufficient credit available considering your income. Our credit decision was based in whole or in part on information obtained in a report from Experian, National Consumer Assistance Center, P.O. Box 2002, Allen, TX 75013-0036, 1-888-297-2472, www.experian .com/reportaccess.
>
> If you have any information that may enable us to reconsider this decision, please write to MBNA, P.O. Box 15023, Wilmington, DE XXXXX-XXXX.
>
> Sincerely,
>
> Don Hamilton, Credit department
>
> Please see the next page of this letter for important information.

The second page of the letter contained various notices and, in relevant part, informed Plaintiff that she had a right to a free copy of her credit report from Experian if she requested it within sixty days from receipt of the letter, and if she discovered any inaccurate or incomplete information in her credit report, she could dispute the matter with Experian.

Plaintiff does not dispute that as of May 2, 2006, she was a student, nor does she dispute that she had a total revolving line of credit from a variety of sources in the amount of $26,596, or that she had balances due on such revolving credit in the amount of $13,285, leaving her $13,311 in available credit. Rather, her dispute with MBNA arises out of the language used by MBNA in its letter. She contends that the reasons provided by MBNA indicating that her American Express credit card application was being denied because she had "sufficient balance on [her] revolving credit lines and [because she had] sufficient credit available considering [her] income" were "incoherent [and] illogical," and, this, she contends, constitutes a violation of the Equal Credit Opportunity Act, 15 U.S.C. §1691(d).

. . .

The ECOA was originally enacted in 1974 to prohibit discrimination in credit transactions. Treadway v. Gateway Chevrolet Oldsmobile, Inc., 362 F.3d 971, 975 (7th Cir. 2004). The Act's principal purpose is "to eradicate discrimination against women, especially married women whom creditors traditionally refused to consider for individual credit." Midkiff v. Adams County Regional Water District, 409 F.3d 758, 771 (6th Cir. 2005) (citation and internal punctuation omitted). The statute was amended in 1976 to require creditors to furnish written notice of the specific reasons why an adverse action was taken against a consumer. See Fischl v. General Motors Acceptance Corp., 708 F.2d 143 (5th Cir. 1983); 15 U.S.C. §1691(d)(2), (3). As explained in the Senate report accompanying the 1976 amendments to the ECOA, Congress viewed the notice requirement as:

> . . . a strong and necessary adjunct to the antidiscrimination purpose of the legislation, for only if creditors know they must explain their decisions will they effectively be

discouraged from discriminatory practices. Yet this requirement fulfills a broader need: rejected credit applicants will now be able to learn where and how their credit status is deficient and this information should have a pervasive and valuable educational benefit. Instead of being told only that they do not meet a particular creditor's standards, consumers particularly should benefit from knowing, for example, that the reason for the denial is their short residence in the area, or their recent change of employment, or their already over-extended financial situation. In those cases where the creditor may have acted on misinformation or inadequate information, the statement of reasons gives the applicant a chance to rectify the mistake.

Fischl, supra, 708 F.2d at 146 (quoting S. Rep. No. 94-589, 94th Cong., 2d sess., 1976 U.S. Code Cong. & Admin. News, pp. 408, 406).

ECOA's notice provisions apply to all loan applicants, not only those who claim to have been denied credit due to discrimination. See Jochum v. Pico Credit Corp. of Westbank, 730 F.2d 1041, 1043 n. 3 (5th Cir. 1984) (finding that the plaintiffs did not need to state a claim of discrimination to assert a cognizable claim under §1691(d)); Diaz v. Paragon Motors of Woodside, Inc., 424 F. Supp. 2d 519, 532 n. 22 (E.D.N.Y. 2006) ("The [ECOA] notification requirement extends to all applicants, and does not require specific allegations of discrimination.").

A credit denial is referred to as an "adverse action" under the ECOA. 15 U.S.C. §1691(d)(6). A written letter informing an applicant that credit has been denied is referred to as an "adverse action notice." With regard to the content of adverse action notices, §1691(d) of the ECOA provides as follows:

(1) Within thirty days (or such longer reasonable time as specified in regulations of the Board for any class of credit transaction) after receipt of a completed application for credit, a creditor shall notify the applicant of its action on the application.

(2) Each applicant against whom adverse action is taken shall be entitled to a statement of reasons for such action from the creditor. A creditor satisfies this obligation by —

(A) providing statements of reasons in writing as a matter of course to applicants against whom adverse action is taken; or

(B) giving written notification of adverse action which discloses (i) the applicant's right to a statement of reasons within thirty days after receipt by the creditor of a request made within sixty days after such notification, and (ii) the identity of the person or office from which such statement may be obtained. Such statement may be given orally if the written notification advises the applicant of his right to have the statement of reasons confirmed in writing on written request.

(3) A statement of reasons meets the requirements of this section if it contains the specific reasons for the adverse action taken.

15 U.S.C. §1691(d).

The regulations which implement the ECOA, "Regulation B," 12 C.F.R. §202.1 et seq., provide only as follows with regard to the content of adverse action notices:

[(a)] (2) Content of notification when adverse action is taken. A notification given to an applicant when adverse action is taken shall be in writing and shall contain a statement of the action taken; the name and address of the creditor; a statement of the provisions of §701(a) of the Act; the name and address of the federal agency that administers compliance with respect to the creditor; and . . . (i) A statement of specific reasons for the action taken. 12 C.F.R. §202.9(a)(2)(i).

[ED. NOTE—The CFPB reissued Regulation B with different numbering that begins with §1002. The content is identical to the prior regulations and Official Staff Interpretation from the Federal Reserve Board.]

Paragraph (b) of the regulation further provides with regard to the statement of reasons:

> Statement of specific reasons. The statement of reasons for adverse action required by paragraph (a)(2)(i) of this section must be specific and indicate the *principal reasons* for the adverse action. Statements based on the creditor's internal standards or policies or that the applicant, joint applicant, or similar party failed to achieve a qualifying score on the creditor's credit scoring system are insufficient.

12 C.F.R. §202.9(b)(2) (emphasis added). While an Appendix to Regulation B sets forth some sample forms intended for use in notifying an applicant that adverse action has been taken on a credit application, the regulations make clear that "[t]he sample forms are illustrative and may not be appropriate for all creditors. They were designed to include some of the factors that creditors most commonly consider." 12 C.F.R. §202, App. C, ¶ 2.

The Official Federal Reserve Board interpretations of Regulation B, 12 C.F.R. §202 Supp. I, further make clear that there is no statutory or regulatory prohibition against a creditor's wording of its reasons. With regard to Section 202.9's notification requirements, the Official Staff Interpretation states, "In notifying an applicant of adverse action as defined by §202.2(c)(1), a creditor may use any words or phrases that describe the action taken on the application." 12 C.F.R. §202 Supp. I.

The Official Staff Interpretation further states that "[a] creditor need not describe how or why a factor adversely affected an applicant." Id.

In this case, MBNA's notice to Plaintiff provided her with two principal reasons that her credit application was denied. The first principal reason given was "you have sufficient balances on your revolving line of credit." The statement is a "specific reason for the action taken." Furthermore, as Defendant notes, and Plaintiff does not dispute, the statement is consistent with the information provided by Plaintiff and Experian. Having "sufficient balances on her revolving lines of credit" meant that Plaintiff could have charged additional amounts on her existing credit accounts at any time causing her to max out her existing credit lines, which would be a concern for a lender.

The second principal reason that Plaintiff's credit was denied was "you have sufficient credit available considering your income." This, too, is a "specific reason for the action taken." While Plaintiff indicated in applying for credit that her "household" income was $70,000, Plaintiff personally had no income source; she was a student. Being able to charge additional amounts on her existing lines of credit and to max out on those credit lines without having any personal source of income is legitimate concern for any lender.

Plaintiff, however, finds MBNA's stated reasons to be "incoherent" and "illogical." She argues that Regulation B requires that the stated reasons be "clearly and conspicuously" explained in "reasonably understandable" terms. There is, however, no such requirement in the statute or the regulations. In fact, the only mention of "clear and conspicuous" is in Section 202.4(d) of the regulation. §202.4 provides:

> (d) Form of disclosures—
> (1) General rule. A creditor that provides in writing any disclosures or information required by this regulation must provide the disclosures in a clear and conspicuous manner and, except for the disclosures required by §§202.5 [requests for information] and 202.13 [information for monitoring purposes], in a form the applicant may retain.

12 C.F.R. §202.4(d). As the Official Staff Interpretations make clear, however, the "clear and conspicuous" requirement set forth in this section deals, not with the content of the notice, but rather with the format:

> 1. Clear and conspicuous. This standard requires that disclosures be presented in a reasonably understandable format in a way that does not obscure the required information. No minimum type size is mandated, but the disclosures must be legible, whether typewritten, handwritten, or printed by computer.

12 C.F.R. §202 Supp. I. The only statutory/regulatory requirement is that the "format" must be "reasonably understandable."

. . .

In sum, the Court finds that the allegations in Plaintiffs Complaint do not make out a cognizable claim for violation of the ECOA. MBNA's adverse action notice clearly and conspicuously presented the creditor's specific reasons for its denial of Plaintiffs credit card application.

For all of the foregoing reasons, the Court finds that Plaintiff has failed to state a claim upon which relief may be granted.

While the content may be of limited use to consumers, the adverse action notice requirement has surprising reach. It applies even when a creditor grants credit, if there is some possible more favorable type of credit that could be issued, because of the broad definition of adverse action.

ECOA's notice rules protect all consumers, even those who are not alleging discrimination. It provides basic procedural fairness whenever adverse action is taken. In this way, ECOA supplements the rights with regard to credit reporting to give consumers' greater insight into lending decisions.

Problem Set 8

8.1. Sunshine State Bank operates branches in areas that attract a high proportion of "snowbirds," retired Americans who leave their homes each winter. Sunshine offers low-cost accounts to these partial-year residents but profitability has been a problem due to the relatively small balances that people keep in these accounts. To boost profits, Sunshine is proposing charging a fee to any new applicants for checking accounts who wish to obtain debit cards. The fee will only be charged to people 55 years or older because

Sunshine's records show that these people often have irregular incomes and thus overdraw their accounts, requiring Sunshine to extend overdraft protection. Sunshine's experience is also that snowbirds are unlikely to heavily use debit cards, preferring instead to be served in person at a branch location. Can Sunshine ask applicants for their year of birth to determine if it will impose the fee? 15 U.S.C. §§1691(a)(1); 1691a(d); 12 C.F.R. §§1002.2; 1002.6(b).

8.2. Todd and Allison Smith own a 4-bedroom house that they purchased brand new when it was built in 2006. Like all their neighbors, they are "upside down" on the loan, owing $100,000 more than their house's value. Todd and Allison applied for a loan modification under their mortgage company's program. They carefully completed all forms and submitted all information. Yesterday, they received a letter stating that "we regret to inform you that a loan modification was not granted." The letter gave no reason for the denial but invited them to reapply if their circumstances change. Todd and Allison are devastated and worry they will soon lose their home to foreclosure. They are also furious that the mortgage company required them to submit extensive documentation, to the tune of 100 pages, and yet they received only a one-line denial. Did the mortgage company violate ECOA in its dealings with Todd and Allison? *See* 15 U.S.C. §§1691(d)(6); 1691a.

8.3. Cherokee Credit Tribe is a community organization devoted to serving members of the Cherokee Nation. They provide policymaking expertise on issue affecting Native Americans and operate some direct service programs, including a zero-interest student loan fund for members of the Cherokee Nation. The amount of loan is dependent on the degree of relation to the Cherokee Nation, and applicants are required to submit a family tree with full family names that are verified against tribal records. Financial need is not a factor in determining eligibility for the loan or its amount. Your stepsister, Shanna, is a member of the Sioux tribe; her paternal grandfather was a tribal elder. There is no equivalent organization for members of the Sioux. Shanna is thinking that maybe a lawsuit (with a quick settlement) might also be a way to find funds for college. Is the Cherokee Credit Tribe violating ECOA? *See* 15 U.S.C. §1691; 12 C.F.R. §1002.8.

8.4. Dollars on Demand is an Internet start-up focusing on person-to-person credit extensions. On its website, consumers can post a request for a loan that does not exceed $1,000 for a period of one year or less. The loan seeker can supply additional information, including the desired interest rate, the reason they seek the loan, their financial characteristics, and a picture. Loan suppliers, who are also individual consumers can search or browse these profiles and make any loans they wish to fund. Dollars on Demand takes a cut of the loan and makes money off advertising on its site. To date, over 50,000 loans have been funded. The typical person supplying a loan has done so four times in the last year, lending an average of $400 per transaction.

You are the newly hired in-house counsel for Dollars on Demand. As part of your compliance review, you are checking for consumer law violations. You already have determined there are no problems with false advertising, the Fair Credit Reporting Act, or the Truth in Lending Act and are now ready to consider the Equal Credit Opportunity Act and parallel laws on credit discrimination. Do you have any concerns? Please also identify any information that you might request from the business department as part of your review. *See* 15 U.S.C. §1691a(e); 12 C.F.R. §§1002.2(l); 1002.4.

Part Three. Doing the Deal: Terms and Financing

Assignment 9. Unfair or Deceptive Acts or Practices

At the heart of consumers' complaints is often a sense that they have been "scammed" or "ripped off." The most apt legal doctrine for such situations is often the laws that prohibit unfair or deceptive acts or practices. Because the statutes are broad and cover all aspects of a transaction, they always merit consideration — both by a consumer rights litigator and a business lawyer advising on the legality of a practice. Prior assignments have given some consideration to these laws, noting that they may be the basis for liability for misleading advertising, oppressive sales practices, or privacy violations.

This assignment delves into how the unfair or Deceptive Acts and Practices laws (UDAP, pronounced U-dap) apply to the terms of deals and the conduct of businesses. Because U.S. law puts few substantive limits on consumer contracts, UDAP statutes are often the primary tool to achieve a remedy when a consumer has entered into a bad contract or had a business breach a contract. UDAP statutes also provide lower thresholds for plaintiffs to assert that a business engaged in fraudulent activity. In this way, UDAP helps compensate for gaps or shortcomings in common law doctrines. Even when substantive regulation exists, UDAP statutes can be useful because they may have longer statutes of limitations, broader scope of coverage, and more generous remedies.

A. Common Law Actions

The common law of both contracts and torts offer multiple legal theories to challenge practices that a consumer believes are unfair or deceptive. Before the enactment of the UDAP laws, these were the exclusive remedies for consumers. If a business's conduct did not fit into the fairly tight bounds of a common law theory and no specific statute proscribed the behavior, the consumer was out of luck. Even with the UDAP laws permitting a private right of action, common law theories sometimes are still useful given particular facts or situations. Savvy consumer lawyers will nearly always plead a common law action in addition to a statutory UDAP violation.

The equivalent contract doctrines to unfairness and deception, respectively, are unconscionability and misrepresentation. The Uniform Commercial Code's requirement of good faith is also important for contract actions. See U.C.C. §1-203; U.C.C. revised §1-304. Warranties may also apply to certain contracts, such as when a consumer has purchased goods. (Warranties are covered in the next Assignment.) In tort, the applicable theories are fraud and its kissing cousins: fraud by omission, negligent or innocent misrepresentation, concealment, and the like. Those variants generally have lesser requirements for pleading and proof than an action for civil fraud.

Consumers trying to use contract and tort theories often face difficulty in proving intent or damages. The law draws distinctions, such as between a statement of fact or an opinion, that often trip up plaintiffs. Another example is the way in which liability differs for an explicit or implicit representation. Courts were sometimes sympathetic to plaintiffs' plight and often condemned defendants' actions, but ultimately were constrained by precedents to dismiss a consumer's lawsuit.

B. Federal Unfair and Deceptive Acts and Practices Laws

Traditionally, the FTC was the leader in the identification and enforcement of unfair and deceptive acts and practices at the federal level. Its statute is long-standing and has been applied to a broad range of conduct. While several financial regulators, such as the Federal Reserve Board, had the authority to determine that banks' practices were unfair or deceptive, they rarely exercised such power. In the wake of the subprime lending meltdown, the Dodd-Frank Act imbued the Consumer Financial Protection Bureau with UDAP authority. Its exclusive consumer focus means that it does not face the agency capture or conflict of interests that prudential banking regulators apparently suffered. Those agencies were focused on safety and soundness—which means profitability of banks—and as you might guess, unfair and deceptive conduct can generate outsized revenue.

The FTC retains its UDAP authority over most businesses and trades, while the CFPB is limited to financial services to consumer financial services or products. Because Dodd-Frank also enhanced the UDAP power available to the CFPB, the two laws are different. There is also more precedent and certainty around the FTC's interpretation and application of the law, given its longer history. For these reasons, the FTC and CFPB are discussed separately below.

1. Federal Trade Commission's UDAP Statute

The federal UDAP statute is mercifully short. It also has not been amended. (Two cheers for law students trying to master this area!) Congress passed the unfair and deceptive part of the statute in 1938, as the federal government was expanding its control of businesses under the Commerce Clause. "Unfair methods of competition in or affecting commerce, and unfair or deceptive acts or practices in or affecting commerce, are hereby declared unlawful." 15 U.S.C. §45(a)(1). Unfair and deceptive are separate elements with distinct meanings, although some conduct may meet the criteria for both categories.

Initially, the statute did not define deceptive. The FTC interpreted the standard generously to consumers. This led some to complain that almost any statement has the capacity to deceive the most gullible consumers and the resulting risk of legal liability was too high. In 1983, the FTC issued a policy statement that established three elements of deception:

1) there must be a representation, practice, or omission likely to mislead consumers;
2) the consumers must be interpreting the message reasonably under the circumstances; and
3) the misleading effects must be material; that is, likely to affect consumers' decisions or conduct.

See Appendix to Cliffdale Associates, 103 F.T.C. 110 (1984). Evidence of actual false belief or evidence that a threshold fraction of consumers hold a certain interpretation are not needed for the second element; the threshold is the likelihood or reasonable possibility that consumers are misled. As to the third element, the Commission assumes that "all express claims are material, and that implied claims are material if they pertain to the central characteristics of the product, such as its safety, cost, or fitness for the purpose sold." *In re Int'l Harvester Co.,* 104 F.T.C. 949 (1984).

Like deception, unfairness initially was undefined in the statute. In 1994, Congress passed the FTC Reauthorization Act, which included a set of principles that bounded what the FTC could declare to be unfair.

> The Commission shall have no authority . . . to declare unlawful an act or practice on the grounds that such act or practice is unfair unless the act or practice causes or is likely to cause substantial injury to consumers which is not reasonably avoidable by consumers themselves and not outweighed by countervailing benefits to consumers or to competition. In determining whether an act or practice is unfair, the Commission may consider established public policies as evidence to be considered with all other evidence. Such public policy considerations may not serve as a primary basis for such determination.

The Federal Trade Commission Act Amendments of 1994, Pub. L. No. 103-312 §9 (adding a new 15 U.S.C. §45(n) (Aug. 26, 1994)). The legislative history helps flesh out the meaning of the key elements of the test. For example, the criteria of substantial injury can be met through a relatively small harm to a large number of consumers or a grave harm to a lesser number of consumers.

The cost-benefit test imbedded in the unfairness principle is a major difference from the deception standard, as false or misleading statements are assumed to have no benefits. The benefit analysis need not be mathematical or based on quantifiable factors but should reflect a careful evaluation after a collection and consideration of reasonably available evidence. Sen. Rep. No. 130, 103d Cong., 2d Sess. 12 (1994).

Another important distinction between unfairness and deception is that unfairness does not require a misrepresentation or omission. Therefore, unfairness can reach a wider variety of conduct than deception, including post-sale practices that do not involve any communication with a consumer.

The Director of the FTC's Bureau of Consumer Protection explained the logic of the three-element test for unfairness:

> The primary purpose of the Commission's modern unfairness authority continues to be to protect consumer sovereignty by attacking practices that impede consumers' ability to make informed choices. . . . Thus, the modern unfairness test reflects several common sense principles about the appropriate role for the Commission in the marketplace. First, the Commission's role is to promote consumer choices, not second-guess those choices. That's the point of the reasonable avoidance test. Second, the Commission should not be in the business of trying to second guess market outcomes when the benefits and costs of a policy are very closely balanced or when the existence of consumer injury is itself disputed. That's the point of the substantial injury test. And the Commission should not be in the business of making essentially political choices about which public policies it wants to pursue. That is the point of codifying the limited role of public policy.

J. Howard Beales, III., "The FTC's Use of Unfairness Authority: Its Rise, Fall and Resurrection," https://www.ftc.gov/public-statements/2003/05/ftcs-use-unfairness-authority-its-rise-fall-and-resurrection.

2. CFPB's UDAAP Statute (no, the additional "A" is not a typo; read on)

When the CFPB assumed responsibility for enforcing federal consumer laws related to financial products and services, it inherited authority over many existing laws, such as the Fair Credit Reporting Act and the Equal Credit Opportunity Act. (See Assignment 3 for more discussion.) The CFPB did get some new authority, however, that prior financial regulators had lacked. Can you spot the difference in the below language from the FTC statute?

> The Bureau may take any action authorized under Part E to prevent a covered person or service provider from committing or engaging in an unfair, deceptive, or abusive act or practice under Federal law in connection with any transaction with a consumer for a consumer financial product or service, or the offering of a consumer financial product or service.

12 U.S.C. §5531(a). The statute created a new federal standard: UDAAP, where the first "A" stands for "Abusive." The addition of abusive may seem subtle, but it produced many sleepless nights for bankers and their lawyers.

The Dodd-Frank law made no effort to define deceptive. Most commentators believe the definition of deceptive developed in the FTC context will be applicable to the CFPB's lawmaking because the definition of unfair is nearly identical to that in the FTC context. On the other hand, perhaps the failure to adopt the FTC's guidance definition of deceptive was an implicit rejection of that standard. Notice too that the definition is worded as a constraint on the CFPB's power, rather than an affirmative authority.

> The Bureau shall have no authority under this section to declare an act or practice in connection with a transaction with a consumer for a consumer financial product or service, or the offering of a consumer financial product or service, to be unlawful on the grounds that such act or practice is unfair, unless the Bureau has a reasonable basis to conclude that—
>
> (A) the act or practice causes or is likely to cause substantial injury to consumers which is not reasonably avoidable by consumers; and
> (B) such substantial injury is not outweighed by countervailing benefits to consumers or to competition.

12 U.S.C. §5531(c). One difference between the language is that the CFPB needs only a "reasonable basis" to support its conclusion that the elements of unfairness are met. Arguably, the FTC statute lacks that qualifier, suggesting that perhaps a greater level of certainty is required to declare a practice unfair.

The term "abusive" does not have a counterpart in the FTC's UDAP law. The addition of abusive to the CFPB's arsenal has provoked considerable debate. Financial service providers argued that the tried-and-true unfair and deceptive standards were sufficient, but they ultimately failed to alter the bill. After its passage, the financial industry switched to complaining that meaning of abusive was unclear, subjecting them to unchecked and roving enforcement. A leading law firm created a client bulletin about the CFPB's abusive power termed "Know It When You See It." Morrison & Foerster webinar, http://www.mofo.com/resources/events/2015/01/150122cfpbudaapaknowitwhenyouseeit (Jan. 22, 2015). Despite these laments, abusive is, in point of fact, defined at length in Dodd-Frank. Like unfairness, it is worded as a check on the CFPB's power.

> The Bureau shall have no authority under this section to declare an act or practice abusive in connection with the provision of a consumer financial product or service, unless the act or practice—
>
> (1) materially interferes with the ability of a consumer to understand a term or condition of a consumer financial product or service; or
> (2) takes unreasonable advantage of—
>   (A) a lack of understanding on the part of the consumer of the material risks, costs, or conditions of the product or service;
>   (B) the inability of the consumer to protect the interests of the consumer in selecting or using a consumer financial product or service; or
>   (C) the reasonable reliance by the consumer on a covered person to act in the interests of the consumer.

12 U.S.C. §5531(d). The CFPB has used its abusive power sparingly, sometimes charging that practices were only unfair and/or deceptive without mention of abusive. Prior to 2015, just five enforcement orders identified the conduct as abusive. The CFPB has begun to use the standard more frequently, as years have now elapsed since it has enacted rules or has exercised supervisory authority over entities. As a general matter, the CFPB seems to charge that conduct is abusive when the consumers are vulnerable or when the company did not

provide consumers with the information needed to understand the product. As of 2015, the CFPB had alleged abusive practices against debt collectors, credit card companies, mortgage servicers, and payday lenders. A central theme of its complaints were that the company interfered with a consumer's ability to understand the product or service; for example, by "burying" a term in a contract or by giving consumers incorrect information about the applicable law. The lynchpin of "abusive" seems to be a business creating and leveraging an information disadvantage to entrap consumers.

Some of the CFPB's actions also suggest that a company need only be negligent to commit a UDAAP violation. In 2015, JPMorgan Chase & Co. paid out approximately $186 million in a settlement with the CFPB and state Attorneys General. The complaint did allege an intention to harm consumers but instead documented the failure of Chase to develop or implement procedural checks and appropriate systems to verify the validity and amount of debts that were sold to debt collectors. The fact that the conduct was not necessarily intentional or willful but was nonetheless challenged as unlawful is a reminder that UDAAP statutes are designed to soften the intent and proof requirements of the common law.

UDAAP litigation generally is rare; settlement via consent order is king. As of July 2015, there was only one case in which a court had ruled on the merits of UDAAP liability. *CFPB v. Chance Gordon*, Minute Order, CV12-6147 (C.D. Cal. June 26, 2013). As more judicial opinions arise, the UDAAP standards may become clearer. The very reason for UDAAP, however, is to have broad authority to challenge new and emerging practices; the authority reflects the dynamic and free market for financial services.

C.   State UDAP Laws

The state UDAP statutes are sometimes called mini-UDAPs. This is a misnomer because each of the fifty states' laws are more powerful than the federal UDAP statute in one regard: they permit a private right of action for enforcement, which the FTC Act does not grant.

Each state's UDAP law is different in its scope, level of detail, and its remedies. *See* National Consumer Law Center, *Unfair and Deceptive Acts and Practices* (8th ed. 2012), App. A. State law may directly prohibit certain practices, either in the statute or by regulation. Some of these are themselves fairly general, while others legislate extremely specific practices (residential water treatment sales scams, radon testing, dance studios, vacation promotions, etc.). In addition, some state laws specify that violations of a federal FTC rule or guidance are violations of the state's UDAP law.

If a consumer can show the business committed the specific prohibition in the UDAP's "laundry list" of misbehavior, there is a per se violation. If no specified prohibitions exist or the conduct does not fall into one of the categories, the alternative is trying to prove that the alleged conduct falls under broader contours of unfair and deceptive behavior. Some states laws are exclusively, or nearly exclusively, lists of prohibitions. Others contain only a generalized prohibition against unfair or deceptive behavior.

California is an illustrative example of these two approaches, although it is unusual in having two statutes that are characterized as UDAP laws. Most states have only a single statute, resulting in less reach than California's double-coverage system.

The Consumers Legal Remedies Act prohibits two dozen enumerated practices as unfair or deceptive practices in California. Cal. Civ. Code §1770. Prohibitions include: misrepresenting the source of goods; advertising goods or services without the intent to sell them as advertised; making false or misleading statements about the reasons for, existence of, or amounts of price reductions; representing that a repair is needed when it is not; and inserting an unconscionable provision in a contract. The law applies to any transactions that are intended to result or that do result in a sale or lease of goods or services to a consumer. The major exclusions are definitional. What constitutes a "good or service?" Was the plaintiff a "consumer" in the transaction? There are also a few statutory exclusions. *See* Cal. Civ. Code §§1750-1785. As its name suggests, this statute provides for ample private remedies to consumers: actual damages, punitive damages, injunctions, restitution, attorneys' fees for prevailing plaintiffs, and an ability to bring class actions. *See* Cal. Civ. Code §§1780-1784.

The California Unfair Competition Law applies broadly to prohibit unfair, deceptive, untrue or misleading advertisements or methods of competition. *See* Cal. Bus & Prof. Code §§17200-17594. People often refer to it in shorthand as a "17200 action" or a "UCL" case. This law has no specified exclusions; its scope is sweeping. Private litigants can obtain relief such as injunctions or restitution to remedy harm, and a prevailing plaintiff may be awarded attorneys' fees. Except for certain enumerated prohibited practices for which treble or punitive damages are available, however, a victory for a consumer does not result in the award of actual or statutory damages to consumers. Not surprisingly, then, private enforcement is rare. Section 17200 is the workhorse of public enforcement, including the California Attorney General and certain city officials who are authorized to bring actions under the statute.

Many courts have ruled that a state UDAP statute is to be interpreted expansively. The fact that UDAP statutes were enacted as a remedial tool for consumers who were without common law remedies seems to motivate these more generous readings of the statutes' applicability.

Rhonda Bosland v. Warnock Dodge, Inc.

964 A.2d 741 (N.J. 2009)

Hoens, Justice.

The Consumer Fraud Act (CFA), N.J.S.A. 56:8-1 to -20, affords broad protections to New Jersey consumers. From 1960, when the Legislature first enacted the CFA in its original form and when it only authorized actions by the Attorney General, see L.

1960, c. 39, until its most recent amendment in 2007, L. 2007, c. 14, (amending N.J.S.A. 56:8-1.1 as it relates to transportation for temporary service workers), the history of the Act demonstrates a strong and consistent pattern of expanding the rights of consumers and protecting them from a wide variety of marketplace tactics and practices deemed to be unconscionable.

This matter calls upon this Court to consider whether a plaintiff, prior to instituting litigation pursuant to the CFA, must first request a refund of a claimed overcharge from an allegedly culpable merchant. Our reading of the plain language of the statute and our understanding of the Legislature's overall intent, both in enacting the CFA and in expanding its scope, compels us to answer this question in the negative. We therefore conclude that the CFA does not require a consumer, who has been victimized by a practice which the statute is designed to remedy, to seek a refund from the offending merchant as a prerequisite to filing a complaint. . . .

The facts that give rise to this dispute are not complicated. On March 13, 2003, plaintiff Rhonda Bosland purchased a new 2003 Jeep Grand Cherokee from defendant Warnock Dodge, Inc. She did not arrange for financing through the dealer, instead paying the full purchase price listed in the Retail Buyer's Order that served as defendant's invoice. That Retail Buyer's Order included a $117 charge that was described only as a "Registration Fee."

Plaintiff asserts that she later learned that the applicable title and registration fees charged by the Motor Vehicle Commission at the time of her purchase were less than the $117 fee the dealer required her to pay. Although there were two ways to calculate what that $117 sum might have represented, plaintiff discovered that the applicable fee could only have been either $77 (comprised of a $74 registration fee and a $3 temporary registration fee) or $97 (representing the sum if an additional $20 title fee could properly be included as a "registration fee"). She therefore reasoned that, regardless of how the $117 charge had been calculated, it must have included an additional documentary service fee that was neither disclosed nor itemized as required by the applicable automobile sales regulations. See N.J.A.C. 13:45A-26B.1, -26B.2(a)(2)(i).

Rather than demanding that defendant refund to her the amount that she had been overcharged, plaintiff filed a complaint, seeking relief both individually and on behalf of a class of similarly situated car buyers. Plaintiff's complaint included three separate causes of action. Two were statutory claims, one asserting that defendant had violated the CFA, and the other relying on the provisions of the Truth-in-Consumer Contract, Warranty, and Notice Act (TCCWNA), N.J.S.A. 56:12-14 to -18. The third cause of action was based upon an alternative quasi-contractual theory of unjust enrichment.

· · ·

We granted defendant's petition for certification in order to decide whether an attempt to obtain a refund from a merchant is an essential prerequisite for a CFA claim. 194 N.J. 262, 944 A.2d 25 (2008). We thereafter granted leave to the New Jersey Coalition of Automotive Retailers, Inc. (NJCAR), the New Jersey Lawsuit Reform Alliance (NJLRA), and the Consumers League of New Jersey (CLNJ) to submit briefs as amici curiae.

II.

Defendant asks us to reverse the Appellate Division's conclusion that a pre-suit demand for a refund is not a prerequisite to a CFA complaint, relying on three arguments. First, defendant urges us to conclude that the Appellate Division erred by departing from the rationale expressed by the court in *Feinberg* and in failing to appreciate that, even though an attempt to secure a refund is not explicitly required under the CFA, there can be no ascertainable loss in the absence of having made that effort. Second, defendant argues that we should reject plaintiff's claimed cause of action on the ground that the alleged $20 overpayment, when compared to the value of the vehicle plaintiff has used and enjoyed without any complaint, is not the type of loss that the CFA was intended to remedy. Finally, defendant contends that the Appellate Division's decision will lead to an inequitable result, contrary to the purposes and goals of the CFA because instead of promoting truth and fair dealing in the marketplace, and instead of providing a remedy for those who have no option but to resort to the court system, it will encourage consumers to litigate, in the hope of obtaining awards of treble damages and attorneys' fees, rather than simply asking for a refund that would make them whole.

Plaintiff responds by arguing that there are only three elements necessary to establish a cause of action for relief pursuant to the CFA, none of which is a requirement that a claimant first ask for a refund. Plaintiff argues that imposing on consumers a pre-litigation requirement that they seek direct relief from an offending merchant would subvert the CFA's purposes, because merchants would be free to violate the CFA, providing refunds only to those consumers savvy enough to request them while reaping unfair profits from unconscionable practices committed against all other consumers without fear of reprisal.

Amicus NJCAR argues that the Appellate Division's analysis would permit the CFA to be used to punish merchants for accidental violations or honest mistakes as opposed to affirmative misconduct, thus expanding the remedies of the statute beyond the scope intended by the Legislature. NJCAR urges this Court to conclude that the remedial purposes of the CFA are most properly effectuated when a consumer is required to make a demand for a refund first because the consumer can then be made whole without the need for court intervention.

· · ·

B.

The CFA, in its original form, authorized only the Attorney General to seek redress for violations of its provisions. As we have explained, "[t]he Legislature enacted the CFA in 1960 to address rampant consumer complaints about fraudulent practices in the marketplace and to deter such conduct by merchants." Thiedemann v. Mercedes-Benz USA, L.L.C., 183 N.J. 234, 245, 872 A.2d 783 (2005).

In 1971, the Legislature amended the CFA, expanding it significantly to include a private right of action through the enactment of L. 1971, c. 247, §7, the provision subsequently codified at N.J.S.A. 56:8-19. That section, which is central to the dispute before this Court, provides as follows:

> Any person who suffers any ascertainable loss of moneys or property, real or personal, as a result of the use or employment by another person of any method, act, or practice declared unlawful under this act or the act hereby amended and supplemented may bring an action or assert a counterclaim therefor in any court of competent jurisdiction. In any action under this section the court shall, in addition to any other appropriate legal or equitable relief, award threefold the damages sustained by any person in interest. In all actions under this section, including those brought by the Attorney General, the court shall also award reasonable attorneys' fees, filing fees and reasonable costs of suit. [N.J.S.A. 56:8-19.]

Although the legislative history surrounding this enactment is sparse, it is clear that the intention was to greatly expand protections for New Jersey consumers. The sponsor of the amendments, then-Assemblyman Thomas H. Kean, was quoted at the time as saying that "the amendments represent an enlightened approach to provide greater protection for the consumer against fraud." Governor's Press Release for Assembly Bill No. 2402, at 1 (Apr. 19, 1971) (issued in support of the introduction of the bill containing amendments). Echoing that sentiment, Governor William Cahill described these amendments to the CFA as being intended to "give New Jersey one of the strongest consumer protection laws in the nation." Ibid. Upon signing the bill into law, the Governor further explained that he believed that the amendments would "provide easier access to the courts for the consumer, [would] increase the attractiveness of consumer actions to attorneys and [would] also help reduce the burdens on the Division of Consumer Affairs." Governor's Press Release, at 2 (June 29, 1971).

There are distinctions between the CFA requirements that govern claims pursued by the Attorney General and those permitted to be brought by private parties. In particular, a private party seeking to recover must demonstrate that he or she has suffered an "ascertainable loss." Meshinsky v. Nichols Yacht Sales, Inc., 110 N.J. 464, 472-73 (1988). In addition, the CFA requires a consumer to prove that the loss is attributable to the conduct that the CFA seeks to punish by including a limitation expressed as a causal link. See id. at 473, 541 A.2d 1063; Daaleman v. Elizabethtown Gas Co., 77 N.J. 267, 271 (1978). In considering these requirements, we have been careful to interpret the CFA, and its prima facie proof requirements, so as to be faithful to the Act's broad remedial purposes. . . . In particular, we have recognized that "[t]he history of the [CFA] is one of constant expansion of consumer protection." Gennari v. Weichert Co. Realtors, 148 N.J. 582, 604 (1997). Similarly, our Appellate Division has noted that we "construe the [CFA] broadly, not in a crabbed fashion." New Mea Constr. Corp. v. Harper, 203 N.J. Super. 486, 502 (App. Div. 1985).

We have traditionally recognized that CFA claims brought by consumers as private plaintiffs can be divided, for analytical purposes, into three categories. See Cox, supra, 138 N.J. at 17. Broadly defined, the categories are claims involving affirmative acts, claims asserting knowing omissions, and claims based on regulatory violations. Ibid. To some extent, the proofs required will vary depending upon the category into which any particular claim falls. For example, we have concluded that if a claimed CFA violation is the result of a defendant's affirmative act, "intent is not an essential element." Id. at 17-18. Likewise, intent is not an element if the claim is based on a defendant's alleged violation of a regulation, because "the regulations impose strict liability for such violations." Id. at 18; see Fenwick v. Kay Am. Jeep, Inc., 72 N.J. 372, 378 (1977). In contrast, we have required that a plaintiff seeking to recover based on a defendant's omission, "must show that the defendant acted with knowledge, and intent *is* an essential element of the fraud." Cox, supra, 138 N.J. at 18 (emphasis in original). Viewed against this framework, we can evaluate the dispute before us.

C.

We turn then to the nature of the proofs required of plaintiff and their relationship to the need to demand a refund prior to filing suit. Plaintiff's CFA claim is straightforward; it is premised on her assertion that the single, unified charge in the invoice for a "registration fee" exceeded the amount, however calculated, that was permitted to be charged for such a fee and therefore included an undisclosed "documentary service fee" in violation of the applicable regulations. See N.J.A.C. 13:45A-26B.1, -26B.2(a)(2)(i). Because plaintiff's complaint is based on a claimed regulatory violation, she is not required to prove defendant's intent. See Cox, supra, 138 N.J. at 18.

In analyzing claims under the CFA, we have found that there are only three elements required for the prima facie proofs: 1) unlawful conduct by defendant; 2) an ascertainable loss by plaintiff; and 3) a causal relationship between the unlawful conduct and the ascertainable loss. Int'l Union of Operating Eng'rs Local No. 68 Welfare Fund v. Merck & Co., Inc., 192 N.J. 372, 389, 929 A.2d 1076 (2007) (explaining three prima facie elements); see Weinberg, supra, 173 N.J. at 247-48, 801 A.2d 281 (declining to abolish ascertainable loss requirement for private cause of action); Meshinsky, supra, 110 N.J. at 473, 541 A.2d 1063 (recognizing that private plaintiff, unlike Attorney General, must demonstrate "ascertainable loss [. . .] as a result of" unlawful conduct); Daaleman, supra, 77 N.J. at 271, 390 A.2d 566 (explaining that private plaintiff must show that he or she "suffers a loss due to" defendant's unlawful practice). Each of the elements of the prima facie case is found within the plain language of the statute itself; each is, without any question, a prerequisite to suit.

The plain language of the CFA does not, however, impose upon any putative plaintiff the requirement that he or she first seek a remedy directly from the offending merchant. Instead, it refers to the right of "any person who suffers any ascertainable loss . . . as a result of" defendant's violation of the CFA to file an action. N.J.S.A. 56:8-19. On its face, then, the statute makes no demand upon plaintiff to try to obtain a refund first as a pre-condition of instituting suit. The question, however, is whether the term "ascertainable loss" or the causal nexus requirement embodied in the statutory phrase "as a result of" or the public policy considerations that underlie the CFA suggest that a pre-suit refund demand is implicit in the CFA.

We have previously considered the meaning of the term "ascertainable loss," and have concluded that it means that plaintiff must suffer a definite, certain and measurable loss, rather than one that is merely theoretical. Thiedemann, supra, 183 N.J. at 248. We found it appropriate to resort to the definition of the words, noting that "'[a]scertain' is defined as 'to make (a thing) certain; establish as a certainty; determine with certainty;' and 'ascertainable,' the adjective, is similarly defined as 'capable of being ascertained.'" Ibid. (quoting Webster's Third New International Dictionary 126 (1981)). "The certainty implicit in the concept of an 'ascertainable' loss is that it is quantifiable or measurable." Ibid.

Apart from relying on the definition of the term, we have further considered a variety of issues that relate to the meaning of the "ascertainable loss" requirement. We have held that a consumer who had repairs to a vehicle performed under warranty at no cost did not sustain such a loss. Id. at 251-52, 872 A.2d 783. Nor does it exist for a customer who considered, but never purchased, a product and thus suffered no damages because of a fraudulent loan application submitted by the merchant in anticipation of a sale. Meshinsky, supra, 110 N.J. at 475 n. 4. On the other hand, we have described our understanding of the ascertainable loss requirement generally in terms that make it equivalent to any lost "benefit of [the] bargain." Furst, supra, 182 N.J. at 11-13 (quantifying lost benefit of the bargain by reference to out-of-pocket expenses for purposes of ascertainable loss analysis).

Even so, we have not always equated an ascertainable loss with one that is demonstrated by an immediate, out-of-pocket expense suffered by the consumer. See Thiedemann, supra, 183 N.J. at 248. For example, we have found that a consumer who had not paid for repairs nonetheless suffered an ascertainable loss caused by a home improvement contractor's failure to comply with applicable regulations requiring the work to be inspected. Cox, supra, 138 N.J. at 22. We analyzed the ascertainable loss requirement by evaluating the consumer's proofs about the reasonable cost of repair in the context of damages that had been awarded by the jury. Id. at 22-24. We held that requiring a consumer to actually make the expenditures needed to incur the loss would be contrary to the remedial purposes of the CFA. Id. at 22, 647 A.2d 454. The CFA does not demand that a plaintiff necessarily point to an actually suffered loss or to an incurred loss, but only to one that is "ascertainable."

· · ·

There are sound reasons why a pre-suit demand requirement is not implicit in the CFA. This dispute in particular illustrates how reading such a requirement into the CFA would potentially permit practices, that the statute is designed to deter, instead to continue unabated and unpunished. Plainly, if we require plaintiffs, as a precondition to filing a complaint under the CFA, to first demand a refund, we will create a safe harbor for an offending merchant. A merchant could rely on the pre-suit refund demand requirement, boldly imposing inflated charges at no risk, and planning to refund the overcharges only when asked. Such an analysis of the CFA would limit relief by making it available only to those consumers who are alert enough to ask for a refund, while allowing the offending merchant to reap a windfall. We see in the broad remedial purposes of the CFA a strong contrary expression of public policy. We discern in the CFA a clear expression of the Legislature's intent to empower consumers who seek to secure relief for themselves and for others who may not be aware that they have been victimized. Because reading a pre-suit demand for refund requirement into the CFA would thwart those salutary purposes, we will not endorse it.

———————

The definitions of unfairness and deception under state law are often more generous than the FTC standards. For example, a few states add "unconscionable" as an additional term, presumably giving separate meaning to unfairness. *See e.g.*, Mich. Comp. Laws §445.903. Seventeen states substitute the term "unconscionable" for "unfairness." *See e.g.*, Tex. Bus. & Com. Code Ann. Tit. 2, §17.50. Query whether the intended or actual effect of the substitution is for "unconscionable" to be a higher or lower standard than "unfairness."

In another example, many states have case law adopting the criteria for unfairness in the Supreme Court's decision in *Federal Trade Comm'n v. Sperry and Hutchinson Co.*, 405 U.S. 233 (1972). This approach to unfairness requires substantial injury to consumers, as well as consideration of whether the challenged practice "offends public policy," as outside "at least the penumbra of some common law, statutory, or other established concept of unfairness." Alternatively or in addition, a practice can be appropriately challenged if it is "immoral, unethical, oppressive, or unscrupulous." These criteria are called the "S&H standard" based on the case name in which the phrase first appeared. That standard reflects the FTC's interpretation before the 1994 FTC Authorization Act imposed the more stringent three-prong test. The interplay between federal and state law on unfairness is discussed further in Michael Greenfield, *Unfairness Under Section 5 of the FTC Act and Its Impact on State Law*, 46 Wayne L. Rev. 1869 (2000).

D.   UDAP in Context

One of the greatest strengths of UDAP statutes is their flexibility. Rather than legislative efforts at regulating specific scams, which can resemble the game "whack-a-mole," UDAP statutes stand at the ready to challenge emergent practices. Public or private enforcement by alleging UDAP violations provides faster marketplace intervention and corrective remedies than waiting for the legislature to recognize and address the situation.

For students of consumer law, however, the broad applicability of UDAP statutes is a challenge. It is easy to either over- or under-estimate the ways the laws may be useful or it may be difficult to imagine the types of practices that may be addressed with UDAP allegations. This section presents excerpts from several cases to illustrate some of the factual contexts of UDAP litigation. The focus here is more on the factual settings than on the legal standards. The examples do not include any violations based on credit transactions, but as the cases in the upcoming assignments will illustrate, UDAP is frequently a tool to challenge lending or banking practices.

———————

1. Landlord-Tenant Law

Pierce v. Reichard

593 S.E.2d 787 (N.C. Ct. App. 2004)

HUDSON, Judge.

Plaintiff Ricky Pierce ("Pierce") owns a house located at 107 Beech Street, Roanoke Rapids, North Carolina. On 5 April 1999, defendant Tammy Reichard ("Ms. Reichard") signed a lease in which she agreed to rent the house from Pierce for $300 per month, plus a $300 security deposit. Approximately two weeks after Ms. Reichard moved into the house, the roof over the living room began to leak after a heavy rainfall. Ms. Reichard and her husband immediately taped up the ceiling to try to stop the leaking. After a period of disputing over the leaks and other matters, Pierce filed a complaint for summary ejectment, claiming that Ms. Reichard had not paid her rent, and also sought money damages for repairs to his truck. The Magistrate ruled in favor of Pierce on both issues. Ms. Reichard appealed to district court and filed a counterclaim seeking retroactive rent abatement for Pierce's breach of the implied warranty of habitability and compensation for personal and property damage. After a bench trial, the court awarded Ms. Reichard treble damages of $14,950, property damages of $200 for a broken windshield, a $200 refund of excessive late fees, the return of her $300 security deposit and attorney's fees of $4,085. The trial court awarded Pierce $318.07 for damage to his truck. Pierce appeals. For the reasons discussed here, we affirm in part, vacate in part and remand for further proceedings.

Ms. Reichard testified in district court that she notified plaintiff of the roof leaks right away and that plaintiff said he would get to it as soon as he could. However, Pierce's evidence tended to show that Ms. Reichard first complained about the leaks in August or September of 2000, and that he hired a repair person at that time to apply a coat of "Koolseal" to the roof. Ms. Reichard did not notice any reduction in the severity of the leaks after its application. Ms. Reichard further testified that she complained about the leaks and water damage each time she paid her rent. In August 2001, Pierce had the old roof removed and new shingles installed, but did not repair any of the water damage inside the house.

During the time it took to repair the roof a dispute arose between the parties over damage to Pierce's dump truck, sustained when it was parked in front of the house to contain roof debris. Ms. Reichard admitted that her four-year-old son may have sprayed water into the truck's open gas tank. Ms. Reichard and her husband agreed to siphon all of the gas out of the tank, and put in enough gas to get the truck to a gas station. They also agreed to reimburse Pierce for the cost of refilling the tank, but Pierce claimed that the truck broke down within a few yards of leaving the house and that the repairs cost him over $300. Pierce demanded that Ms. Reichard pay the repair bill, and she refused.

During her tenancy, Ms. Reichard complained to Pierce about a rotten tree on the property that she thought endangered her and her family. After Pierce failed to address this issue, a limb broke off the tree during a storm and damaged Ms. Reichard's car. . . . After reviewing the entire record, we find competent evidence to support this finding of fact. Ms. Reichard testified that about two weeks after she moved into the two-bedroom house, water leaked through the ceiling in the back bedroom and portions of the living room during a strong rain storm. In an effort to stop the leaks, she and her husband put contact paper and duct tape over the leaks, and notified Pierce about the ceiling's condition. Ms. Reichard also testified that ceiling debris often fell through holes in the ceiling where the water leaked, and that when they took down the old tape to replace it, rotten wood fell from the ceiling. Water leaked into the back bedroom, causing mold on the carpets and ruining a mattress. Ms. Reichard was forced to move her daughter out of that bedroom, which she then used to store "junk."

. . .

Plaintiff next argues that the trial court erred by awarding defendant treble damages for rent abatement on her claim of unfair and deceptive trade practices. We disagree.

A trade practice is unfair within the meaning of G.S. §75-1.1 "when it offends established public policy as well as when the practice is immoral, unethical, oppressive, unscrupulous, or substantially injurious to consumers." Creekside Apartments v. Poteat, 446 S.E.2d 826, 833 (citations omitted), disc. review denied, 451 S.E.2d 632 (1994). Chapter 75 applies to residential rentals because the rental of residential housing is commerce pursuant to §75-1.1. Love v. Pressley, 239 S.E.2d 574, 583 (1977), cert. denied, 241 S.E.2d 843 (1978).

In *Allen v. Simmons*, 394 S.E.2d 478 (1990), this Court held that a jury could find that plaintiff committed an unfair trade practice where defendant's evidence was that plaintiff leased defendant a house which contained numerous defects throughout defendant's tenancy and which rendered the house uninhabitable. Id. at 484. Plaintiff failed to respond to numerous notices about the uninhabitable state of the house. Despite the condition of the house, plaintiff attempted to collect rent after defendant discontinued payments. We held that plaintiff's behavior can be considered "immoral, unethical, oppressive, unscrupulous, or substantially injurious to consumers." Id. at 484. See also Creekside Apartments, 446 S.E.2d 826, 833; Foy v. Spinks, 414 S.E.2d 87 (1992).

Here, Ms. Reichard testified that she complained about significant leaks in the back bedroom and living room of the house for more than two years and that Pierce continued to collect rent until the day he demanded she vacate the house. Pierce's argument that he had no notice of damage to the interior of the house is to no avail. "[W]here a tenant's evidence establishes the residential rental premises were unfit for human habitation and the landlord was aware of needed repairs but failed to honor his promises to correct the deficiencies and continued to demand rent, then such evidence would support a factual finding . . . that the landlord committed an unfair or deceptive trade practice." Foy, 414 S.E.2d at 89-90. Here, Pierce was aware that the roof was leaking and that repairs were necessary, yet did not perform necessary repairs until approximately two years after the defective condition was brought to his attention. Thus, as in *Allen* and *Foy*, the trial court correctly concluded that plaintiff's actions in collecting rent after having knowledge of the uninhabitable nature of part of the house constituted unfair trade practices and was thus a violation of G.S. §75-1.1.

2. Unauthorized Practice of Law

Sussman v. Grado
746 N.Y.S.2d 548 (Dist. Ct. 2002)

ASARCH, Judge.

The plaintiff had obtained a judgment against a debtor on November 14, 2001 for $1,472.00. When the plaintiff attempted to enforce the judgment, he learned that there were two joint bank accounts at different banks in the names of the judgment debtor and his wife, for which the Sheriff's Department required a turnover order.

The plaintiff went to the defendant, "an independent paralegal" and president/sole shareholder of Accutech Consulting Group, Inc., and explained what he needed. He paid the defendant $45 for the services. Despite the defendant's claim that she did not know what a turnover order was, she accepted the case and the fee.

The plaintiff alleged that the papers prepared by the defendant were deficient and, as a result, the "Sheriff's Department closed the case." He sues to recover the amount of the judgment plus the fee paid to the defendant (which she admittedly would refund). In fact, by letter dated February 21, 2002, the defendant sent the plaintiff a check for $45 (which he denied receiving), refunding the $45 for the turnover order which "was executed in good faith by this office. You indicated an error and we did not ever refuse to make the correction. This is not a usual type of court order. In fact, the three attorneys that we did speak with about it understood the relevance, but had never heard of it or done such an order." The defendant indicated that because the plaintiff had challenged the "integrity" of the defendant's office, his business "will not be welcome here." . . .

The defendant testified that she's a graduate from a paralegal certificate program and has been a paralegal for 13 years and she "help[s] a lot of people."

In response to the Court's question: "Do you work under the authority of an attorney?" The defendant answered: "I'm an independent. I assist the general public. I assist attorneys with work. And Mr. Sussman came to me of his own free will and asked me to do this work for him."

To this Court, there is a difference between assisting someone to fill out a form and preparing a form on a subject with which the "assistance" is unfamiliar. Instead of referring this plaintiff to an attorney, the defendant allegedly asked three (3) attorneys about what a turnover order was ("none of them had ever heard of it") and called the Sheriff's office who informed her that "they needed something to direct the bank to research it's [sic] files and find out the assets of the debtor."

"So I prepared for Mr. Sussman the turn over order that you're looking at."

When asked by the Court how she got the form, the defendant answered: "I patterned it based upon what I know of other orders petitioning money from the court." . . .

The American Bar Association has defined an independent paralegal as "a person who is not supervised by a lawyer, provides services to clients with regard to a process in which the law is involved, is not functioning at the time as a paralegal or a document preparer, and for whose work no lawyer is accountable," Nonlawyer

Practice in the United States: Summary of the Factual Record before the American Bar Association Commission on Nonlawyer Practice (1994). However, New York State bar associations have not recognized the "legal technician/ independent paralegal" for reasons obvious from this case — the independent paralegal, working without the supervision of an attorney, may cross the line between assisting a person in need to hurting a person in need through lack of knowledge and supervision, see e.g. N.Y. County Lawyers Association Ethics Committee opinion 641 (1975), Association of the Bar of the City of New York Ethics Committee opinion 1995-11 ["Supervision within the law firm thus is a key consideration."]. . . .

The defendant has, in this Court's opinion, crossed the line between filling out forms and engaging in the practice of law by rendering legal services, Judiciary Law §478; People v. Jakubowitz, 184 Misc. 2d 559 (Supreme Court Bronx County, 2000). The defendant "was going to attempt to prepare an order that would hopefully affect the bank turning over the portion of the account of [the judgment-debtor]'s assets to Mr. Sussman on his judgment. That was the intention" (defendant's testimony). "The practice of law involves the rendering of legal advice and opinions directed to particular clients (citations omitted)," Matter of Rowe, 604 N.E.2d 728 (1992). . . . This Court finds that the defendant used independent judgment on a subject with which she had insufficient knowledge. As indicated above, the defendant did not follow proper procedure with respect to the turnover proceeding. Failure to comply with CPLR 5225 and/or 5227 prevented the Court from issuing a turnover order. Such document preparation was not "customary and innocuous practices," Spivak v. Sachs, 211 N.E.2d 329 (1965), nor were the turnover order documents the preparation of legal forms or text simply designed to say what the law is, see New York County Lawyers Association v. Dacey, 234 N.E.2d 459 (1967). Rather, the defendant herein purported to "give personal advice on a specific problem" with respect to the turnover proceeding vis a vis the plaintiff's judgment, Id. at 28 A.D.2d 161 (dissent by Justice Stevens, adopted by the Court of Appeals majority).

Regardless of her intentions to help the plaintiff, this independent paralegal operated without the supervision of an attorney. She tried to create a legal document without the required knowledge, skill or training. As a result the plaintiff may have lost the ability to execute against two bank accounts. Just as a law school graduate, not admitted to practice law, cannot undertake to collect overdue accounts on behalf of prospective clients, so is an independent paralegal barred from attempting to collect a judgment.

There is no doubt that the public needs assistance in navigating the court system. This is one reason for the Chief Judge's work in creating offices for the self-represented in the courts. The hundreds of thousands of hours which the practicing bar devotes annually in voluntary pro bono services also go a long way to protecting the rights of those who cannot afford legal representation. However, the guidance of an attorney and his or her professional staff seems much preferable to an "independent paralegal" who has not gone through law school, has not passed the bar exam and who is not licensed in New York State (it should be noted that an attorney's license to practice law is subject to discipline if ethical standards are not met). Section 484 of the Judiciary Law is designed "to protect the public in this State from 'the dangers of legal representation and advice given by persons not trained, examined and licensed for such work, whether they be laymen or lawyers from other jurisdictions' (citation omitted)," El Gemayel v. Seaman, 533 N.E.2d 245 (1988).

This Court finds that the actions of the defendant constituted a deceptive act "likely to mislead a reasonable consumer acting reasonably under the circumstances," Oswego Laborers' Local 214 Pension Fund v. Marine Midland Bank, 647 N.E.2d 741 (1995) and that "the acts or practices have a broader impact on consumers at large," Id. . . . [T]he Court finds that the accepting of the assignment was misleading in a material respect to the consumer and that the consumer was injured—he was unable to collect his judgment from the two restrained bank accounts. Accordingly, the Court finds that the plaintiff is entitled to treble damages, Gen. Bus. Law §349(h), in the sum of $135.00.

---

3. Towing Practices

Waters v. Hollie

642 S.W.2d 90 (Tex. App. 1982)

JORDAN, Justice

Suit was brought by appellant under the Deceptive Trade Practices Act, and after trial to a jury resulted in a verdict for appellant in the amount of $800.00 actual damages plus attorney's fees through the Supreme Court. Appellant moved for judgment on the verdict and appellee moved the court to disregard the jury's findings and in the alternative for judgment for defendant. . . .

There is no statement of facts in this case, but the facts, as stated in both briefs, are not in dispute and they are some-what unusual. On or about the night of November 27, 1978, appellant's car broke down on the South Freeway in Fort Worth in the area of East Berry Street as appellant was on her way home from work as a waitress. It was somehow moved the same night to the parking lot of the Treasure City Department Store located at East Berry and the South Freeway. It remained there overnight and the next morning the manager of the store had it towed away by appellee, who operated a wrecking and towing service and storage facility. Appellant's car was then stored at appellee's place of business for over three months, before she learned where it was. Appellant reported her car as stolen to the Fort Worth Police who located the car at Hollie's Garage. Appellee never did notify appellant that he had her car.

When appellant finally saw her car at Hollie's Garage, the contents, consisting of a C.B. radio, tape deck, fish locator, a gold crucifix, a gold medal and various fishing equipment, worth approximately $800.00, were missing. She thereafter filed this suit for recovery of the value of the missing articles under the Deceptive Trade Practices Act only. She did not sue on any common law negligence, conversion, or a bailor-bailee theory.

We disagree with the holding of the trial court that under the facts of this case appellant was not a consumer under [Tex. Bus. & Comm. Code] §17.45(4) of the Act and that she therefore cannot recover thereunder.

Mouse-Trapping on Internet

FTC Press Release, "Cyberscam Targeted by FTC" (Oct. 1, 2001)
re FTC v. Zuccarini, Civ. Action No. 02C 7456.C.A. No. 01-CV-4854
(E.D. Pa. filed Sept. 25, 2001)

A cyberscammer who used more than 5,500 copycat Web addresses to divert surfers from their intended Internet destinations to one of his sites, and hold them
captive while he pelted their screens with a barrage of ads, was charged by the
Federal Trade Commission with violating federal laws. At the request of the FTC,
a U.S. District Court enjoined his activities pending further order of the court. The
FTC will seek a court order to force the defendant to give up his ill-gotten gains.

"Schemes that capture consumers and hold them at sites against their will while
exposing Internet users, including children, to solicitations for gambling, psychics,
lotteries, and pornography must be stopped," said Timothy J. Muris, Chairman of
the FTC. "In addition to violating the trademark rights of legitimate Website owners, the defendant may have placed employees in peril by exposing them to sexually explicit sites and gambling sites on the job, in violation of company policies.
With more than 63 previous law suits against him for the identical practices, we
believe the court will shut down the defendant's schemes permanently."

According to the FTC, the scheme works like this: The defendant registers Internet domain names that are misspellings of legitimate domain names or that incorporate transposed or inverted words or phrases. For example, he registered 15
variations of the popular children's cartoon site, www.cartoonnetwork.com, and
41 variations on the name of teen pop star, Britney Spears. Surfers looking for a site
who misspell its Web address or invert a term — using cartoonjoe.com, for
example, rather than joecartoon.com — are taken to the defendant's sites. They
then are bombarded with a rapid series of windows displaying ads for goods and
services ranging from Internet gambling to pornography. An FTC investigator
entered one of the defendant's copycat domain names, annakurnikova.com, and
29 browser windows opened automatically. In some cases, the legitimate site to
which the consumer was attempting to go is also launched, so that consumers may
think the hailstorm of ads to which they are being exposed is from a legitimate
Web site.

Once consumers are taken to one of the defendant's sites, it is very difficult for
them to exit. In a move called "mousetrapping," special programming code at the
sites obstructs surfers' ability to close their browser or go back to the previous page.
Clicks on the "close" or "back" buttons cause new windows to open. "After one FTC
staff member closed out of 32 separate windows, leaving just two windows on the
task bar, he selected the "back" button, only to watch as the same seven windows
that initiated the blitz erupted on his screen, and the cybertrap began anew,"
according to papers filed with the court.

These examples show the flexibility and breadth of the UDAP approach to
protecting consumers. In some of these instances, the plaintiff could also have
used either a subject-matter-specific statute or common law to challenge the
conduct. The choice to use UDAP sometimes reflects a desire to avail oneself of

enhanced remedies, such as the treble damages referenced in *Pierce v. Reichard*. Other times, the consumer may benefit by alleging something is "unfair" or "deceptive," rather than a violation of an obscure statutory provision because such claims create more grave reputational risks or terrible publicity. The remedial focus and broad sweep of UDAP statutes tend to get the attention of the defendant company's legal department and help provoke a settlement.

Problem Set 9

9.1. Bid Big runs online auctions for new merchandise. Unlike other popular Internet auction sites, Bid Big is selling items that it has purchased specifically for retail sale. The auctions use a novel bidding structure. Every bid is an increment of one penny, with an opening price of one cent. This allows many people to get in on the action, often bidding hundreds of times for the item as time counts down. The ultimate price paid by the winning consumer is often very low in relationship to the value of the item, such as $128 for a tablet computer that retails for $1,199. Bid Big makes profits from such auctions because it charges users 50 cents to place each bid. High-interest items like a Nikon camera attract about 12,000 bids, generating $6,000 in revenue for the company. After Bid Big pays for the camera and its operating costs such as advertising and site hosting, it still handsomely profits.

Bored of the long Massachusetts winter and looking for a distraction, your spouse has been bidding big. He has confessed to placing 100 or more bids each day on various items, which required spending over $1,000 this month in bid fees, while failing to win a single item. You've asked your spouse to stop, but you were met with a pointed allegation that you have some expensive hobbies yourself—golf membership, spa retreats, etc. You plan to call your state's Attorney General and the FTC to try to entice them to investigate Bid Big. Are these practices unfair or deceptive or both? You expect the AG or FTC will be more persuaded if you can analogize to other UDAP suits and if you are versed in the legal standard. 15 U.S.C. §45; Mass. Genl. Law. §93A.

9.2. It took nearly two years for Cassie Grey to land a new job when the call center that employed her was off-shored to cut costs. During that period, Cassie collected unemployment but also spent on credit cards to make ends meet. She now owes more than $33,000 and is struggling to make even the minimum payments on her cards. Her annual salary at her new position is $27,000, which is enough for Cassie to meet ongoing expenses but leaves nothing leftover to pay down her debts or save. She's cut up all her credit cards but needs a solution for the debts. She says that bankruptcy is "absolutely out." Her least-favorite uncle is a bankruptcy trustee in her community and is certain to tell her entire family about her situation. Instead, Cassie has contacted Death to Debt, a company that promotes itself with the following statements:

> "When you are enrolled in our program, you will not have to make payments to all of your creditors anymore."
> "We help 100 percent of the people who enter this program attack their debts."

"Settle your debts for less than half of what you owe and avoid the stigma of bankruptcy."

Cassie obtained a preliminary plan for her debts, reproduced below. She has asked you, her long-time best friend, for your advice on whether Death to Debt is a legitimate operation. Her new job is with a public relations company, and she doesn't want to get mixed up with any "shady deals." Is Death to Debt engaged in an unlawful activity? If you are concerned, where should you report Death to Debt? Consider only federal law. 15 U.S.C. §45; 12 U.S.C. §5531.

Client ID:

** Please Note : This page must be returned in order for the set up of your file to be completed.

CSA™ Estimated Plan Cost		Settlement CSA™ Service Fee Schedule	Payment	Estimated Personal Savings Plan for Payments to Creditors	
Total Unsecured Debt:	$ 33,551.23	CSA™ Total Service Fee:	$ 5,032.88	Estimated Settlement (Approx. 40%):	$ 13,420
Estimated Settlement Amount (Approx 40%)	$ 13,420.49	2 Initial Deposit Payment(s) of:	$ 512.58	Savings Budget During Initial Payments	* Optional *
CSA™ Service Fee:	$ 5,032.88	1 Remaining Deposit Payment(s) of:	$ 380.00	Minimum Savings During 20 Service Fee Payments:	$ 198.62
Adjusted Total Debt Elimination Cost:	$ 18,453.17	CSA Initial Payment Total:	$ 1,405.16	Minimum Personal Savings Deposits After Service Fee Payments:	$ 380.00
Total Debt Savings:	$ 15,098.06	Remaining Service Fee Balance:	$ 3,627.52	Total Payments towards Savings After All Payments:	25
Adjusted Estimated Monthly Budget Payments:	$ 380.00	20 Monthly Service Fee Payments of:	$ 181.38	Estimated DEBT FREE Time Frame	48 Months
		Total Months to Payoff Service Fee:	23		

** NOTE: The estimated saving plan is the minimum suggested for payoff of your enrolled accounts. CSA™ highly recommends that any additional funds, which may become available, be allocated towards your personal savings account. You are encouraged to add as much towards savings as possible, as it is to your advantage to do so. The quicker you save money, the sooner you can get your enrolled debts resolved.

Updated ACH Debit Service Fee Summary / Personal Savings Summary			
Program Start Date:	1/29/2007	2 Initial Payments of:	$ 512.58
Remaining Deposit Payments Start Date:	3/29/2007	1 Initial Payments of:	$ 380.00
Remaining Service Fee Start Date:	4/29/2007	20 Monthly Service Fee Payments of:	$ 181.38
Personal Savings Start Date:	12/29/2008	25 Personal Savings Deposits of:	$ 380.00
Personal Savings During Service Fee:	4/29/2007	20 Personal Savings Deposits of:	$ 198.62
			Date:

Client Signature:
Important: The above debt schedule is the updated recommended payment and personal savings budget. Any debit changes of your scheduled ACH Debit. CSA™ service fee payments, requires a minimum of five(5) business days notice .

Service Fee Addendum : I acknowledge and confirm the above tables represents an adjustment of fees to be paid to CSA™ due to an addition and/or deletion of an enrolled account(s). This new fee schedule is hereby incorporated into the Service Agreement by reference. This addendum in no way changes any other provision of the Agreement. All other provisions of the Agreement shall remain in full force and effect.

Client signature _____   Date _____

Address, City, Zip Code ████████████████████

** NOTE : If adding a new account, a Creditor Information Sheet for the new account being added must accompany this page.

9.3. Universal University has operated a top-tier law school for more than 100 years. Its reputation for excellence recently was marred. The school published inaccurate statistics on the grades and LSAT scores of its most recent incoming class and disseminated the statistics by mailing the publication to more than two thousand prospective students for next year. The admissions office obtained the individuals' grades and LSAT scores from an outside organization as part of the application process but itself computed the statistical information on average and 25th and 75th quartiles. The information has not appeared outside of the law school's publication; it was not reported to the American Bar Association or any news organizations. The University has hired you to advise it on how to handle this situation. At your recommendation, it has immediately suspended all admissions staff and sent a letter to all brochure recipients advising them to disregard entirely the grade and score information that "should not have been printed." Are you worried about an unfair or deceptive practices lawsuit? Given that your report will be made to the dean of the law school and the university's general counsel, be prepared to explain your analysis and defend your conclusion. 15 U.S.C. §45(a)(4).

9.4. Identify a practice that you have experienced that left you feeling wronged as a consumer. Look up your state's UDAP statute. (If you have trouble finding the statute and wind up at the library reference desk for help, consider how consumers without attorneys or legal education fare.) Does the practice fit within the reach of your state's UDAP law? Why or why not? What will be the most difficult aspect of using UDAP to address the practice?

9.5. Your partner, Luz, earned a two-year college degree about five years ago. Since then she has worked as a teacher's assistant, supporting your household while you were in law school. In your third year of law school, Luz applied to three colleges for admission to earn a bachelors' degree. She was admitted to a local state university, rejected at an out-of-state public university, and was waitlisted at a private school, Williston College. She has her heart set on Williston because it offers excellent financial aid packages and ranks among the top 25 small private colleges. In late July, Luz refused to enroll in the state university, missing the first deadline for tuition payments and course selection, because she wanted to see if Williston admits her. You return home on August 1 to find her sobbing. She received a rejection letter from Williston and called to ask if there was any chance she could still be admitted. The admission officer explained that the entering class of 415 was fully enrolled at this time, and that they had admitted only 27 students off the wait list all summer. In response to her question about how close she came to being among the admitted students, the officer explained, "We waitlisted 300 students. Those 27 kids are lucky, and I'm sorry you were not one of them. I do wish you the best." Luz is devastated, but you are angry that Luz "waited" with such low odds. Do you think Williston engaged in an unfair or deceptive act or practice? Which is the better legal claim? Outline the elements of the cause of action and the supporting facts.

Assignment 10.   Warranties

Like many aspects of consumer law, warranties have origins in both tort and contract law. Products liability law in tort allows recovery for physical injuries to people or property if a product is not made with reasonable care. Breach of contract allow consumers to sue if the good is not as promised and to recover even if the only loss is economic.

Modern warranty law has two major sources. State warranty law primarily consists of Article 2 of the Uniform Commercial Code (U.C.C.), adopted in every state except Louisiana. A federal statute, the Magnuson-Moss Warranty Act, regulates the disclosure of warranties and provides remedies for warranty breaches. Together, they create a framework of warranty law that provides substantially more protection for consumers than common law tort or contract.

A.   Uniform Commercial Code

The U.C.C. creates a statutory scheme of warranties that applies to all sales of goods. It codifies the common law ideas of "express" and "implied" warranties.

Article 2 of the U.C.C. applies only to the sale of "goods," U.C.C. §2-102. Goods are broadly defined to include "all things . . . which are movable at the time of identification to the contract for sale." U.C.C. §2-105(1). The big exclusions are real property, which is not a good, and leases rather than sales, which are governed by U.C.C. 2A, including its warranty provisions. The other important exclusion is services; even if they are "defective" in the sense of highly unsatisfactory, there is no warranty and no U.C.C. coverage. Instead, poor services are often challenged as "unfair acts" under UDAP law. In Texas, for example, the Deceptive Trade Practices Act can be used to sue a cleaning service that bleached areas of carpets. Also, note that the U.C.C. applies to all goods, whether sold for consumer or business purposes, so what you learn here is applicable to nearly all sales of personal property.

The warranty rules are subject to the U.C.C.'s extensive rules on performance, breach, and remedies. These are taught in Contracts, or a specialized Sales course. For consumer law, one of the most important rules is the statute of limitations for breach of warranty. Generally, actions must be commenced within four years after the cause of action accrued—normally when the goods are tendered for delivery and accepted by the consumer. U.C.C. §2-725. Because the U.C.C.'s remedies are limited, some states have expanded the protection. In California, the Song-Beverly Act, allows consumers who demonstrate a breach of express or implied warranties to recover judgments for actual damages (such as the cost of repairs), costs and expenses, attorney's fees based on reasonable actual time expended, and for willful violations, a civil penalty not to exceed two times the actual damages. Cal. Civ. Code §1790 et seq.

1. Express Warranties

An express warranty is one established by the sellers' conduct, rather than by the law. Sellers can create express warranties orally, by advertising, or by product packaging. An express warranty can exist even without the use of the word "warranty" or similar words, and even if the seller had not intent to create an express warranty.

The U.C.C. establishes three types of express warranties. These arise from 1) an affirmation of fact or promise that relates to the goods; 2) any description of the goods; or 3) any sample or model of the goods. U.C.C. §2-313(1). Much of the case law interpreting express warranties arises in the context of auto sales, where statements that a vehicle will be "trouble-free" or in "tip-top" shape have been held to be express warranties.

To be an express warranty, the affirmation, description, or sample must have become part of the basis of the bargain between buyer and seller. This does not require a showing that the buyer actually relied on the warranty. Instead, the basis of bargain approach looks to the overall transaction and the understanding of the parties, focusing on whether the seller's actions created an express warranty. Because express warranties are deemed to be central to the bargain, express warranties cannot be disclaimed. U.C.C. §2-313, Cmt. 1. This rules prevents burying a disclaimer of a salesperson's statements that constituted an express warranty in the fine print of the sales contract.

The following case considers what constitutes an express warranty and the elements of proving a breach of such warranty.

Sanders v. Apple Inc.
672 F. Supp. 2d 978 (N.D. Cal. 2009)

FOGEL, District Judge.

Plaintiffs Chandra Sanders ("Sanders"), Keith Yonai ("Yonai"), and Bonnier Corporation ("Bonnier") (collectively, "Plaintiffs") bring this putative class action on behalf of themselves and all persons who purchased a 2007 twenty-inch Aluminum iMac desktop computer designed, manufactured, and sold by Defendant Apple Inc. ("Apple"). Apple moves to dismiss the complaint pursuant to Federal Rules of Civil Procedure 12(b)(1) and 12(b)(6) and to strike all of the purported class claims. The Court has considered the briefing submitted by the parties as well as the oral arguments of counsel presented at the hearing on November 14, 2008. For the reasons set forth below, the motion will be granted, with leave to amend.

I. BACKGROUND

Apple is a leading manufacturer of personal computers and consumer electronics. One of Apple's most successful products is a personal desktop computer known as the iMac. Since its introduction in 1998, the iMac has undergone numerous revisions and updates. The most recent version of the iMac ("Aluminum iMac") was released in August 2007. Aluminum iMacs are available with a twenty-inch active-matrix liquid crystal display ("20-inch Aluminum iMac") or a twenty-four-inch active-matrix liquid crystal display ("24-inch Aluminum iMac").

The 20-inch Aluminum iMac and the 24-inch Aluminum iMac utilize different technologies to display digital images. All digital images consist of pixels, the smallest components of a digitalized picture. Each pixel is comprised of three "channels," which correspond to the three main colors used to display digital images: red, blue, and green. Every channel contains a certain number of "bits" — the smallest measure of digital information. A bit can take the value of either zero or one, or "on" or "off." The particular combination of "on" and "off" bits in each channel results in the desired color of that pixel. The number of bits in each pixel determines the total number of colors a computer monitor is capable of displaying.

The 24-inch Aluminum iMac utilizes an "eight-bit" monitor, capable of displaying 16,777,216 colors. The previous generation of 20-inch iMacs, which the Aluminum iMacs replaced, also used an "eight-bit" monitor. However, the new 20-inch Aluminum iMac uses a "six-bit" monitor that is able to display only 262,144 colors. To create the same effect as the "eight-bit" monitor, the "six-bit" monitor uses color simulation processes known as "dithering," and "frame rate control" ("FRC"), which causes the brain to perceive a particular color shade by perceiving many nearly identical shades. Specifically, dithering uses a combination of adjacent pixels to produce the desired shade. Through the FRC process, a single pixel displays alternating shades of color that are almost identical to the desired shade. When run at a high speed, these processes give the illusion of the desired color shade. Plaintiffs allege that the "emulation of true colors" through dithering can cause the appearance of transverse stripes in smooth color gradients and can result in flickering on particular images. They also assert that the 20-inch Aluminum iMacs have a narrower viewing angle, less color depth and accuracy, and are more susceptible to washout across the screen. Plaintiffs contend that these flaws are "particularly crippling" when displays that use this technology are used for image and video editing.

Plaintiffs allege that Apple markets both its 20-inch and 24-inch Aluminum iMacs for editing movies and photos and describes the display of both Aluminum iMacs as though they were interchangeable. Plaintiffs assert that at a press conference announcing the new Aluminum Macs on August 7, 2007, Apple CEO Steve Jobs claimed that photos and movies "look way better on these glossy, beautiful, crisp displays." In a press release issued that same day, Apple stated that the new iMac line "featured gorgeous 20-and 24-inch widescreen displays" that provide "incredibly crisp images, ideal for photos and movies. . ." Plaintiffs also assert that on its website, Apple states that: "[n]o matter what you like to do on your computer — watch movies, edit photos, play games, even just view a screen saver — it's going to look stunning on an iMac." Plaintiffs allege that Apple made each of these representations without revealing that the 20-inch Aluminum iMac uses "a significantly inferior display" to the display found in both the 24-inch Aluminum iMac and the

20-inch prior generation iMac. Plaintiffs also allege that in the "Technical Specifica-tions" for both the 20-inch and 24-inch Aluminum iMacs, the Apple website states: "[m]illions of colors at all resolutions" without disclosing that the 20-inch Alumi-num iMac is actually capable of displaying only 262,144 true colors.

Between January and March 2008, Plaintiff Bonnier purchased sixteen 20-inch Aluminum iMacs for various departments of its magazine publishing business. Bon-nier asserts that it purchased these computers based on its "positive experience and satisfaction with the two previous generations of iMacs that it owned." Yonai pur-chased his 20-inch Aluminum iMac in August 2007 for his graphics design business. Yonai alleges that he made his purchase based on "the information presented by . . . Apple on its website" and recommendations by friends in the graphics arts industry who owned previous generation iMacs. Bonnier and Yonai both allege that after purchasing their 20-inch Aluminum iMacs, they noticed color shifting on the screen. Yonai asserts that this color-shifting caused "problems with his graphics work." Plaintiffs allege that they "would not have acted as they did if they had known of the concealed material facts." Plaintiffs filed the instant action on March 31, 2008 on behalf of themselves and all persons or entities in the United States who own a 20-inch Aluminum iMac, alleging fraudulent concealment, breach of express warranty, violation under Unfair Competition Law ("UCL"), and unjust enrichment. [ED. NOTE—UCL is California's UDAP statute, as discussed in Assignment 9.]

. . .

C. CLAIM FOR BREACH OF EXPRESS WARRANTY

To plead an action for breach of express warranty under California law, a plaintiff must allege: (1) the exact terms of the warranty; (2) reasonable reliance thereon; and (3) a breach of warranty which proximately caused plaintiffs injury. Williams v. Beechnut Nutrition Corp., 185 Cal. App. 3d 135, 142, 229 Cal. Rptr. 605 (1986). A plaintiff also must plead that he provided the defendant with pre-suit notice of the breach. California Commercial Code §2607.

Yonai contends that Apple's representation that the 20-inch Aluminum iMac was capable of displaying "millions of colors" constituted an express warranty between the manufacturer and the Plaintiffs. He alleges that the inability of the 20-inch Alu-minum iMac to display "millions of colors" natively is a breach of this warranty, and that his reasonable reliance on this representation proximately caused damages. At issue is whether the phrase "millions of colors" constitutes an express warranty, whether a breach occurred, and whether reliance and notice are required to state a claim.

1. Whether Apple's Representation that the 20-inch Aluminum iMac Displays "Millions of Colors" Constitutes an Express Warranty

Statements constituting "mere puffery" cannot support liability under a claim for breach of warranty. See, e.g. Pulvers v. Kaiser Foundation Health Plan, Inc., 99 Cal. App. 3d 560, 565, 160 Cal. Rptr. 392 (1979). The distinguishing characteristics of puffery are "vague, highly subjective claims as opposed to specific, detailed factual assertions." Haskell v. Time, Inc., 857 F. Supp. 1392, 1399 (E.D. Cal. 1994).

Apple contends that "millions of colors at all resolutions" is a vague superlative as opposed to a specific, detailed factual assertion. "[C]ourts have held that such comparative claims, often involving large numbers, are puffing because a consumer cannot reasonably believe that there is a test behind the claim." In re General Motors Corp. Anti-Lock Brake Products Liab. Litig., 966 F. Supp. 1525 (E.D. Mo. 1997), aff'd, 172 F.3d 623 (8th Cir. 1999), see Avon Products, Inc. v. S.C. Johnson & Son, Inc., Case No. 94CIV3958, 1994 WL 267836, *7 (S.D.N.Y. Jun. 15, 1994) (stating that when the alleged representation contains a "round number one advertiser might select at random for the purpose of demonstrating a product's superiority, (e.g. 100 or 1,000), such a statement constitutes puffery.") (parenthetical in original). Apple notes that the San Diego Superior Court recently held that "vague superlatives are puffery and not actionable . . . [and t]his includes statements like MacBook supports 'millions of colors.'" See Exhibit A: December 13, 2007 San Diego County Superior Court Ruling in Case No. 37-2007-00066199-CBT-CTL.

Yonai asserts that "puffery is distinguishable from misdescriptions or false representations of specific characteristics of a product," Castrol Inc. v. Pennzoil Co., 987 F.2d 939, 945 (3d Cir. 1993), and that by using the phrase "millions of colors" in the "Technical Specifications" section on Apple's website, Apple made an actionable statement about the specific characteristics of the 20-inch Aluminum iMac. Yonai notes that other details provided within the technical specifications of the iMac include the amount of memory, processor speed, hard drive size, and electrical and operating requirements. Pl.'s Opp. to Mot. to Dismiss 14. Yonai also points out that the "round numbers" cases cited by Apple involved comparative assertions that a particular product was 100 or 1,000 times better than another product. Such statements were held to be non-actionable puffery because a consumer could not reasonably believe that there was a test behind the assertion that a product was 100 times better than another, see In re GMC, 966 F. Supp. at 1531, or because the comparative claim contained a round number conjured up by an advertiser. See Avon Products, Inc., Case No. 94CIV3958, 1994 WL 267836.

Here, Apple states that its monitors display "millions" of colors in a list of other technical specifications on which the consumer is expected to rely. Although in an advertising context the phrase "millions of colors" might be considered a vague superlative, the fact that the phrase was used in the technical specifications section of Apple's website transforms it into an express warranty upon which a potential buyer might rely in deciding whether to purchase the computer.

2. Whether a Breach Occurred

A claim for breach of an express warranty requires an actual breach. See Williams, 185 Cal. App. 3d at 142, 229 Cal. Rptr. 605. Yonai argues that Apple breached the express warranty that the 20-inch Aluminum iMac could display "millions of colors" because the computer does not "natively" display millions of colors, and instead can display only 262,144 colors. Yonai also alleges that the process of dithering used in the 20-inch Aluminum iMac monitor can trick the human eye into seeing certain colors and that it is able only to *approximate the number of colors possible on an 8-bit display.*

Apple argues that Yonai makes no factual allegation that he cannot *perceive* "millions of colors" on his 20-inch Aluminum iMacs and points to Yonai's concession that the purpose behind Apple's use of dithering is to approximate the number of colors appearing on the "eight-bit" display. Apple contends that it never represented that its monitors could "natively" display anything. Yonai alleges that Apple expressly warranted the capability of its 20-inch Aluminum iMac to display "millions of colors," and that providing the emulation of millions of colors through dithering does not satisfy this warranty. Yonai must allege in greater detail why the emulation of "millions of colors" generated by the dithering process amounts to a breach of the express warranty that the computer displays "millions of colors."

3. Whether Reliance Is Required

Yonai asserts that reliance is not required to support a claim for breach of express warranty, but rather that the statements become "part of the basis of the bargain" under California Commercial Code §2313. See Keith v. Buchanan, 220 Cal. Rptr. 392 (1985). However, another court this district has dismissed express warranty claims brought by a plaintiff who never saw the warranted statement, stating that "California courts have held that '[u]nder the law relating generally to express warranties a plaintiff must show reliance on the defendant's representation.'" Moncada v. Allstate Ins. Co., 471 F. Supp. 2d 987, 997 (N.D. Cal. 2006) (dismissing claim because plaintiffs presented no evidence that they actually read or relied upon the representations in the website). Although Yonai — the only named plaintiff with standing to sue — asserts that he looked at Apple's website, he fails to allege reasonable reliance on any specific representations Apple made with respect to the 20-inch Aluminum iMac.

. . .

Apple contends that Yonai may not base a nationwide class action on fraud and warranty claims because individual issues with respect to reliance overwhelmingly will predominate the litigation. Yonai responds to this argument by asserting that reliance is not a required element of fraudulent concealment or breach of express warranty.

As discussed above, reliance *is* a necessary element of a claim for breach of express warranty. . . . This requirement inquires into the specific facts surrounding each buyer's transaction, and is functionally equivalent to the "reliance element." If the proposed class were to be certified, the Court would be forced to engage in individual inquiries of each class member with respect to materiality of the statement, whether the member saw Apple's advertisements or visited Apple's website, and what caused the member to make the purchase. Moreover, since Yonai purports to bring a nationwide class action, these individual inquiries very likely would be subject to the differing state laws that may or may not apply.

Courts routinely hold that both fraud and warranty claims are difficult to maintain on a nationwide basis and rarely are certified. See Cole v. Gen. Motors Corp., 484 F.3d 717, 724-30 (5th Cir. 2007) (discussing at length why warranty claims are inappropriate for class treatment); Castano v. Am. Tobacco Co., 84 F.3d 734, 745 (5th Cir. 1996) ("a fraud class action cannot be certified when individual reliance is an issue."). In light of the foregoing, it is not clear that a nationwide class action is the "superior" method for adjudication of rights. Accordingly, the class allegations will be stricken, with leave to amend. The Court urges Plaintiffs to consider whether a more narrowly defined class might be appropriate.

Good cause therefore appearing, the motion to dismiss and to strike is granted, with leave to amend. Any amended complaint shall be filed within thirty (30) days of the date of this order.

The court also ruled that Yonai, the plaintiff, had failed to give notice to Apple, "within a reasonable time after he discover[ed] or should have discovered any breach, [a buyer must] notify the seller of breach or be barred from any remedy." Cal. Civ. Code §2607(3)(A). Under California law, there is an exception to the notice requirement: when a consumer brings an action against a manufacturer, which he or she did not deal with directly. Yonai shopped at Apple's online store and Apple was the manufacturer. Therefore, the court held that he was unable to use the exception. With the rise of Internet sales and the demise of general brick-and-mortar retail, the notice requirement may be applicable to more consumers. While avoiding the "middle man" may sound good, consumers will deal with more manufacturers, triggering the notice requirement.

2. Implied Warranties

In many transactions, both express and implied warranties exist and cover the same aspects of a good. Implied warranties arise regardless of seller conduct. For consumer goods, the two most important implied warranties are those of merchantability, U.C.C. §2-314, and fitness for a particular purpose, U.C.C. §2-315.

The warranty of merchantability applies only when the seller is a merchant, "a person who deals in goods of the kind or otherwise by his occupation holds himself out as having knowledge or skill peculiar to the practices or goods involved in the transaction . . ." U.C.C. §2-104(1). It imposes a promise that the goods are fit for the ordinary purpose for which they are to be used. In short, the goods cannot be so defective as to not be useful. Factors such as safety, efficiency, and comfort help determine whether goods meet their ordinary purpose.

The warranty of fitness applies to all sellers (not just merchants). It requires the goods to be suitable for the buyer's particular purpose. This warranty is narrower and more precise than the warranty of merchantability; both will often exist. Whereas with express warranties the focus was on the seller's conduct, with the implied warranty of fitness the focus will be on whether the buyer communicated the purpose of the purchase to the seller. The seller needs a "reason to know" of the particular purpose and that the buyer "is relying on the seller's skill or judgment to select or furnish suitable goods." U.C.C. §2-315.

Unlike express warranties, implied warranties can be disclaimed under certain circumstances. In general, the U.C.C. permits disclaimers of implied warranties but requires such disclaimers to be conspicuous and meet other standards. Despite a salesman representing that a car was "a good car" and "reliable," a court held that a sales contract stating that the car was "as is" was sufficient to disclaim the implied warranty of merchantability. The plaintiffs, whose car's engine blew less than a week after the sale, had no U.C.C. remedy. *Lester v. Wow Car Co.*, 2014 WL 2567097 (S.D. Ohio 2014). By contrast, the Magnuson-Moss Warranty Act, discussed below, prohibits the disclaimer of implied warranties if a "written warranty" or a "service contract" is provided.

B. Magnuson-Moss Warranty Act

Along with the UDAP statute, the Magnuson-Moss Warranty Act (M-M Act) is one of the cornerstones of consumer protection law. Like many of these archetypal consumer laws, it was enacted in the 1970s and focuses on empowering consumers by giving them information. For the novice, the major surprise about the M-M Act is that it does not require warranties in any circumstances. This is a major difference between the U.C.C. and the M-M Act. Instead, the M-M Act regulates disclosures by requiring that written warranties — if chosen to be offered — meet certain standards. The key legal concept in the M-M Act is the "written warranty." 15 U.S.C. §2301(6). A written warranty is a form of express warranty; it arises from a written affirmation of fact or written promise, or an undertaking in writing to refund, repair, replace, or provide another remedy if the product fails to meet specifications.

Written warranties must meet myriad requirements to comply with the M-M Act. At the most basic level, a written warranty must be in "simple and readily understood language" and disclose "fully and conspicuously" the terms and conditions of the warranty. 15 U.S.C. §2302(a). The FTC, which writes rules for the M-M Act, has stated that the warranty disclosures must be in a single document. 16 C.F.R. §701.3(a). The warranties also have to lay out made the identity of the parties, the scope of the warranty, the procedures to use the warranty, and the remedies available to the consumer. Note that in contrast to the U.C.C., the M-M Act only applies to consumers who are purchasing "consumer products" — tangible personal property normally used for personal, family, or household purposes. 15 U.S.C. §2301(1).

The M-M Act provides a cause of action for failure to comply with obligations under a written warranty or the failure to comply with an implied warranty created by state law. 15 U.S.C. §2310(d). Disclosure violations may also give rise to liability, although with all M-M Act claims the consumer must show that they were "damaged by the failure" in compliance. The remedies under M-M have some limitations but generally permit individual or class actions.

The M-M Act requires the labeling of written warranties as either "full" or "limited." A particular item may be covered with a full warranty as to some of its aspects and a limited warranty — or even no warranty — as to other aspects. 15 U.S.C. §2305. A full warranty must remedy a defect or malfunction of a consumer product within a reasonable time and without charge. While the full warranty may be only for a certain duration, which must be clearly stated, the offering of a full warranty carries with it the requirement that the seller may not impose any limitation of any implied warranty, such as those arising under the U.C.C. 15 U.S.C. §2304. A limited warranty can curtail the duration of implied warranties.

The case below shows the complex interaction between M-M, the U.C.C., and supplementary state warranty laws, such as California's Song-Beverly Act. Despite all those laws, the plaintiff found herself washed up.

Smith v. LG Electronics USA, Inc.

83 UCC Rep. Serv. 2d 92 (N.D. Cal. 2014)

Hamilton, District Judge.

This is a case filed as a proposed class action by plaintiff Laury Smith, against LG Electronics U.S.A., Inc., and Sears Holding Corp., asserting claims related to the design, manufacture, sale, and service of six models of top-loading LG brand and Kenmore brand automatic clothes-washing machines (three models of LG brand, and three models of Kenmore brand), which plaintiff alleges are defective.

Plaintiff alleges that the washing machines were labeled and advertised as "High Efficiency" machines featuring "extra high" spin speeds of 1050–1100 RPM, along with a system that prevents or minimizes vibrations, for smooth, quiet operation during use. Plaintiff claims, however, that the washing machines have inherent design defects that cause them to shake and vibrate excessively during use due to unbalanced loads, which in turn causes internal parts to become loose. Cplt ¶ 2.

Plaintiff alleges that she purchased a Kenmore Elite Model No. 29272 in November 2011, based on defendants' representations that the product was a "High Efficiency" machine, capable of "extra high" spin speed cycles at 1050 RPMs, which would help her dry her laundry faster than washing machines that do not have high efficiency capabilities. Cplt ¶¶ 6, 40-42. . . .

Plaintiff asserts that "from the very beginning," she experienced unbalanced loads that caused the machine to shake violently, make banging noises, rock from side to side, and move or "walk" itself away from the wall against which it was positioned. Cplt ¶¶ 6, 43-44. Indeed, she claims that the "violent movement" of her "defective machine" was so severe that the machine "would actually shift or 'walk itself' away from the wall on which it was positioned." Cplt ¶ 44. She alleges that to keep the machine from damaging the dryer positioned next to it, she used a plastic trash can as a "buffer" to help absorb the "shock of the shaking machine" and "attempt to keep it in place." Cplt ¶ 44. Nevertheless, she did not complain to Sears about the alleged defects until more than a year had passed after her purchase of the machine.

On December 18, 2012, the United States Consumer Products Safety Commission recalled the LG/Kenmore washing machines due to the risk of personal injury and property damage as a result of these alleged design defects. The recall announcement stated that "[a]n unbalanced load can cause the washing machine to shake excessively and the drum to come loose during use, posing a risk of injury to consumers and property damage to the surrounding area." The six models of recalled LG/Kenmore washing machines were manufactured between

February 2010 and November 2011, and were sold between April 2010 and December 2012. Cplt ¶¶ 2-3.

According to the recall announcement, as of the recall date, defendants had sold approximately 457,000 of the allegedly defective machines, and had received at least 343 reports of washing machines vibrating excessively, of which at least 187 involved property damage, and one report of minor injury. Cplt ¶ 25.

As part of the recall, customers were instructed to immediately contact LG or Sears for a free in-home repair, consisting of the installation of a software "upgrade" on the washing machines. Plaintiff asserts, however, that the software "upgrade" implemented by defendants was not an upgrade at all, but instead "fixed" the problem by capping the spin speed of the washing machines, such that the washing machines were no longer capable of operating at the advertised "extra high" spin speed setting of 1050–1100 RPM. Cplt ¶¶ 4, 26-27. Plaintiff contends that fast speed cycles are a desirable feature because they remove water from clothing faster, thereby shortening washing machine time, and leave consumers with drier clothes, thus shortening the time the clothes need to spend in the dryer. Thus, plaintiff alleges, the "upgrade" rendered the machines useless for the purpose for which they were advertised. Cplt ¶¶ 26-31.

Plaintiff asserts further that along with the software "upgrade," consumers were provided with a new caution label to be affixed to the washing machines, listing a number of washables that the washing machines are no longer capable of washing — items such as waterproof or water-resistant clothing, mattress covers, outdoor gear, and plastic mats. Cplt ¶ 32.

Plaintiff requested an in-home repair after hearing about the recall, and her washing machine was serviced in March 2013. However, she claims that after this repair, her machine no longer functions as represented in the product advertising, marketing, and Use & Care Guide; that it fails to wring out her clothing; and that it can no longer be used to launder certain machine-washable items. Cplt ¶¶ 45-46.

The washing machines are covered by a limited warranty. The Kenmore Use & Care Guide ("Kenmore Guide") and the LG Owner's Manual ("LG Manual") both provide an express limited warranty that "covers only defects in materials and workmanship," for one year from the date of purchase. The warranty further provides that the customer's exclusive remedy is repair (in the case of the Kenmore models) and repair or replacement at LG's option (in the case of the LG models). Furthermore, the warranty included in both the Kenmore Guide and the LG Manual limits the duration of the limited warranty, where allowed by law, to the shortest period allowed by law.

The Kenmore Guide and the LG Manual also contain specific instructions regarding how to operate the washing machines, including what users should avoid doing. For example, the Kenmore Guide cautions users against loading the washing machines with waterproof items.

Plaintiff filed the present action on September 19, 2013, asserting nine causes of action — (1) violation of the Magnuson–Moss Warranty Act, 15 U.S.C. §2301, et seq.; (2) breach of express warranty; (3) breach of the implied warranty of merchantability; (4) breach of the implied warranty of fitness for a particular purpose; (5) unjust enrichment; (6) violation of the Consumers Legal Remedies Act, Cal. Civ. Code §1750, et seq. ("CLRA"); (7) unlawful, unfair, and fraudulent business practices, in violation of the Unfair Competition Law, Cal. Bus. & Prof. Code §17200, et seq.; (8) false advertising, in violation of the False Advertising Law, Cal. Bus. & Prof. Code §17500, et seq.; and (9) violation of the Song-Beverly Consumer Warranty Act, Cal. Civ. Code §1790, et seq.

Defendants now seek an order dismissing all causes of action alleged in the complaint pursuant to Federal Rules of Civil Procedure 12(b)(6) and 9(b).

. . .

1. Breach of Express Warranty

Defendants assert that the complaint fails to state viable claims for breach of express warranty (first, second, and ninth causes of action), because the limited warranty does not cover alleged design defects and because plaintiff fails to allege facts sufficient to state a claim for breach of express warranty.

To state a claim for breach of express warranty, a plaintiff must allege that the defendant's statements constituted an affirmation of fact or promise or a description of one of the goods; that the statement was part of the benefit of the bargain; and that the warranty was breached. Weinstat v. Dentsply Int'l, Inc., 180 Cal. App. 4th 1213, 1227 (2010).

Plaintiff contends that her claims in this case are based on the express warranty, not on the limited warranty; at the hearing on the present motion, plaintiff's counsel confirmed that her claims were not based on the limited warranty in the manuals. Instead, plaintiff lists six statements she claims were "express warranties" that defendants breached. These are statements that the washing machines (a) were "High Efficiency" washers and "HE" compliant; (b) were Energy Star® compliant and thus water- and energy-efficient; (c) helped dry clothes faster using the "Extra High" spin cycles of 1050-1100 RPMs; (d) were safe for residential use and fit for everyday laundering needs; (e) "will provide many years of reliable service;" and (f) are "designed and manufactured for years of dependable service." Cplt ¶¶ 63, 72.

Defendants contend that plaintiff fails to plead facts sufficient to support the requisite elements of a breach of express warranty claim as to any of the six statements. First, defendants argue that the statements that the washers were "High Efficiency," would "provide many years of reliable service," "were designed and manufactured for years of dependable service," and were safe for residential use and fit of everyday laundering needs are non-actionable statements of opinion, not affirmations of fact or promise, or a description of one of the goods.

Under California law, "an affirmation merely of the value of the goods or a statement purporting to be merely the seller's opinion or commendation of the goods does not create a warranty." Cal. Com. Code §2313; Cal. Civ. Code §1791.2(a)(2)(b). Thus, to constitute a warranty and be actionable, the statement must be "specific and unequivocal." Johnson v. Mitsubishi Digital Elecs. Am., Inc., 578 F. Supp. 2d 1229, 1236 (C.D. Cal. 2008). Defendants assert that plaintiff's express warranty claims fail to the extent they are based on such generalized and vague statements of opinion and sales puffery.

Second, defendants contend that plaintiff has failed to plead facts showing that the statements at issue formed "the basis of the bargain." For a statement to form the basis of the bargain, the plaintiff must allege facts showing that she was exposed to the alleged statement prior to making the decision to purchase the product.

Sanders v. Apple Inc., 672 F. Supp. 2d 978, 988 (N.D. Cal. 2009); Moncada v. Allstate Ins. Co., 471 F. Supp. 2d 987, 997 (N.D. Cal. 2006). Here, defendants assert, plaintiff alleges only that the statements were printed in the user guides that accompanied the machines—not that she reviewed the guides and relied on the statements in deciding to make the purchase. Defendants also contend that the statement "High Efficiency" cannot have formed the basis of the bargain because plaintiff does not allege with sufficient particularity that she knew what this statement meant at the time of purchase.

Finally, defendants assert that plaintiff has failed to allege facts sufficient to show that defendants breached any express warranty. For example, they contend that the complaint does not relate to whether the washing machines were "High Efficiency," able to operate at the "Extra High" spin cycle," or whether they were Energy Star® and/or HE compliant, and that plaintiff does not allege that these statements were untrue at the time of purchase or during the one-year warranty period. They argue that plaintiff appears to be resting her warranty claims on alleged failures that manifested after the recall repair, and that the claim fails because an express warranty does not cover repairs after the applicable time period has elapsed.

In opposition, plaintiff argues that she has adequately pled facts supporting all elements of the claim of breach of express warranty. First, she asserts that the six statements were affirmations and promises. She concedes that product superiority claims that are vague or highly subjective may amount to non-actionable puffery, but argues that misdescriptions of specific or absolute characteristics of a product are actionable, and in particular, that representations as to the safety of consumer products are generally found to be affirmative statements of fact rather than opinions.

With regard to the representation that the washers would provide "many years of dependable service," plaintiff contends that this is an affirmative promise that can be objectively verified with the passage of time; and with regard to the representation that the washers were "High Efficiency," plaintiff asserts that "High Efficiency" is simply the long form of "HE," and that defendants do not challenge that the use of the "HE" logo has a precise meaning within the industry and can be considered an affirmative promise that constitutes an express warranty.

With regard to the second element—that the affirmation or promise was part of the basis of the bargain—plaintiff contends that affirmations, promises, and descriptions given at the time of purchase (including product manuals and other materials given to the purchaser at the time of delivery) can become part of the basis of the bargain, and can be fairly regarded as part of the contract.

With regard to the third element—that the seller breached the warranty—plaintiff argues that defendants breached the warranties that the machines were "HE" compliant, that they were Energy Star® compliant, that they functioned with a spin cycle of 1050-1100 RPMs, that they were "safe for residential use," and that they would provide "years of dependable service," because a design defect caused the washing machines to shake violently and pose a risk of property damage and personal injury. Moreover, she argues, the breach continued following the recall, because the "upgrade" capped the spin speeds at 700 RPMs, which prevented the machines from drying the clothes faster, saving energy, or operating as "High Efficiency" machines.

The court finds that the motion must be granted. Vague statements regarding reliability, dependability, and safety are not actionable express warranties. District courts within the Ninth Circuit have found that words such as "reliable" and "dependable" are inherently vague and general, and therefore are non-actionable, and that words regarding "safety" and "fitness for use" are not the unequivocal sorts of statements that can give rise to contractual obligations. See, e.g., Viggiano v. Hansen Natural Corp., 2013 WL 2005430, at *10-11 (C.D. Cal. May 13, 2013); Casteneda v. Fila USA, Inc., 2011 WL 7719013, at *4 (S.D. Cal. Aug. 10, 2011); Tietsworth v. Sears, 720 F. Supp. 2d 1123, 1136–37 (N.D. Cal. 2010); Johnson, 578 F. Supp. 2d at 1236 (C.D. Cal. 2008); Sanders, 672 F. Supp. 2d at 987.

Thus, statements that the machines were safe for residential use and fit for everyday laundering needs, that they would provide many years of reliable service, and that they were designed and manufactured for years of dependable service — are not statements of affirmation and promise, but rather non-actionable puffery. Such generalized advertisements say nothing about the specific characteristics or components of the machine, and include no guarantee, for example, that the machine will not require a repair within a specified period of time. Virtually identical statements have been found non-actionable by other courts. See, e.g., Oestreicher v. Alienware Corp., 544 F. Supp. 2d 964, 973 (N.D. Cal. 2008) (noting that statements of product superiority based on being "faster, more powerful, and more innovative," "higher performance," and having a "longer battery life" are "non-actionable puffery").

Moreover, of the statements that plaintiff has posited as the actionable "express warranties," she has not alleged facts showing that at the time of sale, the machines were not "High Efficiency," that they were not Energy Star® compliant, or that did not utilize spin cycles of 1050–1100 RPMs. Indeed, it appears from the allegations in the complaint that all these features were in fact present in the machines at the time of sale. Following the recall and the "fix" provided by defendants, the spin speed was lowered. However, this fact does not render false the statements made at the time of sale regarding efficiency and spin speed.

Finally, plaintiff fails to allege facts showing a *breach* of any express warranty. Plaintiff's position as set forth in the opposition appears to be that the statements at issue were independent express warranties with an unlimited duration — not that defendants breached the written express limited warranty. The general rule, however, is that a "seller may limit its liability for defective goods by disclaiming or modifying a warranty," and that an express warranty does not cover defects after the applicable warranty period has elapsed. *See* Daugherty v. American Honda Motor Co., Inc., 144 Cal. App. 4th 824, 830 (2006). In addition, "[w]ords or conduct relevant to the creation of an express warranty and words or conduct tending to negate or limit warranty shall be construed wherever reasonable as consistent with each other." Cal. Com. Code §2316(1).

Here, the only reasonable and consistent reading of the warranty and the alleged express warranty statements is to consider the warranty — including the one-year durational limitation — to apply to limit the duration of the six alleged express warranty statements at issue. The only alternative reading would be that the statements "created an express warranty . . . of indefinite duration" — which would be "wholly untenable," and "leave [Defendants] susceptible to a breach of warranty claim for every [machine] which, at any time, required repairs. . . ." Long v. Hewlett-Packard Co., 2007 WL 2994812, at *6 n.4 (N.D. Cal. Jul. 27, 2007).

To the extent that plaintiff's claims are based on what defendants refer to as the "recall efficiency issue" — the alleged reduction in efficiency following the software "upgrade" — plaintiff is alleging defects that first manifested after the recall repair, which resulted in the washing machines operating at slower spin speeds and purportedly neutralizing the benefits of the HE and Energy Star@ designations. See Cplt. ¶ 31. However, there was no breach as to any of the six alleged express warranties because plaintiff has not alleged that the recall efficiency issue rendered the alleged express warranties untrue during the applicable one-year warranty period.

It is clear from the allegations in the complaint that the recall efficiency issue surfaced only after the one-year warranty period expired. Plaintiff has not alleged that the washing machines did not perform as warranted by the HE logo, the Energy Star@ designation, and the spin speed throughout the warranty period. See Cplt ¶¶ 3-6 (alleging November 2011 purchase and December 2012 recall). In California, an express warranty does not include malfunctions that occur after the warranty has ended. See Elias v. Hewlett-Packard Co., 903 F. Supp. 2d 843, 850 (N.D. Cal. 2012). Thus, any warranty claim based on the recall efficiency issue fails.

Moreover, plaintiff alleges no facts to support her assertion that the alleged recall efficiency issue warranties were breached at any time. While plaintiff alleges that "High Efficiency" and "HE-compliant" are "affirmative promises" regarding the washing machines' water savings — that is, that they "use from 20% to 66% of the water used by traditional agitator washers," see Cplt ¶ 21 n.3 — the complaint contains no allegations of the machines' actual water usage at any time before or after the recall, much less a comparison to "traditional agitator washers." See Cplt ¶¶ 27, 45.

Similarly, although plaintiff claims that the Energy Star@ logo represents that the washing machines "use 40 to 50 percent less energy and about 55 percent less water than standard washers," Cplt ¶ 21 n.4, she pleads no facts regarding how much energy and water the washing machines consumed either before or after the recall, let alone any facts sufficient to support an inference that the washing machines no longer qualify for the Energy Star® designation.

2. Breach of Implied Warranties

Defendants argue that plaintiff fails to allege facts sufficient to support the elements of a claim for breach of implied warranties (third and fourth causes of action for breach of implied warranty of merchantability and breach of implied warranty of fitness for a particular purpose).

There exists in every contract for the sale of goods by a merchant a warranty that the goods shall be merchantable. Atkinson v. Elk Corp. of Texas, 142 Cal. App. 4th 212, 228 (2006). The core test of merchantability is fitness for the ordinary purpose for which such goods are used. Cal. Com. Code §2314(2); see also Hauter v. Zogarts, 14 Cal. 3d 104, 117-18 (1975) ("merchantability" requires that a product conform to its ordinary and intended use). Thus, to prevail on an implied warranty of merchantability claim, the plaintiff must demonstrate that the alleged defect renders the subject goods unfit for their ordinary purpose. See Southern Cal. Stroke Rehabilitation Assocs., Inc., 782 F. Supp. 2d 1096, 1112 (S.D. Cal. 2011).

To state a claim for breach of the implied warranty of fitness for a *particular* purpose, a plaintiff must allege facts showing that (1) at the time of purchase, the buyer intended to use the product for a particular purpose; (2) the seller had reason to know this; (3) the buyer relied on the seller's judgment to select suitable goods for that purpose; (4) the seller had reason to know that the buyer was relying on seller in this way; and (5) the product failed to suit buyer's purpose and subsequently damaged the buyer. Keith v. Buchanan, 173 Cal. App. 3d 13, 25 (1985).

A "particular purpose" differs from "the ordinary purpose for which the goods are used" in that it "envisages a specific use by the buyer which is peculiar to the nature of his business whereas the ordinary purposes for which goods are used are those envisaged in the concept of merchantability and go to uses which are customarily made of the goods in question." American Suzuki Motor Corp. v. Superior Court, 37 Cal. App. 4th 1291, 1295 n.2 (1995) (quoting Cal. Com. Code §2315, UCC Code Comment 2).

Under California law, implied warranties are "co-extensive in duration with an express warranty" and "in no event shall . . . have a duration of . . . more than one year following the sale." Cal. Civ. Code §1791.1(c). Thus, any implied warranties for the washing machines were valid for a period of no more than one year from the date of purchase. See Tietsworth, 720 F. Supp. 2d at 1142; In re Sony Grand Wega KDF–E A10/A20 Series Rear Projection HDTV Television Litig., 758 F. Supp. 2d 1077, 1100 (S.D. Cal. 2010).

Defendants contend that plaintiff has failed to allege facts showing that the washing machines were unfit for their *ordinary* purpose (washing clothes) during the applicable one-year warranty period (or that even if they were, that she notified defendants within a reasonable time); and has failed to allege that the washing machines were unfit for her *particular* purpose because she has pled no facts showing that her purpose was anything other than the ordinary one of washing clothes.

In response, plaintiff contends that the complaint adequately pleads that the washing machines are not merchantable, and that a washing machine that vibrates and makes excessive noise, and does not wring out clothes, is not fit for its intended purpose. She also asserts that the particular purpose for which she purchased the machine was the ability to operate it at 1050-1100 RPMs, and for the benefit of the specified efficiency standards. She argues that her claim is not barred by the one-year limitation on claims for breach of implied warranties, because the alleged defect was "latent" and "hidden from consumers who could not have identified the defect."

The court finds that the motion must be granted. As stated above, in California, implied warranties are "co-extensive in duration with an express warranty," and "in no event shall . . . have a duration of . . . more than one year following the sale." Cal. Civ. Code §1791.1(c). Here, plaintiff purchased the washing machine in November 2011. While she alleges that she had problems with the washing machine "from the very beginning," Cplt ¶ 43, she nonetheless bases her warranty claims on events that occurred more than a year after the date of purchase. She requested an in-home repair well after the one-year period had elapsed, but based on the allegations in the complaint, that request was prompted only by the recall announcement.

In addition, with regard to the claim for breach of the implied warranty of merchantability, the ordinary purpose of a washing machine is to wash clothes. Plaintiff has not alleged facts showing that defendants breach of the implied warranty of merchantability, which requires that a product conform to its ordinary and intended use. As for the claim for breach of the implied warranty of fitness for a particular purpose, plaintiff has identified no "particular purpose" for which she purchased the washing machine. She purchased it to wash her laundry, which is the "ordinary" purpose of a washing machine.

———————————

Perhaps the most important function of the U.C.C.'s warranty provisions are in the shadow of the law. Many retailers have "no-questions-asked" policies that permit exchanges or refunds for goods. As a practical matter, these voluntary responses to unsatisfied consumers dramatically reduce the need for formal legal charges that a product fails to meet the U.C.C. warranties. Similarly, rather than deal with the procedural requirements of making a claim with the manufacturer under the M-M Act consumers simply line up at the customer return counter of a local retailer. The law cannot hold a candle to a merchant's best customer service in terms of remedying problems with products, but it is also true that the law has influenced the rise of such policies.

C. Statutory Warranties

Certain products, usually high-dollar transactions or high-risk goods, have specific statutory warranties. Such laws generally address perceived weaknesses or gaps in coverage of the U.C.C. and the M-M Act and are explicitly pro-con-sumer. (Recall that the U.C.C. warranty rules apply to both businesses and consumers, and that M-M does not require any warranty at all.)

The classic example of a statutory warranty is a "lemon law," which requires manufacturers to try to repair defective cars, and if that proves ineffective to provide the consumer with a remedy. A car is not a lemon merely because a consumer identifies some flaws. Most statutes require a substantial impair-ment of value, use, or safety. Lemon laws obligate only the manufacturer, and not the dealer, to provide redress to consumers. The lemon laws typically limit the number of repair attempts that a manufacturer is allowed before the consumer is entitled to the better remedy of replacement or refund.

All fifty states have such laws that cover new cars and other new vehicles; only a half dozen states have lemon or similar laws for used cars. With used vehicles, the major remedies remain the express and implied warranties under the U.C.C. Other examples of products covered by statutory warranties are wheelchairs and other assistive devices, and manufactured homes, which sometimes escape from coverage under the U.C.C. if they are sold as part of a transaction with underlying real property.

The consumer in the upcoming case relied on the multiple warranty laws to seek relief, as did the plaintiff in *Smith v. LG Electronics*. With the addition of the lemon law and M-M Act, however, the plaintiff cruised to victory.

———————————

Milicevic v. Fletcher Jones Imports, LTD

402 F.3d 912 (9th Cir. 2005)

BEA, Circuit Judge.

Defendants-Appellants Fletcher Jones Imports and Mercedes-Benz USA (collectively "Mercedes") appeal from the district court's judgment in favor of Plaintiff-Appellee Marina Milicevic following a bench trial. Milicevic sued for damages due to defects in the Mercedes S-500 automobile she purchased from Fletcher Jones Imports. Her Nevada state court complaint alleged breach of express warranty, breach of the implied warranties of merchantability and fitness, violation of Nevada Revised Statute §§597.600-597.680 (2000) (Nevada's "lemon law"), and violation of the federal Magnuson-Moss Warranty Act, 15 U.S.C. §§2301-2312 (1998). Mercedes removed the case to federal court based on federal question jurisdiction.

The district court found that Mercedes breached its written warranty and violated both the Nevada lemon law and the Magnuson-Moss Warranty Act. The district court awarded Milicevic damages under the Nevada lemon law and attorneys' fees under the Magnuson-Moss Warranty Act.

Mercedes contends the district court incorrectly found a violation of the Nevada lemon law. Mercedes also contends that the district court incorrectly applied the Magnuson-Moss Warranty Act and that its award of attorneys' fees under the act was improper. Milicevic cross-appeals the amount of attorneys' fees awarded as insufficient. She also claims Mercedes' appeal is moot because Mercedes paid the judgment and, therefore, there is no longer a "case or controversy" between the parties. We have jurisdiction and affirm.

BACKGROUND

Milicevic purchased a new Mercedes S-500 from Fletcher Jones Imports on May 11, 2001, for $98,722.25. From day one, the car exhibited a number of aesthetic and mechanical problems. Within the first seven months, the following repairs were made: all four brake rotors were warped and required replacement at 6,000 miles; after locking Milicevic out of the car, the remote entry system was replaced; the motor for the passenger side window was replaced; the passenger side mirror was replaced due to a thumb print in the paint; and the rear window seal and molding were unsuccessfully repaired three times. All repairs were made under Mercedes' limited written warranty. By the end of seven months, the car had spent 55 days at Fletcher Jones' repair shop.

At that point, Milicevic wanted Mercedes to replace the car or to reimburse her for the purchase price and take the car back. Her attorney and then-fiancé, Christopher Gellner, wrote a letter to Mercedes-Benz to that effect, explaining the series of problems and repairs. Aside from a cursory letter notifying Gellner that he would be contacted by a local representative of Mercedes-Benz in the near future, Mercedes-Benz did not respond to Gellner's letter, even though he made a series of unreturned phone calls. Milicevic sued Mercedes-Benz and Fletcher Jones Imports. . . .

The contested issues addressed at trial were whether: (1) the brakes on Milicevic's car were "defective"; (2) it was necessary for Milicevic to leave the car at Fletcher Jones for an extended period while parts were on order for the rear window repair; and (3) the unsuccessful repair of the rear window was "significant." Ultimately, Milicevic testified at trial that she found the car's use and value impaired: "I feel like I am stranded. I cannot feel comfortable to take the car on a trip. I do not feel comfortable to drive because I don't know what next will come. [E]very day is a new problem."

. . .

NEVADA LEMON LAW

The district court did not commit clear error when it found a violation of the Nevada lemon law. There was sufficient evidence to support the district court's finding that after a reasonable number of attempts at repair had been made, a reasonable person would have found the use and value of the car substantially impaired, as did Milicevic.

The Nevada lemon law states that if an automobile manufacturer, its agent or its authorized dealer is not able to conform a vehicle to its warranty after a reasonable number of attempts to repair the vehicle have been made, and the nonconformity substantially impairs the use and value of the vehicle to the buyer, it must replace the vehicle or give the purchaser a refund of the purchase price, including taxes and fees, less a deduction for the reasonable use of the vehicle. Nev. Rev. Stat. §597.630(1). If within the first year, or within the time the warranty is in effect, whichever is less, the same condition is subject to repair four or more times or the vehicle is out of service for repair more than 30 calendar days for reasons not beyond the control of the manufacturer, its agent or its authorized dealer, it is presumed that a reasonable number of attempts to repair the vehicle have been made. Nev. Rev. Stat. §597.630(2). When the vehicle is out of service more than 30 calendar days, the nonconformity does not have to be ongoing. See id.

Here the presumption that a reasonable number of attempts at repair had been made was appropriate because Milicevic's car was subject to repair four or more times within the first year for the condition both of the brakes and of the rear window, conditions which Fletcher Jones never successfully repaired. Additionally, the district court did not clearly err in finding that Milicevic's car was out of service for repair a cumulative total of 55 days during the first year.

Although Mercedes claims that the vehicle was only "out of service" for repair 24 days, discounting 31 days Milicevic's car was at Fletcher Jones awaiting the arrival of parts needed to fix the rear window seal, Fletcher Jones ordered the wrong part for the repair. When a repair is delayed by the unavailability of a part, the time under section 597.630(2)(b) is not tolled. Cf. Ayer v. Ford Motor Co., 200 Mich. App. 337, 503 N.W.2d 767, 770 (1993) ("To allow a defendant to assert the unavailability of parts as a reason for failing to make timely repairs would defeat the statute's intent to place the risk of inconvenience and monetary loss on the manufacturer rather than the consumer."). Milicevic had no control over the ordering of the parts, nor was she in a position to know how long the necessary parts would take to arrive. She left her car at Fletcher Jones while the parts were on order because she was told the repair would take only a few days. The responsibility for the timeliness of the repair rested with Fletcher Jones.

ATTORNEYS' FEES UNDER THE MAGNUSON-MOSS WARRANTY ACT

A. The Magnuson-Moss Warranty Act Creates a Federal Private Cause of Action for a Warrantor's Failure to Comply with the Terms of a Written Warranty

Subject to certain conditions with which Milicevic complied, the Magnuson-Moss Warranty Act creates a federal private cause of action for a warrantor's failure to comply with the terms of a written warranty: "[A] consumer who is damaged by the failure of a warrantor to comply with any obligation under a written warranty may bring suit for damages and other legal and equitable relief in an appropriate district court of the United States." 15 U.S.C. §2310(d)(1)(B). To the extent Mercedes argues to the contrary, the cases on which it relies are inapposite.

First, Mercedes cites the following language from *Skelton v. General Motors Corp.*, 660 F.2d 311 (7th Cir. 1981): "The district court properly rejected plaintiffs' argument that the Act's draftsmen intended in [Section 2310(d)] to create a federal private cause of action for breach of *all* written express warranties." Id. at 316 (emphasis added). The context for the Seventh Circuit's statement, however, is essential. The district court had held that the written promises at issue were not "written warrant[ies]" as defined in Section 2301(6), and the plaintiffs did not appeal that holding. Id. at 316 n. 7. Rather, the plaintiffs argued that all written promises constituted written warranties for the purposes of Section 2310(d)(1). The Seventh Circuit rejected the plaintiffs' argument, holding that the definition of "written warranty" provided in Section 2301(6) applied wherever "written warranty" was used throughout the Magnuson-Moss Warranty Act. Id. at 322. Unlike General Motors' written promises, which the Seventh Circuit presumed not to amount to warranties under Section 2301(6), as we explain below, the express limited warranty given by Mercedes does qualify as a written warranty.

In *Walsh v. Ford Motor Co.*, 807 F.2d 1000 (D.C. Cir. 1986), the D.C. Circuit held: "[E]xcept in the specific instances in which Magnuson-Moss expressly prescribes a regulating rule, the Act calls for the application of state written and implied warranty law, not the creation of additional federal law." Id. at 1012. Again, however, the context is crucial. There, the plaintiffs sought certification of three classes in an action brought under the Magnuson-Moss Warranty Act for breach of written and implied warranties. Id. at 1002. Despite the fact that the plaintiffs resided in several different states and that there were variations in state laws governing the interpretation of written and implied warranties, the district court "apparently believed that the federal Act alone, uncomplicated by 'any State law variations,' covered the class members' 'claims for breach of written warranty,'" id. at 1011, and, as for the claims for breach of implied warranty, interpreted the Magnuson-Moss Warranty Act as mandating a "somewhat looser application of Rule 23." Id. at 1003-05. The D.C. Circuit granted interlocutory appeal on the issue of class certification, concluded the district court improperly construed the Magnuson-Moss Warranty Act, and instructed the district court to reexamine whether the variance in state warranty laws prohibited the finding (required for class certification) that common questions of law predominated.

Id. at 1012. However, at no point did the D.C. Circuit suggest that there was no federal cause of action under the Magnuson-Moss Warranty Act.

Thus, it is clear from the statutory language that the Magnuson-Moss Warranty Act creates a private cause of action for a warrantor's failure to comply with the terms of a written warranty, and none of the cases cited by Mercedes support a contrary position. Finally, in this regard, whether the written warranty is full or limited makes no difference. Although the Magnuson-Moss Warranty Act distinguishes between full and limited warranties, it nonetheless refers to each as a written warranty. 15 U.S.C. §2303(a)(1)-(2). Likewise, Section 2301(6) defines a "written warranty" without limiting it to either full or limited warranties, and Section 2310(d)(1) does not limit its application to either full or limited warranties.

B. Milicevic Had a Limited Written Warranty and the District Court's Findings Support the Conclusion that Mercedes Was in Breach of that Warranty

As defined in the Magnuson-Moss Warranty Act, a written warranty is a writing made by the supplier of a product relating to the nature of the material or workmanship of the product, which warranty promises that the product is defect free or will meet a certain level of performance for a given period of time, or a writing in which the supplier agrees to refund, repair, replace, or take other remedial action in the event that the product fails to meet its specifications. 15 U.S.C. §2301(6). Here, Mercedes supplied such a limited written warranty, which by its terms "warrants to the original and each subsequent owner of a new Mercedes-Benz passenger car that any authorized Mercedes-Benz Center will make any repairs or replacements necessary to correct defects in material or workmanship" at no charge for parts or labor.

The district court did not clearly err in finding that two significant nonconformities — the rear window seal and the brakes — were not corrected. A Fletcher Jones mechanic admitted that the rear window seal was a "factory defect," and Mercedes never corrected the defect. And even after the brake pads and rotors were replaced, Milicevic testified the brakes still did not work properly. The district court also found that all of the defects, conditions and non-conformities complained of by plaintiff, which Fletcher Jones was unable to repair, were covered by Mercedes-Benz's said warranty. We are not firmly convinced this was in error. Even though the warranty provides that "normal maintenance" of items was the owner's responsibility, it also states:

> Our intention is to repair under warranty, without charge to you, anything that goes wrong with your car during the warranty period which is our fault? Please note the difference between "defects" and "damage" as used in the warranty. Defects are covered since we, the manufacturer or distributor are responsible.

The rear window seal and brakes were repaired under warranty at no cost to Milicevic. By attempting to repair the rear window seal and the brakes under warranty, Mercedes admitted the defective nature of these conditions. Thus, when it failed to correct the defects in the rear window seal and brakes, Mercedes breached the terms of its limited written warranty in violation of Section 2310(d)(1).

C. The District Court Did Not Abuse Its Discretion
in Its Award of Attorneys' Fees

Having made out a claim for relief under the Magnuson-Moss Warranty Act, Milicevic may be awarded reasonable costs and attorneys' fees. 15 U.S.C. §2310(d)(2). With respect to attorneys' fees, the Magnuson-Moss Warranty Act gives courts discretion to award "reasonabl[e]" attorneys' fees "based on actual time expended." Id. The district court did not abuse its discretion when it concluded that the hourly rate requested by Milicevic's attorneys was not reasonable and, thus, eliminated hours it thought were unnecessarily duplicative. American Law Center PC v. Stanley (In re Jastrem), 253 F.3d 438, 443 (9th Cir. 2001). The evidence in the record supports the conclusion that it was not necessary to have both Gellner and Haley prepare for trial in this case. Mercedes informed Gellner of its intent to call Gellner as a witness in advance of trial. Once Gellner knew he might be called to testify, the district court found Gellner could have turned over to Haley the task of trial preparation. Such a finding was well within the discretion of the district court. Further, the case was not overly complicated and did not require any special expertise. Last, the district court was well within its discretion in reducing the hourly rate and hours upon which Milicevic based her attorneys' fee request.

CONCLUSION

For the foregoing reasons, we affirm the district court's judgment and its award of attorneys' fees.

The M-M Act provided the attorney with fees. The "actual time expended" language is designed to prevent a cost-benefit analysis of attorneys' fees in which a court concludes that it is not "reasonable" for an attorney to charge ten thousand dollars pursuing a remedy for a car that cost only a few thousand dollars. While purchasing a nearly six-figure car is one way to ensure that the remedy is worth the candle, we cannot all drive a Mercedes. Consumer laws aim to keep people out of lemons.

Problem Set 10

10.1. Willett Bird loves to bargain hunt and frequents yard sales in Brooklyn. These are often called "stoop" sales due to the lack of any real yard and are held on the steps of brownstones. Willett recently came across a top-of-the-line, new model eFone for sale for only $15. He visually inspected the product, noting that it was free of scratches, dents, or other obvious problems. He noticed the eFone did not turn on when he pushed the power button. He asked the seller, Kami, if the eFone worked, saying that he really wanted to replace his Robot phone. Kami explained that it probably had a dead battery but that she had thrown out the charger. Willett asked why she was selling the eFone rather than buying a new charger. Kami explained that the eFone was a gift from her former girlfriend and that she wanted to get rid of everything that reminded her of her lost love—charger, phone, everything. Kami offered to throw in a Yankees T-shirt along with the eFone if Willett made the purchase for $15, reassuring him that the eFone was "fine as far as she knew." Willett paid up and later spent $30 purchasing a charger at a retail store. The eFone, however, only held a charge for 10 seconds, no matter how long Willett allowed it to charge. Willett remembers where Kami lives, and he is not happy that his bargain turned out to be a bust. Does a warranty cover this product? If so, what are Willett's remedies? *See* 15 U.S.C. §§2301 and 2310(d); U.C.C. §§2-104(1), 2-313, 2-314, and 2-315, and 2-608; 2-714(2).

10.2. You are an associate at Virginia's largest plaintiff-side law firm. The senior partner has jetted off (literally, he owns a jet due to the firm's lucrative profit from suing businesses in the last few years) and left you with a research project. TechTown, a big-box retailer, sells consumer electronics. For any purchases over $1,000, TechTown requires consumers to complete a warranty information form at the point-of-sale either using the electronic keypad or if the consumer balks, a paper form. The form collects information about the consumer and clearly states the terms of the warranty, including all information in section 2302(a) of the M-M Act. The warranty is labeled "Full Warranty for 5 Days." Is TechTown violating the law? You know the partner will want your advice on maximizing the firm's recovery in a case against a deep-pocket defendant such as TechTown. *See* 15 U.S.C. §§2302(b); 2304; 16 C.F.R. §700.7.

10.3. About a year ago, Everett was driving his Kruz car home from work when he heard a clunking noise in his car. It's a long commute and the freeway was packed. Fearing a breakdown, Everett pulled over and went to the nearest automobile shop with reliable Internet reviews. The mechanic quickly replaced a part, charged $39.99, and got Everett back on the road. Six months later, when the Kruz would not start, despite an effort to jump the battery, Everett called the Kruz dealer where he purchased the car as a new vehicle two years ago. At the service appointment, the Kruz dealer's mechanic, Kris, explained the problem was with the transmission. He quoted $2,178 to fix it, inclusive of parts and labor. Everett was shocked as the car was covered by a "bumper-to-bumper" three-year warranty. Kris stated that Everett had voided the warranty entirely, and handed him the warranty booklet for his vehicle, pointing to this paragraph:

> Have maintenance and repair work performed by your Kruz dealer. Make sure that all work is noted by the repair person in this booklet. These entries are evidence of your vehicle maintenance and are a requirement for warranty claims.

Everett asked to speak to the dealer's owner and questioned whether the transmission problem was related to the part replacement. "Probably not," replied the Kruz dealer, "but you gotta read the fine print in life. We don't want incompetent mechanics ever touching Kruz cars. It's part of how we track problems and ensure quality." Does Everett have any remedy against Kruz? What is the possible extent of Kruz's liability? 15 U.S.C. §§2302; 2310.

10.4. Sohee loves her boyfriend Brian but their relationship is stuck. Sohee resists spending the night at Brian's house, deeming it unusual for its minimalist furnishings. While Sohee doesn't mind bringing things such as travel size Kleenex and a water cup in her overnight bag, she is grossed out by sharing one towel. When the two got into an argument in the middle of Taco Tuesday at a local restaurant, Sohee whipped out her phone and ordered towels from Happy Home using its mobile site. "Problem solved," she announced, particularly pleased that if three towels were purchased together, the price was only $36 total. When the towels arrived, however, Sohee's bliss disappeared. After one washing, most of the fluff disappeared and the towels became threadbare. Sohee contacted Happy Home but they refused to provide a refund. Happy Home directed her to a section on the bottom right of its homepage entitled "Warranty Information." That link forwards to a webpage with this text: "Happy Home disclaims the warranty of merchantability for all products sold on this site. Goods are never returnable." Are the towels covered by a warranty? Does Happy Home's conduct raise liability under any other laws? See U.C.C. §§2-314, 2-316; 16 C.F.R. §702.

Assignment 11. Usury

In nearly every consumer purchase, price is a key term. With goods, there are generally no limits on what a business can charge, assuming it is avoiding anti-competitive pricing that would violate the antitrust laws. With financial products such as loans, price is nearly always regulated. The interest rate that can be charged prevents expensive borrowing.

If that last statement seems wrong to you, it's likely because you have been living in the United States in the last thirty years. Across history, cultures, and geography, the statement is correct that law limits interest rates. It is flatly wrong, however, with respect to the United States today. In most instances, the price of consumer credit is not curbed. Interest rates reflect what lenders believe that consumers are willing to pay to borrow. The modern U.S. approach of unconstrained credit cost is unusual in historical and comparative context.

Usury is the term to describe charging an illegally (or unacceptably) high interest rate. This assignment examines the usury laws that exist in the U.S. and why they have only narrow applicability. We then look at the ongoing policy debates about usury and the reluctance of lawmakers to limit interest rates directly.

A. Historical and Comparative Contexts of Usury

Usury laws are one of the most ancient and primal forms of consumer protection. Steven Mercatante, *The Deregulation of Usury Ceilings, Rise of Easy Credit, and Increasing Consumer Debt*, 53 S.D. L. Rev. 37, 39 (2008). The basic tension is between historical beliefs that charging interest is morally wrong and the fact that money lending is necessary for economic growth. The moral issue came into sharp context because of harsh debt collection laws that allowed a creditor to enslave a borrower. The injunctions against usury date back to at least 3000 B.C., and can be found in the Old Testament. The Catholic Church condemned usurious lending, and indeed charging interest was not clearly legalized in England until the mid 1500s. The rate was capped at 10 percent, and later lowered to 5 percent by the Statute of Anne enacted in 1713. A longstanding example of usury can be found in Sharia law, which is based on Islamic teachings.

Exceptions and workarounds were and are common, however, as lenders want to skirt price limits on credit. Some exceptions drew boundaries based on the borrower. For example, traditionally while one Jew could not charge to lend to another, a Jew could make loans with interest to Christians and other non-Jews. Business people lending to each other also were sometimes exempted from usury limits. Other strategies involved characterizing loans as other kinds of transactions; the "interest" was restructured to be a "fee" or the like. Examples are assignments of rents or investments with guaranteed returns. In his book, *Pious Property: Islamic Mortgage in the United States* (2006), Bill Maurer describes how U.S. consumers who follow Sharia law effectively obtain the equivalent of mortgages at an approximate market rate of interest using lease-to-own arrangements or cost-plus contracts for home purchases.

From the colonial period onward, every U.S. state had some form of law limiting the interest rate on at least some categories of loans. The thirteen colonies had annual rates limits between 5 and 8 percent at the time of the Declaration of Independence. Christopher Peterson, *Usury Law, Payday Loans, and Statutory Sleight of Hand: Salience Distortion in American Credit Pricing Limits*, 92 Minn. L. Rev. 1110, 1118 tbl. 1 (2008). Usury laws remain on the books in most states today.

Despite the federalization of many laws governing consumer credit, the United States has never had a federal usury law that applied to all consumers. Most other nations do have such a law. Examples are South Africa and Thailand. A useful comparison point for the U.S. is the European Union. At least 14 member states have ceilings on contractual interest rates; these states as well as several others also cap default or penalty interest rates. The maximum rate is usually based on a reference rate that fluctuates with economic conditions, including the nation's central bank policies. The rates also often vary by credit product, from low ceilings in the single digit for mortgages to double digits for shorter-term loans or loans without collateral.

Usury statutes can be civil or criminal. The latter approach reflects the hefty moral component to these laws. Canada has a national usury law that limits the interest rate to 60 percent per year. Canada Criminal Code R.S.C. 1985, c. C-46. An offense is a crime punishable by imprisonment for a term not exceeding five years, or a fine of up to $25,000 or to imprisonment not exceeding six months or both, if found liable on summary conviction. Violating a usury statute, civil or criminal, also typically results in courts refusing to enforce collection of the debt, or at least eliminate the interest component of the debt. Because usury is a defense to the legality of a loan, it is usually raised by people who have not paid. Most violations of usury requirements are not detected, however, because people simply pay the stated rate. It is particularly difficult to enforce usury laws in informal lending, or consumer-to-consumer loans. Ask yourself what rate you charged the last time you agreed to make a loan to your youngest sibling?

B.   State Statutes

Most states do have usury laws, but these statutes have a sharply limited reach. The following case describes the Supreme Court decisions that dismantled state usury protections and shows a court trying to look elsewhere in the law to address a perceived wrong that amounts to charging too high of a price for credit.

Citibank (South Dakota), N.A. v. Rosemary Walker DeCristoforo

28 Mass. L. Rptr. 139 (Jan. 4, 2011)

CORNETTA, Judge.

INTRODUCTION

The plaintiff, Citibank (South Dakota), N.A. ("Citibank"), filed the current action for account stated to recover a debt the defendant, Rosemary Walker DeCristoforo ("DeCristoforo"), purportedly owes it with respect to two delinquent credit card accounts. In response, DeCristoforo filed a counterclaim, alleging Citibank charged her interest in an amount greater than allowed by federal law. The matter is currently before the court on the parties' cross motions for summary judgment. . . .

FACTUAL BACKGROUND

The material facts do not appear to be in dispute. Citibank is a national banking association located in South Dakota. DeCristoforo is an individual residing in Beverly, Massachusetts.

On October 1, 1984, DeCristoforo opened a credit card line of credit with Citibank, which has a current account number ending in 8960 (the "1984 Account"). Almost ten years later, on March 14, 1994, DeCristoforo opened a second credit card line of credit with Citibank, which has a current account number ending in 6865 (the "1994 Account"). DeCristoforo used the 1984 and 1994 Accounts to obtain credit from Citibank to acquire goods, services, and/or cash advances.

Citibank mailed periodic billing statements for the 1984 and the 1994 Accounts to the address DeCristoforo provided. The last payment posted to the 1994 Account on August 14, 2008 in the amount of $316.15. The last payment posted to the 1984 Account on August 20, 2008 in the amount of $812.36. As of March 12, 2009, the outstanding balance on the 1994 Account, as reflected on its monthly statement, was $8,465.69. As of May 7, 2009, the outstanding balance on the 1984 Account, as reflected on its monthly statement, was $25,870.44.

With respect to all unpaid amounts owed under the 1984 Account, as asserted in monthly statements to DeCristoforo, dated January 8, 2001 thru May 7, 2009, Citibank charged interest at annual rates of no less than 14.4% and no greater than 32.24%, exclusive of late fees and other charges. With respect to all unpaid amounts owed under the 1994 Account, as asserted in monthly statements to DeCristoforo, dated July 13/August 13, 2001 thru February 12/March 12, 2009, Citibank charged interest at annual rates of no less than 10.65% and no greater than 54.7333%, exclusive of late fees and other charges.

DISCUSSION

. . .

In support of summary judgment on her counterclaims, DeCristoforo argues 12 U.S.C. §85 ("Section 85") caps interest at seven percent and that Citibank violated this provision by charging interest, on the 1984 Account, between 14.4% and 32.24%, and on the 1994 Account, between 10.65% and 54.7333%. In response, Citibank contends Section 85 is not applicable in this case because, in accordance with the Supreme Court's holding in *Daggs v. Phoenix Nat'l Bank*, 177 U.S. 549 (1900), this provision only applies where the bank's home state does not allow for any interest. Since Citibank is headquartered in South Dakota and South Dakota allows interest at any rate agreed upon in writing, according to Citibank, it can charge interest at any rate agreed upon between it and its credit card customers. This dispute highlights an issue of national concern — mounting credit card debt and unregulated interest rates, which make paying that debt next to impossible.

A. Section 85

To help finance the Civil War, in 1861, then Treasury Secretary, Salmon P. Chase, recommended the federal government establish a national banking system whereby national banks could be chartered by the federal government and authorized to issue bank notes secured by government bonds. This idea came to fruition a few years later, in 1864, when the National Banking Act was enacted. Section 85 was included in the National Banking Act to protect against usurious interest rates.

Section 85 provides, in relevant part, that

> [a]ny association may . . . charge on any loan . . . or upon . . . other evidences of debt, interest at the rate allowed by the laws of the State . . . where the bank is located . . . and no more, except that where by the laws of any State a different rate is limited for banks organized under State laws, the rate so limited shall be allowed for associations organized or existing in any such State under title 62 of the Revised Statutes. When no rate is fixed by the laws of the State . . . the bank may . . . charge a rate not exceeding 7 per centum . . .

12 U.S.C. §85. No decisions interpreting this provision, pertinent to the resolution of the current dispute, were decided until 1900 when the Supreme Court decided *Daggs*.

In *Daggs*, a national bank located in Arizona sought to enforce promissory notes bearing a ten percent interest rate. Id. at 549. In response, Daggs argued Section 85 limited the interest rate to seven percent, if no rate was "fixed" by the laws of the state or territory where the national bank was located. Id. at 554. Because, in Arizona, the interest rate was not "fixed" by the laws of the territory, but by the parties to the notes, Daggs contended the notes were usurious. Id. The Supreme Court disagreed. Id. at 555.

The Supreme Court concluded that the phrase "fixed by the laws," from the second sentence of Section 85, should be construed to mean "allowed by the laws." Id. It reasoned that the "national banks 'were established for the purpose, in part, of providing a currency for the whole country, and in part to create a market for the loans of the general government. It could not have been intended, therefore, to expose them to the hazard of unfriendly legislation by the states, or to ruinous competition with state banks.'" Id. at 555, quoting Tiffany v. National Bank, 18 Wall. 409, 85 U.S. 409 (1873). Under this interpretation, Section 85's interest rate cap is only applicable when the laws of the bank's home state allow no interest rate. See Hawkins v. Citicorp Credit Servs., Inc., 665 F. Sup. 2d 518, 523 (2009).

For all practical purposes, *Daggs* eliminated the protections afforded by Section 85. Following *Daggs*, the national banks were able to charge interest at whatever rate was allowed by the state in which they were located and there was very little uniformity from state to state. Interest rates were lower in states concerned with consumer protection, but much higher in states trying to lure large commercial banks into doing business within their borders. This went on until 1978, when the Supreme Court decided *Marquette v. First Omaha Serv. Corp.*, 439 U.S. 299 (1978).

Marquette involved two banks: Marquette National Bank of Minneapolis ("Marquette"), where the state's usury law capped interest rates for loans at twelve percent; and the First National Bank of Omaha ("First National") in Nebraska, where state laws allowed an interest rate of up to eighteen percent. Id. at 301-03. To make up for the low cap in Minnesota, banks in Minnesota could charge an annual fee, which Marquette did. Id. at 304-05. First National then started marketing its credit cards to Minnesota residents as "no-fee" cards. Id.

Perceiving itself to be at a disadvantage, Marquette sued First National, arguing it was violating Minnesota's usury law. Id. The Supreme Court made two important rulings. First, it concluded that state usury laws do not apply to nationally chartered banks based in other states. See id. at 308. Second, it decided that nationally chartered banks can "export" the interest rates allowed in their home states to customers throughout the country. Id. at 313-14. Under this holding, when a bank from a state without limits on interest issues credit cards to people living in states, which cap credit card interest, the costumer can be charged any rate of interest. See id.

The *Marquette* decision caused unprecedented expansion in the consumer credit industry as large national banks relocated to states with lender-friendly interest rate provisions. Today, all of the major credit card companies are located in a handful of states such as South Dakota, Utah, Arizona, and Delaware where the interest rate caps are either extremely high or nonexistent. Citibank is no exception.

In 1980, during a time of great economic strife in South Dakota, Citibank executives approached the then governor, William Janklow, with a plan. Citibank would move its headquarters to South Dakota, providing hundreds of high-paying white-collar jobs, if South Dakota quickly passed legislation eliminating its interest rate cap. South Dakota responded by passing a new interest rate provision, which provides, in pertinent part, that "[u]nless a maximum interest rate or charge is specifically established elsewhere in the code, there is no maximum interest rate or charge, or usury rate restriction, between or among persons, corporations . . . associations, or any other entities if they establish the interest rate or charge by written agreement. A written agreement includes the contract created [between a card holder and a card issuer]."

Thereafter, Citibank relocated from New York to South Dakota. Ultimately, this arrangement succeeded beyond the parties' expectations. Citibank's agreement with South Dakota brought 3,000 high-paying jobs to the state and enabled Citibank to become a credit card giant, exporting South Dakota's unregulated interest rate provision to customers around the country, including DeCristoforo. Merely because Citibank is able to charge interest premised on South Dakota law, which does not cap interest, does not, however, mean Citibank can charge any interest rate. Citibank's interest rate must still comport with common-law concepts of fairness such as unconscionability.

In this case, the parties have not provided the court with a contract identifying a choice of law provision. Thus, the court must use the factors set forth in the Restatement to determine whether South Dakota or Massachusetts has the most significant relationship to the transactions at issue. None of the above factors weigh in favor of applying South Dakota law. Citbank purposely chooses to market its credit card products to Massachusetts residents. DeCristoforo is a resident of Massachusetts. Any contract or agreement between Citibank and DeCristoforo would have been executed in Massachusetts. Most importantly, Massachusetts has a strong public policy interest in ensuring its residents are protected against predatory lending practices, which is more significant than any countervailing interest South Dakota may have in the current dispute.

B. Unconscionability

"The doctrine of unconscionability has long been recognized by common law courts in this country and in England." Waters v. Min Ltd., 412 Mass. 64, 66, 587 N.E.2d 231 (1992), and cases cited. As the Appeals Court aptly explained more than three decades ago:

> Historically, a bargain was considered unconscionable if it was "such as no man in his senses and not under delusion would make on the one hand, and as no honest and fair man would accept on the other." Hume v. United States, 132 U.S. 406, 411 (1889), quoting 38 Eng. Rep. 82, 100 (Ch. 1750). Later, a contract was determined unenforceable because unconscionable when "the sum total of its provisions drives too hard a bargain for a court of conscience to assist." Campbell Soup Co. v. Wentz, 172 F.2d 80, 84 (3d Cir. 1948).

Covich v. Chambers, 8 Mass. App. Ct. 740, 750 n. 13, (1979).

Unconscionability is a matter of law decided by the court and must be determined on a case-by-case basis. Zapatha v. Dairy Mart, Inc., 381 Mass. 284, 291, 408 N.E.2d 1370 (1980). Particular attention is addressed to "whether the challenged provision could result in oppression and unfair surprise to the disadvantaged party." Waters, 412 Mass. at 68, quoting Zapatha, 381 Mass. at 292-93, 408 N.E.2d 1370. "The principle is one of prevention of oppression . . . and not of disturbance of [the] allocation of risks because of superior bargaining power." Zapatha, 381 Mass. at 292, quoting U.C.C. §2-302, cmt. 1. "Oppression" is a matter of the substantive unfairness of the contract; "unfair surprise" means procedural unfairness in the manner in which the contract was concluded. See Id. at 293-95.

Substantive unconscionability occurs when contract terms are unreasonably favorable to one party. See Gilman v. Chase–Manhattan Bank, N.A., 73 N.Y.2d 1 (N.Y. 1988) (stating the question of substantive unconscionability "entails an analysis of the substance of the bargain to determine whether the terms were unreasonably favorable to the party against whom the unconscionability is urged . . ."). When "a provision of the contract is so outrageous as to warrant holding it unenforceable," unconscionability can be based on the substantive component alone. Id. Meanwhile, procedural unconscionability "requires an examination of the contract formation process and the alleged lack of meaningful choice." Id. at 828.

Although the facts pertaining to the formation of DeCristorforo's credit card agreements are not set forth in the record, the court can fully grasp the one-sided nature of those proceedings. Nevertheless, even putting procedural unconscionability aside, the court concludes this is an instance where unconscionability can be based on the substantive component alone. Id. at 829. The court acknowledges that Citibank's interest rate charges are not always unreasonable. For example, at times, Citibank charged DeCristoforo as little at 10.65%. As time went by, however, Citibank continually increased its rate, especially as DeCristoforo began to fall behind with her payments, until it reached rates as high as 54.7333%. Substantial interest rate hikes such as this have greatly contributed to the consumer credit crisis in America.

With interest rates as high as forty and fifty percent, a significant portion of the debtor's monthly payment goes toward paying interest without touching the underlying debt. At these rates, individuals must make monthly payments for years before putting a dent in their debt, especially when one owes credit balances in excess of $25,000, as is the case with DeCristoforo. Interest charges at these rates drain needed resources and slow economic growth. Citibank's charges, in excess of eighteen percent, "drives too hard a bargain for a court of conscience to assist." Campbell Soup Co., 172 F.2d at 84. The court concludes interest rate charges above eighteen percent are unconscionable and "so outrageous as to warrant holding [them] . . . unenforceable." Gilman, 537 N.Y.S.2d 787 at 829.

· · ·

Here, it is undisputed that Citibank mailed, to DeCristoforo, monthly statements for the 1984 and the 1994 Accounts. Further, DeCristoforo does not appear to dispute that she made the purchases or accepted the cash advances listed on the account statements. At an initial glance this would seem to support summary judgment in Citibank's favor. However, in her counterclaim, which is discussed above, DeCristoforo objects to the interest rate Citibank charged. Although DeCristoforo is clearly liable for the goods, services, and/or cash advances she incurred under each account, there is no agreement between the parties as to what DeCristoforo actually owes Citibank. Therefore, Citibank's Cross Motion for Summary Judgment will be DENIED.

———————

While unconscionability—that pesky common law—remains a theoretical threat to lenders, as a practical matter, it has not taken hold as a remedy to high credit costs. In response to the above decision, and the court's subsequent judgment against the plaintiff consumer, Citibank appealed. Not content with the principal (the $28,000 awarded), Citibank pursued the principle of the matter. The appellate court noted that the plaintiff had not pleaded unconscionability as an affirmative defense and that the court, acting *sua sponte*, had not even reviewed the credit card agreement (noting without irony that an action for "account stated" does not even require a creditor to produce the debt contract). *Citibank (S.D.) v. DeCristoforo*, 2013 Mass. App. Unpub. LEXIS 576; 2013 WL 2111637, *8 (Mass. App. 2013) (unpublished decision that per court rules may be cited as persuasive but is not precedential).

The court vacated the court's finding that the interest rate charges were unconscionable and remanded for entry of a judgment calculated using the credit card's 18 percent interest rate. Citibank collected $6,000 in additional debt but the moral victory was "priceless" for credit card companies that could return to business as usual.

The current regime still allows nationally-chartered banks to charge what the market will bear for loans, credit cards, and the like to most consumers. But of course, not all loans are made by national banks. The Supreme Court's decision in *Marquette* was an interpretation of the National Banking Act; many smaller lenders are outside its scope. What about state-chartered financial institutions, credit unions, and others? Do state usury laws substantially curb the interest rates they can charge?

A handful of states, including Delaware, Nevada, South Dakota, and Utah, have repealed their usury laws entirely, but most states have some law that limits interest rates. The two statutes below illustrate the framework of usury regulation.

VA. Code. Ann. §6.2-1817. Rate of interest, loan fee, and verification fee.

A. A licensee may charge and receive on each loan interest at a simple annual rate not to exceed 36 percent. A licensee may also charge (i) a loan fee as provided in subsection B and (ii) a verification fee as provided in subsection C.

B. A licensee may charge and receive a loan fee in an amount not to exceed 20 percent of the amount of the loan proceeds advanced to the borrower.

C. A licensee may charge and receive a verification fee in an amount not to exceed $5 for a loan made under this chapter. The verification fee shall be used in part to defray the costs of submitting a database inquiry [of the borrower's payday loans].

N.C. Gen Stat. §53-173.

(a) Maximum Rate of Interest. — Every licensee under this section may make loans in installments not exceeding three thousand dollars ($3,000) in amount, at interest rates not exceeding thirty-six percent (36%) per annum on the outstanding principal balance of any loan not in excess of six hundred dollars ($600.00) and fifteen percent (15%) per annum on any remainder of such unpaid principal balance. Interest shall be contracted for and collected at the single simple interest rate applied to the outstanding balance that would earn the same amount of interest as the above rates for payment according to schedule.

(a1) Maximum Fee. — In addition to the interest authorized in subsection (a) of this section, a licensee making loans under this section may collect from the borrower a fee for processing the loan equal to five percent (5%) of the loan amount not to exceed twenty-five dollars ($25.00), provided that such charges may not be assessed more than twice in any 12-month period.

(b) Computation of Interest. — Interest on loans made pursuant to this section shall not be paid, deducted, or received in advance. Such interest shall not be compounded but interest on loans shall (i) be computed and paid only as a percentage of the unpaid principal balance or portion thereof and (ii) computed on the basis of the number of days actually elapsed; provided, however, if part or all of the consideration for a loan contract is the unpaid principal balance of a prior loan, then the principal amount payable under the loan contract may include any unpaid interest on the prior loan which have accrued within 90 days before the making of the new loan contract. For the purpose of computing interest, a day shall equal 1/365th of a year. Any payment made on a loan shall be applied first to any accrued interest and then to principal, and any portion or all of the principal balance may be prepaid at any time without penalty.

While these statutes seem pretty sweeping, their scope is limited. One limit comes from the definition of "licensee" found in both laws. Licensee in this context refers to a person (individual or business) who has registered with the state to be in the business of making small-dollar loans. The statutes also permit a variety of charges other than interest. "Processing fees" and "loan fees" are excluded from the rate calculation. Functionally, these charges to consumers increase the return on the loan. Just like interest, they compensate the lender for the cost of originating and extending the loan.

The Supreme Court also waded into the fee-for-all (sorry). It clarified fees charged by lenders are "interest" under the National Banking Act. *Smiley v. Citibank (South Dakota) N.A.*, 517 U.S. 735 (1995). Banks could therefore charge consumers living in all states the fees that would be permissible in the state of their headquarters. The Court included as "interest" a large swath of fees, including late fees, annual fees, over-the-limit fees, cash advance fees, and non-sufficient funds fees. In reaching this conclusion, the Court noted that it was reviewing—with appropriate deference—the regulatory guidance of the Office of the Comptroller of the Currency, the national bank's prudential regulator for safety and soundness. As discussed earlier, fees drive profits, and the OCC was—at best—conflicted on whether curbing fees was sound policy.

Another limit comes from "parity" rules. Arguing that the little guy was getting worse treatment, lenders that were not covered by the National Banking Act, such as state-chartered banks and credit unions, lobbied hard. Through a series of maneuvers, these financial institutions got what they wanted. In 1980, Congress passed the Depository Institutions Deregulation and Monetary Control Act of 1980 (DIDMCA), 12 U.S.C. §1735f-7a(a)(1). It stated that the constitution or laws of any State that limited the interest rate or other charges shall not apply to first-lien residential mortgages. The FDIC chimed in with a General Counsel Opinion that DIDMCA allowed federally insured (but state-chartered) institutions to charge the same interest rates as a national bank could. State-chartered banks can now charge a customer whatever interest rates the national banks could charge. Gramm-Leach-Bliley was the final nail in the coffin of state usury laws. It allows a state-chartered bank to charge the greater of the state usury limit or the rate charged by an out-of-state bank that has a branch in Arkansas. Under current law, if a national bank headquartered in South Dakota was charging 38 percent interest to a credit card customer living in Arkansas, a state-chartered bank based in Arkansas can charge the same rate. Despite a state usury statute that capped rates at 17 percent, the state-chartered bank could charge double the rate to an Arkansas resident, simply because a South Dakota-based national bank could charge that rate.

These changes were enacted without a significant public debate about whether usury laws were necessary in a modern consumer credit market. But because parity laws kept intact usury laws (they just dramatically limited their applicability), legislatures can say they did not change the usury limit. They can simply point to the incorrigible Supreme Court and rascally Congress. The result has been described as a *trompe l'oleil*, a deception. James J. White, *The Usury Trompe l'Oleil*, 51 S.C. L. Rev. 445 (2000).

The difficulty in creating a debate about usury laws has another dimension: the ways in which the laws are written. Christopher Peterson explains his concept of "salience distortion."

> Because currency is numerical, in any statute that caps the price of a loan, the legislature must at some point pick a number or numbers. While this is true of every usury law, the specific number a legislature chooses only has meaning in relation to other variables associated with the law in question. For example, one legislature might adopt a usury limit of 8% per year while another might adopt a cap of 8% per month. Both legislatures would have chosen to feature the same number in the language of the statute, but the latter cap is twelve times higher than the former because there are twelve months per year. . . . The point here is simply that if it chooses to do so, a legislature can pick a small number and create a relatively high price limit. Or, it can pick a large number and create a relatively low price limit. Legislatures can feature whatever number they want in a usury law.

Christopher Peterson, *Usury Law, Payday Loans, and Statutory Sleight of Hand: Salience Distortion in American Credit Pricing Limits*, 92 Minn. L. Rev. 1110, 1136 (2008). To see this effect, compare the Virginia and North Carolina usury laws on the preceding pages. Which rate cap is lower? Is it possible to answer in the abstract?

In his article, Peterson calculates the annual percentage rate of interest for a $325 payday loan in all states and looks at how the cost of credit would differ from the most prominent (that is, salient) number in the statute. He concludes that "[t]odays' legislature refuse to use numbers transparently reflective of actual credit prices," because triple-digit figures would offend the moral and social norms that have long animated usury laws. *Id.* at 1150.

C. Federal Law

The United States does have a federal usury law that applies to only one group of consumers: servicemembers on activity duty and their dependents. It restricts the cost of credit for loans made on or after October 1, 2007, when the statute and the Department of Defense regulations became effective. The Talent-Nelson amendment, enacted as part of a defense appropriations bill, caught lenders by surprise, although there were a number of reports and hearings focused on predatory lending to servicemembers. National Consumer Law Center, *In Harm's Way At Home: Consumer Scams and the Direct Targeting of America's Military and Veterans* (2003). One particular concern is that financial trouble, such as filing bankruptcy or collection suits, can prevent or eliminate national security clearance. The ostensible fear is that financially-troubled servicemembers are at risk of being bribed to commit treason or similar crimes to scrape up money to pay debts.

The statute imposes a 36 percent cap, called the "military annual percentage rate."

> (a) Interest. A creditor who extends consumer credit to a covered member of the armed forces or a dependent of such a member shall not require the member or dependent to pay interest with respect to the extension of such credit, except as—
> (1) agreed to under the terms of the credit agreement or promissory note;
> (2) authorized by applicable State or Federal law; and
> (3) not specifically prohibited by this section.
> (b) Annual Percentage Rate. A creditor described in subsection (a) may not impose an annual percentage rate of interest greater than 36 percent with respect to the consumer credit extended to a covered member or a dependent of a covered member.

10 U.S.C. §987(i). Congress gave authority to the Department of Defense to define "consumer credit" but made clear that mortgages and car loans were to be excluded from the rate limit. The latter restriction was a source of controversy since used-car lots ring military bases and often charge much higher interest rates than what is typically available farther from base. But without a car at all, it is hard for servicemembers to shop in areas distant from base. In its regulation, the Department of Defense limited "consumer credit" to mean only closed-end loans. 32 C.F.R. §232.3. The difference between closed-end and open-end credit is complex, but essentially open-end credit is freely available at will up to a certain dollar limit. The balance goes up and down, as the account stays open. The credit card is the classic example. The regulations went on to exclude any purchase-money loans from the term "consumer credit." Purchase-money transactions are when the loan is being taken out to buy an item, and the item is securing the loan as collateral. U.C.C. §9-103.

Consumer advocates were displeased at this narrow definition. The Department of Defense revised its definition to include all forms of credit other than home mortgages and purchase money loans. The new definition is effective on October 1, 2016, except that credit card lenders have another year to comply (and a possible loophole whereby the Secretary of Defense has discretion to further extend the time before credit cards are subject to the MAPR).

In another respect though, the Department of Defense went much further than the statute arguably required. It not only capped the rate at 36 percent, it also prohibited securing the loan by a check, automobile title, bank account or military allotment. Effectively, payday loans and car title loans, which are the subject of upcoming assignments, are completely banned for servicemembers and their dependents. While it is possible that the industry would not have been willing to offer payday or title loans at 36 percent, Congress foreclosed an experiment with what the market would bear. If Congress had stayed silent on the rate and payday or title loans were not profitable at 36 percent, the Department of Defense could have adjusted the rate cap incrementally to the point at which credit became available. Instead, Congress enacted the rate cap structured as a hard limit, without the ability for the Department of Defense to adjust it. Perhaps it would have been better to for Congress to have crisply and broadly defined "consumer credit," which reflects more of a policy choice than the exact appropriate number for an interest rate.

D.   Usury as Economic and Social Policy

The moral concerns about interest center on a belief that it is ungodly and uncharitable to profit from another person's need for money. Note the assumptions in this approach: that the lender and borrower are individuals, that the interest rate would be sufficiently high to generate a profit, and that a borrower is a person in dire financial straits. None of these assumptions may hold in the modern U.S. consumer finance market. Most families carrying a credit card balance, and paying 25 percent interest, earn incomes well above the poverty line. Nevertheless, the concerns about high interest rates leaving people mired in chronic poverty continue. Payday loans are a focal point of debate because of eye-popping annualized percentage rates that result from an expensive short-term loan. Nathalie Martin, *1,000% Interest—Good While Supplies Last: A Study of Payday Loan Practices and Solutions*, 52 Az. L. Rev. 563 (2010).

The morality debate about usury also continues, albeit with some twists. Despite the Biblical traditions disfavoring lending money at interest, usury restrictions are non-existent or minimal in locations with states that are politically conservative. As a result, payday lenders thrive in the places where evangelical churches are concentrated, lending to people who are particularly committed to Biblical values. Christopher L. Peterson & Steven M. Graves, *Usury Law and the Christian Right: Faith-Based Political Power and the Geography of the American Payday Loan Regulation*, 57 Catholic Univ. L. Rev. 637 (2008).

At the heart of the debate are two questions: Do usury laws reduce credit, and if so, is this an undesirable outcome? Several studies have examined the first question, which is purely empirical in nature, and the weight of the evidence is that interest rate caps—at least at some level—do limit credit. One solution proffered is to make the usury law a floating cap, set a certain percent above a baseline rate. As the baseline changed, the usury rate would move. While this addresses the serious problem that occurred in the 1970s when interest rates skyrocketed and usury laws remained unchanged, it does not answer the question about the optimal level for a cap.

Setting a usury limit ultimately involves a judgment about the amount of credit that consumers should be able to access. Usury laws likely will limit credit, at least to some degree. But is less borrowing a bad or a good outcome? Some have argued that usury functions as a crude social insurance scheme, protecting people from becoming irretrievably mired in debt. Edward L. Glaeser & Jose Scheinkman, *Neither a Borrower Nor a Lender Be: An Economic Analysis of Interest Restrictions and Usury Law*, 41 J.L. & Econ. 1 (1998). Creditors are not willing to lend to high-risk consumers at a cost that does not cover the risk of nonpayment and generate a profit. Usury laws can substitute for underwriting guidelines that require an assessment of a consumer's ability to repay. Post to

Credit Slips blog by Adam J. Levitin, *Usury Laws Are Dead. Long Live the New Usury Laws. The CFPB's Ability to Repay Mortgage Rule*, Jan. 11, 2013, at http://www.creditslips.org/creditslips/2013/01/usury-laws-are-dead-long-live-the-new-usury-law-the-cfpbs-ability-to-repay-mortgage-rule.html. Rather than looking at creditworthiness on a scale that is matched to price, lenders would simply not make loans when the usury limit did not exceed the anticipated risk and desired profit.

A major study of European Union interest rate regulations found that concerns about reduced access to credit are overreliant on US-based studies where usury laws were not benchmarked to a market rate and were quite low. Study on interest rate restrictions in the EU, Final Report for the EU Commission DG Internal Market and Services, Project No. ETD/2009/IM/H3/87, iff/ZEW (2010). European states typically set rates with reference to a publicly available rate. The EU study also concluded that there is "no convincing" evidence that usury laws lead to a growth in illegal lending or loan sharking, or result in higher default rates. One of the authors summed up the challenge with usury:

> It's about the level at which the ceiling is set. The art or science of this policy issue revolves around establishing an interest rate ceiling sufficiently high to permit borrowers with little security to obtain access to credit but sufficiently low so that lenders do not lend to the most fragile borrowers whose precarious position would be made worse by a larger amount of interest to repay.

Ultimately, the usury debate is probably more normative than empirical, although better empirical evidence about how low-income or financially distressed families use and perceive credit would be helpful. One study found that fifty low-income women had "a profound ambivalence towards the relationship between access and usury caps" and that these consumers were more interested in designing credit products that allowed them to self-direct their use of credit than in the price of credit. Angela Littwin, *Beyond Usury: A Study of Credit Card Use and Preference Among Low-Income Consumers*, 86 TEX. L. REV. 451 2008.

Congress has made very clear that it disdains usury. The Dodd-Frank Act passed in 2010 prohibits the Consumer Financial Protection Bureau from enacting an interest rate limit applicable to state banks and specifies that the current system for national banks of interest rate exportation is undisturbed. *See* §§1027(o); 1044(a).

As discussed in the next assignments, the focus of the current U.S. legal environment is on price disclosure, not price limits. Notwithstanding that, the problems below show that usury can still trip up lenders and their lawyers. Usury is likely to remain a battleground for consumer protection in upcoming decades. Timothy Goldsmith & Nathalie Martin, *Interest Rate Caps, State Legislation, and Public Opinion: Does the Law Reflect the Public's Desires?* 89 CHICAGO KENT L. REV. 115 (2013). While Ohio repealed its usury law in 1995, the legislature reinstated the cap in 2008. In response, lenders sought alternative licenses that let them avoid the 28 percent usury limit. In part because of these evasive tactics and in part because of online lending, scholars continue to point to a federal usury law as a comprehensive and sensible strategy. Brian M. McCall, *Unprofitable Lending: Modern Credit Regulation and the Lost Theory of Usury*, 30 CARDOZO L. REV. 549 (2008).

Problem Set 11

11.1. You take your younger sister Annie out for dinner, and after a couple of cocktails, she blurts out that she needs a loan. You would never charge a family member interest or require a written contract, but you felt compelled as an older sibling to poke into her shenanigans. She confessed that she ran up a number of large credit card bills a couple of years ago when she was "wardrobing" herself for her new job as a photographer's assistant. After juggling minimum payments for a while, her boyfriend Willow offered to lend her $20,000 to pay off the debts so she could "hang" and "chill" with him without being stressed about the debts. Annie and Willow split up, however, when his family summoned him back to become Ward, the scion of a family-owned private equity firm run. Things have soured between them, and Ward is threatening to sue Annie if she doesn't return the $20,000. She produces what appears to be a copy of a cocktail napkin, upon which is scrawled "In exchange for $20,000, Annie Chang will repay to Ward Elliot 12 percent per month for 12 consecutive months beginning 12 months from the date below as an investment profit." Does Annie have a way out of repaying this debt? Your state's usury statute (Florida) is below.

> Unless otherwise specifically allowed by law, any person making an extension of credit to any person, who shall willfully and knowingly charge, take, or receive interest thereon at a rate exceeding 45 percent per annum, or the equivalent rate for a longer or shorter period of time, whether directly or indirectly, or conspires so to do, commits a felony of the third degree to take interest exceeding 45 percent per annum.

Florida Statute §687.071.

11.2. You are the legislative director for a newly elected Senator, Monica Mendieta, who is planning her first-term agenda. Financial services companies of various types, such as brokerage firms and mutual fund companies, are a major employer in your home state. The Senator breezed in yesterday and dropped an article with this introduction on your desk:

> "Independence Bank's only branch in Nevada, opened last month, is tucked into the end of a run-down strip mall next to an auto parts store. It has just one ATM, four employees, and is open only Monday to Friday, 9 A.M. to 3 P.M. It will now be the Independence Bank's official address for 'regulatory reasons.'"

You avoided the Senator yesterday but you know she'll be back. Independence Bank has its name on the stadium in your state's largest city, and a shiny office building downtown. It employs more than 20,000 people and is the largest depository financial institution. In fact, Senator Mendieta's account and her election account are held there. (You bank at a credit union.) Prepare at least four talking points for the Senator on this issue, including one statement that you would offer to her communications director for media use. Is this legal? Is it moral? Is it politically wise?

Assignment 12. Credit Cost Disclosures

As substantive limits, such as usury, have receded, laws mandating disclosures of the cost of credit have multiplied. The Truth in Lending Act (TILA) is the cornerstone of consumer credit law. It was enacted in 1968 with the hope of improving consumers' knowledge of the cost of borrowing and allowing them to shop on price when borrowing. The statute is primarily designed to be preventative. With a better understanding of the deal before them, consumers can make well-informed decisions and avoid credit problems. Lenders face substantial compliance burdens to complete and disseminate TILA disclosures, but should be rewarded with a more competitive market. Additional information should promote robust competition by letting consumers choose the best loan for their circumstances.

TILA represents a major shift in the orientation of consumer lawmaking. Its focus on disclosure reflects a vision of consumers as empowered actors who can shape a marketplace with their behavior. The goal of law is not to place substantive bounds on credit products but to improve the borrowing process. This approach resists substantive regulation as paternalistic and welfare-reducing and instead focuses on consumers as rational actors who should be allowed to make their own decisions. The role of the law is to ensure that consumers have the necessary information to make their own choices, not to limit their options.

A lively debate exists about the efficacy of disclosure statutes, including TILA, and whether substantive limits such as bans on certain fees or product terms accomplish better outcomes. Consumer advocates and lenders are not necessarily on opposite sides of the disclosure issue. Some advocates advance disclosure as an important consumer remedy, while others see it as a distraction from "real" regulation of credit. Similarly, the financial industry has sometimes proffered additional disclosures in response to consumer protection concerns, while other times lamented disclosure as costly and useless.

A. Basic Concepts in Truth in Lending

Despite a so-called "simplification amendment," TILA remains among the most complex consumer law statutes. It is long, dense, and hard to apply in certain contexts. Because of this, the rules that implement TILA, Regulation Z, are particularly important and useful. Regulation Z includes more than a dozen appendices; the most important of these are model disclosures and permissible language. A substantial body of commentary, most importantly in the form of Official Staff Commentary, also exists for TILA. Upon its creation, the CFPB assumed rulemaking responsibility for Regulation Z, previously held by the Federal Reserve Board. The numbering of Regulation Z was basically kept intact, with only the initial digits changing. So, for example, 12 C.F.R. §226.1 became 12 C.F.R. §1026.1; §226.2 became §1026.2, etc. The cases in this Assignment predate the CFPB and so cite the Federal Reserve Board's Regulation Z and refer to the Federal Reserve Board's authority. Remember that now the CFPB is the agency with TILA authority.

Assignment 3, on the scope of consumer law, examined an important aspect of TILA, which is how it limits its scope to consumer credit transactions. Briefly, the limitations are exclusionary; all credit transactions are subject to TILA unless they are extended "primarily for a business, commercial, or agricultural purpose" or to "other than a natural person." 15 U.S.C. §1603. Large transactions, even to individual persons acting as consumers, also are exempt from TILA, although lenders may comply for the avoidance of any doubt. The dollar threshold is adjusted annually based on an inflation index. The start point for adjustment, doubled in 2010 from its original limit that endured from the passage of TILA in 1968, is now $50,000 for non-mortgage credit. All loans that relate to a consumer's principal dwelling are covered, regardless of amount.

TILA contains different rules for the two major kinds of credit: closed-end and open-end borrowing. It also contains special rules for certain types of loans, most notably home mortgages and credit cards. Part A of TILA, 15 U.S.C. §§1601-1615, provides the key tools for disclosing the cost of credit. It defines the price aspects of credit using three fundamental concepts: finance charge, amount financed, and annual percentage rate.

1.   The Finance Charge

The finance charge is the cost of credit as a dollar amount. One can understand it as the price tag for a loan. The other key aspect of a loan is the amount financed. This can be thought of as a price tag for the merchandise (here, a loan) that is being purchased. For example, if I borrow $10,000, that is the amount financed. If the loan is provided at 10 percent simple interest, calculated and payable one year from the loan's origination, the finance charge is $1,000. TILA regulates what goes in each category; the finance charge and the amount financed are mutually exclusive categories. The result is a standardized way of assessing loans and their costs.

A finance charge is defined broadly as "sum of all charges, payable directly or indirectly by the [borrower], and imposed directly or indirectly by the creditor as an incident to the extension of credit." 15 U.S.C. §1605; 12 C.F.R. §1026.4(a). The definition is broad, so as to capture nearly all the costs of the credit. The finance charge reflects both the interest rate and other charges for the transaction. It is a more complete measure of the expense of a loan than the interest rate by itself. The focus is on the borrower's cost, not the creditor's recovery. Charges by third parties (not the creditor) are to be included in the finance charge if the creditor requires the use of a third party for the credit extension or retains a portion of the third-party charge. 12 C.F.R.

§1026.4(a)(1). Regulation Z gives a long list of examples of things that are finance charges. 12 C.F.R. §1026.4(b). The list is illustrative, not exclusive.

Regulation Z also gives a long list of things that are *not* finance charges. 12 C.F.R. §1026.4(c)-(e). These are not examples but rather definitive exclusions. Items not on the list are usually finance charges if the basic definition applies. The simplest way to exclude something from the finance charge is to determine that the cost would be "payable in a comparable cash transaction." 15 U.S.C. §1605. This is redundant, however, because the definition of a finance charge requires that the charge be imposed as an "incident to the extension of credit." *Id*. Examples of charges that would be imposed by the creditor in either cash or credit sales are sales tax and a license fee for the purchase of a vehicle. These are not finance charges (although keep reading to see how they appear in a TILA disclosure).

The definitional boundaries of the finance charge remain contested. Forty years after the enactment of TILA, such disputes still make their way to the Supreme Court.

Household Credit Servs. v. Pfenning

541 U.S. 232 (2004)

THOMAS, Justice.

Congress enacted the Truth in Lending Act (TILA), in order to promote the "informed use of credit" by consumers. 15 U.S.C. §1601(a). To that end, TILA's disclosure provisions seek to ensure "meaningful disclosure of credit terms." Ibid. Further, Congress delegated expansive authority to the Federal Reserve Board (Board) to enact appropriate regulations to advance this purpose. §1604(a). We granted certiorari, 539 U.S. 957 (2003), to decide whether the Board's Regulation Z, which specifically excludes fees imposed for exceeding a credit limit (over-limit fees) from the definition of "finance charge," is an unreasonable interpretation of §1605. We conclude that it is not, and, accordingly, we reverse the judgment of the Court of Appeals for the Sixth Circuit.

I.

Respondent, Sharon Pfennig, holds a credit card initially issued by petitioner Household Credit Services, Inc. (Household), but in which petitioner MBNA America Bank, N. A. (MBNA), now holds an interest through the acquisition of Household's credit card portfolio. Although the terms of respondent's credit card agreement set respondent's credit limit at $2,000, respondent was able to make charges exceeding that limit, subject to a $29 "over-limit fee" for each month in which her balance exceeded $2,000.

TILA regulates, *inter alia*, the substance and form of disclosures that creditors offering "open end consumer credit plans" (a term that includes credit card accounts) must make to consumers, §1637(a), and provides a civil remedy for consumers who suffer damages as a result of a creditor's failure to comply with TILA's provisions, §1640. When a creditor and a consumer enter into an open-end consumer credit plan, the creditor is required to provide to the consumer a statement for each billing cycle for which there is an outstanding balance due. §1637(b). The statement must include the account's outstanding balance at the end of the billing period, §1637(b)(8), and "[t]he amount of any finance charge added to the account during the period, itemized to show the amounts, if any, due to the application of percentage rates and the amount, if any, imposed as a minimum or fixed charge," §1637(b)(4). A "finance charge" is an amount "payable directly or indirectly by the person to whom the credit is extended, and imposed directly or indirectly by the creditor as an incident to the extension of credit." §1605(a). The Board has interpreted this definition to exclude "[c]harges . . . for exceeding a credit limit." See 12 C.F.R. §226.4(c)(2) (2004) (Regulation Z). Thus, although respondent's billing statement disclosed the imposition of an over-limit fee when she exceeded her $2,000 credit limit, consistent with Regulation Z, the amount was not included as part of the "finance charge."

On August 24, 1999, respondent filed a complaint in the United States District Court for the Southern District of Ohio on behalf of a purported nationwide class of all consumers who were charged or assessed over-limit fees by petitioners. Respondent alleged in her complaint that petitioners allowed her and each of the other putative class members to exceed their credit limits, thereby subjecting them to over-limit fees. Petitioners violated TILA, respondent alleged, by failing to classify the over-limit fees as "finance charges" and thereby "misrepresented the true cost of credit" to respondent and the other class members. Petitioners moved to dismiss the complaint pursuant to Federal Rule of Civil Procedure 12(b)(6) on the ground that Regulation Z specifically excludes over-limit fees from the definition of "finance charge." 12 C.F.R. §226.4(c)(2) (2004). The District Court agreed and granted petitioners' motion to dismiss.

On appeal, respondent argued, and the Court of Appeals agreed, that Regulation Z's explicit exclusion of over-limit fees from the definition of "finance charge" conflicts with the plain language of 15 U.S.C. §1605(a). The Court of Appeals first noted that, as a remedial statute, TILA must be liberally interpreted in favor of consumers. 295 F.3d 522, 528 (6th Cir. 2002). The Court of Appeals then concluded that the over-limit fees in this case were imposed "incident to the extension of credit" and therefore fell squarely within §1605's definition of "finance charge." Id., at 528-529. The Court of Appeals' conclusion turned on the distinction between unilateral acts of default and acts of default resulting from consumers' requests for additional credit, exceeding a predetermined credit limit, that creditors grant. Under the Court of Appeals' reasoning, a penalty imposed due to a unilateral act of default would not constitute a "finance charge." Id., at 530-531. Respondent alleged in her complaint, however, that petitioners "allowed [her] to make charges and/or assessed [her] charges that allowed her balance to exceed her credit limit of two thousand dollars," putting her actions under the category of acts of default resulting from consumers requests for additional credit, exceeding a predetermined credit limit, that creditors grant. The Court of Appeals held that because petitioners "made an additional extension of credit to [respondent] over and above the alleged 'credit limit,'" id., and charged the over-limit fee as a condition of this additional extension of credit, the over-limit fee clearly and unmistakably fell under the definition of a "finance charge." 295 F.3d, at 530. Based on its reading of respondent's allegations, the Court of Appeals limited its holding to "those instances in which the creditor knowingly permits the credit card holder to exceed his or her credit limit and then imposes a fee incident to the extension of that credit." Id., at 532, n.5.

II.

Congress has expressly delegated to the Board the authority to prescribe regulations containing "such classifications, differentiations, or other provisions" as, in the judgment of the Board, "are necessary or proper to effectuate the purposes of [TILA], to prevent circumvention or evasion thereof, or to facilitate compliance therewith." §1604(a). . . . [T]wice since the passage of TILA, Congress has made this intention clear: first by providing a good-faith defense to creditors who comply with the Board's rules and regulations, 88 Stat. 1518, codified at 15 U.S.C. §1640(f), and, second, by expanding this good-faith defense to creditors who conform to "any interpretation or approval by an official or employee of the Federal Reserve System duly authorized by the Board to issue such interpretations or approvals," 90 Stat. 197, codified as amended, at §1640(f). 444 U.S., at 566-567.

Respondent does not challenge the Board's authority to issue binding regulations. Thus, in determining whether Regulation Z's interpretation of TILA's text is binding on the courts, we are faced with only two questions. We first ask whether "Congress has directly spoken to the precise question at issue." Chevron U.S.A. Inc. v. Natural Resources Defense Council, Inc., 467 U.S. 837, 842 (1984). If so, courts, as well as the agency, "must give effect to the unambiguously expressed intent of Congress." Id., at 842-843. However, whenever Congress has "explicitly left a gap for the agency to fill," the agency's regulation is "given controlling weight unless [it is] arbitrary, capricious, or manifestly contrary to the statute." Id., at 843-844.

A.

TILA itself does not explicitly address whether over-limit fees are included within the definition of "finance charge." Congress defined "finance charge" as "all charges, payable directly or indirectly by the person to whom the credit is extended, and imposed directly or indirectly by the creditor as an incident to the extension of credit." §1605(a). The Court of Appeals, however, made no attempt to clarify the scope of the critical term "incident to the extension of credit." The Court of Appeals recognized that, "'[i]n ascertaining the plain meaning of the statute, the court must look to the particular statutory language at issue, as well as the language and design of the statute as a whole.'" Id., at 529-530 (quoting Kmart Corp. v. Cartier, Inc., 486 U.S. 281, 291 (1988)). However, the Court of Appeals failed to examine TILA's other provisions, or even the surrounding language in §1605, before reaching its conclusion. Because petitioners would not have imposed the over-limit fee had they not "granted [respondent's] request for additional credit, which resulted in her exceeding her credit limit," the Court of Appeals held that the over-limit fee in this case fell squarely within §1605(a)'s definition of "finance charge." 295 F.3d, at 528-529. Thus, the Court of Appeals rested its holding primarily on its particular characterization of the transaction that led to the over-limit charge in this case.

The Court of Appeals' characterization of the transaction in this case, however, is not supported even by the facts as set forth in respondent's complaint. Respondent alleged in her complaint that the over-limit fee is imposed for each month in which her balance exceeds the original credit limit. If this were true, however, the over-limit fee would be imposed not as a direct result of an extension of credit for a purchase that caused respondent to exceed her $2,000 limit, but rather as a result of the fact that her charges exceeded her $2,000 limit at the time respondent's monthly charges were officially calculated. Because over-limit fees, regardless of a creditor's particular billing practices, are imposed only when a consumer exceeds his credit limit, it is perfectly reasonable to characterize an over-limit fee not as a charge imposed for obtaining an extension of credit over a consumer's credit limit, but rather as a penalty for violating the credit agreement.

The Court of Appeals thus erred in resting its conclusion solely on this particular characterization of the details of credit card transactions, a characterization that is not clearly compelled by the terms and definitions of TILA, and one with which others could reasonably disagree. Certainly, regardless of how the fee is character-ized, there is at least some connection between the over-limit fee and an extension of credit. But, this Court has recognized that the phrase "incident to or in conjunc-tion with" implies some *necessary* connection between the antecedent and its object, although it "does not place beyond rational debate the nature or extent of the required connection." Holly Farms Corp. v. NLRB, 517 U.S. 392, 403, n. 9 (1996) (internal quotation marks omitted). In other words, the phrase "incident to" does not make clear whether a substantial (as opposed to a remote) connection is required. Thus, unlike the Court of Appeals, we cannot conclude that the term "finance charge" unambiguously includes over-limit fees. That term, standing alone, is ambiguous.

Moreover, an examination of TILA's related provisions, as well as the full text of §1605 itself, casts doubt on the Court of Appeals' interpretation of the statute. A consumer holding an open-end credit plan may incur two types of charges — finance charges and "other charges which may be imposed as part of the plan." §§1637(a)(1)-(5). TILA does not make clear which charges fall into each cate-gory. But TILA's recognition of at least two categories of charges does make clear that Congress did not contemplate that *all* charges made in connection with an open-end credit plan would be considered "finance charges." And where TILA does explicitly address over-limit fees, it defines them as fees imposed "in connection with an extension of credit," §1637(c)(1)(B)(iii), rather than "inci-dent to the extension of credit," §1605(a). Furthermore, none of §1605's specific examples of charges that fall within the definition of "finance charge" includes over-limit or comparable fees. See, e.g., §1605(a)(2) ("[s]ervice or carrying charge"); §1605(a)(3) (loan fee or similar charge); §1605(a)(6) (mortgage broker fees).

As our prior discussion indicates, the best interpretation of the term "finance charge" may exclude over-limit fees. But §1605(a) is, at best, ambiguous, because neither §1605(a) nor its surrounding provisions provides a clear answer. While we acknowledge that there may be some fees not explicitly addressed by §1605(a)'s definition of "finance charge" but which are unambiguously included in or excluded by that definition, over-limit fees are not such fees.

B.

Because §1605 is ambiguous, the Board's regulation implementing §1605 "is binding in the courts unless procedurally defective, arbitrary or capricious in substance, or manifestly contrary to the statute." United States v. Mead Corp., 533 U.S. 218, 227 (2001).

Regulation Z's exclusion of over-limit fees from the term "finance charge" is in no way manifestly contrary to §1605. Regulation Z defines the term "finance charge" as "the cost of consumer credit." 12 C.F.R. §226.4 (2004). It specifically excludes from the definition of "finance charge" the following:

"(1) Application fees charged to all applicants for credit, whether or not credit is actually extended.

"(2) Charges for actual unanticipated late payment, *for exceeding a credit limit*, or for delinquency, default, or a similar occurrence.

"(3) Charges imposed by a financial institution for paying items that overdraw an account, unless the payment of such items and the imposition of the charge were previously agreed upon in writing.

"(4) Fees charged for participation in a credit plan, whether assessed on an annual or other periodic basis.

"(5) Seller's points.

"(6) Interest forfeited as a result of an interest reduction required by law on a time deposit used as security for an extension of credit.

"(7) [Certain fees related to real estate.]

"(8) Discounts offered to induce payment for a purchase by cash, check, or other means, as provided in section 167(b) of the Act." §226.4(c).

The Board adopted the regulation to emphasize "disclosures that are relevant to credit decisions, as opposed to disclosures related to events occurring after the initial credit choice," because "the primary goals of the [TILA] are not particularly enhanced by regulatory provisions relating to changes in terms on outstanding obligations and on the effects of the failure to comply with the terms of the obligation." 45 Fed. Reg. 80 649 (1980). The Board's decision to emphasize disclosures that are most relevant to a consumer's initial credit decisions reflects an understanding that "[m]eaningful disclosure does not mean *more* disclosure," but instead "describes a balance between 'competing considerations of complete disclosure . . . and the need to avoid . . . [informational overload].'" Ford Motor Credit Co., 444 U.S., at 568 (quoting S. Rep. No. 96-73, p. 3 (1979)). Although the fees excluded from the term "finance charge" in Regulation Z (*e.g.,* application charges, late payment charges, and over-limit fees) might be relevant to a consumer's credit decision, the Board rationally concluded that these fees — which are not automatically recurring or are imposed only when a consumer defaults on a credit agreement — are less relevant to determining the true cost of credit. Because over-limit fees, which are imposed only when a consumer breaches the terms of his credit agreement, can reasonably be characterized as a penalty for defaulting on the credit agreement, the Board's decision to exclude them from the term "finance charge" is surely reasonable. . . .

Congress has authorized the Board to make "such classifications, differentiations, or other provisions, and [to] provide for such adjustments and exceptions for any class of transactions, as in the judgment of the Board are necessary or proper to effectuate the purposes of [TILA], to prevent circumvention or evasion thereof, or to facilitate compliance therewith." §1604(a). Here, the Board has accomplished all of these objectives by setting forth a clear, easy to apply (and easy to enforce) rule that highlights the charges the Board determined to be most relevant to a consumer's credit decisions. The judgment of the Court of Appeals is therefore reversed.

It is so ordered.

———————

The court's opinion illustrates the deference to Regulation Z that is typical in TILA litigation. With the CPFB now in charge of TILA, these regulations may change in ways that are more favorable to consumers. The emphasis on a rule that is easy to apply seems likely to persist, however, given the huge number of transactions and creditors to which TILA applies.

As a reminder, TILA does not limit the amount of a finance charge. It can be low or high; it must only be accurately calculated and correctly disclosed to the consumer.

2.   *Amount Financed*

The "amount financed" is the second key component of TILA's price disclosures. TILA suggests labeling the amount financed as "the amount of credit provided to you." 12 C.F.R. §1026.18(b). The principal of the loan is usually the largest component of the amount financed. But in the same way that the interest rate is part of the finance charge but not fully equivalent to that term, the principal amount of a loan is not the entirety of the amount financed. A simple construction of the amount financed is that it is the principal loan amount plus financed fees that are not part of the finance charge. An example of charges that are included in the amount financed (and excluded, as noted earlier, from the finance charge) are sales tax and license fees that are being financed as part of a vehicle purchase. Other aspects of a transaction that are not part of the amount financed are down payments or trade-in value, or any prepaid finance charges.

3.   *Annual Percentage Rate*

The annual percentage rate (APR) is derived from the finance charge, the amount financed, and the payment schedule. It is a mathematical transformation of those numbers into the cost of the credit expressed as a yearly rate. The APR will almost never be identical to the stated interest rate in a promissory note because charges other than interest are included in the finance charge upon which APR is based. While some people explain the APR as the finance charge expressed as a percentage, that definition is not accurate. The amount financed and the payment schedule both influence APR. In its *Truth-in-Lending Examination Manual* (April 2015), the CFPB offers an illustrative example of how APR is not merely a transformation of the finance charge.

- For loan 1, the amount financed is $5,000 with a payment schedule of 36 equal monthly payments of $166.07 each.
- For loan 2, the amount financed is $4,500, and the payment schedule is 35 equal monthly payments of $152.18 and 1 final payment of $152.22.

Begin by calculating the finance charge for each loan. (Hint: For loan 1, take 36 x 166.07, and subtract 5,000 from the result. Repeat process for loan 2.) Notice anything? (If what you are noticing is feelings of anxiety about math, rest assured that this is about the deepest this book goes into credit calculations.)

The amount financed for each loan is identical ($978.52). But if you were to calculate the APR for each loan, it would be different. It would be 12 percent for loan 1, but 13.26 percent on loan 2. The difference reflects the amount being financed and the payment schedule, specifically when the loan would be amortized (the balance brought to zero through payments). The determination of APR is complex enough that federal banking regulator, the Office of the Comptroller of the Currency, offers an entire downloadable program to calculate it, and many vendors sell APR software to lenders. Because today nearly all creditors use computer programs to calculate APRs, errors in APR disclosures usually mirror an underlying error in determining the finance charge or the amount financed, rather than a mathematical mistake.

B.   Distinguishing Closed-End Credit and Open-End Credit

The disclosure requirements differ for closed-end and open-end credit. Generally, more information is required to be disclosed in a closed-end transaction and the disclosure gives consumers a more detailed and complete breakdown of the loan's cost.

TILA does not use the term "closed-end" credit; instead, it refers only to credit "other than open-end credit." If the finance charge can be conclusively determined at the time of the transaction, it is a closed-end loan. To be open-end credit, the credit plan must provide for a finance charge that may be computed from time to time on an outstanding unpaid balance. TILA also defines open-end credit to arise when a creditor "reasonably contemplates" repeated transactions. 15 U.S.C. §1602(i). A creditor cannot simply deem something to be open-end credit to reduce its compliance burden. Rather, it is a question of fact whether a transaction is open-end or closed-end. 12 C.F.R. §1026, Supp. I, §(a)(20)(3).

Closed-end credit transactions require the disclosure of six main items. Three of these are discussed above: the finance charge, the amount financed, and the APR. The other three items are the payment schedule, the total of the payments, and information about a security interest, if applicable because the creditor is taking collateral on the loan.

Open-end credit transactions require initial disclosures and periodic disclosures. Because at the time of the account opening, it is not known how much credit the consumer will use, the open-end disclosures provide a less definitive price tag for borrowing than closed-end disclosures. The terms and structure of open-end loans tend to vary significantly, and TILA requires disclosure of items only if applicable to the transaction. 12 C.F.R. §1026.6. The following should be disclosed in an initial disclosure on an open-end loan:

1) The conditions under which a finance charge may be imposed, including whether there is a grace period for a consumer to pay to avoid a finance charge and if so, the length of that period;
2) the method of determining the balance upon which the finance charge will be imposed;
3) the method of determining the amount of the finance charge;
4) all "periodic rates," and the corresponding nominal annual percentage rates, and the balance amounts that trigger the applicability of a particular rate; and
5) other charges that may be imposed, such as penalty fees, account fees, and minimum finance charges.

As with closed-end credit, if a security interest is being taken as part of the transaction, that fact and information about the security interest must be given.

The periodic statements for open-end credit provide detail on the state of the open-end credit plan in the prior period and where it stands as of the billing date. 12 C.F.R. §1026.7. For example, the statement shows the beginning and ending balance, the due date, and the creditor's address. Detail on the amount and date of each credit extension also is required. 12 C.F.R. §1026.8.

The accuracy of the finance charge and APR calculations need not always be perfect. The threshold for errors varies for open-end and closed-end credit. Here are a few of the most important rules. With regard to the finance charge, it must be completely accurate with regard to open-end credit, while for closed-end credit, the finance charge is accurate if it is within $10 in either direction of the exact finance charge if the amount financed exceeds $1,000 and within $5 in either direction if the amount financed is less than or equal to $1,000. 12 C.F.R. §1026.18(d)(2). For APR, the rules are even more complicated, in part because there are tolerances for both open-end and closed-end credit, as well as special tolerances for mortgage loans (which are covered in Assignment 16). The easiest rule is that for an open-end account the disclosed APR is accurate if it is within 1/8th of one percentage point of the correctly calculated APR. Closed-end credit is more complicated, distinguishing between "regular" and "irregular" transactions. The general proposition is that there is a higher tolerance for irregular loans because the APR calculation is more complex. 15 U.S.C. §1606(c); 12 C.F.R. §1026.22(a)(2).

C. Disclosure Design and Delivery

For closed-end credit, the APR and the finance charge must be disclosed "more conspicuously" than other disclosures required by TILA. 12 C.F.R.

§1026.17(a)(2). While you may wonder how something becomes *more* conspicuous, TILA mandates that all its disclosures should be "clear and conspicuous." 15 U.S.C. §1632(a); 12 C.F.R. §1026.17(a)(1). The idea is that these two key price-tag disclosures stand out. For open-end credit, the finance charge need only be garden-variety conspicuous, rather than more conspicuous. 12 C.F.R. §1026.5(a)(1). This rule is simple enough for the law student who need only memorize the different standard for the exam; the tough part is for creditors to figure out how to actually design and deliver disclosures that are in compliance. Then there is the seemingly simple process of delivering the disclosure to the consumer, even if all the numbers are calculated correctly.

Smith v. Cash Store Mgmt., Inc.

195 F.3d 325 (7th Cir. 1999)

FLAUM, Circuit Judge.

Valerie Smith sued The Cash Store, Ltd.; The Cash Store Management, Inc.; and The Cash Store Management, Inc.'s officers and directors (collectively "Cash Store") on behalf of a putative class for violations of the Truth in Lending Act ("TILA"), 15 U.S.C. §1601 et seq., and Illinois state contract law and consumer fraud statutes. This is an appeal from the district court's dismissal of Smith's suit for failure to state a claim under TILA. For the reasons set forth below, we affirm in part and reverse in part.

BACKGROUND

Cash Store operates at least sixteen loan establishments in Illinois. These establishments specialize in making short-term, high interest "payday loans," typically two weeks in duration and carrying annual percentage rates greater than 500%. When a Cash Store customer is granted a loan, the customer writes out a check, post-dated to the end of the loan period, for the full amount that he is obligated to pay. At the end of the two-week period, the customer has the option of continuing the loan for an additional two-week period by paying the interest.

Between June 13, 1998 and September 19, 1998, Smith obtained eight such loans from Cash Store. On each occasion she signed a standard "Consumer Loan Agreement" form. Each loan agreement stated an annual interest rate of 521%. Each loan agreement also contained the statement: "Security. Your post-dated check is security for this loan." Upon entering into or renewing each loan, Cash Store stapled to the top of the loan agreement a receipt which labeled the finance charge in red ink as either a "deferred deposit extension fee" or a "deferred deposit check fee," depending on whether the transaction was a renewal or an original loan.

The details of the loan agreement are important because the content and presentation of such agreements are regulated under TILA, 15 U.S.C. §1601 et seq., and implementing Federal Reserve Board Regulation Z ("Regulation Z"), 12 C.F.R. §226. Congress enacted TILA to ensure that consumers receive accurate information from creditors in a precise, uniform manner that allows consumers to compare the cost of credit from various lenders. 15 U.S.C. §1601; Anderson Bros. Ford v. Valencia, 452 U.S. 205, 220 (1981). Regulation Z mandates that: "The creditor shall make the disclosures required by this subpart clearly and conspicuously in writing, in a form that the consumer may keep. The disclosures shall be grouped together, shall be segregated from everything else, and shall not contain any information not directly related to the [required] disclosures. . . ." 12 C.F.R. §226.17(a)(1). The mandatory disclosures, which must be grouped in a federal disclosure section of a written loan agreement, include, among other things, the finance charge, the annual percentage rate, and any security interests that the lender takes. 12 C.F.R. §226.18.

On March 16, 1999, Smith filed a class action complaint, amended on April 6, 1999, against Cash Store in the United States District Court for the Northern District of Illinois. She sued on behalf of a putative class for violations of TILA, for relief from an unconscionable loan contract, and for violations of the Illinois Consumer Fraud Act. The district court dismissed with prejudice the TILA claims for failure to state a claim upon which relief can be granted, Fed. R. Civ. P. 12(b)(6), and then exercised its discretion to dismiss without prejudice the remaining supplemental state claims, as permitted by 28 U.S.C. §1367(c)(3).

DISCUSSION

Smith argues on appeal that two of Cash Store's practices violate TILA, and that the district court's dismissal of the claims was therefore erroneous. The first practice relates to the receipts that Cash Store routinely stapled to the top of Smith's loan agreements. Smith contends that the receipts physically obscured the required federal disclosures and that they characterized the finance charges in a misleading way. The second practice relates to the security interest disclosures, which Smith contends were inaccurate. We address each of these allegations in turn.

The Receipt Claim

TILA requires that a creditor make the required disclosures "clearly and conspicuously in writing. . . ." 12 C.F.R. §226.17. Smith alleges that the cash register receipt that Cash Store stapled to the upper left-hand corner of the loan agreements physically covered up some of the required disclosures. Furthermore, on her receipts were printed, in red, the terms "deferred deposit extension fee" or "deferred deposit check fee," whereas the term "finance charge" is used in the federal disclosure box. Smith argues that both of these practices render the required disclosures on the loan agreement neither "clear" nor "conspicuous."

The district court dismissed the claim relating to the Cash Store receipt on the ground that the allegations did not state a cause of action. It held that neither Cash Store's stapling of a receipt to the loan documents nor the printed contents of the receipt violated TILA, having found that "Cash Store's practice of stapling a small receipt to its TILA disclosures could not reasonably confuse or mislead Smith as to the terms of the loan." Smith v. Cash Store Mgmt., Inc., No. 99 C 1726, (N.D. Ill. June 8, 1999).

A complaint should not be dismissed for failure to state a claim unless it appears beyond doubt that the plaintiff can prove no set of facts to support his claim which would entitle him to relief. Conley v. Gibson, 355 U.S. 41, 45-46 (1957). . . . As we recently stated, "Rule 12(b)(6) should be employed only when the complaint does not present a legal claim." Johnson v. Revenue Mgmt. Corp., 169 F.3d 1057, 1059 (7th Cir. 1999). Because the district court may not dismiss the complaint under Rule 12(b)(6) unless it is legally insufficient, we review that decision de novo. Caremark, 113 F.3d at 648.

As noted above, Regulation Z requires that "[t]he creditor shall make the disclosures required by this subpart clearly and conspicuously." 12 C.F.R §226.17. The "sufficiency of TILA-mandated disclosures is to be viewed from the standpoint of an ordinary consumer, not the perspective of a Federal Reserve Board member, federal judge, or English professor." Cemail v. Viking Dodge, 982 F. Supp. 1296, 1302 (N.D. Ill. 1997).

Whether or not Cash Store's practices run afoul of Regulation Z is a factual issue, and the district court therefore erred in dismissing the receipt claims under Rule 12(b)(6). In her amended complaint, Smith contends that the stapled receipt contradicted and obfuscated the required disclosures. Am. Compl., ¶ 19. Her claim may fail on the facts, "but assessing factual support for a suit is not the office of Rule 12(b)(6)." Johnson, 169 F.3d at 1059. Although our holding does not preclude Cash Store from arguing, at the summary judgment stage, that Smith cannot prove her claims, Smith's complaint alleging that the stapled receipt obscured the disclosures and that the printed contents of the receipt were confusing or misleading states a valid legal claim under TILA, and that is sufficient to pass Rule 12(b)(6) scrutiny.

The Security Interest Claim

Smith also contends that the district court erred in holding that Cash Store's statement, "Your post-dated check is security for this loan," was a lawful disclosure under TILA. TILA requires creditors to disclose accurately any security interest taken by the lender and to describe accurately the property in which the interest is taken. 15 U.S.C. §1638; 12 C.F.R. §226.18. Regulation Z defines "security interest" as "an interest in property that secures performance of a consumer credit obligation and that is recognized by state or federal law." 12 C.F.R. §226.2(a)(25). Smith contends that Cash Store's statement in the loan agreement violates TILA because, under Illinois law, the check does not serve as security.

Subject to narrow exceptions, "hypertechnicality reigns" in the application of TILA. Cowen v. Bank United of Texas, FSB, 70 F.3d 937, 941 (7th Cir. 1995). Regulation Z specifies that certain federal disclosures must be grouped together in the loan agreement and also directs that the agreement "not contain any information not directly related to the [required] disclosures." 12 C.F.R. §226.17(a)(1). In Bizier v. Globe Financial Services Inc., the First Circuit explained that overinclusive security interest disclosures "cannot be dismissed as de minimis or hypertechnical." Overinclusive disclosures might deter a borrower's "future borrowing or property acquisition out of an exaggerated belief in the security interest to which they would be subject, or [give] a lender an apparent right which, even if ultimately unenforceable, could serve as a significant bargaining lever in any future negotiations concerning rights or obligations under the loan." 654 F.2d 1, 3 (1st Cir. 1981); see also Tinsman v. Moline Beneficial Fin. Co., 531 F.2d 815, 818-19 (7th Cir. 1976) (holding that an overbroad disclosure of security interests violated TILA). All TILA disclosures must be accurate, Gibson v. Bob Watson Chevrolet-Geo, Inc., 112 F.3d 283, 285 (7th Cir. 1997), and lenders are generally strictly liable under TILA for inaccuracies, even absent a showing that the inaccuracies are misleading, Brown v. Marquette Savings and Loan Assoc., 686 F.2d 608, 614 (7th Cir. 1982). Smith contends that if the check that Smith handed over upon agreeing to the loan does not give Cash Store a security interest, then its statement to that effect violates TILA.

Cash Store first responds that the check acts as "security" because it gives Cash Store alternate routes to collect its debt. The check might facilitate payment because the loan agreement provides that Cash Store may deposit it on the loan due date if another form of payment is not made. If the check were to bounce, Cash Store could sue Smith under Illinois "bad check" statutes. According to Cash Store, the check then "secures" the loan by making repayment easier or by placing Cash Store in a stronger litigating position under Illinois law if Smith does not pay back the loan. Hence, the statement "Security: Your post-dated check is security for this loan" is accurate, and perhaps even required under TILA.

This argument, standing alone, is incomplete because it confuses "security" with "security interest." True, Cash Store may be in a better position with the check than without it, and in that sense it may regard its loan as more "secure." But this is a broader sense of "security" than that contemplated by Regulation Z. The regulations define "security interest" — which is a term of art referring to a specific class of transactions — as "an interest in property that secures performance of a consumer credit obligation and that is recognized by state or federal law." 12 C.F.R. §226.2(a)(25). Illinois commercial law, in turn, defines it as "an interest in personal property . . . which secures payment or performance of an obligation." 810 ILCS 5/1-201(37). By creating a security interest through a security agreement, a debtor provides that a creditor may, upon default, take or sell the property — or collateral — to satisfy the obligation for which the security interest is given. 810 ILCS 5/9-105(1)(c) ("'Collateral' means the property subject to a security interest, and includes accounts and chattel paper which have been sold"). Because TILA restricts what information a lender can include in its federal disclosures, the question before us is not simply whether the post-dated check makes repayment more likely ("security") but whether it can meet the statutory requirements of "collateral" ("security *interest*").

Cash Store also maintains that Article 9 of the Illinois Uniform Commercial Code ("Illinois U.C.C."), which governs secured transactions, applies "to any transaction (regardless of its form) which is intended to create a security interest in personal property . . . including . . . instruments." 810 ILCS 5/9-102(1)(a). Because the check is an instrument, it can be used to create a security interest by the terms of the Illinois U.C.C. See In re Brigance, 234 B.R. 401, 404-05 (W.D. Tenn. 1999) (holding that, under Tennessee's U.C.C., a borrower's personal check can serve as collateral in which a security interest can be obtained).

We again believe that this argument is incomplete. While Article 9 of the Illinois U.C.C. generally authorizes the use of instruments as collateral to secure a loan, it is not immediately clear whether this provision applies to a post-dated check issued by the *borrower*.

Neither the ease of recovery in the event of default nor the simple fact that a check is an instrument are sufficient to create a security interest. It is the economic substance of the transaction that determines whether the check serves as collateral. Cf. Cobb v. Monarch Finance Corp., 913 F. Supp. 1164, 1177-78 (N.D. Ill. 1995) (distinguishing between a mechanism set up to facilitate repayment of a loan and an interest that secures a loan in the event of default). Therefore, in turning to our resolution of whether Cash Store took a security interest, our analysis must focus on the economic substance of Smith's pledged check. . . .

Smith argues that, having already promised contractually through the loan agreement to pay the amount printed on the check, the pledged check gives Cash Store no interest that it did not already have. The Illinois U.C.C. expressly provides that a check does not operate as an assignment of the bank account on which it is drawn. 810 ILCS 5/3-408. And the check itself has no intrinsic value beyond the minuscule value of a scrap of paper. According to Smith, then, the post-dated check does not secure the loan because it merely restates the promise to pay already contained in the loan agreement. Hitner v. Diamond State Steel Co., 176 F. 384, 391-92 (C.C.D. Del. 1910) ("It hardly admits of discussion that the mere duplication or multiplication of a promise to pay or of an acknowledgment of liability to pay a certain sum representing the total real indebtedness to a creditor, whatever may be its effect in furnishing in certain exigencies alternative or cumulative evidence of the real demand, cannot constitute collateral security.").

Smith may be correct that a second promise to pay, identical to the first, would not serve as collateral to secure a loan, because the second promise is of no economic significance: in the event that the borrower defaults on the first promise, the second promise to pay provides nothing of economic value that the creditor could seize and apply towards repayment of the loan. In this case, however, the post-dated check is not merely a second, *identical* promise. It is, indeed, a promise to pay the same amount as the first, but it has value to the creditor in the event of default beyond the value of the first promise. That is because a holder of both the loan and the check has remedies available to him that a holder of only the loan agreement does not. For example, the holder of the check has available remedies created by the Illinois bad check statute, 810 ILCS 5/3-806, which mandates that if a check is not honored, the drawer shall be liable for interest and costs and expenses incurred in the collection of the amount of the check.

Smith's own statement that the check is of no intrinsic value is instructive: it is its extrinsic legal status and the legal rights and remedies granted the holder of the check, like the holder of a loan agreement, that give rise to its value. Upon default on the loan agreement, Cash Store would get use of the check, along with the rights that go with it. Cash Store could simply negotiate it to someone else. Cash Store could take it to the bank and present it for payment. If denied, Cash Store could pursue bad check litigation. Additional value is created through these rights because Cash Store need not renegotiate or litigate the loan agreement as its only avenue of recourse.

It is not important that, as Smith argues, by the time Cash Store gets use of the check it might be clear that Smith would not or could not make good on a promise for that amount. Cash Store's likelihood of, for example, successfully pursuing bad check litigation goes to the issue of valuation of the check (one might roughly calculate it as its face value plus supplementary awards created by the bad check statute, discounted by the probability of successfully pressing the claim) not the issue of whether the check has *any* value beyond the promise contained in the original loan agreement. In the same way, there is the chance that Smith would call her bank and cancel the post-dated check before the loan's due date, but this potentiality, depending on how the loan agreement might affect her legal right to do so, goes to how much holding the check is worth, not whether it has any value at all. Some additional value is created by the bad check statute and other legal provisions governing instruments.

This is not to say that by putting up a check as collateral, a lender like Cash Store necessarily takes a security interest in the *amount* printed on the face of the instrument. Rather, the rights created by state commercial law can, and in this case do, create some value in the instrument. We are therefore satisfied that Cash Store could lawfully assert under TILA that Smith's post-dated check was security for the loan.

CONCLUSION

For the reasons stated above, we affirm the district court's dismissal of the security interest claim, and we reverse and remand the district court's dismissal of the receipt claim for further proceedings consistent with this opinion.

MANION, Circuit Judge, concurring in part and dissenting in part.

I certainly agree with the court regarding the security issue. The Cash Store did not violate the Truth in Lending Act by informing Smith that it was holding her post-dated check as security for her loan. While possessing a post-dated check does not create a "security interest" as that term is usually understood, possession of the check nevertheless provided the Cash Store with added security for the loan. Although the Cash Store was not obligated under TILA to inform Smith that it held this check as security, lenders that seek to provide more information than is necessary under TILA should not be penalized for following the spirit of the statute. Thus, this court correctly affirmed the district court on this, the most substantive issue before this court on appeal.

The court's decision to reverse the district court on Smith's "receipt" claim is a concern. It is important to note that there are two facets to this claim. Smith asserts that stapling a small receipt to "the top of the 'Consumer Loan Agreement'" violated TILA by (1) contradicting the TILA-mandated disclosures; and (2) obscuring the required disclosures. Complaint ¶ 19. Smith possibly stated a claim regarding the "obfuscation" assertion because there could be a fact question as to exactly where the receipt was stapled and what it specifically obscured. But on its face the receipt clearly does not "contradict" the finance charge and the annual percentage rate, and it should cause no confusion regarding the terms of the agreement itself.

With respect to Smith's contention that the receipt obscured the required disclosures, for starters it appears that no court has ever held that obstructing a borrower's immediate view of the TILA disclosures violates TILA. The text of the statute and the regulations interpreting the statute do not indicate that this constitutes a violation. This is literally a matter of first impression, on a claim that is weak at best. For that reason alone the district court's dismissal of this claim has merit. See 15 U.S.C. §1638; 12 C.F.R. §226.17(a)(1) & n. 37 ("The disclosures may include an acknowledgment of receipt. . . ."). That aside, the documents attached to Smith's complaint include an 8.5 × 11 inch disclosure form and a 4.5 × 3 inch receipt that supposedly obstructed some of the mandated disclosures. Perhaps there is a plausible set of facts regarding the obstruction claim that could require looking beyond the complaint to determine if Smith would be entitled to any relief. The complaint states that the receipt was stapled to the "top" of the agreement. The court's opinion refers to stapling to the "upper left-hand corner." The district court noted that the staple mark was on the upper left-hand corner of the receipt and the loan document itself had no marks. If "top" could mean "front" and if Smith could show that the receipt was consistently stapled in the middle of the page covering the boxes boldly labeled "Annual Percentage Rate" and "Finance Charge," perhaps she would have a claim. But if this relatively small receipt is routinely stapled to the upper left-hand corner with the lowest part barely covering one of the boxes and which could easily be lifted, there would not be any material obscuring of the TILA disclosures. More importantly, even assuming that an unsophisticated borrower would not lift up the receipt to see the small portion of the loan agreement covered by the receipt, such a borrower would still be able to clearly see the portions of the loan agreement which specify the annual percentage rate, the finance charge, the amount financed, the total of payments, the payment schedule, the security posted for the loan, the penalty for late payment, and a notice telling the borrower to examine the other side of the agreement for important information. Congress enacted TILA to ensure that consumers had access to this information so that they could comparatively shop for loans. See Walker v. Wallace Auto Sales, Inc., 155 F.3d 927, 930 (7th Cir. 1998) (citing Brown v. Marquette Sav. & Loan Ass'n, 686 F.2d 608, 612 (7th Cir. 1982) (Congress enacted TILA to "provide information to facilitate comparative credit shopping and thereby the informed use of credit by consumers.")). So by clearly communicating these terms, the Cash Store complied with the Act. The two pieces of information that the receipt would obstruct (if stapled to the upper left-hand corner), the lender's name and the borrower's own name, are not material to comparing interest rates and the like (and the names were printed on the receipt anyway). Accordingly, unless the Cash Store attached the small receipt to the middle of the loan agreement, implicitly to purposely obstruct and prevent an easy review of this information, there is no violation of TILA's requirements that the mandated disclosures be clear and conspicuous, and plaintiff fails to state a claim under the Act.

Smith also contends that the contents of the receipt contradicted the TILA-mandated disclosures. An obvious contradiction of a material term would constitute a violation of TILA. See Rodash v. AIB Mortgage Co., 16 F.3d 1142, 1146 (11th Cir. 1994). Thus, when a lender informs a borrower of his right to rescind, but also contradicts this notice by telling the borrower that he had waived his right to rescind, the borrower may state a claim under the Act. Id. But Smith has not made such an assertion here. In assessing a complaint under Rule 12(b)(6) we again look at the exhibits attached to the complaint, and the receipts attached to Smith's complaint on their face do not contradict the disclosures in the loan agreement. The receipts here contain the amount borrowed on the same line as the words or word fragments: "DEFERRED CHECKS" or "DEFERRED DEPOSIT EXTENSION." As there are no assertions made in the receipt, these words in no way contradict the information contained in the loan agreement. Furthermore, as the district court stated:

> The receipt is an insignificant and unofficial-looking document in comparison with the attached loan document. The "deferred deposit check fee" is a single, small entry on the receipt. The loan agreement, on the other hand, disclosed the finance charge and interest rate in large, boldface type in a conspicuous position on the front of the loan document. Even an unsophisticated borrower, receiving the two documents together, could not be confused as to the terms of the loan.

Perhaps the 500% interest rate is an "unconscionable" exploitation of the needs of the unsophisticated consumer as Smith's claim under state law asserts. As with the purchase of lottery tickets or cigarettes, consumers of payday loans likely know a bad deal when they see it but ignore the risks and take the loan anyway. A new state or federal law could eliminate these loans regardless of market demand. Until then TILA should not be stretched beyond its terms to restrict a product sophisticated consumers don't like. Because Smith's complaint and the exhibits attached thereto indicate that there was no contradiction (much less an obvious contradiction of a material term), she has failed to state a claim under TILA. Accordingly, the district court also correctly dismissed this part of the claim under Rule 12(b)(6).

While the *Smith* court ruled that the clarity of disclosure is a question of fact and some courts have agreed, *see Roberts v. Fleet Bank (R.I.) N.A.,* 342 F.3d 260 (2003), a split of authority exists. *See Rubio v. Capital One Bank,* 613 F.3d 1195 (9th Cir. 2010) (holding as a matter of law that Capital One had failed to show that its APR disclosure was made in a reasonably understandable form and readily noticeable to the consumer). Even the Seventh Circuit seems to be unclear on the question of clarity. In *Hamm v. Ameriquest Mortg. Co.,* 506 F.3d 525 (7th Cir. 2007), it held that whether a TILA disclosure is clear and conspicuous is a question of law.

For both closed- and open-end credit, the disclosures must be written and given in a form that consumers can retain. Model forms exist for many typical transactions in the Appendices to Regulation Z, but the creditor still has the obligation to choose the appropriate form, complete it correctly, and deliver it timely. 15 U.S.C. §1604(b). Many of the disclosures for open-end transactions, including account-opening forms credit or charge card applications, and change-in-terms notices, must be made in tabular form, with the information presented in boxes in a prescribed order. 12 C.F.R. §1026.5(a)(3).

The disclosure applicable in closed-end credit must be given "before the credit is extended," 15 U.S.C. §1638(b)(1), or in the parlance of Regulation Z, "before consummation." 12 C.F.R. §1026.17(b). Similarly, the initial disclosure for open-end credit must occur before the first transaction that obligates the consumer to repay an amount. 12 C.F.R. §1026.5(b)(1).

This Assignment gives the general rules for credit disclosure. The special requirements for certain types of transactions, such as credit cards and home mortgage loans, are considered in upcoming Assignments. As with other topics considered in the book, the enforcement options and liability rules are considered in Part IV of this book. This Assignment focuses the general and enduring concepts of lending disclosure—such as the APR term and the distinction between open-end and closed-end credit and highlights disclosure as a workhorse of consumer protection.

Despite its legal importance, the research on credit disclosure is surprisingly sparse. Back when TILA was enacted, a few studies exploited the new requirements to see if consumers' knowledge of loan terms increased. A measurable fraction of consumers had improved awareness of the interest rate, but still only just more than half of consumers had an accurate understanding of the cost of the loan. *See e.g.,* Lewis Mandell, *Consumer Perception of Incurred Interest Rates: An Empirical Test of the Efficacy of Truth-in-Lending Laws,* 26 J. OF FIN. 1143 (1971). Part of the issue is a widely-held (although perhaps incorrect) belief that more information is always beneficial, so there was relatively little questioning of whether disclosure works as desired. Remember that the goal of TILA is not just to increase knowledge, but to prompt consumers to comparison shop for credit using that information. Behavioral economics, which emphasizes what people actually do — rather than what a perfectly rational actor can be assumed to do — suggests that disclosures may be of limited value. The book *More Than You Wanted to Know* surveys the evidence before concluding that mandatory disclosure rarely works, in part because disclosures are complex, obscure, and dull. Omri Ben-Shahar & Carl E. Schneider, *More Than You Wanted to Know: The Failure of Mandated Disclosure* (2014). Provocatively, the authors conclude that plain English and improved design cannot solve the ultimate issues — that the transactions at issue are complex and that consumers make decisions by stripping away information to lower the cognitive burden. This new research continues to fuel the controversy about the relative merits of disclosure to substantive regulation.

Problem Set 12

12.1. Auto Advance makes loans to people purchasing used cars. It offers borrowers the option of purchasing life insurance that runs for the length of the car loan. Over 99 percent of borrowers purchase this life insurance. The cost of the policy is added to the loan and paid for in the regular monthly installments. Auto Advance gives the consumer an insurance information sheet that gives the amount of the premiums and makes clear that Auto Advance's subsidiary, Insure Advance, is the insurance company that will provide the insurance. Does Auto Advance have to include the insurance premiums in the finance charge? *See* 12 C.F.R. §1026.4.

12.2. Arnie Winger is the best salesmen at BottomsDown, a store specializing in high-end home office furniture for the Silicon Valley telecommuter set. He has taken a real interest in mentoring the store's new salesperson, Sally Roberts. Arnie keeps joking about how he has taken Sally "under his wing" and is teaching her the tricks of the trade. Part of Arnie's success is that he convinces nearly all customers to finance their furniture purchase. The problem is that Arnie likes to talk, not to write, and so is constantly leaving Sally with a big stack of paperwork to finish up in the evening. Today, he asked her to complete a TILA disclosure for a customer that looked at a desk, a chair, and other office furniture components and has promised to come back first thing tomorrow morning to finalize the deal. How should Sally complete the disclosure that Arnie started? What, if anything, goes in the missing boxes?

ANNUAL PERCENTAGE RATE The cost of your credit as a yearly rate.	FINANCE CHARGE The dollar amount the credit will cost you.	Amount Financed The amount of credit provided to you or on your behalf.	Total of Payments The amount you will have paid after you have made all payments as scheduled.	Total Sale Price The total cost of your chase on credit, including your downpayment of $ _1500._00_
_14.84_ %	$ _1496.80_	$ _6104_	$ _7604.30_	$ _9104.30_

You have the right to receive at this time an itemization of the Amount Financed.

☐ **I want an itemization.**   ☒ **I do not want an itemization**

Your payment schedule will be:

Number of Payments	Amount of Payments	When Payments are Due
_36_	_211 12_	_Monthly, starting 10/1_
	_263.01_	

12.3. Haynes always has been the most financially responsible (and morally superior) of his five siblings. The other day, his sister Clarice, asked him for advice. She received a credit card solicitation and is about to get her first credit card. Clarice is 23 years old and employed full-time at her first job as a sales associate at an auto dealer. Having heard Haynes rib their siblings for foolish financial and investment decisions, Clarice asks Haynes to choose between the two cards offered to her in a solicitation. Which card should Haynes recommend, assuming that Clarice identifies her priorities as a card with the lowest cost and the least risk of fees?

12.4. You are deputy compliance counsel for a non-bank mortgage lender, Upworthy Loans. Your role is to prepare the lender for state and federal examinations to determine if Upworthy is following all consumer laws. Last week, the CFPB released a new mortgage loan disclosure, including a model form for a fixed-rate loan (reproduced below). While the operations team has been working hard to deploy the new form before its effective date in three months, Upworthy's general counsel has given you a side project. She explains that she heard from a former CFPB employee, who now works for a competing lender, that CFPB "improved the law itself" with its form. "Of course, Upworthy will use the new form," she says, "but just in case an examiner finds an 'opportunity to improve' and we catch regulatory fire, I want to have some ammunition to challenge the required disclosure." What is your analysis? Focus on the three main elements of TILA disclosure. 15 U.S.C. §§1632(a); 1638(a); 12 C.F.R. §§1026.17(a); 1026.19(f); 1026.38.

Credit Card Disclosure		
	Kryptonite Card	Titanium Card
Interest Rates & Charges		
Annual Percentage Rate (APR) for Purchases*	**13.9%**	**7.75%** **Variable Rate**
Balance Transfers APR*	**4.9%***	**4.9%***
Cash Advance APR*	**13.9%**	**17.75%**
How to avoid paying interest	To avoid paying interest, simply pay the entire New Balance shown on your monthly statement within 25 days from the closing date of that statement.	
Minimum Finance Charge	None	None
Fees		
Annual Fee	None	$99
Balance Transfer Fee	None	$12 up to $10,000 transferred; otherwise $20.
Late Payment Fee	**5%** Or a minimum of $20	**10%** Or a minimum of $38
Returned Check Fee	$28	$47
International Transaction Fee	2.5% of transaction	1% of transaction
Cash Advance Fee	None	None
To obtain information about shopping for and using Credit Cards	To learn more about factors to consider when applying for or using a cred card, visit the website of the Consumer Financial Protection Bureau at: www.consumerfinance.gov/credit-cards.	
Interest and Fee Information for Checks		
APR for Check Transactions*	**13.9%**	**17.75%**
Use by Date	You must use the check within one year.	
Paying Interest	We will begin charging interest on these checks on the transaction date.	
Billing rights: Information on your rights to dispute transactions and how to exercise those rights is provided in your account agreement.		
***How We Will Calculate Your Balance**: We use a method called "Average Daily Balance, including New Purchases". See your account agreement for more details		
****Variable Rate:** The Variable rate is calculated by adding 4.50% to the Prime Lending rate in the Wall Street Journal, and will not exceed 18%.		
*****Balance Transfers:** This rate will apply for the first six months and then standard purchase rates will apply thereafter.		

Closing Disclosure

This form is a statement of final loan terms and closing costs. Compare this document with your Loan Estimate.

Closing Information

Date Issued	4/15/2013
Closing Date	4/15/2013
Disbursement Date	4/15/2013
Settlement Agent	Epsilon Title Co.
File #	12-3456
Property	456 Somewhere Ave
	Anytown, ST 12345
Sale Price	$180,000

Transaction Information

Borrower	Michael Jones and Mary Stone
	123 Anywhere Street
	Anytown, ST 12345
Seller	Steve Cole and Amy Doe
	321 Somewhere Drive
	Anytown, ST 12345
Lender	Ficus Bank

Loan Information

Loan Term	30 years
Purpose	Purchase
Product	Fixed Rate
Loan Type	☒ Conventional ☐ FHA
	☐ VA ☐ _____
Loan ID #	123456789
MIC #	000654321

Loan Terms

Loan Terms		Can this amount increase after closing?
Loan Amount	$162,000	**NO**
Interest Rate	3.875%	**NO**
Monthly Principal & Interest *See Projected Payments below for your Estimated Total Monthly Payment*	$761.78	**NO**
		Does the loan have these features?
Prepayment Penalty		**YES** • **As high as $3,240** if you pay off the loan during the first 2 years
Balloon Payment		**NO**

Projected Payments

Payment Calculation	Years 1-7		Years 8-30	
Principal & Interest		$761.78		$761.78
Mortgage Insurance	+	82.35	+	—
Estimated Escrow *Amount can increase over time*	+	206.13	+	206.13
Estimated Total Monthly Payment		**$1,050.26**		**$967.91**

Estimated Taxes, Insurance & Assessments *Amount can increase over time* *See page 4 for details*	**$356.13** a month	**This estimate includes** ☒ Property Taxes ☒ Homeowner's Insurance ☒ Other: Homeowner's Association Dues *See Escrow Account on page 4 for details. You must pay for other property costs separately.*	**In escrow?** **YES** **YES** **NO**

Costs at Closing

Closing Costs	$9,712.10	Includes $4,694.05 in Loan Costs + $5,018.05 in Other Costs – $0 in Lender Credits. *See page 2 for details.*
Cash to Close	$14,147.26	Includes Closing Costs. *See Calculating Cash to Close on page 3 for details.*

Closing Cost Details

Loan Costs	Borrower-Paid At Closing	Borrower-Paid Before Closing	Seller-Paid At Closing	Seller-Paid Before Closing	Paid by Others
A. Origination Charges	**$1,802.00**				
01 0.25 % of Loan Amount (Points)	$405.00				
02 Application Fee	$300.00				
03 Underwriting Fee	$1,097.00				
04					
05					
06					
07					
08					
B. Services Borrower Did Not Shop For	**$236.55**				
01 Appraisal Fee to John Smith Appraisers Inc.					$405.00
02 Credit Report Fee to Information Inc.		$29.80			
03 Flood Determination Fee to Info Co.	$20.00				
04 Flood Monitoring Fee to Info Co.	$31.75				
05 Tax Monitoring Fee to Info Co.	$75.00				
06 Tax Status Research Fee to Info Co.	$80.00				
07					
08					
09					
10					
C. Services Borrower Did Shop For	**$2,655.50**				
01 Pest Inspection Fee to Pests Co.	$120.50				
02 Survey Fee to Surveys Co.	$85.00				
03 Title – Insurance Binder to Epsilon Title Co.	$650.00				
04 Title – Lender's Title Insurance to Epsilon Title Co.	$500.00				
05 Title – Settlement Agent Fee to Epsilon Title Co.	$500.00				
06 Title – Title Search to Epsilon Title Co.	$800.00				
07					
08					
D. TOTAL LOAN COSTS (Borrower-Paid)	**$4,694.05**				
Loan Costs Subtotals (A + B + C)	$4,664.25	$29.80			

Other Costs	Borrower-Paid At Closing	Borrower-Paid Before Closing	Seller-Paid At Closing	Seller-Paid Before Closing	Paid by Others
E. Taxes and Other Government Fees	**$85.00**				
01 Recording Fees Deed: $40.00 Mortgage: $45.00	$85.00				
02 Transfer Tax to Any State			$950.00		
F. Prepaids	**$2,120.80**				
01 Homeowner's Insurance Premium (12 mo.) to Insurance Co.	$1,209.96				
02 Mortgage Insurance Premium (mo.)					
03 Prepaid Interest ($17.44 per day from 4/15/13 to 5/1/13)	$279.04				
04 Property Taxes (6 mo.) to Any County USA	$631.80				
05					
G. Initial Escrow Payment at Closing	**$412.25**				
01 Homeowner's Insurance $100.83 per month for 2 mo.	$201.66				
02 Mortgage Insurance per month for mo.					
03 Property Taxes $105.30 per month for 2 mo.	$210.60				
04					
05					
06					
07					
08 Aggregate Adjustment	– 0.01				
H. Other	**$2,400.00**				
01 HOA Capital Contribution to HOA Acre Inc.	$500.00				
02 HOA Processing Fee to HOA Acre Inc.	$150.00				
03 Home Inspection Fee to Engineers Inc.	$750.00			$750.00	
04 Home Warranty Fee to XYZ Warranty Inc.			$450.00		
05 Real Estate Commission to Alpha Real Estate Broker			$5,700.00		
06 Real Estate Commission to Omega Real Estate Broker			$5,700.00		
07 Title – Owner's Title Insurance (optional) to Epsilon Title Co.	$1,000.00				
08					
I. TOTAL OTHER COSTS (Borrower-Paid)	**$5,018.05**				
Other Costs Subtotals (E + F + G + H)	$5,018.05				
J. TOTAL CLOSING COSTS (Borrower-Paid)	**$9,712.10**				
Closing Costs Subtotals (D + I)	$9,682.30	$29.80	$12,800.00	$750.00	$405.00
Lender Credits					

CLOSING DISCLOSURE   PAGE 2 OF 5 · LOAN ID # 123456789

Calculating Cash to Close	Use this table to see what has changed from your Loan Estimate.		
	Loan Estimate	Final	Did this change?
Total Closing Costs (J)	$8,054.00	$9,712.10	**YES** · See **Total Loan Costs (D)** and **Total Other Costs (I)**
Closing Costs Paid Before Closing	$0	− $29.80	**YES** · You paid these Closing Costs **before closing**
Closing Costs Financed (Paid from your Loan Amount)	$0	$0	**NO**
Down Payment/Funds from Borrower	$18,000.00	$18,000.00	**NO**
Deposit	− $10,000.00	− $10,000.00	**NO**
Funds for Borrower	$0	$0	**NO**
Seller Credits	$0	− $2,500.00	**YES** · See Seller Credits in **Section L.**
Adjustments and Other Credits	$0	− $1,035.04	**YES** · See details in **Sections K and L**
Cash to Close	$16,054.00	$14,147.26	

Summaries of Transactions — Use this table to see a summary of your transaction.

BORROWER'S TRANSACTION

K. Due from Borrower at Closing	$189,762.30
01 Sale Price of Property	$180,000.00
02 Sale Price of Any Personal Property Included in Sale	
03 Closing Costs Paid at Closing (J)	$9,682.30
04	
Adjustments	
05	
06	
07	
Adjustments for Items Paid by Seller in Advance	
08 City/Town Taxes to	
09 County Taxes to	
10 Assessments to	
11 HOA Dues 4/15/13 to 4/30/13	$80.00
12	
13	
14	
15	

L. Paid Already by or on Behalf of Borrower at Closing	$175,615.04
01 Deposit	$10,000.00
02 Loan Amount	$162,000.00
03 Existing Loan(s) Assumed or Taken Subject to	
04	
05 Seller Credit	$2,500.00
Other Credits	
06 Rebate from Epsilon Title Co.	$750.00
07	
Adjustments	
08	
09	
10	
11	
Adjustments for Items Unpaid by Seller	
12 City/Town Taxes 1/1/13 to 4/14/13	$365.04
13 County Taxes to	
14 Assessments to	
15	
16	
17	

CALCULATION	
Total Due from Borrower at Closing (K)	$189,762.30
Total Paid Already by or on Behalf of Borrower at Closing (L)	− $175,615.04
Cash to Close ☒ From ☐ To Borrower	**$14,147.26**

SELLER'S TRANSACTION

M. Due to Seller at Closing	$180,080.00
01 Sale Price of Property	$180,000.00
02 Sale Price of Any Personal Property Included in Sale	
03	
04	
05	
06	
07	
08	
Adjustments for Items Paid by Seller in Advance	
09 City/Town Taxes to	
10 County Taxes to	
11 Assessments to	
12 HOA Dues 4/15/13 to 4/30/13	$80.00
13	
14	
15	
16	

N. Due from Seller at Closing	$115,665.04
01 Excess Deposit	
02 Closing Costs Paid at Closing (J)	$12,800.00
03 Existing Loan(s) Assumed or Taken Subject to	
04 Payoff of First Mortgage Loan	$100,000.00
05 Payoff of Second Mortgage Loan	
06	
07	
08 Seller Credit	$2,500.00
09	
10	
11	
12	
13	
Adjustments for Items Unpaid by Seller	
14 City/Town Taxes 1/1/13 to 4/14/13	$365.04
15 County Taxes to	
16 Assessments to	
17	
18	
19	

CALCULATION	
Total Due to Seller at Closing (M)	$180,080.00
Total Due from Seller at Closing (N)	− $115,665.04
Cash ☐ From ☒ To Seller	**$64,414.96**

Additional Information About This Loan

Loan Disclosures

Assumption

If you sell or transfer this property to another person, your lender

☐ will allow, under certain conditions, this person to assume this loan on the original terms.

☒ will not allow assumption of this loan on the original terms.

Demand Feature

Your loan

☐ has a demand feature, which permits your lender to require early repayment of the loan. You should review your note for details.

☒ does not have a demand feature.

Late Payment

If your payment is more than *15* days late, your lender will charge a late fee of *5% of the monthly principal and interest payment.*

Negative Amortization (Increase in Loan Amount)

Under your loan terms, you

☐ are scheduled to make monthly payments that do not pay all of the interest due that month. As a result, your loan amount will increase (negatively amortize), and your loan amount will likely become larger than your original loan amount. Increases in your loan amount lower the equity you have in this property.

☐ may have monthly payments that do not pay all of the interest due that month. If you do, your loan amount will increase (negatively amortize), and, as a result, your loan amount may become larger than your original loan amount. Increases in your loan amount lower the equity you have in this property.

☒ do not have a negative amortization feature.

Partial Payments

Your lender

☒ may accept payments that are less than the full amount due (partial payments) and apply them to your loan.

☐ may hold them in a separate account until you pay the rest of the payment, and then apply the full payment to your loan.

☐ does not accept any partial payments.

If this loan is sold, your new lender may have a different policy.

Security Interest

You are granting a security interest in

456 Somewhere Ave., Anytown, ST 12345

You may lose this property if you do not make your payments or satisfy other obligations for this loan.

Escrow Account

For now, your loan

☒ will have an escrow account (also called an "impound" or "trust" account) to pay the property costs listed below. Without an escrow account, you would pay them directly, possibly in one or two large payments a year. Your lender may be liable for penalties and interest for failing to make a payment.

Escrow		
Escrowed Property Costs over Year 1	$2,473.56	Estimated total amount over year 1 for your escrowed property costs: *Homeowner's Insurance Property Taxes*
Non-Escrowed Property Costs over Year 1	$1,800.00	Estimated total amount over year 1 for your non-escrowed property costs: *Homeowner's Association Dues* You may have other property costs.
Initial Escrow Payment	$412.25	A cushion for the escrow account you pay at closing. See Section G on page 2.
Monthly Escrow Payment	$206.13	The amount included in your total monthly payment.

☐ will not have an escrow account because ☐ you declined it ☐ your lender does not offer one. You must directly pay your property costs, such as taxes and homeowner's insurance. Contact your lender to ask if your loan can have an escrow account.

No Escrow		
Estimated Property Costs over Year 1		Estimated total amount over year 1. You must pay these costs directly, possibly in one or two large payments a year.
Escrow Waiver Fee		

In the future,

Your property costs may change and, as a result, your escrow payment may change. You may be able to cancel your escrow account, but if you do, you must pay your property costs directly. If you fail to pay your property taxes, your state or local government may (1) impose fines and penalties or (2) place a tax lien on this property. If you fail to pay any of your property costs, your lender may (1) add the amounts to your loan balance, (2) add an escrow account to your loan, or (3) require you to pay for property insurance that the lender buys on your behalf, which likely would cost more and provide fewer benefits than what you could buy on your own.

CLOSING DISCLOSURE

m   n   (x)

Loan Calculations

Total of Payments. Total you will have paid after you make all payments of principal, interest, mortgage insurance, and loan costs, as scheduled.	$285,803.36
Finance Charge. The dollar amount the loan will cost you.	$118,830.27
Amount Financed. The loan amount available after paying your upfront finance charge.	$162,000.00
Annual Percentage Rate (APR). Your costs over the loan term expressed as a rate. This is not your interest rate.	4.174%
Total Interest Percentage (TIP). The total amount of interest that you will pay over the loan term as a percentage of your loan amount.	69.46%

Questions? If you have questions about the loan terms or costs on this form, use the contact information below. To get more information or make a complaint, contact the Consumer Financial Protection Bureau at **www.consumerfinance.gov/mortgage-closing**

Other Disclosures

Appraisal
If the property was appraised for your loan, your lender is required to give you a copy at no additional cost at least 3 days before closing. If you have not yet received it, please contact your lender at the information listed below.

Contract Details
See your note and security instrument for information about
- what happens if you fail to make your payments,
- what is a default on the loan,
- situations in which your lender can require early repayment of the loan, and
- the rules for making payments before they are due.

Liability after Foreclosure
If your lender forecloses on this property and the foreclosure does not cover the amount of unpaid balance on this loan,
☒ state law may protect you from liability for the unpaid balance. If you refinance or take on any additional debt on this property, you may lose this protection and have to pay any debt remaining even after foreclosure. You may want to consult a lawyer for more information.
☐ state law does not protect you from liability for the unpaid balance.

Refinance
Refinancing this loan will depend on your future financial situation, the property value, and market conditions. You may not be able to refinance this loan.

Tax Deductions
If you borrow more than this property is worth, the interest on the loan amount above this property's fair market value is not deductible from your federal income taxes. You should consult a tax advisor for more information.

Contact Information

	Lender	Mortgage Broker	Real Estate Broker (B)	Real Estate Broker (S)	Settlement Agent
Name	Ficus Bank		Omega Real Estate Broker Inc.	Alpha Real Estate Broker Co.	Epsilon Title Co.
Address	4321 Random Blvd. Somecity, ST 12340		789 Local Lane Sometown, ST 12345	987 Suburb Ct. Someplace, ST 12340	123 Commerce Pl. Somecity, ST 12344
NMLS ID					
ST License ID			Z765416	Z61456	Z61616
Contact	Joe Smith		Samuel Green	Joseph Cain	Sarah Arnold
Contact NMLS ID	12345				
Contact ST License ID			P16415	P51461	PT1234
Email	joesmith@ ficusbank.com		sam@omegare.biz	joe@alphare.biz	sarah@ epsilontitle.com
Phone	123-456-7890		123-555-1717	321-555-7171	987-555-4321

Confirm Receipt

By signing, you are only confirming that you have received this form. You do not have to accept this loan because you have signed or received this form.

_____   _____   _____   _____
Applicant Signature   Date   Co-Applicant Signature   Date

CLOSING DISCLOSURE

Assignment 13. Home Purchases

A home is the largest purchase that most consumers make. Homeownership is a vehicle for building wealth and promoting stable neighborhoods. For decades, the federal government has encouraged homeownership as a matter of policy. For these reasons, you might expect robust laws for consumers as they buy and finance homes. Historically, that has not been the situation. Until very recently, the laws that govern homeownership were a patchwork of uneven protection. In some areas, such as warranty, home buyers have even fewer consumer protections than apply to less expensive purchases. With regard to credit, consumer protection also was curtailed. Most usury laws never applied to home mortgages, for example. Concerns about providing access to credit held sway in shaping consumer laws for mortgages because homeownership was seen as socially and economically beneficial. Additionally, regulatory oversight for mortgages was fractured among federal and state agencies, and further complicated by the roles of entities such as Fannie Mae.

The financial crisis that began in 2008 essentially shut down the residential real estate and lending markets. While the liquidity problems of large institutions such as Lehman Brothers, Bear Stearns, and AIG involved complexities such as repo/swap agreements, shadow banking, and capital requirements, a root cause was home mortgages. The Financial Crisis Inquiry Commission Report explains:

> In this report, we detail the events of the crisis. But a simple summary, as we see it, is useful at the outset. While the vulnerabilities that created the potential for crisis were years in the making, it was the collapse of the housing bubble — fueled by low interest rates, easy and available credit, scant regulation, and toxic mortgages — that was the spark that ignited a string of events, which led to a full-blown crisis in the fall of 2008. Trillions of dollars in risky mortgages had become embedded throughout the financial system, as mortgage-related securities were packaged, repackaged, and sold to investors around the world. When the bubble burst, hundreds of billions of dollars in losses in mortgages and mortgage-related securities shook markets as well as financial institutions that had significant exposures to those mortgages and had borrowed heavily against them. This happened not just in the United States but around the world.

p. xvi. http://fcic.law.stanford.edu/report. In the decade preceding the onset of the financial crisis, an increasing proportion of loans were "subprime." This undefined term generally means loans of lower quality than "prime" loans; in fact, the lack of definitional clarity and data on subprime loans hampered careful monitoring of the mortgage market. Businesses "peddled a cornucopia of risky nontraditional mortgage products to borrowers during the housing bubble: hybrid ARMs (adjustable-rate mortgages), interest-only loans, pay-option ARMS, and loans with negative amortization." Kathleen C. Engel &

Patricia A. McCoy, *The Subprime Virus* 34 (2011). Underwriting standards loosened too, giving rise to some colorful monikers. A "NINJA" loan was funded without lender verification of a consumer's financial prospects. These no-income, no-job, no-asset loans were later called "liar's loans," although it is likely that both borrowers and mortgage professionals were engaged in misconduct. Some people who took out home mortgages were in default less than a year later—or never made a single payment. By 2006, over 80 percent of home loans were to refinance previous loans, not to help a family into a house.

In 2010, the Dodd-Frank Act fundamentally reshaped the laws relating to home purchase and finance for consumers. Congress enacted new laws, amended dozens of existing statutes, and directed the CFPB to issue new regulations. The new homeownership laws were complex to write and to implement. The most important rules became effective in 2015. Other issues, such as the federal government's role in financing the mortgage market, still remain unsettled as of 2016. It is an understatement to say that the law is uncertain; case law is essentially non-existent and will take years to develop.

In the meantime, however, consumers continue to want homes, and businesses continue to want to sell and lend. This book describes the legal landscape with an eye to the future, but there is a certain amount of educated guessing about how the market will evolve. To make learning more manageable, coverage of homeownership is divided. This assignment discusses how consumers get homes and their rights in a purchase transaction. A primary goal is understanding the actors, vocabulary, and structure of the homeownership market. The next assignment covers the rules on home mortgages and repayment.

A. Anatomy of a Home Purchase

Most consumers lack the cash to buy a home outright. If a consumer is so lucky (aka rich, or the "1 percent"), the issues that might arise are largely limited to choosing a home, negotiating the price and terms with the seller, and trying to ensure against problems with the house. These issues are covered later in this section.

For the rest of us (let's say, the "99 percent"), buying a home is inextricably linked with financing the purchase price. This means that many consumers start by looking for credit, and then select a home that is priced in the range of the loan for which they qualify. This section lays out a typical home purchase in some detail but it does not cover the law that governs underwriting mortgages. That is saved for the next assignment, after you have more background on residential real estate.

1. Qualifying for a Mortgage

After deciding that they want a home, consumers need to figure out what they can afford to spend. Instead of checking their wallets for cash or their credit card limits, consumers have to make a prospective ask to lenders. Will you give me a home loan, and if so, for how much money? As a practical matter, many consumers rely on lenders to determine what they can afford, rather than making an independent calculation. Recognizing this reality and to curb some of the unaffordable loans of the 1990s and 2000s, federal law now has underwriting requirements. Lenders today must assess a potential mortgage borrower's "ability to repay." This legal standard is detailed in the next assignment.

Perhaps the most important factor in the cost of the loan is the interest rate—and the biggest driver of this is nothing particular to consumers. It is the lender's cost of funds. Most lenders borrow money in order to lend money (or have to pay interest on deposits, which they can then lend out). The market rate of interest is always their starting point in pricing a loan. The other key factors are the type of loan that the consumer requests or is offered. This varies along several parameters, each of which changes the cost of the loan—and the lender's profit and risk.

- Fixed- or adjustable-rate of interest. A fixed rate of interest will not change, providing certainty that principal and interest payments will be steady. Adjustable-rate loans may be lower than fixed-rate loans initially but may change. Often the rate changes based on a market index (commonly the LIBOR, the London Inter Bank Offer Rate); there is usually a rate floor and cap.

- Points. These are costs paid at the time of the home purchase and are expressed as a percentage of the loan amount (normally less than 1 percent). They are essentially prepayment of interest, in return for a lower interest rate on the loan. Consumers can pay points in cash at closing or the lender can pay points but then credit the consumer that amount toward closing costs. A zero-point loan means that the consumer just pays the stated interest rate and any costs to actually close the loan (see next section of this assignment).

- Fully amortizing or balloon payment. Amortization means that the amount owed is paid down to zero by the end of the loan term. Negative amortization occurs when the payments are not sufficient to even cover interest and fees, leading to an increasing balance over time. Sometimes the loan payments are calculated as if the loan is fully amortized over a long term but the loan itself is shorter. This produces a balloon payment, often quite large, at the end of the loan term.

- Prepayment penalty. Usually mortgage loans can be paid off at the consumer's will for the payoff balance—the outstanding principal and accrued interest since the last payment. A prepayment penalty is an additional fee that is owed if the loan is paid off earlier than the loan term (or a determined period, such as the first ten years of the loan). A prepayment penalty can apply upon refinance or home sale. It compensates the lender for the profits from the lost interest that would have been earned if all payments were made over time.

- Down payment. This is the amount of money that a consumer pays to the seller at the time of the home purchase. It is usually expressed as a percentage of the home's value. A traditional residential loan requires a 20 percent down payment. Some government programs, such as the

Veterans Administration, permit 0 percent down loans. When the down payment is less than 20 percent, some lenders will require the consumer to pay for private mortgage insurance (PMI). This covers the lender's loss if the consumer fails to pay the mortgage.

An "originator" arranges, assists, or offers a consumer a home loan or a home loan application in expectation of direct or indirect compensation or monetary gain. 12 C.F.R. §1026.36. Mortgage originators are required to be registered and licensed by either state or federal law. 15 U.S.C. §1639(b). Originators can be large depository banks, non-banks, or individual people. A person who shops for a loan to present to a consumer is commonly called a "mortgage broker" while a person who works for a financial institution that offers a loan to a consumer is often called a "mortgage banker" or "loan officer."

There is no law that requires a consumer to be offered the best or lowest-priced loan for which he or she may qualify. Consumers can choose who originates their loan and select from any offered loan. This is why consumers are urged to shop for loans, either online or in person, and either on their own or with help. Originators are prohibited from steering or directing consumers to a particular lender or loan because the originator will receive greater compensation. 15 U.S.C. §1639b(c). Generally, originators must show consumers at least three types of loans. Often consumers will get "pre-qualified" or "pre-approved" with a lender to get an idea of the amount of loan that is likely to be made. The lender is not required to make a particular loan at a particular rate to that consumer but is doing some underwriting on the consumer, such as checking a credit score and verifying income.

A real estate broker, unless also being compensated for the loan, is not a mortgage originator. While brokers sometimes recommend lenders, that is not their primary function and they are not to be compensated by lenders. The job of a real estate broker is to sell a house that is listed for sale. A real estate broker is compensated by the seller based on a percentage of the house's sale price. A higher-priced home generates more revenue for the real estate broker. Real estate brokers also help buyers locate homes for sale. A related term, real estate salesperson, usually connotes someone who works for a broker or who has less experience in real estate sales. *See, e.g.* Fla. Stat. §457.17 (requiring a person seeking to be licensed as a broker to have had at least 24 months of an active real estate license as a sales associate). Real estate brokers are not mere middlemen but the exact nature of their duties is often misunderstood.

Horiike v. Coldwell Banker Residential Brokerage Co.

225 Cal. App. 4th 427 (2014)

KRIEGLER, Appellate Judge.

A broker represented both the buyer and the seller in a real property transaction through two different salespersons. The buyer brought several claims against the broker and the salesperson who listed the property for sale, including breach of fiduciary duty. The trial court granted a nonsuit on the claim for breach of fiduciary duty against the salesperson on the ground that the salesperson who listed the property did not have a fiduciary duty to the buyer. The court also instructed the jury that the broker had no liability for breach of fiduciary duty based on the salesperson's acts. The jury returned a verdict in favor of the defense on the remaining causes of action.

The buyer contends that the salesperson had a fiduciary duty equivalent to the duty owed by the broker, and the trial court incorrectly granted the nonsuit and erroneously instructed the jury. We agree. When a broker is the dual agent of both the buyer and the seller in a real property transaction, the salespersons acting under the broker have the same fiduciary duty to the buyer and the seller as the broker. The buyer was prejudiced by the erroneous rulings, because the jury's findings of fact did not resolve the omitted issues concerning breach of fiduciary duty. Therefore, we reverse the judgment and remand for a new trial.

FACTS

Defendant Chris Cortazzo is a salesperson for defendant Coldwell Banker Residential Brokerage Company (CB). In 2006, the owners of a residential property in Malibu engaged Cortazzo to sell their property. The building permit lists the total square footage of the property as 11,050 square feet, including a single-family residence of 9,224 square feet, a guest house of 746 square feet, a garage of 1,080 square feet, and a basement of unspecified area.

Cortazzo listed the property for sale on a multiple listing service (MLS) in September 2006. The listing service provided Cortazzo with public record information for reference, which stated that the living area of the property was 9,434 square feet. The listing that Cortazzo created, however, stated the home "offers approximately 15,000 square feet of living areas." Cortazzo prepared a flier for the property which stated it "offers approximately 15,000 square feet of living areas."

In March 2007, a couple made an offer to purchase the property. They asked Cortazzo for verification of the living area square footage. Cortazzo provided a letter from the architect stating the size of the house under a current Malibu building department ordinance was approximately 15,000 square feet. Cortazzo suggested the couple hire a qualified specialist to verify the square footage. The couple requested the certificate of occupancy and the architectural plans, but no architectural plans were available. In the real estate transfer disclosure statement, Cortazzo noted from his visual inspection that adjacent parcels were vacant and subject to development. He repeated his advice to hire a qualified specialist to verify the square footage of the home, stating that the broker did not guarantee or warrant the square footage.

When the couple learned architectural plans were not available, they requested a six-day extension to inspect the property. The sellers refused to grant the extension and the couple cancelled the transaction at the end of March 2007. In July 2007, Cortazzo changed the MLS listing to state that the approximate square footage was "0/O.T.," by which he meant zero square feet and other comments.

Plaintiff Hiroshi Horiike was working with CB salesperson Chizuko Namba to locate a residential property to purchase. Namba saw Cortazzo's listing for the

Malibu property and arranged for Cortazzo to show the property to Horiike on November 1, 2007. Cortazzo gave Horiike a copy of the flier stating the property had 15,000 square feet of living areas. Escrow opened on November 9, 2007. Cortazzo sent a copy of the building permit to Namba. Namba provided a copy of the permit to Horiike with other documents.

The parties to the transaction signed a confirmation of the real estate agency relationships as required by Civil Code section 2079.17. The document explained that CB, as the listing agent and the selling agent, was the agent of both the buyer and the seller. Cortazzo signed the document as an associate licensee of the listing agent CB. Namba signed the document as an associate licensee of the selling agent CB.

Horiike also executed a form required under Civil Code section 2079.16 for the disclosure of three possible real estate agency relationships. First, the form explained the relationship of a seller's agent acting under a listing agreement with the seller. The seller's agent acts as an agent for the seller only and has a fiduciary duty in dealings with the seller. The seller's agent has obligations to both the buyer and the seller to exercise reasonable skill and care, as well as a duty of fair dealing and good faith, and a "duty to disclose all facts known to the agent materially affecting the value or desirability of the property that are not known to, or within the diligent attention and observation of, the parties."

The second type of relationship, which is not at issue in this case, involves the obligations of an agent acting for the buyer only. An agent acting only for a buyer has a fiduciary duty in dealings with the buyer. A buyer's agent also has obligations to the buyer and the seller to exercise reasonable care, deal fairly and in good faith, and disclose material facts.

The third relationship described was an agent representing both the seller and the buyer. "A real estate agent, either acting directly or through one or more associate licensees, can legally be the agent of both the Seller and the Buyer in a transaction, but only with the knowledge and consent of both the Seller and the Buyer." An agent in a dual agency situation has a fiduciary duty to both the seller and the buyer, as well as the duties to buyer and seller listed in the previous sections.

Horiike signed the disclosure form as the buyer and Cortazzo signed as an associate licensee for the agent CB. In the visual inspection disclosure that Cortazzo provided to Horiike, he noted adjacent vacant lots were subject to building development. He did not add a handwritten note of advice to hire a qualified specialist to verify the square footage of the home, as he had in the previous transaction. Horiike completed the property transaction.

In preparation for work on the property in 2009, Horiike reviewed the building permit. He asked Cortazzo to verify that the property had 15,000 square feet of living areas. Horiike's expert testified at trial that the living areas of the home totaled 11,964 square feet. The defense expert testified the home's living areas totaled 14,186 square feet.

PROCEDURAL BACKGROUND

On November 23, 2010, Horiike filed a complaint against Cortazzo and CB for intentional and negligent misrepresentation, breach of fiduciary duty, unfair business practices in violation of Business and Professions Code section 17200, and false advertising in violation of Business and Professions Code section 17500. The parties agreed that the claims based on violations of the Business and Professions Code would be determined by the court following the jury trial.

After the presentation of Horiike's case to the jury, Cortazzo moved for nonsuit on the cause of action for breach of fiduciary duty against him. The trial court granted the motion on the ground that Cortazzo had no fiduciary duty to Horiike. . . .

The trial court determined the jury's findings resolved the remaining claims in favor of Cortazzo and CB. Therefore, on October 30, 2012, the court entered judgment in favor of Cortazzo and CB. Horiike filed a motion for a new trial on the ground the verdict was internally inconsistent, which the court denied. Horiike filed a timely notice of appeal.

DISCUSSION

. . .

Duty of a Salesperson Acting for a Dual Agent

Horiike contends that Cortazzo, as an associate licensee of CB, owed a fiduciary duty to him equivalent to the fiduciary duty owed by CB. We agree.

The duties of brokers and salespersons in real property transactions are regulated by a comprehensive statutory scheme. Civ. Code, §2079 et seq. Under this scheme, an "agent" is a licensed real estate broker "under whose license a listing is executed or an offer to purchase is obtained." Id., §2079.13, subd. (a). An "associate licensee" is a licensed real estate broker or salesperson "who is either licensed under a broker or has entered into a written contract with a broker to act as the broker's agent in connection with acts requiring a real estate license and to function under the broker's supervision in the capacity of an associate licensee." Id., subd. (b). "'Dual agent' means an agent acting, either directly or through an associate licensee, as agent for both the seller and the buyer in a real property transaction." Id., subd. (d).

"The agent in the real property transaction bears responsibility for his or her associate licensees who perform as agents of the agent. When an associate licensee owes a duty to any principal, or to any buyer or seller who is not a principal, in a real property transaction, that duty is equivalent to the duty owed to that party by the broker for whom the associate licensee functions." Civ. Code, §2079.13, subd. (b).

"[A] broker's fiduciary duty to his client requires the highest good faith and undivided service and loyalty." Field v. Century 21 Klowden-Forness Realty, 73 Cal. Rptr. 2d 784 (1998). "[A] dual agent has fiduciary duties to both the buyer and seller." Assilzadeh v. California Federal Bank, 98 Cal. Rptr. 2d 176 (2000).

CB acted as the dual agent of the buyer and the seller in this case, as was confirmed on the disclosure forms provided to Horiike. The disclosure form explicitly stated that a dual agent has a fiduciary duty of utmost care, integrity, honesty, and loyalty in dealings with either the seller or the buyer. See Assilzadeh v. California Federal Bank, supra, 82 Cal. App. 4th at p. 414. Cortazzo executed the forms on behalf of CB as an associate licensee. Under Civil Code section 2079.13, subdivision (b), the duty that Cortazzo owed to any principal, or to any buyer who was not a principal, was equivalent to the duty owed to that party by CB. CB owed a fiduciary duty to Horiike, and therefore, Cortazzo owed a fiduciary duty to Horiike.

Miller & Starr explains: "When there is one broker, and there are different sales-persons licensed under the same broker, each salesperson is an employee of the broker and their actions are the actions of the employing broker. . . . When one salesperson obtains the listing and represents the seller, and another salesperson employed by the same broker represents the buyer, they both act as employees of the same broker. That broker thereby becomes a dual agent representing both parties." 2 Miller & Starr, Cal. Real Estate (3d ed. 2011) §3:12, p. 68. Miller & Starr notes: "Salespersons commonly believe that there is no dual representation if one salesperson 'represents' one party to the transaction and another salesperson employed by the same broker 'represents' another party to the transaction. The real estate industry has sought to establish salespersons as 'independent contractors' for tax purposes, and this concept has enhanced the misunderstanding of salespersons that they can deal independently in the transaction even though they are negotiat-ing with a different salesperson employed by the same broker who is representing the other party to the transaction." Id. at fn. 29.

Cortazzo, as an associate licensee acting on behalf of CB, had the same fiduciary duty to Horiike as CB. The motion for nonsuit should have been denied and the cause of action against Cortazzo for breach of fiduciary duty submitted to the jury. The jury was also incorrectly instructed that CB could not be held liable for breach of fiduciary duty based on Cortazzo's actions. . . .

"A broker's fiduciary duty to his client requires the highest good faith and undi-vided service and loyalty. 'The broker as a fiduciary has a duty to learn the material facts that may affect the principal's decision. He is hired for his professional knowl-edge and skill; he is expected to perform the necessary research and investigation in order to know those important matters that will affect the principal's decision, and he has a duty to counsel and advise the principal regarding the propriety and rami-fications of the decision. The agent's duty to disclose material information to the principal includes the duty to disclose reasonably obtainable material informa-tion.'" Assilzadeh v. California Federal Bank, supra, 82 Cal. App. 4th at pp. 414-415, quoting Field v. Century 21 Klowden-Forness Realty, supra, 63 Cal. App. 4th at pp. 25-26.

"A fiduciary must tell its principal of all information it possesses that is material to the principal's interests. A fiduciary's failure to share material information with the principal is constructive fraud, a term of art obviating actual fraudulent intent." Michel v. Moore & Associates, Inc., 67 Cal. Rptr. 3d 797 (2007).

"'Constructive fraud is a unique species of fraud applicable only to a fiduciary or confidential relationship. . . . Most acts by an agent in breach of his fiduciary duties constitute constructive fraud. The failure of the fiduciary to disclose a material fact to his principal which might affect the fiduciary's motives or the principal's decision, which is known (or should be known) to the fiduciary, may constitute constructive fraud. Also, a careless misstatement may constitute constructive fraud even though there is no fraudulent intent.'" Salahutdin v. Valley of California, Inc., 29 Cal. Rptr. 2d 463 (1994). . . .

A trier of fact could conclude that Cortazzo was aware of material information that he failed to provide Horiike, even though he did not have a fraudulent intent. Cortazzo knew the square footage of the property had been measured and reflected differently in different documents. When a potential purchaser sought to confirm the square footage, Cortazzo gave handwritten advice to have the square footage verified by a specialist. He subsequently changed the listing for the property to reflect that the square footage required explanation. He did not explain to Horiike that contradictory square footage measurements existed. A trier of fact could conclude that although Cortazzo did not intentionally conceal the information, Cortazzo breached his fiduciary duty by failing to communicate all of the material information he knew about the square footage. He did not even provide the handwritten advice given to other potential purchasers to hire a specialist to verify the square footage. . . .

The judgment is reversed. Appellant Hiroshi Horiike is awarded his costs on appeal.

Not all states permit "dual agency," in part because of concerns about conflicting duties. *See e.g.*, Fla. Stat. §§475.278; 275.272. A buyer will want to pay the lowest price for the home but a broker is compensated based on a percentage of the sales price, creating a potential conflict. As with warranty law, the more information that a consumer provides, the higher the duty to disclose.

2.   Closing on a Home

When a consumer is interested in a home, he or she makes a written offer. There will be conditions to the offer, such as the buyer obtaining a loan or the seller perhaps making certain repairs. The offer will normally be accompanied by "earnest money," essentially a very small down payment toward the purchase price to indicate that the buyer is serious. The seller then must accept the offer—just like you learned in first-year law school. At this point, the parties have a tentative deal. Before the home is actually purchased, there are additional steps each party must take. If the buyer fails to do the required steps, the earnest money may be forfeited to the seller, who took the property off the market to allow the buyer to proceed.

The consummation and transfer of ownership will occur at the "closing." This is when the parties will sign and exchange all necessary documents, and everybody either pays or gets paid—as befits the situation.

There are several distinct documents related to a home purchase. These are greatly simplified definitions but even at this level, they expose some of the complex aspects of home purchase.

- Loan Estimate. This disclosure must be given to a consumer no later than the third business day after he or she submits a loan application and at least four business days prior to the consumer's being committed to the loan (called "consummation"). The form provides key information on the loan terms, projected payments, and closing costs. 12 C.F.R. §1026.37.
- Deed. This is the real estate document that transfers ownership of the home from the seller or the buyer. It is recorded in the county land records. The statute of frauds and other state laws impose formalities, such as a notary or witnesses, on the signing of deeds.

- Promissory Note. This is the contract to borrow money. It is signed by the lender and the borrower (the buyer of the house). It will set forth the key loan terms, such as the amount borrowed, the length of the loan, and the interest rate. The note is usually a "negotiable instrument," which means it can be transferred to others who can then collect on it.
- Mortgage or Deed of Trust or Security Instrument. The particular type of document used depends on state law but each document has the same purpose. When signed by the homeowner/borrower, it grants the lender a contingent, non-possessory security interest in the home. The mortgage will cause the house to be collateral for the loan, specify the terms of default, and give the right to foreclose (to take ownership) of the house if the loan is unpaid.
- Closing Disclosure. The Truth in Lending Act and the Real Estate Settlement Procedures Act require a disclosure of all costs related to the mortgage loan and to closing the transaction. 12 C.F.R. §1026.38. These are integrated into a Closing Disclosure. Creditors must provide the document no later than three business days before "consummation" of the loan. See Problem 12.4 in the preceding assignment for an example.

The CFPB has promulgated sample loan estimates for compliance purposes with Regulation Z, which implements the Truth in Lending Act. An example, Ficus Bank, is on the next page.

Note that unless the buyer is paying cash for the home or the seller is financing the purchase (both rare), there are two important contractual relationships being created. The first is between the current owner of the home (seller) and its new owner (buyer); the second is between the lender (mortgagee) who is financing the transaction and the borrower (buyer/mortgagor). The Closing Disclosure contains information about both contracts. It describes the principal, interest rate, length of loan, and the like. It also describes the costs of certain closing transactions and who is being paid for the work, such as the recording fee for the deed, the appraisal fee, etc. Because both closing costs and financing costs affect the price of a home, consumers can review only one document (albeit five pages) to see the key terms in both contracts.

There are a number of other participants, at least in the background, at closing. A title company representative might attend, or at least will have prepared a title report. This is an examination of the history of ownership of the property. A "clean" title report means that the seller has the right to transfer the property, as described, subject to any listed obligations—such as the seller's own mortgage company. Types of title problems can include a problematic past conveyance in the chain of title, or a previously undiscovered but valid lease, easement, or similar encumbrance on the land. Lenders usually require title insurance as protection if someone later challenges ownership or asserts a superior right to the property. Sometimes, particularly in the Western United States, owners also may have title policies to protect themselves.

A buyer may have the home inspected between making the offer and closing, and have made the closing contingent on a satisfactory inspection. This is for the buyer's benefit in assessing the home's condition, and can include specialized inspections such as for radon or lead paint. The appraiser, on the other hand, is largely for the lender's benefit. The appraiser is to exercise judgment to estimate the home's value. A buyer may be paying more or less than the appraisal, depending on market conditions and the down payment. The most visible person at a closing is called, handily enough, a "closing agent." This person may work for either the lender or the title company or may be the buyer's realtor, all depending on state law. The easiest way to recognize a closing agent is to see who is constantly proffering a pen to the homebuyer for signatures.

FICUS BANK
4321 Random Boulevard · Somecity, ST 12340

Save this Loan Estimate to compare with your Closing Disclosure.

Loan Estimate

DATE ISSUED	2/15/2013
APPLICANTS	Michael Jones and Mary Stone
	123 Anywhere Street
	Anytown, ST 12345
PROPERTY	456 Somewhere Avenue
	Anytown, ST 12345
SALE PRICE	$180,000

LOAN TERM	30 years
PURPOSE	Purchase
PRODUCT	Fixed Rate
LOAN TYPE	☒ Conventional ☐ FHA ☐ VA ☐ _____
LOAN ID #	123456789
RATE LOCK	☐ NO ☒ YES, until 4/16/2013 at 5:00 p.m. EDT

*Before closing, your interest rate, points, and lender credits can change unless you lock the interest rate. All other estimated closing costs expire on **3/4/2013** at 5:00 p.m. EDT*

Loan Terms

		Can this amount increase after closing?
Loan Amount	$162,000	**NO**
Interest Rate	3.875%	**NO**
Monthly Principal & Interest *See Projected Payments below for your Estimated Total Monthly Payment*	$761.78	**NO**

		Does the loan have these features?
Prepayment Penalty		**YES** · **As high as $3,240** if you pay off the loan during the first 2 years
Balloon Payment		**NO**

Projected Payments

Payment Calculation	Years 1-7	Years 8-30
Principal & Interest	$761.78	$761.78
Mortgage Insurance	+ 82	+ —
Estimated Escrow *Amount can increase over time*	+ 206	+ 206
Estimated Total Monthly Payment	**$1,050**	**$968**

		This estimate includes	In escrow?
Estimated Taxes, Insurance & Assessments *Amount can increase over time*	$206 a month	☒ Property Taxes ☒ Homeowner's Insurance ☐ Other:	YES YES
		See Section G on page 2 for escrowed property costs. You must pay for other property costs separately.	

Costs at Closing

Estimated Closing Costs	$8,054	Includes $5,672 in Loan Costs + $2,382 in Other Costs – $0 in Lender Credits. *See page 2 for details.*
Estimated Cash to Close	$16,054	Includes Closing Costs. *See Calculating Cash to Close on page 2 for details.*

Visit **www.consumerfinance.gov/mortgage-estimate** for general information and tools.

LOAN ESTIMATE

PAGE 1 OF 3 · LOAN ID # 123456789

One final term of art with regard to homeownership is "escrow." This is a way of handling payments that are required for the home purchase, other than the principal and interest due on the promissory note. For any given home, there will be property taxes, homeowner's insurance, specialized flood or earthquake insurance, and mortgage insurance. With escrow, the borrower makes advance payments to the lender, who in turn is responsible for paying these obligations. The benefit to the borrower of escrow is one simplified payment; the benefit to the lender is that it ensures that these bills are being timely paid, which reduces its risk if the borrower defaults or calamity strikes.

The rules surrounding escrow, and closing generally, as found in the Real Estate Settlement Procedures Act (RESPA), 12 U.S.C. §2601 et. seq., and its corresponding Regulation X. The major purpose of RESPA is to provide transparency in pricing around closing real estate deals. It prohibits kickbacks from lenders to companies that provide closing services, including title insurance or appraisals. The consumer is allowed to select the most important services, such as the title insurer, rather than being steered to a particular insurer, who overcharges and then returns part of the overcharge to the lender as a "nice doing business with you" treat. Lenders typically provide suggested companies, however, which is partly why the Closing Disclosure breaks down costs into "Services Borrower Did Not Shop For" and "Services Borrower Did Shop For." The idea is presumably to remind the borrower that overcharges could be occurring if the consumer did not question or compare costs.

Consumer lawyers, as you may be gathering, need to be vocabulary and acronym whizzes to navigate homeownership transactions. If you are feel overwhelmed, consider how a non-English speaking, non-college-educated, first-time homebuyer might feel during closing. It is precisely these feelings of confusion and information overload that prompt consumers to rely — sometimes to their detriment — on mortgage and real estate professionals to "sum it up" or "point to where to sign."

3. *Housing Finance System*

As a consumer is unpacking moving boxes, rearranging furniture, and throwing a housewarming party, the lender is only halfway done with its work. Very few home loans remain owned by the originating lenders. Instead, they are sold on the secondary market. This process generates immediate cash (and profit) to the originating lender, which can then use to fund more lending. The housing finance system, which includes public, quasi-public, and private actors, is the economic engine that makes homeownership possible.

The reasons that lenders sell loans are myriad. A major reason, especially for stand-alone mortgage companies, is simply to generate additional funding for another round of loans. Other important reasons that mortgage loans are usually not held in the originator's portfolio including the need to diversify risks and balance short- and long-term obligations. One obvious risk for anyone holding a mortgage loan is default. Even in the best of times, unemployment and family break-up make it impossible for some people to pay their mortgages. To mitigate such risk, especially on loans with low down payments, lenders sometimes require mortgage insurance. Private mortgage insurance (PMI) is offered by companies for a fee and adds to the consumer's monthly payment on the loan. The government also insures mortgage loans. In the simplest form, the lender can make a claim to be reimbursed for its losses if a loan goes to foreclosure. This is how Federal Housing Administration (FHA) and Veterans Administration (VA) loans work. To make a reimbursement claim, the lender certifies to the government that it carefully followed all rules and procedures in originating the loans. In the years after the foreclosure crisis, FHA became more aggressive in challenging banks' claims, sometimes pursuing them for False Claims Act liability on the grounds that defects in the origination process made the loan ineligible for government reimbursements that lenders sought and were paid.

One major reason that depository institutions sell the mortgages that they originate is the tremendous interest-rate risk with a typical fixed-rate mortgage. If a bank makes a 30-year loan at 5 percent interest, but only five years later is paying out 7 percent to its depositors as interest, there is a problem. It's called losing money, and it's not something we want from our banks. To hedge against this risk, and others such as the consumer paying off the loan early (and therefore eliminating a lot of the interest that the bank expected to make on the loan), lenders sell the loans.

This market for mortgages is called the "secondary market." The government was the original player, beginning in 1930s with a panoply of institutions such as the Federal Home Loan Banks, which continue to provide liquidity to mortgage lenders today. Government support of funding for homeownership evolved to focus on two quasi-private institutions, Fannie Mae and Freddie Mac. Known as "government sponsored enterprises" (GSEs), these entities purchase mortgage loans and sell them to investors. In 2015, Fannie and Freddie function a lot like Coke and Pepsi in the market for soda (or pop, for those from certain parts of the country); they are a duopoly that controls the market. The other important player, which functions like a button that dispenses all the other brands of soda pop, is Ginnie Mae. Its system creates mortgage securities for investors from loans originated by the VA, USDA, FHA, and similar government agencies. In 2015, mortgages implicitly or explicitly guaranteed by the government are 90 percent of all loans originated, compared with about two thirds before the 2008 financial crisis.

Fannie and Freddie originally purchased mortgage from private lenders and held them in their portfolios. Pension funds and others invested in mortgages by purchasing bonds issued by Fannie and Freddie. While these organizations had features of private corporations, including shareholders, they were federally chartered. Investors believed that the federal government would stand behind their bonds, as it explicitly does with U.S. Treasury bonds. In the 1970s, Fannie, Freddie, and Ginnie began to "securitize" mortgage loans, a finance tool that further increased liquidity for homeownership investment.

> The agencies would purchase home mortgages, deposit large numbers of them in "pools," and sell participation in the pools to investors on Wall Street. With these new pass-through investment vehicles, investors could hold a share of large (and diversified) numbers of mortgages insured by the government in the case of Ginnie Mae, or guaranteed by the large stable government sponsored enterprises (GSEs) in the case of Freddie Mac and Fannie Mae. Because the

agencies still guaranteed the principal and interest income of their securities even when mortgagors defaulted, investors saw the securities as a low risk investment. . . .

Christopher L. Peterson, *Fannie Mae, Freddie Mac, and the Home Mortgage Foreclosure Crisis*, 10 LOYOLA J. OF PUBLIC INTEREST L. 149, 156 (2009). Private institutions, such as investment banks, saw the profit potential of creating mortgage-backed securities for loans outside the GSE's bailiwick. These included "jumbo" loans that exceed the GSE's "conforming loan limits" and subprime loans that did not meet the underwriting guidelines for purchase by the two GSEs. In the 1990s and 2000s, the types and terms of mortgage loans increasingly deviated from the 30-year, fixed-rate rate, 20 percent down payment loans of the GSEs. Professor Peterson continues the story of securitization of non-conforming loans.

> [I]nvestment banking firms developed pricing models that allowed prospective investors to anticipate the value and liquidity of private-label mortgage backed securities. Investment banks also began partitioning risk into different investments with a variety of credit risks, all drawing on the same income stream from a pool of mortgages. Where earlier residential mortgage backed securities would merely pass through income to investors, *tranched* securities divided payments into different income streams suited to the time and risk preferences of investors. . . .

Id. at 159. In 2003, Fannie and Freddie began to invest in these private-label securities, giving them exposure to the profits—and perils—of riskier mortgages. These bets were losers, and in 2008, the federal government put the GSEs into conservatorship and created a new stronger regulator, the Federal Housing Finance Agency. At this time, Congress has not acted with regard to the future of the GSEs. Some have called for their dismemberment, arguing their functions can and should be provided by private institutions. Others have doubled-down on the public option, arguing that there should be an explicit government guarantee of mortgage-backed securities. In the meantime, the Federal Housing Finance Agency has focused on updating its technology and creating a common securitization platform, which produce a "single security" that puts Fannie and Freddie on parity with each other in the bond market. It also provides the potential for private label securitizers to eventually use the same infrastructure. As of 2016, private securitizations remain rare, however, and the government is the exclusive secondary market for mortgages.

　　The fact that loans are sold, and ultimately owned by trusts as part of the securitization process, creates confusion among homeowners. A consumer may have dealt with Lender Q, but any effort to get in touch with Lender Q when there are problems with repayment is met with "we sold your loan." When the consumer calls the trust, a chipper receptionist explains that the trust is a "passive entity" and that the homeowner must call the loan servicer. These companies are on the front lines of dealing with consumers, and as a result are the subject of much consumer and regulatory ire. Servicing is discussed at length in the next assignment, but mentioned here because it is the secondary market for mortgages that creates the need for a company to work with the consumer. The real loan owners are hundreds or thousands of investors in tranched securities who each own only a sliver of the loan.

B.   Liability for Homes

Shopping for a home is fundamentally different from buying personal property. A primary reason is that homes are not sold by retailers as inventory, but by owners as a one-off transaction. Shopping is much more involved than walking down an aisle and browsing products, or even reading reviews on a website. The law treats a piece of real property as unique, rather than as a fungible good. The U.C.C. rules on warranties do not apply, and state law is not uniform. In general, consumers have many fewer rights with regard to home quality than any other purchase. While that legal rule may have made sense when what was being purchased was bare land for use in farming or ranching, few consumers can reliably assess construction or property defects when buying a home.

1.   Caveat Emptor

"The maxim 'caveat emptor' (let the buyer beware) expresses a rule of the common law applicable to sales of property which implies that the buyer must not trust blindly that he will get value for his money, but must take care to examine and ascertain the kind and quality of the article he is purchasing, or, if he is unable to examine it fully or intelligently, or lacks the knowledge to judge accurately of its quality or value, to protect himself against possible loss by requiring an express warranty from the seller." *McClurkin v. DeGaigney,* 251 S.W. 617, 619 (Ky. 1923). Quoting this language nearly a century later, the court put the rule of liability for real property more succinctly: "The Court Will Not Protect Unwise Decisions." *Manning v. Lewis,* 400 S.W.3d 737, 741 (2013). Even for sales to unsophisticated first-time home buyers, the general rule is caveat venditor, or "seller beware." From a consumer protection standpoint, it is a harsh rule.

Douglas v. Visser
295 P.3d 800 (Wa. Ct. App. 2013)

Appelwick, Judge.

FACTS

In 2007, Nigel and Kathleen Douglas were looking for a home in Blaine, Washington. They are Canadian citizens and wanted a second home in the area. In the course of the search, they discovered a property owned by Terry and Diane Visser. Terry Visser is a licensed real estate agent and listed the property himself.

The Vissers purchased the property in 2005. At the time, it needed significant work. The Vissers intended to renovate and rent the property. They demolished bungalows that were located on the property. In the main house, they renovated the bathroom, repaired portions of rot, insulated the exterior walls, fixed wall paneling, insulated the ceiling, installed Styrofoam ceiling tiles, and replaced the exterior bellyband. During the course of repairs, the Vissers realized that the renovations would take more time and money than they expected, and they decided to sell the house.

After the Douglases made an offer, the Vissers filled out a seller disclosure statement. But, they answered "don't know" or simply failed to respond at all to many questions that the Douglases felt should have had a clear "yes" or "no" answer. Perplexed, the Douglases sent a list of follow-up questions. In addition to seeking clarification, they requested a copy of the inspection report prepared before the Vissers purchased the property. Diane Visser handwrote responses to the questions, but the Douglases continued to think the answers were inadequate. The Vissers never provided a copy of the inspection report. Nevertheless, the Douglases did not ask for any further clarification.

Dennis Flaherty performed a prepurchase inspection for the Douglases. He discovered a small area of rot and decay near the roof line, and caulking that suggested a previous roof leak in the area. Beneath the home, he found an area of rotted sill plate that sat below the section of water damaged exterior siding. . . . In his inspection report, he noted that those areas did not pose a structural threat but should be repaired if the condition degraded rapidly.

The Douglases did not discuss the report with Flaherty or the Vissers. They purchased the house without discussing the issue of rot with the Vissers. The sale closed in April 2007. The parties agreed on a purchase price of $189,000. The Douglases paid $40,000 cash and gave the Vissers a promissory note secured by a deed of trust for the remaining $149,000. The total amount was due on August 1, 2008.

After purchasing the house, the Douglases began to notice a damp smell and a constant presence of potato bugs around the perimeter of the house and in the bathroom. In an effort to keep out the potato bugs, they caulked the baseboards in the bathroom. Eventually, they noticed that the ceiling tiles were gradually separating in the living room, master bedroom, and second bedroom.

Flaherty returned to inspect the home again. When he removed a ceiling tile, insulation and water came down from behind it. In response to what they found, the Douglases requested a bid from a mold abatement company. The company was unable to guarantee the removal of all mold because of the house's pristine mold-growing conditions. Without a guarantee, the Douglases elected to take no action.

In July 2008, the pay-in-full date was quickly approaching. Because it was uninhabitable, they requested an additional month to investigate the extent of the mold. The promissory note's due date was pushed back to September 1.

In the meantime, the Douglases removed the bellyband. They discovered substantial rot and pest issues underneath. In fact, there was virtually nothing behind the bellyband and they did not encounter any resistance in removing the boards. The Douglases defaulted on the promissory note.

In September 2008, Flaherty returned to the house a third time. He determined that the rim joists had 50 percent to 70 percent wet rot and pest damage that could not be seen from the crawl space without removing insulation. Similarly, he concluded the sill plate had 50 percent to 70 percent wet rot and pest damage. He opined that "installation of the siding was within the last two years and the extent of damage to the sill and rim joist could not have occurred since the installation of the skirt boards siding. Therefore, whoever installed the skirt board siding would have known that structurally damaged portions of the framing would have been concealed." He further stated, "It is my professional opinion that the installation of the pink fiberglass insulation in the crawl space stud bays between the floor joists and firmly packed against the rim joists may have been installed to reduce the probability that damaged rim joists and sill would be discovered during a standard home inspection."

Another inspector, Kirk Juneau, also inspected the damage. He determined that a new trim was used on the house's exterior that is intended only for interior use. The trim covered and concealed damage, and had been installed within the previous two to three years. In the house's interior, he noted that where subflooring had been replaced the person who made the patches should have discovered the damage beneath. Beneath the house, he determined that some joist damage was visible, because it was not covered by insulation, and that once insulation was removed more damage was visible.

The Douglases shut off the water, drained the lines, and turned off the electricity. They obtained a bid from a contractor who determined it would cost more to repair the home than to tear it down and rebuild.

The Douglases sued the Vissers. They claimed fraudulent concealment; negligent misrepresentation; violation of the Consumer Protection Act, ch. 19.86 RCW; breach of contract; and violation of Terry Visser's statutory duties as a real estate agent.

Kelly Hatch, who assisted Visser with some of the repairs, testified that he had difficulty fixing the floors in the bathroom, because the wood was too soft to install screws. When he advised Terry Visser to rip out the plywood to inspect the joists underneath, Visser said he could not put any more into it and told Hatch to find a way to attach the wood. On the house's exterior, Hatch discovered that wood underneath the bellyband was rotted. Visser instructed him to cover it up with trim. Specifically, Visser said they could cover it in caulking, use a bunch of nails, paint it, and seal it. When Hatch nailed the trim up, it was so rotted that he could not get the nails to stay in. Visser himself testified that he added a new piece of wood to a rotted joist, although he asserted he could not see the rot.

Flaherty explained that the rot he discovered in the first inspection was "[n]ot necessarily" a sign that the building's whole sill plate was rotted. He testified that the concealed rot he discovered in his last inspection was the worst he had ever seen. Juneau testified that at the time of the Douglases' purchase there was readily observable damage that warranted further inspection or inquiries.

The trial court found that the Vissers discovered significant wood rot to the sill plate and rim joist, as well as to the floor joists. It determined that, instead of correcting the defects, the Vissers made superficial repairs and concealed the damage. It ruled in favor of the Douglases on all claims. The court awarded the Douglases $103,000 to tear down and rebuild the house; $3,000 to cover the cost of inspections; $1,500 in moving expenses; $12,000 for emotional distress; and $25,000 as treble damages pursuant to the Consumer Protection Act. It also awarded the Douglases their fees and costs in the amount of $49,838. It offset those damages against the principal and interest the Douglases still owed on the promissory note. Judgment was entered for the Douglases in the amount of $24,245.

DISCUSSION

. . .

The Vissers challenge several of the trial court's findings that are central to its conclusions. Specifically, they argue that there is no substantial evidence to support findings that the Vissers discovered and concealed defects before selling the home or a finding that the defects were unknown and undiscoverable to the Douglases. The trial court found:

> During the course of renovating the house, the Vissers discovered significant wood rot to the sill plate and rim joist that connects the concrete foundation to the frame.

It further found:

> Rather than correct these defects, the Vissers or their hired help made superficial repairs to the visible damage and covered up the rest.

Two inspectors independently concluded that extensive damage was covered up during the period of time that the Vissers owned the house. Flaherty determined that the damage could not have occurred after the repair work, and Juneau determined that damage beneath the flooring should have been discovered when the subflooring was repaired. Hatch corroborated the inspectors' reports. He testified that he and Terry Visser covered rot with new trim and new subflooring. The inspection reports, together with Hatch's testimony, amply support the trial court's findings that the Vissers discovered and concealed rot.

The trial court also found:

> The defects were unknown to the Douglases and were not discoverable by a careful and reasonable inspection.

When a buyer is on notice of a defect, it must make further inquiries of the seller. In *Puget Sound Service Corp. v. Dalarna Management Corp.,* an apartment building had chronic water leaks. 752 P.2d 1353 (1988). . . . We concluded that where "an actual inspection demonstrates some evidence of water penetration, the buyer must make inquiries of the seller." Id. at 215. The buyer knew there was a defect but did not make any inquiries or establish that inquiries would have been fruitless. Id. The extent of the damage itself was not a separate defect, and it was no defense that the defect was worse than the buyer anticipated. Id. at 214-15. Accordingly, its claim could not proceed. Id. at 215.

In contrast, in *Sloan v. Thompson* the buyers had extensive knowledge of various defects. 128 Wn. App. 776, 781 (2005). Before they purchased it, the Sloans rented the home for three years and discovered that the roof leaked, the decks were rotted, some electrical outlets did not work, and the toilets did not flush properly. Id. After the sale was completed, an earthquake revealed that the septic tank was defective and the foundation was structurally unsound due to "'extremely faulty construction.'" Id. at 782, 786. Because the defective septic tank and structurally unsound foundation were separate defects from the extensive problems the buyers knew of, the buyers succeeded on their claim for fraudulent concealment. Id. at 789, 791.

Here, Flaherty identified an area of rot and decay near the roofline, an area of rotted sill plate, and sistered floor joists. The Douglases and their inspector were on notice of the defect and had a duty to make further inquiries. The Douglases argue that "they had no idea that 50 to 70% of the sill plate and rim joist were destroyed" and that the area of rot that Flaherty discovered was not unusual. That, however, is the precise argument we rejected in *Dalarna*. Once a buyer discovers evidence of a defect, they are on notice and have a duty to make further inquiries. They cannot succeed when the extent of the defect is greater than anticipated, even when it is magnitudes greater.

The Douglases suggest, without citation to the record, that they did in fact make further inquiries, asserting that "[n]either a reasonable inspection, *nor the Douglases' reasonable questions*, put them on notice" of the extent of damage. (Emphasis added.) But, Nigel Douglas explicitly testified that after the prepurchase inspection report, which was the source of notice of the defects, he did not ask the Vissers or Flaherty any questions about the rot that Flaherty identified. Instead, they were content to let the report speak for itself.

Prior to the inspection, the Douglases asked follow-up questions to the Vissers' perplexing responses in the seller disclosure statement. But none of those questions expressly addressed the rot issue, and the Douglases did not ask any specific questions about rot or the house's foundation. More significantly, both the seller disclosure statement and the Vissers' responses to the Douglases' inquiries predate the prepurchase inspection report. Inquiries made before the prepurchase inspection cannot be construed as inquiries regarding the rot discovered during the inspection.

As in *Dalarna*, there is no evidence that the Douglases made further inquiries once they were on notice of the defect. *Dalarna* recognizes that further inquiry is not necessary where it would have been fruitless. 51 Wn. App. at 215. While the Vissers' overt attempts to cover up the defects prior to listing the property and their preinspection evasiveness may support an inference, if not a conclusion, that such inquiry would have been fruitless, the trial court did not enter any such findings. Accordingly, despite the egregious nondisclosure and concealment by the Vissers, an essential element of each of the Douglases' claims is not satisfied.

A claim for fraudulent concealment exists when (1) the residential dwelling has a concealed defect, (2) the seller has knowledge of the defect, (3) the defect presents a danger to the property or health or life of the buyer, (4) the defect is unknown to the buyer, and (5) the defect would not be disclosed by a careful, reasonable inspection by the buyer. Alejandre v. Bull, 159 Wn.2d 674, 689 (2007). A statutory claim for breach of a real estate agent's duties exists when the agent does not disclose all material facts known to the agent that are not apparent or readily ascertainable. RCW 18.86.030(1)(d). A claim for negligent misrepresentation exists when (1) the seller makes a false statement, (2) to induce a business transaction, and (3) the buyer justifiably relies on the false statement. Amtruck Factors v. Int'l Forest Prods., 59 Wn. App. 8, 18 (1990). A violation of the Consumer Protection Act exists when there is (1) an unfair or deceptive act or practice, (2) occurring in trade or commerce, (3) with a public interest impact, (4) that proximately causes, (5) injury to a plaintiff in his or her business or property. Svendsen v. Stock, 143 Wn. 2d 546, 553 (2001); Indoor Billboard/Wash., Inc. v. Integra Telecom of Wash., Inc., 162 Wn. 2d 59, 83-84 (2007).

Because the Douglases were on notice of the defect and had a duty to make further inquiry, it cannot be said that the defect was unknown to the Douglases, that it could not have been discovered by a reasonable inspection, that the Douglases justifiably relied on the Vissers' misrepresentations, or that the Vissers committed an unfair or deceptive act that caused the Douglases' injury. The Douglases breach of contract claim was based upon fraudulent concealment and negligent misrepresentation claims. When those claims fail, so does the breach of contract claim.

The Vissers' efforts in concealing the defects of the house they were selling are reprehensible, even more so because Visser is a licensed real estate agent. Nonetheless, the law retains a duty on a buyer to beware, to inspect, and to question. We caution that the Douglases did not have a duty to perform exhaustive invasive inspection or endlessly assail the Vissers with further questions. They merely had to make further inquiries after discovering rot or at trial show that further inquiry would have been fruitless. The only evidence of when the Douglases first learned of rot in the house is the report issued after Flaherty conducted his prepurchase inspection. Despite that discovery, on top of the Vissers' previous evasive and incomplete answers and the Vissers' ongoing failure to provide their own prepurchase inspection report, either of which should have caused concern and further inquiry, there is no evidence that the Douglases made any inquiries whatsoever after the inspection. They obtained no finding from the trial court that further inquiry would have been fruitless. Under *Dalarna*, the Douglases' failure means they were not entitled to maintain these claims.

The Douglases defaulted on the promissory note. The interest rate in the event of default is 18 percent. The Douglases owe the principal and interest at 18 percent. Further, the purchase and sale agreement provides an attorney fee provision. When an action in tort is based on a contract containing an attorney fee provision, the prevailing party is entitled to attorney fees. Brown v. Johnson, 109 Wn. App. 56, 58 (2001). We award the Vissers their reasonable attorney fees.

We reverse.

Where should a consumer buy a dream home? Hawaii? Florida? California? If what you seek is protection from home defects, the answer is clear: Louisiana. It has a unique cause of action, "redhibition," that applies when a property has a defect or "vice" that renders the home useless or so inconvenient that a buyer would not have purchased it had the defect been known. *See Jessup v. Ketchings*, 482 F.3d 336, 342 (5th Cir. 2007). While defects that were known or could have been discovered are excluded, consumers seem to fare better in Louisiana under its civil law tradition than at common law.

2.   *Warranties on New Property*

If Louisiana isn't your place, the other way to obtain more protection is to buy a new home. You get a warranty and that new paint smell (along with the fun of having to install towel racks and curtain rods and an endless other number of items you rarely give thought to.)

Davencourt at Pilgrims Landing Homeowners Ass'n v. Davencourt at Pilgrims Landing LC

221 P.3d 234 (Utah 2009)

Durham, Chief Judge.

. . .

Davencourt at Pilgrims Landing (the Project) is a planned unit development. The Project is the result of the design and development efforts by Davencourt at Pilgrims Landing, LC (Developer) . . .

In selling the units, the Developer used a standard form real estate purchase contract for residential construction in each transaction. Also, the Developer represented and warranted that the Project (1) complied with the building code and had been inspected for such; (2) consisted of high-quality structures; (3) was in good condition and properly and fully maintained; (4) had no faulty workmanship; (5) had no water intrusion, moisture problems, or other material defects; and (6) the Association's budget and monthly assessments were accurate and adequate for future maintenance, repair, and replacement.

A few years after turnover of the Association to the Unit Owners, the Association learned of significant problems with the Project. Water began to seep into the buildings through the foundation, floors, porches, stucco, sidewalls, exterior walls, doors, windows, window boxes, and roofs. The water intrusion caused damage to the buildings in the form of dryrot, mold, staining, and degradation of the stucco. Upon hiring a building envelope specialist, the Association learned that the water intrusion and resulting damage stemmed from faulty design, faulty workmanship, defective materials, improper construction, and/or noncompliance with building codes. The building envelope specialist informed the Association that these flaws and defects, evident in all the buildings, were present in several latent construction defects, including: improper installation of stucco; improper stucco termination points at slabs and foundations; window boxes designed without a drainage plane, allowing water into the building cavity; improper integration of the stucco; missing or inadequate control joints in the stucco to prevent cracking; missing or improper flashings; and missing, incomplete, or improperly installed waterproofing at the foundations and walls of the units.

The Association also learned that before construction began, the Developer and the Builder had obtained a geo-technical study on the soil and subsurface soils of the Project. The report from the study warned that the Project would rest on collapsible subsurface soils that would cause land subsidence without proper preparation. Following construction, the land subsided. This land subsidence caused severe structural defects to the stucco and cement work and contributed to the water intrusion through the foundation, floors, porches, stucco, sidewalls, exterior walls, windows, window boxes, and roofs.

The Association repeatedly requested that the Developer and the Builder repair the defects, but they refused to do so.

. . .

ANALYSIS

The Association next asserts that the district court erred by dismissing the claim for breach of implied warranties. The district court correctly noted that this court has yet to recognize such a claim in the sale of a new residence; we do so now.

Utah courts have historically refused to recognize an implied warranty of workmanlike manner and habitability in the context of new residential sales. In *American Towers Owners Ass'n v. CCI Mechanical, Inc.,* the court explained its refusal:

> The main policy reasons behind extending an implied warranty of habitability to residential leases are the unequal bargaining position of the parties and the prospective tenant's limited ability to inspect and repair the property. *These policy reasons are not present to the same degree in the purchase of residential property.* The purchaser has the right to inspect the house before the purchase as thoroughly as that individual desires, and to condition purchase of the house upon a satisfactory inspection report. Further, if there are particular concerns about a home, the parties can contract for an express written warranty from the seller. Finally, if there are material latent defects of which the seller was aware, the buyer may have a cause of action in fraud. Therefore, *the circumstances presented to the purchaser of a residence are not closely analogous to those of a relatively powerless lessee. . . .*

930 P.2d 1182, 1193 (Utah 1996) (omission in original) (quoting Maack v. Res. Design & Constr., Inc., 875 P.2d 570, 582–83 (Utah Ct. App. 1994)).

After reviewing the state of the case law from around the country, we conclude that our rule has become an anachronism.

During the first half of the twentieth century, the doctrine of caveat emptor in new residential construction led courts to reject implied warranties. Underlying this almost universal doctrine was the theory of equal bargaining power in contract and the ability and opportunity to inspect. 12 Thompson on Real Property §99.06(a)(2) (David A. Thomas ed., 2d Thomas ed. 2008). With the boom in post-World War II construction, the tide changed. Id. In the late 1950s, the first American court recognized an implied warranty in the sale of a new home. Vanderschrier v. Aaron, 103 Ohio App. 340 (1957). Other courts followed suit in the 1960s. By the 1980s, the minority became the majority. See Conklin v. Hurley, 428 So. 2d 654, 656 n.2 (Fla. 1983) (citing to thirty-three states that recognize an implied warranty of habitability of new homes).

Today, by common law or statutory law, an overwhelming majority of jurisdictions recognize an implied warranty in the purchase of new residential property. Forty-five states have adopted an implied warranty in some form and Hawaii appears to have done so in dicta. Forty-three states provide for an implied warranty of habitability. Besides the four states that do not recognize any implied warranty, only Delaware, Nebraska, and Ohio expressly reject the implied warranty of habitability; yet those three states each provide for an implied warranty of workmanlike manner. Out of the four states that have not adopted any implied warranty, two states, New Mexico and North Dakota, have not directly addressed or answered the issue. The two remaining states, Georgia and Utah, have expressly rejected implied warranties. But Georgia does so because it allows recovery under negligence theory. This leaves Utah in a minority of one.

Although the implied warranties adopted by courts "are known by various names such as 'habitability,' 'quality,' 'workmanship,' or 'fitness,'" courts rely on similar reasons and public policy considerations in adopting the warranties. Courts recognize that "[b]uilding construction by modern methods is complex and intertwined with governmental codes and regulations." Tavares v. Horstman, 542 P.2d 1275, 1279 (Wyo. 1975). For a builder-vendor or developer-vendor engaged in the business of selling houses, the construction and/or sale of a new home is a daily event, whereas for a buyer the purchase of a new home is a significant and unique transaction. See Bethlahmy v. Bechtel, 415 P.2d 698, 710 (1966) ("The purchase of a home is not an everyday transaction for the average family, and in many instances is the most important transaction of a lifetime. To apply the rule of caveat emptor to an inexperienced buyer, and in favor of a builder who is daily engaged in the business of building and selling houses, is manifestly a denial of justice."). Given these modern realities and this disparity, "[a] home buyer should be able to place reliance on the builder or developer who sells him a new house." Tavares, 542 P.2d at 1279. Some courts reason that the implied warranty will "inhibit the unscrupulous, fly-by-night, or unskilled builder and . . . discourage much of the sloppy work and jerry building that has become perceptible over the years." Capra v. Smith, 372 So. 2d 321, 323 (Ala. 1979) (internal quotation marks omitted). An implied warranty also takes into account the equitable consideration that between two innocent parties, the one in the better position to prevent the harm ought to bear the loss. See Chandler v. Madsen, 642 P.2d 1028, 1031 (1982). . . . Hence, in protecting the innocent home purchaser by holding the responsible party accountable, the law has come to recognize that no longer does the purchaser of a new residence stand on an equal bargaining position with the builder-vendor or developer-vendor.

Moreover, the concept of an implied warranty is "consistent with the expectations of the parties." Sloat v. Matheny, 625 P.2d 1031, 1033 (Colo. 1981). "[T]he essence of the transaction is an implicit engagement upon the part of the seller to transfer a house suitable for habitation." Yepsen v. Burgess, 525 P.2d 1019, 1022 (1974). If the purchaser expected anything less, there would be no sale. See Sloat, 625 P.2d at 1033. The creation of an implied warranty, therefore, causes "no more uncertainty or chaos than the warranties commonly applied in sales of personal property." Bethlahmy, 415 P.2d at 707. Also, we are not convinced that an express written warranty provides sufficient protection where concerns regarding latent defects exist. "A buyer who has no knowledge, notice, or warning of defects, is in no position to exact specific warranties. Any written warranty demanded in such a case would necessarily be so general in terms as to be difficult to enforce." Id.

These sound reasons and policy considerations "lead[ ] logically to the buyer's expectation that he be judicially protected." Tavares, 542 P.2d at 1279. Although we rejected an implied warranty in *American Towers,* we agree with the following statement.

> The law should be based on current concepts of what is right and just and the judiciary should be alert to the never-ending need for keeping its common law principles abreast of the times. Ancient distinctions which make no sense in today's society and tend to discredit the law should be readily rejected. . . .

Schipper v. Levitt & Sons, Inc., 207 A.2d 314, 325 (1965). Recognizing that *American Towers* no longer represents what is right and just as to implied warranties in the purchase of a new residence, we now join the overwhelming majority of states. Under Utah law, in every contract for the sale of a new residence, a vendor in the business of building or selling such residences makes an implied warranty to the vendee that the residence is constructed in a workmanlike manner and fit for habitation.

We recognize that "[t]he expansion of implied warranties has resulted in a blurring of the 'distinction, if any, between an implied warranty of habitability and an implied warranty of good quality and workmanship . . . in decisional law throughout the country.'" Albrecht, 767 N.E. 2d at 45 n. 7. Some courts define the implied warranty of workmanlike manner as "'the quality of work that would be done by a worker of average skill and intelligence.'" Id. Other courts define the implied warranty of habitability in the sense that if a new residence does not keep out the elements because of a defect of construction, such a residence is not habitable or that the new residence must "provide inhabitants with [a] reasonably safe place to live, without fear of injury to person, health, safety, or property." Id. In Utah, the scope of the implied warranty should be construed broadly to comport with the public policy considerations. . . . Nor can the implied warranty "be waived or disclaimed, because to permit the disclaimer of a warranty protecting a purchaser from the consequences of latent defects would defeat the very purpose of the warranty." Albrecht, 767 N.E.2d at 47.

The implied warranty, however, does not require perfection on the part of the builder-vendor/developer-vendor or "make them an insurer against any and all defects in a home." Id. "No house is built without defects," Bethlahmy, 415 P.2d at 711, and the implied warranty does not "protect against mere defects in workmanship, minor or procedural violations of the applicable building codes, or defects that are trivial or aesthetic." Albrecht, 767 N.E.2d at 47. Nor is the implied warranty intended to alleviate purchasers of their due diligence and opportunity to inspect a residential construction or the incentive to negotiate for express warranties.

Therefore, to establish a breach of the implied warranty of workmanlike manner or habitability under Utah law a plaintiff must show (1) the purchase of a new residence from a defendant builder-vendor/developer-vendor; (2) the residence contained a latent defect; (3) the defect manifested itself after purchase; (4) the defect was caused by improper design, material, or workmanship; and (5) the defect created a question of safety or made the house unfit for human habitation. See id.

The implied warranty is not infinite. A claim for breach of the implied warranty must be brought in accordance with Utah Code section 78B–2–225. That section imposes periods of limitation and repose for "all causes of action by or against a provider arising out of or related to the design, construction, or installation of an improvement." Utah Code Ann. §78B-2-225(2)(e) (2008). "An action by or against a provider based in contract or warranty shall be commenced within six years of the date of completion of the improvement or abandonment of construction." Id. §78B-2-225(3)(a).

Finally, we emphasize that this implied warranty does not abrogate the doctrine of caveat emptor in the sale of existing or used residences. See Utah State Med. Ass'n v. Utah State Employees Credit Union, 655 P.2d 643, 645 (Utah 1982) ("The doctrine [of caveat emptor] has eroded in the sale of new residential housing.

However, the doctrine appears to prevail in the sale of used property whether homes or commercial.").

We now turn to the Association's claim for breach of the implied warranty. We hold that because Utah now recognizes the implied warranty of workmanlike manner and habitability, the district court erred in dismissing the Association's claim for breach of the implied warranty. . . . Accordingly, because Utah now recognizes an implied warranty of workmanlike manner and habitability, we reverse the district court's dismissal of the Association's claim.

. . .

All fifty states recognize an implied warranty in the sale of a new home. The warranty is usually framed as requiring either "habitability" or "built in a workmanlike manner." The latter is broader, encompassing defects that an ordinarily prudent builder would not have created. It is similar to malpractice, requiring that the construction was done with customary skill and care in accordance with accepted standards. Many successful cases focus on major problems, such as a lack of proper site preparation or a defective foundation. *See, e.g., Hildebrand v. New Vista Homes II, LLC*, 253 P.3d 1159 (Colo. App. 2010).

A few states, notably California, have statutory implied warranties for new homes. Cal. Civ. Code §§896-945.5. These are often limited to one year for most defects but up to ten years for structural defects. *See, e.g.*, N.J. Stat. §§46:3B-2, 46:3B-3 (permitting actions for up to ten years for major defects identified in the statute). An advantage of the common law warranty for a new home is that these are of uncertain duration, often held to extend for a reasonable time or a similarly flexible standard.

3.   Manufactured Homes

Over 17 million Americans live in manufactured homes; these are no longer called "mobile" homes, in recognition of the fact that many are never, in fact, moved from their sites. Depending on the circumstances and state law, a manufactured home may be either real or personal property. Regardless, TILA covers manufactured homes that are a consumer's principal dwelling regardless of real or personal property designation. The applicability of other laws, such as RESPA, is less clear. Whether a manufactured home is real or personal property is particularly important if a consumer alleges a warranty problem. Common manufacturing defects include leaking roofs (such as where the two halves of a double-wide mobile home are sealed), improperly installed windows or doors, sagging roofs and ceilings, and defective flooring. The Department of Housing and Urban Development (HUD) has issued nationwide standards for quality building of manufactured homes. 42 U.S.C. §§5401-5426. Manufacturers often offer a one-year home warranty, and about half of states provide such protection through statutes. While these are of short duration, they provide more protection during that period than the real property rules discussed above, particularly for resale homes.

The distinction between real and personal property is also critical if the homeowner defaults. As discussed *infra* in the Assignment on creditors' rights, real property requires many more procedural steps for a creditor to exercise the right to possession and sale than personal property. About three-quarters of states have statutes that elaborate a procedure by which a consumer may convert a manufactured home from personal to real property. Consumers generally enjoy greater consumer protections if they take this step.

Problem Set 13

13.1. Emily Ling prides herself on attention to detail. In her role as a compliance officer for a mortgage lender, she deals every day with questions about procedure. Alberto, a loan officer working in Albuquerque asked her to review his process for providing mortgage loan disclosures for home purchases, based on a recent transaction with Pam and Bubba Kirk. On Wednesday, December 30th, he met in person with potential borrowers and collected a mortgage application. It included estimates of the value of the home to be purchased and the amount of the loan needed. When he returned to the office on Monday, January 4th, he mailed two copies of the completed Loan Estimate to the Kirks. The Kirks decided to proceed with the loan, so Alberto emailed them the Closing Disclosure on Friday January 15th. The Kirks immediately replied back to that message, "Thanks! See you at the closing Tuesday." On January 19th, Tuesday, the Kirks signed the promissory note and mortgage, and the lender funded the loan. Did Alberto comply with the disclosure rules for a closed-end mortgage? *See* 12 C.F.R. §§1026.2(a)(3) and (a)(6); 1026.19(e)(1) and (f)(1).

13.2. Barret and Amanda's family is growing, and they have decided to purchase a bigger home. They found a three-bedroom on a half-acre in a lovely suburban development. As tidy people, Barret and Amanda particularly liked the covenants that required identical mailboxes and a neutral paint palette. Their agent, Hillary, works for Clinton Realty. Hillary and Amanda are friends from volunteering at the local animal shelter and are constantly swapping pictures of their numerous, adopted "fur babies."

The home was listed with Clinton Realty with Bill as the selling agent. Bill and the seller, Hubert, are poker buddies. Notwithstanding the kind of friendship that develops in late-night poker, Bill was careful to have Hubert sign all paperwork, including a Disclosure Agreement that required Hubert to "disclose matters reasonably discoverable affecting the property value or desirability." When the parties agreed on a sale price, both buyers and sellers signed a Consensual Dual Agency Agreement that acknowledged that one Clinton Realty agent was representing the buyer and another Clinton Realty agent was representing the seller. The agreement also provided that Clinton would disclose all "material defects" in the property.

At closing, Barret and Amanda were devastated to note that the title opinion disclosed a restrictive covenant on the property limiting dog ownership to one per property. Barret and Amanda could not bear the thought of giving up one of their four dogs and walked away from the deal. Hubert was furious, asking

Bill and Hillary why this didn't come up earlier. Who, if anyone, is liable for the deal falling through and on what theory?

13.3. Alan Suspinsky is the best consumer financial services lawyer in America, at least if you are a "covered person" subject to the CFPB. He has relentlessly pointed out problems and warned of the dangers of overregulation. Today, when you saw Alan in the hallway, he was purple with rage. He shook the form below under your nose.

Loan Estimate

DATE ISSUED 10/04/2015
APPLICANTS ▮▮▮▮▮▮▮

PROPERTY ▮▮▮▮▮▮

EST. PROP. V ▮▮▮▮

LOAN TERM 30 years
PURPOSE Refinance
PRODUCT Fixed Rate
LOAN TYPE ☒ Conventional ☐ FHA ☐ VA ☐ _____
LOAN ID # ▮▮▮▮
RATE LOCK ☐ NO ☒ YES, until 11/18/2015 11:59 PM EDT

Before closing, your interest rate, points, and lender credits can change unless you lock the interest rate. All other estimated closing costs expire on 10/16/2015 11:59 PM EDT

Loan Terms

		Can this amount increase after closing?
Loan Amount	$750,000	NO
Interest Rate	4.125%	NO
Monthly Principal & Interest See Projected Payments below for your Estimated Total Monthly Payment	$3,634.88	NO
		Does the loan have these features?
Prepayment Penalty		NO
Balloon Payment		NO

Projected Payments

Payment Calculation	Years 1 - 30
Principal & Interest	$3,634.88
Mortgage Insurance	+ 0
Estimated Escrow Amount can increase over time	+ 1,300
Estimated Total Monthly Payment	$4,935

Estimated Taxes, Insurance & Assessments Amount can increase over time	$1,300 a month	This estimate includes ☒ Property Taxes ☒ Homeowner's Insurance ☐ Other: See Section G on page 2 for escrowed property costs. You must pay for other property costs separately.	In escrow? YES YES

Costs at Closing

Estimated Closing Costs	$12,559	Includes $5,324 in Loan Costs + $7,235 in Other Costs - $0 in Lender Credits. See page 2 for details.
Estimated Cash to Close	$150,712	Includes Closing Costs. See Calculating Cash to Close on page 2 for details. ☐ From ☒ To Borrower

Visit www.consumerfinance.gov/mortgage-estimate for general information and tools.

LOAN ESTIMATE
Document ID Number:
Wolters Kluwer Financial Services © 2014

PAGE 1 OF 3 • LOAN ID # 3347979449

VMP3311A (1407)

"Do you see the error? Do you? How can a lender do business with disclosure rules like this!" he sputtered. Not wanting to seem dumb, you nodded along. "Every number is correct!" he screeched. "But now VestCo won't buy our client's mortgages because they could be sued by a consumer years from now even after the loan is securitized," Alan continues. "I'm calling Congress members and I want a solution." And off Alan went, mumbling to himself about the demise of democracy as the Founders intended it.

Safely back in your office, you pull up the client's disclosure from the firm's file. What is the purported error that VestCo has identified? (Hint: Do a visual comparison with the model Loan Estimate in the assignment and look at 12 C.F.R. §1026.37(o)(3).) If there is a problem, what is the tolerance for liability? Why doesn't Alan's client just fix the Loan Estimate to look the way VestCo believes that it must? 12 C.F.R. §1026.19(e)(3); 15 U.S.C. §1640(a).

Assignment 14. Home Mortgages

The law on home loans changed dramatically in the wake of the foreclosure crisis. Federal law now requires lenders to consider a consumer's ability to repay a residential mortgage. The new underwriting standards, along with the rules on mortgage broker compensation and improved loan disclosures discussed in the prior assignment, were designed to eliminate the egregious practices that preceded the foreclosure crisis.

Because most homes are financed with long-term loans, the consumer laws stretch into the years that follow the initial purchase. The process of collecting payments, and if necessary, addressing defaults in payment is called mortgage servicing. If a homeowner does not pay a mortgage loan, the lender can foreclose causing the family to lose the home. High default and foreclosure rates revealed serious problems in mortgage servicing and sparked reforms to encourage foreclosure prevention. Servicers that deal with homeowners must adhere to extensive standards of conduct.

Because homes are so important to a family's social and financial security, consumers are particularly likely to seek legal help in avoiding foreclosure. Mistakes in underwriting are often only recognized or addressed as defenses to foreclosure. In mortgage lending, *finis origine pendet*. After you brush up on your Latin, consider how this phrase is true both for the consumer in terms of home retention and the lender in terms of liability.

A. Making Mortgage Loans

In the prior assignment, the lender was portrayed as basically an agreeable sort who was happy to dole out money and spent time fretting about disclosure and closing forms. That was a caricature, for certain. Lenders today must carefully consider loan applications. This new environment comes, in part, from strict new rules and tougher regulatory scrutiny. But it also comes from the market. Investors want to avoid the losses of the foreclosure crisis and scrutinize the behavior of all actors: real estate agents, mortgage brokers, appraisers, underwriters, investment banks, government sponsored enterprises, servicers, and certainly, not least, consumers. The excerpt below is the kind of cautionary tale that undergirded efforts to tighten underwriting.

> Lacey Phillips and Erin Hall are a couple. Phillips is a hairdresser, Hall a barber. In the spring of 2006, just as — unbeknownst to them — the housing bubble was deflating, they found a house they wanted to buy priced slightly below $250,000. Like countless American couples during the housing bubble they

mistakenly believed they could afford the house they wanted. They had never owned a house, had only a high-school education (Hall had some college but no degree), and were financially unsophisticated.

They applied to Associated Bank for a mortgage. The bank turned down their application because Hall had a recent bankruptcy and because the bank deemed the couple's joint monthly income of $3,800 too meager to justify the loan of more than $200,000 that they needed. After this rebuff Hall turned to a mortgage broker named Brian Bowling whom he knew and admired (Hall had been Bowling's barber) for help in obtaining a mortgage loan. Bowling—a crook who brokered fraudulent loans (but there is no indication that either Phillips or Hall knew or suspected that he was a crook)—steered the couple to a federally insured bank of dubious ethics named Fremont Investment & Loan. Had Fremont been the bank that had turned the defendants down the first time, this might have shown that they realized they didn't meet the bank's criteria for a loan and so would be able to obtain a loan only by lying. But it was of course a different bank that had previously turned them down.

Associated Bank was a reputable bank. Fremont was not. See *Commonwealth v. Fremont Investment & Loan,* 897 N.E.2d 548, 551-55 (2008). Fremont's specialty was making "stated income" loans—known to the knowing as "liars' loans" because in a stated-income loan the lender accepts the borrower's statement of his income without trying to verify it. Such loans, which played a significant role in the financial collapse of September 2008—the doleful consequences of which continue to plague the U.S. and world economies—were profitable despite the high risk of default because lenders sold them as soon as they'd made them. Many of the loans were repackaged by the buyers into ill-fated mortgage-backed securities whose holders lost their shirts. This was musical-chairs financing.

Fremont went broke when the music stopped in June 2008. Its collapse was a harbinger of the worldwide financial collapse that occurred three months later when Lehman Brothers suddenly declared bankruptcy. "[The] very terms [of Fremont's loans]—short-term interest rates followed by payment shock, plus high loan-to-value and high debt-to-income ratios—were likely to lead to default and foreclosure." Megan Woolhouse, "Lender Settles with State for $10m," *Boston Globe,* Business, p. 7, June 10, 2009, www.boston.com/business/ articles/2009/06/10/subprime_lender_settles_suit_with_mass_for_0m/ (visited Sept. 3, 2013) (quoting Attorney General of Massachusetts).

The defendants soon lost their home, being unable—despite valiant efforts to keep up their mortgage payments by working second jobs—to make the monthly payments of principal and interest required by the terms of the mortgage. The interest rate was adjustable; it reset automatically after two years, doubtless at a higher rate. "A large majority of Fremont's subprime loans [the loan to the defendants was subprime] were adjustable rate mortgage (ARM) loans, which bore a fixed interest rate for the first two or three years, and then adjusted every six months to a considerably higher variable rate for the remaining period of what was generally a thirty-year loan." *Commonwealth v. Fremont Investment & Loan, supra,* 897 N.E.2d at 552. Though hapless victims of Bowling, the defendants were convicted in part on the basis of his testimony; for he turned state's evidence and was rewarded for helping to convict his victims by being given a big slice off his sentence.

United States v. Hall, 731 F.3d 649, 650-651 (7th Cir. 2013) Although the Seventh Circuit went on to reverse the consumer's conviction for making false statements to a federally insured bank, the facts illustrate that the fallout from the mortgage crisis spread far and wide. The foreclosure crisis wreaked havoc on consumers but also on businesses, government, communities, courts, and the economy.

1.   Underwriting the Loan (QM)

The next decade of mortgage lending will be a sharp break from the practices in the late 1990s and early 2000s. The contours of that future, however, are unknown. The law has created some lines that cannot be crossed when underwriting a loan, and other paths that can be traversed but that carry more risks.

Congress imposed an obligation on mortgage lenders to consider the likelihood of repayment for most residential mortgage loans. 12 C.F.R. §1026.43(a). The requirement does not apply to reverse mortgages, timeshares, bridge or construction loans of 12 months or less, and home equity lines of credit. "Ability to repay" is an absolute that allows creditors to make loans only after a reasonable and good faith determination that the consumer is likely to be able to repay. 15 U.S.C. §1639c(a). Sounds simple enough but regulatory lawyers—always the type to jump in with commas and clauses—have added hundreds of pages to Regulation Z. The rule provides a minimum of eight underwriting factors that must be considered but does not proscribe a particular underwriting model or specify how the factors should be weighted.

Ability to repay is only one of two key terms in mortgage underwriting. As an alternative to assessing and documenting ability to repay, lenders may make a "qualified mortgage." 15 U.S.C. §1639c(b). These "QM" loans enjoy protection from challenge as failing the ability-to-repay standard. A qualified mortgage must have or avoid the following characteristics:

- A loan term of not greater than 30 years
- No negative amortization
- No interest only loans
- No balloon payments
- Documentation of borrower's income and assets
- Underwriting at the fully amortized rate
- Total points and fees that are not more than 3 percent of the total loan amount
- A borrower debt-to-income ratio of 43 percent or less (measured off monthly pre-tax income)

15 U.S.C. §1639c(b)(2).

These rules sound pretty exciting, with lots of potential work for lawyers. But as of early 2016, the system is a snooze. With no private secondary market, mortgage lenders make loans that the government sponsored agencies will buy. The CFPB created a years-long "temporary" exemption until 2021 that deems as a qualified mortgage any loan that is eligible for purchase, guarantee, or insurance by a GSE, FHA, VA, or USDA under those entities' underwriting standards. The exemption holds regardless of the debt-to-income ratio, which is widely considered the most difficult criteria for most consumers to meet. (If the GSEs exit federal conservatorship or a federal agency issues its own qualified mortgage rules before January 10, 2021, then those actions trump this "GSE-QM" category). The GSEs do have affordable lending products that permit down payments below the traditional 20 percent and relax income eligibility requirements. *See, e.g.,* Lisa Prevost, Fannie Mae Revamps Mortgage Program, N.Y. TIMES, Sept. 4, 2015, http://www.nytimes.com/2015/09/06/realestate/fannie-mae-revamps-mortgage-program.html?_r=0.

Non-qualified mortgages exist but they are rare. Their infrequency, combined with the fact that these rules went into effect in January 2014, means that there is no litigation testing what a reasonable, good-faith determination of a consumer's ability to repay actually is. Agency loans are deemed QM loans, and QM loans presumptively meet the ability-to-repay standard. The CFPB is examining institutions on non-QM loans, but today most ability-to-repay loans are jumbo loans (for expensive houses for which the loan exceeds the GSE's conforming loan limit) to borrowers with excellent credit and high percentage down payments. These prime non-QMs have not had early defaults and would probably satisfy ability to repay, even if challenged. At this time, ability to repay is likely sound policy on paper and a hot mess in practice.

The unknown — and potentially profitable — category of loans is subprime loans that do not meet the QM definition. Assuming these loans do not meet the eligibility standards for sale to a GSE or for insurance by a government agency, they must be underwritten for ability to repay. This is a tricky task for lenders who want to serve subprime customers. Most commonly, these loans will have payments that trigger the 43 percent limit on debt-to-income ratio, or will be made to those with volatile incomes, such as medical residents, small business owners, and the self-employed. The non-prime, non-QM market is very small as of 2016, and it is uncertain whether lenders will expand the credit box to make more subprime loans. More clarity on the ability to repay standard is a likely prerequisite for subprime QM.

Lenders face substantial liability for underwriting errors. First, lenders stay on the hook, even if the loan is assigned if the violation is apparent on the face of the disclosure documents. No longer can lenders sell loans in the secondary market and enjoy freedom from future litigation over origination practices. Liability is joint and several with the originating mortgage company and the assignee of the loan at the time of challenge.

Regular QM and GSE-QM loans have a safe harbor from liability; they are conclusively presumed to comply with the ability-to-repay requirement. 12 C.F.R. §1026.643(e). There is also a lesser protection for "higher-priced covered transactions." The definitional trigger is if the otherwise-qualified mortgage's APR exceeds the APOR by 1.5 percentage points for first liens, and 3.5 percentage points for Subordinate liens. 12 C.F.R. §1026.43(b)(3). APOR is the average prime offer rate for a comparable transaction as of a given date, as published by the CFPB. In easier language, the loan has a relatively high interest rate but otherwise meets the qualified mortgage rules. These higher-cost QM loans enjoy a "rebuttable presumption" that the creditor satisfied the ability-to-repay requirement. 15 U.S.C. §1639c(b). The consumer may later argue that the consumer's income and debt obligations were insufficient for ability to repay when the loan was made, but this litigation will be riskier and costlier for the consumer who has an uphill climb. Because of the overlap between qualified mortgages and ability to repay, the smart money (and we all hope the too-big-to-fail people are smart money this time around) will underwrite these higher-cost covered loans with care. That likely requires meeting both the QM standard (to enjoy the rebuttable presumption) and the ability-to-repay standard (in case the consumer defeats the presumption and the lender must demonstrate the sufficiency of its underwriting process).

2.   Special Rules for High-Cost Mortgages (HOEPA)

Even in the early days of subprime mortgage lending, there were rules that intended to protect subprime borrowers. *See* Cathy Lesser Mansfield, *The road to 'HEL' Was Paved with Good Congressional Intentions*, 51 S. CAR. L. REV. 473 (2000). The Home Ownership and Equity Protection Act of 1994 (HOEPA) forbade certain terms in higher-cost loans such as prepayment penalties. The problem was that virtually nothing turned out to be a higher-cost loan. For starters, the pre-Dodd-Frank HOEPA statute only applied to non-purchase, closed-end mortgages (i.e., refinances). But even among those loans, the definition was easy to evade by adjusting other terms. The result was that there were gaping holes in HOEPA, and lenders easily avoided its application.

Some states enacted laws to guard against predatory mortgage lending to shore up HOEPA's weaknesses. Raphael W. Bostic et al., *State and Local Anti-Predatory Lending Laws: The Effect of Legal Enforcement Mechanisms*, 60 J. ECON. & BUS. 47 (2008). These laws were relatively limited because the federal government asserted that its role as prudential banking regulator preempted most underwriting laws. The case below is an example of a state statute that attempted to curb lending practices and illustrates how the common law was applied to predatory lending.

––––––––––

Bishop v. Quicken Loans, Inc.
2011 WL 1321360 (S.D. W. Va. 2011)

COPENHAVER, JR., District Judge.

I. BACKGROUND AND PROCEDURAL HISTORY

Plaintiff William Bishop is a veteran and retired coal miner. His wife, plaintiff Juanita Bishop, was primarily a homemaker, raising the couple's six children. Both Mr. and Mrs. Bishop are high school graduates. They earn a fixed monthly income of approximately $4,165, consisting of retirement pensions and Social Security benefits.

In 1994, plaintiffs purchased their home in Beckley, West Virginia, for $60,000. Plaintiffs co-own the Beckley property. They refinanced the property twice with Bank One Corporation, once in 2002 and again in 2004 (the "Bank One Loans"). From May 2005 to December 2006, plaintiffs refinanced their home three times with defendant Quicken Loans. Each time only Mr. Bishop signed the note or notes, but both Mr. and Mrs. Bishop signed the deed of trust securing the obligation.

Plaintiffs' dealings with Quicken Loans are at the center of this dispute. Four counts are alleged in the second amended complaint. In Count I, Unconscionable Conduct, plaintiffs ask that the third Quicken loan be declared unconscionable. In Count II, Illegal Loan, plaintiffs allege that Quicken (1) imposed illegal origination and investigation fees twice within a twenty-four month period and (2) issued two mortgage loans (the second and third loans) that exceeded the fair market value of plaintiffs' property. Count III, Fraud, relates to the rate of interest imposed on the third loan. Count Four, Fraud, relates to an inflated appraisal furnished by an appraiser from Quicken Loans' sister corporation for the second and third loans.

A. The May 2005 Notes

In the spring of 2005, after seeing an advertisement on television, Mrs. Bishop (who handled the couple's finances) contacted Quicken Loans about refinancing the Beckley property. Plaintiffs were current on their mortgage payments at the time but indicated to Quicken Loans that they were interested in paying off their credit card debt and lowering their monthly mortgage payments. To facilitate plaintiffs' attempt to refinance, Quicken Loans obtained an appraisal from appraiser William Whitehair of Whitehair Appraisals, Inc., an independent appraisal company located in Elkins, West Virginia. On April 21, 2005, Mr. Whitehair valued plaintiffs' property at $112,500.

On May 18, 2005, Mr. Bishop executed two Quicken Loans promissory notes in order to refinance the Beckley property (the "May 2005 notes"). The first was a Fixed Rate Note in the amount of $84,000, payable in 360 monthly installments beginning in July 2005 with an interest rate of 6.375%. Exclusive of tax or insurance escrows, plaintiffs' monthly payment under the Fixed Rate Note was $524.06. The second note was a Fixed Rate Balloon Note in the amount of $15,000. The Fixed Rate Balloon Note had a fixed interest rate of 6.80%, resulting in a monthly payment of $97.79 and a balloon payment of $11,113.63 due after fifteen years. The May 2005 notes were secured by deeds of trust on the Beckley property executed by both plaintiffs.

By refinancing, plaintiffs satisfied their preexisting mortgage loan in the amount of $66,870.93, as well as certain unsecured debt in the amount of $1,840. Plaintiffs also secured a lower interest rate as compared to their prior mortgage loan and obtained $26,910.97 in cash. The settlement charges incurred by plaintiffs in connection with the May 2005 notes totaled approximately $3,700.

B. The July 2006 Notes

In 2006, John Snively of Quicken Loans contacted plaintiffs by e-mail about refinancing their property. Mr. Snively, who e-mailed plaintiffs approximately once per month, apparently indicated to plaintiffs that they could obtain a lower monthly mortgage payment by refinancing the May 2005 notes. After plaintiffs expressed interest, Quicken Loans requested that TSI Appraisal Services ("TSI"), an appraisal management company, arrange for a full appraisal of plaintiffs' property. TSI, which, like Quicken Loans, is a subsidiary of Rock Holdings Inc., arranged for an appraisal of plaintiffs' property to be completed by Kirk Riffe of Mountaineer Appraisals. On April 20, 2006, Mr. Riffe prepared an appraisal of the property, indicating that its fair market value at the time was $153,000. Quicken Loans reviewed and approved Mr. Riffe's appraisal and conditionally approved plaintiffs' loan application.

On July 6, 2006, Mr. Bishop again executed two Quicken Loans notes (the "July 2006 notes"), totaling $122,400. The first was an Interest First Note in the amount of $112,400 with an interest rate of 6.5%. The Interest First Note provided for interest-only payments in the amount of $608.83 per month for the first 120 months, followed by monthly payments of $838.03 for the next 240 months. The second note was a Fixed Rate Balloon Note in the amount of $10,000 with a fixed interest rate of 9.375%. The Fixed Rate Balloon Note had monthly payments of $83.18, with a balloon payment of $8,104.43 due after fifteen years. The July 2006 notes were secured by deeds of trust on the Beckley property executed by both plaintiffs

Plaintiffs used the proceeds from the July 2006 notes to satisfy the balance of the May 2005 notes and certain unsecured debt in the amount of $9,885. Plaintiffs also received $5,536.28 in cash. The settlement charges accompanying the July 2006 notes totaled approximately $8,300.

C. The December 2006 Note

In September 2006, Mr. Snively called Mrs. Bishop about refinancing the property for a third time. Mr. Snively represented to Mrs. Bishop that by obtaining an adjustable rate note, plaintiffs could lower their mortgage payment to approximately $450 per month. Mrs. Bishop explained that she and her husband did not want an adjustable rate note, to which Mr. Snively responded that Quicken Loans would refinance the home again before the interest rate on the proposed note would increase. Based on Mr. Snively's representations, plaintiffs applied for another mortgage loan. On September 12, 2006, plaintiffs were conditionally approved for a seven-year, adjustable rate loan in the amount of $131,600. On September 24, 2006, Kirk Riffe prepared another appraisal of the property for Quicken Loans, again indicating that its fair market value was $153,000.

On November 15, 2006, Mrs. Bishop expressed concern that the proposed seven-year loan included private mortgage insurance, which would protect Quicken Loans in the event of default by plaintiffs and result in higher monthly payments. As a result, on December 15, 2006, Mr. Bishop instead obtained from Quicken Loans a thirty-year Option Adjustable Rate Note in the amount of $133,600, with an initial interest rate of 6.250% (the "December 2006 note"). The December 2006 note, signed by Mr. Bishop only, gave plaintiffs the option to select among a variety of payment methods, including a fully amortizing repayment structure calculated over fifteen- and thirty-year terms, as well as the option of making a minimum monthly payment of $361.83. Quicken specified in the December 2006 note, however, that the loan was subject to "negative amortization," such that a minimum monthly payment "will not be sufficient to pay interest at

[6.250%]" and that the deferred interest will both increase the loan balance and accrue additional interest. Both Mr. and Mrs. Bishop executed the deed of trust securing the December 2006 note.

The proceeds from the December 2006 note satisfied the balance of the July 2006 notes; plaintiffs also received $1,265.35 in cash. The settlement costs accompanying the December 2006 note amounted to approximately $8,300.

D. The Procedural History of this Action

Plaintiffs began making monthly payments on the December 2006 note of approximately $450, which equaled the minimum monthly payment plus escrow payments. At some point in 2008, they learned that the minimum monthly payment under the December 2006 note "would more than double within 5 years" after the adjustable interest rate increased. In March 2008, plaintiffs contacted Quicken Loans and attempted to refinance their property to reduce the monthly payment. In April 2008, Brett Brotherton of the Southern West Virginia Appraisal Group prepared an appraisal of plaintiffs' property for Quicken Loans, indicating that the value of the house was $137,000. Inasmuch as the balance on the December 2006 note exceeded the property's appraised value, Quicken Loans denied plaintiffs' 2008 loan application.

Plaintiffs allege that they learned the "true value" of their property in 2009. Specifically, in June 2009, plaintiffs hired Robert Wilson of Wilson and Associates, Inc., to perform a retrospective appraisal of the property. On June 30, 2009, Mr. Wilson provided plaintiffs with his appraisal, which retrospectively valued the property at $100,000 as of December 2006.

Plaintiffs instituted this action in the Circuit Court of Kanawha County on September 2, 2009. Quicken Loans removed on October 2, 2009, invoking the court's diversity jurisdiction.

• • •

ANALYSIS

A. Count I: Unconscionability

Count I of the complaint seeks a declaration that the conduct engaged in by Quicken Loans was unconscionable, rendering the December 2006 note void and unenforceable. In addition to actual damages, plaintiffs seek civil penalties under §46A-5-101 of the West Virginia Consumer Credit and Protection Act.

In West Virginia, the basic test for unconscionability is:

> [W]hether, in the light of the background and setting of the market, the needs of the particular trade or case, and the condition of the particular parties to the conduct or contract, the conduct involved is, or the contract or clauses involved are so one sided as to be unconscionable under the circumstances existing at the time the conduct occurs or is threatened or at the time of the making of the contract.

Arnold v. United Cos. Lending Corp., 204 W. Va. 229 (1998).

[Ed. Note — The court ruled that the evidence did not demonstrate indisputably that the Bishops were sophisticated customers, despite Quicken's assertion that they had refinanced their home five times in four years. The court also noted that rapid escalation in refinance fees from $3,700 in May 2005 to $8,300 for both the July and December 2006 notes could support a finding of excessive fees that were unreasonably favorable to Quicken. Finally, the court noted that evidence of the 36 percent increase in property value between the appraisals in April 2005 and April 2006 raised at least a question of fact concerning the fairness of the transaction. It ruled that summary judgment was inappropriate on the count of unconscionability.]

. . .

B. Count II: Illegal Loan

1. West Virginia Code §31-17-8(d)

Plaintiffs first allege in Count II that, within a twenty-four month period, Quicken Loans twice imposed loan origination fees and investigation fees upon them, in violation of West Virginia Code §31-17-8(d). That provision prohibits lenders from imposing such fees twice within a twenty-four month period, "unless the new loan has a reasonable, tangible net benefit to the borrower considering all of the circumstances, including the terms of both the new and the refinanced loans, the cost of the new loan, and the borrower's circumstances." W. Va. Code §31-17-8(d). Quicken Loans does not dispute that it imposed origination and investigation fees twice within a twenty-four-month period. Rather, it contends that plaintiffs received a tangible net benefit from the loans, precluding liability under §31-17-8(d).

Without question, plaintiffs received a reasonable, tangible net benefit from the May 2005 notes. Specifically, plaintiffs received $26,910.97 in cash and the payment of $1,840 in unsecured debt out of the loan proceeds, compared to settlement charges totaling approximately $3,700. Whether plaintiffs received a similar net benefit from the second and third Quicken loans remains in question. The settlement costs accompanying the July 2006 notes increased significantly to $8,300, or more than half of the amount plaintiffs realized in cash and debt relief ($15,421.28) from the July transaction. Similarly, the settlement costs incurred as a result of the December 2006 note totaled approximately $8,300, yet plaintiffs received only $1,265.35 in cash from that loan. To be sure, a cost-benefit analysis of a consumer loan must consider more than simply settlement costs. A borrower may well benefit from a loan, despite the presence of such high fees, if the loan, for example, secures a lower interest rate or more affordable payment terms for the borrower. As a result of the July 2006 and December 2006 notes, however, plaintiffs were forced to pay higher interest rates and, according to their deposition testimony, face increasing payments that will soon be unaffordable.

In such circumstances, the court cannot conclude at this juncture that plaintiffs received a reasonable, tangible net benefit from the second and third Quicken loans. Accordingly, there remains a question of fact as to whether Quicken improperly imposed origination and investigation fees twice within a twenty-four month period. Summary judgment on plaintiffs' §31-17-8(d) claim is thus not appropriate.

2. West Virginia Code §31-17-8(m)(8)

Plaintiffs also allege in Count II that Quicken Loans violated West Virginia Code §31-17-8(m)(8). That provision prohibits mortgage lenders from securing "a primary or subordinate mortgage loan in a principal amount . . . that exceeds the fair market value of the property." The statute provides that a lender

> may rely upon a bona fide written appraisal of the property made by an independent third-party appraiser, duly licensed or certified by the West Virginia real estate appraiser licensing and certification board and prepared in compliance with the uniform standards of professional appraisal practice.

W. Va. Code §31-17-8(m)(8). In Count II, plaintiffs contend that Quicken Loans violated this provision by granting them a loan that far exceeded the market value of the property. To support this claim, plaintiffs proffer the retrospective appraisal performed in 2009 that reached a lower value than the appraisals performed in 2006 by Mr. Riffe. In its motion for summary judgment, Quicken Loans apparently does not dispute that the 2009 retrospective appraisal raises a question of fact as to the market value of the house in 2006. Nevertheless, Quicken Loans contends that summary judgment on the §31-17-8(m)(8) claim is appropriate, inasmuch as Quicken Loans relied on the 2006 appraisals of Mr. Riffe, an independent, third-party appraiser who complied with the uniform standards of professional appraisal practice.

In contending that Mr. Riffe was an independent, third-party appraiser, Quicken Loans emphasizes Mr. Riffe's affidavit, wherein he attests that he "did not, at any time, speak with Quicken Loans, Inc. or any representative thereof, or the mortgage banker assigned to the loans relating to [plaintiffs'] property." Mr. Riffe further asserts that he was never "told what value [he] should reach in [his] appraisal of the property." From his affidavit, Quicken Loans asserts that Mr. Riffe was independent and that plaintiffs' §31-17-8(m)(8) claim must be dismissed.

Notwithstanding Mr. Riffe's assertions, the court cannot conclude from this record that he was unquestionably an independent, third-party appraiser. Plaintiffs have introduced evidence indicating a relationship between Quicken Loans and Mr. Riffe's employer, TSI. Specifically, Mr. Clint Bonkowski, a divisional vice president of Quicken Loans, testified that his company and TSI share a parent corporation known as Rock Holdings, Inc. That fact, in and of itself, raises a material question as to whether Mr. Riffe was an independent appraiser.

Even assuming Mr. Riffe's independence, plaintiffs have also presented evidence suggesting that his appraisal did not comply with the uniform standards of professional appraisal practice. Specifically, plaintiffs proffered an appraisal examination conducted by Troy Sneddon, who concluded that Mr. Riffe's 2006 appraisals violated several provisions of the Uniform Standards of Professional Appraisal Practice ("USPAP"). For instance, Mr. Sneddon noted that Mr. Riffe's appraisals failed to include the actual dimensions of the site; misstated the property's acreage; failed to specify the zoning classification; failed to correctly identify the FEMA Special Flood Hazard Area; and failed to note the portion of the property's basement that was finished. According to Mr. Sneddon, these deficiencies contravened at least nine separate provisions of the USPAP, including Standard Rule 1.1(b), which provides that an appraiser must not commit a substantial error of omission, and Standard Rule 2.1(a), which requires that an appraiser's report clearly and accurately set forth the appraisal in a manner that will not be misleading. Mr. Sneddon concluded that, collectively, the deficiencies in Mr. Riffe's appraisals indicate that the appraisals lack credibility and "lack the necessary information for USPAP compliance."

Whether the appraiser was independent and whether the cited failures constitute substantial error remain to be evaluated. Inasmuch as there is are disputed questions of fact as to whether the appraisals relied upon by Quicken Loans complied with industry standards, the court concludes that summary judgment as to plaintiffs' §31-17-8(m)(8) claim is not appropriate.

C. Count III: Fraud

In order to establish a claim for fraud, plaintiffs must prove: (1) that the act claimed to be fraudulent was the act of Quicken Loans or was induced by it; (2) that the act was material and false, and that plaintiffs relied upon it and were justified under the circumstances in relying upon it; and (3) that plaintiffs were damaged because of this reliance. See Kidd v. Mull, 215 W. Va. 151 (2004); Lengyel v. Lint, 167 W. Va. 272 (1981). In the complaint, the Count III fraud allegations, which appear to relate only to the December 2006 note, are as follows:

> 39. At the time of inducement and even at closing, [Quicken Loans] misrepresented and suppressed specific rates and terms to Plaintiffs in the loan, and represented the loan would be refinanced before the Plaintiffs' payments increased.
> 40. Defendants intentionally misrepresented these facts and suppressed the true cost/rate for the purpose of inducing the Plaintiffs to contract.
> 41. The Plaintiffs reasonably relied upon their belief as to the low rate promised.
> 42. Said misrepresentation and suppressions were material.

As a result, plaintiffs allege that they were "damaged by the misrepresentation and suppressions."

As an initial matter, plaintiffs have presented insufficient evidence to demonstrate that Quicken Loans misrepresented or suppressed any specific material terms of the December 2006 note itself. Mrs. Bishop testified during her deposition that she advised Mr. Snively that she and her husband did not want an adjustable rate mortgage. Mr. Snively apparently responded by assuring her that, although the December 2006 note included an adjustable interest rate, Quicken Loans would refinance the mortgage before the initial interest rate expired. Mr. Snively's assurances in this regard were not included in the December 2006 note, which squarely alerted plaintiffs that the initial interest could increase after sixty months. Mrs. Bishop was thus aware that the December 2006 note contained an adjustable interest rate. Furthermore, although plaintiffs allege that they were unaware of the payment options associated with the December 2006 note and the consequences of making only the minimum payment, the mortgage documents that Mr. Bishop signed explain his payment options and the consequence of each. For example, a document entitled "Fixed/Adjustable Rate Note with Payment Options," which Mr. Bishop signed, described each payment option and cautioned as follows:

> The principal balance on your loan will not be decreased by making [the minimum payment]. Additionally, because your [minimum payment] is less than the interest

that has actually accrued on your Note, the Note Holder will subtract the amount of your monthly payment from the amount of the actual accrued interest and will add the difference to your unpaid principal (this is referred to as "negative amortization").

Plaintiffs thus knew or should have known that their loan balance would increase if they paid only the minimum amount.

Nevertheless, plaintiffs have presented sufficient evidence that Quicken Loans materially misrepresented that it would refinance the December 2006 note to a fixed-rate loan before the adjustable interest rate could increase. Ordinarily, fraud "cannot be based on statements which are promissory in nature or which constitute expressions of intention." Croston v. Emax Oil Co., 195 W. Va. 86 (1995). Only if the plaintiff can show that the defendant did not intend to fulfill the promise at the time it was made may a promissory statement serve as the basis of fraud. Id. Here, in response to concerns raised by Mrs. Bishop, Mr. Snively assured plaintiffs that the December 2006 note would be refinanced to a fixed-rate loan before any increase in the adjustable interest rate. That Mr. Snively failed to incorporate this promise into the official loan documents surrounding the December 2006 note (which, of course, bound plaintiffs to pay an adjustable interest rate) raises a question of material fact regarding Quicken Loans' intentions to fulfill the promise at the time it was made. See England v. MG Invs., Inc., 93 F. Supp. 2d 718, 722 (holding that lender's failure to include oral promise concerning interest rate into written loan documents raised question concerning lender's intent to abide by promise). Accordingly, summary judgment as to Count III is inappropriate.

D. Count IV: Fraud

Count IV of the complaint alleges that Quicken Loans intentionally arranged for an inflated market value of plaintiffs' property for the purpose of inducing them to refinance their property. Plaintiffs further allege that Quicken Loans' reliance upon the inflated appraisal was intentional and material, and that plaintiffs "reasonably relied upon the origination of the loan being consistent with prudent lending practices."

Evidence presented to the court in support of Count IV is sparse. One might argue that the wide variance in the Riffe appraisal and the retrospective appraisal conducted in 2009 raises a question of fact not only as to the accuracy of the former but also whether it is so far off the mark as to be a materially false representation of the value of the property.

Even so, plaintiffs have failed to establish a claim for fraud based on an inflated appraisal. As mentioned, plaintiffs must demonstrate that they reasonably relied upon the false representation. See Kidd v. Mull, 215 W. Va. 151 (2004). Although it is "not necessary that the fraudulent representations complained of . . . be the sole consideration or inducement moving the plaintiff," the representations must at least "contribute [ ] to the formation of the conclusion in the plaintiff's mind." Horton v. Tyree, 104 W. Va. 238 (1927). Plaintiffs have failed to introduce any evidence that the Riffe appraisals materially affected their decision to enter into the December 2006 note. Indeed, plaintiffs testified that they never saw any appraisal and did not know what the property had appraised for in connection with the Quicken Loans notes.

Inasmuch as plaintiffs have failed to introduce evidence as to a necessary element of their fraud claim, namely, that they relied on a materially false representation concerning the value of their property, summary judgment on Count IV is appropriate.

. . .

IV.

Pursuant to the foregoing analysis, it is ORDERED as follows:

1. That Quicken Loans' motion for summary judgment be, and it hereby is, granted insofar as it seeks dismissal of Count IV and the claims of plaintiff Juanita Bishop in Counts I and II, and denied in all other respects;

2. That Count IV be, and it hereby is, dismissed; . . .

The CFPB amended Regulation X to expand the types of mortgage loans that are subject to HOEPA's rules. 12 C.F.R. §1026.32. These were previously often called "high-cost" loans but now with the new QM "higher cost covered transactions," the more clear terminology is "HOEPA loans." HOEPA now applies to nearly all mortgages that meet one or more of three triggers. The first trigger is a prepayment penalty test. It has two separate components. Can the lender charge a prepayment penalty more than three years after the loan's origination? Or can the prepayment penalty exceeds more than 2 percent of the amount prepaid? If so, the loan is a HOEPA loan. The second trigger is set off if the APR for the loan exceeds the APOR (remember, "average prime offer rate") by more than 6.5 percentage points for a first-lien mortgage, or 8.5 percentage points for a subordinate-lien or personal property dwelling (manufactured home) mortgage. The third trigger is based on total points and fees. If they exceed 5 percent of the total loan for any loan of $20,000 or more, the transaction is covered by HOEPA. Note to the unwary, this dollar threshold adjusts based on the consumer price index each January 1. For smaller loans, the points and fees cannot exceed 8 percent or HOEPA applies.

Because they are relatively costly, the law provides more consumer protections when a borrower takes out a HOEPA loan. Certain fees are forbidden entirely: prepayment penalties, balloon payments, late fees that exceed 4 percent of the regular payment, and a few others. Appraisers of homes that will be collateral for a HOEPA loan also must be certified or licensed, inspect the interior of the home, and provide a free copy of the appraisal to the borrower. Although there are yet even more exceptions, most HOEPA loans also must be managed with escrow accounts, at least for the first five years of the loan. For HOEPA loans, Regulation X (RESPA rules) requires pre-counseling from a statutorily prescribed housing counselor, who cannot be in the employ of the lender. 12 C.F.R. §1024.20.

3. Creditor Defenses and Borrower Liability

Because the mortgage underwriting rules are part of Regulation Z, liability arises under the general TILA statute. 15 U.S.C. §1640. It provides for actual and statutory damages, and the recovery of attorneys' fees and costs. This statute is discussed in more detail in the upcoming assignment on enforcement but there are special rules for mortgages to note now. A lender may be held liable for "enhanced" damages for violating the ability-to-repay requirement. 15 U.S.C. §1640(a)(4). These damages can equal the sum of all finance charges and fees paid by the consumer on the loan, which especially in the early years of a loan is a huge fraction of the monthly payments. The lender can escape these damages if it can show that its failure to comply is not material. As of now, there are no cases defining and applying "material" in this context. The result for lenders — depending on your perspective — is complete paranoia or strict adherence to consumer law.

A consumer may bring an affirmative lawsuit for monetary damages for up to three years from the loan origination date. If the consumer is in foreclosure, however, the period for asserting violations is not limited. If a creditor, assignee, or anyone acting on their behalf initiates a judicial or non-judicial foreclosure, the borrower may assert, as a defense by set off or recoupment, that the orginating lender did not properly determine ability to repay as a defense. 15 U.S.C. §1640(k). While lenders may prevail in such litigation, it is a powerful weapon for consumers (and their lawyers) to have an ability-to-repay violation that can be a defense to foreclosure.

B. Mortgage Servicing

Mortgage servicing is the collection of payments from borrowers and the disbursement of those payments to the appropriate parties, such as lenders, investors, taxing authorities, and insurers. The rise of servicing as a distinct industry resulted from the widespread use of securitization in the mortgage market. As explained in Assignment 13, securitization is the process of creating debt instruments (bonds or securities) by pooling mortgage loans, transferring those obligations to a trust, and then selling fractional interests in the trust's right to receive payments from the mortgages to investors. Servicers act as intermediaries between the borrower and the other parties to the securitization. A "pooling and servicing agreement" sets out the servicer's responsibilities for collecting and remitting the mortgage payments. It also obligates the servicer to take steps to foreclose in the event of default. The participation of servicers complicates the debtor-creditor relationship and creates the need for specific consumer protections.

Mortgage servicers do not have a customer relationship with homeowners; they work, via the trust, for the investors in the mortgage-backed securities. Borrowers cannot shop for a loan based on the quality of the servicing, and they have virtually no ability to change servicers if they are dissatisfied with the servicers' conduct. The only exit strategy for a dissatisfied borrower is refinancing the mortgage, and even then, the homeowner may find the new loan assigned to the prior servicer — or an even worse entity. This creates what the CFPB's first director, Rich Cordray, called a "deadend," a market in which consumers cannot vote with their feet to address indefensible or unfair tactics.

In fact, servicers have some financial incentives to impose additional fees on consumers. Servicers often are permitted to retain all, or part, of any default fees, such as late charges, that consumers pay. In this way, a borrower's default can boost a servicer's profits, although the costs of servicing a defaulted loan can be very high and exceed the fixed servicing fee, often between 0.25 percent and 0.5 percent of the notes' principals. Because of the revenue structure, a servicer's incentives upon a homeowner's default may not align with investors' incentives or a consumer's needs.

A consumer is only obligated to pay charges if they are permitted by the terms of the mortgage and by state and federal law. To validate such charges, consumers must know how the servicer calculated the amount due and whether such fees are consistent with their loan contracts. Mortgage servicers can exploit consumers' difficulty in recognizing errors or overcharges by failing to provide comprehensible or complete information. Permissible default charges and processes vary by state law, the loan note and mortgage, and the type of loan (GSE, FHA, etc.). The result is a thicket of fees.

Spiking foreclosure rates worsened problems with mortgage servicing. Consumers grew frustrated with customer service representatives who were difficult to reach or provided conflicting information, with poor document handling practices, and with impenetrable statements or letters. Falling real-estate prices also changed the profit calculus of foreclosure. It became clear that at least some investors were better off by modifying the loan rather than foreclosing. The federal government's umbrella of programs, Making Homes Affordable, encouraged lenders to contact delinquent borrowers and provided modest financial incentives to servicers for modifying delinquent loans. Facing political and financial pressure, lenders and servicers struggled to develop cost- and time-effective strategies for helping homeowners. The legal woes of mortgage companies also mounted as consumers and regulators began to challenge servicing practices.

The federal government recently established new stronger protections for servicing, creating a floor that some state laws exceed. The new rules are a recognition that mortgage servicing is a crucial part of the homeownership process. Some rules focus on current borrowers, while others provide procedural protections to delinquent borrowers.

1. Payment Collection

Even in tough times, most homeowners are current on their mortgages. The main job of servicers is to calculate, solicit, and apply payments. The Real Estate Settlement Procedures Act (RESPA) not only governs "settlement" at origination but also imposes ongoing duties on servicers. The CFPB extensively amended RESPA's Regulation X in 2013. It creates both general and specific duties. Section 1024.38 requires servicers to have objective-based policies and procedures to provide timely and accurate information to consumers and to ensure compliance with the detailed rules for servicer transfer and loss mitigation.

Servicers must credit periodic payments as of the date of receipt. 12 C.F.R. §1024.36(c). If a consumer makes less than the amount needed to cover the outstanding principal, interest, and escrow, the servicer may hold that payment in a suspense account. To curb abuses when servicers let thousands of dollars of consecutive payments accumulate in such accounts, leaving the consumer delinquent and subject to late fees or insufficient payment fees each month, Regulation X requires that when a suspense account balance is sufficient to cover a periodic payment, the money to be applied to the consumer's account. Consumers are also entitled to receive an accurate payoff balance no later than seven business days after a servicer receives a written request. In the past, consumers would have to make repeated requests for such statements, often needed for refinancing, and by the time statements were received, they were woefully miscalculated.

The content, timing, and form of billing statements for mortgages are proscribed by Regulation Z, implementing TILA. The billing statements inform consumers of the amount due, fees imposed, transaction activity, and servicer's contact information. 12 C.F.R. §1026.41. Servicers also must notify consumers of interest-rate adjustments in advance and provide an estimate of the new payment. These rules may seem duplicative of those covered with regard to the Fair Credit Billing Act, but until the CFPB acted in 2013, there were no parallel obligations on mortgage servicers. Consumers had to make a "qualified written request" under RESPA if they needed information. If the servicer did not respond, however, the consumer had no right of action to force compliance or create liability. It literally was nothing more than a request.

Servicers have expanded duties with regard to consumer inquiries under the new rules. They have only five days to acknowledge a consumer's request for information or a notice of error, and must respond after investigation within 30 to 45 days. 12 C.F.R. §§1024.35; 1024.36. The servicer can require these requests or notices to be in writing and specify an address for receipt, but they cannot charge for responding or make adverse credit reports based on a notice. Creditors must also exercise care before imposing property insurance on consumers. This force-placed insurance is more expensive than consumer-shopped coverage, and to prevent abuse — such as servicers farming out insurance to affiliates with high rates — the insurance price must bear a reasonable relationship to its actual cost. 12 C.F.R. §1024.37.

2. Default and Loss Mitigation

Functionally, default servicing was the final resting place for illegally originated loans. With no ability to track down the originator lender or mortgage broker or appraiser or realtor, consumers threatened with foreclosure hurled ire at servicers. And in fairness to consumers, servicers were ill prepared to handle the task. For the first few years of the foreclosure crisis, servicers struggled to manage the defaults during the foreclosure crisis. While most companies had home retention departments, there was little communication with foreclosure departments. Consumers suffered the consequences, while servicers pocketed fees and had little regulatory oversight. *See* Katherine Porter, *Misbehavior and Mistake in Bankruptcy Mortgage Claims,* 87 Tex. L. Rev. 121 (2008).

A few of the key default rules are highlighted below, but it should be a telltale sign to you about the comprehensiveness — and comprehensibility — of the rules that the CFPB's own best effort to educate *consumers* on loss mitigation exceed 50 pages. CFPB, *Help for Struggling Borrowers* (Jan. 28, 2014) http://files.consumerfinance.gov/f/201402_cfpb_mortgages_help-for-struggling-borrowers.pdf. Some would say these rules are a poster child for government being unduly prescriptive; others would say that when an industry commits serious and systemic violations that a detailed schema of reform is necessary. These extensive rules may be an effort to paper over a more subtle but serious problem. Investors, not consumers, still control the servicing market, and the law creates absolutely no right to a loan modification. Servicers must follow many rules to implement foreclosure prevention programs, but after the expiration of federal programs, such as HAMP, loan modifications may disappear or be replaced with the less generous forbearance and recapitalization programs.

The key theme of the CFPB's servicing rules is early intervention. As soon as a borrower fails to make a single payment sufficient to cover principal, interest, and any escrow payment, the servicer has the obligation to reach out and try to stay in contact. 12 C.F.R. §1024, Supp. I, Cmts. 39(a)-1(i); 39(b)(1)-1 and 40(a)(3). While the legal standard is a "good faith effort" to reach the borrower by telephone or talk to the borrower in-person, 12 C.F.R. §1024.39(a), the CFPB encourages servicers to make multiple efforts. Leaving a voicemail does not satisfy the good faith effort; the calls must continue.

Once the borrower is reached, the servicer must tell the borrower about loss mitigation options available — with the notable caveat that the servicer may use "reasonable discretion" to decide if it is appropriate to give the consumer such information. 12 C.F.R. §1024, Supp. I, Cmt. 39(a)-3. This information can be in writing, and usually is delivered that way to allow the servicer to prove this requirement was met. The servicer must also facilitate "continuity of contact" by assigning a designated representative, called a single point of contact, to the borrower. 12 C.F.R. §1038(a). This requirement is meant to eliminate the problems consumers experienced during the foreclosure crisis with receiving inconsistent information; essentially, hearing different answers each time they called the servicer. The single point of contact has enumerated duties. 12 C.F.R. §1040(a) & (b). The focus is on assisting the borrower in submitting an application for loss mitigation.

If the application is received 45 days or more before any scheduled foreclosure sale, the servicer must send an acknowledgment to the borrower within five days of its receipt of the documents. That letter must also inform the borrower what documents are needed to complete the application. 12 C.F.R. §1024.41(b)(2)(i)(B). If the application is received fewer than 45 days before the scheduled foreclosure, the servicer does not have to send the five-day acknowledgment but must still "exercise reasonable diligence in obtaining documents and information to complete a loss mitigation document." 12 C.F.R. §1024.41(b). Until the application is complete, however, the foreclosure process can continue. When the application is complete — an endpoint left to the servicer to define — the foreclosure process must halt. The servicer must evaluate the borrower for all appropriate loss mitigation options, explain its decision, and give time to appeal. If the complete application is received 37 days or fewer before the scheduled sale, the servicer does not have to follow the loss mitigation requirements. 12 C.F.R. §1024, Supp. I, Cmt. 41(g)-4.

Some states, most notably California, have loss mitigation statutes. The California Homeowner Bill of Rights was enacted after the nation's attorneys general achieved a $25 billion settlement against the five largest mortgage servicers. One of its primary purposes was to broaden the protections of the settlement to all mortgage servicers and to make the most important protections permanent (the settlement reforms had a three-year window). The statute was also acted before the CFPB promulgated its servicing rules. This is an example both of a state being more nimble but also now of the compliance difficulties for companies that have federal and state rules that are not perfectly aligned.

Valbuena v. Ocwen Loan Servicing, LLC

188 Cal. Rptr. 3d 668 (2015)

GOODMAN, Appellate Judge.

Plaintiffs Amado and Myrna Valbuena sued Ocwen Loan Servicing, LLC (Ocwen), following their lender's purchase of their residence at a nonjudicial foreclosure sale. They allege that Ocwen violated Civil Code section 2923.6, the prohibition on "dual tracking" contained in the Homeowner Bill of Rights, when it conducted a foreclosure sale of their property while their loan modification application was pending. The trial court sustained Ocwen's demurrer, ruling that plaintiffs' failure to allege tender of the loan balance defeated their claims. We disagree, and so reverse the judgment.

FACTUAL AND PROCEDURAL BACKGROUND

Plaintiffs purchased the real property located at 360 East 238th Place in Carson (the property) in 2004. In August 2006, plaintiffs obtained from American Brokers Conduit a $485,000 loan secured by the property; that loan was assigned to Deutsche Bank in September 2011. At that time, plaintiffs were behind in their mortgage payments, having suffered financial difficulties.

On September 26, 2011, T.D. Service Company, as trustee, recorded a notice of default and election to sell under deed of trust on the property. The notice of default stated that plaintiffs were $21,181.11 in arrears as of September 30, 2011. A notice of trustee's sale was recorded on December 22, 2011, setting a foreclosure sale for January 17, 2012. A second notice of trustee's sale was recorded on February 15, 2013, setting the foreclosure sale date for March 14, 2013; the sale was later postponed until March 25, 2013. The lender acquired the property at the foreclosure sale on that date. A trustee's deed upon sale was recorded on October 15, 2013.

As of March 1, 2013, after the second notice of trustee's sale was recorded, Ocwen took over the servicing of plaintiffs' mortgage loan. Ocwen sent plaintiffs a letter dated March 13, 2013, which plaintiffs received on March 18, 2013, stating: "[A]s your loan servicer, we are committed to helping YOU. We offer a full range of mortgage assistance programs, and actively participate in the Obama Administration's Home Affordable Mortgage Program (HAMP). You may be able to lower your monthly payments—APPLY NOW to find out what options are available to you!" The letter explained the application process, and promised "a thorough review of your financial situation." The letter continued: "While we consider your request, we will not initiate a new foreclosure action and we will not move ahead with the foreclosure sale on an active foreclosure as long as we have received all required documents and you have met the eligibility requirements. In the event that a foreclosure sale has been set and is within 30 days from this request for a HAMP application, the foreclosure sale will not be stopped and the sale will take place on the scheduled date unless a complete HAMP application with all required attachments and signatures is delivered to Ocwen no later than 7 business days prior to the scheduled foreclosure sale date."

On March 21, 2013, plaintiffs responded to this letter by submitting paystubs, a W-2, and bank statements to Ocwen. On March 23, 2013, after speaking with an Ocwen representative, plaintiffs submitted additional financial documentation in support of their loan modification application. By letter dated March 25, 2013, the date of the foreclosure sale, Ocwen notified plaintiffs that they were not eligible for a loan modification because "[a]s of the date of this letter your loan has a confirmed sale date within 7 days."

[ED. NOTE—The operative version of plaintiff's complaint on appeal alleged causes of action for breach of contract, negligent misrepresentation, promissory estoppel, unlawful business practices, breach of the implied covenant of good faith and fair dealing, fraud, and violation of the Homeowner Bill of Rights.]

Ocwen again demurred, contending that the second amended complaint failed to state a cause of action upon which relief could be granted. The trial court agreed, stating in its minute order that its grant of leave to amend did not authorize plaintiffs to allege the new causes of action for negligence and intentional infliction of emotional distress, and that the remaining causes of action were defective due to the absence of "pleading of tender or exception to tender requirement even though this is post-foreclosure." The court sustained the demurrer without leave to amend, and subsequently entered judgment in favor of Ocwen.

Plaintiffs timely appealed the judgment of dismissal.

DISCUSSION

"A demurrer tests the legal sufficiency . . . in a complaint. We independently review the sustaining of a demurrer and determine de novo whether the complaint alleges facts sufficient to state a cause of action or discloses a complete defense. McCall v. PacifiCare of Cal., Inc. 25 Cal. 4th 412, 415 (2001). . . .

Plaintiffs frame the issue in this appeal as follows: "[W]hether the Trial Court erred in sustaining the Respondent's Demurrer . . . concluding that the entire case—which, among other things, alleges several statutory violations of the California Homeowner's Bill of Rights ('HBOR')—should be dismissed with prejudice because

Plaintiffs/Appellants did not allege tender of their entire loan balance in their amended complaint."

The Homeowner Bill of Rights (HBOR), effective January 1, 2013, was enacted "to ensure that, as part of the nonjudicial foreclosure process, borrowers are considered for, and have a meaningful opportunity to obtain, available loss mitigation options, if any, offered by or through the borrower's mortgage servicer, such as loan modifications or other alternatives to foreclosure." Cal. Civ. Code §2923.4, subd. (a). Among other things, HBOR prohibits "dual tracking," which occurs when a bank forecloses on a loan while negotiating with the borrower to avoid foreclosure. See Cal. Civ. Code §2923.6. HBOR provides for injunctive relief for statutory violations that occur prior to foreclosure (Cal. Civ. Code §2924.12, subd. (a)), and monetary damages when the borrower seeks relief for violations after the foreclosure sale has occurred (Cal. Civ. Code §2924.12, subd. (b)).

Section 2923.6, the "dual tracking" prohibition in HBOR which plaintiff maintains Ocwen violated, provides in pertinent part as follows:

> (b) It is the intent of the Legislature that the mortgage servicer offer the borrower a loan modification or workout plan if such a modification or plan is consistent with its contractual or other authority.
>
> (c) If a borrower submits a complete application for a first lien loan modification offered by, or through, the borrower's mortgage servicer, a mortgage servicer, mortgagee, trustee, beneficiary, or authorized agent shall not record a notice of default or notice of sale, or conduct a trustee's sale, while the complete first lien loan modification application is pending. A mortgage servicer, mortgagee, trustee, beneficiary, or authorized agent shall not record a notice of default or notice of sale or conduct a trustee's sale until any of the following occurs: (1) The mortgage servicer makes a written determination that the borrower is not eligible for a first lien loan modification, and any appeal period pursuant to subdivision (d) has expired. (2) The borrower does not accept an offered first lien loan modification within 14 days of the offer. . . .
>
> (h) For purposes of this section, an application shall be deemed 'complete' when a borrower has supplied the mortgage servicer with all documents required by the mortgage servicer within the reasonable timeframes specified by the mortgage servicer.

Cal. Civ. Code §2923.6.

HBOR provides remedies for violation of the foregoing statutory provision in section 2924.12: "If a trustee's deed upon sale has not been recorded, a borrower may bring an action for injunctive relief . . . ," which injunction shall remain in place "until the court determines that the mortgage servicer . . . has corrected and remedied the violation or violations giving rise to the action for injunctive relief." Cal. Civ. Code §2924.12, subd. (a)(1)-(2).) After a trustee's deed upon sale has been recorded, a borrower may sue for "actual economic damages." Cal. Civ. Code §2924.12, subd. (b). A material violation found by the court to be intentional or reckless, or to result from willful misconduct, may result in a trebling of actual damages or statutory damages of $50,000. Ibid. "A court may award a prevailing borrower reasonable attorney's fees and costs in an action brought pursuant to this section." Cal. Civ. Code §2924.12, subd. (i).

Nothing in the language of HBOR suggests that a borrower must tender the loan balance before filing suit based on a violation of the requirements of the law. Indeed, such a requirement would completely eviscerate the remedial provisions of the statute. Moreover, the rationale for the tender rule, "[I]t would be futile to set aside a foreclosure sale on the technical ground that notice was improper, if the party making the challenge did not first make full tender and thereby establish his ability to purchase the property," United States Cold Storage v. Great Western Savings & Loan Assn. 165 Cal. App. 3d 1214, 1225 (1995), has no application here, where plaintiffs' lawsuit is not based on the premise of a defect in the giving of notice but on the statutory grounds laid out in HBOR, and seeks monetary damages. Ocwen's citation to case law predating the enactment of HBOR to create a pleading requirement not contained in the statute is unavailing. In short, we agree with plaintiffs that a tender of the amount due under the loan is not required to state a cause of action under section 2923.6.5

Ocwen also contends that the loan modification application submitted by plaintiffs was neither timely nor complete. It argues, "an application is only deemed 'complete' 'when a borrower has supplied the mortgage servicer with all documents required by the mortgage servicer within the reasonable timeframes specified by the mortgage servicer.' Here, [plaintiffs] admit that they did not supply servicer Ocwen with all the documents required per the timeframe specified in the March 13, 2013 Letter ("Offer Letter")." Thus, Ocwen asserts that plaintiffs' allegation that they submitted a "complete" loan modification application is a conclusory allegation insufficient to survive a demurrer, and that the untimeliness of the application is established by the offer letter.

In their second amended complaint, plaintiffs alleged that, after receiving the offer letter on March 18, 2013, they responded by submitting the requested documentation to Ocwen on March 21, 2013. Also around this time, they received notice that the foreclosure sale previously scheduled for March 14, 2013, had been postponed until March 25, 2013. On March 23, 2013, plaintiffs spoke with Ocwen's representative by telephone, and were informed that they "just need to submit some more documents to make their loan modification application 'complete.'" The Ocwen representative did not tell them that, due to the pending sale date, it was already too late to apply for a loan modification. Plaintiffs mailed the additional financial documents requested by Ocwen on that same day, and requested no further documents thereafter. Based on the forgoing facts, plaintiffs alleged that their loan modification application was "complete."

Ocwen relies on the statute's definition of a "complete" submission — that is, all documents required by the mortgage servicer within the reasonable timeframe specified by the mortgage servicer; see Cal. Civ. Code, §2923.6, to argue that the modification application was not complete because it was not received seven or more days before the scheduled foreclosure sale. However, the complaint alleges that the offer letter, dated March 13, 2013, by its own terms required plaintiffs to submit a completed application by March 18, 2013, the same day they received the offer in the mail. Plaintiffs contend that these facts at best create a triable issue of whether Ocwen provided plaintiffs with a "reasonable timeframe" for submission of a complete application, an issue not suitable for resolution on a demurrer. We agree. In short, we conclude that by alleging the submission of the loan modification application three days after receipt of the offer letter, and the transmittal of the additional documents requested by Ocwen on the date of request, plaintiffs have sufficiently alleged that a complete loan modification application was pending at the time Ocwen foreclosed on their home in violation of section 2923.6.

[E]ach of plaintiffs' remaining causes of action (for breach of contract, breach of the implied covenant of good faith and fair dealing, promissory estoppel, fraud, negligent misrepresentation and violations of Bus. & Prof. Code, §17200 et seq.) were dismissed based upon the improper application of the tender rule. Because the sufficiency of the factual allegations to support these causes were not considered below, we reverse the trial court's ruling on demurrer as to each of them.

---

3.   Rescission

Violations of TILA or HOEPA carry a potent remedy: rescission of the mortgage. As a refresher from contracts, rescission means the unwinding of the transaction to return the borrowers to the position before the loan was made. Rescission is a complete defense to foreclosure because it voids the security interest, without which there is nothing to foreclose. Rescission is available only for non-purchase-money mortgages in a consumer's principal dwelling. The case below describes rescission rights and provides a discussion of the process for asserting rescission.

Paatalo v. JPMorgan Chase Bank
___ F. Supp. 3d ___, 2015 WL 7015317 (Or. 2015)

AIKEN, Chief Judge.
Plaintiff William J. Paatalo seeks a declaratory judgment deeming null and void the 2009 foreclosure of his home loan and trustee's sale of the property securing the loan. Defendant JPMorgan Chase, the purchaser of the property at the trustee's sale, moves to dismiss. For the reasons set forth below, defendant's motion is denied.

BACKGROUND

In 2006, plaintiff refinanced the loan on his property ("the property") in Yachats, Oregon. He obtained a $880,000 "Option Arm" loan and a nearly $110,000 (later increased to $155,000) home equity line of credit ("HELOC") from Washington Mutual Bank, F.A. ("WaMu"). Both loans were secured by deeds of trust on the property.

Plaintiff alleges WaMu misapplied payments and reported false derogatory information to credit reporting agencies on the HELOC account. After disputing those actions with WaMu, plaintiff alleges he began to suspect fraud. He alleges WaMu inflated the appraised value of his property, falsified plaintiff's income on his loan application without his knowledge or consent, and committed numerous violations of the Truth in Lending Act ("TILA"), 15 U.S.C. §§1601 et seq., including "fail[ing] to provide proper 'Notices of Rescission' on the 2006 loans[.]" Plaintiff further alleges he sent a written "Notice of Rescission" on both loans to WaMu on or about March 29, 2008. Plaintiff asserts WaMu sent him a letter declining his rescission and attaching a "payoff quote" of just under one million dollars. According to plaintiff, the letter stated he could not rescind unless he first paid off the amount of the debt in full — something he was unable to do. In July 2008, plaintiff filed suit against WaMu. . . .

Plaintiff alleges on April 2, 2009, WaMu recorded a "Notice of Default and Election to Sell" in connection with the property. . . . At the trustee's sale, defendant purchased the property for $410,000 cash, and on August 18, 2009, a Trustee's Deed was issued to defendant for the property. . . .

On July 12, 2011, while the unlawful detainer action was still being litigated, defendant sold the property for $285,000. [ED. NOTE — Take a look back up at the loan amount to get a sense of why "loss severity" is a term that strikes terror into bankers.]

In February 2015, the United States Supreme Court decided Jesinoski v. Countrywide Home Loans, ____ U.S. ____, 135 S. Ct. 790 (2015). After Jesinoski was decided, plaintiff alleges he sent defendant a notice memorializing the March 29, 2008 rescissions. Plaintiff asserts Jesinoski makes clear "[t]he loan and contracts were void as of March 29, 2008, and must be cancelled as a matter of law."

Plaintiff filed this action on July 29, 2015. He asks this court to declare (1) plaintiff is the sole owner of the property; (2) the foreclosure of the Deeds of Trust was null and void; and (3) all documents recorded on or against title to the subject property after the March 29, 2008 notices of rescission are null and void. Defendant moves to dismiss for failure to state a claim.

. . .

DISCUSSION

Defendant argues the complaint should be dismissed for two reasons. First, it asserts plaintiff never completed the steps required to rescind the loans under TILA. Second, it contends even if plaintiff rescinded the loans in March 2008, any rights plaintiff had to the property were cut off by the trustee's sale.

I. RESCISSION UNDER TILA

"Congress enacted TILA 'to assure a meaningful disclosure of credit terms so that the consumer will be able to compare more readily the various credit terms available to him and avoid the uninformed use of credit, and to protect the consumer against inaccurate and unfair credit billing and credit card practices.'" Hauk v. JP Morgan Chase Bank USA, 552 F.3d 1114, 1118 (9th Cir. 2009) (quoting 15 U.S.C. §1601). "To effectuate TILA's purpose, a court must construe 'the Act's provisions liberally in favor of the consumer' and require absolute compliance by creditors." Id. (quoting In re Ferrell, 539 F.3d 1186, 1189 (9th Cir. 2008)). TILA provides special rescission rights for loans secured by a borrower's principal dwelling.

15 U.S.C. §1635(a); Semar v. Platte Valley Fed. Sav. & Loan Ass'n, 791 F.2d 699, 701 (9th Cir. 1986). TILA's "buyer's remorse" provision grants buyers the right to rescind within three days of either "the consummation of the transaction or the delivery of the information and rescission forms required under this section together with a statement containing the material disclosures required under this subchapter, whichever is later[.]" 15 U.S.C. §1635(a). The right to rescind expires "three years after the date of consummation of the transaction or upon the sale of the property, whichever occurs first." Id. §1635(f).

The effect of this provision is to create two separate rescission rights. The first is an "unconditional" right to rescind, good for three business days after the transaction. Jesinoski, 135 S. Ct. at 792. The second is a "conditional" right. Id. If more than three days have passed since the transaction was consummated, the right to rescind exists only if the lender has failed to provide the required information, forms, and disclosures. This conditional right "does not last forever"; it expires after three years or upon the sale of the property "[e]ven if a lender never makes the required disclosures." Id.

Under the statute, rescission triggers an unwinding process. TILA provides "[w]hen an obligor exercises his right to rescind . . . , he is not liable for any finance or other charge, and any security interest given by the obligor, including any interest arising by operation of law, becomes void upon such a rescission." 15 U.S.C. §1635(b). Within 20 days after "receipt of notice of rescission," the lender must "return to the obligor any money or property given as earnest money, down-payment, or otherwise, and shall take any action necessary . . . to reflect the termination of any security interest created under the transaction." Id. At that point, the borrower is required to "tender the property to the creditor." Id.

Plaintiff alleges because WaMu failed to provide the required notices, he possessed a conditional right to rescind in March 2008, and he timely delivered written notice of his intent to rescind as required by 15 U.S.C. §1635(a). He further alleges WaMu told him he would have to tender the full payoff amount of the loan in order to rescind, contrary to 15 U.S.C. §1635(b), which instead required WaMu to take the first steps to unwind the loan.

It is undisputed more than three years have passed since the consummation of plaintiff's 2006 loans and plaintiff's right to rescind, if not yet exercised, has expired. Thus, the viability of plaintiff's claim that WaMu's security interest in his property was voided in March 2008 hinges on the effect of the notices of rescission to WaMu. Taking the allegations in the complaint as true, if those notices actually rescinded the loan, plaintiff's complaint will survive the motion to dismiss. If, on the other hand, notice of intent to exercise the conditional right of rescission did not actually effect the rescission, defendant is entitled to dismissal. The Supreme Court answered this question in *Jesinoski*. A unanimous Court declared "rescission is effected when the borrower notifies the creditor of his intention to rescind." Jesinoski, 135 S. Ct. at 792. Thus, if — as plaintiff alleges — WaMu failed to provide the required disclosures and plaintiff delivered written notice of rescission in March 2008, the rescission was effected and the security interest in plaintiff's property voided at that time.

Defendant disputes this reading, arguing *Jesinoski* concerns the time period in which a borrower must provide written notice of his intent to exercise a right to rescind. The court agrees *Jesinoski*'s holding concerns the three-year life of the rescission right. The question, however, was whether a borrower can exercise her rescission right by sending written notice of rescission within three years, or whether she must also file a lawsuit within that time period to enforce her rescission right. Jesinoski, 135 S. Ct. at 791. The Court had to determine when rescission actually occurred in order to answer that question:

> The language of [the statute] leaves no doubt that rescission is effected when the borrower notifies the creditor of his intention to rescind. It follows that, so long as the borrower notifies within three years after the transaction is consummated, his rescission is timely.

Id. Thus, the *Jesinoski* holding rested on the Court's determination, as a matter of statutory interpretation, that written notice actually effects the rescission. Defendant correctly notes a number of federal appellate courts, prior to *Jesinoski*, distinguished between notice of intent to exercise the rescission right and the rescission itself. See, e.g., Gilbert v. Residential Funding, LLC, 678 F.3d 271, 277 (4th Cir. 2012) ("We must not conflate the issue of whether a borrower has exercised her right to rescind with the issue of whether the rescission has, in fact, been completed and the contract voided."). That distinction, however, cannot survive the Court's clear statement "rescission is effected" at the time of notice. Jesinoski, 135 S. Ct. at 792.

Defendant argues this reading of *Jesinoski* cannot be correct because it means "a borrower's mere notice of rescission automatically converts a secured lender into an unsecured lender, leaving the lender with no other remedy but to file suit to challenge the validity of a borrower's rescission." Essentially, defendant argues rescission cannot be the default rule. Taken to its logical conclusion, defendant's argument would require borrowers to file suit to enforce their right to rescind, rendering no rescission the default rule. The Supreme Court implicitly rejected defendant's argument when it declared "rescission is effected" at the time of notice, without regard to whether a borrower files a lawsuit within the three-year period. Jesinoski, 135 S. Ct. at 792; Alexandra P. Everhart Sickler, And the Truth Shall Set You Free: Explaining Judicial Hostility to the Truth in Lending Act's Right to Rescind a Mortgage Loan, 12 Rutgers J.L. & Pub. Pol'y 463, 481 (Summer 2015) ("As a practical consequence of [the *Jesinoski*] ruling, a lender now bears the burden of filing a lawsuit to contest the borrower's ability to rescind.").

This reading of *Jesinoski* does not, as defendant asserts, amount to holding "the process of unwinding a loan is automatic and complete upon a borrower's written notice of rescission." After WaMu received plaintiff's notice of rescission, it had two options. It could have begun the unwinding process by returning plaintiff's down payment or earnest money and taking action to "reflect the termination of [the] security interest," pursuant to 15 U.S.C. §1635(b). Those actions would, in turn, have triggered plaintiff's obligation to tender a payoff of the remaining loan amount. In the alternative, WaMu could have filed a lawsuit to dispute plaintiff's right to rescind the loan. Plaintiff alleges WaMu did neither of those things. The question here is what happens when the unwinding process is not completed and neither party files suit within the TILA statute of limitations. In such circumstances, *Jesinoski* directs that the rescission and voiding of the security interest are effective as a matter of law as of the date of the notice.

Finally, defendant argues even if *Jesinoski* means rescission is effective upon a borrower's notice, that holding cannot be applied "retroactively" to 2008. But there is no retroactivity issue here. When a court interprets a statute, it is not 'retroactive' to apply the decision to transactions already entered into, because the court is determining what the law has always meant. . . .

[B]ecause plaintiff has adequately alleged (1) he had a conditional right to rescind in 2008; and (2) he exercised that right, he has stated a claim for at least some of the relief he seeks — a declaratory judgment deeming the foreclosure of the Deeds of Trust null and void. . . .

———————

To finalize the rescission, debtors will usually have to find alternate lenders to finance the tender of the loan proceeds, less any prepaid finance charges and loan payments to date, to the creditor. While voiding the security interest frees up the house as collateral, without a lawyer hooked up to a community development lender, consumers may not navigate rescission. Nonetheless, rescission is a crucial example of a self-effectuating, non-judicial consumer remedy — at least to a certain degree.

Problem Set 14

14.1. Badar Khan is counsel to a fintech company (that is "financial technology" for those outside the industry). The company's computer programmers write complex underwriting programs to help loan officers assess whether a loan meets the CFPB's underwriting rules. The programmers have worked since 2013, when the CFPB released rules on the program. About to deliver the product to three large mortgage companies, they are running error traps in the beta software. For each of the loans below, Badar needs to verify if the program correctly categorized the loan. Did it? If there is a problem, identify it. 15 U.S.C. §§1639b and 1939c; 12 C.F.R. §1026.43.

  a. A 40-year mortgage loan for $160,000, with 2 percentage points and fees, which is fully amortized in its payments. The program considered and verified the borrower's mortgage-related obligations, income and assets, employment, other loans and debts, and family support obligations. The borrower has a 750 credit score (on a scale of 800) and the debt-to-income ratio is 42.89 percent. Program result: Qualified Mortgage.

  b. A 15-year mortgage loan for $800,000, with no points or fees, and an adjustable interest rate that starts at 5 percent and grows each of the first ten years by .025 percent. The borrower will make a downpayment equal to 50 percent of the collateral. The program did the underwriting based on the maximum rate at the 10-year mark and considered the borrower's mortgage-related obligations, income and assets, employment, other loans and debts, and family support obligations. The borrower has a 690 credit score (on a scale of 800) and the debt-to-income ratio is 37 percent. Program result: Qualified Mortgage

  c. A 10-year mortgage loan for $275,000, with 2.5 percentage points and fees, that has a fixed interest rate of 7 percent. The loan payments will be less than necessary to bring the balance to year at the end of the term of the loan, so a final payment of $75,000 will be due. The program considered the borrower's mortgage-related obligations, income and assets, employment, other loans and debts, and family support obligations. The borrower has no credit score because she recently moved to the United States. The debt-to-income ratio is 18 percent. Program result: Ability to Repay.

d. A 30-year mortgage loan for $500,000 with a fixed interest rate of 6.25 percent. Points and fees are equal to 3 percent of the loan. The program considered the borrower's mortgage-related obligations, income and assets, employment, other loans and debts, and family support obligations. The borrower has a credit score of 682 (on a scale of 800); the debt to income ratio is 38 percent. Program result: Qualified Mortgage.

14.2. Felipe Cordwin is a registered lobbyist and lawyer. His client is the nation's largest bank. After the foreclosure crisis, the last thing it wants is bad publicity, including litigation over something as ugly-sounding as problems with "ability to repay." That said, the business line of the bank is insistent that ability-to-repay (ATR) (non-QM) loans can produce good money (query if there such a thing as "bad money" to a banker). The bank's mortgage counsel, Joyce Palazzo, has halted the launch of an ATR loan program because she believes that even if an ATR loan never defaults or goes to foreclosure, a consumer could kick up trouble just to generate money. She notes that these damages could easily erase all bank profits on the loan, plus impose litigation costs. The bank has asked you to conduct outside research. Is Joyce correct on the law? 15 U.S.C. §§1639b(d); 1639c; 1640(a)(4).

14.3. Starbright Co. has rocketed upward in the last few years, fueled by hedge fund money and the desire of larger banks to escape the reputational risk of foreclosing on homeowners. Starbright purchases mortgage servicing rights on defaulted loans and then runs homeowners through its StarSaver program of foreclosure alternatives. The company recently received an inquiry from Middle State's Attorney's General Office about its practices. The inquiry letter alleges consumers have complained that the transfer of servicing — and the concomitant triggering of the StarSaver program — disrupts homeowner's pending loan modification applications with their prior servicer. As general counsel to Starbright, Roger Rood believes the StarSaver program is the most generous in the business in terms of loan modifications but he admits that it requires additional documentation. He notes that Starbright uses the CFPB's model "Notice of Servicing Transfer" letter. The Attorney's General Office stated that the model was deceptive because it stated that "[n]othing else about your mortgage loan will change" upon transfer except a new servicer will collect payments. 12 C.F.R. §1024.33; Appendix MS-2; and 12 C.F.R. §1024.41(a). Is the letter deceptive? If so, what should Starbright change about its practices?

14.4. Maeve Zinner is one of the best consumer lawyers in California, and he takes pride in dozens of pictures of families in front of homes saved from foreclosure. But Maeve also has a file of "failures" where homes were lost, and they haunt her. The problem that Maeve faces is establishing when a "complete" application has been submitted. She is disappointed in how the CFPB addressed the issue and wants to amend the California Homeowner Bill of Rights to do better. What would you suggest? 12 C.F.R. §1024.41(b)(1); Cal. Civ. Code §2924.28(d).

Assignment 15. Credit Cards

About three of four adult Americans have at least one credit card, with the typical consumer having an estimated 3.5 active cards. Credit cards also are important because they are particularly likely to be used for high-dollar transactions. Each year, Americans charge about $2 trillion in purchases. Much of the law that governs credit card transactions is contractual; this is particularly true about the relationships between card issuers and merchants and others in the card processing industry. Consumers have contracts with issuers called card agreements. The terms of such agreements, however, are limited by numerous provisions of the Truth in Lending Act (TILA). The Credit Card Accountability Responsibility and Disclosure Act of 2010 (CARD Act) added protections to TILA, addressing many practices with regard to penalty fees that were subject to public enforcement or consumer advocacy.

A. Credit Card Transactions

Credit cards are unusual products because they combine two distinct features: the ability to pay and the ability to borrow. From the consumer's perspective, the merchant is effectively paid at the time the card is swiped, just as if the consumer had handed the merchant cash. It is weeks later when the consumer receives the bill that the consumer decides whether to pay off the entire balance or to finance the purchase by paying only a portion of the balance. This pay-now, buy-later feature of credit cards means that they raise two consumer protection concerns: as a payment system and as a loan.

What most of us think of as a "credit card company" is called an issuer. This is the business, usually a financial institution, that gives the card to the consumer. The issuer develops and advertises card products, solicits consumers to open accounts, and makes initial disclosures. TILA regulates all of these processes. Unlike with mortgages, issuers nearly always service the credit card accounts that they originate. Issuers send consumers monthly statements, apply payments, address billing disputes, and collect from delinquent consumers. TILA also proscribes the rules for these ongoing issues that occur with payment and open-end credit.

Although the consumer deals primarily with the issuer, credit card transactions involve several other parties. When a merchant accepts the card, it uses a card processer to submit the transaction for authorization and payment. These card processors are called "acquirers" because they receive transactions from a merchant and process the transaction to obtain payment from the issuer. The acquirer submits the payment back to the merchant, who is paid for the transaction. Acquirers receive payment, usually a fraction of one percent, of the total purchase price as payment for their work as intermediaries. The best known entities in the credit card world—Visa and Mastercard—are not issuers or acquirers; instead they provide networks and technology for processing that merchants and acquirers use to obtain authorization for transactions and to receive payments from issuers. Visa and Mastercard and issuers also get a fraction (one or two percent) of the total purchase price of credit card transactions. Generically, these costs are called "interchange fees." Like the money that merchants pay to acquirers, the fees to Visa, Mastercard, and similar companies are costs borne by merchants. Ultimately, credit card processing costs are added into the cost of goods and services, despite usually being invisible to consumers.

Although the technology and processing of the payment to the merchant is similar, the borrowing aspect of a credit card distinguishes it from debit cards and charge cards. Debit cards result in immediate or near-immediate deductions from consumers' bank accounts. Charge cards, unlike credit cards, are supposed to be paid in full at the end of each month; the credit extended is limited to the billing cycle. TILA defines a credit card broadly as "any card . . . or other credit device existing for the purpose of obtaining money, property, labor, or services on credit." 15 U.S.C. §1602(k). This obviously sweeps in both cards issued by financial institutions or retailers on the Visa or Mastercard networks, and cards issued by entities with their own processing networks, such as American Express. Regulation Z expands the definition of credit card to make TILA applicable to charge cards. 12 C.F.R. §1026.2(a)(15). The definition of "creditor" with regard to credit cards is also more stringent. Even if finance charges are not frequently imposed, an issuer is covered. 12 C.F.R. §1026.2(a)(17)(iii).

Credit cards are generally subject to many of the laws covered in prior assignments. This includes credit reporting and lending discrimination laws and UDAP statutes. TILA imposes additional rules on credit card advertising and solicitations. One example, which was described in Problem 5.4, is the limitations on credit card marketing on college campuses. Another example is the prohibition on mailing of unsolicited cards; cards must be issued only "in response to a request or application" from a consumer. 15 U.S.C. §1664. Because of these rules, the protections of other laws like those that help consumers deal with unordered merchandise that arrives at their doorstep, are not needed in the credit card context. Similarly, the general framework for false advertising is less useful in challenging the tactics of credit card issuers. The issuers argue that TILA already circumscribes the boundaries of their actions in soliciting consumers. While TILA does not preempt these other actions, courts frequently seem to agree with credit card companies. As a practical matter, if TILA permits the company's actions, that seems to insulate the card company from liability for violating other applicable laws, including UDAP statutes.

The TILA provisions on open-end disclosures apply to credit cards. Disclosures must be given at the time of account opening and included in periodic statements. Such disclosures should be clear and conspicuous and focus on the costs of credit cards. As with mortgages, credit cards have specialized disclosures. Of particular note is the requirement that disclosures in direct mail solicitations for cards contain disclosures using a tabular format. 12 C.F.R.

§1026.5a(a)(2). These disclosures, nicknamed the "Schumer" box after the Senator involved in the legislation, include a requirement that the APR be disclosed using 16-point font.

B. Limitations on Fees and Other Product Terms

TILA imposes significant additional limitations on fees, even if fully disclosed and agreed to in a card agreement. Beyond the usual concerns about adhesion contracts and whether consumers read the fine print, the complexity of cards creates lengthy and difficult contracts. Even when they try, consumers often do not understand the terms of credit cards. For example, one study found that even when offered a choice between just two cards with only two varying terms, consumers chose the suboptimal card 40 percent of the time. Sumit Agarwal et al., *Do Consumers Choose the Right Credit Contracts?*, 4 REV. CORP. FIN. STUDIES 239, 242 (2015). Also some provisions were so flexible and open-ended as to make it impossible for consumers to shop for a good deal among issuers without a crystal ball to perceive the issuers' future decisions. Professor Ronald Mann has called these "unpriceable" terms; other scholars have more colorfully suggested that when many such terms are included, as they typically have been in credit card contracts, the result is "bullshit promises" — defined as promises that are not made with an intention to deceive but nonetheless are insincere because they reserve the right for the company to do as it wishes, which is a complete disregard for norms of honest promise-making. Curtis Bridgeman & Karen Sandrik, *Bullshit Promises*, 76 TENN. L. REV. 379 (2009). The CARD Act took aim at a number of aspects of credit cards that permitted issuers to redesign the product repeatedly and without limitation. For example, TILA now requires that an issuer that offers a "fixed rate" actually provide a fixed rate, which is defined as a rate that "will not change or vary for any reason over the period specified clearly and conspicuously in the terms of the account." 15 U.S.C. §1637(m). If this kind of detailed legislation seems unnecessary, consider that lawsuits trying to challenge "fixed rates" that could change at any time for any reason under the terms of the card agreement under the unfair and deceptive practices laws were unsuccessful.

1. Late Fees and Other Penalty Fees

Late fees are imposed when a consumer fails to make a timely payment, as defined under the card agreement. For many decades, there were virtually no specific rules on the amount of late fees or when late fees could be imposed. Fees increased significantly in the late 1990s and 2000s, with the typical fee charged by a large issuer reaching $39. Such fees generated substantial revenue for card issuers. Before the effective date of the CARD Act, issuers collected about $900 million in such fees each month. The CARD Act reduced late fees substantially, halving them to $427 million in November 2010 in the wake of the legislation.

The premise for charging a late fee is that issuers incur costs from a delay in payment. At least some of these costs are presumably distinct from the cost of money loaned out for a longer than anticipated period, as that it is the purpose of interest being charged on the account. Of course, when a consumer is delinquent, the issuer may worry about the consumer's creditworthiness, and a late fee may be an alternative to increasing the interest rate immediately and without notice, which TILA prohibits. Consumers who pay late also increase servicing costs for issuers, who need to send reminders or initiate a review of the consumer's creditworthiness. A study by the Center for Responsible Lending found only a weak relationship between the imposition of late fees and actual credit losses, however, which suggests that many late fees result from mistakes or disorganization rather than from financial distress. The Center for Responsible Lending, *A Just Fee or Just a Fee? An Examination of Credit Card Late Fees,* (June 8, 2010), http://www.responsiblelending.org/credit-cards/research-analysis/A-Just-fee-or-Just-a-Fee.pdf (last visited Oct. 26, 2015).

The law curbs the imposition of late fees in two ways, both of which reflect concern about whether such fees are appropriately calibrated to their purported purpose. First, issuers are required to use consistent billing practices that could minimize the incidence of late fees resulting merely from consumer confusion. Credit card bills must be due on the same date each month, and that day must give consumers at least 21 days to pay their bills. Payments received by 5:00 p.m. on the due date must be treated as timely, 12 C.F.R. §1026.10(b)(2)(ii), although many a West Coast resident has learned the expensive way that this can be 5:00 p.m. Eastern Time. Before these laws, a due date for a given month might vary by 7 or 10 days, making it hard for the consumer to remember the due date. Or consumers might get tripped up by a late fee even though they made their payment on that month's specified due date, merely because they failed to note the payment was due by 9am, noon, or some other time.

The second change to the law limits late fees and other penalty fees to an amount that is "reasonable and proportional to the omission or violation to which the fee or charge relates." 15 U.S.C. §1665d(a). The implementing rule provides guidance on the costs that issuers may consider in setting a fee. Issuers are excluded from passing along the costs of higher rates of losses from nonpayment (that is credit risk and should be covered by the interest rate) but may include in the fee amount any collection costs, such as sending delinquency notifications and negotiating payment plans. As an alternative to justifying costs, issuers can charge fees below the amount of "safe harbor" fees. Section 1026.52(b) of Regulation Z permits the imposition of a $25 penalty fee for the first violation and a $35 fee for any additional violation of the same type during the next six billing cycles. These amounts, set in 2010, adjust annually based on the Consumer Price Index. If an account becomes seriously delinquent, defined as no payment or less than the required payment for two or more consecutive billing cycles, the late payment fee may be increased to equal 3 percent of the delinquent balance.

TILA also restricts overlimit fees, which like late fees were a major source of industry profit before the CARD Act of 2009. In many ways, the approach to overlimit fees is similar to late fees, eliminating common practices decried as abuses at the time of the legislation. Overlimit fees also must be "reasonable and proportional" in amount and cannot exceed the transaction itself (so if the transaction that puts the consumer over the limit is a $2 charge for coffee; the overlimit fee cannot exceed $2). 12 C.F.R. §1026.52(b). The law also limits when overlimit fees may be imposed. Issuers may not charge more than one overlimit fee per billing cycle, regardless of the number of times the consumer exceeds the limit. The justification for this approach is that the issuer could decline to approve further transactions once learning that the customer has exceeded the limit, and that if the issuer wishes to authorize such transactions, it should not be at additional expense to the consumer.

To give consumers an additional tool to control the imposition of overlimit fees, the law requires issuers to obtain the express consent of the issuer to impose overlimit transactions. Such "opt-ins," so-named because the default rule is that without consent there may not be overlimit charges applied to accounts, may be revoked at any time by the consumer. 15 U.S.C. §1637(k). One year after the CARD Act's effective date, these legal changes have dramatically reduced — if not virtually eliminated — overlimit fees in the credit card industry. The number of accounts charged an overlimit fee dropped from approximately 12 percent to 1 percent. Many issuers decided not to bother with trying to convince consumers to opt-in, instead forgoing the right to charge overlimit fees (although such issuers may still allow consumers to exceed their limits).

2. Rate Changes

Credit cards are open-end, revolving loans. While there is a set credit limit, the amount of credit used each month varies, and the card may have been issued years prior to the instant charges. A major weapon that card issuers have to protect themselves against changes in market conditions, such as their cost of funds, and against erosion of a consumer's creditworthiness, is changing the APR. Until recently, the norm in the industry was "any time, any reason" repricing. This practice was criticized for being unfair. It made it nearly pointless for a consumer to shop for credit because it was uncertain if and under what conditions issuers might reprice. The changes also were retrospective, effectively changing the cost of the toaster bought on a credit card with a balance after the consumer decided to buy the toaster.

Despite an outcry from the card industry, Congress enacted limits on when issuers can increase interest rates. TILA prohibits retrospective rate increases. A higher APR can be applied only to new purchases; the old balance is protected from the rate increase. If the cardholder has missed two consecutive payments, however, she loses this protection. If the cardholder makes six consecutive timely payments of at least the minimum amount, she can earn back the prior rate on the remaining protected balance. 12 C.F.R. §226.55(b)(4). This complicated scheme reflects the policy tension at issue. Issuers assert that the flexibility to increase rates is a crucial reason that they can extend ample credit to a range of consumers, including those whose creditworthiness may erode over time. For consumers, however, the changes can translate into escalating fees and rates that make repayment increasingly difficult and can spiral into serious financial distress.

Issuers must give cardholders notice of a rate increase 45 days before it takes effect. 15 U.S.C. §1637(i). The prior law required 30 days of notice. The 45-day notice rule also applies to changes to certain fees, including annual fees and cash advance fees. In the notice of the increase, issuers must tell cardholders that they have a right to cancel the card, rather than be subject to the rate increase. If a cardholder chooses to cancel the card instead of accept the higher fee, an issuer can close the account and increase the monthly payment to accelerate the balance being brought to zero. 12 C.F.R. §1026.55(c). TILA also requires issuers to consider resetting rates downward beginning six months after a rate increase. The law requires creditors to reduce the APR if a reduction is "indicated" by the review but also states that no specific amount of reduction is required. 12 C.F.R. §1026.59.

C.   Defenses to Liability for Charges

In the early years of credit cards, there was considerable concern about the potential of the products to harm consumers. Cards were new compared to cash and checks, and the mysterious "swiping" and electronic payment processing was less tangible. Whereas in recent years that harm has focused on fees, interest rates, and the role of cards in consumers' accumulating unmanageable debt, the initial regulation of credit cards focused on their use as payment devices and on fraud. These laws, described below, generally make credit cards more favorable to consumers than cash, checks, or debit cards.

1.   Claims Against Merchants

TILA allows cardholders to withhold payment from the card issuer for a transaction for which the cardholder has a defense that it could assert against the merchant that accepted the card. 15 U.S.C. §1666i. This means that if a person purchases defective merchandise using a credit card, the person may refuse to pay the amount of the credit card bill that pertains to the defective merchandise. The law does impose several limitations to this right. As a prerequisite, TILA requires cardholders to make a "good faith attempt to obtain satisfactory resolution of an agreement or problem relative to the transaction from the person honoring the credit card." 15 U.S.C. §1666i. The transaction must have exceeded $50 in amount and have occurred in the cardholder's state of residence or within 100 miles thereof. More subtly, the law limits the time by which the cardholder can use the provision to her advantage. TILA gives a right to withhold payment, not to seek a refund from the issuer at a later date after the bill has been paid. This means that those who carry card balances (and pay interest on them, of course) will have a longer period to assert a defense.

These legal protections are undoubtedly of real benefit to consumers. VISA and Mastercard and card issuers have gone out of their way to educate consumers about these advantages of credit cards to encourage their adoption and use. Indeed, issuers in the card agreements may allow consumers to dispute charges without meeting these requirements. This is one instance in which the law seems to be setting a floor for consumer protection that businesses have exceeded as a matter of providing customer service and competition. While hundreds, if not thousands, of consumers contact card companies to dispute charges every day, there are only a few dozen court opinions on this TILA provision. *See, e.g., Citibank (South Dakota), N.A. v. Mincks*, 135 S.W.3d 545 (Mo. Ct. App. 2004); *Hyland v. First USA Bank*, 1995 WL 595861 (E.D. Pa. Sept. 28, 1995). Accessing the TILA protections against merchants is only a toll-free call to the card issuer away, as compared to many consumer protections that require learning about the law, hiring a lawyer, filing a suit, and prevailing on the merits.

2. Unauthorized Charges

As with all payment systems, credit cards create risks of errors or fraud. These are not just, or even mainly, consumer protection problems. Merchants, acquirers, and issuers all need to prevent erroneous or unauthorized charges to reduce the costs of the system. While the other parties protect themselves through allocation of loss using contracts, TILA focuses on the risk of harm to cardholders. Part D of TILA, enacted as the "Fair Credit Billing Act," permits a consumer to challenge credit card charges. The first step is that the consumer alleges a "billing error" on a statement. Billing errors, as the name suggests, are primarily errors—the creditor failed to credit a payment, a merchant made a mistake in transmitting the amount of a charge, etc. A different challenge comes from unauthorized charges. The problem is not innocent error but malfeasance. The case below begins with a consumer who did not keep track of the whereabouts of his card. Many disputes concern situations when someone lent a card to another person, often a friend or family member, who goes on a spending spree well beyond what the cardholder intended to authorize.

Crestar Bank, N.A. v. Cheevers

744 A.2d 1043 (D.C. 2000)

REID, Associate Judge.

The central issue presented in this case is whether, under the Truth in Lending Act ("TILA"), 15 U.S.C. §§1601 et seq. (1994), a credit cardholder is required to avail himself of the billing dispute procedures of 15 U.S.C. §1666 by notifying the creditor of disputed charges, in order to invoke the liability protections of 15 U.S.C. §1643 against unauthorized charges to a credit card. Appellant Crestar Bank ("Crestar") filed a civil action against appellee Eric L. Cheevers alleging that Mr. Cheevers owed an outstanding credit card balance of $4,231.76, plus interest. Mr. Cheevers claimed that he did not make or authorize most of the charges alleged. The trial court concluded that the disputed charges were "unauthorized" within the meaning of 15 U.S.C. §1643, and thus, Mr. Cheevers was not liable for them. We affirm, concluding that §1666 imposes no mandatory notification requirement on the credit cardholder, and that Crestar failed to satisfy its burden of proof under §1643 by showing that the charges on Mr. Cheevers' credit card were authorized, or that if unauthorized, the statutory conditions imposed on Crestar were not met.

FACTUAL SUMMARY

The evidence at trial established that on April 3, 1992, Mr. Cheevers entered into an agreement with Crestar for use of a Visa credit card. At the time, he resided in the 1600 block of Kenyon Street, N.W., but notified Crestar in December 1992 of his move to another address. Crestar received regular and timely payments from Mr. Cheevers from April 1992 until December 1993. Mr. Cheevers made additional charges on his account in January, February and April 1994. After his April 1994 charge, he took the credit card out of his wallet to avoid further use because he was experiencing financial difficulties. He could not recall what he did with the card, but thought it may have been lost during his move from Kenyon Street.

When Mr. Cheevers' account became two months past due in June 1994, Crestar blocked the account from further transactions and mailed Mr. Cheevers a statement informing him that his privileges had been suspended. Despite the block on Mr. Cheevers' account, in October and November, 1994, charges totaling $3,583.92 were posted to Mr. Cheevers' card from Amtrak automated ticket machines.

In August 1994, Mr. Cheevers moved again and filled out a postal forwarding address card. On November 29, 1994, Crestar sent Mr. Cheevers a billing statement which included the charges from October and November. Mr. Cheevers testified that he never received the statement. Crestar's litigation department also sent a letter to Mr. Cheevers, but the letter was returned by the postal service to Crestar on December 14, 1994. At that time, Crestar charged the matter off as bad debt, turned it over to its attorneys, and stopped mailing monthly statements to Mr. Cheevers.

Sometime around November 1994, Crestar contacted the Amtrak Police Department about the charges on Mr. Cheevers' credit card. Raymond E. Wright, then a criminal investigator with the Amtrak Police, investigated the matter. He testified that the machines used to purchase the Amtrak tickets required no signature nor other identifying information, and took no photograph of the purchaser. He stated that the transactions amounting to thousands of dollars on Mr. Cheevers's card were unusual. He concluded that the ticket transactions were irregular and fraudulent.

In the early part of 1995, Crestar continued its efforts to collect from Mr. Cheevers the sums charged to his account. On March 8, 1995, an entry made by the Crestar collector assigned to the account stated: "This is probably fraud, no idea, real mess." On March 22, 1995, Crestar's attorneys called Mr. Cheevers and left a message on his machine. When they called back on April 8, 1995, the number was disconnected. On April 26, 1995, the attorneys contacted Mr. Cheevers' place of employment but were informed that he had been fired. On May 2, 1995, Crestar filed suit against Mr. Cheevers.

Mr. Cheevers testified that after changing jobs in April 1995, which resulted in his making more money, he contacted Crestar on July 24, 1995, without knowledge either of the October and November charges on his credit card or the lawsuit against him, because he wanted to pay off his balance which he believed was about $400. When the Crestar representative told him that the balance was about $4,500, Mr. Cheevers "became very alarmed and asked her why the amount was so high." The Crestar representative stated that fraud was suspected and suggested that he call Amtrak and Crestar's attorneys. Mr. Cheevers called Officer Wright and the attorneys. Subsequently, in January 1996, he notified Crestar, the bank's attorneys, and the Amtrak Police in writing that he disputed the October and November 1994 charges. He testified that he did not make the Amtrak charges, that he did not receive any benefit from the charges, that neither he nor his family traveled during that period of time, that he did not give tickets to anyone, and that he does not know who made the charges.

After the bench trial, the trial court ruled "for Mr. Cheevers as to all of the matters in dispute" and in favor of the bank for the undisputed amount of $617.84, plus prejudgment interest from September 1994. In particular, the court concluded that Crestar had failed to carry its burden of proof to show that the charges made on Mr. Cheevers' credit card were authorized,[1] and that Mr. Cheevers could not be assessed the statutory $50 fee "because the bank ha[d] not provided a method whereby the use[r] of the card can be identified as the person authorized to use it with respect to the charges that were incurred." Relying on Stieger [v. Chevy Chase Sav. Bank, F.S.B., 666 A.2d 479 (D.C. 1995),] the trial court also determined that TILA precluded "a finding of apparent authority where the transfer of the card was without the cardholder's consent as in cases involving theft, loss or fraud."

ANALYSIS

Crestar cites 15 U.S.C. §1666, known as the Fair Credit Billing Act ("FCBA"), and contends that the trial court erred by ruling that Mr. Cheevers was not liable for the disputed charges on his credit card, and that §1666 obligated him to notify Crestar, in writing, within sixty (60) days of receipt of the billing statement that the October and November 1994 charges were unauthorized. Moreover, Crestar argues, Mr. Cheevers had a contractual and common law duty to notify the bank that his credit card had been lost or stolen. In response, Mr. Cheevers argues that §1666 does not bar him from raising an unauthorized charge defense under 15 U.S.C. §1643 of TILA, and that Crestar failed to sustain its burden of proof under §1643, the credit agreement and the common law, to show that the disputed charges were authorized.

---

1. More specifically, the court stated:

I just think that this case turns on the burden of proof and the bank didn't know who was fooling around with this card, Union Station, Amtrak after investigating it couldn't figure out who was involved in the unauthorized use of this card. Looking at the statements for October and November, there's really nothing that quite jumps out that makes it plain that it must have been Mr. Cheevers who was running up these charges and then selling the tickets on the street to get some money.

At the outset of this opinion, we set forth certain principles that guide our decision. We recognize that: "The Truth-In-Lending Act was enacted 'in large measure to protect credit cardholders from unauthorized use perpetrated by those able to obtain possession of a card from its original owner.'" Stieger, supra note 2, 666 A.2d at 482 (quoting Towers World Airways Inc. v. PHH Aviation Sys., Inc., 933 F.2d 174, 176 (2d Cir.), cert. denied, 502 U.S. 823 (1991)). Moreover, "[TILA] is to be liberally construed in favor of the consumer." Martin v. American Express, Inc., 361 So. 2d 597, 600 (Ala. Civ. App. 1978). In keeping with Congress' intent to protect cardholders, §1643(b) of TILA places the burden of proof on the card issuer, in this case Crestar bank, to show that the disputed charges were authorized: "In any action by a card issuer to enforce liability for the use of a credit card, the burden of proof is upon the card issuer to show that the use was authorized. . . ." If certain statutory conditions are met, the limit of liability for unauthorized charges is $50 under §1643(a)(1)(B). "However, [TILA] does not limit liability for the cardholder for third party charges made with 'actual, implied or apparent authority.'" Stieger, 666 A.2d at 482 (quoting 15 U.S.C.A. §1602(o)). While §1666 of the FCBA refers to a sixty day notice to the bank of a billing error and the steps the bank must take if a cardholder notifies it of a billing error, notice of such billing error by the cardholder is not required to trigger the protections of §1643. See Regulation Z, 12 C.F.R. §226, Supp. I, at 354 (1999). Indeed, "the legislative history of . . . [the FCBA] shows that it amended [TILA] for the purpose of protecting the consumer against 'unfair and inaccurate credit billing and credit card practices.'" Jacobs v. Marine Midland Bank, N.A., 124 Misc. 2d 162, 475 N.Y.S.2d 1003, 1005 (N.Y. Sup. Ct. 1984); see also Saunders v. Ameritrust of Cincinnati, 587 F. Supp. 896, 898 (S.D. Ohio 1984) ("Section 1666 sets out the mechanisms by which an obligor is to notify a creditor of a billing error, and the steps a creditor must take once it receives notice of a billing error.").

We turn first to Crestar's argument that: "In its simplest form, 15 U.S.C. §1666 (1998) requires cardholders to inform card issuers of any errors on their statements, in writing, within sixty (60) days of the receipt of the statement." Crestar seeks to impose a notification requirement on Mr. Cheevers that does not exist either under the plain words of §1666 or its legislative history. Rather, §1666 requires the bank or a creditor to take certain action after the cardholder notifies it of a billing error.[2] Thus, §1666 recognizes that a cardholder may inform the bank of a billing error, but

---

2. Section 1666 provides in pertinent part:
    (a) . . . If a creditor, within sixty days after having transmitted to an obligor a statement of the obligor's account in connection with an extension of consumer credit, receives at the address disclosed under section 1637(b)(10) of this title a written notice . . . from the obligor in which the obligor—
    . . .
        (2) indicates the obligor's belief that the statement contains a billing error and the amount of such billing error, and
        (3) . . . the creditor shall, unless the obligor has, after giving such written notice . . ., agreed that the statement was correct—
            (A) not later than thirty days after the receipt of the notice, send a written acknowledgement thereof to the obligor . . ., and
            (B) not later than two complete billing cycles of the creditor . . . after the receipt of the notice and prior to taking any action to collect the amount . . . either—
                (i) make appropriate corrections in the account of the obligor . . . ; or
                (ii) send a written explanation or clarification to the obligor, after having conducted an investigation . . .

does not mandate such notification. See Gray v. American Express Co., 240 U.S. App. D.C. 10, 13 (1984) ("'If the [cardholder] believes that the [billing] statement contains a billing error . . . , he then may send the creditor a written notice setting forth that belief, indicating the amount of the error and the reasons supporting his belief that it is an error.'") (quoting American Express Co. v. Koerner, 452 U.S. 233, 235-36 (1981)). In addition, §1666 imposes on the card issuer or the bank an obligation to acknowledge and investigate the alleged billing error. Id.

This reading of the statute is consistent with the legislative history of §1666 which reveals Congress' intent to protect the consumer against the creditor's unfair and inaccurate billing practices. Moreover, it is consistent with Federal Reserve Board staff interpretation of the unauthorized use provision of §1643 and the billing error provision of §1666 of Regulation Z, 12 C.F.R. pts. 226.12 and 226.13, regulations promulgated by the Board of Governors of the Federal Reserve System to implement TILA. In interpreting the notice to card issuer provision, the staff of the Board stated:

> Notice of loss, theft, or possible unauthorized use need not be initiated by the cardholder. . . .
>
>   The liability protections afforded to cardholders in §226.12 do not depend upon the cardholder's following the error resolution procedures in §226.13. For example, the written notification and time limit requirements of §226.13 do not affect the §226.12 protections.

12 C.F.R. §226, Supp. I, at 354. Courts must give deference to agency interpretations of TILA and its implementing regulations. See Anderson Bros. Ford v. Valencia, 452 U.S. 205, 219 (1981) ("[A]bsent some obvious repugnance to [TILA], the Board's regulation implementing this legislation should be accepted by the courts, as should the Board's interpretation of its own regulation."); Ford Motor Credit Co. v. Milhollin, 444 U.S. 555, 565 (1980) ("[D]eference is especially appropriate in the process of interpreting the Truth in Lending Act and Regulation Z."). Consequently, we conclude that §1666 imposed no requirement on Mr. Cheevers to notify Crestar of a billing error before he could invoke the protections of §1643. We turn now to §1643.

Crestar maintains that Mr. Cheevers' "failure to object to the [disputed] charges within a reasonable time, even if not his, constituted ratification and acceptance of those charges," and that under contractual and common law, "if the cardholder fails to notify the bank of any dispute within a reasonable period, he is deemed to have admitted the authenticity of the charges." In essence, Crestar reads into §1643 a presumption that if the cardholder fails to notify the bank that the disputed charges are not his, they will be deemed to have been authorized by the cardholder. This presumption is at odds with the plain words of §1643 which impose on the bank the burden to show authorized use of the card, or liability of the cardholder for unauthorized use. As the trial court concluded, nothing in the record demonstrated that Mr. Cheevers authorized the charges on his credit card in November and December 1994. In fact, he emphatically denied authorizing the purchase of any Amtrak tickets on his credit card. Nor was there any evidence in the record that Mr. Cheevers voluntarily transferred his card to a third person. "'[TILA] clearly precludes a finding of apparent authority where the transfer of the card was without the cardholder's consent as in cases involving theft, loss, or fraud.'" Stieger, 666 A.2d at 482 (quoting Towers World Airways Inc., 933 F.2d at 177). Similarly, the record in this case provided no support for the proposition that Mr. Cheevers transferred his card to a third person who had apparent authority to charge the Amtrak tickets. Therefore, we agree with the trial court that Crestar failed to carry its burden of proof to show that the disputed charges were authorized.

The only other way Crestar could prevail under §1643(a)[3] is to show that the conditions of liability for unauthorized use of Mr. Cheevers' card have been met: "[I]f the use was unauthorized, then the burden of proof is upon the card issuer to show that the conditions of liability for the unauthorized use of a credit card . . . have been met." 15 U.S.C. §1643(b). Six statutory conditions are imposed upon the card issuer or the bank. We agree with the trial court that Crestar did not satisfy at least one of these conditions, §1643(a)(1)(F): "The card issuer has provided a method whereby the user of such card can be identified as the person authorized to use it." Mr. Wright, the Amtrak Police criminal investigator in this matter, testified that the machines used to purchase the Amtrak tickets required no signature, took no photograph of the purchaser, and did not identify the purchaser by any other means. In fact, it was impossible to determine who had used Mr. Cheevers' credit card to purchase the Amtrak tickets. Consequently, no evidence was introduced at trial to show that Crestar "provided a method whereby the user of [Mr. Cheevers'] card can be identified as the person authorized to use it," and thus, Crestar did not sustain its burden to show that it met the conditions for Mr. Cheevers' liability for unauthorized use of his credit card.

Accordingly, for the foregoing reasons, we affirm the judgment of the trial court.

D.   Payments from Consumers

The Assignment previously discussed some of the rules pertaining to processing payments from cardholders, including the rules on late fees. The law also controls how issuers bill and collect from consumers. It generally requires that

---

3. Section 1643(a) provides:

(1) A cardholder shall be liable for the unauthorized use of a credit card only if —
   (A) the card is an accepted credit card;
   (B) the liability is not in excess of $50;
   (C) the card issuer gives adequate notice to the cardholder of the potential liability;
   (D) the card issuer has provided the cardholder with a description of a means by which the card issuer may be notified of loss or theft of the card, which description may be provided on the face or reverse side of the statement required by section 1637(b) of this title or on a separate notice accompanying such statement;
   (E) the unauthorized use occurs before the card issuer has been notified that an unauthorized use of the credit card has occurred or may occur as the result of loss, theft, or otherwise; and
   (F) the card issuer has provided a method whereby the user of such card can be identified as the person authorized to use it.

(2) For purposes of this section, a card issuer has been notified when such steps as may be reasonably required in the ordinary course of business to provide the card issuer with the pertinent information have been taken, whether or not any particular officer, employee, or agent of the card issuer does, in fact receive such information.

issuers apply any payment in excess of the minimum required payment to the balance carrying the highest interest rate. This helps consumers reduce the amount of interest that they accrue while they are carrying a balance. Issuers are also prohibited from using a practice called "double-cycle billing," in which interest was imposed on amounts owed during both the current and prior billing cycles. In simple form, the law caps the interest cost to a single month for those who only sporadically carry a balance (or who may carry a balance inadvertently by missing a payment date).

The monthly billing statements are peppered with required disclosures. Credit card statements must contain warnings about making late payments and illustrations of the costs of paying off a balance over time. The law requires the issuer to show, if the cardholders made only the required minimum payment, how much interest would be charged and how long it would take to pay off the balance. These calculations presume the cardholder does not make any additional charges. The same disclosures are then made under a proposed faster payment schedule, showing the amount needed to be paid to reduce the balance to zero in three years and the estimated savings from this payment schedule as opposed to the minimum payment. 15 U.S.C. §1637(b)(11).

The early research on the effectiveness of these changes is mixed. A study commissioned by the Consumer Financial Protection Bureau found that 77 percent of consumers noticed the late payment warnings and that 70 percent of consumers noticed the disclosures about the costs of minimum payments. If consumers react to those warnings in the expected fashion is less clear. One study of credit union customers found that while more cardholders began making payments the amount on the statement that corresponded to eliminating the balance in three years, that the people attracted to that three-year schedule made smaller payments than a similar cohort of cardholders before the disclosure, who began to pay down balances even faster. The three-year schedule seemed to be an anchor that attracted some consumers but those consumers may have put themselves on even more stringent payment plans without such a disclosure. *See* Consumer Financial Protection Bureau, *CARD Act conference: Key findings*, http://www.consumerfinance.gov/credit-cards/credit-card-act/card-act-conference-key-findings (last visited Oct. 26, 2015).

A further practical problem with the new disclosures exists. Under the existing regulation, the three-year payment amount is recalculated each month; this means that if the consumer keeps paying the amount shown as the "three-year amount," they will remain three years away from a zero balance. To give an example, a cardholder with a 15.32 percent APR carrying a balance of $3900 who makes no new charges and pays the disclosed three-year amount each month will take 150 months to eliminate the debt, not the 36 months that seem to be contemplated by the disclosure. This issue highlights the difficulty of designing credit disclosures that are accurate and effective for credit products with many moving parts. Credit cards are the poster child for the complexity in financial products; the law mirrors that complexity in its myriad regulations.

Problem Set 15

15.1. After a grueling year of practice, you joined a consulting firm that specializes in helping businesses identify and exploit "strategic market opportunities." The firm has put you in charge of coming up with ideas to help its financial services clients use the changes imposed by the CARD Act to their advantage. Your research has revealed that in advance of the CARD Act, issuers hiked rates on cards and are now less willing to issue cards because of the limitations on future rate increases and penalty fees. You also have read that consumers are feeling the pinch of the economic downturn and are struggling to make ends meet.

Your idea is to develop a specialty line of cards for high-risk consumers, including the unemployed or those with foreclosures on their credit reports. To offset credit risk, the issuer would collect an upfront fee of $150 for every $500 of credit line that it approved for a consumer. The issuer would not open the account or issue a card until the upfront fee was paid in full. The issuer would implement special servicing procedures to handle its high-risk customer base, including the ability to text, call, or email its customers on a daily basis if they became delinquent or engaged in other behavior that seemed to indicate a decline in creditworthiness. The issuer would charge a late fee of $50 but not permit consumers to go over the pre-set limit unless the consumer contacted the issuer by telephone and agreed to a $50 overlimit fee. You are pretty sure this product will make money. Your remaining question is whether it violates the law. Does it? *See* 15 U.S.C. §1637(n); 12 C.F.R. §§1026.51, 52, and 56.

15.2. Pamela Simmons travels a great deal for her job as a sales consultant. To maximize the perks of the job, she has used her More for Me Mastercard for her purchases for the last decade. The More for Me card gives her a variety of rewards, combining a cash back feature and travel rewards points rather than making her choose between these rewards. The APR on the card is 18.99 percent, a variable rate pegged to the prime rate of the U.S. Treasury. Pamela has been late a few times in recent years when travel caused her to be away from home when the statement arrived. The issuer of More for Me never increased her rate but she did pay some late fees and accumulated interest charges. After she noticed in 2011 that her due date was the same date each month, Pamela set up her account to have her entire credit card statement balance paid automatically out of her checking account one day before the due date.

On one of her recent short stays in her own home, Pamela opened her More for Me Mastercard bill and found a notice that her interest rate is increasing to 28.99 percent effective immediately as of the date of the letter. There was also a paragraph in the letter advising that the company is eliminating the airline rewards aspect of the card but that any earned rewards remain valid to the extent of the airline's expiration policy. The notice justified the rewards change based on consolidation in the airline industry making the cost of providing the rewards more expensive to the issuer. It did not provide any reason for the increase but it did tell Pamela that she could cancel her card. Pamela had previously paid the entire balance off by auto-debit from her bank account and she rarely carries a balance. Nonetheless, she is incensed that More for Me Mastercard seems to be out to get more for itself, and finds its behavior particularly distasteful given her years as a loyal More for Me cardholder. Has More for Me violated the law in making or implementing these changes? *See* 15 U.S.C. §1637(i); 12 C.F.R. §§1026.9(c)(2) and 1026.55.

15.3. Roger Holt lives in El Paso, Texas. He recently purchased a kit from Honey Heaven to grow bees for honey production and plans to sell the honey at local farmers' markets. Holt made the purchase online, paying the $89 cost with his bank-issued credit card. While he was waiting for the kit to arrive, he saw a report on television that Honey Heaven, located outside of Austin, Texas, was shut down by animal control after weeks of demonstrations by animal rights activists concerned about the ethical treatment of bees. Holt tried to contact Honey Heaven but the emails keep bouncing and the phone message says that Honey Heaven is closed "indefinitely." It has been two weeks, and the kit has not arrived. Holt's credit card bill, on the other hand, is in his hand and due in three weeks. Holt contacted his credit card company and told them that he disputes the charges. The card company apologized for this inconvenience but informed him that they were not obliged to remove the charges by law. They admitted that they used to remove such charges as a courtesy but said that in this tough economic environment, it was all the bank could do to make ends meet by complying with the tons of regulations that apply to it. Holt has a bee in his bonnet, so to speak, about the bank refusing to remove the charge. Has the bank violated TILA in this situation? *See* 15 U.S.C. §1666(i), 12 C.F.R. §§1026.12 and 13.

15.4. Lydia Gomez bought a used scooter from Slim's Scooters for $3,700. Neither the salesman nor the sale paperwork made any mention of warranties. She paid using her Wish credit card, which had no balance on it at the time of the scooter purchase. Two weeks after she bought the scooter, when she was riding it to work, one wheel fell off. Lydia was thrown to the ground and suffered a head injury, requiring $300 in doctor's bills and medical treatment. She also had to pay $400 to Ronny's Repair to have the wheel reattached to her scooter. Lydia is furious at Slim's Scooters. She phoned up Slim, the owner of Slim's Scooters, yelling that she wants her $3,700 back. Slim told her, "I already got paid," and when she wouldn't calm down and have a conversation, he eventually hung up on her. Frustrated, Lydia has written to the address provided on her Wish credit card and explained the issue in great detail. Her letter described the accident with the scooter wheel and her shouting match with Slim, and then stated:

> "It is a mistake to bill me $3,700 for a scooter that was defective. I refuse to pay anything for the scooter."

You represent Wish, the card issuer. It has asked you the following questions: Is the above-quoted statement by the consumer correct? If so, under what authority? Can the consumer refuse to pay the entire $3,700? What, if anything, must the issuer do now or avoid doing now? *See* 15 U.S.C. §1666; 12 C.F.R. §§1026.12 and 13.

Assignment 16.   Automobile Transactions

Car ownership is an important indicator of economic success. Research has indicated that car ownership is linked to higher employment and earnings, lower absenteeism, better health, and improved access to goods and services. Buying a car has long been the largest purchase most Americans will make short of buying a home. In April 2015, the average price of a new car was $33,560. Used car prices were at their highest in 2014, with the average price reaching $16,800.

Car buyers use one of three methods (or a combination thereof) of paying for these big-ticket purchases: self-financing (i.e., saving money to pay the purchase price or borrowing from a family member), direct lending (when the consumer arranges for a loan from a bank, credit union, or finance company without the involvement of the automobile dealer), or dealership financing (when the dealership either provides the financing, or more commonly, serves as an intermediary between a buyer and a lender). Dealership financing can take the form of a loan or a lease.

The combination of the expense of automobiles and the importance of car ownership results in a keen need for consumer protection. Laws regulate car quality, sales practices, and vehicle financing. At the federal level, the main laws are the federal UDAP statute and the Truth in Lending Act, although laws such as the Fair Credit Reporting Act and the Equal Credit Opportunity Act also apply to car financing. The auto industry successfully lobbied Congress to exclude automobile dealers from the purview of the CFPB. 12 U.S.C. §5519. The CFPB does regulate car loans made by large banks and credit unions, and under its so-called larger participant rule, it has extended its authority to nonbank auto finance companies that make, acquire, or refinance 10,000 or more loans or leases annually. These companies, often affiliates of auto manufacturers, provide much of the credit to dealerships, so that the CFPB now indirectly reaches most mainstream dealerships. With fewer responsibilities for consumer protection after the CFPB's creation, the FTC also may be able to devote more resources to consumer complaints about automobile dealers. Used car dealerships, particularly when they provide financing for customers, are perhaps the least regulated actors in the industry and yet prompt the most concerns about consumer protection. Some of these are "buy-here, pay-here" dealerships, named because consumers are required to return in person, with the car, to make payments. One in four borrowers defaults. A three-part series on the industry covers the economies and customer base, including the investors in these dealerships. Ken Bensinger, *A Vicious Cycle in the Used-Car Business*, L.A. Times (Oct. 30, 2011).

A.   Automobile Sales

Car purchases are large-dollar transactions for both the salesperson earning a commission and the consumer spending thousands of dollars. This can lead to high-pressure sales tactics and concerns about unfair and deceptive practices. This section considers two specific legal responses to sales practices of cars. In one situation, the remedy is disclosure. In the other, it is a right to unwind the deal.

1.   Odometer Laws

Federal law mandates certain disclosures to consumers shopping for a car. The Automobile Information Disclosure Act (the Monroney Act) requires labels on all new vehicles for sale, disclosing such information assembly location, price, and safety data. 15 U.S.C. §1232. To the extent consumers read these disclosures and find the information useful, these disclosures can improve the efficiency of the automobile market. However, at least one court has held that while the law carries criminal penalties, it does not imply a private right of action. *Reiff v. Don Rosen Cadillac-BMW, Inc.*, 501 F. Supp. 77, 80 (E.D. Pa. 1980).

Dealers also are obliged to disclose the mileage of cars. The Federal Odometer Act requires an accurate written disclosure of the mileage. 49 U.S.C. §32701 *et seq.* The statute's reach is arguably broader than that, however, as this case illustrates.

Owens v. Samkle Automotive Inc.
425 F.3d 1318 (11th Cir. 2005)

Per Curiam.

Glendale Owens appeals the dismissal of her amended complaint alleging that Samkle Automotive violated the federal Vehicle Information and Cost Savings Act (the "Odometer Act" or the "Act"), 49 U.S.C. §32701 et seq. [It] permits a private party to recover treble damages or $1,500, whichever is greater, from "[a] person who violates [the Odometer Act] or a regulation prescribed or order issued under [the Odometer Act], with intent to defraud[.]" 49 U.S.C. §32710(a). The parties do not dispute that Owens properly alleged that Samkle violated the Odometer Act, and that it did so with the intent to defraud her. However, Owens did not allege that Samkle intended to defraud her specifically with respect to the vehicle's mileage, a fact the district court found fatal to her Odometer Act claim. The district court held that "recovery under the Odometer Act is permissible only when a plaintiff can allege and prove intent to defraud with the respect to a vehicle's mileage."

Owens argues that the plain language of §32710(a) contains no such restriction, and an allegation of intent to defraud in connection with an Odometer Act violation sufficiently states a claim under that subsection. We agree, and accordingly reverse and remand this case to the district court for further proceedings.

I. BACKGROUND

Owens' amended complaint alleges the following facts. Samkle operates a car dealership in Miami, Florida, known as "Marlin Mazda," from which Owens sought to purchase a used car. Salespersons at the dealership showed her a 2002 Mazda 626, and told her that the vehicle was in "excellent" condition. Based on this representation, Owens bought the car.

At the time of sale, the dealership required Owens to sign a battery of forms — a power of attorney, an odometer disclosure statement, a motor vehicle reassignment supplement, and an application for certificate of title (collectively, the "Transfer Forms") — but not the car's original title, as required by the Odometer Act. See 49 U.S.C. §32705(a); 49 C.F.R. §580.5. The Transfer Forms were not the official, secured forms issued by the State of Florida as required by the Odometer Act, see 49 C.F.R. §580.4, and did not contain certain mandatory disclosures. See id. §580.5. By having Owens sign the Transfer Forms, Marlin Mazda transferred ownership of the car to Owens without ever showing her the car's original title.

Owens alleges that the dealership used the Transfer Forms, and not the original title, to transfer ownership of the car because it sought to conceal what the title would have revealed — that the car was previously a short-term rental vehicle owned by Hertz. She alleges that she would not have bought the car at $25,858.00 had she known it had been a Hertz rental vehicle.

II. DISCUSSION

We review a district court's grant of a motion to dismiss *de novo,* taking as true the facts as they are alleged in the complaint. Sosa v. Chase Manhattan Mortgage Corp., 348 F.3d 979, 983 (11th Cir. 2003).

The Odometer Act allows private parties to recover money damages from those that violate its provisions with the intent to defraud: "A person that violates this chapter or a regulation prescribed or order issued under this chapter, with intent to defraud, is liable for 3 times the actual damages or $1,500, whichever is greater." 49 U.S.C. §32710(a). There is no dispute that Owens has properly alleged violations of the Odometer Act. The complaint alleges that Marlin Mazda, with the intent to defraud Owens, violated a "regulation prescribed . . . under" the Odometer Act. Specifically, Owens alleged the violation of 49 C.F.R. §580.5(c), which provides that "[i]n connection with the transfer of ownership of a motor vehicle, each transferor shall disclose the mileage to the transferee in writing *on the title. . . .*" (emphasis added). The Act defines "title" as "the certificate of title or other document issued by the State indicating ownership." 49 U.S.C. §32702(7). Thus, the complaint alleged all of the necessary elements required for a private cause of action pursuant to this statute: (1) that the defendant violated the Act or its regulations, (2) with intent to defraud.

Samkle argues that although it may have acted "with intent to defraud" Ms. Owens when it concealed the title from her, the complaint still fails to state a cause of action because the fraud referenced in the statute can only relate to the vehicle's mileage. However, to accept this argument would violate the first canon of statutory construction, which requires that courts give effect to the plain and unambiguous language of a statute. 525 U.S. 432, 438 (1999). . . .

On its face, this statute's meaning is direct, clear and unambiguous. No language limits the meaning of the clause "with intent to defraud." Absent any such limitation, the statute's meaning is clear — if you violate the Odometer Act, and you do so with the intent to defraud your victim in any respect relating to the Odometer Act or the regulations passed pursuant to it, you are liable. Thus, the statute's plain language does not admit to the district court's limiting construction, which reads words into the statute that do not exist. U.S. v. Fisher, 289 F.3d 1329, 1338 (11th Cir. 2002) ("If the statute's meaning is plain and unambiguous, there is no need for further inquiry. The plain language is presumed to express congressional intent and will control a court's interpretation."). To augment the statutory language with an additional element, never mentioned by Congress, that the fraud must be "with respect to the vehicle's mileage" violates the cardinal rule of statutory construction.[1]

Nor do we agree with Ioffe's construction of the "intent to defraud" language of §32710(a) as a "shorthand designation for specific acts or omissions which violate [the regulation]." Id. (citing U.S. v. Int'l Minerals & Chem. Corp., 402 U.S. 558 (1971)). In *Int'l Minerals*, the Supreme Court held that, in order to preserve the rule that ignorance of the law is no excuse, a statute punishing the "knowing" violation of the regulation in question (covering description of transported hazardous material) must be construed to apply not to knowledge of the regulation but to knowledge of facts which violated the statute or regulation. Under §32710(a), however, "intent to defraud" does not fall within the same "narrow zone" in which the "mens rea" issue was raised in *Int'l Minerals*. See id. at 560. In this case, "intent to defraud" is not an element of the prohibited conduct, but an independent requirement for a private claim arising out of the violation.

We do note, however, that a plain-language reading is also consistent with the general principle that the Odometer Act is remedial legislation that should be "broadly construed to effectuate its purpose," Ryan v. Edwards, 592 F.2d 756, 760 (4th Cir. 1979) (construing the predecessor to §32710(a)), and a plain reading is not inconsistent with the Act's stated purposes. Title 49, section 32701 of the United States Code ("Findings and purposes") indicates that the Odometer Act, as its title suggests, is aimed at preventing odometer tampering and odometer fraud:

(a) Findings. Congress finds that —

(1) buyers of motor vehicles rely heavily on the odometer reading as an index of the condition and value of a vehicle;

---

1. For this reason, we disagree with the court in Ioffe v. Skokie Motor Sales, 414 F.3d 708 (7th Cir. 2005) ("[A]n Odometer Act claim that is brought by a private party and is based on a violation of §580.5(c) requires proof that the vehicle's transferor intended to defraud a transferee with respect to mileage."). We believe the Seventh Circuit failed to apply the statute's plain language, which unambiguously requires that a transferor of a motor vehicle disclose the actual mileage to the transferee *on the title*.

(2) buyers are entitled to rely on the odometer reading as an accurate indication of the mileage of the vehicle;

(3) an accurate indication of the mileage assists a buyer in deciding on the safety and reliability of the vehicle; and

(4) motor vehicles move in, or affect, interstate and foreign commerce.

(b) Purposes. The purposes of this chapter are —

(1) to prohibit tampering with motor vehicle odometers; and

(2) to provide safeguards to protect purchasers in the sale of motor vehicles with altered or reset odometers.

49 U.S.C. §32701.

Consistent with these purposes and findings, Congress established a remedial scheme that not only punished violators, but also deterred would-be violators through a complex regulatory system that made even sophisticated odometer fraud difficult to attempt unnoticed. The regulations include, as one would expect, a flat prohibition on odometer tampering. 49 U.S.C. §32703. However, Congress also mandated standardized disclosure requirements and record-keeping procedures formulated to provide consumers with transparent information about a vehicle's background, to ease investigation and prosecution of violators, and to prevent would-be violators from taking advantage of titling and registration loopholes to perpetrate odometer fraud. See, e.g., 49 U.S.C. §32705 (setting forth disclosure requirements for transferring ownership of a motor vehicle); 49 C.F.R. §580.1 et seq. (specifying, among other things, the content of odometer information disclosures and record keeping procedures, and requiring titles and power of attorney forms to be printed using a secure printing process); *see also* 49 U.S.C. §32706 (conferring investigatory authority and the power to require car dealers or distributors to keep records of motor vehicle sales available for inspection by the Secretary of Transportation).

In particular, the disclosure and title regulations that Samkle allegedly violated aim in part to thwart "title laundering," a practice unscrupulous sellers employ to falsify the mileage listed on a car's title to conform with an altered odometer reading:

> Title laundering is a scheme commonly used by dealers involved in odometer fraud. The main purpose of title laundering is to get a low mileage title from a State motor vehicle titling office in exchange for a high mileage title. The most basic form of title laundering is to simply alter the high odometer reading on the title to a low odometer reading and apply for and receive a title containing the lower reading. A more sophisticated scheme involves sending the high mileage title to a State not requiring odometer readings on title documents and obtaining a new title which does not contain an odometer reading.

Odometer Disclosure Requirements, 52 Fed. Reg. 27022, 27023 (proposed July 17, 1987).

Requiring mileage disclosures to be made on a securely printed title proved critical to fighting title laundering. Prior to the 1988 revisions establishing the present-day regulations, federal law required mileage disclosure only on a "federal odometer statement." Odometer Disclosure Requirements, 52 Fed. Reg. at 27023. A piece of paper separate from the title, the odometer statement could be easily altered or discarded and did not travel with the title. Id. Consequently, it did not warn subsequent purchasers about the vehicle's mileage and ownership history, and did little to curb title laundering. Id. at 27022-23. On the other hand, when the title itself must contain the mileage disclosure and be shown to the buyer, a seller will find it difficult to conceal the vehicle's history and true mileage. Id. Also, to require the mileage disclosure directly on the title establishes a "paper trail" for consumers and law enforcement to deter potential violators and help apprehend sellers that break the law. Id. Similarly, the rule that requires sellers to print titles and power of attorney forms using a secure process, and states to issue power of attorney forms by the state, see 49 C.F.R. §580.4, makes alteration or forgery of titles more difficult and creates an official paper record tracing the vehicle's ownership.

In other words, the regulations at issue in this case are the "safeguards" designed "to protect purchasers in the sale of motor vehicles with altered or reset odometers" that are contemplated by the Act's purposes. See 49 U.S.C. §32701(b)(2). They prevent unscrupulous dealers from using their own procedures to mislead a purchaser about a vehicle's mileage — not only with respect to the actual number of miles driven, but *where* those miles were driven and *by whom*. See 49 C.F.R. §580.2 ("The purpose of this part is to provide purchasers of motor vehicles with odometer information to assist them in determining a vehicle's condition and value. . . ."); Yazzie v. Amigo Chevrolet, Inc., 189 F. Supp. 2d 1245, 1248-49 (D.N.M. 2001) (holding that allegations of specific intent to defraud with respect to the vehicle's mileage are not required to bring suit under §32710(a) when a dealer manipulated title procedures in violation of the Odometer Act to hide the identity of the vehicle's prior owner). The identity of former owners, of critical import to the consumer, is also critical to law enforcement, who rely on the chain of title to ascertain the true ownership and mileage of a vehicle. See Odometer Disclosure Requirements, 53 Fed. Reg. at 29468-69 ("Congress noted that '[o]ne of the major barriers to decreasing odometer fraud is the lack of evidence or "paper trail" showing incidence of rollbacks[.]' . . . Under [the title disclosure requirements], the integrity of the paper trail has been maintained since the disclosure will be on the title and consumers will be able to see the disclosures and examine the titles for alterations, erasures, or other marks. Furthermore, consumers will learn the names of previous owners that appear on the title.") (quoting H.R. Rep. No. 99-833, at 18 (1986) (committee report for the Truth in Mileage Act of 1986, Pub. L. No. 99-579, (1986), which modified the original federal odometer laws in the Motor Vehicle Information and Cost Savings Act of 1972, Pub. L. No. 92-513, §§401-13).

Thus, the success of the complex remedial scheme Congress has created depends on compliance with a multitude of interdependent and seemingly "technical" provisions, such as those Samkle allegedly violated. Violations of these "technical" regulations can defeat the entire remedial scheme — even if they are not committed with the intent to defraud with respect to the vehicle's mileage — by creating gaps in the vehicle's "paper trail" that: (1) thwart investigation of future violations; and (2) make it difficult for future purchasers of a vehicle to spot odometer fraud by preventing them from accurately assessing the vehicle's ownership history.

Moreover, the language of §32710(a) reflects Congressional intent to use civil suits by private individuals to enforce compliance with even the most "technical" provisions of the Odometer Act. To be sure, violators are subject to both civil and criminal penalties for "technical" violations even if they commit them without intent to defraud, see 49 U.S.C. §32709(a)-(b), as well as to suits for injunctive relief by the United States and the fifty States. Id. §§32709(c), (d)(1)(A). But, as the former Fifth Circuit recognized, "unless a violation of the [Odometer] Act can lead to [private] civil liability, the Act is toothless." Nieto v. Pence, 578 F.2d 640, 643 (5th Cir. 1978); see also H.R. Rep. No. 99-833, at 18 (1986) (justifying making odometer fraud a felony because "[t]he Department of Transportation (DOT) believes that evidence indicates that current criminal penalties for odometer tampering are not a sufficient deterrent. According to DOT, many prosecutors are reluctant to prosecute misdemeanor offenses and place very low priority on odometer cases because they are misdemeanors."). Although a violator faces potential punishment from the government, "such relief, although theoretically available, is unlikely. Private prosecution is needed to make the Act effective." Nieto, 578 F.2d at 643. Accordingly, Congress provided a private civil remedy to punish violators of the Odometer Act, so that it would be "largely self-enforcing." H.R. Rep. No. 92-1033, at 20 (1972).

Therefore, to limit private civil suits under §32710(a) only to instances where the defendant intended to defraud the victim with respect to the vehicle's mileage runs counter to the purposes of the private civil remedy-to compensate victims for harm suffered, *and* to ensure strict compliance with the Odometer Act's provisions. Both purposes are also reflected in the text of §32710(a). The violator must make the victim whole, but also must pay an additional price — either double the actual damages or up to $1,500 — as a penalty for violating the Act. 49 U.S.C. §32710(a). It would therefore be inimical to the private civil remedy's function as the Act's primary enforcement mechanism to limit its reach to instances where the defendant intended to defraud his victim "with respect to the vehicle's mileage." Such a reading neither comports with the statute's plain language, nor accords with its remedial purpose.

Consequently, the district court erred when it required Owens to "allege and prove intent to defraud with respect to a vehicle's mileage." Owens has alleged violations of the Odometer Act committed with the intent to defraud, and that is enough to state a claim under §32710(a).

Some states have enacted statutes that expand the federal protection from odometer fraud. Washington, for example, requires knowledge rather than intent to defraud, making it easier for consumers to win actions. *See Quinn v. Cherry Lane Auto Plaza, Inc.*, 225 P.3d 266, (Wash. App. 2009). Other states, like Ohio, treat it as a strict liability offense, removing any question of dealer motive. *See State v. Burrell*, No. 1-07-52, 2008 WL 1700417 (Ohio App. 2008).

2. *Lemon Laws*

Even if lenders make the required disclosures and consumers digest them, the transaction can go awry for the consumer if the car fails to perform as expected. All fifty states and the District of Columbia have some form of "lemon law." This term references the car ownership experience souring for the consumer when the car has persistent, serious defects. The typical statute requires the consumer to give notice to the manufacturer of the problem, and if the car cannot be made reasonably serviceable after a specified number of attempts at fixing the problems, to replace the motor vehicle with a comparable "non-lemon" or to return the purchase price to the consumer.

Most lemon laws are limited to new vehicles, although some are slightly broader, sweeping in things like demonstration vehicles. And there is the issue of what is a covered motor vehicle—do motorcycles, motor homes, or all-terrain vehicles fall under the statute? The basic elements of a lemon law claim are a violation of an applicable warranty *and* a nonconformity that results in a substantial impairment of the vehicle's value, use, or safety. Examples of such problems include cars that routinely fail to start, that have structural defects in the chassis that leak fluid, and the like.

Only a handful of states apply their lemon laws to used vehicles. However, the usual warranty laws, including the Magnuson-Moss Act that were discussed in Assignment 10, apply to the purchase of new or used cars.

B. Automobile Financing

Most Americans do not pay cash for a car but instead finance its purchase. Either method of financing—borrowing or leasing—raises issues of consumer protection. One major concern with financing is the cozy relationship of dealers and financers at the expense of consumers. The result can be dealer markups, which less charitably are viewed as kickbacks. The Center for Responsible Lending estimates that dealer markups increase the cost of automobile loans by $25.8 billion over the lives of the loans. Center for Responsible Lending, *Under the Hood: Auto Loans Interest Rate Hikes Inflate Consumer Costs and Loan Losses,* 2 (2011), http://www.responsiblelending.org/other-consumer-loans/auto-financing/research-analysis/Under-the-Hood-Auto-Dealer-Rate-Markups.pdf. Dealer markups come in two main flavors: dealer reserves and loan packing.

1. Dealer Reserves

"Dealer reserves" refers to the practice of a dealer submitting a customer's financial information to a lender, which replies with a quote of the lowest terms and maximum loan the customer is qualified to receive. The lender and the dealer have an arrangement by which the dealer is compensated for "brokering" the loan for the lender, and additional compensation for negotiating a higher interest rate with the customer, often 2 to 2.5 percent higher. The dealer knows what rate the customer is qualified for, but the customer does not. If the dealer is able to negotiate a higher rate, the dealer and the lender typically share the resulting overage on the interest rate. This often goes by the innocuous description of "dealer participation."

Beaudreau v. Larry Hill Pontiac

160 S.W.3d 874 (Tenn. Ct. App. 2004)

SUSANO JR., Judge.

This is a class action lawsuit filed by a consumer, Patrick Beaudreau, against a car dealer, Larry Hill Pontiac/Oldsmobile/GMC, Inc. ("Hill Pontiac"). Beaudreau purchased an automobile from Hill Pontiac and the purchase was financed through General Motors Acceptance Corporation ("GMAC"). Beaudreau alleges, inter alia, that Hill Pontiac violated the Tennessee Consumer Protection Act and the Tennessee Trade Practices Act ("the TTPA") in that it failed to reveal to Beaudreau that it had an arrangement with GMAC by the terms of which Hill Pontiac received a portion of the interest rate charged to Beaudreau. The trial court dismissed Beaudreau's claims. Beaudreau appeals. We affirm.

I.

On April 12, 1999, Beaudreau agreed to purchase an automobile from Hill Pontiac in Sevierville. In order to purchase the vehicle, Beaudreau obtained financing — with the help of Hill Pontiac representatives — through GMAC. The Hill Pontiac representatives informed Beaudreau that the financing would be subject to a per annum interest rate of 13.5%, which Beaudreau accepted. Sometime later, Beaudreau learned that GMAC had quoted Hill Pontiac an interest rate of 11.25% and that Hill Pontiac had added 2.25% to that rate, thus arriving at the 13.5% interest rate. This practice of a car dealer receiving a certain percentage of the financing it arranges for its customers is commonly referred to as the "dealer reserve" or a "dealer participation" agreement.

On March 8, 2000, Beaudreau filed a complaint against Hill Pontiac, alleging that Hill Pontiac's practice of dealer reserve violated the Tennessee Consumer Protection Act. As additional grounds, Beaudreau raised the issues of unjust enrichment, money had and received, and civil conspiracy, among others. In his complaint, Beaudreau sought class certification for all Hill Pontiac customers similarly situated.

. . .

Finding that the cases relied upon by Beaudreau were easily distinguishable from his case, and holding that an unpublished California trial court opinion provided good insight, the trial court reasoned that there was nothing unlawful about the practice of dealer reserve.

From this ruling, Beaudreau appeals.

II.

As previously stated, the trial court granted Hill Pontiac's motion to dismiss Beaudreau's claims. Hill Pontiac's motion was premised on the failure of the complaint to state a claim upon which relief can be granted. See Tenn. R. Civ. P. 12.02(6). "Such a motion challenges the legal sufficiency of the complaint." Trau-Med of Am., Inc. v. Allstate Ins. Co., 71 S.W.3d 691, 696 (Tenn. 2002). Our role on this appeal is clear. We "must construe the complaint liberally, presum[e] all factual allegations to be true and giv[e] the plaintiff the benefit of all reasonable inferences." Id. A complaint should be dismissed only if "it appears that the plaintiff can prove no set of facts in support of [its] claim that would entitle [it] to relief." Cook v. Spinnaker's of Rivergate, Inc., 878 S.W.2d 934, 938 (Tenn. 1994). Our review is de novo with no presumption of correctness attaching to the trial court's judgment, Trau-Med, 71 S.W.3d at 696-97, because the question before us is one of law: Does the complaint state a cause of action?

III.

The plaintiff raises four issues on appeal, which can be succinctly stated as follows:

1. Did the trial court err in finding that Beaudreau failed to state a cause of action under the Tennessee Consumer Protection Act?
2. Did the trial court err in finding that Beaudreau failed to state a cause of action for civil conspiracy?
3. Did the trial court err in finding that Beaudreau failed to state a cause of action under the TTPA?
4. Did the trial court err in finding that Beaudreau failed to state a cause of action for unjust enrichment and/or money had and received?

IV.

A.

Beaudreau first asserts that the trial court erred in finding that he failed to state a cause of action under the Tennessee Consumer Protection Act. Specifically, Beaudreau claims that Hill Pontiac had a duty to disclose the "real" interest rate, i.e., the 11.25% rate, to him. We disagree.

The Tennessee Consumer Protection Act was enacted, in part, "[t]o protect consumers . . . from those who engage in unfair or deceptive acts or practices in the conduct of any trade or commerce . . . within this state." Tenn. Code Ann. §47-18-102(2). Beaudreau alleges that Hill Pontiac's practice of "secretly inflating the real interest rates consumers are charged when financing their car purchases" is a deceptive practice under the meaning of the Tennessee Consumer Protection Act and is thus unlawful. (Emphasis in original omitted). See Tenn. Code Ann. §47-18-104(b)(27) (stating that engaging in an act that is deceptive to the consumer is unlawful). In support of his position, Beaudreau points to the following allegations in his second amended complaint:

> During the course of the transaction, [Beaudreau] was told by Hill Pontiac representatives that financing for him could and would be arranged by Hill Pontiac through GMAC "at the lowest rates offered" by GMAC. Financing of [Beaudreau's] vehicle was ultimately provided by GMAC. When the Hill Pontiac representative, who at all times was acting as [Beaudreau's] agent, returned with what he characterized as "the best rate they could give us," [Beaudreau] believed he had negotiated the "best rate" with GMAC on his behalf.

However, Hill Pontiac secretly, and without [Beaudreau's] knowledge, added 2.25 percentage points to [Beaudreau's] real interest rate (consequently arriving at the 13.50% rate). [Beaudreau] was specifically told by Hill Pontiac representatives, including the salesman and finance department personnel, that Hill Pontiac had dealt with GMAC on [Beaudreau's] behalf and that the 13.50% rate was the best rate GMAC could offer. However, Hill Pontiac knew GMAC had agreed to finance [Beaudreau's] purchase at a rate lower than 13.50%, which would have consequently led to lower monthly payments.

[Beaudreau] was never told and did not understand that Hill Pontiac was going to receive any of the 13.5% interest rate that he was charged. The real interest rate was never disclosed to [Beaudreau]. Specifically, [Beaudreau] also did not know that the interest rate at which the automobile was financed—and which he paid—was *secretly* inflated by and for the economic benefit of Hill Pontiac by utilizing the dealer reserve scheme described herein.

GMAC arranges for its automobile dealers to act as intermediaries between the consumer and GMAC in order to finance the sale of automobiles. This arrangement is set out in a "dealer participation" agreement between Hill Pontiac and GMAC. According to the agreement between GMAC and Hill Pontiac, the dealership is specifically authorized by GMAC to overcharge consumers by inflating the interest rate charged.

(Numbering in original omitted) (emphasis in original).

This is an issue of first impression in Tennessee. While the issue of dealer reserve was involved in the case of Pyburn v. Bill Heard Chevrolet, 63 S.W.3d 351 (Tenn. Ct. App. 2001), that case centered solely on the issue of an arbitration agreement; the issue of whether the practice of dealer reserve violated the TCPA was never reached. Beaudreau relies upon the unreported case of Adkinson v. Harpeth Ford-Mercury, Inc., No. 01A01-9009-CH00332, 1991 WL 17177 (Tenn. Ct. App. M.S., filed February 15, 1991), in which the concept of dealer reserve, among many other issues, was involved. In *Adkinson*, the court made the following finding with respect to dealer reserve:

We are also of the opinion that *under the circumstances* it was proper for the jury to base a finding of unfair or deceptive acts and practices on the evidence at trial which shows that Harpeth kept for itself 2.5% of the 16.5% annual percentage rate financing which plaintiff was led to believe was charged by [Ford Motor Credit Company] to finance the transaction. Harpeth told plaintiff that FMCC was financing the transaction but failed to disclose to plaintiff that it had secretly imposed the 2.5% additional charge.

Id., at *7 (emphasis added). Relying upon this language, Beaudreau advances the position that the Court of Appeals has "specifically held that the practice [of dealer reserve] . . . violates the TCPA." However, Beaudreau overlooks the limiting language of "under the circumstances." In *Adkinson*, the court found evidence of oral misrepresentations that induced the plaintiff into signing a written contract, as well as evidence that the dealership "used high-pressure tactics" to pressure the plaintiff into purchasing a car when she simply wanted to pay off her lease of the vehicle. Id. Based upon these events, the court went on to find that "[t]here is substantial material evidence that Harpeth engaged in unfair or deceptive acts or practices under the [TCPA] and that it also made negligent misrepresentations to plaintiff." Id. The court did state that the jury could have based its findings on the "deceptive act" of dealer reserve — *under the circumstances* of the case, which included numerous acts which were clearly deceptive under the TCPA. Id. Indeed, this court has previously interpreted this language to mean that "a dealer's failure to disclose 'dealer reserve' was actionable *when the dealer engaged in a pattern of deceptive conduct.*" Harvey v. Ford Motor Credit Co., 8 S.W.3d 273, 275 (Tenn. Ct. App. 1999) (emphasis added). By contrast, there are no allegations of such deceptive or misleading acts in the instant case — the only allegation is that Hill Pontiac engaged in the practice of dealer reserve. We find that the facts in *Adkinson* are distinguishable from those in the case at bar. Accordingly, we conclude that *Adkinson* does not have precedential value in the instant case.

Beaudreau also relies upon another unreported case, *Baggett v. Crown Auto. Group, Inc.*, No. 01A01-9110-CV00401, 1992 WL 108710 (Tenn. Ct. App. M.S., filed May 22, 1992), to support his position that the practice of dealer reserve is unlawful. This case contains evidence of the dealership engaging in egregious fraudulent conduct, which included the dealership making alterations to the original sales contract without the plaintiff's knowledge. Id., at *7. When the plaintiff signed the sales contract on the purchase of his automobile, he agreed to an annual percentage rate of 14.75%. Id., at *3. However, when the dealership realized that Ford Motor Credit Company was not going to approve the financing on the terms agreed upon by the plaintiff and the dealership, the dealership unilaterally increased the annual percentage rate to 15.3% in order to obtain the financing. Id., at *3-*5. The dealership then induced the plaintiff's wife to sign a new contract, in the absence of the plaintiff, without telling her of the changes in the contract. Id., at *4-*5. This court held that increasing the interest rate without informing the plaintiff constituted an unfair or deceptive act as contemplated by the TCPA. Id., at *10. However, the actions by the dealership in increasing the rate of interest in the *Baggett* case do not constitute the practice of dealer reserve such as we have in the instant case. Further, as in *Adkinson*, the actions of the dealership in *Baggett* were clearly deceptive, as well as fraudulent. We have no such conduct in the case at bar.

The only other instance in which dealer reserve has been addressed in Tennessee is in the case of *Harvey v. Ford Motor Credit Co.*, 8 S.W.3d 273 (Tenn. Ct. App. 1999), in which we held that the plaintiff's complaint did not state a cause of action against Ford Motor Credit Company for a violation of the TCPA, based upon the practice of dealer reserve. Id. at 276. Because the plaintiff filed suit against the automotive financing company only and not the dealership involved, we did not reach the issue of the dealership's liability, if any, for engaging in the practice of dealer reserve. Id. However, in our opinion on Harvey's petition for rehearing, this court held as follows:

> Although the Amended Complaint alleges that the plaintiff was "required to pay hidden fees," he was clearly informed of the total interest rate, which he was free to accept or reject. Regardless of how payment was allocated between the dealer and defendant, the plaintiff was aware of what his overall payment and total interest rate would be.

Harvey v. Ford Motor Credit Co., No. 03A01-9807-CV-00235, 1999 WL 486894, at *2 (Tenn. Ct. App. E.S., filed July 13, 1999). The court went on to point out that the plaintiff was "free to seek financing from other sources." Id. There is no allegation in the instant case that Hill Pontiac prevented Beaudreau from considering other financing options.

Because there is no case that is squarely on point in Tennessee, we have looked to the case law outside of our jurisdiction for guidance. While our research has revealed that only a handful of jurisdictions have addressed the legality of dealer reserve, the cases in those jurisdictions are indeed instructive.

The United States Court of Appeals for the Seventh Circuit addressed the issue of dealer reserve in the context of the plaintiff's allegation that the dealership was acting as his agent when it arranged the financing:

> [A]n automobile dealer is not its customers' agent, obviously not in selling cars but only a little less obviously in arranging financing. If the buyer pays cash and arranges his own financing, the dealer is not in the picture at all. If the buyer wants to buy on credit, he recognizes that his decision does not change the arms' length nature of his relation to the dealer. He knows, or at least has no reason to doubt, that the dealer seeks a profit on the financing as well as on the underlying sale.
>
> . . .
>
> [T]here is no suggestion that the dealer here represented that he would act as the buyer's agent in dealing with the finance company, no indication therefore that an agency relationship was created. If there were such a relationship it would mean that the buyer could tell the dealer to shop the retail sales contract among finance companies and to disclose the various offers the dealer obtained to him, and no one dealing with an automobile dealer expects that kind of service.

Balderos v. City Chevrolet, 214 F.3d 849, 853-54 (7th Cir. 2000).

The Alabama Supreme Court adopted similar reasoning when it addressed the issue of dealer reserve:

> Although this case specifically involves lenders and interest rates, interest is nothing other than the cost or price of borrowing money. The [dealer reserve] agreement at issue here is nothing more than [the dealership's] profit on the loan transaction, which had a wholesale price and a retail price. We decline to recognize a common law duty that would require the seller of a good or service, absent special circumstances, to reveal to its purchaser a detailed breakdown of how the seller derived the sales price of the good or service, including the amount of profit to be earned on the sale.

Ex parte Ford Motor Credit Co., 717 So. 2d 781, 787 (Ala. 1997) (internal citation omitted).

Finally, the California Court of Appeal has made the following statements with respect to the legality of dealer reserve:

> The [plaintiffs] effectively assert that payment of the dealer reserve is deceptive merely because it is not disclosed to consumers. However, disclosure is not required by law, and indeed the Federal Reserve Board long ago rejected the proposition that

such disclosure would be useful to consumers.[2] Moreover, the [plaintiffs] allege no facts suggesting why a reasonable person would believe that the financing rate in his or her contract with the dealer is the same rate at which a lender would make a direct loan. Indeed, a reasonable person would likely believe the opposite; the Federal Reserve Board thought so, and several courts have agreed. . . . Accordingly, we conclude payment of the dealer reserve as alleged in the complaints does not constitute a fraudulent business practice.

. . .

The claim that consumers pay higher interest rates than they would if no dealer commission existed may be true, but that is scarcely unfair. Dealers, like any other retailer, seek a profit on the credit services they provide. We are compelled to agree with [the defendant] that the "unfair" prong of the unfair competition law was not intended to eliminate retailers' profits by requiring them to sell at their cost, whether the product is automobiles or automobile financing. In short, we discern no offense to public policy, and no unfairness to be weighed. Payment of the dealer reserve is not an unfair practice under the unfair competition law.

Kunert v. Mission Fin. Servs. Corp., 110 Cal. App. 4th 242 (2003) (internal citations omitted); see also Geller v. Onyx Acceptance Corp., No. 728614, 2001 WL 1711313, at *2, *6 (Cal. Superior, filed November 13, 2001) (noting that the practice of dealer reserve has been "an integral part of the indirect auto finance market since at least the 1960's" and finding that dealer reserve does not constitute an unfair or deceptive business practice).

We find the approach to dealer reserve followed by these other jurisdictions to be well-reasoned and adopt it as our own. Each of the aforementioned cases holds, in essence, that a reasonable consumer should be aware that a for-profit retailer, in arranging for financing for a consumer, would expect to receive some sort of remuneration for its efforts; that the consumer is free to seek financing elsewhere if he or she is unhappy with the terms quoted by the dealer; that the practice of dealer reserve need not be disclosed to the consumer, as previously found by the Federal Reserve Board; and that the practice of dealer reserve is in no way unlawful. It appears that this court was contemplating a similar reasoning in *Harvey*, when it noted that the plaintiff was "free to accept or reject" the quoted interest rate and that the plaintiff was no doubt aware of the total payment and interest rate. Harvey, 1999 WL 486894, at *2.

2. At this point in the opinion, the California court refers the reader to an earlier footnote, which states as follows:

In 1977, the Federal Reserve Board issued a decision interpreting Regulation Z (12 C.F.R. Part 226), which implemented the federal Truth in Lending Act. The Board ruled that a dealer participation need not be identified or disclosed in Truth in Lending disclosures as a separate component of the finance charge. At the same time, the Board withdrew a proposal that would have required separate disclosure of the existence, but not the amount, of a dealer participation. The Board concluded that disclosure of the total finance charge and widespread advertisement of credit terms afforded consumers "the most important information with which to comparison shop for credit." Also, the Board believed the addition of another disclosure requirement would result in more complex disclosure statements and could lead to confusion or misunderstanding by consumers. 42 Fed. Reg. 19124-19125 (Apr. 12, 1977).

Kunert, 1 Cal. Rptr. 3d at 599 n. 10.

There is no factual predicate in the complaint before us which gives rise to a legal duty on Hill Pontiac to disclose to the plaintiff that it is to receive a portion of the interest charged by GMAC. The plaintiff was aware that his contract called for interest at the rate of 13.5% per annum. There is nothing in the complaint indicating that this information or the amount of his monthly payment was hidden from him. Regardless of whether GMAC was to receive all or only a portion of the stated interest of 13.5%, the fact remains that the plaintiff knew that he was paying 13.5% interest to borrow the money to finance the purchase of his car. He was, at all times, free to reject GMAC financing and look elsewhere for a loan to pay for his vehicle.

Accordingly, we find, in the instant case, that Hill Pontiac's dealer participation agreement with GMAC does not constitute a deceptive act or practice and that Hill Pontiac had no duty to disclose the existence of the agreement to Beaudreau. We conclude that the practice of dealer reserve, standing alone, does not violate the TCPA.

. . .

C.

Next, Beaudreau argues that the trial court erred in finding that he failed to state a claim under the TTPA. With respect to this issue, Beaudreau specifically asserts that Hill Pontiac conspired with lenders "to lessen competition and/or to advance the costs of auto financing."

The TTPA provides, in pertinent part, as follows:

> All arrangements, contracts, agreements, trusts, or combinations between persons or corporations made with a view to lessen, or which tend to lessen, full and free competition in the importation or sale of *articles* imported into this state, or in the manufacture or sale of *articles* of domestic growth or of domestic raw material, and all arrangements, contracts, agreements, trusts, or combinations between persons or corporations designed, or which tend, to advance, reduce, or control the price or the cost to the producer or the consumer of any such *product or article,* are declared to be against public policy, unlawful, and void.

Tenn. Code Ann. §47-25-101 (2001) (emphasis added).

Despite Beaudreau's attempts to argue that Hill Pontiac provided a product when it arranged the financing for Beaudreau's automobile, the transaction at issue clearly involves a service. This court has previously held that the TTPA is not applicable to workers' compensation insurance premiums, "which [are] an intangible contract right or service" rather than a product or article. Jo Ann Forman, Inc. v. Nat'l Council on Comp. Ins., Inc., 13 S.W.3d 365, 373 (Tenn. Ct. App. 1999); see also McAdoo Contractors, Inc. v. Harris, 439 S.W.2d 594, 597 (1969) (holding that the TTPA does not apply to the award of a building construction contract). Likewise, the arranging of financing constitutes a service, not a product. We therefore hold that the TTPA has no applicability in the instant case. Furthermore, even if the arranging of financing was deemed to fall under the purview of the TTPA — and we do not believe that it does — we find that the practice of dealer reserve is not an arrangement made to lessen "full and free competition," as contemplated by the statute.

D.

Finally, Beaudreau contends that the trial court erred in finding that he had not stated a cause of action for unjust enrichment and/or money had or received. We disagree.

In order to recover under a theory of unjust enrichment, the plaintiff must prove the following: "A benefit conferred upon the defendant by the plaintiff, appreciation by the defendant of such benefit, and acceptance of such benefit under such circumstances that it would be inequitable for him to retain the benefit without payment of the value thereof." Paschall's, Inc. v. Dozier, 407 S.W.2d 150, 155 (1966). While the first two prongs of this test have been satisfied, Beaudreau cannot prove that it would be inequitable for Hill Pontiac to retain the 2.25% dealer reserve commission. Indeed, as discussed earlier in this opinion, a consumer cannot expect a dealership to assist that consumer in obtaining financing without receiving some sort of payment for its services. Under the circumstances, we cannot say that it was inequitable for Hill Pontiac to retain the 2.25% dealer reserve.

With respect to the claim of money had and received, such an action "may be maintained where one receives money or its equivalent under such circumstances that in equity and good conscience he ought not to retain and in justice and fairness it belongs to another." Steelman v. Ford Motor Credit Co., 911 S.W.2d 720, 724 (Tenn. Ct. App.1995) (citing Interstate Life & Accident Co. v. Cook, 86 S.W.2d 887, 891 (1935)). Again, we find that there is nothing inequitable in allowing Hill Pontiac to retain the dealer reserve. Accordingly, Beaudreau's claims for unjust enrichment and money had and received must fail.

As *Beaudreau* illustrates, courts seem to bless the practice of dealer markups, absent additional issues or additional inappropriate dealer conduct.

The legal landscape on dealer markups may be poised to change. In 2012, the CFPB began investigating and warned several companies of potential lawsuits. The focus was on credit discrimination. Customers with lower credit scores likely have higher rate markups. This could be a sign that dealers are targeting the customers with the least bargaining power — those who are worried they won't be approved for any loan and who thus have less leverage to negotiate a lower rate. Because the law does not require the collection of data on the race of auto loan borrowers (see Assignment 8), any evidence would have to rely on proxies for race such as surnames and addresses. The U.S. Department of Justice Office of Civil Rights and the CFPB recently reached a settlement valued at an estimated $25 million with Honda Finance that included an agreement to lower the amount that dealers could mark up a loan. Despite these suits, the CFPB has said that it does not consider dealer markups to be intrinsically unlawful. Consumers or state attorneys general, however, may go after dealer markups on grounds other than discrimination such as UDAP statutes. Challenges to dealer markups may have more success now that Congress has prohibited the analogous practice in mortgage loans — yield spread premiums that let mortgage loan brokers capture as profit the additional money paid when homeowners took on higher cost loans than lenders' best offers.

2.   Loan Packing

Loan packing refers to the practice of adding additional items or services on top of the price of the automobile, thereby increasing the amount of the loan. The dealer and the lender may have an arrangement that incentivizes the dealer to increase the loan amount. If these items are then financed, the profit from the additional finance charge on the loan goes to the lender. The dealer also increases its profit because the additional items or services that are bundled with the vehicle sale are typically priced significantly above market rates. *See Guinn v. Hoskins Chevrolet*, 361 Ill. App. 3d 575 (Ct. App. Ill. 2005) (car dealership and bank not required to disclose participation in shared profit arrangement under Truth in Lending Act, dealership sufficiently disclosed that it was retaining a portion of life insurance premium, dismissal of unjust enrichment claim was warranted).

3.   Leases

The alternative route to acquiring a car, leasing, carries its own potential problems for consumers. Open-end leases are structured to compensate the lessor for the vehicle's depreciation with, of course, a profit on the transaction as well. This potentially benefits the consumer because monthly payments are typically lower than in a conventional financing sale. For example, a dealer might offer a $20,000 car on a four-year lease. If the dealer estimates the vehicle will be worth $8,000 at the end of the lease, the dealer would be expected to base its open-end lease on the depreciation ($12,000), not the full new value of the vehicle ($20,000). This lowers the monthly payments, even at the same interest rate, because the equivalent "amount financed" is lower in a lease. At the end of the lease's term, however, the consumer has zero equity and no car. The vehicle still belongs to the dealer that can sell it again, hopefully with profitable used-car financing.

Evaluating the economics of leasing requires an accurate estimation of the vehicle's end-of-term value. However, under typical leases, if the vehicle's actual end-of-term value is lower than the estimate, the consumer is responsible for the difference. The opposite is also true; if the vehicle's actual end-of-term value is higher than expected, the lessee is entitled to a refund of the excess. This virtually never happens because the dealer has an incentive to inflate the estimated end-of-term value to lower the monthly payments and further entice the customer. Altering the above example, the dealer might state that the vehicle's estimated end-of-term value is instead $10,400, resulting in expected depreciation of $9,600, allowing for monthly payments of $200. When at the end of the lease term the vehicle is actually worth only $8,000, the consumer has to come up with the extra $1,600, at a time when she likely also needs to buy or lease a replacement vehicle.

By the end of the transaction, the dealer is not receiving any more or less money by inflating the estimated end-of-term value, except for the likelihood that a consumer will lease a vehicle she could not afford without the artificially-lowered payments. If she realized she would be responsible for a large balloon payment at the end of the lease, she might not sign the lease, so the primary problem with these contracts is one of information. This issue is among those addressed by Regulation M, which implements the consumer leasing provisions of the Truth in Lending Act. The laws try to address the risks of leasing using three main strategies:

1. Warning consumers before they sign leases about potential liability at the end of the term;
2. Giving consumers the right to challenge lessors' end-of-term estimates of residual value (if the vehicles are not sold to establish such value) with professional independent appraisals; and
3. Making it financially unprofitable for lessors to sue consumers for "unreasonable" end-of-term liability.

Regulation M effectuates these strategies in many ways, including disclosure requirement. If the consumer is liable at the end of the lease term for the difference between the residual value of the car and its realized value, the consumer gets informed of certain rights. For example, the consumer must be given a statement that the lessee and lessor are permitted, after termination of the lease, to make any mutually agreeable final adjustment regarding excess liability. 12 CFR §213.4(m). The consumer also must be told about the law's intervention in setting residual value. Regulation M creates a rebuttable presumption that the residual value of the leased property is unreasonable and not in good faith to the extent that the residual value exceeds the realized value by more than three times the base monthly payment. Regulation M is unusual in tackling the leverage that businesses have over consumers in taking enforcement action. It provides that the lessor cannot collect the excess amount above the rebuttable presumption amount unless the lessor brings a successful court action and pays the lessee's reasonable attorney's fees. There is an important exception if the excess of the residual value over the realized value is due to unreasonable or excessive wear or use of the leased property. This leads to heated battles about what is reasonable wear and tear. This is a concept consumers can grasp, however, and debate with lessors to reach a fairer outcome.

The rebuttable presumption in Section 2 is an important consumer protection. It provides that any overage at the end-of-lease is unreasonable if it is greater than three times the monthly payments. Thus, in the hypothetical example above, the dealer would only be able to collect $600 (three times the $200 monthly payment) of the $1,600 overage without going to court and showing that the overage was not unreasonable. That is a pretty tough standard for lessors. *See Wilson v. World Omni Leasing, Inc.*, 540 So. 2d 713 (Ala. 1989) (where consumer's truck was destroyed in an accident, unreasonability presumption is rebutted because difference between actual value and estimated residual value was caused by damage beyond reasonable wear and use).

C. Title Loans

Automobile loans, like mortgage loans of recent years, have a subprime market and a prime market. The interest rate spread is even greater in car loans, in part because the collateral depreciates more rapidly, and in part because unlike a house and the land it sits on, cars can disappear. A specialized kind of car loan with very high interest rates is a title loan. These do not help consumers purchase cars but rather give a consumer who owns a car access to cash in return for offering up the car's title as collateral. The description below illustrates how a title loan works and its economics.

> In her complaint, the plaintiff alleges that she is a Pennsylvania resident who traveled to Claymont, Delaware, where, on November 9, 2009, she borrowed $800 from defendant Dominion. [The debtor, in April 2009, borrowed a similar amount from Dominion, on identical terms. She repaid this loan, with interest, prior to November 2009.] This loan was secured by a lien on her vehicle: a 1997 Jeep Grand Cherokee. Under the terms of this loan, the debtor was obligated to repay monthly at least the accrued interest on the loan, which interest rate was disclosed at 0.9863% daily and 360% annually. Interest accrues at the rate of $7.8904 per day. Monthly interest is thus $236.71. The debtor further alleges that she tendered monthly payments to Dominion for approximately one year with little or no principal reduction. Interest payments for one year would be $2,840.54 unless some principal reduction payments were made. Thereafter, she stopped tendering payments (she asserts that Dominion informed her that she could do so) and her vehicle was repossessed in Pennsylvania without notice.

In re Pfeiffer, 2011 WL 4005504 (Bankr. E.D. Pa. 2011). Why did the consumer travel to Delaware to borrow $800? The answer is that Pennsylvania sharply limits the interest rates on small dollar loans, whereas Delaware has no usury law. For individuals with risky credit profiles, loans are more readily available in Delaware. This consumer filed bankruptcy as a result of her financial problems—at that point, she had paid 3.5 times the amount that she borrowed ($800) and had lost her car.

Some of the objections to title loans parallel their unsecured cousin in the high-yield lending market, payday loans (the subject of the next Assignment). The rates are high, disclosures may be ineffective in revealing the costs and risks of the loans, and consumers may find themselves in a cycle of debt because of the loan. The additional harm of title loans, however, is that the loss of a car can often mean the loss of a job, particularly in places where there is no public transportation. People are often so desperate to get a new car after losing one to repossession that they are willing to buy from unscrupulous dealers. The data on the auto title lending's effects on consumers are contested. *Compare* Kathryn Fritzdixon, Jim Hawkins & Paige Marta Skiba, *Dude, Where's My Car Title?: The Law, Behavior and Economics of Title Industry Markets*, 2014 U. ILL. L. REV. 1013 (2014) *with* Susanna Motezemolo, *Car-Title Lending*, Center for Responsible Lending (July 2013). Part of the disagreement is about how to interpret the data. Because many title loans are rolled over each month (which technically creates a new loan), the repossession rate looks much lower if calculated based on the number of loans as compared to the number of borrowers. The Center for Responding Lending reports that 17 percent of borrowers incurred a repossession fee, although some of these may have scraped up the cash to get their car back. *Id.* at 8. The Fritzdixon, Hawkins & Skiba paper estimates a 10 percent repossession rate.

In most states, title lenders operate with the protection of the law. There are some state laws that sharply limit auto-title loans, usually by imposing interest rate caps of 36 percent or below. *See, e.g.,* Iowa Code §537.2403 ("A lender shall not contract for or receive a finance charge exceeding twenty-one percent per year on the unpaid balance of the amount financed for a loan of money secured by a certificate of title to a motor vehicle used for personal, family, or household purpose except as authorized under chapter 536 or 536A."). Even when the law places limitations on auto title lenders, however, they have proven adept at evading regulation. Many transactions are restructured to disguise the loans in order to exploit loopholes in existing laws—for example calling the loans "pawns" or "motor vehicle equity lines of credit" or setting them up as a sale to the lender with a leaseback to the consumer.

Problem Set 16

16.1. BDD is an automobile manufacturer that focuses on mid-price vehicles. After several successful products, it expanded its line to a high-end vehicle, loaded with the latest technology. Jack Tutz purchased the Opal from the Bluebell BDD dealership for $57,539. After about ten months, the Opal began to have warning lights flash. Each time Jack returned the car to Bluebell, it reset the lights and assured him everything was fine but "this extremely sophisticated technology is very sensitive."

The other day when a low tire sensor came on, Jack ignored it as another false alarm. Thirty miles later, he had a blow out on the freeway. While the Opal was undamaged, Jack's swerving caused another car to hit the median, with a concussion for its driver. The car was towed to Bluebell, and a livid Jack really let Bluebell's sales manager, Evan, have it. When Jack produced a sheaf of repair slips from the Opal's glove box and mentioned a lawsuit for a defective car, Evan offered him a solution. Bluebell would credit Jack with $2,000 toward any car on the lot plus the market value trade-in on his Opal. Jack accepted, and left happy.

Two days later, after a thorough evaluation and repair of the Opal's central computer, Bluebell sold the Opal that formerly belonged to Jack to Amber, a young law firm associate making her first vehicle purchase. Amber was delighted to find such a low-mileage luxury vehicle, as she worried about the mechanical problems that come with used cars and the sales tactics of used car dealers but she could not afford a brand-new car. Amber paid $43,000 cash for the car, and received a copy of the dealership's certificate of quality—a list of all the aspects of the car that were checked and in working order at the time of the sale. Amber parked the Opal at her firm next to her supervising partner, Jack Tutz, who exclaimed, "I can't believe you bought a lemon! I thought you had better judgment." Amber has identified the following lemon statutes. Did Bluebell BDD or BDD Manufacturing violate the law? Tex. Occ. Code Ann. §2301.601 et seq.

16.2. Cathy Cho's small business in Reno went bust, and in her mind she lost "everything," including the car that she had offered as collateral on a bank line of credit for the business. On Monday morning, she starts a new job with a stable but low income but needs a car to avoid an unpredictable and lengthy commute. On Saturday afternoon, Cathy visited Wonder Wheels, a local used car dealer and selected a "well-loved" (a.k.a. high-mileage, beat-up) Civic. The finance guy, Hubert, collected details on Cathy's new job and income on the credit application, and said he was confident that "it would all work out" despite Cathy's poor credit. The written sales contract disclosed a 17 percent APR and contained a clause that Wonder Wheels "would exercise all due diligence to obtain financing as stated and to consummate the transaction." Cathy paid the required $500 downpayment in cash, signed the contract, and drove off in the Civic.

On Monday morning, Hubert presented Cathy's loan to his boss, who frowned a lot while flipping through the paperwork. He had Hubert offer the loan to several buyers, all of whom declined to purchase the loan at a rate that would be profitable for Wonder Wheels. Hubert was instructed to call Cathy back, tell her that the financing had "fallen through" and give her a choice: she could sign a new contract agreeing to a loan with a 24 percent APR (and correspondingly higher payments) or give up the car and her downpayment. Cathy is devastated to get Hubert's call. That downpayment was her last cash, and if she returns the car, she has no way to get to work. Does Cathy have any options? Nevada Rev. Stat. §482.554.

16.3. You are outside counsel to a small chain of used car dealerships in Alaska. It takes cars on trade for the majority of sales. The dealership believes that consumers often fail to disclose damage to the cars that they offer for sale or trade. It buys about 50 percent of its cars from a Hawaiian wholesaler that ships in used cars on a container ship. Does the dealership have any liability to consumers who purchase the cars and later learn, upon a mechanic's inspection or the like, that the car was previously damaged? What would you recommend to the dealership as strategies to limit its liability? Alaska Stat. §45.25.465; Haw. Rev. Stat. §481J-4.

16.4. You are a lawyer working for a labor union that represents low-to-moderate income service employees in a Midwestern state. You have been asked by a member of the state legislature whether the labor union believes this statute would help its members. Assume that there is no state law on point at all, but that the state does have a UDAP Act that covers "unfair and unconscionable acts and practices."

A title loan lender shall not:

I. Make more than one outstanding loan that is secured by one title.

II. Make a title loan without providing the borrower within the title loan agreement the right to cancel the title loan at any time before the close of business of the next business day following the date of the transaction by repaying to the lender in cash the amount advanced to the borrower.

III. Offer, advertise, or make a loan with a rate of interest that is lower in the original period than in subsequent renewals.

IV. Make a loan to a borrower who currently has an outstanding or who has had an outstanding payday or title loan within the previous 60-day period. As part of its application process for such a loan, a lender shall obtain a written statement under oath from the borrower certifying the borrower does not currently have an outstanding and has not had an outstanding payday loan or title loan within the previous 60-day period.

V. Charge interest at higher than 25 percent per month, however actual costs incurred by the lender may be passed through to the borrower.

Assignment 17. Payday Loans

The prior assignments have focused on financial products that are widely used by American families such as mortgages, credit cards, and car loans. While recent years have seen significant segmentation in these markets, these products are generally thought of as mainstream or middle class. In contrast, there are "fringe" credit products. These are usually designed for and used by people who may lack access to mainstream credit products, may prefer them for particular reasons, or may be steered to use them. Fringe products nearly always carry high interest rates and charge high fees. For this reason, some people refer to this market as "high-yield" lending because it can generate significant revenue for lenders. Others categorize some or all fringe credit products as "predatory," a considerably less favorable moniker. Examples of fringe products are rent-to-own transactions, automobile title loans, and pawn loans.

This assignment focuses on payday loans as an exemplar of the legal issues presented by high-cost credit. Payday loans illustrate a variety of approaches to consumer protection strategies and are the locus of a fierce debate about which approach is most effective. Payday loans also highlight the policy tensions in credit, including the difficulty of determining whether consumers benefit from legal protections if the consequence is a significant reduction in access to credit.

A. Payday Loan Industry

Despite being categorized as fringe credit, payday loans are not rare. There are at least 22,000 storefront payday lenders nationwide, more than many ubiquitous retail establishments such as McDonald's or Starbucks. Chris Peterson & Steve Graves, *Predatory Lending and the Military: The Law and Geography of 'Payday' Loans in Military Towns*, 66 Ohio St. L.J. 653 (2005). Analysts estimate that payday lenders extend somewhere between $25 billion and $40 billion in loans each year. It is difficult to get reliable estimates on the popularity of payday loans at the household level. In a 2013 survey, only 4.2 percent of families said they had taken out a payday loan in the last year. Federal Reserve Bulletin, Changes in U.S. Family Finances from 2010 to 2013: Evidence from the Survey of Consumer Finance 30 (Sept. 2014), http://www.federalreserve. gov/pubs/bulletin/2014/pdf/scf14.pdf. Other research estimates the number of payday borrowers at 19 million, which would be closer to 8 percent of adults.

Payday borrowers are disproportionately female and are often single women with dependent children. Amy Schmitz, *Females on the Fringe: Considering*

Gender in Payday Lending Policy, 89 Chicago-Kent L. Rev. 65 (2014). Payday lenders tend to have less income and fewer assets than families without payday loans, but notably they also have less debt. One-quarter of payday borrowers identified themselves as savers, compared to half of those who did not recently take out a payday loan. *See* Amanda Logan & Christian Weller, *Who Borrows From Payday Lenders?* 12 (2009), at http://www.americanprogress.org/issues/2009/03/pdf/payday_lending.pdf.

The demographic profiles of payday borrowers have more meaning when one understands how the product works. The key aspects of payday loans are that they are small dollar and short term. In return for the loan, the borrower gives the lender a post-dated check or an authorization for a bank account withdrawal called an automated clearing house (ACH). If the consumer does not repay the loan, the lender could cash the check or debit the consumer's bank account. An example of a typical product would be a $400 loan for 14 days with a $100 transaction or processing fee. The consumer would receive $400 and authorize a $500 bank withdrawal on the borrower's payday. The lender would exercise the withdrawal unless the borrower paid the $500. If the consumer gave a check instead, postdated to payday, this is called a deferred presentment because the lender will wait to seek payment from the consumer's bank on the check. If the borrower does not pay or want the check cashed / debit made, the loan is sometimes renewed or rolled over into a new loan, as explained below.

The process for obtaining such a loan is fairly simple and quick. A borrower will complete a short application form and be asked to provide proof of identification, evidence of income such as a recent paystub, and a bank statement. The lender may use a software program to check the borrower's history with the lender or consult a database for bad checks or other collection activity, but FICO scores are not widely used the way they are for mortgages or cars.

B.   Regulatory Approaches to Payday Loans

A number of federal consumer laws apply to payday loans, including federal unfair and deceptive acts and practices laws, the Truth in Lending Act, and the Fair Debt Collection Practices Act. These are generally applicable to most credit, however, and do not take aim at the specific practices of payday lending. Historically states have been active in regulating payday loans and have used approaches from disclosure requirements to product limitations to outright bans. Lenders chafe at the variety of tactics used by state regulators and attorneys general. Certainly, the heteroge of state laws increases compliance costs and creates greater uncertainty about litigation risk for payday lenders.

Payday loans have not yet been regulated at the federal level. The Consumer Financial Protection Bureau put out preliminary proposed regulations, but as of December 2015, these have not yet been moved into the rulemaking process; they are only released for study on their potential impacts on small businesses. Consumer Financial Protection Bureau, *Outline of Proposals Under Consideration and Alternatives Considered (2015),* http://files.consumerfinance.gov/f/201503_cfpb_outline-of-the-proposals-from-small-business-review-panel.pdf. The next few years may see a major reform of payday loans by the federal government.

The *Quik Payday* case below illustrates the creativity of the lawyers for the payday industry in challenging the boundaries of state regulation. The case centers on a constitutional challenge to a consumer lending law but is included here for its useful overview of a payday loan business and the types of state laws that apply to it.

Quik Payday, Inc. v. Stork
549 F.3d 1302 (10th Cir. 2008)

HARTZ, Circuit Judge.

Quik Payday, Inc., which used the Internet in making short-term loans, appeals from the district court's rejection of its constitutional challenge to the application of Kansas's consumer-lending statute to those loans. Defendants were Judi M. Stork, Kansas's acting bank commissioner, and Kevin C. Glendening, deputy commissioner of the state's Office of the State Bank Commission (OSBC), both in their official capacities.

Quik Payday argues that applying the statute runs afoul of the dormant Commerce Clause by (1) regulating conduct that occurs wholly outside Kansas, (2) unduly burdening interstate commerce relative to the benefit it confers, and (3) imposing Kansas requirements when Internet commerce demands nationally uniform regulation. We disagree. The Kansas statute, as interpreted by the state officials charged with its enforcement, does not regulate extraterritorial conduct; this court's precedent informs us that the statute's burden on interstate commerce does not exceed the benefit that it confers; and Quik Payday's national-uniformity argument, which is merely a species of a burden-to-benefit argument, is not persuasive in the context of the specific regulation of commercial activity at issue in this case. We have jurisdiction under 28 U.S.C. §1291 and affirm the district court.

I. BACKGROUND

From 1999 through early 2006, appellant Quik Payday was in the business of making modest, short-term personal loans, also called payday loans. It maintained an Internet website for its loan business. The prospective borrower typically found this website through an Internet search for payday loans or was steered there by third-party "lead generators," a term used for the intermediaries that solicit consumers to take out these loans. In some instances Quik Payday sent solicitations by e-mail directly to previous borrowers.

Once on Quik Payday's website, the prospective borrower completed an online application form, giving Quik Payday his or her home address, birthdate, employment information, state driver's license number, bank-account number, social

security number, and references. If Quik Payday approved the application, it electronically sent the borrower a loan contract, which the borrower signed electronically and sent back to Quik Payday. (In a small number of cases these last few steps
took place through facsimile, with approved borrowers physically signing the contracts before faxing them back to Quik Payday.) Quik Payday then transferred the
amount of the loan to the borrower's bank account.

Quik Payday made loans of $100 to $500, in hundred-dollar increments. The loans
carried $20 finance charges for each $100 borrowed. The borrower either paid back the
loans by the maturity date — typically, the borrower's next payday — or extended
them, incurring an additional finance charge of $20 for every $100 borrowed.

Quik Payday was headquartered in Logan, Utah. It was licensed by Utah's
Department of Financial Institutions to make payday loans in Utah. It had no offices,
employees, or other physical presence in Kansas.

Between May 2001 and January 2005, Quik Payday made 3,079 payday loans to
972 borrowers who provided Kansas addresses in their applications. Quik Payday
loaned these borrowers approximately $967,550.00 in principal and charged some
$485,165.00 in fees; it collected $1,325,282.20 in principal and fees. When a
Kansas borrower defaulted, Quik Payday engaged in informal collection activities
in Kansas but never filed suit. [ED. NOTE — This is different than the Uniform
Commercial Code.]

Kansas regulates consumer lending, including payday lending, under its version
of the Uniform Consumer Credit Code. See Kan. Stat. Ann. §§16a-1-101 through
16a-9-102 (KUCCC). The KUCCC defines payday loans, or "supervised loans,"
as those on which the annual percentage interest rate exceeds 12%. Id.
§16a-1-301(46). Under the KUCCC a payday lender (other than a supervised financial organization — in essence, a bank with a federal or state charter) must obtain a
license from the head of the consumer-and-mortgage-lending division of the OSBC
before it can make supervised loans in Kansas. See id. §§16a-1-301(2), 16a-2-302.
Obtaining a license requires paying an application fee of $425 (and a further $325
to renew each year), posting a surety bond costing approximately $500 per year,
and submitting to a criminal-background and credit check. Supervised lenders may
not charge more than 36% per annum on unpaid loan balances of $860 or less, and
may not charge more than 21% per annum on unpaid balances of more than $860.
See id. §16a-2-401(2). Supervised lenders are required to schedule installment payments in substantially equal amounts and at substantially regular intervals on loans
of less than $1,000 and on which the finance charge exceeds 12%. Id. §16a-2-308.
When such loans are for $300 or less, they must be payable within 25 months, while
such loans of more than $300 must be payable within 37 months. Id. §16a-2-
308(a)-(b). Quik Payday was never licensed to make supervised loans by the OSBC.

In 1999 Kansas amended the provision of the KUCCC that governs the statute's
territorial application. See id. §16a-1-201. Before that year a consumer-credit transaction was deemed to have been "made in th[e] state," and to come under the
KUCCC, if either (a) the creditor received in Kansas a signed writing evidencing the
consumer's obligation or offer, or (b) "the creditor induces the consumer who is a
resident of this state to enter into the transaction by face-to-face solicitation in this
state." 1993 Kan. Sess. Laws ch. 200 §3. The 1999 legislation amended paragraph
(1)(b) to say that the transaction is deemed to have been made in Kansas if "the
creditor induces the consumer who is a resident of this state to enter into the

transaction by solicitation in this state by any means, including but not limited to: Mail, telephone, radio, television or any other electronic means." Kan. Stat. Ann. §16a-1-201(1)(b). No party or amicus questions that the catch-all "other electronic means" includes the Internet.

Under the KUCCC a consumer's residence is the address given by the consumer as his or her address "in any writing signed by the consumer in connection with a credit transaction." Id. §16a-1-201(6). The statute does not define "solicitation." Defendants conceded in district court, however, that merely maintaining a website accessible in Kansas that advertises payday loans is not solicitation in Kansas under §16a-1-201(1)(b). See Quik Payday, Inc. v. Stork, 509 F. Supp. 2d 974, 982 n. 7 (D. Kan. 2007).

In June 2005 the OSBC received a complaint from a Kansas consumer about a loan transaction with Quik Payday. The agency responded by ordering Quik Payday, which was not on its list of licensed supervised lenders, to produce documents regarding its loans to Kansas residents. Quik Payday submitted the requested documents, which revealed the above-mentioned 3,079 payday loans to 972 Kansas residents. On March 13, 2006, the OSBC issued a summary order that required Quik Payday to stop all payday lending to Kansas residents, halt any collections on outstanding loans, pay a civil penalty of $5 million, and return to the borrowers the interest, service fees, and profits from the 3,079 loans. The order also barred Quik Payday from applying in the future to become a licensed payday lender in Kansas. Quik Payday timely requested an administrative hearing to challenge the order.

On May 19, 2006, shortly before the scheduled date of the administrative hearing, Quik Payday filed this lawsuit under 42 U.S.C. §1983 against Defendants in the United States District Court for the District of Kansas. (Quik Payday requested and was granted a stay of the administrative hearing; as a result, no final order has been entered in that proceeding.) Quik Payday's complaint in district court sought a declaratory judgment that Kansas could not regulate Quik Payday's loans and an injunction barring such regulation. It claimed that both Kan. Stat. Ann. §16a-1-201(1)(b) itself and Kansas's application of its consumer-credit laws to Quik Payday under this provision of the statute are unconstitutional under the Commerce Clause and Due Process Clause.

Quik Payday moved for summary judgment, offering three arguments under the dormant Commerce Clause: (1) the statute is an impermissible extraterritorial regulation; (2) the statute impermissibly burdens interstate commerce under the balancing test of *Pike v. Bruce Church, Inc.*, 397 U.S. 137 (1970); and (3) the statute subjects Internet lending to inconsistent state regulations. On the same day, Defendants moved for summary judgment on Quik Payday's constitutional claims, including its contentions under the Due Process Clause that Kansas lacked the power to regulate it and that Kan. Stat. Ann. §16a-1-201 is unconstitutionally vague and overbroad. (Quik Payday did not seek summary judgment on these due-process claims.) The parties stipulated to the facts to be considered by the district court in deciding their motions.

The district court denied Quik Payday's motion for summary judgment and granted Defendants' cross-motion. It rejected each of Quik Payday's three Commerce Clause challenges to the Kansas statute and its application to Quik Payday. It rejected the contention that Kansas was seeking to regulate conduct entirely outside its borders because the Kansas statute is triggered only if there is both solicitation in Kansas and a loan to one of its residents. Quik Payday, 509 F. Supp. 2d at 981. With regard to *Pike* balancing, the court cited our decision in Aldens, Inc. v. Ryan, 571 F.2d 1159 (10th Cir. 1978), for the proposition that "a state's regulation of the cost and terms on which its residents borrow money from an out-of-state creditor is not outweighed by the burdens on interstate commerce." Quik Payday, 509 F. Supp. 2d at 979. And as to national uniformity, the court determined that Quik Payday had not shown that "internet payday lending specifically represents the type of commerce that should only be subject to nationally-uniform standards," id. at 983; its regulated conduct was aimed specifically at Kansas and did not necessarily implicate other states or their regulations. The court also entered summary judgment for Defendants on Quik Payday's due-process claims. Id. at 984-85.

Quik Payday appeals the district court's grant of summary judgment to the Defendants and the denial of summary judgment to itself. It does not challenge the district court's due-process rulings but only those regarding the Commerce Clause.

II. DISCUSSION

We review a district court's decision to grant summary judgment de novo, viewing all facts in the light most favorable to the party opposing summary judgment. See Jacklovich v. Simmons, 392 F.3d 420, 425 (10th Cir. 2004). We will affirm a grant of summary judgment if there is no genuine issue of material fact and the prevailing party is entitled to judgment under the law. See id. At 426; Fed. R. Civ. P. 56(c). Likewise, we conduct de novo review of legal issues, including challenges to the constitutionality of statutes. See Hoffmann-Pugh v. Keenan, 338 F.3d 1136, 1138 (10th Cir. 2003).

A. The Dormant Commerce Clause

The Supreme Court "long has recognized that th[e] affirmative grant of authority to Congress [to regulate interstate commerce] also encompasses an implicit or 'dormant' limitation on the authority of the States to enact legislation affecting interstate commerce." Healy v. Beer Inst., 491 U.S. 324, 326 n. 1 (1989); see Dennis v. Higgins, 498 U.S. 439 (1991) ("[T]he Commerce Clause does more than confer power on the Federal Government; it is also a substantive restriction on permissible state regulation of interstate commerce."). State statutes may violate the dormant limitation in three ways:

> First, a statute that clearly discriminates against interstate commerce in favor of intrastate commerce is virtually invalid per se and can survive only if the discrimination is demonstrably justified by a valid factor unrelated to economic protectionism. Second, if the statute does not discriminate against interstate commerce, it will nevertheless be invalidated under the *Pike* [397 U.S. at 142] balancing test if it imposes a burden on interstate commerce incommensurate with the local benefits secured. Third, a statute will be invalid per se if it has the practical effect of extraterritorial control of commerce occurring entirely outside the boundaries of the state in question.

KT & G Corp. v. Att'y Gen. of Okla., 535 F.3d 1114, 1143 (10th Cir. 2008).

Although Quik Payday treats the need for national uniformity as an additional ground for determining that a state law violates the Commerce Clause, concerns about national uniformity are simply part of the *Pike* burden/benefit balancing analysis. When assessing the burden of a state law on interstate commerce, "the practical effect of the statute must be evaluated not only by considering the consequences of the statute itself, but also by considering how the challenged statute may interact with the legitimate regulatory regimes of other States and what effect would arise if not one, but many or every, State adopted similar legislation." Healy, 491 U.S. at 336. For example, in Southern Pacific Co. v. Arizona ex rel. Sullivan, 325 U.S. 761 (1945), the Supreme Court declared that states may not "regulate those phases of the national commerce which, because of the need of national uniformity, demand that their regulation, if any, be prescribed by a single authority." Id. at 767. But its holding that a state law could not limit train lengths was supported by what amounts to *Pike* balancing — namely, (1) a thorough analysis of the problems that would be created for interstate railroad transportation if each state could regulate train lengths and (2) an assessment that such state regulation would confer little, if any, local benefit. Id. at 771-79; cf. ACLU v. Johnson, 194 F.3d 1149, 1160 (10th Cir. 1999) ("[T]he Supreme Court has long recognized that certain types of commerce are uniquely suited to national, as opposed to state, regulation.").

Quik Payday does not argue that the Kansas statute discriminates against interstate commerce in favor of the local variety. Rather, it challenges the Kansas statute only under the extraterritorial-impact and *Pike*-balancing tests. To the extent that it also argues what it terms the "national unity" test, we will treat that issue as part of the balancing process.

B. Extraterritoriality

Quik Payday argues that the Kansas statute regulates interstate commerce that happens entirely outside Kansas. It contends that the Kansas statute reaches cases in which a Kansas resident is "solicited" while using a work computer in Missouri and accepts the loan through the same computer. In support, it points to census data on the number of Kansas residents who work in metropolitan Kansas City, Missouri, and thus likely use computers that lie in Missouri. Additionally, it asserts that "lenders, having no ability to determine the physical location of the consumer at the time of the solicitation, are forced as a practical matter to abide by the K[U]CCC for all transactions with Kansas residents or refuse to lend to such residents altogether." Aplt. Br. at 43.

Defendants, however, have stipulated that such a transaction would not be governed by the Kansas statute. In district court they conceded that a website advertisement does not trigger application of Kan. Stat. Ann. §16a-1-201(1)(b), even though the website is accessible in Kansas. See Quik Payday, 509 F. Supp. 2d at 982 n. 7. . . .

Quik Payday has failed to show that this possible extraterritorial effect of the statute is more than speculation. It has provided no evidence of any loan transaction with a Kansas resident that was effected totally outside Kansas. Even if the Kansas resident applied for the loan on a computer in Missouri, other aspects of the transaction are very likely to be in Kansas — notably, the transfer of loan funds to the borrower would naturally be to a bank in Kansas. Although the Kansas statute would not apply to such a loan transaction (because the solicitation was not in Kansas), the transaction would not be wholly extraterritorial, and thus not problematic under the dormant Commerce Clause. Moreover, Quik Payday has not explained how it would be burdensome to it simply to inquire of the customer in which state he is located while communicating with Quik Payday. In this circumstance, we will not hold that the KUCCC has a prohibited effect on extraterritorial commerce. . . .

C. *Pike* Balancing

A state law that does not discriminate against interstate commerce may still be invalidated under the dormant Commerce Clause if it puts a burden on interstate commerce that is "clearly excessive in relation to the putative local benefits." Pike, 397 U.S. at 142. Although evidence regarding a particular company may be suggestive, the benefit-to-burden calculation is based on the overall benefits and burdens that the statutory provision may create, not on the benefits and burdens with respect to a particular company or transaction. "[T]he [Commerce] Clause protects the interstate market, not particular interstate firms, from prohibitive or burdensome regulations." Exxon Corp. v. Governor of Md., 437 U.S. 117, 127-28 (1978); see Pharm. Research & Mfrs. of Am. v. Concannon, 249 F.3d 66, 84 (1st Cir. 2001).

. . .

Aldens governs the analysis under the *Pike* test in this case. To begin with, we note that our review of the KUCCC is limited. Although Quik Payday might be burdened by statutory provisions regarding interest rates, repayment schedules, and loan renewals, we need not concern ourselves with provisions that have never been applied to Quik Payday (and which, because Quik Payday no longer operates as a payday lender, never will be). Perhaps some of those unapplied provisions are unconstitutional and must be stricken. But striking them would not entitle Quik Payday to relief if the provisions that were applied withstand a Commerce Clause challenge. Here, the sanction imposed on Quik Payday was based solely on its failure to obtain a license as a lender of supervised loans. Thus, we address only the burdens and benefits of the license requirement.

The stipulated facts show that the burden of obtaining a license is limited to a $425 fee, a surety bond whose annual cost would be roughly $500, and a criminal-background check, for which there is no fee. Quik Payday presented no evidence of other expenses that it would incur. The burden on Quik Payday of obtaining a license would not be materially greater than the burden on *Aldens*. Aldens, Inc. v. Ryan, 571 F.2d 1159 (10th Cir. 1978). And on the other side of the ledger, Defendants point to significant benefits from the licensing requirement: the criminal-background check protects Kansas consumers from providing felons their financial data and access to their bank accounts; and the surety-bond requirement ensures that Kansas residents will have a meaningful remedy if they are harmed by a lender. We follow our decision in *Aldens* in holding that the burden of acquiring a license does not outweigh the benefit from that requirement.

Quik Payday tries to distinguish *Aldens* by suggesting that regulating Internet lending cannot, as a practical matter, protect Kansas residents, because such lenders can go offshore to avoid the reach of the state's law. In support, Quik Payday relies on our opinion in *Johnson*. That case involved constitutional challenges to a New Mexico statute that criminalized "dissemination of material that is harmful to a minor by computer." 194 F.3d at 1152. The challenged statute defined the offense as

> the use of a computer communications system that allows the input, output, examination or transfer of computer data or computer programs from one computer to another, to knowingly and intentionally initiate or engage in communication with a person under eighteen years of age when such communication in whole or in part depicts actual or simulated nudity, sexual intercourse or any other sexual conduct.

N.M. Stat. §30-37-3.2(A) (1998). . . .

Our case is readily distinguishable from *Johnson* in this respect. An offshore lender may well have incentives to comply with Kansas law. *Johnson* did not involve credit transactions. One who sent pornography to New Mexico from Amsterdam needed nothing in the future from the New Mexico resident. Payday lending, however, would not be very profitable if the borrowers refused to repay, or were prevented from repaying, their loans. Regulators can educate borrowers regarding their rights not to repay loans, and they may have authority to control lenders by seizing assets (such as a bank account) from which a lender expects to be repaid. We are not persuaded that Kansas would be powerless to protect its residents from offshore payday lenders who refused to comply with applicable Kansas laws.

Quik Payday also relies on national-uniformity arguments to support its Commerce Clause challenge. It contends that the nature of the Internet requires any regulation of Internet operations to be national in scope, not state-by-state. . . . Quik Payday also quotes our comment in *Johnson* that "[t]he Internet, like rail and highway traffic, requires a cohesive national scheme of regulation so that users are reasonably able to determine their obligations." *Johnson*, 194 F.3d at 1162 (ellipses and internal quotation marks omitted).

But Quik Payday reads too much into these statements. The courts have not held that certain modes of interstate commerce always require uniform regulation. They have examined particular types of regulation and made individual determinations. For example, the Supreme Court has not held that all regulation of interstate railroads must be national in scope. In *Southern Pacific* the Court held that the length of interstate trains could not be regulated state by state, see 325 U.S. at 781-82, but it did not retreat from its prior decisions allowing individual states to impose some safety measures, such as limitations on the size and composition of crews on interstate trains, see id. at 779, 782.

. . .

Thus, we turn to Quik Payday's argument based on the specifics of the KUCCC. It contends that subjecting it to regulation by multiple states will in fact create inconsistency that would unduly burden interstate commerce. Quik Payday's briefs present a compilation of payday-loan laws in various states that, in its view, reveal how unmanageable its business would be if Kansas and other states could each enforce its own rules. Our review of those laws raises doubts about the merits of Quik Payday's argument. But we need not resolve the matter. Quik Payday is not being penalized by Kansas for the way it renews loans, or even for the interest rate it charges. Its misconduct was a simple failure to get a Kansas license. And requiring

se in each state does not impose an undue burden. The Supreme Court
~~d~~ an analogous argument in American Trucking Associations, Inc. v. Mich-
~~blic~~ Service Commission, 545 U.S. 429 (2005). In that case, interstate truck-
~~s~~ challenged Michigan's flat fee on trucks engaged in intrastate hauling (i.e.,
~~-point~~ deliveries within Michigan) under the dormant Commerce Clause.
~~... ...~~ at 431-32. . . . The Supreme Court rejected the challenge on several
grounds, among them that every state could legitimately assess such a fee without
putting interstate commerce at a disadvantage:

> We must concede that here, as [the challengers] argue, if all States did the same, an
> interstate truck would have to pay fees totaling several hundred dollars, or even
> several thousand dollars, were it to "top off" its business by carrying local loads in
> many (or even all) other States. *But it would have to do so only because it engages in
> local business in all those States.*

Id. At 438 (emphasis added). If some future Internet payday lender were to point to
potential inconsistency among the states in some other component of the
KUCCC — say the handling of renewals — then a court could address whether
the Commerce Clause bars this type of regulation. For this case, however, we
need not undertake that task.

III. CONCLUSION

We AFFIRM the judgment of the district court.

How did you like Quik Payday's revenue from lending to Kansans? Based on
the numbers in the opinion, Quick Payday charged fees in an amount equal to
50 percent of the total principal it lent. Put another way, on average, for every
$2 a consumer borrowed from Quick Payday, he or she incurred a $1 fee.

1. *Disclosure Requirements*

The Truth in Lending Act (TILA) applies to payday loans to require the disclosure of the amount financed, the finance charge, and the APR. See Turner v. E-Z
Check Cashing of Cookeville, TN, Inc., 35 F. Supp. 2d 1042, 1047 (M.D. Tenn.
1999) ("Courts that have addressed the issue have held, without exception,
that deferred presentment transactions are extensions of 'credit' under
TILA."). As noted in Assignment 12, however, the fact that a consumer is
given a cost disclosure does not mean that it was used to shop for the lowest
cost credit, or that it was even reviewed or understood. In her study of consumers exiting payday lenders in New Mexico, researchers found that customers selected the lender based on convenient location rather than price. *See*
Nathalie Martin, *1,000% Interest — Good While Supplies Last: A Study of Payday
Loan Practices and Solutions,* 52 Ariz. L. Rev. 563 (2010). Most customers also
were unable to give the APR on their loans, even as they held freshly minted

TILA disclosures in their hands. Another separate concern is that the APR may be an ineffective way to describe the cost of a payday loan. An annual rate may confuse consumers in the context of short-term loans with a maturity of only one or two weeks. A 5 percent interest rate for a loan of a week sounds reasonable but annualized that is a triple-digit rate. Additionally, businesses may be particularly motivated to skirt compliance because the high APR figures would deter consumers or tarnish their reputations. Indeed, it is hard to imagine businesses competing with signs advertising, "Avoid that 300 percent APR; we offer 250 percent. Rush in today for this great offer." APRs may be inapt for loans lasting only a fraction of a year, despite the benefit of standardizing rates.

2. Limits on Interest Rates and Costs

With such high interest rates, usury laws might seem an obvious obstacle to payday lenders. As noted in Assignment 11, a handful of states have repealed their usury laws, while others have set limits on interest rates that are very high. As a result, payday lending continues with little differentiation between states based on usury laws. Many states have carved out exceptions for payday lending in their usury laws, often making rate caps inapplicable to payday loans, which are described in the statutory exceptions by less-recognizable names, such as "cash advance loans" or "presentment transactions." For example, Michigan has a usury law that caps interest at 10 percent but characterizes the charges related to payday loans as "service fees" rather than interest, such that the usury law is inapplicable.

Another strategy to limit the application of usury restrictions is to make only small-dollar loans. Many states have minimum threshold amounts below which the usury law does not apply. The logic here seems to be that even though the interest rate may be high, if the dollar amount of the loan is small, then the financial harm of payday loans is moderated. The payday lenders' trade association has a model bill that includes a provision limiting a loan to $500. Of course lenders themselves may not want to risk more than $500 on any one consumer transaction. That is, this model law may merely parrot the state of the market, in which $500 is already the maximum available payday loan, rather than affirmatively curb the market.

3. Limits on Numbers of Transactions

Although any given payday loan is short-term in nature, the practical reality of this type of borrowing is different. Many consumers seem to routinely renew existing loans, or more commonly, take out new loans that follow immediately upon the expiration of a prior loan. These "rollovers" can create a cycle of debt, with consumers paying fees for each renewal. They never eliminate the underlying debt, which grows with each rollover. The financial effect of rollovers is to dramatically drive up the costs; a consumer might pay $360 to maintain a $100 debt over a period of six months. Every two weeks at payday when the consumer renews the loan, she would pay a $30 fee; none of that amount would reduce the $100 of outstanding debt. On the other hand, in this form of rollover, the debt does not negatively amortize. The consumer will have paid many dollars in fees but even after a dozen rollovers still only has $100 in outstanding principal. This can make payday loans look as safe as a preschool toy compared to the standard credit card that requires only a 3 percent minimum monthly payment and continues to accrue interest at a much higher rate; the result is that the total owed balloons over time.

The problem is partially one of framing. At each transaction, the consumer may focus on the $30 fee, perceiving it as a reasonable charge. But as the example above illustrates, the cost of the loan over time can mushroom well beyond the benefit to the consumer. In dollar terms, a consumer has paid three times the loan amount. Because of these concerns, the majority of states have limits on repeated transactions. These are typically designed in one of two ways. They either limit rollovers of the same loan to a fixed number, or more restrictively, attempt to prohibit any subsequent back-to-back loan.

These laws seem to have limited effect. A study by the FDIC found that about 46 percent of all payday loans are either renewals of existing loans or new loans that immediately follow the payoff of a prior loan. Mark Flannery & Katherine Samolyk, *Payday Lending: Do the Costs Justify the Price?* 1 (2005), *at* http://www.fdic.gov/bank/analytical/cfr/2005/wp2005/CFRWP_2005-09_Flannery_Samolyk.pdf. To get around the latter problem, some states have enacted cooling off periods that must elapse before a consumer can take out a new payday loan. Nearly all of these are much shorter than two weeks, however, meaning that consumers can still have every payday check encumbered by a loan. Consumers themselves may skirt the rollover bans by going from lender to lender. If a roll-over is not available from Payday Store 1, the consumer simply takes out a loan from Payday Store 2, crosses the street and pays off Payday Store 1. There is no financial difference between this strategy and merely rolling over the loan at Payday Store 1. Consumers simply are doing some additional work to manage their loans. Lenders may respond to this flip-flop strategy by flouting the law on rollovers; what business wants to embrace a law that sends its customers to a competitor on a regular basis? The emerging solution that may more effectively regulate rollovers is state-wide databases of all payday loans outstanding at any time. Before a lender can make a loan, the law requires it to check whether the consumer has any existing loan, from any lender, or that the cooling off period has elapsed from a prior loan. Thus far, a small handful of states have such databases, and some consumers cross state lines to evade these "protections."

4. Bans on Payday Lending

In response to the perceived danger of lenders preying on desperate consumers, some states have taken legislative steps to restrict payday lending. Thirteen states have set low interest rate caps on small value loans, limiting the profits a lender can obtain by offering payday loans. North Carolina's Consumer Finance Act illustrates the typical approach:

(a) Maximum Rate of Interest. — Every licensee under this section may make loans in installments not exceeding three thousand dollars ($3,000) in amount, at interest rates not exceeding thirty-six percent (36%) per annum on the outstanding principal balance of any loan not in excess of six hundred dollars ($600.00) and fifteen percent (15%) per annum on any remainder of such unpaid principal balance. Interest shall be contracted for and collected at the single simple interest rate applied to the outstanding balance that would earn the same amount of interest as the above rates for payment according to schedule.

> (a1) Maximum Fee.—In addition to the interest authorized in subsection (a) of this section, a licensee making loans under this section may collect from the borrower a fee for processing the loan equal to five percent (5%) of the loan amount not to exceed twenty-five dollars ($25.00), provided that such charges may not be assessed more than twice in any 12-month period.

N.C. Gen. Stat. §53-173. While this may look like a rate cap, the effect has been to eliminate payday lending. The industry has ceased to do business in these states, asserting that the rate cap prevents them from being profitable.

A few of these thirteen states have gone one step further and have expressly banned the practice of making loans on the basis of post-dated checks. These states include Maine (with an exemption for "supervised lenders"), Massachusetts, New York, New Jersey, and Pennsylvania.

While capping interest rates on small loans and banning payday lending outright has intuitive appeal, some researchers are less optimistic that state regulation of payday loans—even outright bans—can effectively prevent lenders from charging excessive interest fees. Because state statutes usually target loans with certain characteristics (e.g. loans for $3000 or less, issued for a period of 14 to 31 days, using a post-dated check as collateral), payday lenders circumvent the statutory restrictions by tweaking the loan to bring it just outside the scope of the regulation (e.g. by issuing it for 32 days, or not requesting a post-dated check but instead using a bank account withdrawal authorization). New Mexico's attempt to curb payday lending serves as a cautionary tale:

> The New Mexico law, like many other [states] around the country, capped interest rates at a generous 417%, yet payday lenders regarded this as an insufficient return. In order to reclaim the "tremendous profits" to which it had become accustomed, the industry invented new products such as the payday loan without the post-dated check and the installment loan . . . which earn higher lender fees. One conclusion resonates strongly from this game of legislative cat-and-mouse, namely that these types of legislative efforts do not reduce short-term lending, interest rates, or fees for such loans. While the payday lending industry itself claims that payday legislation *can* effectively protect consumers, the industry's actions tell a different story. The new products offered by short-term lenders suggest what the industry denies, namely that the only type of regulation that really ends the abusive practice of charging 500% or more in interest over long periods of time is an absolute interest rate cap. Any other solution is subject to further end runs.

Martin, *1000% Interest*, at 23. Martin's proposal for a federal usury law is explicitly barred by the Dodd-Frank Act. It would take Congressional action to reverse that position and that seems very unlikely. A bill in the House, H.R. 1214, the Payday Loan Reform Act of 2009, did not include a usury cap, focusing instead on expanding TILA disclosures for payday loans. Even that bill died in committee. Advocates objected it was too weak, and the industry was not going to lobby for more paperwork.

States have continued to actively regulate payday loans, however, and much of the advocacy is at state capitols. The laws change frequently, and some states have bills introduced by consumer advocates and by industry nearly every legislative session. The takeaway is that payday loans are likely to be the subject of lively debate and state lawmaking in future years. This is all on top of the CFPB's movement toward regulation of small-dollar loans that was described earlier in the assignment. The most certain thing that can be said about payday loans is that the legal landscape is certain to change.

C.   Policy Debates on Payday Lending

The policy debate about payday and other fringe credit is fierce. Part of that is typical industry versus advocate but there are a number of points of empirical disagreements that impede consensus. This section looks at three of the most contentious issues. While these issues apply to all credit, the payday loan context deepens the disagreement.

1.   Product Substitution

A ban on payday loans does not, of course, provide extra income to families who run short on cash or guard against unexpected expenses exploding the family's budget. If payday loans are not available, what will consumers do?

A frequent point offered in defense of payday loans is that they are better for consumers than the alternative options. Lenders or staunch critics of regulation often suggest that but for payday loans, families would be borrowing from unsavory loan sharks who may have criminal ties—or more obliquely put, an interesting relationship with the law. Consumer advocates respond that such characterizations are a matter of perspective. They may see storefront payday lenders themselves as unsavory establishments whose practices routinely flaunt the law. Not surprisingly, few people list "loan sharks" as their occupation on tax returns or Census forms, making it impossible to even guess at the availability of such lenders to the families who currently use payday loans. In her study of the credit practices of low-income women in Boston, Professor Angela Littwin found that credit cards, a type of borrowing strongly associated with mainstream or middle-class credit, were viewed more negatively than fringe alternatives like pawn shops. *See* Angela K. Littwin, *Testing the Substitution Hypothesis: Would Credit Card Regulations Force Low-Income Borrowers into Less Desirable Lending Alternatives*, 2009 ILL. L. REV. 403, 442 (2009). Because her study was in a state that prohibited payday loans (Massachusetts), we do not know how payday lenders would fare in such comparisons. More of this kind of research may produce data to help untangle the product substitution issue.

Another product substitute for payday loans is bounced checks. These also are expensive and poorly understood by consumers, the very same criticisms that are made of payday loans. The policy goal is not just to switch consumers to another product but to move them to a better product. One possible strategy is enlisting credit unions and other financial institutions serving low-income consumers (such as community development financial institutions) to offer lower-cost alternatives to payday loans. This is a market-driven solution that rests upon consumers becoming aware of these alternatives and choosing them, despite perhaps their requiring more paperwork or travel to a less convenient location.

Reduced availability of payday loans could also lead to deprivation for financially-strapped consumers. The alternative to payday loans may be doing without. Whether this is a serious policy problem depends to a large degree on what people do with the proceeds of payday loans. If people use payday loans to obtain medical care or to repair cars that are needed to travel to jobs, the elimination of such loans could worsen the situations of consumers. One study found that consumers used them primarily to meet regular, recurring expenses — or to pay off other payday loans. Emergency purposes were less common. *See* Martin, *1,000% Interest*, 52 Ariz. L. Rev. 563 (2010). One's perspective on the "necessity" of payday loans to help families in tough situations also may depend on the perceived availability and adequacy of the social safety net, including access to free health care, subsidized housing, food stamps, and other types of benefits to prevent severe hardships.

2. Relationship of Payday Lending to Financial Distress

People who take out payday loans are in worse financial condition than the typical American, with lower incomes and net worths. The research suggests a correlation between payday borrowing and debt problems. A study found that "relative to all U.S. adults, three times the percentage of payday loan customers are seriously debt burdened and have been denied credit or not given as much credit as they applied for in the last 5 years." Michael A. Stegman, *Payday Lending*, 21 J. Econ. Perspectives 169, 173 (2007). The same study found that "[p]ayday loan customers are also four times more likely than all adults to have filed for bankruptcy." Id.

These are correlations, however, and do not necessarily show causation. On that question, academic researchers disagree. An examination of states banning payday lending found that consumers in those locations experience a higher rate of chapter 7 bankruptcy filings, bounce more checks, and file more complaints with the Federal Trade Commission against lenders and debt collectors. *See* Donald P. Morgan & Michael Strain, *Payday Holiday: How Households Fare After Payday Credit Bans* 26, (Fed. Reserve Bank of N.Y. Working Paper, Paper No. 309, 2008), *available at* http://newyorkfed.org/research/staff_reports/sr309.pdf. Researchers have asserted a causal link between payday loans and bankruptcy, finding that "for first-time payday applicants near the 20th percentile of the credit-score distribution, access to payday loans causes chapter 13 bankruptcy filings over the next two years to double." *See* Paige M. Skiba & Jeremy Tobacman, *Do Payday Loans Cause Bankruptcy?*

1 (2009), *available at* http://papers. ssrn.com/sol3/papers.cfm?abstract_id=
1266215.

On the other hand, payday loans may decrease the incidence of bankruptcy
by providing desperate debtors with a final source of funds after they have
exhausted their alternative resources. A study has failed to find evidence
that the availability of payday lending increases the rate of bankruptcy.
See Petru S. Stoianovici & Michael T. Maloney, *Restrictions on Credit: A Public
Policy Analysis of Payday Lending* 1 (2008), *available at* http://ssrn.com/
abstract=1291278 (concluding, based on their study of state data collected
between 1990 and 2006, that there is no empirical evidence to support the
proposition that payday lending leads to more bankruptcy filings). These
conflicting findings could be partially explained by differences in methodology between the various studies. The studies finding no causation between
payday loans and bankruptcy tend to focus on state-level trends (e.g. contrast-
ing the total number of bankruptcies filed in states with and without payday
lenders), while the studies that support a connection usually rely on a case-by-
case analysis of individual bankruptcy debtors in a particular jurisdiction and
their shared characteristics. Given the present state of research, those opposing
or supporting payday loans can find studies to support their views.

3. *Regulatory Arbitrage*

The lack of federal regulation and the wide variation in state approaches has
led to a situation of regulatory arbitrage for lenders. The most egregious situation was pejoratively called "rent-a-charter," in which payday lenders part-
nered with national banks to avoid state usury laws by taking advantage of the
preemption standards applicable to federal banks. Regulators shut this practice
down by 2006, however, and it seems very unlikely to spring back up with the
CFPB responsible for examining national banks for consumer law compliance
and able to pressure banks' prudential regulators.

Online payday lenders present even greater regulatory challenges. It is difficult to learn much about these providers, including their states of incorpo-
ration or whether banks are involved in providing financing. As Professors Jim
Hawkins and Ronald Mann note, "the only information of significance about
the lawfulness of the transactions is an assertion that the transactions are governed by the law of the lender's location." Ronald J. Mann & Jim Hawkins, *Just
Until Payday*, 54 UCLA L. Rev. 855, 870 (2007). The FTC and several states have
targeted online payday lenders with enforcement actions but the low costs of
setting up such a business make it relatively easy for new providers to spring up
in the wake of shuttered sites. As commerce becomes more global, off-shore
payday loans may increase, adding to enforcement difficulties.

Problem Set 17

17.1. Alba Gonzales enters Money Madness, a payday lender operating in
Salinas, California to obtain a $300 loan. She needs to get an infected tooth
removed, and her dentist requires cash payment at the time of the procedure.

Money Madness tells her that the fee for such a loan will be $45, plus a $5 registration and background check fee. Money Madness gives Alba a written contract that states this is a deferred deposit transaction and lays out these costs. She also receives a Truth in Lending disclosure that shows an APR of 260 percent. Alba writes a check to Money Madness to cover the cost of the transaction; the check is dated 20 days from today's date on her next payday. You are an attorney with the California Department of Business Oversight who is reviewing this transaction as part of the licensing renewal of Money Madness. Did either Alba or Money Madness violate the law? *See* California Civil Code §§1789.30-1789.38.

17.2. Staid Bank is a nationally-chartered depository bank. It has branches in three New England states but is headquartered in the community of Thayer, Massachusetts, a seaside hamlet. Thayer is an old-fashioned company town; over 80 percent of the adult population works for the "Factory," a manufacturer of paperclips. The company has tried to treat its employees well, but the reduction in paper caused by email and increased competition from binder clips have eroded profits. Today, the average worker gets a take-home paycheck of $2,000 every month, an amount that is lower in real dollars than workers at the factory earned thirty years ago. As a result of the low wages and rising costs for essentials such as gas and health care, many of Staid Banks' customers struggle to save money. They lack a cushion against unexpected expenses, a problem the bank has noticed as it tracked a sharp uptick in overdrafts on accounts in recent years.

To address this problem, Staid Bank is offering a new product called Tomorrow Now. Account holders who are employed at the factory and have their paychecks directly deposited can contact Staid Bank by phone and obtain an instant line of credit up to $1,000. When the factory deposits the customer's next paycheck, Staid Bank will repay itself by deducting the loan balance, plus a fee of $19 for every $100 of the loan used by the customer. You are the new risk and compliance officer for Staid Bank. Assuming all disclosures are properly designed and delivered, does Tomorrow Now violate any federal or state consumer law that is applicable to Staid Bank? Does it pose any other risks that to Staid Bank's general business approach? *See* Regulation E, 12 C.F.R. §1005.10; Mass. Gen. Laws ch. 140, §96; and Office of the Comptroller of Currency, Guidance on Supervisory Concerns and Expectations Regarding Deposit Advance Products.

17.3. You are Vice President for Strategic Operations for Fun Funds, a large national payday lending operation. You are increasingly worried that the CFPB will take action to make payday loans unprofitable and you continue to be distressed at the inability to operate in all fifty states because some states such as New York have laws that limit interest rates on payday loans below profitability. You were recently approached by Rosanna Ayer, the chief of a federally recognized tribe of Native Americans. The Tribe would like to buy Fun Funds to take advantage of its technology infrastructure, customer service staff, and brand recognition. The proposed sale agreement that you are reviewing makes clear that all employees — including senior staff such as yourself — get guaranteed employment contracts after the sale. It also contains a clause that allows the deal to be unwound within the first five years after the sale date if the Tribe becomes "subject to any payday lending laws that are not currently

Assignment 18. Student Loans

You may be wondering why there is a chapter on student loans when it seems your legal education is a three-year study of the topic. For many currently in college, federal and private student loans may seem to be the norm. However, prior to World War II, American students typically received financial aid directly from the colleges. National Consumer Law Center, *Student Loan Law* 3 (2015). Congress has enacted and phased out several laws in the last fifty years that collectively have significantly increased the degree to which higher education is a debt-driven experience. Adjusting for inflation, the average cost of tuition and fees for a public four-year college have increased 225 percent since the 1984-1985 academic year. For the private four-year college, the average has increased 146 percent. Student loans are the second largest component of consumer debt, surpassed only by mortgages. The volume of outstanding federal student loan debt has gone from $516 billion in 2007 to greater than $1.2 trillion in the third quarter of 2015. *Id.* at 8. While this is a huge figure, student loans are unlikely to be the source of systemic risk that mortgages were in 2007. Jonathan Glater, *Student Debt and the Siren Song of Systemic Risk* (Oct. 15, 2015), http://papers.ssrn.com/sol3/papers.cfm?abstract_id=2674718. Student loans have peculiar qualities compared to most consumer debt, in part because they are an investment in education, which should be an appreciating asset. (Compare to the depreciation on a new car when you drive it off the lot. One hopes your mind continues to grow during higher education.)

Over 41 million Americans have student debt, and most of these consumers are in the early or middle years of their careers. Americans under age 39 are responsible for 65 percent of outstanding student loans. Consumer Financial Protection Bureau, *Student loan servicing: Analysis of Public Input and Recommendations for Reform* 3 (2015), http://files.consumerfinance.gov/f/201509_cfpb_student-loan-servicing-report.pdf. On some level, the policy crisis is about public investment in higher education and changing labor demographics, not borrowing. Although the Bureau of Labor Statistics found in 2012 that only 27 percent of jobs require an associate degree or higher, employers increasingly seek college graduates for positions that traditionally did not require one. Patricia Cohen, *For-Profit Colleges Accused of Fraud Still Receive U.S. Funds,* N.Y. Times, Oct. 12, 2015, http://www.nytimes.com/2015/10/13/business/for-profit-colleges-accused-of-fraud-still-receive-us-funds.html?_r=0. With tuition on the rise and their parents facing the financial consequences of the economic recession that began in 2008, students are increasingly relying on student loans to finance their educations and their futures.

This assignment is organized along the central divide between public and private student loans. The two types of credit differ in their costs, risks, and use, and, of course, are the subject of different laws and regulatory actors.

A.   Federal Student Loans

Compared side-by-side, federal student loans are hands-down the better financial decision than private loans. Federals loans do not look at the student's creditworthiness but instead have eligibility requirements that apply to all borrowers. The rate and other terms also are favorable to the borrower as a matter of higher-education policy. With private loans, the lender underwrites the loan to reflect the perceived risk from an individual's credit history. For both students and parents, the terms of the loan and most importantly the interest rate are determined by creditworthiness. The worse an individual's credit, the less favorable the terms of the loan. For students with poor credit or students whose parents have poor credit, private loans are either not an option or an exorbitantly expensive option.

1.   Types of Federal Student Assistance

Federal student loans can be subsidized or unsubsidized. With a subsidized loan, the student, the borrower, is not charged any interest before the repayment period begins on the loan, or during deferment. For unsubsidized loans, interest is charged from the time the loan is disbursed and continues until it is paid in full. Subsidized federal student loans are awarded based upon the student's financial need, whereas unsubsidized loans are not.

Ignoring federal loans made before 1994 and the designated-for-extinction Perkins Loan Program, there are two main types of federal student loans: Stafford and PLUS. These loans are available through the Direct Loan Program, which means the government itself makes the loan without an intermediary funder. Prior to 2010, some Stafford or PLUS loans made may be a Federal Family Education Loan (FFEL) and not a Direct Loan. FFEL loans differ in repayment options, but are otherwise identical in loan limits, deferment, and cancellation provisions.

Stafford loans can be subsidized or unsubsidized, and are available to both undergraduate and graduate students. The annual borrowing limits are determined by the Department of Education and, as of July 1, 2012, graduate and professional students are not eligible for subsidized loans. PLUS loans offer higher loan limits and are available to a larger slice of the population. A parent or legal guardian wishing to borrow for a dependent undergraduate student who is enrolled in school at least part time can take out a PLUS loan to fund the child's education. Graduate students and professional students are also eligible for PLUS loans, although annual limits cap the maximum loan amount.

Both Stafford and PLUS loans can be consolidated. A student can consolidate some or all of his loans without limit to the size of the consolidated loan. But there are limitations on consolidation, including the ability to 'reconsolidate' — consolidating a loan that has previously been consolidated. The benefits of consolidation are procedural and substantive. Consolidation means one monthly payment, which eases the administrative burden on the student. Consolidation also reduces the interest rate. This does not necessarily save the student money, however, because consolidation may extend the term of some loans such that with the added years of interest the total amount repaid is more than it would have been without consolidation. Also, consolidation of federal loans together with private loans results in the loss of many of the options and protections federal loans provide.

In addition to federal student loans, a student can apply for a federal grant. The Federal Pell Grant Program provides grants to low-income students. The grant amount varies based upon the amount the student's family can contribute, the cost of attendance, whether the student is full-time or part-time, and the length of the student's attendance. Unlike student loans, grants are not repaid. They are essentially need-based scholarships from the public. There are a number of federal grant programs, in addition to the Pell grant, including "specialty grants" with study and work requirements. An example is the TEACH grant that requires the borrower to agree to teach full-time in a high-need subject in a school that serves low-income students.

2. Loan Limits, Interest Rates, Fees, and Disclosures

Under the Higher Education Act the federal government limits the amounts that students can borrow in federal loans. These limits vary depending on the type of the loan. For Stafford loans, the limits are different for students who are classified as dependent versus those who are independent. 34 C.F.R. §685.203. The Higher Education Act also sets the interest rates for federal student loans. Before July 1, 2006, loans could have variable rates with an upper limit of 8.25 percent. Most federal student loan rates are now fixed under the Bipartisan Student Loan Certainty Act of 2013, which uses a formula to determine the interest rate. But once determined, the rate is fixed for the life of the loan. Unlike mortgages, borrowers cannot refinance their loans if the market interest rates fall. The Higher Education Act preempts usury laws, with the exception of the Servicemember Civil Relief Act.

In other assignments we have discussed origination fees, late charges, and prepayment penalties. These are important aspects of determining the cost of a loan. As of July 1, 2010 (when the government became the direct lender), federal student loans no longer have origination fees. If all or a portion of the monthly loan payment is not paid, a late charge of up to six cents for each dollar that is late may be charged. Although these late fees are in the loan contracts, the servicing contracts, as of 2014, state that these fees should not be assessed "at this time." The servicing contracts are instructions from the lender, the federal government, to the private companies about how to interact with borrowers. Prepayment penalties are not allowed. These consumer-friendly terms are a major advantage of federal loans over private student loans as you will see when we discuss private student loans below.

In one consumer protection aspect, student loans are arguably less protective than other products. Federal student loans are exempt from TILA and state disclosure laws.[1] Instead, federal student loans are governed by the Higher Education Act. 20 U.S.C. §1001 et seq. Disclosures must be provided in "simple and understandable terms, in a statement provided to the borrower at or prior to the beginning of the repayment period," with additional disclosures made at least 30 days, but not more than 150 days before the first payment is due. 34 C.F.R. §682.205. This differs from TILA, which requires disclosure before credit is extended.

The initial disclosure must include:

(i) The lender's name, a toll-free telephone number accessible from within the United States that the borrower can use to obtain additional loan information, and the address to which correspondence with the lender and payments should be sent;

(ii) The scheduled date the repayment period is to begin, or a deferment under §682.210(v), if applicable, is to end;

(iii) The estimated balance, including the estimated amount of interest to be capitalized, owed by the borrower as of the date upon which the repayment period is to begin, a deferment under §682.210(v), if applicable, is to end, or the date of the disclosure, whichever is later;

(iv) The actual interest rate on the loan;

(v) An explanation of any fees that may accrue or be charged to the borrower during the repayment period;

(vi) The borrower's repayment schedule, including the due date of the first installment and the number, amount, and frequency of payments based on the repayment schedule selected by the borrower;

(vii) Except in the case of a Consolidation loan, an explanation of any special options the borrower may have for consolidating or refinancing the loan and of the availability and terms of such other options;

(viii) The estimated total amount of interest to be paid on the loan, assuming that payments are made in accordance with the repayment schedule, and if interest has been paid, the amount of interest paid;

(ix) A statement that the borrower has the right to prepay all or part of the loan at any time, without penalty;

(x) Information on any special loan repayment benefits offered on the loan, including benefits that are contingent on repayment behavior, and any other special loan repayment benefits for which the borrower may be eligible that would reduce the amount or length of repayment; and at the request of the borrower, an explanation of the effect of a reduced interest rate on the borrower's total payoff amount and time for repayment;

(xi) If the lender provides a repayment benefit, any limitations on that benefit, any circumstances in which the borrower could lose that benefit, and whether and how the borrower may regain eligibility for the repayment benefit;

---

1. One caveat is that loans made under the Health Education Assistance Loan program are subject to TILA. These loans are for medical school.

(xii) A description of all the repayment plans available to the borrower and a statement that the borrower may change plans during the repayment period at least annually;

(xiii) A description of the options available to the borrower to avoid or be removed from default, as well as any fees associated with those options; and

(xiv) Any additional resources, including nonprofit organizations, advocates and counselors, including the Department of Education's Student Loan Ombudsman, the lender is aware of where the borrower may obtain additional advice and assistance on loan repayment.

34 C.F.R. §682.205 (a)(2). Compare these disclosure requirements to those required by TILA (see Assignment 12). Do they strike you as more or less consumer friendly?

Once the loan enters repayment, additional disclosures are required, and if the student is struggling to make repayments, there are specific disclosures required based upon the difficulty. 34 C.F.R. §682.205(c). For example, for a student who is 60 days delinquent in making a payment, a disclosure describing the options available to avoid default must be sent within 5 days of the date the student becomes 60 days delinquent. 34 C.F.R. §682.205(c)5.

3. Postponing Repayment

You've finished up school, you're looking for a job in a highly competitive market, and you have thousands, if not tens or hundreds of thousands, of dollars of student loan debt. The first bit of good news in this scenario is what is called a "grace period." For Stafford loans, the borrower has six months to begin repayment either 1) after graduation, 2) after a student leaves school, or 3) after the student is less than part-time enrolled in school. 34 C.F.R. §§682.207, 685.209. Remember, however, that with unsubsidized loans, however, remember that interest has been accruing since the loan was disbursed and continues to accrue during this grace period.

The law explicitly contemplates that borrowers will not even be able to make their first payments. (This might tip you off to why student loans present serious consumer protection concerns.) Depending on the type and size of the loan, deferment is available as an option to avoid default. For subsidized loans, the deferment delays not only payment of the loan but also accrual of interest. For unsubsidized loans, the borrower is still liable for the interest during the deferment period, and the lender may capitalize it after the deferment period ends. Capitalization means adding the accrued interest to the loan balance and recalculating the payments to reflect the higher amount due. When a borrower seeks deferment, the lender must notify the borrower of the option to pay the accruing interest or cancel the deferment and make loan payments.

Once a borrower is in default, deferment is not an option. But if you aren't yet in default, how do you defer repayment of your student loans? It is done by requesting deferment and providing documentation. Eligibility and qualification requirements vary based upon the type of deferment sought. Unemployment, military service, economic hardship, and in some cases continued education and graduate fellowships are all circumstances that may qualify a borrower for deferment.

Forbearance is when a loan holder agrees to a temporary hold on payments, an extension of time for making payments, or an acceptance of smaller payments. This is normally either a last resort before default, or a way of hopefully giving the defaulted borrower a little breathing room, after which hopefully payment will resume. When the borrower is already in default, the loan holder has the discretion to stop collection actions. Although a useful tool for some borrowers needing short-term relief, the interest in both federal and private loans continues to accrue, and may be capitalized, with forbearance. Again, capitalized means that the outstanding balance can grow during forbearance leading to further financial problems down the road.

4. Servicing

"Servicers manage borrowers' accounts, process monthly payments, and communicate directly with borrowers." Consumer Financial Protection Bureau, *Student loan servicing: Analysis of public input and recommendations for reform* at 11. Essentially, "[a] loan servicer . . . handles the day-to-day management of loans." William J. Cox, *The Student Borrower: Slave to the Servicer?* 27 Loy. Consumer L. Rev. 189 at 191 (2015). The servicer is not necessarily the lender. "[T]he federal government originates all federal loans while contracting out servicing work to the largest student loan servicers." *Id.* Further, the company acting as the servicer, for both federal and private student loans, can change. This is something the borrower has little to no control over.

The Department of Education and the Consumer Financial Protection Bureau (CFPB) regulate the federal student loan servicers. The Department of Education has oversight due to the contracts between the federal government and the servicers. The CFPB has oversight authority under the Dodd-Frank Act. 12 U.S.C. §5514. Despite the regulatory framework in place for federal student loans, "there is no existing, comprehensive federal statutory or regulatory framework providing consistent standards for the servicing of all student loans." Consumer Financial Protection Bureau, *Student Loan Servicing: Analysis of Public Input and Recommendations for Reform* at 11.

In 2015 the CFPB and the Department of Education launched a public inquiry into student loan servicing practices, and received more than 30,000 comments. *See generally* Consumer Financial Protection Bureau, *Student Loan Servicing: Analysis of Public Input and Recommendations for Reform.* The CFPB issued a report describing existing servicing practices and how they affect repayment, while also considering how protections, such as those in place for consumers with mortgages and credit cards, could be used in the student loan market. *Id.* The report found significant problems in servicing stemming from a lack of consistency, clarity and oversight. Id.

Consumers complained to the CFPB about difficulties in receiving objective counseling about options, getting basic account information, consolidating loans, and even just ensuring payments were applied to their loans. Unlike credit cards and mortgages, there are few laws protecting borrowers from servicer misconduct. The Higher Education Act requires due diligence in servicing a loan, but speaks to FFEL loans and not to Direct Loans. 34 C.F.R. §682.208. This section includes notice requirements for when a loan is assigned or transferred to another servicer. 34 C.F.R. §682.208(e). These regulations do not necessarily apply to Direct Loans. The Direct Loan program has benefits for consumers, but it is a no-man's land for servicing protections.

Even things as basic as access to original loan document or a payment history are left to the whims of servicers. For medical records and consumer lending, there are record retention laws. No federal regulations exist regarding record retention for student loans servicers following a servicing transfer. Even the accuracy of the information provided to the borrower by the servicer is unregulated. Consumer Financial Protection Bureau, *Student Loan Servicing: Analysis of Public Input and Recommendations for Reform* at 64.

If a borrower fails to make a payment when it is due, and fails to make these payments or to meet other terms of the federal loan agreement for 270 days, the borrower is in default. 34 C.F.R. §685.102(b). During this roughly nine-month period, the borrower should be working with the servicer to avoid default.

5. *Repayment Programs*

With federal student loans, a student has many repayment options. Unless a student chooses another option, the student will be automatically enrolled in the standard repayment plan. Certain consolidated loans aside, standard repayment plans have the highest monthly payments. Those payments are usually the same amount each month, with some variety if there is a variable interest rate. Under the standard repayment plan, the borrower has ten years to repay the loan.

Graduated repayment plans start out at a low monthly payment and increase over the life of the repayment period. Graduated repayment plans still have a repayment period of ten years. The rationale with graduated repayment is that the borrower will see a marked increase in earnings within a few years. Extended repayment plans are available for those with outstanding principal and interest over $30,000. The extended repayment plan allows repayment over a longer period of time, not more than 25 years. Typically the monthly payments in an extended repayment plan are less than the standard plan, but the borrower pays much more in interest over the life of the loan.

Income-based repayment (IBR), income-contingent repayment (ICR), pay as you earn (PAYE), and income-sensitive repayment (ISR)[2] are four types of repayment plans tied to the borrower's income. These repayment plans calculate the monthly payment using the borrower's income but they differ in the formula used to determine the payment. Monthly payment amounts are governed by statute. These plans generally require a minimum monthly payment that is a percentage of the borrower's discretionary income. "Discretionary income" is the amount the borrower's adjusted gross income exceeds the

---

2. An ISR plan applies only to FFEL loans.

poverty guidelines about in the borrower's state of residence. U.S. Department of Education, Federal Student Aid Glossary, https://studentaid.ed.gov/sa/glossary#Discretionary_Income. Like with other repayment options with lower monthly payments, income-based repayment plans take longer to payoff and may cost the borrower more in interest. These options are designed to prevent default, but the percentage of borrowers taking advantage of these repayment plans remained low through 2013, with only 6 percent of federal borrowers enrolled in an IBR plan. David Leonhardt, *A Quiet Revolution in Helping Lift the Burden of Student Debt,* The N.Y. Times (Jan. 24, 2015), http://nyti.ms/1uHSdtB. By the end of 2014, 11.8 percent of federal borrowers were enrolled in an IBR, indicating a growing awareness by borrowers of the options available. *Id.*

These repayment options have existed in some form since the 1990s, when borrowers had the option to enroll in a repayment plan limiting the month payments to 20 percent of the borrower's income. After 25 years, the remaining balance of the loan was forgiven. In recent years, the repayment plans have been revamped to allow for even lower monthly payments, capping at 15 percent beginning in 2007, and 10 percent beginning in 2016. The law governing federal loan forgiveness has changed as well and is discussed later in this assignment.

Borrowers are not always aware of the changes in the federal student loan law and are often unaware of their options. Lack of oversight and transparency in student loan servicing coupled with uninformed borrowers has created an opportunity for some third-party "debt relief" companies to profit off of struggling borrowers. These companies offer to enroll the borrower in income-based repayment plans and other free federal programs for a high one-time upfront charge, or monthly payments. Consumer Financial Protection Bureau, *Student Loan Servicing: Analysis of Public Input and Recommendations for Reform* at 99. The CFPB has taken steps to end these scams, largely by raising awareness that they are scams and by attempting to educate borrowers of their repayment options. *Id.* at 100.

B.   Private Student Loans

For the student needing to borrow more than the federal loan limits, there are private student loans. For private loans, the student can go directly to a bank and avoid involving the school in the process as the recipient of funds. For federal loans, schools are required to provide counseling to students. For private loans, a student usually only needs to involve their schools to verify enrollment.

Generally private student loans are subject to even less oversight than their federal cousins, and thus less consumer protection. The CFPB does have some authority over private student loans. The Higher Education Act (HEA) does not apply to private student loans. This is both good and bad news. HEA protections such as the grace period are not available. But state laws are no longer specifically preempted, and borrowers can find protections and remedies under TILA.

1. *Disclosures*

TILA defines "private education loans" as a loan provided by a private education lender that is not made, insured or guaranteed under title IV of the Higher Education Act, and is issued expressly for postsecondary educational expenses. *See* 15 U.S.C. §1650(a)(7). TILA requires special disclosures for private student loans. *See* 15 U.S.C. §1638(e). The Higher Education Opportunity Act of 2008 also includes disclosure requirements for private student loans. 12 C.F.R. §§1026.5-1026.9. Additionally, some states have enacted their own requirements.

TILA requires different disclosures at the following stages of the loan process: application and solicitation; loan approval; and final disclosure before disbursement of funds. With each disclosure, the lender must provide information about federal student financial assistance, including the interest rates available on federal loans. The idea here is to encourage students to exhaust federal borrowing before private borrowing by revealing the fact that the federal rates are lower. The lender must also notify the borrower of the right to accept the terms of the loan within 30 days of the offer, and that during this time the rates and terms of the loan cannot be changed. 15 U.S.C. §1638(e)(1)(O).

2. *Repayment*

The multitude of repayment options available for federal student loans has no parallel with private student loans. Borrowers are left to negotiate with the bank — or more likely their loan servicers — if they find themselves in financial trouble. Despite the lack of federal law requiring private student loan creditors to offer deferments or forbearances, many lenders previously provided in-school deferment of payments. National Consumer Law Center, *Paying the Price: The High Cost of Student Loans and the Dangers for Student Borrowers* (Mar. 2008), available at www.studentloanborrowerassistance.org. Of course, during many of these "deferments," interest was accruing. *Id.* Since the financial crisis in 2008, the availability of forbearance has been restricted. Fitch Ratings, *Private Education Loans: Time for a Re-Education* 6 (Jan. 28, 2009). Some lenders allow for cancellation of the loans in the event of the borrower's death, or permanent and total disability, but generally this is done on a case-by-case basis requiring documentation. A loan modification or restructured payment plan is typically only an option if the borrower is in default and after extensive process.

C. Default and Collections

The definition of default varies depending on the type of student loan. For federal student loans under the FFEL or Direct loan programs, default occurs if the borrower fails to make required payments for 270 days for loans for monthly installment loans, or 330 days for loans on a less-than monthly repayment schedule. 34 C.F.R. §§682.2000, 685.102(b). In private student loans, default is defined by the loan contract. That nearly always means a shorter period. Typically private student loans are in default when the borrower fails to make a payment for 120 days, or 3 months. Consumer Financial Protection Bureau, *What does it mean to "default" on my private student loans?* (July 4, 2012), http://www.consumerfinance.gov/askcfpb/ 665/what-does-it-mean-default-my-private-student-loans.html. The entire balance of the private student loan becomes due in full, immediately, upon default.

The ramifications of default vary depending on if you have a federal or private student loan. For all the protections a federal student loan affords the borrower before default, the federal government's power to collect once the borrower is in default is far greater than a private lender's. After 2008 the default rate on student loans has increased. This increase has been more significant in the private sector, largely because of the lack of options available to struggling borrowers. In recent years, as the economy has recovered, the default rates have stabilized. The default rate for federal student loans dropped from 14.7 percent for students entering repayment in the 2010 fiscal year to 13.7 percent for the 2011 fiscal year. U.S. Department of Education, *New Data Shows a Lower Percentage of Students Defaulting on Federal Student Loans* (Sept. 24, 2014), http://www.ed.gov/news/ press-releases/new-data-shows-lower-percentage-students-defaulting-federal-student-loans.

There are many reasons borrowers default on their student loans. There is a dearth of research attempting to predict which borrowers are more likely to default. There is a correlation between students completing their education and earning a degree, and paying back their loans. "A study of student loan debtors who entered repayment in 2005 found that 33 percent of those who did not earn a credential became delinquent and another 26 percent defaulted." Katherine Porter, *Broke* 95 (2012) (citing Alisa F. Cunningham and Gregory S. Kienzl, *Delinquency: The Untold Story of Student Loan Borrowing.* Washington, DC). In fact, this seems so obvious it hardly seems worth noting. But determining the risk that a borrower will fail to graduate, as well as determining the default risk of those who do graduate, is complicated.

The federal government has far-reaching avenues for collecting on a defaulted student loan. The Department of Treasury states that it uses demand letters, telephone calls, wage garnishment and the Treasury Offset Program (to retain your tax refund for example) before resorting to private collection agencies. U.S. Dept. of the Treasury, *Private Collection Agencies: Debt Collection Contract*, available at fmsq.treas.gov/debt/pca.html. Private student loan creditors generally rely upon third-party debt collectors. If unable to collect through a debt collector, private student or federal creditors can sue the borrower to obtain a judgment. In both federal and private student loans, the creditor can seek to recover reasonable fees associated with the collection process. These fees should be related to the actual expenses incurred for collection. *See Bottoni v. Sallie Mae, Inc.*, 2011 WL 635272 (N.D. Cal. Feb 11, 1011) (denying summary judgment because there was a genuine dispute about whether Sallie

Mae would add 25 percent of the outstanding principal and interest, regardless of the actual collection cost incurred, to the loan balance before sending the loans to a third-party debt collector.)

In the following case, a creditor attempted to assess collection costs against a borrower who had previously defaulted on her loan, but then entered into a repayment agreement, which the borrower satisfied. The court also discusses a recurring claim by creditors that the HEA preempts state laws that give rise to private causes of action such as breach of contract.

Bible v. United Student Aid Funds, Inc.

799 F.3d 633 (7th Cir. 2015)

HAMILTON, Circuit Judge.

Plaintiff Bryana Bible obtained a student loan under the Federal Family Education Loan Program. She defaulted in 2012 but promptly agreed to enter into a rehabilitation agreement that required her to make a series of reduced monthly payments. She timely made all of the payments that were required of her under this agreement, and she remains current on her loan payments. Although Bible complied with her obligations under the repayment agreement, a guaranty agency assessed over $4,500 in collection costs against her. [ED. NOTE — A guaranty agency repays the loan if the borrower does not, but in return has the rights under the loan to recover from the borrower.]

The terms of Bible's loan were governed by a form document known as a Federal Stafford Loan Master Promissory Note (MPN). This form has been approved by the U.S. Department of Education and is used in connection with many student loans across the country. The MPN incorporates the Higher Education Act and its associated regulations. In pertinent part, the MPN provides that Bible must pay "reasonable collection fees and costs, plus court costs and attorney fees" if she defaults on her loan. As we will see, "reasonable collection fees and costs" are defined by regulations issued by the Secretary of Education under the authority expressly conferred by the Higher Education Act. The MPN provided that Bible would owe only those collection costs that are permitted by the Higher Education Act and its regulations.

Bible sued the guaranty agency (defendant United Student Aid Funds, Inc.) alleging breach of contract and a violation of the Racketeer Influenced and Corrupt Organizations Act (RICO), 18 U.S.C. §1961 et seq. Her breach of contract theory is that the MPN incorporated federal regulations that prohibit the guaranty agency from assessing collection costs against her because she timely entered into an alternative repayment agreement and complied with that agreement. Her RICO claim alleges that the guaranty agency, in association with a debt collector and a loan service provider, committed mail fraud in violation of 18 U.S.C. §1341 and wire fraud in violation of 18 U.S.C. §1343 when it assessed collection costs of more than $4,500 against her despite its representations that her "current collection cost balance" and "current other charges" were zero and that these costs would be "reduced" once she completed the rehabilitation process.

The district court granted the guaranty agency's motion to dismiss [on the grounds] that both claims were "preempted" by the Higher Education Act. It reasoned that both claims depend on alleged violations of the Act and should not be permitted because the Act does not provide a private right of action. The district court held in the alternative that the amended complaint failed to state a claim that is plausible on its face. It concluded that the breach of contract claim failed because both the MPN and the Higher Education Act expressly permit imposing collection costs against borrowers who default on their loans. The district court also concluded that the RICO claim failed because Bible's amended complaint "has not shown participation in a scheme to defraud; commission of an act with intent to defraud; or the use of mails or interstate wires in furtherance of a fraudulent scheme." Bible v. United Student Aid Funds, Inc., No. 1:13-CV-00575-TWP-TAB, 2014 U.S. Dist. LEXIS 33320, 2014 WL 1048807, at *10 (S.D. Ind. Mar. 14, 2014).

We reverse. Neither of Bible's claims is preempted by the Higher Education Act. Bible's state law breach of contract claim is not preempted because it does not conflict with federal law. The contract at issue simply incorporates applicable federal regulations as the standard for compliance. Accordingly, the duty imposed by the state law is precisely congruent with the federal requirements. A state law claim that does not seek to vary the requirements of federal law does not conflict with federal law.

We apply the Secretary of the Education's interpretation of the applicable statutes and regulations, which is consistent with Bible's. (The Secretary accepted our invitation to file an *amicus* brief addressing the question.) The Secretary interprets the regulations to provide that a guaranty agency may not impose collection costs on a borrower who is in default for the first time but who has timely entered into and complied with an alternative repayment agreement. Nor is Bible's RICO claim preempted. RICO is a federal statute and thus is not preempted by another federal statute, and we see no conflict between RICO and the Higher Education Act. On the merits, both the breach of contract and RICO claims satisfy the plausibility standard under Rule 12(b)(6).

. . .

A. The Higher Education Act and Regulatory Background

Congress enacted the Higher Education Act of 1965 (HEA or the Act), now codified as amended at 20 U.S.C. §1001 et seq., "to keep the college door open to all students of ability, regardless of socioeconomic background." Rowe v. Educational Credit Management Corp., 559 F.3d 1028, 1030 (9th Cir. 2009); see also 20 U.S.C. §1070(a) (identifying purpose of the statute). Among other things, the Act created the Federal Family Education Loan Program (FFELP), "a system of loan guarantees meant to encourage lenders to loan money to students and their parents on favorable terms." Chae v. SLM Corp., 593 F.3d 936, 938-39 (9th Cir. 2010). The Secretary of Education administers the FFELP and has issued regulations to carry out the program.

. . .

In 1986 Congress amended the HEA to require guaranty agencies to assess collection costs against borrowers to prevent these costs from being passed on to federal taxpayers. See Black v. Educational Credit Mgmt. Corp., 459 F.3d 796, 799 (7th Cir. 2006). The relevant statutory provision provides simply that "a borrower who has defaulted on a loan . . . shall be required to pay . . . reasonable collection costs." 20 U.S.C. §1091a(b)(1). Congress chose not to define the meaning of "reasonable collection costs" in the statute and instead "left it up to the Secretary [of Education] to interpret that term through regulations." Black, 459 F.3d at 799; 20 U.S.C. §1082(a)(1) (delegating authority to the Secretary of Education to "prescribe such regulations as may be necessary to carry out the purposes" of FFELP).

The regulations define "reasonable collection costs." Two regulations are central to this lawsuit. We describe these regulations in detail below, and we ultimately agree with the interpretation of the Secretary of Education, which is consistent with Bible's. In short, 34 C.F.R. §682.405 provides that guaranty agencies must create loan rehabilitation programs for all borrowers who have enforceable promissory notes, and 34 C.F.R. §682.410 establishes fiscal, administrative, and enforcement requirements that a guaranty agency must satisfy to participate in the FFELP. One requirement is that a guaranty agency must give a borrower who has defaulted notice and the opportunity to enter into a repayment agreement before it assesses collection costs or reports the default to a consumer reporting agency. 34 C.F.R. §682.410(b)(5)(ii)(D). The guaranty agency is not permitted to charge collection costs to the borrower if (1) this is the first time the borrower has defaulted, (2) she enters into a repayment agreement within 60 days of receiving notice that the guaranty agency has paid the default claim, and (3) she complies with that agreement. Imposing collection costs on a borrower under these circumstances would be "unreasonable" within the meaning of 20 U.S.C. §1091a(b)(1).

B. Bible's Loan, Default, and Decision to Enter into the Rehabilitation Agreement

In June 2006, Bible obtained a student loan. The written agreement governing her loan is the Federal Stafford Loan Master Promissory Note (MPN), which identifies Citibank as the "Lender" and defendant United Student Aid Funds (USA Funds) as the "Guarantor, Program, or Lender." . . .

The contract term covering "late charges and collection costs" states:

> The lender may collect from me: (i) a late charge for each late installment payment if I fail to make any part of a required installment payment within 15 days after it becomes due, and (ii) any other charges and fees *that are permitted by the Act for the collection of my loans*. If I default on any loans, I will pay reasonable collection fees and costs, plus court costs and attorney fees.

The "governing law and notices" term provides: "The terms of this MPN will be interpreted in accordance with the applicable federal statutes and regulations, and the guarantor's policies. Applicable state law, except as preempted by federal law, may provide for certain borrower rights, remedies, and defenses in addition to those stated in this MPN."

In 2012, Citibank determined that Bible was in default and transferred the debt to USA Funds, which paid Citibank's default claim. To comply with its obligations under the HEA and its associated regulations, USA Funds, through its agent General Revenue Corp. (GRC), mailed Bible a form letter dated April 12, 2012 saying that her loan was in default and identifying several options for resolving her debt, including the opportunity for loan rehabilitation. . . . The letter noted that Bible's current total amount due was $18,062.60.

Between April 12 and April 25, Bible and her attorney spoke to GRC on the phone three times to negotiate a loan rehabilitation agreement. Bible and GRC agreed on a rehabilitation plan requiring monthly payments of $50. On April 27, GRC faxed Bible a form rehabilitation agreement. Bible promptly signed the agreement and returned it by fax on April 30, 2012.

The rehabilitation agreement included [a] table. . . .

The agreement also said that Bible's current total amount due was $18,112.85. Accumulating interest accounted for the $50.25 increase in Bible's total balance. The figures for her "current collection cost balance" and "current other charges" remained at all times $0.

Five paragraphs above the signature line, toward the end of the rehabilitation agreement, the following language appears:

> Once rehabilitation is complete, collection costs that have been added will be reduced to 18.5% of the unpaid principal and accrued interest outstanding at the time of Loan Rehabilitation. Collection costs may be capitalized at the time of the Loan Rehabilitation by your new lender, along with outstanding accrued interest, to form one new principal amount.

The paragraph immediately above the signature line states: "By signing below, I understand and agree that the lender may capitalize collection costs of 18.5% of the outstanding principal and accrued interest upon rehabilitation of my loan(s)."

After signing the rehabilitation agreement, Bible made nine on-time payments of $50. Although she fully complied with her obligations under this agreement, USA Funds assessed collection costs against her in the amount of $4,547.44. It applied her monthly payments toward the collection costs rather than the principal. When Bible filed this lawsuit, she had not completed the rehabilitation process. (Her loan had not yet been sold to an eligible lender.) She remains current on her loan under the terms of the rehabilitation agreement.

. . .

II. ANALYSIS

We conclude that (A) Bible has stated a viable breach of contract claim under Indiana law; (B) federal law does not preclude Bible from pursuing this state-law claim; and (C) Bible has stated a viable RICO claim under federal law, though it remains to be seen whether she can support that claim with evidence of fraudulent intent.

A. Breach of Contract Claim

"Under Indiana law, the elements of a breach of contract action are the existence of a contract, the defendant's breach thereof, and damages." U.S. Valves, Inc. v. Dray, 190 F.3d 811, 814 (7th Cir. 1999). The parties agree that the MPN is a valid contract and that it governs the terms of Bible's loan, including the consequences of her default. They disagree, however, about whether the amended complaint has adequately pled a breach of the MPN and resulting damages.

1. Breach

a. Incorporation by Reference

Bible alleges that USA Funds breached the MPN by assessing collection costs even though she timely entered into a repayment agreement and complied with her obligations under that agreement. She argues that the MPN incorporated federal regulations that prohibit guaranty agencies from imposing collection costs against first-time defaulters who promptly agree to repay their loans within 60 days of receiving notice from the guaranty agency that it has paid the lender's default claim and who have complied with that agreement. She relies on 34 C.F.R. §§682.405 and 682.410 and language in the MPN to the effect that the guaranty agency can collect from the borrower only "charges and fees that are permitted by the Act."

We agree with Bible that the MPN incorporated the HEA and its associated regulations. "Other writings, or matters contained therein, which are referred to in a written contract may be regarded as incorporated by the reference as a part of the contract and, therefore, may properly be considered in the construction of the contract." I.C.C. Protective Coatings, Inc. v. A.E. Staley Mfg. Co., 695 N.E.2d 1030, 1036 (Ind. App. 1998). The page of the contract that sets out the terms of the loan refers to the HEA and its regulations no fewer than 16 times, though once would be enough. [T]he specific term covering "late charges and collection costs" states that "[t]he lender may collect from me . . . any other charges and fees that are permitted by the Act." And the contract defines "the Act" as the HEA "and applicable U.S. Department of Education regulations."

USA Funds relies on a sentence in the MPN granting it the right to impose "reasonable collection fees and costs, plus court costs and attorney fees." USA Funds reads this language in isolation to mean that it can impose collection costs at any time after the borrower has defaulted. This interpretation fails to give weight to the preceding sentence, which limits the lender's power to impose only those charges and fees "that are permitted by the Act." Basic principles of contract law require a court to consider a contract's provisions together and in a way that harmonizes them. E.g., Hinc v. Lime-O-Sol Co., 382 F.3d 716, 720 (7th Cir. 2004) (Indiana law). If USA Funds charged Bible collection costs in violation of the HEA and its regulations, then it breached the contract.

b. Requirements for Imposing Collection Costs

Bible has plausibly alleged a breach of the MPN by alleging that USA Funds assessed collection costs that were not authorized by the Higher Education Act and its regulations. This conclusion is supported by two independent grounds. . . .

i. The Statutory and Regulatory Requirements

Beginning with interpretation without deference to the agency, Bible acknowledges that guaranty agencies are required to impose collection costs on borrowers who have defaulted in certain circumstances. Both the HEA itself and the implementing regulations make this clear. See 20 U.S.C. §1091a(b)(1) ("[A] borrower who has defaulted on a loan . . . shall be required to pay . . . reasonable collection costs."); id. §1078-6(a)(1)(D)(i)(II)(aa) (upon successful rehabilitation, a guaranty agency may, in order to defray collection costs, "charge to the borrower an amount not to exceed 18.5 percent of the outstanding principal and interest at the time of the loan sale"); 34 C.F.R. §682.410(b)(2) ("[T]he guaranty agency shall charge a borrower an amount equal to reasonable costs incurred by the agency in collecting a loan."). Bible argues, however, that the regulations prohibit USA Funds from imposing collection costs in her circumstances: a first-time defaulter who she promptly agreed to enter into a rehabilitation agreement within 60 days of receiving notice that USA Funds had paid her lender's default claim, and who has complied with that agreement. She contends that imposing collection costs in these circumstances is "unreasonable" under 20 U.S.C. §1091a(b)(1).

Two key regulations define the phrase "reasonable collection costs" in §1091a(b)(1). The first regulation, 34 C.F.R. §682.405, requires guaranty agencies to create loan rehabilitation programs for all borrowers that have enforceable promissory notes. These programs are designed to give eligible borrowers an opportunity to rehabilitate defaulted loans so that, upon successful rehabilitation, the loans may be purchased by eligible lenders and removed from default status. 34 C.F.R. §682.405(a).

A loan is considered rehabilitated only after two requirements are met: (1) the borrower has timely made nine out of ten payments required under a monthly repayment agreement, and (2) the loan has been sold to an eligible lender. 34 C.F.R. §682.405(a)(2)(i)-(ii). Subsection (b) of this regulation then establishes specific requirements for terms that must be included in the rehabilitation agreement. For example, the guaranty agency must provide the borrower with a written statement confirming the borrower's "reasonable and affordable payment amount" and "inform[ing] the borrower of the amount of the collection costs to be added to the unpaid principal at the time of the sale." 34 C.F.R. §682.405(b)(1)(vi).

The second regulation, 34 C.F.R. §682.410, is even more specific. It establishes fiscal, administrative, and enforcement requirements that a guaranty agency must satisfy to participate in the FFELP. Paragraph (b)(2) addresses collection costs:

> Collection charges. Whether or not provided for in the borrower's promissory note and subject to any limitation on the amount of those costs in that note, the guaranty agency shall charge a borrower an amount equal to reasonable costs incurred by the agency in collecting a loan on which the agency has paid a default or bankruptcy claim. These costs may include, but are not limited to, all attorney's fees, collection agency charges, and court costs. [Subject to certain exceptions not relevant here], the amount charged a borrower must equal the lesser of—
>   (i) The amount the same borrower would be charged for the cost of collection under the formula in 34 C.F.R. [§]30.60; or
>   (ii) The amount the same borrower would be charged for the cost of collection if the loan was held by the U.S. Department of Education.

34 C.F.R. §682.410(b)(2). This paragraph makes clear that guaranty agencies must charge a borrower reasonable collection costs, and it establishes a cap on the

maximum *amount* that can be charged by the guaranty agency. Paragraph (b)(2), however, does not specify the *circumstances* under which these costs may be assessed. That issue is addressed by other portions of §682.410, which create procedural safeguards for student borrowers.

First, some context. Guaranty agencies have two primary ways of pushing student-borrowers to repay their defaulted loans: (1) reporting the delinquent account to a consumer reporting agency (which lowers the borrower's credit rating) and (2) assessing collection costs against the borrower. Because the Department of Education was concerned about recent graduates facing these adverse consequences without first being given an opportunity to cure their defaults, it created protections in §682.410(b)(5)(ii). . . .

Subparagraph (b)(5)(ii) effectively creates a safe harbor for borrowers who find themselves in default for the first time. When a borrower is first notified that a guaranty agency has paid a default claim on her loan, she has a 60-day window to request administrative review of the debt or to enter into a repayment agreement with the agency. If she does not take either action, the guaranty agency can then take collection actions against her, report her default to a consumer reporting agency, and assess collection costs against her in the amount specified by §682.410(b)(2).

To be sure, subparagraph (b)(5)(iv)(B) mentions the opportunity to request administrative review of the loan obligation, not the opportunity to enter into a repayment agreement with the agency. But that is not a problem for Bible. Her point is that subparagraph (b)(5)(ii) requires the guaranty agency to provide the borrower with all four things before reporting the debt to a consumer reporting agency or assessing collection costs, and one of those things (administrative review) triggers a waiting period of at least 60 days. The regulations do not force the borrower to choose between requesting administrative review and entering into a repayment program. The borrower has a right to request administrative review and then to decide whether to enter into a repayment agreement. Accordingly, the borrower has at least 60 days to enter into an alternative repayment agreement. That Bible did not request administrative review of her loan obligation in this case is beside the point; she had at least 60 days to do so, and before that time ran out, she entered into the rehabilitation agreement.

This understanding is confirmed by §682.410(b)(6)(ii), which requires the guaranty agency to inform the borrower "that if he or she does not make repayment arrangements acceptable to the agency, the agency will promptly initiate procedures to collect the debt," such as garnishing her wages, filing a civil suit, or taking her income tax refunds. 34 C.F.R. §682.410(b)(6)(ii). What would be the point of warning the borrower that declining to make repayment arrangements would trigger costly debt collection activities if the guaranty agency could initiate these procedures and assess those costs regardless of whether she agrees to repay?

That the regulations create this sort of safe harbor is not surprising. Under USA Funds' interpretation of the regulations, a guaranty agency could assess collection costs against a borrower even though it was *never* forced to "initiate procedures to collect the debt." This would allow the guaranty agency to charge for costly actions that it might never need to take, such as wage garnishment or filing a civil suit. This case illustrates the point. USA Funds assessed over $4,500 in collection costs even though it merely sent one letter, sent and received one fax, spoke to Bible and her attorney on the phone several times, and cashed Bible's monthly checks.

The safe harbor of subparagraph (b)(5)(ii) also creates an incentive for first-time defaulters to rehabilitate their loans by voluntary repayment. If first-time defaulters knew that they would face collection costs regardless of whether they agree to repay, they would have less incentive to enter into the repayment program voluntarily. These regulations are designed to reward cooperation.

. . .

Subparagraph (b)(5)(ii) discusses credit reporting and the assessment of collection costs in the exact same way: "but before it reports the default to a consumer reporting agency or assesses collection costs against a borrower. . . ." USA Funds has given us no persuasive reason to treat one of the stated adverse consequences of default (a bad credit report) differently from the other (collection costs). Yet that is precisely what its interpretation of the statutory framework and related regulations would do.

This conclusion is based on the text of the applicable statutory provisions, regulations, and the MPN itself. USA Funds does not squarely address the textual basis of Bible's claim but responds with three arguments. First, it argues that §682.410(b)(2) allows it to impose collection costs, and the regulations do not explicitly prohibit the imposition of collection costs against a borrower who has defaulted but promptly entered into a repayment agreement. This argument is not persuasive. Paragraph (b)(2) merely establishes the background rule that the guaranty agency must assess "reasonable collection costs" against the borrower and establishes the cap on the maximum amount of costs that can be charged. It does not say anything about the circumstances under which these costs can be imposed. As explained, other parts of the regulation such as subparagraph (b)(5)(ii) impose more specific requirements about the circumstances in which collection costs may be assessed.

Second, USA Funds contends that Bible's interpretation of §682.410(b)(5)(ii)(D) ignores the fact that the repayment agreement must be "on terms satisfactory to the agency." It appears to argue that under this language the guaranty agency retains the discretion to assess collection costs whenever it wants. But this interpretation is inconsistent with the introductory paragraph of the regulation, which makes clear that the agency must provide the borrower an opportunity to enter into a repayment agreement *before* collection costs are assessed. Guaranty agencies do not have unfettered discretion to impose whatever collection costs they want, whenever they want, as the argument suggests.

Contrary to USA Funds' arguments, Bible's interpretation still gives meaning to the phrase "on terms satisfactory to the agency." Under her theory, USA Funds retained the discretion to set the terms of the repayment agreement. After all, it transmitted the form document to Bible that became the rehabilitation agreement. It could have insisted on higher monthly payments, for example. USA Funds had the power to set the initial terms of its offer and to reject any proposed counteroffer. It did not have the power, though, to impose collection costs in contravention of §682.410(b)(5)(ii).

Third, USA Funds points to another provision in the MPN: "If I default, the guarantor may purchase my loans and capitalize all then-outstanding interest into a new principal balance, and collection fees will become immediately due and payable." This provision, however, does not displace the guaranty agency's obligations under

34 C.F.R. §682.410. The collection fees become "immediately due and payable" only after the guaranty agency has first provided the borrower with (1) written notice that meets the requirements spelled out in subparagraph (b)(5)(vi), (2) an opportunity to inspect and copy agency records pertaining to the loan obligation, (3) an opportunity for administrative review of the enforceability or past-due status of the loan obligation, and (4) an opportunity to enter into a repayment agreement. See 34 C.F.R. §682.410(b)(5)(ii)(A)-(D). Interpreting the provision as USA Funds suggests would contradict §682.410(b)(5)(ii). Recall, moreover, that USA Funds had told Bible that she owed zero collection costs when she first defaulted. It was not until after she signed the rehabilitation agreement that she finally learned about the costs.

ii. Deference to the Secretary of Education's Interpretation

Even if the preceding analysis does not provide the best interpretation of the statutory framework and accompanying regulations . . . the same result would still be correct based on the deference we owe to the Secretary of Education, who is tasked with administering the FFELP and issuing the implementing regulations.

. . .

The Secretary's interpretation of "reasonable collection costs" in 20 U.S.C. §1091a(b)(1) is reasonable. The Secretary interprets "reasonable" to mean that similar costs must be assessed against borrowers who are at similar stages of delinquency. Under the Secretary's view, a borrower who promptly enters into a voluntary repayment agreement and complies with that agreement, thereby obviating the need for the guarantor to initiate costly debt collection procedures, is not similarly situated to someone who does not, thereby forcing the guarantor to undertake costly debt collection procedures. . . .

To summarize, Bible has alleged sufficiently that USA Funds breached its contract with her by assessing over $4,500 in collections costs after she timely entered into and complied with a monthly repayment agreement, in violation of the applicable regulations that were incorporated into the parties' contract.

2. Damages

We next address whether Bible has adequately pled damages. USA Funds argues she has not because she defaulted on her loan and continues to owe money on that obligation. This argument is meritless. Of course Bible continues to owe money under her loan obligation. That does not mean she has not been damaged by USA Funds' imposing over $4,500 in unauthorized collection costs. These costs represent new charges that have been added to her accrued interest and principal, thereby increasing the total amount she owes on her account. Because these charges were not permitted by her contract, she has plausibly alleged damages, even if the remedy might take the form of a credit to her account rather than cash in her pocket. Bible has plausibly alleged a viable breach of contract claim under state law.

B. Preemption & the "Disguised Claim" Theory

We next examine whether federal law preempts or otherwise displaces Bible's state law claim. "Preemption can take on three different forms: express preemption, field preemption, and conflict preemption." Aux Sable Liquid Products v. Murphy, 526 F.3d 1028, 1033 (7th Cir. 2008). USA Funds relies on conflict preemption. It also argues that the breach of contract claim is nothing more than a "disguised claim" for a violation of the Higher Education Act and is thus "preempted" by the HEA. Neither theory has merit. Federal law does not preempt or otherwise displace Bible's breach of contract claim.

1. Conflict Preemption

Conflict preemption can occur in two situations: (1) when "it is impossible for a private party to comply with both state and federal requirements," or (2) when "state law stands as an obstacle to the accomplishment and execution of the full purposes and objectives of Congress." Freightliner Corp. v. Myrick, 514 U.S. 280, 287 (1995) (citations and internal quotation marks omitted). USA Funds does not contend that it would be impossible, without violating federal law, for it to comply with the state law duty Bible's suit seeks to impose. Instead, it invokes the second species of conflict preemption known as "obstacle" preemption. USA Funds argues that entertaining Bible's breach of contract claim would frustrate Congress's goal of "uniformity" because it would require many state and federal courts to interpret HEA regulations in potentially inconsistent ways. We reject this contention.

. . .

The real question is whether entertaining Bible's breach of contract claim actually conflicts with the HEA and its associated regulations. It does not. We begin with Wigod v. Wells Fargo Bank, N.A., 673 F.3d 547 (7th Cir. 2012), where we dealt with a nearly identical issue in the context of the federal Home Affordable Mortgage Program (HAMP). In Wigod, the plaintiff brought state law claims against her mortgage service provider, including a breach of contract claim alleging that the defendant breached a written agreement that incorporated the HAMP requirements. Like USA Funds in this case, the defendant in Wigod argued that the state law claims were preempted by the federal guidelines under principles of conflict preemption. We rejected the argument. 673 F.3d at 577-81.

Although Wigod dealt with a different regulatory framework, its reasoning applies directly here. Bible's claim is that USA Funds breached the MPN by acting contrary to the federal regulations incorporated into the contract. Just as in Wigod, "the state-law duty allegedly breached is imported from and delimited by federal standards." Wigod, 673 F.3d at 579. In this situation, federal law simply provides the standard of compliance, and the parties' duties are actually enforced under state law. See id. at 579-80. There is no conflict.

The Fourth Circuit reached the same conclusion regarding the HEA in College Loan Corp. v. SLM Corp., 396 F.3d 588 (4th Cir. 2005). In that case, the plaintiff sued Sallie Mae and its affiliates under state law, alleging that they had a contract that incorporated the requirements of the HEA and its regulations. The district court held that the state law claims were preempted. The Fourth Circuit reversed. The court held that the plaintiff's state law claims were not preempted even though they relied on establishing a violation of the HEA and its regulations:

> This point is particularly obvious in relation to [plaintiff's] contract claim. As parties to the Agreement, [the parties] voluntarily included federal standards (the HEA) in their bargained-for private contractual arrangement. Both *expressly agreed* to comply with the HEA. In that context, [defendants'] argument that enforcement of the Agreement's terms is preempted by the HEA boils down to a contention that it was free to enter into a contract that invoked a federal standard as the indicator of compliance, then to proceed to breach its duties thereunder and to shield its breach by pleading preemption. In this case at least, federal supremacy does not mandate such a result.

Id. at 598 (citations omitted). The Fourth Circuit's reasoning applies with equal force here.

Unable to distinguish *Wigod* or *College Loan Corp.* in meaningful ways, USA Funds seeks help from *Chae v. SLM Corp.*, 593 F.3d 936 (9th Cir. 2010). But *Chae* actually reinforces our conclusion. There, borrowers sued Sallie Mae under state law for its handling of their student loans. Applying principles of conflict preemption, the Ninth Circuit held that the claims were preempted by the HEA because "[p]ermitting varying state law challenges across the country, with state law standards that may differ and impede uniformity" would pose an obstacle to Congress's purpose in creating the FFELP. *Chae*, 593 F.3d at 945. The Ninth Circuit, however, carefully distinguished *College Loan Corp.* on grounds directly applicable here, saying that the plaintiff in *College Loan Corp.* had "sought to enforce FFELP rules, not to vary them." Id. at 946, citing 396 F.3d at 591-94. In *Chae*, though, the plaintiffs were "not seek[ing] to buttress the FFELP framework, but rather to alter it in their home state." Id. They were asking the court to impose a higher standard of compliance than was required by federal law. Such claims are preempted, held *Chae*, but that reasoning does not apply here.

Like the plaintiff in *College Loan Corp.* and unlike those in *Chae*, Bible is not attempting to require more of the defendant than was already required by the HEA and its regulations. She seeks only to enforce the federal standards that the parties agreed to in their contract. This case is therefore not different from *Wigod*, where we held that state law claims attempting to enforce the requirements of the HAMP guidelines were not preempted by federal law. In *Wigod*, *College Loan Corp.*, and now this case, the plaintiffs' state law claims were complementary to, not in conflict with, the federal requirements. Bible's claim is not preempted by federal law.

2. The "Disguised Claim" Theory

In addition to its formal preemption argument, USA Funds argues that Bible's state law claim is "preempted" because it is nothing more than a "disguised claim" for a violation of the HEA, and the HEA does not provide a private right of action. We considered and rejected this same theory in *Wigod*. There the defendant-lender referred to it as an "end-run" theory rather than a "disguised claim" theory. The difference is merely semantic. The defense theory in both cases is that the lack of a private right of action under a regulatory statute necessarily preempts or otherwise displaces a state law cause of action that makes the violation of that regulatory statute an element of the claim. This theory is mistaken at its core: "The absence of a private right of action from a federal statute provides no reason to dismiss a claim under a state law just because it refers to or incorporates some element of the federal law. To find otherwise would require adopting the novel presumption that where Congress provides no remedy under federal law, state law may not afford one in its stead." Wigod, 673 F.3d at 581.

. . .

We reiterate the lesson from *Wigod*. The absence of a private right of action under federal law provides no reason to dismiss a state law claim just because the claim refers to or incorporates some element of the federal law. Congress's decision not to supply a remedy under federal law does not necessarily mean that it also intended to displace state law remedies. The lack of a private right of action under the HEA itself does not preclude Bible's breach of contract claim.

. . .

CONCLUSION

Neither of Bible's claims is preempted or otherwise displaced by federal law, and she has plausibly alleged all of the elements of both claims. The judgment of the district court is REVERSED and the case is REMANDED for further proceedings.

D.   Discharging Student Loans

1.   Statutory Discharge

Absent from the following discussion of statutory discharge is private student loan debt. As you will see, statutory discharge is only available for federal student loans. The HEA allows for discharge, or cancellation, of a federal student loan in six instances, three of these are school related discharges. 34 C.F.R. §§682.402, 674.33(g), 684.214. The other three relate to the borrower and can be sought if the borrower dies, suffers a permanent and total disability, or if the borrower's profession — teaching, or military or public service — qualifies the borrower for discharge. Obtaining statutory discharge under the HEA can be a lengthy and complicated process, sometimes with unforeseen drawbacks. For instance, under the Public Service Loan Forgiveness Program, it is possible for a person to have a significant portion of their debt discharged, but when the debt is discharged, it can be taxed as income. For a public servant earning $38,000 a year, having $100,000 of student loan debt forgiven could result in ten or twenty thousand dollars of taxes.

The Public Service Loan Forgiveness Program only applies to Direct Loan borrowers. *See* 34 C.F.R. §682.219. To qualify, borrowers must not be in default and must have made 120 monthly payments on their loans after October 1, 2007. 34 C.F.R. §682.219(c). Public service employment that qualifies for this program includes a federal, state, local, or tribal government organization, agency or entity, certain non-profit organizations, a tribal college or university, or certain private organizations providing specific public services. 34 C.F.R. §682.219(b).

When a school closes, falsifies the certification of the borrower's eligibility, or fails to pay a refund owed to a student, then the borrower can seek to have the debt discharged under the HEA. 34 C.F.R. §§682.402, 684.33(g), 684.214. These statutory remedies do not apply equally to all loans. In the case of Direct Consolidated loans, relief is more complicated, as discharge may apply to part but not all of the loan. The school closure discharge is not as straightforward as it may seem. Discharge is available only if the borrower was unable to "complete the program of study for which the loan was intended because the school . . . closed, or the borrower withdrew from the school not more than 90 days prior to the date the school closed." 34 C.F.R. §682.402(d). If the *program* closes, but the school continues to provide other educational instruction, then the school has not "closed" and this provision does not apply. *Id.*

A borrower can seek discharge if the school: 1) falsified the certification of the borrower's eligibility for a FFEL Program with regard to the ability of the borrower to benefit from the schools' training and the student did not meet the statutory requirements; 2) signed the borrower's name without authorization on the loan application or promissory note; or 3) certified the borrower's eligibility for a FFEL program loan as a result of identity theft, in some situations. 34 C.F.R. §682.402(e). When a school, opened or closed, fails to pay a borrower an owed refund, the borrower can seek discharge, although the process to apply for discharge differs depending on whether the school is currently open or closed. *See* 34 C.F.R. §682.402(l).

All of these statutory discharge options require the borrower to apply and supply various types of documentation. As with any application, there is a chance of denial. If the application for discharge was dismissed for lack of evidence, and there is new evidence available, the borrower can resubmit an application with the new documentation. In some cases, the applicant can, or must, seek administrative review of the denial before seeking judicial review of the decision.

2. Bankruptcy

Bankruptcy is an important consumer remedy and is covered in Assignment 22 The treatment of student loan debt in bankruptcy, however, is quite unusual compared to most consumer debts. Bankruptcy law imposes a general rule that student loans are nondischargeable. 11 U.S.C. §523(a)(8). The rule applies equally to public and private student loans. A consumer in bankruptcy can ask the court to discharge student loans, which has the effect of permanently barring the creditor or servicer from making any collection efforts or even inquiring about voluntary payment. To get this relief, the consumer must litigate to prove that the repayment of the student loans would impose an "undue hardship" on the debtor or dependents. 11 U.S.C. §523(a)(8). While undue hardship is an undefined standard in the statutes, and courts give it varying interpretations, the consensus is that it is a high standard. Many courts require that a consumer show that she has made good faith efforts to repay the loans, that the debtor cannot maintain a "minimal" standard of living, and that the debtor's financial situation is likely to persist for a significant portion of the repayment period. *Brunner v. New York State Higher Education Services Corp.,* 831 F.2d 395 (2d Cir. 1987). As much as consumers have difficulty winning a discharge, the bigger effect of the standard may be to discourage bankruptcy as an option to address unmanageable student loans. Jason Iuliano, *An Empirical Assessment of Student Loan Discharges and the Bankruptcy Undue Hardship Standard,* 86 AM. BANKR. L.J. 495 (2012) (finding that 39 percent of student loan borrowers were, in fact, successful in receiving a full or partial discharge of student loans). The limitations on bankruptcy relief have increased the need for effective non-bankruptcy remedies for student loan debt.

E.   For-Profit Schools

1.   Scholarship Scams and Diploma Mills

The College Scholarship Fraud Prevention Act is aimed at creating national awareness by requiring an informational website. 20 U.S.C. §1092d. The law targets the scholarship scams in which companies take advanced payment from a student, or their families, in exchange for finding a scholarship or grant with private companies. Another problem facing consumers are unaccredited schools offering specialty degrees or certificates with little or no education or training. These businesses are called "diploma mills," a pejorative that now is incorporated into federal law. 20 U.S.C. §1003(7). Some students are directed to diploma mills by for-profit schools if they lack a high school diploma. The diploma mills will generate a "high school diploma" after the student takes an online test, all for a fee of course. Often these diplomas are invalid. These services tend to prey upon non-English speaking students or immigrants, who might not know that the diploma is invalid.

2.   Government Discharge and Reimbursement Programs for School Misconduct

As discussed above, borrowers can seek statutory discharge of their student loan debt for school-related problems. When statutory discharge is not available, a borrower may find relief from state tuition recovery funds that may reimburse a defrauded borrower. These programs, and their requirements and regulations, vary by state. Some states also have bond programs, but both may be used to reimburse a defrauded borrower. While California is a notable example of a state tuition recovery fund. If a borrower would be entitled to reimbursement under the fund, the borrower also likely would be entitled to a statutory discharge.

3. Legal Claims

For-profit schools have been cropping up in the news as the Department of Education, the CFPB, and state attorneys general crack down fraudulent schools receiving federal funding. To receive federal funds, for-profit schools must be approved or licensed by the state where they operate. Each state has its own regulatory framework for the oversight of private higher education institutions, so borrowers victimized by a fraudulent or bad-acting institution may have state law remedies. The federal government has the ability to pull the purse-strings of many for-profit schools through regulation by refusing to extend federal aid to its enrollees, but for the borrower who is the victim of school fraud, that step offers no debt relief. The HEA sets out standards, violations of these standards, and misrepresentation, are not grounds for private right of action.

Borrowers wishing to challenge a school generally must proceed under a state unfair and deceptive acts and practices law (UDAP), or a Fair Debt Collection Practice Act violation. (The latter is the subject of Assignment 23.) There are a handful of other laws that can support a UDAP claim or provide an avenue for relief. The Federal Trade Commission has guidelines concerning the representations made by private vocational and distance education schools. 16 C.F.R. §254.0-254.7. A violation of these guidelines may strengthen a borrower's UDAP claim or be a per se violation as defined in a state's UDAP law. The Racketeer Influenced and Corrupt Organization Act (RICO) is another option for recovering damages in a private action against a school. A RICO claim may be particularly useful because of the amount of damages the borrower can recover. For a more thorough discussion of RICO, see the omitted sections of the *Bible* case. As occurred in *Bible,* borrowers often are confronted with the federal preemption argument from lenders. The HEA does explicitly preempt some state laws, such as usury laws, statutes of limitation, and disclosure requirements, to name a few. Most courts have ruled that these specific preemptions do not support a determination that the HEA preempts *all* state laws.

State common law contract and tort claims, such as misrepresentation, breach of contract or fraud, also may be valid courses of action against schools that engage in misconduct. But even if the borrower prevails in a lawsuit against a private educational institution that does not necessarily mean the borrower will then be "made whole" by having the debt erased or paid. This suit could yield money damages that are less than the debt. Therefore finding a claim that supports punitive damages is vital to pay off the debt.

A borrower also can file a private suit against a school under the False Claims Act (FCA) in the name of the United States if the school made false or fraudulent claims to the federal government in receiving federal aid. Typically FCA cases assert theories of promissory fraud or false certification of various regulatory requirements that are prerequisites for funneling federal loans to students.

Problem Set 18

18.1. Four years ago your cousin Bobby Copper received a glossy course catalogue from Premier Protection College, a for-profit school touting a three-year program preparing its elite students for careers in law enforcement, including jobs as police officers, sheriffs, correction officer and FBI agents. On the third page of the mailer were statistics about Premier Protection College's alumni. Bobby was excited to see that 90 percent of alumni found work in criminal justice jobs within one year of graduation. The college boasted that its career development team had connections in the FBI, the CIA, and several top-notch private security firms.

Premier Protection College's three-year degree program came with the hefty price tag of $75,000, but Bobby was able to take out a subsidized federal loan as well as a private loan from Western Coach Bank. Since graduating from Premier Protection College, Bobby hasn't been able to secure a job beyond working part-time as a security guard in a local mall. His current job barely pays his rent, let alone his multiple student loan payments.

A few nights ago, while sitting in the security office located near the bathrooms in the basement, Bobby received an email from a fellow alumni complaining about the job placement rates for Premier Protection College. According to an article attached the email, only 4 percent of Premier Protection College graduates are employed as sworn law enforcement officers or correctional officers. In fact, the most common job for Premier Protection College grads are retail store guards like Bobby's. In the wake of this bad publicity, enrollment has plummeted. Now it seems Premier Protection College may file for bankruptcy. The article states that the school received over $100 million in federal aid in the last school year.

Bobby calls you up, livid. He's heard that the government is cracking down on for-profit schools under a new rule requiring school graduates to achieve "gainful employment." He knows you have your own student loan worries as a law student, but wants to know if there is any way out of his debts using this "gainful employment rule." *See* 34 C.F.R. §§668.401-.403.

18.2. After law school, you accept a position working for the California Office of the Attorney General. A few weeks into your new job, you go out at lunch with some co-workers, including your legal assistant Darren. Come to find out, Darren went to law school in Louisiana seven years ago before chasing his aspiring actress girlfriend — you've already heard all about her toothpaste commercial — to California. Although Darren had intended to take the bar exam years ago, he finds working for the Attorney General less stressful than a corporate gig and it lets him catch the surf before sundown.

While discussing the outrageous living expenses in Los Angeles, Darren tells you that he plans to work a few more years for the AG and then use the Public Service Loan Forgiveness Program to wipe out his significant student loan debt. Darren explains he borrowed as much as he possibly could during law school and currently has three different loans with names he can't remember.

Something about FFEL, another is Direct something, and then a 'regular old' loan from his bank. Once he doesn't have student loan debt hanging over his head, he plans to start saving some money and stop living paycheck to paycheck. As you walk back to work, Darren asks you what you think of his plan. *See* 20 U.S.C. §1087(e)(m); 34 C.F.R. §685.219.

18.3. National United Bank has decided to expand its lending to include student loans. Hoping to grab market share, the head of marketing has created a direct mail advertisement that features a nearby state university's mascot and school seal near the bank's logo. The flier announces that National United Bank is offering competitive rates for student loans. For National United Bank customers with existing checking accounts, variable interest rates can be as low as 2.95 percent APR and fixed interest rates start at 5.2 percent.

Before sending out the new glossy brochure, the CEO of the bank wants legal's stamp of approval before marketing sends the flier design to the printer. He lets slip that the flier may boast interest rates far below those actually projected to be offered to most customers. As deputy corporate counsel, do you have legal concerns about the mailer? *See* §§12 C.F.R. 1026.47(a); 1026.48(a)&(b); Official Interpretation to 47(a)(1)(i).

18.4. Student loan debt is the second largest amount of consumer debt in the U.S. economy. It totals an estimated $1.2 trillion. Mortgage debt is first. In the years after the 2008 housing crisis, policymakers began to discuss the country's outstanding student loans as a "bubble" or a looming crisis. These alarms pointed to regulation and reform that could limit the overall damage of the rising default rate on student loans. The annual three-year national cohort default rate in 2014 was 11.8 percent. U.S. Department of Education, *Three-year Official Cohort Default Rates for Schools*, http://www2.ed.gov/offices/OSFAP/ defaultmanagement/cdr.html (last visited Nov. 18, 2015). Are you persuaded that today's student loan debt is similar to the mortgage debts that pushed the economy to near-collapse? What are the similarities and differences between student loan debts and mortgage debts? Consider things such as underwriting, securitization, government backing or guarantees, the nature and amount of debt, and the like.

Assignment 19.   Banking Transactions

The last several assignments examined the laws that govern different types of borrowing: mortgages, car loans, credit cards, and payday lending. Of course, not every purchase is financed. Many consumers pay using cash, check, debit cards, or other forms of payment. While these are immediate transactions that lack the "buy now, pay later" feature of credit, consumer issues still arise. Banking transactions are every day and routine, which may lead to consumers paying insufficient attention to the costs and risks. Banking transactions also have a complex infrastructure that may be invisible or confusing to consumers. Finally, technology has prompted innovations in payments that have introduced new conveniences, but also loopholes in the consumer protection law.

"Banks" are creatures of law, not unlike corporations or public utilities in the sense that the designation carries with it both benefits and burdens. This Assignment uses bank as shorthand for companies that perform payment functions, although many of these companies are not legally "banks." The central concern of banking law is safety and soundness, and this is the traditional focus of banking regulators. For example, the Federal Deposit Insurance Corporation (FDIC) provides deposit insurance on accounts that insure consumers against the bank being unable to provide deposits back upon customer demand.

This Assignment focuses on payment law — the how, what, and when of a consumer making a payment to another. It explores how the law allocates responsibility for fraud, theft, mistake, accounting error between banks and consumers, and it also studies the approach to regulating fees and costs. The checking account remains the foundational product, even though paper checks are declining sharply in use. Debit cards and other means of electronic fund transfers now dominate. New payment tools such as mobile payments and gift cards illustrate how consumer protection in banking continues to confront issues of transparency and fairness, regardless of platform.

A.   Bank Accounts

Deposit and payment functions are newer businesses for banks than lending. Traditionally, banks were creatures of the nation-state and had issuing and backing money currency as their primary responsibility. This idea of payment processing as a public good remains today, although banks themselves are private, for-profit institutions. The Federal Reserve, the FDIC, and the U.S. Treasury have vital roles in banking, and by extension in consumer protection. In part because of a perceived conflict between protecting consumers and banks profiting from them, the Consumer Financial Protection Bureau

380

(CFPB) now has authority over the aspects of banking that are "consumer protection functions." 12 U.S.C. §5581. Included in the CFPB's enumerated "federal consumer financial law" are the Electronic Funds Transfer Act, the Truth in Savings Act, and the part of the Federal Deposit Insurance Act that proscribes disclosures for non-FDIC-insured institutions. 12 U.S.C. §§5481(12) and (14). By statute, the CFPB has limited authority over banks and credit unions with $10 billion or less in assets. 12 U.S.C. §5516. The purpose of this restriction was to reduce the regulatory burden on smaller institutions. One result is that the "regulation by institution" approach lingers in banking, rather than the "regulation by product" approach that provides more comprehensive oversight.

1. Checking Accounts

The slow demise of paper checks continues, and its end may be nigh. Check use is dwarfed by debit cards, credit cards, and cash. Scott Schuh & Joanna Stavins, *The 2013 Survey of Consumer Payment Choice: Summary Results,* Federal Reserve Bank of Boston (2015), https://www.bostonfed.org/economic/rdr/2015/rdr1504.pdf.

Number and share of consumer payments in a typical month, by type of payment instrument

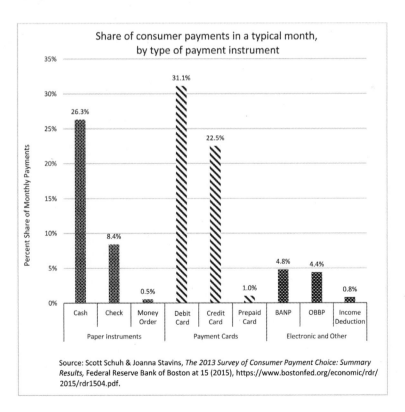

Source: Scott Schuh & Joanna Stavins, *The 2013 Survey of Consumer Payment Choice: Summary Results,* Federal Reserve Bank of Boston at 15 (2015), https://www.bostonfed.org/economic/rdr/2015/rdr1504.pdf.

Id. at 15. The trends in the graph do not make checking accounts obsolete; indeed the transformation from paper to electronic payments may create new consumer protection issues as the law lags behind the market. Professor Ronald Mann astutely observes that the move from paper to electronic systems is also a crucial policy shift from heavily regulated, government-subsidized systems to less regulated, private systems. Ronald Mann, *Payment Systems and Other Financial Transactions* 7 (5th ed. 2011). The law relating to liability for checks is well developed compared to newer payment technologies and also permits study of accounts themselves.

A checking account reflects an agreement by a bank to hold money and dispose of it as the consumer directs. State and federal laws override these contracts if their provisions are contrary to law. Articles 3 and 4 of the Uniform Commercial Code (U.C.C.) are the key state laws, with several federal statutes addressing specific issues.

Money arrives in bank accounts in a variety of ways. Money inbound to the customer's account may be a cash deposit, a fund transfer from another person's account at the same bank, or the deposit of a check drawn on a geographically distant bank. These deposits carry different levels of risk for a bank, but consumers tend to want to access the money regardless. To create consistency and bring a consumer-friendly approach to this issue, Congress passed the Expedited Funds Availability Act, 12 U.S.C. §§4001-4010. Its Regulation CC establishes a framework of deadlines by which a depository bank must release money to a customer. The rules vary by the perceived riskiness of the deposit and by the method by which the consumer wants to access the funds.

The law obligates banks to pay properly presented items. But a bank's liability for failure to do so runs to its customer, not the payee. The consumer is left holding an unpaid check and needing to track down the person who wrote the check to secure alternate payment.

Banks may dishonor a check if the account balance is smaller than the check presented. U.C.C. §4-401(a). Alternatively, the bank may pay the check and charge the consumer a fee, called an insufficient fund or non-sufficient funds (NSF) fee. The rules for ATM withdrawals or debits are different. A consumer must have opted in to overdraft protection to be charged a fee for allowing such a transaction to process. Several banks have faced lawsuits for failing to disclose adequately the costs associated with overdraft protection programs. The CFPB may attempt to improve the disclosures related to overdraft protection, although the industry has suggested that consumers simply want the charges paid, even at a cost. Note that if a bank has agreed to pay the overdraft, then the bank must pay according to its contract with the customer. To limit liability, most banks have some bounds on what overdraft protection does cover.

A major controversy has erupted about whether banks should be obligated to process transactions in the order that reduces any overdraft charges. A bank may have its program set up to deduct items by descending order of amount. By paying the largest debit first, each subsequent smaller transaction could create a separate overdraft item, and consequential fee to a consumer. Banks can pay items in "any order." U.C.C. §4-403(b), and a CFPB report found a wide variety of practices, including some banks that processed certain types of transactions first, such as bill payments, and some banks that processed transactions of all kinds together from smallest to largest. CFPB, *Study of Overdraft Programs* (June 2013), http://files.consumerfinance.gov/f/201306_cfpb_whitepaper_overdraft-practices.pdf. The lack of standardized processing means that consumers will not be able to anticipate whether a particular transaction will create an overdraft. The only sure way to avoid trouble is to have all the money currently available for all types of deductions.

Banks have good reason to worry about check fraud. Its costs amount to about $1 billion per year. The law generally puts the loss on the party that engaged in negligence, if there was one.

Marx v. Whitney Nat'l Bank

713 So. 2d 1142 (La. 1998)

MARCUS, Justice.

David Marx filed suit against the Whitney National Bank (hereinafter "Whitney") asserting that Whitney was obligated to restore to his checking account a total of $10,000 for five checks drawn on his account by a person whose signature was unauthorized. . . . Whitney declined to restore the funds paid out on the forged checks to the plaintiffs' account. It answered asserting that the failure of David Marx to exercise reasonable care in the handling of the account precluded relief.

The facts underlying this matter are undisputed by the parties. . . . David Marx maintained a checking account at Whitney for which he received monthly statements. His January 1995 statement contained evidence of five forged checks totaling $2,373.00. He did not review his January 1995 statement. Nor did he review his statements for the months of February, March, and April of 1995. Had he reviewed the January through April 1995 statements, he would have discovered seventeen forged checks totaling almost $13,000.00. On April 24, 1995, two children of David Marx, Stanley Marx and Maxine Marx Goodman, were added as joint owners to the same account. Five additional checks were forged on the account in March, April, and May 1995 which first appeared on the May 1995 statement. Stanley Marx noticed these forged instruments when he reviewed the bank statement dated May 16, 1995 and the enclosed cancelled checks. At the behest of Stanley Marx, David Marx reported the forgeries to Whitney and executed an "Affidavit of Forgery, Alteration, Loss or Theft of Instrument and Subrogation and Hold Harmless Agreement" in which he identified his grandson, Joel Goodman, as both the maker and payee of the forged instruments. Plaintiffs asked Whitney to credit back to their account the funds paid out on the last five forgeries discovered and reported upon receipt of the May 1995 statement. The parties stipulated that Joel Goodman had access to David Marx's checkbook whenever he visited his grandfather, that he was the party who had forged all of the checks in question, and that David Marx was negligent for failing to review his January, February, March, and April 1995 statements.

The trial judge granted plaintiffs' motion for summary judgment, rendering judgment in plaintiffs' favor for $10,000, plus legal interest from date of judicial demand, and all costs of the proceedings. The court of appeal affirmed. We granted certiorari to review the correctness of that decision.

The sole issue for our review is whether the stipulated negligence of David Marx precludes recovery against Whitney by all joint owners on the account for the five forged checks honored by Whitney which were discovered and reported upon receipt of the May 1995 statement.

The law applicable to this case is found in Chapters Three and Four of the Louisiana Commercial Laws. Pursuant to Louisiana's Commercial Laws as well as the established jurisprudence prior to their adoption, the relationship between a bank and its depositor is a debtor-creditor relationship that is contractual in nature. Fidelity Nat'l. Bank of Baton Rouge v. Vuci, 68 So. 2d 781 (1953). The initial deposit of funds gives rise to the contract between bank and depositor; the subsequent creation of rights of others to an interest in an account involves an amendment of the original contract.

During the course of the contract with its depositor, a bank has the right to use the funds on deposit and, in consideration thereof, it covenants to pay funds out of the depositor's account only on the depositor's orders. First Nat'l. Bank v. Pine Belt Producers Co-op, 363 So. 2d at 1204. La. R.S. 10:3-401 specifically provides that a person is not liable on an instrument unless the person signed the instrument. La. R.S. 10:3-403 further provides that an unauthorized signature is ineffective except as the signature of the unauthorized signer in favor of a person who in good faith pays the instrument or takes it for value. Accordingly, the general rule is that a bank is liable when it pays based upon a forged signature. Colonial Bank v. Marina Seafood Market, Inc., 425 So. 2d 722 (La. 1983). A charge against a customer's account based on a forged instrument is not an authorized charge under the contract between the parties because the order to pay was not given by the customer. For that reason, a banking customer can insist that the drawee bank recredit to his account any funds paid out on a forged instrument. James V. Vergai & Virginia V. Shue, Checks, Payments, and Electronic Banking 458 (Practicing Law Institute 1986); Fidelity Nat'l. Bank of Baton Rouge v. Vuci, 68 So. 2d 781 (1953).

Notwithstanding the general rule that imposes the risk of loss for payment of a forged instrument on the drawee bank, the law provides that under certain circumstances a bank's customer may be *precluded* from asserting rights against the bank in connection with a forged check. Pursuant to La. R.S. 10:3-406 and 10:4-406, a customer is precluded from having funds paid out on a forged instrument restored to his account if his failure to exercise reasonable care in handling the account, either *before or after* the forgery, substantially contributed to the loss. [Ed. Note— emphasis added] In this case, Whitney asserted both statutory defenses in response to plaintiffs' motion for summary judgment.

· · ·

La. R.S. 10:3-406 precludes a bank's customer from asserting a claim when the customer's conduct *before* a forgery substantially contributes to the making of the forgery. The burden of proving that the customer's handling of the account precludes recovery is on the bank. In this case, the bank asserted that David Marx substantially contributed to the forgeries and was precluded from making a claim against the bank by La. R.S. 10:3-406(a) because his grandson had access to his checkbook each time he visited the residence. No further facts were stipulated by the parties concerning where or how the checkbook was kept, the manner in which the grandson obtained blank checks of his grandfather, the frequency of his visits, or whether the grandfather had reason to be suspicious that his checks might be taken and his name forged on them. The mere fact that one family member has access to checks at the residence of another family member, without more, does not establish a failure to exercise ordinary care substantially contributing to the making of a forged signature so as to preclude recovery on a forged instrument. Accordingly, Whitney did not carry its burden of proof that plaintiffs were precluded from recovery pursuant La. R.S. 10:3-406.

Whitney also defended against plaintiffs' motion for summary judgment by asserting that David Marx failed to discover and report the initial forgeries upon receipt of the January 1995 statement, thereby precluding recovery for any subsequent forgeries on the account by the same wrongdoer. La. R.S. 10:4-406 provides in pertinent part:

(c) If a bank sends or makes available a statement of account or items pursuant to Subsection (a), *the customer must exercise reasonable promptness in examining the statement or the items to determine whether any payment was not authorized* because of an alteration of an item or because a purported signature by or on behalf of the customer was not authorized. If, based on the statement or items provided, the customer should reasonably have discovered the unauthorized payment, the *customer must promptly notify the bank* of the relevant facts.

(d) *If* the bank proves that *the customer failed, with respect to an item, to comply with the duties imposed on the customer by Subsection (c), the customer is precluded from asserting against the bank:*

(1) the customer's unauthorized signature or any alteration on the item, if the bank also proves that it suffered a loss by reason of the failure; and

(2) *the customer's unauthorized signature* or alteration *by the same wrong-doer on any other item paid* in good faith by the bank *if the payment was made before the bank received notice* from the customer of the unauthorized signature or alteration and *after the customer had been afforded a reasonable period of time, not exceeding thirty days, in which to examine the item or statement of account and notify the bank.* [Emphasis added].

The rule stated in Subsection (d)(2) imposes on the customer the risk of loss on all subsequent forgeries by the *same wrongdoer* after the customer had a reasonable time to detect an initial forgery if the bank has honored subsequent forgeries prior to notice. Even before the adoption of the Uniform Commercial Code, case law throughout the country reflected the view that the suppression of forgery required a cooperative approach. Rules developed which shifted the risk of loss on certain forgeries to a customer who failed to give notice to the bank of forgeries and alterations. Out of the duty imposed on the customer to review his statement grew the rule that successive forgeries result from the failure of the customer to discover and report the initial forgeries which he could have detected had he acted in accord with the duty imposed by law upon him. . . .

In this case, plaintiffs have stipulated that David Marx did not review the January 1995 bank statement for his account and that if he had done so the unauthorized signature of his grandson on several checks would have been detected. Since he did not do so, plaintiffs are precluded from asserting against the bank *all subsequent forgeries* by the *same* unauthorized signatory. That being the case, plaintiffs are not in a position to recover against Whitney for the five forged checks that were discovered in the May 1995 statement which were forged by the same wrongdoer.

Plaintiffs argue that the "same wrongdoer" rule results in absurd consequences because a very minor undetected forgery would preclude a later claim with respect to a potentially large forged instrument drawn by the same wrongdoer. However, in our view plaintiffs' protest illustrates precisely the risk that La. R.S. 10:4-406 allocates to the customer, who is in the best position to discover and report small forgeries before the wrongdoer is emboldened and attempts a larger misdeed.

Plaintiffs further suggest that the prior conduct of David Marx should have no effect on the claims of Stanley Marx and Maxine Marx Goodman, who were not added to the account as owners until April 24, 1995 and who noticed and promptly reported the five checks sued upon after examination of the first statement sent to them. We do not agree.

Plaintiffs concede that if new owners had not been added to the account in April 1995, the failure of David Marx to examine and report the initial forgeries after receipt of the January 1995 statement would serve as an absolute bar to *his* recovery on the subsequent forgeries disclosed in the May 1995 statement. If plaintiffs' argument were accepted and the prior conduct of an account owner was deemed irrelevant to claims of new owners on the same account, a bank customer could subvert the operation of the "same wrongdoer" preclusion rule set forth in La. R.S. 10:4-406 simply by adding another person to the account, thereby defeating the system for allocation of risk adopted by our legislature. Indeed, in this case, plaintiffs' argument would allow David Marx to avoid operation of the preclusion rule and recover on the five checks at issue. Official Code Comment 7 to U.C.C. §4-406, which has been adopted in Louisiana, provides:

> Section 4-406 evidence[s] a public policy in favor of imposing on customers the duty of prompt examination of their bank statements and the notification of banks of forgeries and alterations and in favor of reasonable time limitations on the responsibility of banks for payment of forged or altered items.

We do not believe that the public policy embodied in La. R.S. 10:4-406 is furthered by allowing a customer to cleanse an account in which forgeries have occurred and avoid operation of the "same wrongdoer" preclusion rule by the simple device of adding another party to the same account. Moreover, the contract with respect to the account in question was confected between Whitney and David Marx when David Marx first deposited funds into the account. The addition of new owners to the account constituted an amendment to the account contract, which left in place all defenses already acquired by the bank. Whitney's defense to recrediting the account for funds paid out pursuant to checks forged by the same wrongdoer vested no later than thirty days after David Marx received the January 1995 statement containing instruments forged by Joel Goodman. La. R.S. 10:4-406. The addition of new owners to the account in April 1995 could not defeat defenses which had already attached in favor of the bank. Whitney carried its burden of proof to defeat plaintiffs' motion for summary judgment on the basis of the preclusion defense afforded pursuant to La. R.S. 10:4-406. The court of appeal erred in affirming the trial judge's grant of summary judgment in favor of plaintiffs. We must reverse.

DECREE

For the reasons assigned, the judgment of the court of appeal is reversed. Plaintiffs' motion for summary judgment is denied. The case is remanded to the district court for further proceedings.

Wrongdoing is not only the province of third parties, who fall neatly into categories of awful relative or thief. As the case below illustrates, checks are not the iron-clad evidence of proper payment that we might assume. Technology has sped up the checking process but also created new confusion.

In re Burrier

399 B.R. 258 (Bankr. D. Colo. 2008)

BROOKS, Judge.

. . .

OVERVIEW

This appears to be an ordinary case where Debtors claimed they made certain mortgage payments, but the creditor disagrees and maintains the payments were not made and it has no record of the payments being made. It is an extraordinary case, however, in that the evidence strongly suggests that the payments were indeed made by Debtors, but the creditor—here, Wells Fargo—has no record of the payments and has not credited the debtors' payments to their mortgage account. The payments have, evidently, been lost in a black hole of the creditor's organization or through accounting mismanagement.

This case illustrates three things. First, it reflects a significant and problematic imbalance between a creditor, the mortgage holder, and debtors, homeowners who are timely making their mortgage payments, and who are not knowledgeable about banking procedures and check processing.

Second, this case illustrates a major lender mortgage company whose operations and collections practices are seemingly disconnected from its own technologies. Or, put another way, this is a major lender/mortgage loan servicer where the left hand does not know what the right hand is doing—the collection department does not know what the check processing and accounting departments are doing.

Third, this dispute might portend a widespread abuse of collection practices or creditor overreaching—demanding of debtors what it, the creditor itself, is unable to provide: accurate and reliable record keeping and billing practices.

BACKGROUND

On June 18, 2004, the Debtors executed a Deed of Trust and Note with NBank, N.A. which provided the Debtors with a loan for $183,126.00.

The Note and Deed of Trust were subsequently negotiated to Wells Fargo Bank, N.A.

On February 21, 2007, Debtors filed for relief under Chapter 13 of the United States Bankruptcy Code at which time they also filed a Chapter 13 Plan. The Plan provided that Debtors . . . would pay regular post-petition mortgage payments directly to Wells Fargo. The Plan was confirmed on August 21, 2007 by Order of this Court. . . .

On February 26, 2008, Wells Fargo filed a Motion for Relief from Automatic Stay ("Motion") based upon the Debtors' alleged failure to make certain of their post-petition, post-confirmation monthly mortgage payments (June, July, October, and December 2007). On March 20, 2008, Debtors filed a Response to Wells Fargo's Motion. In Debtors' Response, they denied that they failed to make payments and asserted that "at least three of the payments referenced in Paragraph 7 of the Motion have been made."

On April 11, 2008, the Debtors and Wells Fargo agreed to the terms of a Stipulation For Resolution of Motion for Relief From Automatic Stay and Motion For Acceptance of Stipulated Terms ("Stipulation"). On April 14, 2008, the Court issued an Order approving the Stipulation.

The Stipulation . . . *provided that, with regard to the four postpetition payments Wells Fargo said had not been made, if Debtors could show that the payments had, indeed, been made, then the Debtors' account would be credited with the payments.* The Stipulation specifically provided, in pertinent part, that:

> Creditor has been provided with alleged proof of certain payments by the Debtors. At this time, insufficient information has been provided to Creditor to research the alleged payments. In the event that Debtors provide "*sufficient information*" (as defined below) to Creditor to determine pursuant to the Colorado Uniform Commercial Code and other applicable law that all of the alleged payments contemplated by this stipulation were negotiated, cleared, and were paid by the Debtors' banking institution and, therefore, the payments should be credited to the loan secured by the Deed of Trust then: (a) Creditor will amend the stipulation to reflect that these payments have been credited to Debtors' account; and (b) Creditor will reimburse Debtors' counsel $400.00. *Under this Stipulation, the term "sufficient information" describes only valid, accurate, and true copies of the front side and back side of all negotiable instruments (e.g. personal banking checks) executed by the Debtors that indicate clearly and unequivocally that such negotiable instruments were negotiated by the Debtors' banking institution.*

In other words, per the Stipulation, if the Debtors could produce true copies of their personal banking checks which demonstrated the "missing" payments had, indeed, been paid, then Wells Fargo would appropriately credit the Debtors' mortgage debt.

On August 21, 2008, Wells Fargo filed a Verified Motion For Court to Enforce Terms of Stipulation and for Relief from the Automatic Stay ("Verified Motion"). Wells Fargo, by its Verified Motion asserts that Debtors have failed to comply with the terms of the Stipulation and requests an order of relief from stay. Debtors have filed a Response opposing the Verified Motion asserting that they were unable to comply with the terms of the Stipulation (i.e., produce ". . . true copies of all negotiable instruments (e.g. personal banking checks)") due to the fact that the mortgage payments were not processed by Wells Fargo in a manner in which cancelled checks were made available. Thus, Debtors maintain they were unable to comply due to impossibility of performance.

The Court held an evidentiary hearing on this matter on October 28, 2008. The Debtor, Ms. Burrier, testified that she asked her bank multiple times for proof that the payments were actually made to Wells Fargo, but was unable to obtain documentation — copies of their checks — because, according to her testimony, the checks were processed electronically and not negotiated in the more conventional manner — through the Federal Reserve System.

Ms. Burrier testified that she went to her bank, Academy Bank, on several occasions, seeking to obtain proof that the checks cleared and payments were debited from her account, but that such documentation — cancelled checks — was unavailable. Debtors did not present during their case a corroborating witness representative from Academy Bank. Nevertheless, the parties stipulated to the admission of Debtors' Exhibits A-D, which were copies of the Debtors' bank account statements for June, July, October, and December of 2007 (the months during which Wells Fargo claims payments were not made to it by the Debtors). Exhibits A-D reflected the following:

- Exhibit A reflected that a check numbered 4230 in the amount of $1,470.00 was processed electronically by "WFHM" on June 15, 2007.
- Exhibit B reflected that a check numbered 4238 in the amount of $1,470.00 was processed electronically by "WFHM" on July 16, 2007.
- Exhibit C reflected that a check numbered 4245 in the amount of $1,600.00 was processed electronically by "WFHM" on October 16, 2007.
- Exhibit D reflected that a check numbered 4182 in the amount of $1,600.00 was processed electronically by "WFHM" on December 17, 2007.

In addition, during the testimony of Ms. Burrier, Debtors' Exhibits E, F, G, and H were offered and admitted, without objection, during her testimony. Exhibits E-H reflected the following:

- Exhibit E is a check carbon for check number 4230 reflecting that the sum of $1,470.00 was paid to Wells Fargo.
- Exhibit F is a check carbon for check number 4238 in the amount of $1,470.00 payable to Wells Fargo.
- Exhibit G is a check carbon for check number 4245 in the amount of $1,600.00 payable to Wells Fargo.
- Exhibit H is a check carbon for check number 4182 in the amount of $1,600.00 payable to Wells Fargo.

Debtors maintain that they tried multiple times to comply with the Stipulation by obtaining copies of their check payments, front and back side, as required. However, Debtors assert that due to the method by which the payments were negotiated, Debtors were unable to obtain the documentation required by the Stipulation, specifically, cancelled checks.

Instead, the Debtors provided documentation to Wells Fargo of the alleged missed payments in the form of the Debtors' Academy Bank statements and carbon copies of checks. The Debtors' bank statements, which were not objected to by Wells Fargo and thus were admitted by this Court, indicate that payments in the identified amounts were debited from Debtors' bank account and sent to "WFHM." The Debtors' bank statements and carbons of the respective checks are persuasive evidence that payments were made by Debtors to Wells Fargo for the mortgage payments in question. . . .

CONCLUSIONS OF LAW

. . .

To this Court's surprise and consternation, neither party addressed the Check Clearing for the 21st Century Act. This is especially troubling since Wells Fargo was one of the proponents of this cost saving Act and modernization of banking. According to the Federal Reserve website regarding the Check Clearing for the 21st Century Act:

> The Check Clearing for the 21st Century Act (Check 21) was signed into law on October 28, 2003, and became effective on October 28, 2004. Check 21 is designed to foster innovation in the payments system and to enhance its efficiency by reducing some of the legal impediments to check truncation. The law facilitates check truncation by creating a new negotiable instrument called a substitute check, which permits banks to truncate original checks, to process check information electronically, and to deliver substitute checks to banks that want to continue receiving paper checks. A substitute check is the legal equivalent of the original check and includes all the information contained on the original check. The law does not require banks to accept checks in electronic form nor does it require banks to use the new authority granted by the act to create substitute checks.

For the uninitiated, such as was this Court before conducting its research in this matter, "check truncation" means:

> The conversion of data on a check into an electronic image after a check enters the processing system. *Check truncation eliminates the need to return canceled checks to customers.*

Moreover, the term "truncate" as defined by 12 U.S.C. §5002(18) means:

> to remove an original paper check from the check collection or return process and send to a recipient, in lieu of such original paper check, a substitute check, or, by agreement information relating to the original check (including data taken from the MICR line of the original check or an electronic image of the original check), whether with or without subsequent delivery of the original paper check.

Based upon this Court's own research, it appears that the "*sufficient information*" as required by Wells Fargo in the subject Stipulation may no longer be valid — and may no longer even be available — in today's marketplace. That is, Wells Fargo's demanded proof of payment, which was "*only valid, accurate, and true copies of the front side and back side of all negotiable instruments (e.g. personal banking checks) executed by the Debtors that indicate clearly and unequivocally that such negotiable instruments were negotiated by the Debtors' banking institution,"* may no longer be required or available in the banking industry.

Key to this case and interpretation of the issues before the Court is *"what is the generally applicable industry standard"* with respect to electronically processed checks. The burden on this issue is on Wells Fargo as the party attempting to enforce the Stipulation. In particular, 12 U.S.C. §5002(18), which provides for "truncation," permits a bank to remove and destroy an original paper check and process it by transferring information, among other ways, "by agreement" evidently between banking institutions. *This Court has heard no testimony with respect to the practices and procedures of Wells Fargo with respect to the Check Clearing for the 21st Century Act and Wells Fargo's electronic check processing procedures. . . .*

The Debtors argue that "impossibility of performance" precludes the enforcement of the Stipulation. Specifically, Debtors argue that the terms of the Stipulation required them to provide documents that were *not available* to them — and possibly do not exist — due to the method by which Wells Fargo processed the payments. The most reasonable inference the Court can draw from the evidence is that the payments were processed electronically — that is, the checks were processed and cleared via the Check Clearing for the 21st Century Act processes. As a result, the mortgage payment checks sent by the Debtors to Wells Fargo were not returned to their bank, Academy Bank, and therefore the Debtors could not provide canceled checks to satisfy the "sufficient information" mandate of the Stipulation.

The Court concludes that the defense of "impossibility of performance" is subject to a very high standard, but that it *was* reached here. A party asserting an affirmative defense has the burden of proving the affirmative defense. In Colorado, an affirmative defense must be established by the party who asserts it. In order to establish the defense of impossibility of performance, it is necessary to demonstrate changed circumstances, which have made the "promise vitally different from what reasonably should have been within the contemplation of both parties when they entered into the contract." In this case, when the Stipulation was entered into, the evidence demonstrates that, *at least the Debtors,* did not have knowledge that the canceled checks — specifically *"valid, accurate, and true copies of the front side and back side of all negotiable instruments (e.g. personal banking checks) executed by the Debtors that indicate clearly and unequivocally that such negotiable instruments were negotiated by the Debtors' banking institution"* — as demanded in the agreement were unavailable. Generally, if the occurrence is reasonably foreseeable, the courts typically take the position that the promissor has assumed the risk of impossibility or frustration. However, no evidence was presented demonstrating that the Debtors could have reasonably foreseen the risk here. . . . If anything, Wells Fargo, being in the banking industry and more knowledgeable about and facile with the technology and the compliance features of the Check Clearing for the 21st Century Act, could have foreseen this risk. Nevertheless, Wells Fargo did not present to this Court any expert who could testify as to how electronic transfers occur.

Ms. Burrier's testimony regarding her reasonable efforts to obtain the cancelled checks is persuasive. The stipulated Debtors' Exhibits A-D show that certain payments were made to "WFHM." The Debtors' account was shown on the bank statements to have been debited in favor of "WFHM" for each of the months Debtors allegedly failed to make the respective mortgage payments. Moreover, the unrefuted evidence as contained in Debtors' Exhibits E-H, reflects that the corresponding checks were written by the Debtors for each of the respective months. The Court would have been greatly aided if material evidence, preferably expert testimony, explaining the process and mechanics of "paperless" electronic mortgage payments of the sort here performed, was provided. Wells Fargo provided no such evidence. Wells Fargo did not carry its burden of going forward, refuting Debtors' evidence of payment, or otherwise demonstrating lack of payments by the Debtors. . . .

It is evident from the testimony that neither party fully anticipated the difficulty of tracing checks in an electronic age. In this electronic age, the requirement that "sufficient information" constitutes *only* "valid, accurate, and true copies of the front side and back side of all negotiable instruments (e.g. personal banking checks) executed by the Debtors that indicate clearly and unequivocally that such negotiable instruments were negotiated by the Debtors' banking institution" may be obsolete. If Wells Fargo requires such precision, such precision will be required of it in enforcing stipulations. Wells Fargo did not meet its burden in this case and relief will be denied accordingly. . . .

The Court was correct in identifying the Check 21 Act as rendering it impossible for consumers to obtain the actual, deposited checks. Banks may legally destroy paper checks. Substitute checks, however, bear language that reads, "This is a legal copy of your check. You can use it the same way you would use the original check." The Debtors produced no substitute checks, and unfortunately for all parties, nothing about the Check 21 Act eliminates good ol' fraud. After losing its motion, Wells Fargo brushed up on its knowledge of check records and asked the Court to revisit the situation. The Court did so, beginning by giving more detail on Debtors' testimony in the first hearing.

Debtor, Denon Arae Burrier, testified that she wrote checks for the post-petition months of June, July, October and December, 2007, and that these payments cleared her checking account with Academy Bank.

When asked whether she altered or changed the July, 2007 check carbon copy that Debtor contended evidenced payment to Wells Fargo, Debtor replied:

Absolutely not. Well, I wrote 'cleared' on it when it cleared the bank. And then, I wrote July of '07 when I was sending them over to Keven [counsel].

In support of her testimony, Debtor submitted evidence to the Court of bank statements showing debits from Debtors' Academy Bank account in the amount of the alleged mortgage payments for the months of June, July, October and December 2007.

Debtor further testified that it was impossible to produce "sufficient information," as set forth under the terms of the Stipulation, to evidence payment to Wells Fargo because the alleged checks were "processed electronically."

Debtor was adamant in her testimony that Wells Fargo debited her checking account for the alleged amounts in dispute. In regards to the alleged October, 2007 payment, Debtor's counsel asked Debtor on direct: "So the bank took the money out of your account and gave it to Wells Fargo Home Mortgage?" Debtor replied, "Absolutely."

Debtor's counsel specifically asked Debtor whether she forged any of the carbon copies of the alleged checks. Debtor's counsel asked:

So, in order to forge these, you would have had to write the check somewhere else, have the payment somewhere else come out of the bank or come up with a whole new set of carbon checks that had exactly the same check numbers and use those. Did you do that?

Debtor replied:

No, I don't have time to do that. I have two small children.

In re Burrier, 403 B.R. 714, 717 (Bankr. D. Colo. 2009). The Court then summarized the new evidence and explained it was . . . ahem, adjusting . . . its prior ruling:

Debtor, Denon Arae Burrier, appeared at the hearing. Debtor, Brandon Michael Burrier, failed to appear. Ms. Burrier indicated that both she and Mr. Burrier were invoking their Fifth Amendment right to not self-incriminate. Accordingly, Ms. Burrier did not sit for cross-examination or offer any evidence at the hearing.

Katherine Lynn Works testified as the custodian of records from Academy Bank with regard to the subpoenaed bank records submitted with Wells Fargo's Supplement to Motion.

Ms. Works testified that the subpoenaed bank records from Academy Bank were the true and correct bank records pertaining to the Debtors' checking account with Academy Bank. Specifically, with regard to the alleged payments made for the post-petition months of June, July, October and December, 2007, Ms. Works testified that:

With respect to the alleged post-petition payment[s] allegedly payable to WFHM, referenced by Debtors [by] check number at the prior hearing, Academy Bank's records reflect that no such check number[s] were presented or negotiated on the account.

Ms. Works further testified that it would be impossible for a payment to appear on an Academy Bank statement and then disappear from a later version of the same month's statement. She testified that based upon her personal knowledge, the only way a payment could appear differently on one version of a statement versus another would be if a customer were to retrieve a statement upon request from a branch, and then alter the statement themselves.

As further evidence that the bank statements previously submitted to the Court were altered, Ms. Works testified that one of the entries on the previously submitted June statement occurred on a Saturday, and no checks are presented for payment on any Saturday because the Federal Reserve is not open.

Id. at 719-720. The Court wrapped up the mess with a bow on top for the Debtors.

The Debtors misled the Court and Wells Fargo by submitting fraudulent evidence to the Court. The Debtors' fraudulent evidence was the product of careful, deliberate, specific and repeated acts. The Debtors intended to and did mislead the Court. Further, the Debtors made a calculated and an effective effort to mislead the Court; clearly, it was no accident.

The Debtors fraudulent testimony and evidence resulted in a misplaced and incorrect criticism of Wells Fargo's procedures and record keeping in the Court's prior opinion. The Court's prior criticism towards Wells Fargo was a mistake. It was a mistake based upon incorrect factual conclusions, as a result of what appears to be, and for which there is no other plausible explanation, than Debtors fabricated and altered evidence submitted in support of their position at the prior hearing. It is evident that the Debtor, Ms. Denon Arae Burrier, provided false testimony to the Court on October 28, 2008.

The testimony from Academy Bank was effective in overcoming and overwhelming the evidence submitted by the Debtors at the prior hearing. Moreover, the testimony from Academy Bank revealed the intrinsic fraud which led to a prior judgment founded on perjured testimony and altered evidence. In sum, the testimony of Academy Bank proved that the Debtors prior testimony was nothing more than a fabricated story — a lie. No payment was ever presented for payment or negotiated to Wells Fargo in June, July, October, or December, 2007.

Additionally, the testimony of Academy Bank proved that Debtors manipulated and lied to the Court and Wells Fargo during the course of this matter, beginning with the September 3, 2008 hearing and continuing for the duration of this matter. They specifically advised the Court and counsel that they could not obtain proof from Academy Bank that the alleged payments were paid to Wells Fargo because the payments were "electronically processed" and no copies were available. Ms. Works testified that Academy Bank would have a specific record of any payment processed through Academy Bank and that such evidence is routinely provided to customers at no charge or for a nominal $2.00 fee. Contrary to Debtor's testimony, the only impediment to obtaining proof of payment was the fact that the payments were never made.

As the prior judgment in this matter was premised upon false and misleading evidence supplied to the Court by the Debtors, it is

ORDERED as follows:

> 1. Wells Fargo Bank, N.A.'s Motion for Relief from Order Entered December 22, 2008 Entitled: Memorandum Opinion and Order Denying Wells Fargo Bank N.A.'s Motion for Court to Enforce Terms of Stipulation and For Relief from the Automatic Stay is GRANTED and the prior order is VACATED.
>
> · · ·
>
> 4. The United States Trustee shall advise the Court on or before April 10, 2009, as to its intentions with regard to this case and any necessary referrals to the United States Attorney upon due investigation.
>
> 5. Wells Fargo may seek sanctions for attorneys' fees and costs against the Debtors by separate motion filed on or before April 17, 2009.

Id. at 720-721.

Despite technology, all payment systems are vulnerable to fraud to at least some degree. The relevant consumer protection issue is how the risk of fraud is allocated. As the sections, *infra*, on electronic transfers and stored value cards illustrate, consumer's vulnerability varies by payment method.

2. Account Disclosures

In some ways, consumer protection related to bank accounts is theoretically similar to the investor protection bent of the Securities and Exchange Commission. The Truth in Savings Act regulates the disclosure of fees and costs, which can significantly erode the financial benefits of saving. Despite the "savings" in its name, the law and its corresponding Regulation DD, apply to both checking and savings accounts for consumers. 12 C.F.R. §1030.2(a). Required disclosures include descriptions of minimum balance requirements, applicable interest rates, and fees. These disclosures are supplemented by those required by the Gramm-Leach-Bliley Act related to privacy, those required by the Expedited Funds Availability Act related to withdrawals, and those required by the Electronic Funds Transfer Act related to electronic transactions. The result is cumulative, creating checking account disclosures that routinely exceed 100 pages. Pew Trust, *Hidden Risks: The Case for Safe Checking* (Apr. 2011) http://www.pewtrusts.org/en/research-and-analysis/reports/2011/ 04/27/hidden-risks. As with credit cards and mortgages, disclosures may be made more salient by using strong graphic design, but at bottom, innovations in banking have made the disclosures longer. Multiple methods of withdrawal and deposit give consumers flexibility but also produce additional terms, fees, and scenarios to disclose.

Keeping on top of disclosures is not an easy job, and the potential liability is large. These allegations against Bank of America are illustrative. In 2010, Plaintiffs Harold C. Rose and Kimberly Lane, filed a Class Action Complaint against Bank of America, N.A. alleging:

> On or about April 30, 2009 Defendants made available the following announcement to Plaintiffs Rose and Lane on their written account statements regarding their checking accounts with Defendant Bank of America:
>
>> Important Information: Please see the enclosed brochure for information about upcoming pricing changes to some deposit accounts. In addition, we've included information on how to help prevent or minimize deposit fees as well as details on improvements we've made to serve you better. If you would like more information, visit bankofamerica.com/pricingchanges.
>
> However, this announcement to Plaintiffs did not clearly and conspicuously (a) disclose which categories of fees (and their amounts) applicable to Plaintiffs' particular account services were changing; (b) direct Plaintiffs' attention to the particular changes for their accounts; and (c) inform Plaintiffs of the precise date when changes to fees on their accounts would occur. Defendants did not notify Plaintiff Rose in advance in writing that Defendants intended to charge Plaintiff Rose on a precise date on his personal deposit account a "check enclosure fee" of three dollars ($3.00) per each account statement period for returning cancelled checks to Plaintiff. Defendants did not notify Plaintiff Lane in advance in writing clearly and conspicuously that Defendants intended to charge Plaintiff Lane on a

precise date on her personal deposit an increase from $5.95 to $8.95 per month for her monthly service charge. This announcement was also deficient in that it did not clearly differentiate the proposed specific changes in fees to Plaintiffs' account from the fee changes to the accounts of other Class members.

Class Action Complaint for Violations of the California Unfair Competition Law, *Rose v. Bank of America, N.A.*, 2010 WL 1056112 (Cal. Superior Ct. 2010) (No. BC433460). The Plaintiffs' claim under the California unfair competition law (UCL), Cal. Civ. Code §§17200 et seq., was based on the fact that the disclosures did not satisfy the Truth in Savings Act.

> Defendants' acts and practices in announcing pricing changes to the personal deposit accounts of Plaintiffs and other Class members as alleged herein constitute "unfair" business acts and practices in violation of the UCL because of the gravity of harm to Plaintiffs and the Class outweighs the utility of Defendants' practices and/or offends public policy, is immoral, unscrupulous, unethical and offensive, and causes substantial injury to Plaintiffs and the Class in that money was deducted from their personal deposit accounts by Defendants. Moreover, Defendants' wrongful conduct as described herein threatens an incipient violation of the The Truth In Savings Act and Regulation DD, or violates the policy or spirit of such laws because it effects are comparable to or the same as a violation of said laws. . . . Defendants' business acts and practices have caused injury to the Plaintiffs and members of the Class in that Defendants have improperly deducted since on or about June 10, 2009 money for increased service fees from their personal deposit accounts maintained at Defendant Bank of America, including but not limited to three dollars ($3.00) for check enclosures for Plaintiff Rose and from $5.95 to $8.95 for monthly service charges for Plaintiff Lane.

Id. The plaintiffs relied on state law because Congress stripped the Truth in Savings Act of a private right of action. The Ninth Circuit ruled that disobeying a federal law could create liability under a state law giving consumers the right to sue. The Supreme Court denied *certiorari* without comment. The Truth in Savings Act continues to create liability risk, much to the consternation of bankers.

3.   *Account Access*

Consumers have no legal right to a bank account, only to be free from unlawful discrimination under ECOA when they seek an account. An estimated 25 million American adults are unbanked. Shawn Donnan & Demetri Sevastopulo, *U.S. Tries to Boost Access to 25m "Unbanked,"* Financial Times Nov. 30, 2015. These consumers incur hundreds of dollars each year from using alternative financial services, such as check cashers. Consumers may be denied an account based on a bank account reporting agency. As of 2016, the two largest are ChexSystems and Early Warning Services. These function similarly to the credit reporting agencies in terms of most banks being most users and furnishers of information. Designed to help banks avoid fraudulent customers, bank reporting agencies now are routinely used to guide decisions on whether consumers should be given requested accounts. If the report shows overdrafts, a consumer may be given an account with higher fees or more limited features. Jessica Silver-Greenberg, *Over a Million are Denied Bank Accounts for Past Errors*, N.Y. Times, July 30, 2013. Consumer advocates assert that the agencies have evolved into a substantial barrier to mainstream banking access, and need regulation beyond the Fair Credit Reporting Act.

B. Electronic Funds Transfer Act

The Electronic Funds Transfer Act (EFTA) is not as hip as it may sound. It was enacted in 1978 and signed into law by President Jimmy Carter. Its importance has grown in subsequent decades, however, as more and more transactions fall under the definition of an "electronic fund transfer." 15 U.S.C. §1693a(7). While there is uncertainty about whether things discussed *infra* such as prepaid calls or certain mobile payment services fall under the statute as currently drafted, it is clear that the EFTA applies to ATM (automated teller machine) transactions, debit card usage, and ACH transactions.

1. Debit Cards

Despite what my grandmother says, an ATM card and a debit card are the same thing. They are a card-based method for immediate access of bank funds. Hereinafter, this Assignment refers to debit cards. At the time a bank account is established, a consumer will nearly always receive a debit card or authorize the sending of such a card. One major use of the debit card is to facilitate routine transactions with the bank. Note that ATM stands for automated teller machine, and bank branches increasingly are holding facilities for ATMs, more than employee workplaces. Getting consumers to use debit cards to make deposits, withdrawals, balance inquiries, and the like reduces costs for banks. But some aspects of electronic access are costly.

Consumers have lamented ATM fees for years, but the law is clear. The fee itself — (even if $3.50 to withdraw $20 seems unconscionable to most consumers) is permissible, provided that the bank discloses the fee as required by the EFTA. In *Clemmer v. Key Bank Nat'l Ass'n*, 539 F.3d 349 (6th Cir. 2008), the court held that a consumer who pushes "yes" to acknowledge an on-screen notice that a fee "may be charged" has received sufficient notice of the subsequent charge. Interestingly, in *Clemmer*, the consumer got no traction from the fact that Key Bank did not, in fact, charge an ATM fee to certain consumers, including members of the military, non-customers conducting international transactions and non-customers using the ATM in the Cleveland Clinic (the plaintiff in *Clemmer* lived in Ohio). The consumer essentially argued that the bank should determine at the time of the transaction if a fee would actually be charged, and then either display no fee notice or state that the fee "will be charged." This type of real-time notice is precisely what consumers receive when they attempt to withdraw funds without overdraft protection and so is clearly technologically possible. The EFTA renders it legally unnecessary. The easiest EFTA disclosure cases to win, and therefore the ones that enforcement attorneys like to bring, are those where there is a complete omission of fees. The FDIC fined a bank and an affiliate for practices related to loading remaining financial aid money, less tuition, onto debit cards. Students were not informed of fees, such as those related to ATM withdrawals and the availability of no-cost ATMs in certain locations. *See* Kim Janssen, *Feds Fine Payment Card Firm Over College Students' Financial Aid*, CHI. TRIB. Dec. 24, 2015.

Debit cards also are used to pay for goods or services. The processing fees for merchants are lower when a consumer uses a debit card than a credit card, especially if the consumer enters a PIN. These transactions are cleared and settled immediately. Non-PIN debit transactions are authorized immediately at the point of sale, with a hold being placed on funds in the consumers' account, but the merchant gets paid (along with credit card transactions) a few days later. PIN or no-PIN, the EFTA requires that consumer be offered a written receipt for a debit transaction. 15 U.S.C. §1693d.

Fraud from debit card transactions is many multiples less than fraud from credit cards but the chip technology recently added to credit cards may bring the two products more in line. From the other direction, as no-PIN debit card transactions become more popular, their rate of fraud will be more similar to credit cards because they are processed in a similar way. The law, however, continues to differ on a consumer's liability for unauthorized use of a debit card versus a credit card. The EFTA allocates loss between the consumer's bank and the consumer for unauthorized use. 15 U.S.C. §1693g. Regulation E interprets the loss rules to apply to any "series of related unauthorized transfers." 12 C.F.R. §1005.6(b). In a parallel to rule for paper checks explained *supra* in *Marx v. Whitney*, consumers must review bank statements and report unauthorized transactions within 60 days. If the consumer fails to do so, any later transactions that could have been halted if the consumer had reported the unauthorized use fall on the consumer. This can include the entire amount of a consumer's account. Initially, the consumer's loss is limited to $50, even if the consumer wrote their PIN on their debit card with a Sharpie marker (true story from my dad's days as a banker). After two business days from when the consumer learns of the theft or risk of unauthorized use, the consumer's liability may increase to a total of $500 (including the prior $50) if the bank is not alerted. Some states have laws that are even more friendly to consumers, either by extending the deadline to report a lost or stolen card or by lowering the liability amount. *See, e.g.,* Mass. Gen. L. ch. 167B, §18 (limiting liability to $50 in all instances).

2. ACH and Bill Pay Systems

An Automatic Clearing House (ACH) payment is a direct debit from or direct credit to a bank account from another account. ACH payments result from a computerized system that relies entirely on electronic messages for communication. Unlike paper checks, ACHs are not governed by the U.C.C. and are not negotiable instruments under state law. While ACHs are squarely covered by the EFTA, another important source of rules are private agreements. NACHA is a non-profit association of clearinghouses that are themselves composed of banks that process ACH transactions. NACHA's Operating Rules are an important source of rules. From a consumer perspective, the most unfavorable aspects of the ACH rules relate to the finality of payment. After the settlement date, a payment cannot generally be retracted. To challenge a debit entry, the NACHA rules require a consumer to act within 15 calendar days of the statement being sent and must complete an affidavit in a specific form. Even after all that, NACHA says only vaguely that a recredit to the consumer's account should be "promptly" performed. There is also no law or policy that permits a consumer to withhold payment because of dissatisfaction with the purchase. This is a major reason that most retail purchases remain on credit cards, while ACH is used for routine bill pay such as utilities.

Businesses receive ACH payments for bills and initiate ACH payments for salaries, employee reimbursement, and the like. Consumer-initiated ACH payments took off in 2001 when NACHA changed its system to facilitate such transactions via the web. Estimates put the number of consumer ACH payments at more than $3 billion per year. A notable aspect of ACH is that consumers use it for both small routine transactions and large irregular ones. Its ubiquity is similar to credit cards; consumer use of ACH payments is probably more responsible for the decline in checking use than credit cards, which were in wide use for decades before 2001.

ACH systems also can be used to convert a paper check to an electronic image. This can happen either at the point-of-sale (in which case the consumer gets back the check after its image is captured) or in a companies' back offices. Many consumers learned the hard way that checks processed via conversion are processed on the next business day. This process makes it much harder for a consumer to exercise the right to stop payment on a check because the check may clear electronically as a conversion before the consumer can notify the bank of the desire to stop payment.

C.   Other Payment Transactions

Banking is more than the process of payment as it usually includes a way to safeguard and store money, as well as transfer it. Payments are the core of banking in terms of numbers of transactions, however, and there are widely used payment methods that exist outside or at the margins of banking basics: checks and cards. Yet each of these systems present the identical legal issues for consumer protection. (No, not whether that dear lady in Nigeria really needs £1 million pounds in funds today from you, kind sir or madam.) The pervasive legal question is how much money can a consumer lose if something goes wrong from things like fraud, billing error, or mistake. For a good overview of consumer protection across payments, *see* Gail Hillebrand, *Before the Grand Rethinking: Five Things to Do Today with Payments Law and Ten Principles to Guide New Payments Products and New Payments Law*, 83 Chi.-Kent L. Rev. 769 (2008).

1. Money Orders and Remittances

A money order is a check for a specified amount. The consumer pays cash to the issuing institution, which in the United States often is the U.S. Postal Service. The consumer fills in the name of the payee. Money orders are used as check substitutes by those without checking accounts or are used to pay those who refuse to accept cash or credit cards, usually out of concerns about security and processing fees, respectively. A few dozen countries, including Canada and Mexico, accept U.S. money orders, making these a useful cross-border payment method.

Remittances is an umbrella term used that describes consumers' payments to people living overseas. Immigrants frequently send money to family in their countries of origin. The World Bank reported that remittances from the United States exceeded $53 billion in 2014. Remittances can be made to and from commercial banks, wire services, and specialized remittance providers. A fee is charged for each transfer, creating a major industry. Bill Gates has noted that if the transaction costs on remittances worldwide were cut from where they are today at around 10 percent to an average of 5 percent, it would unlock $15 billion a year in poor countries. Bill Gates, *Innovation with Impact: Financing 21st Century Development* 12 (Nov. 2011), http://www.gatesfoundation.org/What-We-Do/Global-Policy/G20-Report.

Federal law now regulates remittances that originate in the United States. 15 U.S.C. §1693o-1. The statute creates baseline protections for remittance senders and requires disclosures of fees. It also creates an error resolution procedure that mimics the Electronic Funds Transfer Act.

2. Stored Value or Prepaid Cards

"Stored value card" is the term that has been coined to describe all of the other useful cards that do not meet the definition of debit or credit cards. (Okay, maybe "value" does not cover your expired rewards card you still have for that sandwich shop that went out of business last year.) Examples of stored value cards are gift cards, health care spending cards, and payroll cards. In fact, the term "prepaid card" is rapidly replacing stored value card as the generic term for these products. These cards may be physical and stored in your wallet, or digital and stored on your phone or accessed online via a code. Stored value cards may or may not be reloadable, and they may work at only a single location, called "closed-loop," or at multiple locations processed via a network such as Mastercard, called "open-loop."

Most stored value cards do not themselves "store" value; instead, they contain coding that permits a contemporaneous authorization of value stored elsewhere, such as in an account held by a prepaid issuer. Technology and consumer preference is evolving to permit transactions that are limited to the merchant and the consumer — without an intermediary. The Starbucks card is perhaps the only widely used system of this type as of 2016, and of course, it is closed-loop, useful only for paying at Starbucks. That said, Ronald Mann reports that Starbucks now loads $4 billion a year on its cards. Ronald Mann, *Payment Systems* 80 (6th ed. 2016). That is a lot of "cash" and caffeine.

The law governing stored value cards is as disparate as the items falling in the definition. The outcome is a number of lawsuits alleging unfair and deceptive practices with decidedly mixed results for consumers. The excerpt below illustrates that broad reach of stored value cards into all areas of law and life.

> The Plaintiff, Robert Reagan, was jailed overnight in the Rockdale, Georgia, County Jail on a charge that later was dropped. When booked, he turned over $764.00 in cash to his jailers. When released the next day, he was given in lieu of his cash a pre-paid debt card worth $764.00 issued by Central National Bank through Stored Value Cards. He had no option to get cash or a check instead. Simultaneously, he received from the jailers a packet of documents that included the Agreement, which was printed in illegible five-point type. The jailers did not tell Reagan that the Agreement was in the packet. And, Reagan did not know that the Agreement was in the packet. This Agreement, which Reagan had no opportunity to read and did not sign, included an arbitration clause. After Reagan brought in state court this punitive class action challenging fees attendant to using the card, Stored Value Card and Central National Bank removed the case to federal district court and filed a motion to compel arbitration.

Reagan v. Stored Value Cards, Inc., 608 Fed. Appx. 895 (11th Cir. 2015). The mandatory arbitration clauses in stored value card agreements are generally enforceable; the result is that most disputes end in a non-public resolution by a private arbiter. The fees that Mr. Reagan challenged were substantial compared with the transactional costs of cash. Getting "cash back" at a point-of-sale in a store costs nearly $1, and even *automated* customer service cost 50 cents. Regardless of whether the released person used the card, a weekly account fee of $3.50 was charged beginning about two days after the person left jail. In the very tiny print, the person learned that there was an option to get a check for the balance on the card — for $9.95.

The move to prepaid cards was animated by businesses' desire to reduce costs for processing checks and credit cards, and to speed up transactions at check out. The preparation and issuance of a paper check for payroll will be several dollars, equal to about an hour of minimum wage pay. With a payroll card, the business pays only a few cents. The government jumped into this system for disbursing benefits such as food stamps and disability benefits. The consumer protections for prepaid cards, however, are much less consistent than their benefits to businesses. Several kinds of fees may be imposed, including charges to check the balance on a card, reach a customer service representative, or obtain a routine or additional account statement.

The CFPB is poised to issue rules that would expressly bring prepaid products within the ambit of the EFTA as prepaid accounts. Its applicability under current law is debatable. The definition of "electronic fund transfer" incorporates broad definitions of "account" and "financial institution," *see* 12 C.F.R. §1005.2(b) and (i), but the explicit addition of "payroll cards" to Regulation E, creates an argument that the exclusion of other stored value cards was intentional. The CFPB's proposed rules would give consumers protection from unauthorized transactions or lost cards by applying the EFTA's provisions on limited liability and error resolution. It would also establish additional origination disclosures and periodic statements. To check whether these rules have been adopted — and to learn some valuable research skills along the way — visit www.ecfr.gov and "Browse" to Title 12, Chapter X, Part 1005.

The type of stored value card with the longest-standing regulatory regime is gift cards. Federal law provides that gift cards must not expire for at least five years from the date of activation and generally limit inactivity fees to certain circumstances, such as if there has been no transaction for at least 12 months. 12 C.F.R. §1025(d) and (e). State laws supplement these protections. In several states, there cannot be any expiration date or any fees associated with a gift card. *See, e.g.*, Fla. Stat. Ann. §501.95 (West). In other states, the emphasis is on additional disclosures. *See, e.g.*, N.Y. Gen. Bus. Law §396-i (McKinney). While more information has its appeal, the size of a gift card makes effective disclosure difficult — a point made in the prior assignment about disclosure on mobile devices.

3. Mobile Payments

Mobile payments refer to using some aspect of a cellular phone to pay. The range of methods is tremendous. In the southern half of the globe, mobile payment often refers literally to paying someone by transferring purchased cell phone minutes to them. In the United States, mobile payments most commonly involve a third-party, non-cellular carrier, although the cell phone companies also have direct carrier billing programs. The latter are used widely to make small charitable contributions via SMS (short messaging service) in partnership between non-profits and wireless carriers. Stephanie Strom, *A Deluge of Donations Via Text Message*, N.Y. Times (Jan. 15, 2010) at http://www.nytimes.com/2010/01/19/us/19charity.html?_r=0. Wireless payment programs generally provide many fewer consumer protections for unauthorized transactions or disputed charges than traditional payments when federal law applies. The California Public Utilities Commission requires that consumers be given the right to withhold payments for disputed charges. Most carriers cap payments at a small amount, limiting the utility of direct payments that appear on a cellular bill.

Applications downloaded onto smart phones are the payment trend that is waiting to take off in the United States. But that sentence could have been written in any of the last ten years, and it is not clear when mobile will truly become widespread. Part of the lag is that smart phone penetration is estimated at about 60 percent; that means many consumers do not have the ability to use mobile payment applications. These apps rely on smart phone technologies such a QRC (quick response codes) or NFC (near-field communication). Even among smart phone users, there is no dominant payment app, despite fierce competition. Given the rapid changes in this area, a useful exercise to update this paragraph is to whip out your smart phone and search for "payment" and see what is popular. (This also gives you an excuse for using your phone in class. Not a good excuse, but better than "I was texting my mom.")

While ApplePay and GoogleWallet garnered brand-name publicity at launch, neither is widely used as of 2016. Similarly big retailers such as Target and Walgreens have implemented point-of-sale terminals that accommodate mobile payment technology, but if you've waited in line recently at these stores, you may have observed that nearly all transactions are still on plastic cards. As a hint that mobile pay remains in the netherworld (a.k.a. Silicon Valley), the buzzword used to describe mobile pay is "ecosystem." This is a sure sign that regulators are far from grappling with the consumer protection issues in mobile pay. Law may need to wait for a bigger market before it can sensibly regulate (although note that some lawmakers seem to think that "sensible regulation" is an oxymoron). On the other hand, law waited to regulate subprime mortgages on the mistaken belief that these mortgages were uncommon and anyone paying attention in 2008 knows how that worked out for the world economy.

Mobile payment applications are tools for transferring currency. They are not innovations in the nature of money itself, although they are moves away from the idea of currency as something physical toward a digital phenomenon. The next advance is to digital currency. A little book with amazingly big ideas about the past and future of money is Bill Maurer, *How Would You Like to Pay? How Technology is Changing the Future of Money* (Duke 2015).

Problem Set 19

19.1. Stephanie French is a bit of a spendthrift, between indulging her 13 cats in kitty daycare and her shoe-shopping problem. Although she makes $60,000 as a nanny, she waits anxiously for her paycheck on the first day of the month. On Wednesday March 1, at 8:37 A.M., as soon as she dropped the older kids at school, Stephanie wheeled the babies in the stroller to the nearest bank branch. She presented her nanny paycheck of $4,025 for deposit and asked for $700 in cash. The teller, Enrique, said that Stephanie could only have $100 and cheerfully described her options of 100 $1 bills, 20 $5 bills, 10 $10 bills, etc. Stephanie interrupted and demanded "at least $500 — that's the minimum that I need to pay the cat sitter." Enrique refused, repeating his offer of $100, but asked if Stephanie had any pictures of her cats. Can Enrique, on behalf of the bank, limit Stephanie's withdrawal to $100? If you are her cat sitter wanting payment, do you have a work around for this situation? *See* 12 C.F.R. §229.12.

19.2. Jonah Rome has a checking account and a savings account at Slumber Bank. He remembers receiving a notification from his bank asking him if he would like the bank to help him "rest easy at night" by having the bank cover overdrafts on his account. The notice from Slumber revealed that the cost of such overdraft protection would be $35 per instance; it also posed the question "What is your reputation worth?" in asking consumers to consider carefully the decision to toss the notice and fail to have overdraft protection. Jonah, however, felt confident that he would always have ample money and tossed the opt-in notice. Since then, he has tried to avoid overdrawing his account, which has become harder since his company quit paying a bonus. Jonah now lives paycheck to paycheck, and the end of the month is tight. On a date last Saturday, Jonah was mortified to have his debit card declined at the restaurant. Luckily, he had enough cash in his wallet to pay the bill, and he satisfied himself that the only damage was to his ego. However, when he got his bank statement the next week, the balance was lower than he expected. A review of the statement revealed that the bank had honored his automatic bill payment of $10 to the United Way charity, even when Jonah had only $5 in his account. The bank had then charged him a $35 fee for overdraft protection. Jonah likes to be generous, but he is fuming that his $10 charitable donation turned into a $45 cost to him. Did the bank violate Regulation E? *See* 12 C.F.R. §§1005.2 and 1005.17.

19.3. Deciding (mistakenly) that the third year of law school is a snooze, Laura recently took a part-time job as a nanny. The family has a stack of prepaid cards from HardCard of $100 each, and every Friday, Laura receives a card as her pay for eight hours of nanny work. She has let the cards accumulate but with the last spring break of her life coming up, Laura went to the mall to load up on suits and sundresses. Unfortunately, the cards were declined . . . every last one of them. The merchant explained that HardCard had been having "technical difficulties" for the last week and that Laura would have to pay a different way. Without enough cash or remaining credit on her credit card, Laura had to leave the store empty-handed, except for her stash of HardCards. When she called the number on the back of the card (not even toll-free), the customer service representative repeatedly assured Laura that the cards had value but that there was an "access delay." Enraged, Laura has had to break her vow to never re-enter the school law library to find out whether she has any legal claims against HardCard. Assume the first source that she scans is this assignment; additionally, *see* 12 C.F.R. §1005.20(b)(2) and (f)(2). What laws might give her a claim against HardCard? Also, does Laura have any claim against the family?

19.4. Robin Gray loves to pay. Specifically, she loves to pay with apps loaded onto her phone. When she woke up in a haze at 11:00 A.M. on Friday morning, she realized that she had left her phone in a bar the prior evening. Efforts to locate the phone on Friday afternoon failed, and Robin's phone has now been missing 18 hours. On Saturday morning, Robin starts trying to contact the mobile payment applications. First problem: she cannot remember all the payment applications loaded on the phone, but she does know that some of them are linked to her primary checking account. Second problem: she cannot locate a phone number for her favorite mobile pay app. Robin has $800 on deposit with application. She has emailed customer service but received an auto response that it is outside business hours and her message will be read Monday through Friday, 9:00 A.M. to 4:00 P.M. What should she do? Is her $800 safe if someone hacks her phone? (Her passcode was 1234.)

Assignment 20. Online Transactions

Consumers can go online to conduct nearly all possible transactions with businesses. From the birth of the World Wide Web, businesses have recognized the sales potential of a platform that is available nearly anytime and anywhere at a consumer's convenience. Generally, consumer protection law is the same whether the transaction is in person or via the Internet. Contract law, including warranty law, applies, as do prohibitions against deceptive advertising or unfair sales practices. Similarly, lending online is regulated by TILA, ECOA, and similar laws.

Online transactions present challenges of information for consumers and therefore require more trust. Disclosures may be hard to display digitally, especially on smaller devices such as mobile phones and tablets. Consumers cannot literally eyeball whether an Internet discount reseller of goods actually has a reasonable quantity for sale, or is merely displaying a picture of the good to drive traffic to its site. This is a digital bait and switch, with the basic problems not unlike the in-person transaction discussed in Assignment 5. Consumers may be easier to fool with a fancy website than in the non-virtual world where they can assess whether a retail business is in a well-run shopping center. Similarly, consumers may find a video sales pitch on a site to be charming, but in real life would find a salesperson to have shifty eyes. As with mail order, consumers take a leap of faith when they input payment and personal information into a web form and hope to receive a timely delivery of quality goods.

Businesses also face risks of identity fraud from consumers who buy online. The odds of getting away with the crime favor the con artist who types a verification code off a stolen credit card into a website over one who shows up in a retail store with a card and must show a stolen or fake photo identification. The ease of online transactions is attractive, but the risk of being scammed is higher for both consumers and businesses.

A. Contracting Online

As with most things in life, transacting online goes best if one uses common sense. Just as a consumer can read context clues at a mall (bare shelves; uninformed staff), online users can use shortcuts or proxies for legitimacy (a domain name suffix other than .com, .gov, or .org; no privacy verification; poor or outdated site design). The actual purchase online versus at a brick-and-mortar is the same at its most basic level. Courts have recognized that commerce is still commerce, applying contract law to digital transactions. "While new commerce on the Internet has exposed courts to many new situations, it has not fundamentally changed the principles of contract." *Register.com, Inc. v. Verio, Inc.*, 356 F.3d 393, 403 (2d Cir. 2004). The Uniform Commercial Code (U.C.C.) and common law of contracts govern online transactions.

When an online transaction requires a written contract, an electronic contract and an electronic signature satisfy the statute of frauds. The fact that a consumer did not put pen to paper to agree to a transaction does not invalidate the contract. Any "electronic sound, symbol, or process, attached to or logically associated with a contract or other record and executed or adopted by a person with the intent to sign the record" counts as a signature. Electronic Signatures in Global and National Commerce Act, 15 U.S.C. §7001 (2000).

Non-virtual transactions usually involve dealing with salespeople and clerks, and conversations can happen about what types of risk the consumer is taking when purchasing a product. Any particularly pertinent information can be vocalized to the consumer at the moment of purchase and things like the terms of a return policy can be disclosed via a "cashwrap" receipt (so-called because it is literally wrapped around a customer's change).

This communication is not as simple online. To communicate the terms and conditions of the transaction online early online retailers took the idea of an End User License Agreement (EULA) from software transactions — where no physical good was being purchased, only a program — and created Terms of Service or Terms of Use. There are two main types of EULAs: clickwraps and browsewraps. Sometimes consumers are confronted with a hybrid agreement. In a clickwrap/browsewrap hybrid, the consumer must still click a box to indicate agreement with the terms, but the consumer is not visually confronted with the text of the agreement, only with a link.

The following case involves a consumer who had filed suit against the social networking platform Facebook. In deciding a motion to transfer venue, the court examines a forum-selection clause contained in Facebook's Terms of Use and discusses the differences between clickwraps, browsewraps, and hybrids.

Fteja v. Facebook, Inc.

841 F. Supp. 2d 829 (S.D.N.Y. 2012)

HOLWELL, District Judge.

. . .

[Plaintiff Mustafa] Fteja, a resident of Staten Island, New York, "was an active user of facebook.com." Fteja "ha[d] been adhering to Facebook['s] terms of service" and "help[ing] build the Facebook community by adding content and signing up new members. . . ." But on September 24, 2010, Facebook allegedly disabled Fteja's account on September 24, 2010 "without warning" and "without reason."

. . .

DISCUSSION

The Court first considers "whether the action could have been brought in the trans-feree forum," here the Atl. Recording Corp. v. Project Playlist, Inc., 603 F. Supp. 2d 690, 695 (S.D.N.Y. 2009). That requires the Court to determine whether the Northern District of California would be a proper venue for this action and whether it would have jurisdiction over this action and over Facebook. See Unlimited Care, Inc. v. Visiting Nurse Ass'n of E. Mass., Inc., 42 F. Supp. 2d 327, 333 (S.D.N.Y. 1999) ("A court electing to transfer an action, may only transfer such action to a district where it might have been brought initially, (i.e., a district where defendant is subject to personal jurisdiction and venue would be proper).").

The Northern District of California would be a proper venue for this action. Venue is proper, inter alia, in "a judicial district in which a substantial part of the events or omissions giving rise to the claim occurred. . . ." 28 U.S.C. §1391(a)(2). The Northern District of California would be such a district in this action because the nub of Fteja's claim is that Facebook wrongfully disabled his account and the employees responsible for disabling accounts work at Facebook's headquarters in Palo Alto, California which is in the Northern District of California.

The Northern District of California would have subject matter jurisdiction over this action on the basis of the parties' diversity of citizenship. And that court would have personal jurisdiction over Facebook because the presence of Facebook's head-quarters in Palo Alto suggests that Facebook has had "continuous and systematic general business contacts" with California. Metro. Life Ins. Co. v. Robertson-Ceco Corp., 84 F.3d 560, 568 (2d Cir. 1996).

The next question, then, is whether Facebook has made a "clear and convincing showing that transfer is proper," Hershman v. Unumprovident Corp., 658 F. Supp. 2d 598, 600 (S.D.N.Y. 2007), that is, that transfer will advance "the convenience of parties and witnesses" as well as "the interest of justice." N.Y. Marine & Gen. Ins. Co. v. Lafarge N. Am., Inc., 599 F.3d 102,112 (2d Cir. 2010).

On that score, the parties devote substantial attention to the forum selection clause contained in the terms and conditions that govern Facebook users' accounts, known as the Terms of Use at the time that Fteja signed up for an account. That clause provides as follows:

> You will resolve any claim, cause of action or dispute ("claim") you have with us arising out of or relating to this Statement or Facebook exclusively in a state or federal court located in Santa Clara County. The laws of the State of California will govern this Statement, as well as any claim that might arise between you and us, without regard to conflict of law provisions. You agree to submit to the personal jurisdiction of the courts located in Santa Clara County, California for the purpose of litigating all such claims.

As an initial matter, Fteja argues that "[t]here is no proof that [he] agreed to a forum selection clause" and that he does "not remember agreeing to [the] forum selection clause or agreeing to any Facebook agreement." Impossible, says Face-book: "a putative Facebook user cannot become an actual Facebook user unless and until they have clicked through the registration page where they acknowledge they have read and agreed to Facebook's terms of use. . . ."

As a matter of logic, Facebook appears to be correct. Declarations filed by Facebook employees, screenshots submitted by Fatouros, and Facebook's current website of which the Court takes judicial notice suggest that the Facebook sign-up process works as follows. A putative user is asked to fill out several fields containing personal and contact information. See http://www.facebook.com. The putative user is then asked to click a button that reads "Sign Up." After clicking this initial "Sign Up" button, the user proceeds to a page entitled "Security Check" that requires a user to reenter a series of letters and numbers displayed on the page. Below the box where the putative user enters that letter-number combination, the page displays a second "Sign Up" button similar to the button the putative user clicked on the initial page. The following sentence appears immediately below that button: "By clicking Sign Up, you are indicating that you have read and agree to the Terms of Service." The phrase "Terms of Service" is underlined, an indication that the phrase is a hyperlink, a phrase that is "usually highlighted or underlined" and "sends users who click on it directly to a new location — usually an internet address or a program of some sort." United States v. Hair, 178 F. App'x. 879, 882 n.3 (11th Cir. 2006).

In order to have obtained a Facebook account, Fteja must have clicked the second "Sign Up" button. Accordingly, if the phrase that appears below that button is given effect, when Fteja clicked "Sign Up," he "indicat[ed] that [he] ha[d] read and agree[d] to the Terms of Policy."

However, "[w]hile new commerce on the Internet has exposed courts to many new situations, it has not fundamentally changed the principles of contract." Register.com, Inc. v. Verio, Inc., 356 F.3d 393, 403 (2d Cir. 2004). And one such principle is that "[m]utual manifestation of assent, whether by written or spoken word or by conduct, is the touchstone of contract." Specht v. Netscape Commc'ns Corp., 306 F.3d 17, 29 (2d Cir. 2002). Hence the threshold requirement that the forum selection "clause was reasonably communicated to the party resisting enforcement." Phillips v. Audio Active, Ltd., 494 F.3d 373, 383 (2 Cir. 2007).

In that regard, the Second Circuit has held that "a consumer's clicking on a . . . button does not communicate assent to contractual terms if the offer did not make clear to the consumer that clicking on the . . . button would signify assent to those terms." Specht, 306 F.3d at 29-30. In Specht, the Second Circuit declined to enforce an arbitration clause to which a user purportedly agreed when he clicked on a button to download software. The terms and conditions were not visible anywhere on the screen containing the download button. Rather, "[t]he sole reference to" the terms and conditions "was located in text that would have become visible to plaintiffs only if they had scrolled down to the next screen where there was the following sentence: 'Please review and agree to the terms of the *Netscape SmartDownload software licensing agreement before downloading and using the software.*'" Id. The just italicized language appeared underlined and if a user "clicked on the underlined invitation to review and agree to the terms, a hypertext link would have taken the user to a separate webpage entitled 'License & Support Agreements.'" Id. at 23-24. That page included the arbitration clause. See id. at 24. "[I]n circumstances such as these, where consumers are urged to download free software at the immediate click of a button," the Court of Appeals held that "a reference to the existence of license terms on a submerged screen is not sufficient to place consumers on inquiry or constructive notice of those terms." Id. at 32.

Specht does not squarely control this case because the second Sign-Up page's reference to the Terms of Use appeared immediately below the "Sign-Up" button. Yet this case does have something in common with *Specht*: the fact that the terms and conditions were not displayed on the page where the user purportedly assented to the terms. Instead, those terms were visible only by clicking on a hyperlink. The Terms of Use therefore appear to be a kind of so-called "browsewrap" agreement, "where website terms and conditions of use are posted on the website typically as a hyperlink at the bottom of the screen." Hines v. Overstock.com, Inc., 668 F. Supp. 2d 362, 366 (E.D.N.Y. 2009). Cf. Pollstar v. Gigmania Ltd., 170 F. Supp. 2d 974, 981 (E.D. Cal. 2000) ("[A] browse wrap license is part of the web site and the user assents to the contract when the user visits the web site.").

Several courts have enforced browsewrap agreements. See, e.g., Ticketmaster L.L.C. v. RMG Technologies, Inc., 507 F. Supp. 2d 1096, 1107 (C.D. Cal. 2007) (plaintiff was "highly likely to succeed in showing that Defendant received notice of the Terms of Use and assented to them by actually using the website" where site displayed a warning that "Use of this website is subject to express Terms of Use" and "[t]he underlined phrase 'Terms of Use' is a hyperlink to the full Terms of Use").

However, several of these cases appear to have turned on the user's constructive knowledge of the hyperlinked terms. Indeed, "[m]ost courts which have considered the issue . . . have held that in order to state a plausible claim for relief based upon a browsewrap agreement, the website user must have had actual or constructive knowledge of the site's terms and conditions, and have manifested assent to them." Cvent, Inc. v. Eventbrite, Inc., 739 F. Supp. 2d 927, 937-38 (E.D. Va. 2010). And at least one court has declined to enforce terms and conditions that "only appear[ed] on [a] website via a link buried at the bottom of the first page" where users "are not required to click on that link, nor are they required to read or assent to the Terms of Use in order to use the website or access any of its content." Id.

Moreover, the cases in which courts have enforced browsewrap agreements have involved users who are businesses rather than, as in *Sprecht* and in this case, consumers. Cf. Mark Lemley, *Terms of Use*, 91 Minn. L. Rev. 459, 472 (2006) ("An examination of the cases that have considered browsewraps in the last five years demonstrates that the courts have been willing to enforce terms of use against corporations, but have not been willing to do so against individuals."). Indeed, one prominent commentator has hypothesized that "[c]ourts may be willing to overlook the utter absence of assent only when there are reasons to believe that the [allegedly assenting party] is aware of the [other party's] terms." Id. at 477. And based on the reasonable supposition that such "awareness may be more likely with corporations than individuals, perhaps because corporations are repeat players," that commentator has argued "that if courts enforce browsewraps at all, enforcement should be limited to the context in which it has so far occurred — against sophisticated commercial entities who are repeat players." Id. at 464, 477.

On the other hand, it is not clear that these countervailing considerations apply to Facebook's Terms of Use. First, Fteja's allegation that he complied with the Terms of Use suggests that he had constructive knowledge of the Terms of Use, though it is not clear from the complaint when he acquired that knowledge and he denies that he read the terms before signing up for his Facebook account.

Second, the Terms of Use were not exactly a true browsewrap license "in which the user does not see the contract at all but in which the license terms provide that using a Web site constitutes agreement to a contract whether the user knows it or not." Lemley, *Terms of Use*, 91 MINN. L. REV. at 460. Indeed, in a pure-form browse-wrap agreement, "the website will contain a notice that — by merely using the services of, obtaining information from, or initiating applications within the website — the user is agreeing to and is bound by the site's terms of service." United States v. Drew, 259 F.R.D. 449, 462 n.22 (C.D. Cal. 2009). In other words, a browse-wrap agreement usually involves a disclaimer that by visiting the website — something that the user has already done — the user agrees to the Terms of Use not listed on the site itself but available only by clicking a hyperlink. Here, by contrast, the second Sign-Up page indicated that additional action beyond merely visiting that page, namely, clicking "Sign-Up," would manifest agreement to the Terms of Use.

In that sense, Facebook's Terms of Use have something in common with so-called "clickwrap" licenses, "in which an online user clicks 'I agree' to standard form terms. . . ." Lemley, *Terms of Use*, 91 MINN. L. REV. 459; Cf. Drew, 259 F.R.D. at 462 n. 22 ("Clickwrap agreements require a user to affirmatively click a box on the website acknowledging awareness of and agreement to the terms of service before he or she is allowed to proceed with further utilization of the website."). A clickwrap agreement "presents the potential licensee (i.e., the end-user) with a message on his or her computer screen, requiring that the user manifest his or her assent to the terms of the license agreement by clicking on an icon." Register.com, Inc. v. Verio, Inc., 356 F.3d 393, 403, 429 (2d Cir. 2004).

"Because the user has 'signed' the contract by clicking 'I agree,'" even commentators who have called for limits on browsewrap agreements find "nothing inherently troubling about enforcing clickwrap licenses." Lemley, *Terms of Use*, 91 MINN. L. REV. at 466. And the courts appear to share that view, for "[c]lickwrap agreements "have been routinely upheld by circuit and district courts." Drew, 259 F.R.D. at 462 n. 22. Indeed, numerous courts, including a number of courts in this Circuit, have enforced forum selection clauses in clickwrap agreements. See, e.g., Segal v. Amazon.com, Inc., 763 F. Supp. 2d 1367 (S.D. Fla. 2011).

Yet Facebook's Terms of Use are not a pure-form clickwrap agreement, either. While the Terms of Use require the user to click on "Sign Up" to assent, they do not contain any mechanism that forces the user to actually examine the terms before assenting. By contrast, in assenting to a clickwrap agreement, "users typically click an 'I agree' box after being presented with a list of terms and conditions of use . . ." Hines, 668 F. Supp. 2d at 366. That aspect of a clickwrap agreement ensures that "potential licensees are presented with the proposed license terms and forced to expressly and unambiguously manifest either assent or rejection prior to being given access to the product." Register.com, 356 F.3d at 429.

Courts have not overlooked this feature. For example, the Second Circuit in *Specht* found a "signal difference" between the software for which the defendant supplied only hyperlinked terms and other software for which users "were automatically shown a scrollable text of that program's license agreement and were not permitted to complete the installation until they had clicked on a 'Yes' button to indicate that they accepted all the license terms." Specht, 306 F.3d at 22-23. In addition, another court has interpreted the clickwrap case law for the proposition that, "[a]s a rule, a clickwrap is valid where the terms of the agreement appear on the same screen with the button the user must click to accept the terms and proceed with the installation of the product." Grosvenor v. Qwest Commc'ns Int'l, Inc.,

No. 09-cv-2848, 2010 U.S. Dist. LEXIS 109884, 2010 WL 3906253, at *2 (D. Colo. Sept. 30, 2010) (declining to enforce arbitration clause in clickwrap agreement where terms did not appear on the same page as the "Yes" box).

Thus Facebook's Terms of Use are somewhat like a browsewrap agreement in that the terms are only visible via a hyperlink, but also somewhat like a clickwrap agreement in that the user must do something else — click "Sign Up" — to assent to the hyperlinked terms. Yet, unlike some clickwrap agreements, the user can click to assent whether or not the user has been presented with the terms.

What result follows? Have terms been reasonably communicated where a consumer must take further action not only, as in a clickwrap agreement, to assent to the terms but also, as in a browsewrap agreement, to view them? Is it enough that Facebook warns its users that they will accept terms if they click a button while providing the opportunity to view the terms by first clicking on a hyperlink?

In answering that question, it is tempting to infer from the power with which the social network has revolutionized how we interact that Facebook has done the same to the law of contract that has been so critical to managing that interaction in a free society. But not even Facebook is so powerful. . . . [T]he Court of Appeals has used a rather simple analogy. "The situation might be compared to one in which" Facebook "maintains a roadside fruit stand displaying bins of apples." Register.com, 356 F.3d at 401. For purposes of this case, suppose that above the bins of apples are signs that say, "By picking up this apple, you consent to the terms of sales by this fruit stand. For those terms, turn over this sign."

In those circumstances, courts have not hesitated in applying the terms against the purchaser. Indeed, in *Carnival Cruise Lines, Inc. v. Shute*, 499 U.S. 585, 587 (1991), the Supreme Court upheld a forum selection clause in fine print on the back of a cruise ticket even though the clause became binding at the time of purchase, and the purchasers only received the ticket some time later. See id.

. . .

There is no reason why that outcome should be different because Facebook's Terms of Use appear on another screen rather than another sheet of paper. What is the difference between a hyperlink and a sign on a bin of apples saying "Turn Over for Terms" or a cruise ticket saying "SUBJECT TO CONDITIONS OF CONTRACT ON LAST PAGES IMPORTANT! PLEASE READ CONTRACT-ON LAST PAGES 1, 2, 3"? Shute, 499 U.S. at 587. The mechanics of the internet surely remain unfamiliar, even obtuse to many people. But it is not too much to expect that an internet user whose social networking was so prolific that losing Facebook access allegedly caused him mental anguish would understand that the hyperlinked phrase "Terms of Use" is really a sign that says "Click Here for Terms of Use." So understood, at least for those to whom the internet is in an indispensable part of daily life, clicking the hyperlinked phrase is the twenty-first century equivalent of turning over the cruise ticket. In both cases, the consumer is prompted to examine terms of sale that are located somewhere else. Whether or not the consumer bothers to look is irrelevant. "Failure to read a contract before agreeing to its terms does not relieve a party of its obligations under the contract." See Centrifugal Force, Inc. v. Softnet Commc'n, Inc., No. 08 Civ. 5463, 2011 U.S. Dist. LEXIS 20536, 2011 WL 744732, at *7 (S.D.N.Y. Mar. 1, 2011) (enforcing clickwrap agreement in breach of contract action). Here, Fteja was informed of the consequences of his assenting click and he was shown, immediately below, where to click to understand those consequences. That was enough.

. . .

[T]he Court concludes that Fteja assented to the Terms of Use and therefore to the forum selection clause therein. If that is so, Fteja agreed to litigate all disputes regarding his Facebook account "exclusively in a state or federal court located in Santa Clara County," California. The federal court for that county is the Northern District of California. . . . Facebook's motion to transfer is granted.

———————

Although courts apply traditional principles of contract law and evaluate whether the consumer manifested assent to the agreement, businesses should be careful when designing their terms of service/EULAs. State and international law varies on what must be included and what will be held enforceable.

The procedural posture of the *Facebook* case illustrates another problem with online transactions: determining the "place" of the transaction. While choice of law clauses can resolve the law of the contract, the harder issues emerge when businesses try to escape the application of criminal or regulatory laws by arguing that the transaction occurs in "their" headquarters. Most courts have held that the substantive law that applies is that of the consumer's location. *See* Erin O'Hara, *Choice of Law in Internet Transactions: The Uneasy Case for Online Consumer Protection*, 153 U. Pa. L. Rev. 1883 (2015). The effect of this for online commerce — and lawyers working in it — is that there are a lot of 50-state surveys of laws and efforts to create operations that comply with the law of all states.

B.   Shopping Online

The FTC's advice for online shopping highlights the similarities of issues with traditional consumer commerce: know who you are dealing with, know what you are buying, and know the terms. The challenge is that with online transactions it can be hard to determine some of these things. Also, there are added costs of shipping, confusion about applicable taxes, and a variety of refund policies.

A few examples of consumer protection issues from online shopping illustrate how the lack of human interaction and information problems can create trouble. Travel discounter Priceline faced a class action lawsuit alleging that it did not adequately inform consumers that, in addition to the price that the consumer "named" and that was accepted, the hotels they stayed in may charge them a "resort fee." According to the plaintiffs, Priceline knew about the hotels' mandatory fees charged and did not disclose this information to consumers to create a misperception of a lower price. Maya Rajamani, *Priceline Can't Escape Resort Fee Suit, Class Says*, Law360.com, (Oct. 26, 2015), http://www.law360.com/articles/718782.

Websites also may get in trouble with policies designed to create "sticky" customers. Some websites offered post-transaction rebates or shipping discounts that required a consumer to agree to a monthly subscription charge. The site used the consumer's previously entered payment information to process these subscription charges. Because the consumer did not enter payment information, they believed this "rebate" or "discount" was free. Under the Restore Online Shoppers' Confidence Act, this practice requires full disclosure of the subscription and forbids reuse of the consumer's payment information from a prior one-off transaction. 15 U.S.C. §8401.

Other websites may border on misleading consumers by nature of their rapid growth. Etsy began as an online marketplace to purchase one-of-a-kind, handmade goods from artists and craftsmen. As it grew, it offered a wider range of goods for sale, including those mass-produced. Etsy modified its terms of use for sellers and its disclosures to consumers, but confusion may continue as its initial reputation endures after changes in business practice. Liz Stinson, *Why Etsy's Future Depends on Redefining "Handmade,"* WIRED.COM (Apr. 19, 2014), http://tinyurl.com/gsz7e7b.

The biggest controversy has come from the biggest business. Amazon.com began as an online bookstore and expanded into an online megastore offering nearly anything a person could want to purchase. The business offers goods not only from its own warehouses, but also through third-party sellers. A consumer may go to Amazon.com, find a product that is offered by "Amazon" and place an order. The product arrives but with a defect. When the customer contacts Amazon support, the company reveals that the order was fulfilled by a third-party vendor via Amazon's online sales platform, and that any problems are the responsibility of this third-party vendor. In essence, the consumer believed that they picked an item off the shelf in Amazon's store and paid Amazon at the register upon checkout, but that the "store" has no liability because it is only a conduit. This is the modern equivalent of the historic debate about whether to make traditional merchants liable for warranty issues created by manufacturers.

Given the breadth of shopping options at Amazon.com, the retailer has run into several consumer problems. For example, Amazon.com allegedly has engaged in price discrimination based on a consumer's physical location, gathered from the digital nature of the transaction. *See* Anita Ramasastry, Web sites change prices based on customers' habits, CNN.com (June 24, 2005), http://www.cnn.com/2005/LAW/06/24/ramasastry.website.prices. As another example, consumers felt wronged when Amazon removed previously purchased e-book titles from consumer's digital libraries without notice. Consumers who paid an annual fee to be "Prime" members who receive additional benefits such as free 2-day shipping have alleged that Amazon engaged in unfair and deceptive practices by encouraging its third-party sellers to raise product prices to cover the costs of shipping. *See Ekin v. Amazon Servs., LLC*, 84 F. Supp. 3d 1172 (W.D. Wash. 2014); Amy Martinez, *Merchants file suit against Amazon.com*, The Seattle Times, (March 15, 2013), http://www.seattletimes.com/business/small-online-merchants-file-suit-against-amazoncom.

Sometimes the controversy arises not from the online nature of the transaction but from what is being sold. Software presents a classification problem for the law. Is software a good, or is it a license? The Uniform Computer

Information Transactions Act (UCITA) was intended to increase uniformity in the law that applies to purchase of software by amending the U.C.C. with regard to software transactions. But ultimately it was only adopted by two states, Virginia and Maryland. Adding further insult to UCITA's creators, some states actually adopted laws to prevent the provisions of UCITA from taking effect in their state. Dorte Toft, *Opponents Blast Proposed U.S. Software Law*, CNN.com, July 12, 1999, http://www.cnn.com/TECH/computing/9907/12/ucita.idg. A major objection to UCITA was its provision that permitted designating, as a matter of state law, that software was a license and not a sale of goods. An anti-consumer effect of this designation was that under a license consumers could be restricted from reselling the software. The ownership of goods, in contrast, carries with it the right to resell.

Reselling is extremely common online. The right to resell a copyrighted product you legally purchased is called the "first sale" doctrine. *See* 17 U.S.C. §109 (limiting a copyright owner's exclusive right to distribute copies of the copyrighted work to give a purchaser the ability to resell). If the purchase of software is a license, it falls outside the doctrine. Online businesses that profit from individuals reselling or auctioning off previously purchased items are major beneficiaries of the first sale doctrine.

The most successful early auction site, eBay, revolutionized how consumers think about online commerce. Its model actually revived an old art — haggling (fixed prices were an invention of the 19th century and the rise of advertising). eBay allows consumers to either bid on an item, or choose the price the consumer thinks is valid for a certain item, and compete with others who may find a higher or lower price more appropriate. This kind of marketplace was wildly successful at first but is dwindling. Some of this may be due to the pervasive online presence of traditional retailers; others think that consumers discovered the allure of bidding led to regret, not unlike that associated with gambling. Another issue was that eBay created unusual policies to attract consumers. Sellers have had issues with dishonest buyers but eBay enforces a "buyer is always right" policy. Jennifer Abel, *Judge Rules Class Action Suit Against eBay and PayPal May Proceed*, Consumer Affairs, (August 14, 2014), http://tinyurl.com/nvx59km. Also, eBay has come under fire for trading in counterfeit merchandise. Like many online merchants, eBay's refrain has been that it is a platform, and that there is no contract other than that between the buyer and the seller. One can question that claim given that eBay charges a fee for each listing based on percentage of the sale. The controversy illustrates the way in which online transactions manifest problems with trust and verification that may exceed in-person deals.

C.   Marketing Online

Marketing is an area of online commerce that is governed by federal law. Businesses use the speed and pervasiveness of email to market to consumers a fraction of traditional costs. Such "spam" advertising messages are a nuisance. Like the flyers stuck under our windshield wipers or the junk mail that comes via

USPS, these emails seldom get read, but given their low cost, they need produce only a few responses to make spamming an effective direct marketing tool. Just like they did not like having their dinner interrupted by telephone solicitors and so enacted the do-not-call registry, Congress did not like spam email and did something about it, despite business's ferocious opposition. In 2003, the Controlling the Assault of Non-Solicited Pornography and Marketing (CAN-SPAM) Act created firm guidelines to businesses on what they can and cannot do when sending generalized commercial messages (as opposed to messages directly resulting from a transaction or a business relationship). 15 U.S.C. §§7701 et al. The business must properly identify itself and offer an opt-out process to allow the consumer prevent further emails. The CAN-SPAM Act is not limited to bulk emails but applies to any commercial message sent by a business. The Federal Trade Commission enforces the CAN-SPAM Act, with violations treated like an unfair or deceptive act or practice. 15 U.S.C. §7706.

Online transactions also ushered in the idea of online reviews. While these were initially prompted by the online seller as a way of easing consumers' concerns about the seller's reliability, the review business is now an area of separate commerce. Sites such as Yelp.com or Angie's List allow reviews of in-person transactions and focus primarily on services, rather than goods. Reviews are a major market innovation that protects consumers. Reviews give consumers more information and are often available right on the commerce site itself so that consumers actually see and use the feedback. Though these reviews should create trust between businesses and consumers, the anonymity of the Internet means that there are few repercussions for someone who posts a snarky or untrue review. In fact, writing false reviews can actually be a career. Websites such as Fiverr.com will pay (unsurprisingly, usually "five" bucks) for users to post reviews on websites about certain products or services. Studies have shown that up to 30 percent of online reviews for certain products, and 10-20 percent of reviews for hotels and restaurants, are fake. Rihannon Lucy Cosslett, *Many Internet Reviews are Bogus — Are You Honestly Surprised?*, THE GUARDIAN.COM, (November 2, 2015), http://www.tinyurl.com/ogez9dr.

Businesses also respond to online reviews in a transparent way at review web sites. By posting a reply that addresses or disputes a consumer's concerns, the online review process creates more information about customer service than a traditional refund that quietly appeases an unhappy consumer. Some businesses have taken their frustrations with negative reviews into their own hands — or at least, their own contracts. Companies ranging from medical providers to cell phone accessory peddlers have included "gag clauses" in their contracts that prohibit consumers from posting negative reviews. Some contracts even ban consumers from threatening to post a negative review or impose penalties on consumers who write a review that a business finds troublesome. In 2015 Congress considered a bill, the Consumer Review Freedom Act, which would ban these gag clauses in consumer contracts. If enacted, it would void any provision that imposed a penalty or fee against an individual for a review or restricted the ability of an individual to engage in "a written, verbal, or pictorial review, performance assessment of, or other similar analysis of, the products, services or conduct of a person." S. 2044, 114th Cong. §2 (2015).

Marketing oneself online is also common. From traditional sites like Match.com and eHarmony.com to the "swipe right" culture of Tinder and Grindr, people looking to get married or simply get lucky are extremely active online. Online dating services take the personal touch out of matchmaking and insert algorithms or rapid human evaluation. This adds another layer of mistrust to those that are inherent in dating. The anonymity of the Internet permits scammers to flourish. "Catfishing" is the act of pretending to be another person (or being yourself, but using false pictures and information to make yourself into someone you aren't) to get another person interested. Some use this power simply to get a first date but others may continue the deception to defraud victims of money.

Sometimes the alleged scam is from the dating website itself. Many sites offer free registration that lets you post your profile on the site. If you want to interact with another member, however, you must pay a membership fee. Some sites have been accused of using fake profiles with attractive photographs or "bots" — computer programs — to induce nonpaying members to pay the membership fee in order to interact with the non-existent person. These sites are subject not just to traditional contract rules and consumer protection statutes, but to specific laws in place for dating services. *See* Cal. Civ. Code §1694.2(b) (requiring that every dating service feature "on its face" a clause informing the consumer of the right to cancel their membership for a refund within three days).

D.   Digital Applications

With the advent of mobile phone and tablets came the rise of the application. These "apps" are programs that perform digital functions without an Internet browser interface. The law governing "apps" is undeveloped, as the law governing online transactions was a few decades ago. Generally, it appears — as with browser-based transactions — that basic contract law will govern, perhaps with specific statutory overlays for consumer protection.

Some apps make the same types of overstatements and false claims made elsewhere in marketing. The FTC sued an app developer for false advertising when the app claimed to be "scientifically proven" to improve a user's eyesight. Federal Trade Commission, *Charges Marketers of 'Vision Improvement' App Deceptive Claims*, September 17, 2015, https://tinyrul.com/ng68l9m. The suit repeats a lesson from this book's first case, *Carbolic Smoke Ball*; the more things change with marketing (from newspaper to TV to apps), the more they stay the same (consumers fall prey to quackery). Other apps have gotten into legal trouble for failing to mention certain things they do, such as hijack your phone to mine cryptocurrency. Federal Trade Commission, *App Developer Settles FTC and New Jersey Charges It Hijacked Consumers' Phones to Mine Cryptocurrency*, June 29, 2015, https://tinyurl.com/pfxw6vh.

An emergent consumer protection problem involves "free" app games. A consumer can download the game at no cost or obligation but then will see offers to make "in-app" purchases. These may allow the consumer to unlock hidden features or advance beyond a certain level in the game. While these purchases can be reasonable or inane, the issue is one of disclosure. Can such a game be fairly called "free?" And how does the game obtain consent to purchase, particularly in a virtual world where the business can claim a certain lack of knowledge of its users.

In re Apple In-App Purchase Litig.

855 F. Supp. 2d 1030 (N.D. Cal. 2012)

DAVILA, District Judge.

Presently before the court is Defendant Apple Inc.'s ("Apple") motion to dismiss Plaintiffs' Consolidated Class Action Complaint ("Complaint") pursuant to Rule 12(b)(6).

Apple, a Delaware corporation with its headquarters and principal place of business in California, is a leading seller of software applications ("apps") that users can download onto their mobile computing devices. Plaintiffs bring the instant class action on behalf of themselves and other similarly situated parents or guardians who (a) downloaded or permitted their minor children to download a supposedly free app from Apple and (b) then incurred charges for game-related purchases made by their minor children, without the parents' and guardians' knowledge or permission.

FACTUAL AND PROCEDURAL BACKGROUND

On April 11, 2011, Plaintiff Garen Meguerian filed a complaint, individually and on behalf of others similarly situated, alleging that Plaintiffs' minor children were able to purchase "game currencies" without their parents' knowledge or authorization while playing game applications ("apps"), provided by Apple and advertised as free. An "app" is a software application that a customer can download from Apple's App Store onto a mobile computing device. "Game currencies" are virtual objects, such as supplies, that are used in connection with gameplay in certain apps. . . . In the Complaint, Plaintiffs allege that minors were able to make in-app purchases of game currency without Plaintiffs' knowledge or permission. The Complaint asserts claims for declaratory judgment, violation of the California Consumers Legal Remedies Act ("CLRA"), Cal. Civ. Code §1750 et seq., violation of California's Unfair Competition Law ("UCL"), Cal. Bus. Prof. Code §17200 et seq., breach of the implied covenant of good faith and fair dealing, and restitution/unjust enrichment/money had and received.

The sale of an app or any game currency is a transaction completed directly between Apple and the consumer. Apple requires users to authenticate their accounts by entering a password prior to purchasing and/or downloading an app or buying game currency. Until early 2011, however, once the password was entered once, Apple permitted users to buy game currency for up to fifteen minutes without re-entering the password. Plaintiffs claim that they were unaware that purchases could be made without re-entering the password. Plaintiffs downloaded and allowed their children to play free or nominal gaming apps, unaware that their children could, for fifteen minutes, purchase game currency without entering a password. Plaintiffs' minor children were able to charge their parents' accounts in amounts ranging from $99.99 to $338.72 at a time.

On August 8, 2011, Defendants filed this instant motion to dismiss Plaintiffs' Complaint. . . .

DISCUSSION

A. Declaratory Judgment

Plaintiffs seek declaratory judgment pursuant to 28 U.S.C. §2201 et seq., seeking a determination that . . . the sales contracts between Apple and the minor children of class members, relating to the purchase of in-app game currency, are voidable at the option of the respective class members on behalf of their minor children. . . . Plaintiffs allege that each in-app purchase constitutes a separate and voidable contract between Apple and Plaintiffs' minor children, which may be disaffirmed by a parent or guardian on behalf of the minors. Plaintiffs allege that a contract between Apple and minor existed each time that (1) Apple offered to sell game currency to a minor playing an app, (2) the minor accepted Apple's offer, and (3) the transaction was supported by consideration, or payment made by the Plaintiffs.[1]

Apple argues that this issue should be dismissed as a matter of law because the relevant contractual relationship governing the in-app purchases is between Apple and Plaintiffs and is based on the original Terms & Conditions signed by Plaintiffs, thus making the individual purchases not voidable. Apple contends that the Terms & Conditions governs the parties' relationships, including all subsequent purchases made using the iTunes account.

However, Plaintiffs contend that the Terms & Conditions are not the contracts at issue. Furthermore, Plaintiffs argue that the Terms & Conditions are subject to interpretation and that the court cannot dismiss the declaratory relief claim because Plaintiffs should be permitted to introduce extrinsic evidence regarding the meaning of the term "unauthorized use" in their contracts.[3] Apple claims that this term is not relevant to Plaintiffs' claim or to Apple's motion to dismiss. . . .

At this point, the court must construe the Complaint in the light most favorable to Plaintiffs, resolving any apparent ambiguity in their favor. . . . Using this standard as a guide, Defendant's request to dismiss Plaintiffs' First Cause of Action must be denied.

1. Apple argues that there is no legal basis for inferring a contract where the alleged offer is made to one party but accepted by another party, and where the consideration is paid by the original offeree, rather than the party who accepted the alleged offer. Plaintiffs contend that their complaint alleges sufficient facts to establish the existence of a contract and that, pursuant to Cal. Civ. Code §1605, consideration for a contract can be conferred upon the promisor by any person, not only the offeree.

3. The Terms & Conditions, which Plaintiffs accepted and agreed to when they opened iTunes accounts, state, "[y]ou are solely responsible for maintaining the confidentiality and security of your Account and for all activities that occur on or through your Account. . . . Apple shall not be responsible for any losses arising out of the unauthorized use of your account."

B. Consumer Legal Remedies Act (CLRA) and Unfair Competition Law (UCL) Claims

. . .

Plaintiffs allege that Apple violated the CLRA by actively marketing and promoting certain gaming apps as free or costing a nominal fee with the intent to induce minors to purchase in-app game currency.[6] Plaintiffs contend that Apple breached its duty to disclose material facts about the game currency embedded in these gaming apps and the ability to purchase such game currency for a fifteen-minute period without re-entering a password. Apple contends that Plaintiffs' CLRA claims fail to meet Rule 9(b)'s heightened pleading standard.

The CLRA proscribes "unfair methods of competition and unfair or deceptive acts or practices." Cal. Civ. Code §1770(a); In re Actimmune Marketing Litig., 2009 U.S. Dist. LEXIS 103408, 2009 WL 3740648, at 16 (N.D. Cal. Nov. 6, 2009). Conduct that is "likely to mislead a reasonable consumer" violates the CLRA. Keegan v. American Honda Motor Co., Inc., 838 F. Supp. 2d 929 (C.D. Cal. Jan. 6, 2012). CLRA claims sounding in fraud must establish reliance and causation. Buckland v. Threshold Enters., Ltd., 155 Cal. App. 4th 798, 809 (2007).

Omissions are actionable under the CLRA only when the omission is contrary to a representation actually made by the defendant or where a duty to disclose exists. Keegan, 2012 U.S. Dist. LEXIS 3007, 2012 WL 75443, at 6. Under California law, a duty to disclose arises in four circumstances: "(1) when the defendant is in a fiduciary relationship with the plaintiff; (2) when the defendant had exclusive knowledge of material facts not known to the plaintiff; (3) when the defendant actively conceals a material fact from plaintiff; or (4) when the defendant makes partial representations but also suppresses some material facts." Id. (quoting Smith v. Ford Motor Co., 749 F. Supp. 2d 980, 987 (N.D. Cal. 2010)). In the instant case, Plaintiffs allege that Apple had a duty to disclose because it concealed and/or omitted facts in the advertising, marketing, and promotion of its apps. For a non-disclosed fact to be material, a plaintiff must show that if the omitted information had been available, the plaintiff would have been aware of it and behaved differently. Id.

Contrary to Apple's argument, Plaintiffs have alleged with specificity which misrepresentations they were exposed to, their reliance on those misrepresentations, and the resulting harm. Plaintiffs pled specific facts that Apple "actively advertis[ed], market[ed] and promot[ed] its bait Apps as 'free' or nominal. . . ." The Complaint explicitly states that at least one Plaintiff downloaded a game app and gave it to her son "[b]ecause it said it was 'free'" and another Plaintiff gave her iPhone to her daughter so that she could "play the 'free' game." Plaintiffs further assert that they were not informed by Apple that once an iTunes account holder entered a password, he or she could make purchases for up to fifteen minutes without re-entering the password. Plaintiffs contend that, "[h]ad any Plaintiff or other member

---

6. Plaintiffs allege that Apple violated three provisions of the CLRA: (1) representing that goods have uses or characteristics they do not have, Cal. Civ. Code §1770(a)(5); (2) representing that goods are of a particular standard or quality when they are of another, Cal. Civ. Code §1770(a)(7); and (3) representing that a transaction confers or involves rights, remedies, or obligations which it does not have or involve, or which are prohibited by law, Cal. Civ. Code §1770(a)(14).

of the Class known what their children were purchasing and for how much, they would not have permitted the sales transaction from being consummated." Finally, the Complaint alleges that as a result of the fraud, Plaintiffs were charged large sums of money after game currency was purchased without their knowledge.

Drawing all inferences in Plaintiffs' favor, the court denies Apple's motion to dismiss Plaintiffs' Second Cause of Action.

iii. Unfair Competition Law

. . .

The UCL, California Business & Professions Code §17200 et seq., prohibits acts of "unfair competition," defined as: (1) unlawful business acts or practices;[7] (2) unfair business acts or practices; (3) fraudulent business acts or practices; and (4) unfair, deceptive or misleading advertising. Each of the three prongs of the UCL ("unfair," "unlawful," and "fraudulent") constitutes an independent basis for liability and fraud is not an essential element of a claim for unfair or unlawful business practices. Actimmune, 2009 U.S. Dist. LEXIS 103408, 2009 WL 3740648, at 7.

Plaintiffs allege that Apple engaged in unlawful, unfair, fraudulent and/or deceptive business acts and practices in violation of the UCL by advertising, marketing, and promoting apps as free or at a nominal cost with the intent to lure minors to purchase game currency. Furthermore, Plaintiffs allege that the Class has suffered substantial actual economic harm. As discussed supra, for claims based on fraudulent conduct, where Rule 9(b)'s heightened pleading standard applies, the court finds that Plaintiffs have sufficiently pled specific facts to support their claims.

Under the "unlawful" prong, Plaintiffs have sufficiently alleged that Apple violated the CLRA. This violation is independently actionable under the UCL.

Under the test for "unfair" business practices, "[a]n act or practice is unfair if the consumer injury is substantial, is not outweighed by any countervailing benefit to consumers or to competition, and is not an injury the consumers themselves could reasonably have avoided." Tietsworth v. Sears, 2009 U.S. Dist. LEXIS 98532, 2009 WL 3320486, at 7. Plaintiffs have shown that they suffered substantial harm by incurring charges that they did not explicitly authorize, ranging from $99 to $338.72 at a time. Plaintiffs contend that no benefit existed and Apple does not claim that there was any benefit to consumers or competition. Plaintiffs also contend that they could not have avoided this harm because they had no way of knowing that for a fifteen-minute window, purchases could be made without re-entering a password.

Under the "fraudulent" prong, Plaintiffs must allege with specificity that Defendant's alleged misrepresentations: (1) were relied upon by the named plaintiffs; (2) were material; (3) influenced the named plaintiffs' decision to purchase the product; and (4) were likely to deceive members of the public. Tietsworth, 2009 U.S. Dist. LEXIS 98532, 2009 WL 3320486, at 8. Following other California courts

---

7. Under the "unlawful" prong, the UCL makes violations of other laws actionable under the UCL. In re Actimmune Marketing Litig., 2009 U.S. Dist. LEXIS 103408, 2009 WL 3740648, at 15 (N.D. Cal. Nov. 6, 2009). Under this prong, "it is not necessary that plaintiffs allege violation of the predicate laws with particularity; they must at a minimum, however, identify the statutory or regulatory provisions that defendants allegedly violated." Id.

and federal courts applying California law, the sufficiency of a plaintiff's UCL fraud claim may be analyzed together with the CLRA claim. Kowalsky v. Hewlett-Packard Co., 2011 U.S. Dist. LEXIS 89379, 2011 WL 3501715 (N.D. Cal. Aug. 10, 2011). As discussed in the analysis of Plaintiffs' Second Cause of Action, Plaintiffs have pled specific facts to support their claim.

Accordingly, drawing all inferences in Plaintiffs' favor, the court denies Apple's motion to dismiss Plaintiffs' Third Cause of Action.

C. Breach of Duty of Good Faith and Fair Dealing

Plaintiffs allege that Apple breached its contractual duty of good faith and fair dealing with Plaintiffs and class. Apple argues that Plaintiffs' claim fails as a matter of law because under California law the implied covenant cannot be used to negate an express contractual provision. Apple further argues that Plaintiffs have not alleged any express provision of their contract that relates to their claim, and an implied covenant claim untethered to an express provision fails as a matter of law.

It has long been recognized in California that every contract contains an implied covenant of good faith and fair dealing that neither party will injure the right of the other party to receive the benefits of the agreement. Wolf v. Walt Disney Pictures & Tel., 162 Cal. App. 4th 1107 (2008). The covenant protects the express covenants or promises of the contract. CarmaDevelopers (Cal.), Inc. v. Marathon Development California, Inc., 826 P.2d 710 (1992). As such, the implied covenant will only be recognized to further the contract's purpose; it will not be read into a contract to prohibit a party from doing that which is expressly permitted by the agreement itself. Id. at 374. However, "breach of a specific provision of the contract is not a necessary prerequisite [for breach of implied covenant of good faith and fair dealing]." Id. at 373.

To establish a claim for breach of the implied covenant of good faith and fair dealing, Plaintiffs must show that Apple lacked subjective good faith in the validity of its act or the act was intended to and did frustrate the common purpose of the agreement. Id. at 372. The Terms & Conditions signed by Plaintiffs expressly provide that Plaintiffs are responsible for activity occurring on or through their accounts and Apple may charge them for any such activity. Thus, the implied covenant cannot negate Apple's ability to charge Plaintiffs.

Plaintiffs have failed to show how Apple's act breached the duty of good faith and fair dealing. Accordingly, the claim for breach of the implied covenant is dismissed with leave to amend.

. . .

For the reasons stated, the court GRANTS in part and DENIES in part Defendant's motion to dismiss.

———————

Vulnerable consumer populations, such as the elderly or children, can be especially prone to misunderstanding (or being misled by) online transactions. In 2014, the Federal Trade Commission alleged that Amazon.com unlawfully charged millions of dollars to customers without obtaining "the account holders' express informed consent" for in-app purchases made because children using devices could make purchases without an adult's affirmative consent. *See FTC v. Amazon.com, Inc.,* 71 F. Supp. 3d 1158, 1160 (W.D. Wash. 2014). A contrary argument might be that the parents consented to their children using their devices, and in so doing, consented to their full use of all applications that the parents decided to download. Another point is that while the age of majority for legal contracts is 18 years, does anybody question a "tween" (between child and teenager) who walks into a convenience store and buys a pack of gum for $0.99? How is this legally distinct from an in-app purchase of another game level? If it is not, why should stores — that can visually assess age — be off the hook, while online companies face lawsuits?

Problem Set 20

20.1. Grandpa calls you up — he knows you've been studying something to do with credit, and he was just denied for a credit card he wanted to open. He has always been extremely careful with his money and has had impeccable credit. Modern technology eludes him, however, and he has several times gotten a virus on his computer. Last month, Grandpa bought anti-virus software from someone who called him from "Window." He reports to you that he felt good about this solution because "Window" is the same name that pops up every time he turns on his computer and so "they should know what they are doing with this Internet stuff." The "Window" representative on the phone helped him install and activate the anti-virus software on his computer. You ask Grandpa what all this cost, and he says, "That's the thing. You do actually get something free in these new days. It's not like old times when everything cost money." You have a bad feeling about this, and start running through the identity theft steps that you learned in consumer law. With his permission, you check his credit report and see nine new credit cards have been opened and maxed out. What could have happened? What recourse does Grandpa have?

20.2. Jess has been shopping online for years and is extremely happy with her "Bestest" service from Pole.com, where she is treated like a preferred customer with special deals emailed directly to her, free shipping, and streaming video. Her sister, Tina, still likes to go to the mall and stroll through shopping districts, and even still pays for cable. Jess and Tina have been trying to find the best price for a birthday gift for their father: a state-of-the-art speaker set for his old school record player.

Pole.com has been showing Jess some great prices, so she chooses a speaker set and has it shipped free to her dad. When she is at Tina's house the next day, Jess hops on Tina's computer to show her the great deal that she got on the speakers from Pole. Tina's never used the site before, and Jess does not bother to log in to her account. She just does a quick search for the speakers on Pole's homepage. She finds the speakers immediately as the top-listed item based on her search but she sees the price is cheaper than she has seen before. At that point, Jess logs into her account to check what she paid and sure enough, she was charged $12 more than the display price. She searches for the speaker listing again, but now the price is back to Jess' purchase price. Angry that Tina's computer showed such a great deal when Jess is a loyal customer, Jess contacts a class action lawyer. I want to sue, she says. "Bestest" simply is not the best. What would be the basis for a lawsuit?

20.3. You are outside counsel to an online payday lender, the OC Moneymen, which is a California corporation. They've been getting a lot of flack lately from consumers who used their services and then been angry when they realized how much debt had mounted. One of their prior customers has started posting angry rants on Eyes, a social media site. The posts are admittedly funny, featuring video of the consumer showing how many pennies it would take to pay even 1 percent of the debt. The posts have gone viral and OC Moneymen are unhappy. Can they change their contract in the future to avoid these problems? If not, how might they challenge or work around any prohibition? Cal. Civ. Code §1670.8.

Part Four. The Deal Goes Awry: Enforcement

Assignment 21. Creditor Remedies

Consumer law is concerned with regulating how businesses attract consumers to deals (Part 2 of this book) and the substantive laws regulating those deals (Part 3). Most of the time, consumers and businesses engage in positive ways. Consumers get goods or services that they desire, and in return, businesses get money from consumers. When deals go awry, however, both parties look to law for remedies. Part 4 of this book considers how businesses and consumers can enforce consumer rights.

A central theme is that enforcement is perhaps the most vexing issue in consumer protection (yes, even worse than designing effective disclosures or writing clear regulations). The disparities between businesses and consumers that prompt the law to protect consumers and to impose duties on businesses are equally present in the enforcement context. Businesses have more resources to spend to learn about the law and have more experience in enforcement. But without enforcement, consumer protections are of little value to people.

It matters dramatically to the design of the remedies whether the business or consumer is more likely to be the party that files the lawsuit. Businesses and consumers have different perspectives on the availability of self-help remedies, the standard for class actions, statutory damages, and attorneys' fees for prevailing parties. These are key issues in designing an enforcement scheme.

This first enforcement Assignment focuses on consumer credit. In this context, businesses file the vast majority of lawsuits or initiate other legal remedies. They do so to collect unpaid debts. Just as consumer credit transactions are an enormous part of the body of substantive consumer law, the rules governing the enforcement for debt collection are among the most widely used laws in America. The Federal Reserve estimates that 14 percent of consumers were contacted by a third-party (not the original creditor) debt collector in 2010. Federal Reserve Bank of New York, *Quarterly Report on Household Debt and Credit* (Feb. 2012), http://www.newyorkfed.org/research/national_economy/householdcredit/DistrictReport_Q42011.pdf. This is double the rate from a decade before. The foreclosure crisis also has sharpened awareness of the policy consequences of debt collection law. With the system facing new pressures, both creditors and debtors are pushing to revisit collection remedies, which are some of the oldest consumer laws on the books. Our study starts with creditors' remedies, in part because most debtors' rights are framed as protective from abuse of these remedies.

As a preliminary note, remember that there must be a default before the creditor can validly take collection action. The loan agreement will typically define default but a creditor may wait until the default is "serious" in its estimation before it begins formal legal collection. Missing even one payment, however, is likely to bring about at least a collection letter. One key provision related to defaults is an acceleration clause. This language allows the creditor to make the entire amount of the debt due and owing upon a default. Without this language, the creditor would have to sue each month (or other repayment date) to get the next payment from the consumer. Acceleration clauses are efficient for creditors and the courts but they also magnify the consequences of a missed payment for a consumer. In many instances, focused as they are on getting paid and keeping accounts in good status, creditors will allow a debtor to cure the default by making any missed payments, reinstating the prior loan payment schedule and de-accelerating the balance due.

A.   Collecting Unsecured Debts

Debts come in two basic flavors: unsecured and secured. Secured debts are those for which the creditor has the right to look to specific property to be paid in the event of a default. Mortgages, auto loans, and tax liens are examples of secured debts. Unsecured debts are those for which the creditor does not have collateral or a remedy in specific property. Medical debts, credit card debts, and student loans are examples of unsecured debts. By dollar volume, secured debts are large on consumers' balance sheets. By number, unsecured debts predominate.

Unsecured and secured debts usually are collected using different techniques. Secured creditors, however, have the best of both worlds. They can use their special remedies — trying to be paid from the property associated with the debt — or they can use the remedies of unsecured creditors. The law also provides mechanisms that allow unsecured debt to be transformed into secured debts, if the creditor is willing to take the required legal steps.

The unsecured framework is common to both types of creditors and is more likely to be familiar to you from your study of civil procedure than the specialized rules for secured debts. We start there.

1.   Lawsuits

When a consumer defaults on an unsecured debt, the creditor does not have any property that is specifically pledged or linked to that debt. Instead, the creditor must begin by obtaining a judgment. (Usually, of course, the creditor will try non-legal mechanism such as phone calls, letters, or hiring a debt collection agency first. The issues raised by these practices are the subject of Assignment 22.)

A judgment is the outcome of litigation. A debt collection lawsuit follows the usual rules of civil procedure. A complaint is filed, and the consumer has the opportunity to answer. There may be discovery, settlement, summary judgment motions, and the like. Ultimately, a trial will be held if needed. For debt collection, however, trials are extraordinarily rare. In fact, it appears that most lawsuits involve no response from consumers at all. Creditors simply obtain default judgments and proceed directly to collecting the judgment. The reality of debt collection lawsuits strays far from the ideals of fact-finding and weighty adjudication on the merits.

One major factor in such lawsuits is the procedural rules of the court hearing the case. Some states permit debt collections to proceed in small claims courts. The small claims process has fewer rules and requirements for plaintiffs to bring cases but it also means that defendants have fewer protections and opportunities to contest the dispute. Originally small claims courts were designed to aid non-lawyers in resolving minor disputes between each other. Today their primary users are collection agencies. Small claims court is a boon for creditors because the debt collectors nearly always hire lawyers to represent them as plaintiffs. The lawyers enjoy the speedy and streamlined process as they pursue consumers who may have less judicial involvement, time, or hurdles to contest the dispute. A Boston Globe investigation concluded that in Massachusetts, "The 'people's court' has become the collectors' court. . . . Debtors often feel intimidated in this arena, and with reason. The system is tilted against them." Beth Healy, *Dignity Faces a Steamroller*, THE BOSTON GLOBE, (July 31, 2006), http://www.boston.com/news/special/spotlight_debt/part2/page1.html.

Another procedural issue for collection cases is the evidentiary burden needed to file a complaint and obtain a default judgment. Debts are often many years old at the time of a lawsuit. The debts may have been sold by the original creditor at the time of origination or assigned to a debt collector upon default. Either way, the creditor may have only limited documentation to support the alleged debt. Because debtors frequently do not appear, the result is that creditors can file and win a judgment with only bare factual assertions. In jurisdictions that do require affidavits in support of complaints or motions for summary judgment, some consumer advocates believe that the affiants frequently lack a basis for knowing the stated facts or that such affidavits are mass-produced without the requisite knowledge.

Obtaining a judgment is frequently easy for a business and a frightening experience for a consumer. In addition to problems learning of the lawsuit or showing up to defend it, consumers often believe wrongly that they must immediately and voluntarily pay a judgment. The judgment does have immediate consequences for the consumer's credit report, where it will appear for seven years as adverse information (see Assignment 7).

2. *Execution and Garnishment*

A judgment is, in the most concrete sense, merely a piece of paper. It does not itself magically transform into paper currency that can be used to repay the creditor's debt. The process for using a judgment to locate and levy on debtors' property is generally called "execution." The creditor, now referred to as the judgment creditor, issues a writ of execution to a public officer. A writ is a document directing someone to do something, in this case, to go out and levy on the judgment debtor's property. When that levy occurs, a lien on the property at issue is created in favor of the judgment creditor. The creditor can then initiate further processes to have that property sold and the proceeds applied toward paying the judgment. The two-step judgment and execution process, if successful, essentially turns unsecured creditors into secured creditors, able to look to specific property for payment. While levy seems straightforward, this classic case illustrates the importance of getting it right. With a deadbeat debtor, there are often other creditors attempting to get paid from the same property.

Credit Bureau of Broken Bow, Inc. v. Moninger
284 N.W.2d (Neb. 1979)

BRODKEY, Justice.

This is an appeal from an order of the District Court for Custer County which affirmed a judgment entered by the county court of Custer County awarding the proceeds from a sheriff's sale of a 1975 Ford pickup truck. . . . The Credit Bureau of Broken Bow, Inc. (hereinafter referred to as Bureau) obtained a default judgment against John Moninger (hereinafter referred to as Moninger) in the amount of $1,518.27 on October 20, 1977. No appeal was taken from this judgment. . . . On June 27, 1978, at the request of the Bureau, a writ of execution was issued on its judgment in the amount of $1,338.50, the balance remaining due on the judgment.

The deputy county sheriff who received the writ examined the motor vehicle title records on July 7, 1978, to determine if a lien existed as of that date on the pickup owned by Moninger. Finding no encumbrance of record, the deputy sheriff proceeded to Moninger's place of employment to levy on the vehicle. The deputy sheriff found Moninger, served him with a copy of the writ, and informed Moninger that he was executing on the pickup. Moninger testified he informed the officer that there was money borrowed from the Bank against the pickup, and that the Bank had title to the vehicle. Following this conversation, the officer proceeded to the vehicle, "grabbed ahold of the pickup," and stated: "I execute on the pickup for the County of Custer." The officer did not take possession of the vehicle at that time, nor did he ask for the keys to the vehicle.

On July 10, 1978, after being informed of the events which occurred on the 7th, the [State] Bank and Moninger executed a security agreement on the vehicle which was then filed. Notation of the security interest was made on the title to the pickup truck that same day. The vehicle was seized by deputy sheriffs on July 13, 1978, and sold at sheriff's sale on August 14, 1978, for $2,050.

The sheriff filed a motion in the county court for a determination of the division of the proceeds from the sheriff's sale. The Bank joined the action by application for the proceeds of the sheriff's sale, basing its claim on its alleged status as a secured creditor. Prior to a hearing on these matters, a stipulation was entered into by all parties whereby this dispute was limited to the distribution of the proceeds of the sheriff's sale, the pickup having previously been sold.

. . .

The Bureau first assigns as error the ruling of the trial court which found the Bank's security interest in the vehicle to be superior to the execution lien of the

Bureau. Specifically, the Bureau contends that the actions of the deputy sheriff on July 7, 1978, amounted to a valid levy which bound the vehicle for the satisfaction of the Bureau's judgment against Moninger. §25-1504, R.R.S. 1943. On that date, the Bank held only an unperfected security interest in the vehicle. The Bureau contends that since the levy of execution made the Bureau a lien creditor, and since the lien creditor has an interest superior to that of an unperfected secured party, the trial court was in error in ruling that the Bank had a superior interest in the proceeds.

In effect, the Bureau is relying on section 9-301, U.C.C. [ED. NOTE—now §9-317.], which relates to the relative priorities as between unperfected security interests and lien creditors. "[A]n unperfected security interest is subordinate to the rights of . . . a person who becomes a lien creditor without knowledge of the security interest and before it is perfected." §9-301(1)(b), U.C.C. The correctness of the Bureau's position turns on two issues: (1) Whether the Bureau was in fact a lien creditor on July 7, 1978; and (2) whether the Bureau was a lien creditor without knowledge of the Bank's alleged security interest prior to the perfection of such interest by the Bank.

From an examination of the record, we conclude that the Bureau was a lien creditor on July 7, 1978. Section 9-301, U.C.C., defines a lien creditor as "a creditor who has acquired a lien on the property involved by attachment, levy or the like. . . ." A lien on personal property is acquired in this state at the time it is "seized in execution." §25-1504, R.R.S. 1943. Therefore, the Bureau became a lien creditor within the meaning of section 9-301, U.C.C., when the sheriff levied on the vehicle.

The rule by which to test the validity of a levy has been earlier set out by this court. "'A manual interference with chattels is not essential to a valid levy thereon. It is sufficient if the property is present and subject for the time being to the control of the officer holding the writ, and that he in express terms asserts his dominion over it by virtue of such writ.'" Battle Creek Valley Bank v. First Nat. Bank of Madison, 62 Neb. 825, 88 N.W. 145 (1909). We believe a review of the record makes it clear that a valid levy did occur before the Bank had perfected its security interest in the chattel.

The deputy sheriff expressly asserted his dominion over the vehicle by virtue of the writ. He likewise exerted control over the vehicle as against all others at the time of levy. At that time the deputy sheriff informed Moninger that he was sorry that he had to execute on the vehicle but that it was his job. He further stated that he hoped Moninger would straighten the problem out with the Bureau. It should be noted that the officer's report, as well as the return on the writ, clearly indicated that the officer "executed" on the vehicle on July 7, 1978. On the basis of this evidence, we conclude that a valid levy took place at that time.

The Bank would have us hold that the pickup should have been physically seized to make the levy valid. We do not believe that failure to take physical possession in this case goes to the validity of the levy. The deputy sheriff did all that was required by the laws of this state with regard to levying under a writ of execution. Whether or not the officer took physical possession after he levied relates to the ability of the officer to produce the property levied on, and to his possible civil liability for failure to do so, not to the validity of the levy. It is, of course, possible that the failure of a levying officer to protect and preserve the property levied upon might give rise to an action between the officer, or his bonding company, and the judgment creditor. In this connection see 33 C.J.S., Executions, §97, p. 245. We therefore reject the

Bank's contention and conclude that the Bureau was a lien creditor on July 7, 1978, by virtue of the deputy sheriff's levy on the writ of execution.

. . .

Reversed and remanded.

Garnishment is a variation on execution in which the creditor asks a third party to the dispute to pay over money or property in which the debtor has an interest. A writ of garnishment is issued to the third party, most typically an employer or a bank. This party, now a "garnishee," must answer the writ by answering a set of questions about its relationship with the debtors' property. The writ then commands the garnishee to pay the money or turn over the property to the garnishor—the judgment creditor. Procedures exist to give notice of the garnishment to the judgment debtor and to permit the garnishor or judgment debtor to raise defenses. Those defenses usually do not include attacking the underlying validity of the judgment, meaning that even default judgments obtained with minimal procedure, put consumers at the risk of lost wages. The debtor protections against execution and garnishment are the subject of the next assignment. For now, remember that they give creditors tremendous leverage in dunning, even without resort to the actual remedies.

B.   Collecting Secured Debts

Creditors have a number of remedies to deploy when payment is not forthcoming. One major factor is the amount of the debt; it simply is not cost effective to garnish someone for a very small amount, for example. Less comfortably, collection tactics also probably vary based on the collector's assessment of the debtor's class status and education level, in some part because these correlate with the likelihood of the consumer complaining to a regulator or exercising their rights. The biggest distinction in debt collection, however, is that between secured creditors and unsecured creditors. Being a secured creditor is so fabulous that law students endure entire courses on how to create and enforce security interests. *See generally* Robert Lawless, Lynn LoPucki & Elizabeth Warren, SECURED CREDIT: A SYSTEMS APPROACH (7th ed. 2011).

For personal property security interests, Article 9 of the Uniform Commercial Code gives the applicable rules, including for collection. For real property mortgages, the rules come from non-uniform state law. In fact, foreclosure is one of the most varied areas of consumer law.

1. Repossession

As with unsecured creditors, a default that gives rise to remedies is defined in the loan contract. With consumer contracts, the triggering event for a collection effort is nearly always failure to make one or more payments. Another possibility, however, is the consumer's failure to protect the collateral, such as by letting its insurance lapse or misusing it in a way that could diminish its value.

Secured creditors rely on their collateral to improve the chances that they are repaid. If the debtor defaults on the debt, the secured creditor may repossess the collateral. Taking possession of the debtor's property tends to have a "focusing effect" for the consumer on the need to comply with payment obligations, especially if that car was how the consumer planned to get to work tomorrow. Because secured creditors will look to the collateral to be repaid, they try to keep track of it. In the case of auto loans to high-risk consumers, the dealer may even get the consumer to agree to the installation of a GPS device. Barring that, some dealers install mechanisms so that they can lock the car's ignition remotely.

Tradesfolk specializing in repossession are a colorful lot called "repo men." The task is part demographer and part psychological profiler, trying to anticipate what kind of person and attitude might greet the repo man at work. Repo men describe guns on the front seat as a warning to stay away, dogs chained to the bumpers, vehicles parked in the neighbor's garage. Just as for used cars, there are repossession agents for other types of collateral. And the bigger they are, the harder they fall.

It was snowing hard when the bank called Nick Popovich. They needed to grab a Gulfstream in South Carolina now. Not tomorrow. Tonight.

All commercial and private planes were grounded, but Nick Popovich wasn't one to turn down a job. So he waited for the storm to clear long enough to charter a Hawker jet from Chicago into South Carolina. There was just one detail: No one had told Popovich about the heavily armed white supremacist militia that would be guarding the aircraft when he arrived.

But then again, no one had told the militia about Popovich, a brawny and intimidating man who has been jailed and shot at and has faced down more angry men than a prison warden. When Popovich and two of his colleagues arrived that evening at a South Carolina airfield, they were met by a bunch of nasty-looking thugs with cocked shotguns. "They had someone in the parking lot with binoculars," Popovich says, recalling the incident. "When we went to grab the plane, one of them came out with his weapon drawn and tells us we better get out of there." Undeterred, Popovich continued toward the plane until he felt a gun resting on his temple.

"You move another inch and I'll blow your fucking head off," the gravel-and-nicotine voice told Popovich.

"Well, you better go ahead and shoot, 'cause I'm grabbing that plane."

A shot was discharged in the air.

The gravel-and-nicotine voice again. "I'm not kidding."

"Then do it already."

Popovich's first rule of firearms is pretty simple: The man who tells you he's going to shoot you will not shoot you. So without so much as looking back, he got on the plane and flew it right to Chicago. "My job is to grab that plane," Popovich says. "And if you haven't paid for it, then it's mine. And I don't like to lose."

Nick Popovich is a repo man, but not the kind that spirits away Hyundais from suburban driveways. Popovich is a super repo man, one of a handful of specialists who get the call when a bank wants back its Gulfstream II jet from, say, a small army of neo-Nazi freaks.

Marc Weingarten, *The Learjet Repo Man*, Salon.com (Jun. 6, 2009), http://www.salon.com/2009/06/06/lear_jet_repo_man.

The foregoing excerpt demonstrates why secured status of a creditor is so important. If you are behind on your Visa bill, and Visa sends some guy to take your car to "square things up," that's called theft. But if you get behind on your auto loan and some guy takes your car, that's called repossession. It is the ultimate creditor self-help remedy and is almost entirely outside the judicial process. Given this extra-judicial nature and high-friction environment, U.C.C. §9-609 codifies the common law rule that prohibits a repossessor from committing a "breach of the peace." The case law is all over the place on what constitutes a breach of the peace, and the fact patterns are, shall we say, memorable. Generally, the standard is permissive; a repossession agent cannot use fists, weapons, or otherwise threaten violence. Telling lies or entering someone's driveway is fair game. A threat by the *debtor* to breach the peace (for example, by pulling a gun when she sees the tow truck) means the creditor has a duty to back off, even though the debtor is the party stirring up trouble.

Repossession is a rough and tumble world. If the secured creditor cannot stomach such brusquerie, it can invoke the formal legal process by using its secured status to seek a writ of replevin or sequestration, which ends with the sheriff taking the property. Keep in mind that repossession is about "possession." In the context of real property, the process to get possession is called eviction. That means legally dispossessing whomever is living there, be he an owner or tenant or squatter or great-uncle Gerald. Repossession is not about ownership. To get title to the property, the creditor will have to take additional steps.

2. Foreclosure

Foreclosure is the name given to extinguishing a security interest and allowing the creditor to look to the collateral for recovery. While the term is used most frequently with regard to real property, there are analogous procedures for personal property in Article 9 of the Uniform Commercial Code. The legal concept is the same; the debtor no longer owns the property and the creditor can recover from the property's value. The biggest difference is the degree of formality required to foreclose. Under Article 9, creditors can sell collateral in a private sale as long as all aspects of the sale (advertising, bidding, etc.) are "commercially reasonable." U.C.C. §9-610.

The process is quick and driven by creditor preference. In the context of cars, for example, the lender could sell the car to a wholesaler in cash after allowing only a short period to elapse. The law does require notice to the consumer of the disposition, U.C.C. §9-614, and provides special protections to consumers if the creditor proposes to retain the collateral in satisfaction of the debt. U.C.C. §9-620. The logic is that without a sale to determine the value of the collateral, a creditor could pronounce the collateral to be nearly or entirely worthless and then sue the consumer on the debt to get a judgment. The effect, if the collateral had value, would be to boost the creditor's recovery beyond the amount of the debt. While this is a theoretical concern, the bigger problem for most creditors is that the collateral — even if sold to maximize value — does not repay the debt. Bankers call this a "loss severity." The managing director of a bank calls it "somebody-around-here's problem" and will want to recover as near as possible to the balance owed.

A "deficiency" lawsuit is the tool for attempting to recover the difference between what the collateral brought at sale and the amount owed. For residential real property, about half of all states ban the collection of a deficiency after foreclosure. This is a debtor protection, but the flip side — the ability to go after consumers long after the lender has taken possession and sold the house — is a powerful creditor's remedy. The laws on what a creditor must do to collect a deficiency depend on the type of foreclosure process that the creditor used and the state's public policy. Generally, permitting deficiency judgments should ease credit access and lower credit costs. *See, e.g.,* Jihad Dagher & Yanfan Sun, *Borrower Protection and the Supply of Credit: Evidence from Foreclosure Laws* (2014) (finding that anti-deficiency statutes result in higher rejection rates for jumbo mortgage loans). Both effects can be seen as particularly important with regard to homeownership. The contrary policy point, however, is that the goal is sustainable homeownership, not temporary homeownership followed by a foreclosure, and that barring deficiency judgments promotes sound underwriting because it limits creditors to the collateral for payment.

Foreclosure of real property can be either judicial or non-judicial. All states have a judicial foreclosure process; about half of all states permit non-judicial foreclosure as an alternative. If it is an option, a creditor will prefer non-judicial foreclosure because as a general matter, it is faster, cheaper, and presents less risk of legal challenge. Even in non-judicial foreclosure states, the sale process is much more circumscribed by law than with personal property under the U.C.C. Homes are high stakes collateral — for consumers and creditors — and the remedies reflect those consequences. As a result of the foreclosure spike in 2008-2015, the law imposes more duties on creditors before foreclosing than in the past.

The term "judicial foreclosure" suggests the involvement of a judge but judicial activity is limited or infrequent. As in other situations when creditors go to court, vigorous defense by the borrower is rare. Judicial foreclosure does, however, require significant steps by other public actors. To begin, a complaint must be filed that pleads the elements of the foreclosure statute. These typically include that there is a valid mortgage between the parties, that the borrower is in default under the terms of the mortgage, and that any required pre-suit notifications were given. A case number and judge are assigned, and the complaint must be served on the borrower. At that point, many cases will end with a summary judgment motion being granted in favor of the lender. If not, the court will adjudicate the dispute. If it concludes the lender has the legal right to foreclose, the court will issue a judgment that determines the amount owed. If this amount is not paid by the deadline established in the judgment, a sheriff or other public offer will sell the property. In some states, there is post-sale judicial review that confirms the sale but in others, the sale is the final step. If a deficiency judgment is permitted, the order confirming the sale will set that amount and create a judgment that the mortgage company can use to pursue the debtor. Some studies have found most reductions in access to credit in judicial foreclosure states compared to nonjudicial foreclosure states, which is often pinned to higher costs in adhering to the judicial process. *See, e.g.,* Karen Pence, *Foreclosing on Opportunity: State Laws and Mortgage Credit*, 88 Rev. of Econ. & Stat. 177 (2006) (estimating that loan sizes are 3 percent to 7 percent smaller in judicial foreclosure states).

Nonjudicial foreclosure is conducted by private non-state actors. The original mortgage (or deed of trust, which is a similar document commonly used in nonjudicial foreclosure states) will contain a "power of sale" clause that permits the lender to take steps to sell the property if the borrower defaults. To satisfy due process, all nonjudicial statutes require at least some notice and procedure. Personal service of process, a matter of course in judicial foreclosure, is only required in five states. Instead service is by mail, sometimes registered or certified, and also through public notice, such as a newspaper advertisement or posting in a public place (such as the county recorder's office). After notice and an elapsed waiting period, the house may be sold. These are often private auctions, conducted by "trustees" named under the deed of trust. If a homeowner wants to raise a defense to the foreclosure, he or she must file a court action requesting an injunction to halt the sale.

Great finality is given to foreclosure sales, whether judicial or nonjudicial. The goal is to maximize the sale price by minimizing any concerns of the purchaser about the sale being upset. In all states, borrowers have the right to "redeem" the property by paying the entire balance owed after the sale. In some states this is an equitable right, while it others it is a statutory right. If the latter, the borrower may only have to pay the sale price and the costs of the sale to the purchaser. (If the bank had a deficiency judgment, however, redemption does not eliminate that debt; it transfers ownership of the house back to the borrower.)

To minimize the financial and social harms of foreclosure, the law provides several protections to borrowers. Although these are technically "debtor's rights," they are covered here as precedents to the creditor being able to foreclose. Half of the states give borrowers the ability to cure the default, by paying any amounts due, before sale. Even when not an official right, lenders are often delighted to get a chunk of money and avoid the losses that come from a sale that will frequently bring less than the amount due on the mortgage.

Federal and some states' laws impose procedural obligations on actors initiating foreclosure to advise borrowers of possible foreclosure alternatives. As with student loans, collecting payments and addressing defaults is performed by a servicer, who is not usually the original lender. The mortgage servicer bought the right to service the note in return for payment for services rendered. It is the servicer (not the owner of the note that is often a securitized trust or other passive entity) that will be communicating with the borrower. Servicers have no duty to provide any specific loss mitigation options. 12 C.F.R. §1014.41(a). The focus is on communication and procedural protections. The timing for the creditors' obligations is highly structured, based off a series of key dates. Confusingly, the key dates are measured from different events, including delinquency (but that is not explicitly defined in the regulation).

The most important rules, described in more detail in Assignment 15, require good faith efforts to reach the borrower, providing information about loss mitigation options, and delaying foreclosure to evalute a complete application for loss mitigation options.

You may be wondering why these loss mitigations are coming up in an Assignment about creditor remedies; they certainly seem like debtor protections. The foreclosure, however, cannot be filed until 120 days have elapsed to allow for the loss mitigation process. Additionally, the foreclosure cannot begin if a borrower has submitted a complete application. 12 C.F.R. §1024.41(f)(2)(i). This prohibits "dual tracking," so named because of prior practices in which servicers would file a foreclosure (track 1) while the borrower was pursuing a loan modification (track 2). These are substantial curbs on the contractual rights to foreclose and create a major federal overlay on state foreclosure procedure. Before the CFPB's rules, it was possible to foreclose in some states in as little as 37 days. (Can you see now where the 37-day period for evaluating a loss mitigation application derived from? It's still a terrible number from the standpoint of consumer comprehension.)

C. Protection from Debtor Suit

On some levels, creditors are like everybody else — they would like to avoid being sued. A highly technical law, the "holder in due course" rule, gives them a major leg-up in this regard. This rule only applies when a debt is sold to a party that did not originate the debt, but because such assignment is extremely common in consumer financial markets, creditors who meet certain requirements enjoy protection from claims by debtors that arise under state or federal consumer protection laws.

1. *Holder in Due Course Doctrine*

The holder in due course rule limits the liability of assignees or purchasers of credit instruments. In the consumer context, this means that if an originating lender sells a note to a third party, the borrower cannot assert most claims against the third party. The rule, and its qualifying elements, is found in U.C.C. §3-305. It limits the liability of a "holder in due course" to a borrower defense based on four grounds:

(i) infancy of the obligor to the extent it is a defense to a simple contract,
(ii) duress, lack of legal capacity, or illegality of the transaction which, under other law, nullifies the obligation of the obligor,
(iii) fraud that induced the obligor to sign the instrument with neither knowledge nor reasonable opportunity to learn of its character or its essential terms, or
(iv) discharge of the obligor in insolvency proceedings.

These are very limited grounds. Either the factual scenarios are relatively uncommon, such as infancy or duress, or the standard for proving the defense is very hard, such as fraud.

To take advantage of this rule, however, one must qualify as a "holder in due course" of an "instrument." This implicates three definitions in the Uniform Commercial Code. First, one must be a holder. This requires the successful completion of the process of "negotiation," which itself is a defined term. U.C.C. §3-201. There is an important caveat here, which is that the so-called "shelter rule" may protect a transferee who acquired instruments from holders in due course, even if the transferee is not a holder in due course. The key point is to check that a party actually is a holder; it is not enough to wish or assume statuses such as assignees or purchasers nearly always are. (Part of the reason they get away with that, however, is that legal aid and consumer lawyers do not know enough hard-core commercial law to challenge the application of the holder in due course rule. This stuff is tough but it is powerful.)

Second, creditors must have acquired their status "in due course." Uniform Commercial Code §3-302 sets out the requirements for such transactions. The two key provisions are that the "the instrument when issued or negotiated to the holder does not bear such apparent evidence of forgery or alteration or is not otherwise so irregular or incomplete as to call into question its authenticity" and that the holder "took the instrument for value, in good faith, without notice that the instrument is overdue or has been dishonored or that there is an uncured default with respect to payment of another instrument issued as part of the same series, and without other specified problems." The thrust of this rule is that assignees are holders in due course if they lacked knowledge of certain problems.

The third definitional requirement of using the holder in due course doctrine is that the document at issue must be an "instrument." This too is a defined term. U.C.C. §3-104. While most parties intend promissory notes to be negotiable instruments, there are technical requirements for negotiability. If the note at issue is not an instrument, the holder in due course rule does not shield the noteholder (the creditor) from liability. Indeed, some law professor has even tried to assert that the Fannie Mae Uniform Note is not a negotiable instrument. Ronald J. Mann, *Searching for Negotiability in Payment and Credit Systems*, 44 UCLA L. Rev. 951, 971-72 (1997) (suggesting that borrower's right to prepay may impair negotiability).

2.   FTC Preservation Rule

The holder in due course rule applies generally. For consumer transactions, the FTC has passed a rule that reverses the Uniform Commercial Code. The "Preservation of consumers' claims and defenses" rule makes it an unfair or deceptive practice under the FTC Act for any assignee or seller to take or receive a consumer credit contract without a specified "Notice" or to accept the proceeds of any purchase money loan if its contract does not contain the "Notice." 16 C.F.R. §433.2. The "Notice" reads:

> Any holder of this consumer credit contract is subject to all claims and defenses which the debtor could assert against the seller of goods or services obtained pursuant hereto or with the proceeds hereof. Recovery hereunder by the debtor shall not exceed amounts paid by the debtor hereunder.

The notice is, as you may be figuring out, actually reversing the substantive rights of the parties. By reversing the Holder in Due Course doctrine, it "preserves" consumers' claims or defenses against an originator of a loan and allows them to be applied to the assignee or purchaser. For added good measure, the FTC rule also eliminates contractual waivers of a consumer's right to assert a defense against an assignee.

Given the FTC Rule that lets consumers assert claims against the assignees and buyers of consumer credit contracts, why did you endure the torture of learning the holder in due course doctrine? The answer lies in the scope of the FTC Rule. It applies only to consumer contracts that are connected to the sale of goods or services. It does not apply to straight loans for money. So, for example, it does apply to a loan to purchase a used car, but it does not apply to a credit card debt. Also, the FTC Preservation rule does not apply to non-goods—otherwise, commonly known as real property. Because mortgages are nearly always assigned through the securitization process, the application of the holder in due course rule leaves consumers with nobody to sue for most claims relating to the origination of their mortgage loans. If you wondered why the foreclosure crisis was not a feast for consumer lawyers, you have your answer. The company holding the mortgage note enjoyed the protection of the holder in due course and the consumer could not assert claims against the holder except for infancy, duress, and fraud—all of which were inapplicable or impossible to prove.

Deutsche Bank National Trust Co. v. Carmichael (In re Carmichael)

443 B.R. 699 (Bankr. E.D. Pa. 2011)

RASLAVICH, Chief U.S. Bankruptcy Judge.

INTRODUCTION

Before the Court is Plaintiff Deutsche Bank's Motion for Summary Judgment. It is opposed by the Defendants who are the debtors in this bankruptcy case. Briefs were submitted. The Court next took the motion under advisement. For the reasons which follow, the Motion for Summary Judgment will be granted.

PROCEDURAL BACKGROUND

This matter began in state court where Deutsche filed a Complaint in Mortgage Foreclosure. A default judgment was entered and then opened. Debtors filed an Answer and New Matter to which Plaintiffs filed a reply. The New Matter consists of an affirmative defense which makes up the thrust of their opposition.

. . .

The Court turns first to what is required for a movant to be entitled to summary judgment in mortgage foreclosure. Entry of summary judgment is appropriate in a mortgage foreclosure action where mortgagors "admit that the mortgage is in default, that they have failed to pay interest on the obligation, and that the recorded mortgage is in the specified amount." Cunningham v. McWilliams, 714 A.2d 1054, 1057 (Pa. Super. 1998).

. . .

DEBTORS' AFFIRMATIVE DEFENSE IN CONTEXT

Defendants contend that at the loan's inception, AMC induced them to sign the mortgage note with fraudulent representations. Although Deutsche was not the original lender who made the loan, Debtors go on, they may raise their fraud claim against Deutsche's foreclosure complaint.

Were it framed as a counterclaim, such a claim would not be allowed in this context. A defendant in a mortgage foreclosure action can only raise counterclaims which arise from the same transaction or occurrence from which the plaintiff's action arose. See Pa. R.C.P. 1148. That rule, however, governs only counterclaims in mortgage foreclosure action and does not apply to new matter. See First Wisconsin Trust Co. v. Strausser, 653 A.2d 688, 692-693 (Pa. Super. 1995).

DEUTSCHE'S RESPONSE

Deutsche does not dispute the Defendant's claim of fraud with regard to certain representations that the original lender, Ameriquest, may have made. Deutsche's position is that it was not aware of such claims when it purchased the loan from Ameriquest. As a result, Deutsche maintains that it is a holder in due course immune from the Debtors' fraud claims.

THE FTC HOLDER RULE

As a threshold matter, the Defendants assert that Deutsche is precluded from raising defenses under applicable federal regulations. They refer here to the FTC Holder Rule:

> In connection with any sale or lease of goods or services to consumers, in or affecting commerce as "commerce" is defined in the Federal Trade Commission Act, it is an unfair or deceptive act or practice within the meaning of section 5 of that Act for a seller, directly or indirectly, to:
> a. Take or receive a consumer credit contract which fails to contain the following provision in at least ten points, bold face, type:
> NOTICE
> ANY HOLDER OF THIS CONSUMER CREDIT CONTRACT IS SUBJECT TO ALL CLAIMS AND DEFENSES WHICH THE DEBTOR COULD ASSERT AGAINST THE SELLER OF GOODS OR SERVICES OBTAINED PURSUANT HERETO OR WITH THE PROCEEDS

HEREOF. RECOVERY HEREUNDER BY THE DEBTOR SHALL NOT EXCEED AMOUNTS
PAID BY THE DEBTOR HEREUNDER.

or,

b. Accept, as full or partial payment for such sale or lease, the proceeds of any
purchase money loan (as purchase money loan is defined herein), unless any
consumer credit contract made in connection with such purchase money loan
contains the following provision in at least ten point, bold face, type:

[same as above].

16 C.F.R. §433.2 (2005). However, the FTC Holder Rule, by its terms, does not
apply to mortgage loans for the purchase of real estate, as in this case. See 41
F.R. 20024 (Friday, May 14, 1976) (excluding purchases of real estate from affected
transaction); see also In re Woodsbey, 375 B.R. 145, 149-150 (Bankr. W.D. Pa.
2007) citing Kaliner v. MERS (In re Reagoso), 2007 Bankr. LEXIS 2004, 2007 WL
1655376 at *6 (Bankr. E.D. Pa., June 6, 2007) citing Johnson v. Long Beach Mortg.
Loan Trust 2001-4, 451 F. Supp. 2d 16, 55 (D.D.C. 2006). Therefore, Defendants
may not rely on that rule in attempting to assert set-offs or recoupment as against
Deutsche Bank for the claims they have against the original lender. It will be state
law which determines what defenses the Defendants may raise as to Deutsche's
foreclosure rights.

HOLDER IN DUE COURSE UNDER PENNSYLVANIA LAW

Pennsylvania law does recognize that a holder of commercial paper may raise a
defense of good faith. Deutsche asserts innocence as to any claims of fraud
which the Debtor would have against the original lender, here, AMC. As a holder
in due course, Deutsche declares, it is not vicariously liable for its predecessor's torts.
A determination of whether Deutsche has established such status follows.

MORTGAGE LOAN AS NEGOTIABLE INSTRUMENT

The threshold requirement for holder in due course (HDC) status is that the party
asserting that defense be a holder of a negotiable instrument. Thus, the first element for the present analysis is whether what Deutsche holds is a negotiable instrument. A negotiable instrument is defined as [ ] an unconditional promise or order to
pay a fixed amount of money, with or without interest or other charges described in
the promise or order, if it:

(1) is payable to bearer or to order at the time it is issued or first comes into
possession of a holder;

(2) is payable on demand or at a definite time; and

(3) does not state any other undertaking or instruction by the person promising or ordering payment to do any act in addition to the payment of money,
but the promise or order may contain:

(i) an undertaking or power to give, maintain or protect collateral to secure
payment;

(ii) an authorization or power to the holder to confess judgment or realize
on or dispose of collateral; or

(iii) a waiver of the benefit of any law intended for the advantage or protection of an obligor.

13 Pa. C.S. §3104(a). Defendants say that a mortgage cannot be a negotiable instrument. Defendants' Brief, 7. However, it is not a mortgage which Deutsche holds, but a promissory note. The mortgage serves to secure that note. Under Pennsylvania law, a promissory note accompanied by a mortgage may be a negotiable instrument. Mellon Bank, N.A. v. Ternisky, 999 F.2d 791, 796 (4th Cir. 1993) (applying Pennsylvania law to hold that mortgagee was holder in due course).

IS DEUTSCHE A HOLDER IN DUE COURSE

Having determined that the note is a negotiable instrument, the Court turns to whether the record demonstrates that Deutsche acquired the note in good faith (i.e., in due course). The circumstances which indicate innocence are as follows:

(1) the instrument when issued or negotiated to the holder does not bear such apparent evidence of forgery or alteration or is not otherwise so irregular or incomplete as to call into question its authenticity; and

(2) the holder took the instrument:

(i) for value;

(ii) in good faith;

(iii) without notice that the instrument is overdue or has been dishonored or that there is an uncured default with respect to payment of another instrument issued as part of the same series;

(iv) without notice that the instrument contains an unauthorized signature or has been altered;

(v) without notice of any claim to the instrument described in section 3306 (relating to claims to an instrument); and

(vi) without notice that any party has a defense or claim in recoupment described in section 3305(a) (relating to defenses and claims in recoupment).

13 Pa. C.S. §3302(a).

There is no allegation of forgery or alteration (subsection (a)(1)). Likewise, the PSA demonstrates that Deutsche took the loan for value and in good faith (subsection (a)(2)(i), (ii)). Defendants contend that Deutsche's innocence is in question when considering ¶ 2(iii) above. By the time of the assignment, they explain, the loan was already nine months in default. Defendants' Brief in Opposition to Summary Judgment, 3. Deutsche contests that premise arguing that the assignment occurred at least two years earlier. What does the record show?

DEBTORS' DEFAULTS/DEUTSCHE'S KNOWLEDGE

In April 2005, the mortgage loan in question was made by Ameriquest Mortgage Company (AMC) to the Defendants. This much is admitted. See Answer to Foreclosure Complaint, ¶ 3. To demonstrate when Deutsche obtained the loan, Deutsche offers the Affidavit of Ronaldo R. Reyes, V.P. According to Mr. Reyes, AMC, Ameriquest Mortgage Services (AMS), and Deutsche entered into a Pooling and Services Agreement (PSA) on June 1, 2005. Pursuant to the PSA, AMC sold the Debtors' loan to AMS which immediately conveyed the loan to Deutsche. Along with the loan, the PSA provided that AMS would also deliver to Deutsche "an original Assignment assigned in blank" as well as any "original recorded intervening assignment or complete chain of assignment from the original to the person assigning the mortgage to Deutsche." PSA, §2.01(iii), (iv). Although the Assignment from AMC to Deutsche would not be recorded until 3 months after Deutsche filed this foreclosure complaint, the PSA had already conveyed the Debtors' mortgage loan from AMC to AMS and then on to Deutsche 2 1/2 years earlier. For that reason, the Court finds that Deutsche took the loan well before it ever went into default. Accordingly, the Court finds Deutsche to have been a holder in due course.

DEFENSES TO HDC STATUS

Yet even a holder in due course is susceptible to certain prescribed defenses of an obligor/borrower. Section 3305 provides, in pertinent part:

> (b) Right of holder in due course to enforce obligation. — The right of a holder in due course to enforce the obligation of a party to pay the instrument is subject to defenses of the obligor stated in subsection (a)(1), but is not subject to defenses of the obligor stated in subsection (a)(2) or claims in recoupment stated in subsection (a)(3) against a person other than the holder.

13 P.S. §3305(b) (emphasis added). The defenses stated in subsection (a)(1) are:
>   (1) a defense of the obligor based on:
>   (i) infancy of the obligor to the extent it is a defense to a simple contract;
>   (ii) duress, lack of legal capacity or illegality of the transaction which, under other law, nullifies the obligation of the obligor;
>   (iii) fraud that induced the obligor to sign the instrument with neither knowledge nor reasonable opportunity to learn of its character or its essential terms; or
>   (iv) discharge of the obligor in insolvency proceedings;

13 Pa.C.S. §3305(a)(1). Which of those defenses, if any, might apply?

As it turns out, none. There is no claim of infancy, duress or other lack of legal capacity. Neither is there raised a discharge of the obligation. That leaves the fraud defense in subparagraph (iii). This provision does not include fraud in all its forms: it draws a distinction between certain types of fraud-based defenses. Subsection (a)(1)(iii) thus preserves as against the HDC on the claim of fraud that is alleged to have occurred in the execution of the instrument, i.e, fraud in factum. Therefore, it precludes other frauds such as a fraudulent inducement to enter into the transaction. See In re Balko, 348 B.R. 684, 698 n. 18 (Bankr. W.D. Pa. 2006) (explaining that fraud in the inducement is not a real defense to a holder in due course); Exchange Intern. Leasing Corp. v. Consolidated Bus. Forms Co., Inc., 462 F. Supp. 626, 628 (W.D. Pa. 1978) ("Under Pennsylvania only fraud in the factum as opposed to fraud in the inducement, is a defense to a holder in due course"); Catasauqua Nat. Bank v. Miller, 60 Pa. Super. 220, 1915 WL 4398 at *3 (Pa. Super.) ("The great fabric of commercial business in this country rests largely upon the proposition, long recognized and everywhere accepted, that a negotiable note is 'a courier without luggage,' and that innocent holders for value, who take such paper in due course of business, are not to be bound or affected by any secret equities between the maker of such paper and the payee named."); Ternisky, supra, 999 F.2d at 796 (applying Pennsylvania law to hold that where bank held mortgage in due course purchaser could not raise defense of fraud in the inducement). As it turns out, the fraud claim which the Defendants would impute to Deutsche consists of a claim of fraudulent inducement. They maintain that they were fraudulently persuaded to refinance their mortgage loan based on representations that if it would be beneficial for them to refinance, then they would later be permitted to refinance notwithstanding the existence of a prepayment penalty in the note. Simply put, these claims may not be raised as to Deutsche, but they are in no way barred as to AMC, the original lender.

UTPCPL

In addition to the fraud in the inducement claim, Defendants raise the affirmative defense of state consumer protection law, the Unfair Trade Practices and Consumer Protection Law. The UTPCPL protects consumer against unfair or deceptive practices to the text of the note and is thus akin to the fraud in the inducement claims discussed, supra. Indeed, the Defendants' claim even used the predicate "induced" to explain how they were allegedly lured into the mortgage with AMC in the first place. Accordingly, they would likewise be subject to the holder in due course defense. See also In re Reagoso, supra 2007 Bankr. LEXIS 2004, [WL] at *6 citing State Street Bank & Trust Co. v. Strawser, 908 F. Supp. 249, 252 (M.D. Pa. 1995)

BREACH OF CONTRACT

Additionally, Defendants construe the same facts which support their fraud in the inducement claims as a breach of contract They are referring here to certain alleged promises made by an AMC representative with regard to the note's prepayment penalty. Defendants maintain that AMC assured them that in the event that they needed to refinance the note, then such prepayment penalty would be waived. In other words, the original parties to the loan contract (i.e, AMC and the Defendants) orally modified one of its terms and that AMC breached that oral argument. Defendants argue that such breach should be enforced against Deutsche. Is such a claim likewise barred against an HDC?

It is. To repeat, §3305(b) specifically provides that "[t]he right of a holder in due to enforce the obligation of a party to pay the instrument is . . . not subject to the defenses of the obligor stated in subsection (a)(2) . . ." 13 Pa. C.S. §3305(b). The defenses of subsection (a)(2) are:

> a defense of the obligor stated in another section of this division of the note or a defense that would be available if the person entitled to enforce the instrument were enforcing a right to payment under a simple contract

13 Pa. C.S. §3305(a)(2). The Comment to subsection (a)(2) explains:

> Subsection (a)(2) states other defenses that, pursuant to subsection (b), are cut off by a holder in due course. These defenses comprise those specifically stated in Article 3 and

those based on common law contract principles. Article 3 defenses are nonissuance of the instrument, conditional issuance, and issuance for a special purpose (Section 3-105(b)); failure to countersign a traveler's check (Section 3-106(c)); modification of the obligation by a separate agreement (Section 3-117); payment that violates a restrictive indorsement (Section 3-206(f)); instruments issued without consideration or for which promised performance has not been given (Section 3-303(b)), and breach of warranty when a draft is accepted (Section 3-417(b)).

Milton v. Wilshire Credit Corporation (In re Milton), 2005 Bankr. LEXIS 3318, 2005 WL 6508305 at **10-11 (Bankr. E.D. Pa., July 26, 2005) quoting 13 Pa. C.S. §3305 Uniform Commercial Code-Comment 1990. The subsection renders the HDC immune from breach of contract claims. Any promise or agreement by AMC to waive the prepayment penalty which it later would not honor is just such a claim. As such, it may not be raised as a defense to Deutsche's enforcement of the note. In sum, none of the causes of action raised in Defendants' New Matter are viable as to Deutsche.

SUMMARY

Based on the evidence offered by Deutsche and the lack of any contrary evidence from Defendants, Deutsche is entitled to a judgment in mortgage foreclosure. Nothing in the Court's ruling, however, constitutes an adjudication on the merits of Defendants' fraud claim against Ameriquest Mortgage Company.

An appropriate Order follows.

A few other laws help mitigate this harsh effect but they are not widely applicable. If a consumer attempts to rescind a mortgage loan under the Truth in Lending Act (a remedy covered in in Assignment 14), the assignee must cooperate in the rescission process. *See* 15 U.S.C. §1641(c). Assignees of home loans that are covered by the Home Ownership and Equity Protection Act (HOEPA) are "subject to all claims and defenses with respect to that mortgage that the consumer could assert against the creditor." 15 U.S.C. §1641(d)(1). This liability applies whether or not the required notice about assignee liability for HOEPA loans appeared in the note and regardless of whether the current owner is a holder in due course. Similarly, some state predatory lending laws also make assignees liable under their provisions for origination-related claims.

Problem Set 21

21.1. Diane Jacobsen went to District Court last week over a $438 utility bill. She had missed her prior court dates and has never denied to anyone that she owes the money. When she appeared in court, Judge Bill Smith told her to hand over the jewelry that she was wearing to pay the money that day or go to jail. Reluctantly, she surrendered her grandmothers' pearls and spent one month scraping up the money from family and friends to pay the debt. In the Legal

Aid office about her pending separation from her husband, she relayed this story to your family law colleague, who was outraged. The family law lawyer correctly states that debtors' prisons were outlawed centuries ago. She asks you how Judge Smith can get away with his behavior. What do you tell her?

21.2. Lynn LoPucki is the long-suffering assistant to the County Sheriff in Black Hawk County, Iowa. A newly elected sheriff has just arrived for his first day of work and has announced that he will be out all morning "testing out the speed potential" of the sheriff's car to "make sure it is adequate to serve his crime-fighting goals." Lynn rolls his eyes, and hands him the legal document delivered earlier that day. Then Lynn goes back to playing games on his computer. A few minutes later the sheriff is still scratching his head and distracting Lynn. Lynn already opened the envelope before giving it to him (hey, the only perk of the job is the right to be nosy) and knows that it contains a "Writ of Execution" form with all the blanks complete. The total owing is $462 and the judgment debtor's address is only about five blocks from the sheriff's office. If he decides to take pity on the sheriff, what should Lynn advise the sheriff to do? *See* Iowa Code and Iowa Rules of Civil Procedure.

21.3. Bruno Holtry is one of your company's best repossession agents. He's quick at his work, which limits the potential for violent responses from debtors. Bruno just called you to report on his last job of the night. He says that he was headed to the employer of Isabel Fury to repossess her 2000 Honda Accord when she passed him headed home from work. He followed her. She stopped the car in front of a modest ranch house and went to the door. He verified that the address was not her home based on your records but figured since it was a few blocks away that he would repo the car and let her walk home. The job was easy, he reported, because Isabel left the keys in the car and the windows rolled down. He heard her yelling and chasing after him when he was a half-block away, but he knew better than to stop and invite trouble.

At this point, you are wondering why the call when Bruno says that he better call you back "because a helicopter's landing out back." You are nonplussed but can't put the pieces together. Waiting for Bruno to call you back, you flip on the office TV. Across the bottom of the screen is an "Amber Alert" for a missing two-year old, Jermaine Fury. When the telephone rings back, it is a police detective, who explains that when Bruno took the car, Jermaine was asleep in his car seat. Apparently, Bruno did not notice him, but Isabel called 911 to report a stolen child. After launching an intense missing child protocol, the police called Bruno and had him check the car. When the police and Isabel arrived on the scene, Bruno was giving the toddler his first root beer. Is your company in legal trouble based on the day's events? Is Bruno? Is Isabel? Is Jermaine? *See* U.C.C. §9-609.

21.4. You are the Deputy Assistant to the General Counsel for the Consumer Financial Protection Bureau. Your boss has been tasked with a major project on examining whether the FTC's Preservation Rule is appropriate in its scope. The project is just starting, and because of your place in the organization's hierarchy, you have been assigned the "background" section of the report. Specifically, you are supposed to explain the justification for the FTC Preservation Rule. What problems is it thought to be correcting? How does it help improve the marketplace for consumer goods and financial services?

Assignment 22. Debtor Rights

Creditors usually "win" debt collection actions, in the sense that they obtain judgments or are able to take their collateral. But their recovery is often curbed by laws that protect debtors. One type of law gives debtors the right to sue and recover from debt collectors who engage in abusive processes. This is the subject of Assignment 23. The other set of laws, examined below, permit debtors to shield property either temporarily or permanently from creditors or even to avoid liability entirely for some debts.

A. FTC Credit Practices Rule

A specialized set of rules for consumer collections that aims to protect debtors is contained in the FTC Credit Practices Rule. 16 C.F.R. §§444.1-444.5. Passed in 1985 under the authority of the Unfair and Deceptive Practices Act, it prohibits a practice known as "pyramiding" late charges and prohibits practices that may mislead cosigners for consumer debts. Lenders or retail sellers are required to give cosigners a separate document, "Notice to Cosigner," that explains that cosigners may be liable for the full amount of the debt and that the creditor can collect from the cosigner without first attempting to collect from the borrower. 16 C.F.R. §444.3(c). If this notice is provided, the creditor is shielded from liability for misrepresenting the nature or extent of cosigner liability, an act prohibited by 16 C.F.R. §444.3(a)(1).

The Credit Practices Rule also prohibits lenders or retail installment sellers from including certain provisions in contracts that essentially allow the creditor to short-circuit the normal collection process. For example, some consumer credit contracts specified that the debtor — by signing the contract — was giving up her right to be notified of a court hearing and agreeing to allow an attorney to confess a judgment in favor of the creditor. These provisions were called "confessions of judgment" or "cognovits." While they remain legal in some states and are used in commercial lending, the FTC Rule makes it an unfair act or practice to include such clauses in consumer contracts. Similarly, consumer contracts may not contain an "assignment of wages" that is an irrevocable agreement to allow a creditor to take a debtor's wages upon default. The effect of such an assignment was to permit wage garnishment without the normal legal steps of filing a garnishment action, permitting an answer, etc.

These rules were established decades ago, unlike so many areas of consumer credit in which the landscape has changed in the wake of Dodd-Frank. But just because a legal rule is old does not mean that it gets followed — even with the "help" of counsel.

F.T.C. v. Loanpointe

2011 U.S. Dist. LEXIS 104982, 2011 WL 4348304 (D. Utah Sept. 15, 2011)

KIMBALL, District Judge.

This matter is before the court on Plaintiff Federal Trade Commission's Motion for Summary Judgment against Defendants LoanPointe, LLC, Eastbrook, LLC, and Joe S. Strom (collectively, "Defendants"). . . .

BACKGROUND

Plaintiff Federal Trade Commission ("FTC") enforces federal statutes prohibiting unfair or deceptive acts or practices in or affecting commerce, specifically debt collection and credit practices. Defendant Eastbrook, LLC is no longer an operating entity because its books were merged into Defendant LoanPointe, LLC. LoanPointe is a Utah limited liability company doing business as GetECash through its internet website www.GetECash.com. Defendant Joe S. Strom is a manager, officer, principal, and registered agent of both Eastbrook and LoanPointe.

Since at least September 2008, Defendants have used their website to offer short-term, small dollar, unsecured, high-interest rate extensions of credit, commonly referred to as payday loans. The principal of the loans is usually less than $1,000 and the term of the loan is meant to extend only to the next payday. Consumers obtain the loans by completing an online application on Defendants' website. Before receiving the loan, consumers must agree to the Terms of the Application, the Privacy Policy, the Authorization Agreement, and the Loan Note and Disclosure. Consumers indicate their agreement by checking a box, as an electronic signature, next to links to each of those documents.

The version of the Loan Note and Disclosure at issue in this case, which consumers had to accept before receiving a loan, included a clause that read, "NOTICE: I agree to have my wages garnished to pay any delinquent amount on this loan." The clause was written in the fine print and it was in bold and underlined.

Strom knew that the loan agreements contained the wage assignment clause. However, he believed that his companies could lawfully use the wage assignment clause and garnish the wages of borrowers under its authority. Strom had sought and received advice from an attorney before authorizing the loan documents. When the FTC notified Strom that certain documents were not legal, Strom withdrew his approval from those documents.

Using the wage assignment clause as authority, Defendants garnished the wages of consumers who were in default on their loans. Although 80% of the consumers that Defendants attempted to garnish wages from refused to allow the garnishment, the wage assignment clause was used to recover approximately 16% of all loan repayments from approximately 10% of all borrowers.

In order to garnish a consumer's pay from a consumer's employer, Defendants would send a garnishment package to the employer that included the following documents: 1) a "Letter to Employer & Important Notice to Employer"; 2) a "Wage Garnishment" document; 3) a "Wage Garnishment Worksheet"; and 4) an "Employer Certification." These document titles match exactly the document titles that the Treasury Department's Financial Management Service ("FMS") includes in the wage garnishment package that it sends to employers when federal agencies seek to garnish wages.

In addition to the other documents in the wage garnishment package, Defendants would also send copies of the consumer's loan application to the consumer's employer, which included the loan amount. Although Strom's declaration states that "all collection efforts, including the wage assignments . . . sent to employers" were from GetECash, Defendants sent their garnishment package using a fax cover-sheet from LoanPointe, a LoanPointe fax tagline, and the words "LoanPointe Garnishment Manager" as the signature.

In addition to sending a garnishment package with document titles identical to those sent by the FMS, Defendants' "Letter to Employer" also included wording similar to the wording included in the FMS's "Letter to Employer." The FMS's letter states the following:

> One of your employees has been identified as owing a delinquent nontax debt to the United States. The Debt Collection Improvement Act of 1996 (DCIA) permits Federal agencies to garnish the pay of individuals who owe such debt without first obtaining a court order. Enclosed is a Wage Garnishment Order directing you to withhold a portion of the employee's pay each period and to forward those amounts to us. We have previously notified the employee that this action was going to take place and have provided the employee with the opportunity to dispute the debt.

Defendants' letter states the following:

> One of your employees has been identified as owing a delinquent debt to GetECash. The Debt Collection Improvement Act of 1996 (DCIA) permits agencies to garnish the pay of individuals who owe such debt without first obtaining a court order. Enclosed is a Wage Garnishment Assignment directing you to withhold a portion of the employee's pay each period and to forward those amounts to GetECash. We have previously notified the employee that this action was going to take place and have provided the employee with the opportunity to dispute the debt.

After being informed by the Treasury Department that the portion of Defendants' letter referring to the DCIA was inaccurate and unacceptable to the government, Defendants discontinued the use of the challenged documents. Specifically, Defendants removed the language referring to the DCIA and asked the Treasury agent if she had any other concerns with the letter. When Defendants did not get a response, they assumed that the remaining information in the letter was proper.

Prior to undertaking any garnishment of wages, Defendants assert that they attempted to contact the consumers several times by telephone, voice mail, and email. According to Defendants, these communications would inform consumers that their continued failure and refusal to repay loans would result in garnishment of their wages. Despite these communications, the FTC references two consumers who were unaware of the Defendants' ability to garnish their wages until Defendants' made contact with their employers, and it references another consumer who was unaware of Defendants' ability to garnish wages after reviewing the loan application. The FTC also references comments from several consumers suggesting that Defendants' contact with consumers' employers exposed them to embarrassment and risk of adverse action, such as job loss.

Using the loan application with the wage assignment clause, Defendants have made at least 7,121 payday loans to consumers from which they have collected a total of $3,013,044. Of that total, $976,107.54 represents principal that consumers repaid to Defendants. Defendants used wage garnishment to collect $468,020.91 of the total amount.

On March 15, 2010, the FTC filed a Complaint against Defendants claiming that Defendants' practices violated Section 5 of the Federal Trade Commission Act ("FTC Act"), the Fair Debt Collection Practices Act ("FDCPA"), and the FTC's Trade Regulation Rule Concerning Credit Practices ("Credit Practices Rule"). As relief for these violations, the FTC sought a preliminary injunction during the pendency of the action, a permanent injunction to prevent future violations, and any other relief the court finds necessary such as rescission or reformation of contracts, restitution, the refund of monies paid, and the disgorgement of illgotten monies. The parties agreed to the entry of a preliminary injunction in April 2010.

DISCUSSION

. . .

I. Violations of the FTC Act

The FTC argues that Defendants violated the FTC Act by engaging in the following unfair or deceptive practices: misrepresenting to consumers' employers that they were authorized to garnish wages under the DCIA without a court order; misrepresenting to consumers' employers that they had notified consumers and given consumers an opportunity to dispute the debt prior to sending the garnishment request; and communicating with and disclosing the existence and amount of consumers' loans to consumers' employers without consumers' knowledge or consent.

. . .

A. Deceptive Practices

The FTC argues that Defendants were deceptive by making explicitly false claims that the DCIA authorized non-federal entities to garnish wages without a court order and that Defendants provided consumers with an opportunity to dispute their debts before seeking wage garnishment. In addition, the FTC claims that Defendants engaged in unfairness through disclosing consumers' debts to third parties, including their employers.

It is undisputed that Defendants made representations that they had authority under the DCIA and that they had notified consumers and given consumers a chance to dispute the debt. Defendants concede that they did not have authority under the DCIA to garnish wages. In addition, although Defendants argue that they notified consumers prior to contacting consumers' employers to garnish wages, Defendants do not argue that they gave consumers an opportunity to dispute the debt before attempting to garnish wages. Therefore, both statements were false and potentially misleading. Accordingly, the only disputes are whether the representations were likely to mislead consumers and whether they were material.

Defendants argue that the representations were not likely to mislead consumers because they were sent to the consumers' employers. Therefore, the crucial question in this analysis is whether sending misleading information to the consumers' employers qualifies as a deceptive act for purposes of the FTC Act.

Both individuals and businesses can be consumers for purposes of Section 5 liability. See, e.g., FTC v. Inc21.com Corp., 745 F. Supp. 2d 975, 982 (N.D. Cal. 2010). The employers in this case are the consumers to whom Defendants' deceptive garnishment letters were directed. Defendants sent the employers letters that looked identical to a garnishment request from the government. The letter also alleged that Defendants had the right to garnish under the DCIA. While Defendants' business is extending credit and loans and they would be expected to know the applicable law applying to such business, the consumers' employers would be in various fields unrelated to the credit and loan business. Thus, the consumers' employers could be, and likely were, misled by Defendants' letter into believing that Defendants had the right to garnish. Moreover, Defendants' represented to the consumers' employers that they had given the employee a right to dispute the debt. The consumers' employers would not be in a position to know whether that was factually correct. Even if the employer questioned its employee regarding the factual representation, it would not be able to verify which version of the facts was accurate. Defendants' factual misrepresentation, therefore, could, and likely did, mislead reasonable employers into believing that Defendants had given the employees an opportunity to dispute the debt. Therefore, the second prong of the test for whether an act or practice is deceptive is met because Defendants conduct was likely to mislead an individual or an entity in a way that affects commerce.

Under the third element, Defendants' practices will be considered deceptive if they are material. To be material, a misrepresentation would have to be "likely to affect a consumer's choice of or conduct regarding a product." In re Thompson Medical Co., 104 F.T.C. 648, 788 (1984), aff'd, 791 F.2d 189, 253 U.S. App. D.C. 18 (D.C. Cir. 1986). . . .

Here, Defendants expressly stated that they had authority under the DCIA and that they had given consumers an opportunity to dispute their debt. Defendants' claims made the employers more likely to garnish the wages of their employees. The claims indicated to the employers that Defendants had the right to garnish and that they had complied with any prerequisites that may be necessary for such garnishment. The evidence demonstrates that approximately twenty percent of the employers that received the documents with those representations actually garnished wages. Because the misrepresentations affected employers' conduct, the representations were material and violated Section 5 of the FTC Act.

B. Unfair Practices

In addition to alleging that Defendants participated in two deceptive acts or practices under the FTC Act, the FTC also argues that Defendants participated in an unfair act or practice by disclosing consumers' debts to their employers without prior approval from the consumers. To qualify as an unfair practice under the Act, the practice need only cause, or be likely to cause, substantial injury to consumers which is not reasonably avoidable by consumers and not outweighed by countervailing interests to consumers or competition. Disclosing consumers' debts to their employers is likely to cause substantial injury to consumers.

Other courts have recognized that wage assignment clauses and wage garnishment procedures cause substantial harm to consumers. For example, the Circuit Court for the District of Columbia has noted that the FTC "found wage assignments particularly harmful to consumers because they can be invoked without the due process safeguards of a hearing and opportunity to present defenses." Am. Fin. Servs. Assoc. v. FTC, 767 F.2d 957, 974 (D.C. Cir. 1985). The following specific injuries to consumers were mentioned in the rulemaking record for the unfair practices provision:

> Employers are hostile to wage assignments due to added administrative costs and burdens and the fear that the employee's job motivation and performance will suffer as a result of the reduction in wages. Moreover, employers tend to view the consumer's failure to repay the debt as a sign of irresponsibility. As a consequence many lose their jobs after wage assignments are filed. Even if the consumer retains the job, promotions, raises, and job assignments may be adversely affected.
>
> . . . Loss of a substantial portion of wages tends to cause further disruption of family finances and may even put at risk the wage earner's ability to provide necessities for the family. . . . The invocation of a wage assignment or just simply the threat of invocation may lead a debtor to enter into costly refinancing, to improvidently default on other obligations, or to forego valid defenses. . . .

Id. at 974-75. The FTC summarized the injuries to consumers as "severe, substantial disruption of employment, the pressure that results from threats to file wage assignments, and the disruption of family finances." Id. at 975. Based on these findings and conclusions by the FTC, the court concluded that "[t]he harms to consumers resulting from the use of . . . wage assignments identified by the Commission on the basis of the rulemaking record are neither trivial or speculative nor based merely on notions of subjective distress or offenses to taste," and that the "risk of substantial economic and monetary harm to the consumer" is significant. Id. at 975. Therefore, the court concludes that Defendants' practice of disclosing debts and the amount of the debts to consumers' employers qualifies as an unfair practice under the FTC Act.

. . .

III. Violations of the Credit Practices Rule

The FTC further argues that Defendants violated the Credit Practices Rule by including an improper wage assignment clause in their credit contracts. The Credit Practices Rule generally prohibits the use of wage assignment clauses, but it allows such clauses to be included if the wage assignment: (i) is, by its terms, revocable at the will of the debtor; (ii) is a payroll deduction plan or preauthorized payment plan, commencing at the time of the transaction, in which the consumer authorizes a series of wage deductions as a method of making each payment; or (iii) applies only to wages or other earnings already earned at the time of the assignment. 16 C.F.R. §444.2(a)(3).

Defendants' wage assignment clause in its loan application does not meet any of the requirements of the Credit Practices Rule. Even though several consumers refused to allow Defendants to garnish their wages upon request, the wage assignment clause was still not revocable by its terms. Because Defendants' clause was not revocable by its terms, Defendants violated the Credit Practices Rule.

Defendants incorrectly attempt to require the FTC to make an additional showing that the violation is a deceptive or unfair practice. In promulgating the Credit Practices Rule, however, the FTC already found that improper wage assignment clauses are unfair and cause substantial harm to consumers. See Am. Fin. Servs. Ass'n v. FTC, 767 F.2d 957, 974-74 (D.C. Cir. 1985). Therefore, the court concludes that summary judgment is appropriate on the issue of whether Defendants violated the Credit Practices Rule.

Defendants dispute the appropriate remedy for a violation of the Credit Practices Rule. Defendants attempt to assert an affirmative defense to their violation of the Credit Practices Rule because they did not know that their wage assignment clause was illegal. However, good faith is not a defense to liability under the FTC Act, in part because the FTC need not prove intent. See, e.g., FTC v. Cyberspace.com, LLC, 453 F.3d 1196, 1202 (9th Cir. 2006). In addition, reliance on others, including counsel, is no defense to FTC Act liability. Cyberspace.com, 453 F.3d at 1202; Amy Travel, 875 F.2d at 575.

Good faith, however, may be relevant in determining the scope of injunctive relief because permanent injunctions are only appropriate if "there exists some cognizable danger of recurrent violation." United States v. W.T. Grant Co., 345 U.S. 629, 633 (1953). Whether there is a danger of a recurrent violation is determined by looking at two factors: 1) the deliberateness and seriousness of the present violation and 2) the violator's past record with respect to unfair advertising practices, Sears, Roebuck and Co. v. FTC, 676 F.2d 385, 392 (9th Cir. 1982). Good faith on the part of a defendant could be relevant to the first factor. Hang-Ups Art. Enters., 1995 U.S. Dist. LEXIS 21444 at *10-11.

Defendants' ignorance of the Credit Practices Rule does nothing to negate the need for permanent injunction in this case because not knowing that the clause was illegal does not lessen the deliberateness or seriousness of the conduct, see Jerman v. Carlisle, McNellie, Rini, Kramer, & Ulrich LPA, 130 S. Ct. 1605, 1612 (2010), and because Defendants should have been diligent in understanding the law relating to their chosen line of business. Therefore, Defendants' good faith defense reinforces, instead of excuses, the need for permanent injunctive relief to ensure that consumers are not harmed in the future.

· · ·

CONCLUSION

Based on the above reasoning, Plaintiff Federal Trade Commission's Motion for Summary Judgment is granted as discussed above and the FTC shall submit a Judgment in accordance with the court's decision within ten days of the date of this Memorandum Decision and Order.

The FTC Credit Practices Rule also limits creditors' rights to take debtors' property. As background for understanding these rules, recall the general idea of a security interest from the prior assignment. If the debtor offers up property as collateral as part of a transaction, secured creditors can repossess or foreclose on that property upon the debtor's default. The right to take the collateral is contractual. The nature of that relationship means that the law generally assumes that debtors knowingly and voluntarily are giving the creditor a property interest in the collateral, including the right to possess and sell the collateral if a default occurs. The FTC Credit Practices Rule accepts this process but distinguishes it from efforts by creditors to use contractual language to require a debtor to "waive" their rights to protect "exempt", non-collateral property from being seized subject to a writ of execution. 16 C.F.R. §444.2(a)(2). The exemption laws, discussed more below, give debtors a right to keep certain delineated property from being taken to satisfy a judgment. It is not subject to levy or sale by a sheriff. A debtor can offer such property as collateral for a security interest but the rules for the creation and enforcement of a security interest, set out for personal property in Uniform Commercial Code, Article 9, must be followed. The logic of the rule seems to be that debtors will understand the consequences of offering up property as collateral ("If I don't pay, the creditor can take it away") but that debtors will not sufficiently value the protection of the property exemptions at the time of contracting to be able to sensibly decide whether they wish to waive them.

A student who has taken a class on secured credit may see a potential loophole in this scheme. Article 9 of the Uniform Commercial Code allows creditors to take security interests in "all the debtor's property." Because the FTC Credit Practices Rule excludes security interests taken at the time of the consumer loan, why can't a creditor not effectively achieve an executory waiver of the exemption laws by taking as collateral everything that a debtor owns, including property that would be protected by the exemption laws? The reason is the second limitation on collateral in the FTC Credit Practices Rule: lenders or retail installment sellers who take a nonpossessory security interest, other than a purchase money security interest, in household goods are engaging in an unfair act or practice. 16 C.F.R. §444.2(a)(4). Household goods are defined to include items such as clothing, furniture, and "personal effects" (including wedding rings). 16 C.F.R. §444.1(i). These items are frequently of very low resale value but are needed by debtors to maintain a safe and adequate standard of living for themselves and their dependents.

The baby crib is the classic tearjerker example used to illustrate the harm the rule is trying to prevent. A cash-strapped new mother, who desperately needs a loan to make ends meet, cannot offer their babies' cribs as collateral. Without such a security interest, the creditor is prohibited from repossessing the crib upon default, leaving the baby sleeping somewhere unsafe as a result (or perhaps just as direly, the mother doing something desperate to pay the creditor to avoid losing the crib). The purchase money exception to the household goods rule means that items such as a crib can be collateral when a consumer is buying them in a transaction. This facilitates extensions of credit for purchasing household goods, giving families the ability to borrow to obtain basic living items such as furniture.

B. Exemptions

1. Property Exemptions

Every state has one or more laws that specify certain property as exempt from seizure for collection. When a creditor obtains a judgment and the sheriff goes out to levy, this property cannot be taken. Exemptions protect debtors from being left destitute after creditor collection. While this is obviously consumer protection in that sense, exemption laws also provide a societal benefit. If debtors are left with nothing — no clothes, no furniture, no tools of their trade — they will need support from society or the government to live. Alternatively, such debtors could be left to suffer but that creates its own strain on community norms about fairness and justice.

Exemptions are creatures of statutes. State legislatures have very different views on the appropriate scope of exemptions. Nowhere is this more pronounced than in the context of homestead exemptions, protections for debtors' places of residence. A handful of states allow debtors to protect a homestead (often limited to a certain number of acres in size) regardless of its value; another handful of states provide no homestead exemption at all. Most states take an intermediate approach, but even there, the variance is large.

Personal property exemptions nearly always include items such as clothing and basic household goods but beyond that have little consistency in their reach. Some statutes clearly reveal their origins in the days of yore, protecting things like a church pew and an ox. Other states amend their statutes regularly, updating them to clarify that things like personal computers are household goods. Of crucial importance to debtors is whether the state provides any protection for cash, whether on hand or in a bank account. These funds are crucial to the debtor being able to buy food, pay bills, and the like.

While debtors enjoy the protection of exemptions by operation of law, they usually need to assert them at the time of levy or at the latest before judicial sale to satisfy the writ of execution. The exemption statutes result in many writs of execution being returned unfulfilled (sometimes noted by the Latin phrase *nulla bona*). The sheriff surveyed the debtor's property but found no non-exempt property. In effect, the exemption laws sharply limit the practical benefits of obtaining a judgment for debtors with few assets. In place of using such legal process, creditors may use informal collection procedures such as dunning, or if the debtor is employed, use wage garnishment procedures instead.

2. Wage Exemptions

In an analog to the property exemption laws, most states put limits on the amount of a debtor's paycheck that can be garnished. At one extreme is Texas, whose state constitution prohibits garnishment entirely. At the other extreme are states with no garnishment protections, but in those states the debtor has a back-stop: federal garnishment limits. The Consumer Credit Protection Act sets out two alternate tests that limit the amount that may be garnished. This law does not apply to support orders (for children or spouses) or to tax collection efforts. 15 U.S.C. §1673. If the debtor's state of residence has a more protective rule, either in amount or scope, the debtor gets to shield that amount. The federal statute creates a floor, bringing some uniformity to a disparate system and preventing the complete garnishment of wages that left debtors with no money to support themselves. A few states, such as Texas, prohibit wage garnishment entirely. Tex. Const. Art. 16, §28.

Exemptions and protection from garnishment may seem merciful to downtrodden debtors. That is certainly their intent. But in application, the outcomes can be excruciatingly difficult to accept. The statutes typically apply to all creditors with very few exceptions, as this case illustrates.

J.M. v. Hobbs

797 N.W.2d 227 (Neb. 2011)

GERRARD, Justice.

Nebraska law provides that a court may order any property of a judgment debtor, not exempted by law, in the hands of either the debtor or any other person or corporation, or due to the debtor, to be applied toward the satisfaction of the judgment. But the Nebraska State Patrol Retirement Act (the Act) provides, as relevant, that annuities or benefits "which any person shall be entitled to receive under" the Act are not subject to garnishment, attachment, levy, or any other process of law. The question presented in this case is whether a plaintiff who wins a civil judgment against a former state trooper can obtain an order in aid of execution against the trooper's State Patrol retirement benefits.

BACKGROUND

The plaintiff in this case, J.M., is the guardian and conservator for his minor child, C.M. In 1999, when C.M. was 7 years old, her mother married the defendant, Billy L. Hobbs. C.M. lived with her mother and Hobbs. Hobbs sexually assaulted C.M. while she was between 12 and 14 years old. In 2006, Hobbs was convicted of first degree sexual assault of a child and sentenced to 25 to 30 years' imprisonment. And J.M. sued Hobbs on C.M.'s behalf and won a judgment of $325,000.

J.M. filed a motion for an order in aid of execution, alleging that Hobbs was a judgment creditor and, although incarcerated, was receiving a retirement pension from the State Patrol. J.M. requested that Hobbs be asked to pay all nonexempt property and funds that came into his hands on a recurring basis toward satisfaction of the judgment. J.M. also moved for the appointment of a receiver to take control of Hobbs' assets in the event that Hobbs did not comply. Hobbs objected, alleging that his State Patrol retirement benefits were exempt from execution and that the order sought by J.M. would effectively subject his retirement benefits to process of law in violation of §81-2032. The district court agreed and denied J.M.'s motion.

J.M. appealed, and we granted his petition to bypass the Nebraska Court of Appeals.

. . .

ANALYSIS

As noted above, §25-1572 provides that in aid of execution of a judgment, a court "may order any property of the judgment debtor, not exempt by law, in the hands of either himself or any other person or corporation, or due to the judgment debtor, to be applied towards the satisfaction of the judgment." The question in this case is whether Hobbs' State Patrol retirement funds are "exempt by law." J.M. argues that the applicable statute here is Neb. Rev. Stat. §25-1563.01 (Reissue 2008), which provides as relevant that "an interest held under a stock bonus, pension, profit-sharing, or similar plan or contract payable on account of illness, disability, death, age, or length of service" is generally exempt from process "[t]o the extent reasonably necessary for the support of the debtor and any dependent of the debtor." J.M. argues that because Hobbs is imprisoned, he does not need his retirement funds for support, so they are available to satisfy C.M.'s judgment.

But Hobbs relies on §81-2032, which provides:

> All annuities or benefits which any person shall be entitled to receive under [the Act] shall not be subject to garnishment, attachment, levy, the operation of bankruptcy or insolvency laws, or any other process of law whatsoever and shall not be assignable except to the extent that such annuities or benefits are subject to a qualified domestic relations order under the Spousal Pension Rights Act.

Hobbs contends that this provision creates a legal exemption from execution for the funds he receives under the Act. We agree with the district court that §81-2032 precludes J.M. from obtaining the relief requested in this proceeding.

J.M. attempts to draw a distinction between the funds that Hobbs "shall be entitled to receive," as specified by §81-2032, and the funds that Hobbs already has received and which are in his possession. J.M. contends that the words "annuities" and "benefits" in §81-2032 refer to a right to payment, not to the payment or proceeds themselves. So, J.M. claims, §81-2032 is actually intended not to protect the money received by a beneficiary of the Act, but simply to protect the Nebraska State Patrol Retirement System from having to deal with the administrative burdens of execution and garnishment. But J.M.'s argument is inconsistent with the language of the Act and the weight of authority applying similar anti-attachment provisions.

To begin with, we have often said that absent a statutory indication to the contrary, words in a statute will be given their ordinary meaning. The words "annuity" and "benefit" are often used to refer, respectively, to "[a] fixed sum of money payable periodically" and "a cash payment or service provided for under an annuity, pension plan, or insurance policy." And those ordinary meanings for "annuity" and "benefit" are clearly how the terms are used in the Act. For example, the Act describes the authority of the Public Employees Retirement Board to "require repayment of benefits paid" or "offset future benefit payments" in the event of "an overpayment of a benefit," and to compensate a beneficiary in the event of "an underpayment of a benefit." And the Act explains how an officer who has reached retirement age or is disabled is entitled to receive "a monthly annuity" for the remainder of his or her life or disability. There is simply no merit to J.M.'s argument that "annuities" and "benefits" in §81-2032 refer to something other than payments of money.

Nor are we persuaded that §81-2032 no longer applies when the money is paid to the beneficiary. The language of §81-2032 mirrors that of anti-attachment provisions that generally have been held to protect benefits such as those provided under the Act from being used by judgment creditors to satisfy private obligations. J.M. argues that the statutes at issue in those cases are distinguishable, because they contained express language that more clearly applies to, for instance, money "'either before or after receipt by the beneficiary.'" But this distinction has been consistently rejected by courts discussing statutes, such as §81-2032, that do not contain such language. The language of §81-2032 is still clearly intended to protect benefits under the Act from legal process.

As Chief Justice Cardozo explained, when addressing whether payments "'due'" were limited to compensation owing and unpaid, "'due,' like words generally . . . , has a color and a content that can vary with the setting. Compensation due under an act may be a payment presently owing, or one to become due in the future, or one already made, but made because due, i. e., required or commanded." And the 10th Circuit, in addressing a provision of the Civil Service Retirement Act that exempted only "money mentioned by this subchapter," concluded that although the statutory language was "not as precisely drafted" as the provision of the Social Security Act that the U.S. Supreme Court had previously addressed, "the broad language of [the statute] offers no hint that its protections are any narrower than those afforded to Social Security payments or that Congress intended to treat future payments any differently than payments already received." Accordingly, the 10th Circuit concluded that the same protection extended to payments that had already been received.

The same is true here. Although we recognize that the result may often seem inequitable, courts have held that anti-attachment provisions are to be given effect even where a creditor is attempting to collect restitution for a criminal act, or a tort judgment. As the Kansas Supreme Court said, in a case involving strikingly similar facts:

> If we were free to decide the case on public policy or equitable consideration, there could be no strong reason asserted for not permitting the attachment. The language of the relevant federal statutes and the United States Supreme Court decision make it clear that we do not have the luxury of deciding the case on the basis of what is the "right" or desirable result. Plaintiff herein is a judgment creditor. . . . We find no legal basis for holding the funds are not exempt due to some implied exception.

And as the U.S. Supreme Court has more generally explained, it is not appropriate for a court to approve any generalized equitable exception to an antigarnishment provision, even for criminal misconduct, despite a "natural distaste for the result."

> [An antigarnishment provision] reflects a considered congressional policy choice, a decision to safeguard a stream of income for pensioners (and their dependents, who may be, and perhaps usually are, blameless), even if that decision prevents others

from securing relief for the wrongs done them. If exceptions to this policy are to be made, it is for Congress to undertake that task.

As a general matter, courts should be loath to announce equitable exceptions to legislative requirements or prohibitions that are unqualified by the statutory text. The creation of such exceptions, in our view, would be especially problematic in the context of an antigarnishment provision. Such a provision acts, by definition, to hinder the collection of a lawful debt. A restriction on garnishment therefore can be defended only on the view that the effectuation of certain broad social policies sometimes takes precedence over the desire to do equity between particular parties. It makes little sense to adopt such a policy and then to refuse enforcement whenever enforcement appears inequitable. A court attempting to carve out an exception that would not swallow the rule would be forced to determine whether application of the rule in particular circumstances would be "especially" inequitable. The impracticability of defining such a standard reinforces our conclusion that the identification of any exception should be left to Congress.

Guidry v. Sheet Metal Workers Pension Fund, 493 U.S. 365, 376-77 (1990) (superseded by statute in U.S. v. Irving, 452 F.3d 110 (2d Cir. 2006)). We agree with the Court's reasoning, and we likewise find that if an exception to §81-2032 is to be created for circumstances such as these, it is a matter for the Legislature to undertake. But as it stands, §81-2032 clearly provides greater protection to benefits under the Act than does the general pension exemption set forth in §25-1563.01. And it is well established that where general and special provisions of statutes are in conflict, the general law yields to the special, without regard to priority of dates in enacting the same. The district court was correct in relying upon this principle to conclude that Hobbs' retirement benefits, even in his possession, are exempted from execution by §81-2032. . . .

For the sake of completeness, we note that Hobbs could, obviously, voluntarily pay his retirement funds toward C.M.'s judgment if he chose to do so and that his willingness (or unwillingness) to do so could be seen as relevant to many of the factors that the Board of Parole is instructed to take into account when making a determination regarding a committed offender's release on parole. We also note that although this opinion addresses the general applicability of §81-2032, we make no comment on the extent to which the exempt status of Hobbs' retirement funds might be affected by any transformation in their character, such as through spending or investment. And, as suggested above, nothing in this opinion should be construed to comment on whether the Legislature, if it chose to do so, could amend the scope of §81-2032.

CONCLUSION

The district court correctly concluded that §81-2032 foreclosed the relief J.M. sought in this proceeding. The court's judgment is affirmed.

The law on whether exempt funds that are then deposited in bank accounts remain exempt mostly favors debtors, often based on either a close statutory reading or legislative intent to sweep broadly. Debtors may lose their rights in exempt funds if the money becomes commingled and cannot be traced or in some instances, if funds are accumulated beyond the amount needed for daily care and maintenance. *See In re Schoonover*, 331 F3d 575 (7th Cir. 2003) (holding that Illinois exemption does not protect "hoards of cash" of over $75,000 because it was meant to protect "minimum monthly income of beneficiaries").

C. Consumer Bankruptcy

Perhaps the ultimate debtor remedy is bankruptcy. Consumers generally file either chapter 7 bankruptcy or chapter 13 bankruptcy. Chapter 7 is liquidation bankruptcy. A bankruptcy trustee takes any non-exempt property of the debtor and sells it for the benefit of the debtor's creditors. Any unpaid debt is discharged. The entire process usually takes about four months. Chapter 13 is repayment bankruptcy. The debtor can retain all property, regardless of exemptions, but must pay any disposable income (income less certain permissible expenses) to a trustee for a period of three to five years. The trustee collects this income and distributes it to the debtor's creditors. In chapter 13, the debtor can even retain property subject to security interests and can catch up on missed payments over time, although to keep the property the debtor must remain current on the ongoing obligations. If the debtor makes all plan payments, he or she will emerge with their property intact and have any remaining amounts owed to unsecured creditors discharged.

In either chapter, the debtor gets immediate relief from bankruptcy in the form of the automatic stay. Upon the filing of a bankruptcy petition, the law prohibits most collection actions. 11 U.S.C. §362(a). This includes most evictions, shut off of utilities, repossession, and the like. The automatic stay continues until the end of the bankruptcy case. Creditors may seek relief from the stay by asking the bankruptcy court to permit it to take actions prohibited by the stay. If a debtor continues to miss mortgage payments during bankruptcy, for example, the court will frequently lift the stay to allow the mortgage servicer to foreclose.

The definition of the debtor's property in bankruptcy, termed "property of the estate," is very broad. The reason, in part, is to give full effect to the automatic stay. This often comes as a surprise to secured creditors, for whom every repossessed car is a potential trove for recovery of unpaid debt.

Mitchell v. BankIllinois (In re Mitchell)

316 B.R. 891 (Bankr. S.D. Tex. 2003)

Rosenthal, District Judge.

Appellant BankIllinois financed debtor/appellee Georgina Mitchell's purchase of an automobile in 2000. On March 12, 2002, BankIllinois repossessed Mitchell's vehicle for failure to make payments. Later that same day, Mitchell filed for bankruptcy protection under Chapter 13 of the Bankruptcy Code. Mitchell demanded that BankIllinois return her vehicle, but BankIllinois refused. Mitchell filed a Complaint for Turnover and for Damages in the bankruptcy court. The court found that the vehicle was property of the bankruptcy estate under 11 U.S.C. §542(a) and that BankIllinois had violated the automatic stay imposed under 11 U.S.C. §362(a)(3) by failing to return the vehicle in response to Mitchell's demand. The court awarded Mitchell $8,520.97 in actual damages and attorney fees under 11 U.S.C. §362(h). BankIllinois appeals this judgment, arguing that an automobile repossessed prepetition is not property of the estate and that BankIllinois was entitled to hold the vehicle until Mitchell demonstrated that its interest in the vehicle was adequately protected. BankIllinois contends that although Mitchell provided proof of insurance for the automobile, this did not show adequate protection of BankIllinois's interests.

After careful consideration of the parties' submissions and the record on appeal, with the applicable law, this court affirms the bankruptcy court's ruling. The reasons are set out in detail below.

I. BACKGROUND

Mitchell purchased a 1997 Chevrolet Monte Carlo (the "vehicle") on December 5, 2000. BankIllinois financed Mitchell's purchase. BankIllinois repossessed the vehicle on March 12, 2002, after Mitchell failed to make payments. Later that day, Mitchell filed a Chapter 13 bankruptcy petition. Mitchell notified BankIllinois by facsimile of the bankruptcy filing and demanded that BankIllinois return the vehicle. Mitchell included proof of her insurance on the vehicle in this facsimile.

The next day, counsel for BankIllinois replied to Mitchell's facsimile. In the reply, counsel stated that its bankruptcy attorney, John Maloney, was away until March 18, but the office would instruct BankIllinois to protect the vehicle until Maloney's return. BankIllinois's counsel also requested a copy of Mitchell's Chapter 13 plan.

On March 18, Maloney responded by letter. Maloney acknowledged receiving Mitchell's proof of insurance. Maloney contended that Mitchell only retained a right of redemption because the repossession occurred prepetition. Maloney stated that BankIllinois wanted to discuss "what arrangements can be made . . . that would allow your client to reinstate the loan," and to have "some serious Code Section 362 discussions." Maloney repeated BankIllinois's request for a copy of Mitchell's Chapter 13 plan, but made no reference to a need for additional proof of adequate protection.

In a facsimile sent to BankIllinois's counsel on March 19, Mitchell repeated her demand that BankIllinois return her automobile. Mitchell also stated that she had lost time at work and was renting a car in order to travel to work. Mitchell stated that she would file an adversary action for turnover of the automobile if BankIllinois did not return the vehicle.

On March 21, Mitchell filed a Complaint for Turnover and Damages in the bankruptcy court. On March 27, BankIllinois filed a motion for relief from the automatic stay of 11 U.S.C. §362 and for adequate protection. BankIllinois requested that this motion be considered on an emergency basis, but withdrew that request at the hearing on Mitchell's complaint

The bankruptcy court held an evidentiary hearing on Mitchell's motion for turnover on March 28, 2002. In that hearing, BankIllinois took the position that the vehicle was not property of Mitchell's bankruptcy estate and Mitchell had no possessory right in the car because it was repossessed prepetition. The bankruptcy court disagreed. Relying primarily on United States v. Whiting Pools, 462 U.S. 198 (1983), the bankruptcy court held that the vehicle was property of the estate and subject to turnover despite the fact that it was seized prepetition. The court found that under Texas law, ownership of collateral remains with the debtor until sale. Because of this, BankIllinois did not own the repossessed vehicle and the vehicle became property of the estate once Mitchell filed her Chapter 13 bankruptcy petition.

The court ordered BankIllinois to return the vehicle to Mitchell. The court stated that although BankIllinois was entitled to request adequate protection of its interest in the vehicle, BankIllinois did not request adequate protection in its initial correspondence with Mitchell, and only raised the issue of adequate protection six days after Mitchell filed her turnover action. The court concluded that "BankIllinois used possession of the vehicle to coerce [Chapter 13] plan treatment to its liking." The court found that BankIllinois willfully violated section 362(a)(3) and ordered it to pay $8,520.97 actual damages and attorney fees under section 362(h). The court did not award sanctions or punitive damages.

. . .

III. ANALYSIS

BankIllinois argues that the bankruptcy court erred in concluding that the vehicle was property of the estate. BankIllinois also contends that even if the vehicle was property of the estate, BankIllinois did not violate the automatic stay by refusing to return the vehicle on demand because its interest in the vehicle was not adequately protected. . . .

A. The Issue of Whether the Vehicle Was Property of the Estate

BankIllinois contends that the vehicle was not property of the estate because it was repossessed before Mitchell filed her Chapter 13 bankruptcy petition. Mitchell responds that under Texas law, she retained ownership of the vehicle after it was repossessed, so that the vehicle became property of the bankruptcy estate once she filed her Chapter 13 petition.

Under 11 U.S.C. §541(a)(1), a bankruptcy estate is comprised of "all legal or equitable interests of the debtor in property as of the commencement of the case." Section 542(a) requires that an entity in possession of property "that the trustee may use, sell, or lease under section 363" must deliver that property to the trustee. The Supreme Court in *Whiting Pools*, 462 U.S. 198, held that if a secured creditor repossesses the debtor's property prepetition, that property may be included in the estate. "[Section] 542(a) grants to the estate a possessory interest in certain property of the debtor that was not held by the debtor at the commencement of the proceedings." 462 U.S. at 207. *Whiting Pools* involved a Chapter 11 proceeding, and the Court reserved the question whether section 542(a) has the same effect in Chapter 13 proceedings. 462 U.S. at 208 n. 17. However, many courts have applied *Whiting Pools* to Chapter 13 cases. See In re Robinson, 285 B.R. 732, 735 (W.D. Okla. 2002); In re Sharon, 234 B.R. 676, 681-82 (6th Cir. BAP 1999); In re Spears, 223 B.R. 159, 163 (N.D. Ill. 1998); In re Richardson, 135 B.R. 256, 257 (E.D. Tex. 1992); In re Attinello, 38 B.R. 609, 610-11 (E.D. Pa. 1984).

The *Whiting Pools* Court stated that section 542(a) may not apply if the seizure of the property transferred ownership. Ownership under section 541 is determined under state law. Butner v. United States, 440 U.S. 48, 55 (1979); In re Thomas, 883 F.2d 991, 995 (11th Cir. 1989); In re Robinson, 285 B.R. at 735. Once the debtor's state law property rights are determined, federal bankruptcy law applies to establish the extent to which those rights are property of the estate. Butner, 440 U.S. at 55; In re Thomas, 883 F.2d at 995; In re Robinson, 285 B.R. at 735. This court must decide whether BankIllinois's repossession of the vehicle gave it ownership of the vehicle, or whether Mitchell retained ownership after BankIllinois took possession. This is a question of Texas law.

Under Tex. Bus. & Com. Code §9.609, a secured party may take possession of collateral after default without judicial process if it proceeds without a breach of the peace. After repossession, a secured party may sell, lease, license, or otherwise dispose of the collateral, so long as it provides the debtor notification before disposition. Tex. Bus. & Com. Code §§9.610-9.612. Under Tex. Bus. & Com. Code §9.617(a), "a secured party's disposition of collateral after default (1) transfers to the transferee for value all of the debtor's rights in the collateral." A secured party can accept the collateral in satisfaction of the debtor's obligation only with the debtor's consent. Tex. Bus. & Com. Code §§9.620(a). The secured party receives "all of a debtor's rights in the collateral" only after it accepts the collateral in satisfaction of the obligation. Tex. Bus. & Com. Code §9.622(a)(2).

Third parties purchasing repossessed collateral from the secured creditor generally require that the certificate of title reflect their ownership. Under Tex. Bus. & Com. Code §§9.619(b), title can be transferred from the debtor to the third-party purchaser after the secured creditor disposing of the property prepares a "transfer statement." The transfer statement must state: (1) that the debtor has defaulted on an obligation secured by specific collateral; (2) that the secured party has exercised its post-default remedies with respect to the collateral; (3) that, through the secured creditor's exercise of the right to dispose of the collateral, a transferee has acquired the rights of the debtor in the collateral; and (4) the name and mailing addresses of the secured party, the debtor, and the transferee. Tex. Bus. & Com. Code §9.619(a).

Section 9.619(b) provides:

> A transfer statement entitles the transferee to the transfer of record of all rights of the debtor in the collateral specified in the statement in any official filing, recording, registration, or certificate-of-title system covering the collateral.

The "transferee" is the third party purchasing the collateral from the secured party that repossessed it.

Under sections 9.617 and 9.619(b), a third party purchasing the collateral from the secured creditor is entitled to "all of the rights of the debtor" in the collateral. The third-party purchaser obtains more than the right to redeem; it obtains ownership of the collateral. The secured creditor's rights are limited to enforcement of its security interest through disposing of the collateral. All of the debtor's rights in the collateral are transferred to the third-party purchaser when the sale is consummated. The secured party obtains the debtor's rights in the collateral by accepting the collateral in satisfaction of the debtor's obligation or purchasing the collateral. Tex. Bus. & Com. Code §§9.610(c), 9.622(a)(2). In *Comerica Acceptance Corp. v. Dallas Central Appraisal Dist.*, 52 S.W.3d 495, 497 (Tex. App. — Dallas 2001, writ denied), the court interpreted the meaning of the term "owner" under the Texas Tax Code, stating as follows:

> Interpreting "owner" to include a secured party in possession of property for purposes of selling it to recover on a debt does not comport with these rules of statutory construction. Simply stated, a lienholder is not an "owner" of the property within the common meaning of that term. Typically the lienholder does not enjoy any of the common benefits of ownership. A lienholder ordinarily has no legal right to share in any accretions to the collateral's value, or a legal obligation to bear any risk of lost value. A lienholder ordinarily has no right to possession or use of the property; what rights it has to use and possession are only in the context of its right to take possession of the collateral upon default and sell it pursuant to the security agreement.

See also In re Clelland, 268 B.R. 539, 540 (E.D. Ark. 2001) (finding that under Texas law debtor retained ownership of an automobile despite having lost possessory rights); In re Richardson, 135 B.R. 256, 257 (E.D. Tex. 1992) ("It is beyond dispute that Debtor's automobile, while lawfully repossessed prior to the filing of Debtor's bankruptcy petition, continues to be the property of the estate.").

A debtor's rights in repossessed collateral include the right to notification before the disposition of the collateral, Tex. Bus. & Com. Code §9.611; the right to any surplus from the disposition of the collateral, Tex. Bus. & Com. Code §9.615(d)(1); and the right to redeem the collateral, Tex. Bus. & Com. Code §9.623. These rights are transferred to a third-party purchaser on sale of the collateral. In *Whiting Pools*, 674 F.2d 144, 149-150 and n.8 (2d Cir. 1982), aff'd, 462 U.S. 198, (1983), the Court held that the debtor's similar rights in property repossessed prepetition made that property belong to the bankruptcy estate. Under *Whiting Pools*, the property rights Mitchell held in the vehicle under Texas law made it property of the estate. "While there are explicit limitations on the reach of §542(a), none requires that the debtor hold a possessory interest in the property at the commencement of the reorganization proceedings." In re Pluta, 200 B.R. 740, 743 (D. Mass. 1996) (citing Whiting Pools, 462 U.S. at 205-06). The estate had a possessory right in the vehicle under section 542(a).

BankIllinois cites two recent cases, *In re Kalter*, 292 F.3d 1350 (11th Cir. 2002) and *In re Lewis*, 137 F.3d 1280 (11th Cir. 1998), in support of its argument that the estate had no possessory right to the vehicle because it was seized prepetition. Subsequent cases criticize both these cases. See In re Robinson, 285 B.R. at 738 n.6; In re Sanders, 291 B.R. 97, 101 (E.D. Mich. 2003). Moreover, both decisions are distinguishable from the present case.

The *In re Lewis* court looked in part to the Alabama common law of conversion in determining that an automobile seized prepetition is not the property of the estate. Because Mitchell's property rights are based on Texas law, *In re Lewis* is inapposite.

In re Kalter stated that the term "debtor," as defined in the Florida UCC, included the owner of the collateral, even if that party was not liable for payment of the secured obligation. The *In re Kalter* court reasoned that the term "debtor" could refer to either the debtor or the creditor in possession of the collateral. 292 F.3d at 1354. The *In re Kalter* court found the language of the Florida UCC insufficient to establish ownership of vehicles repossessed prepetition, and relied on the Florida Certificate of Title statute to determine ownership. The Texas UCC, by contrast, provides sufficient guidance to determine ownership in this case. The Texas UCC defines "debtor" as "a person having an interest, other than a security interest or other lien, in the collateral." Tex. Bus. & Com. Code §9.102(a)(28). A "secured party" is "a person in whose favor a security interest is created or provided for under a security agreement, whether or not any obligation to be secured is outstanding." Tex. Bus. & Com. Code §9.102(a)(73). The sections of the Texas UCC regarding disposition of collateral seized after default make it clear that the party seizing the collateral is a secured party and that the defaulting party is the debtor. See Tex. Bus. & Com. Code §9.609-9.624. Because of this, the analysis of the Florida UCC in *In re Kalter* is inapposite. The terms of the Texas UCC are sufficient to determine that Mitchell's vehicle became property of the bankruptcy estate after she filed her bankruptcy petition; this court need not rely on Texas title statutes to determine ownership of the vehicle.

Following *Whiting Pools* and the majority of courts that have considered this question, this court finds that Mitchell's vehicle was property of the bankruptcy estate, despite the fact that BankIllinois seized it prepetition.

B. WHETHER BANKILLINOIS VIOLATED THE AUTOMATIC STAY

BankIllinois contends that it did not violate the section 362 automatic stay by refusing to return the vehicle upon demand. BankIllinois argues that the proof of insurance Mitchell provided was not adequate protection of its interest in the vehicle.

Under section 362(a)(3), the filing of a bankruptcy petition acts as a stay of "any act . . . to exercise control over property of the estate." The courts disagree as to whether a creditor violates the automatic stay by refusing to turn over an automobile repossessed before the debtor filed a bankruptcy petition. The majority of courts have held that creditors retaining an automobile repossessed prepetition, after the debtor demands return and tenders adequate protection, violate the section 362(a)(3) automatic stay. See In re Sharon, 234 B.R. 676, 681-682 (6th Cir. BAP 1999); Carr v. Sec. Sav. & Loan Ass'n., 130 B.R. 434 (D.N.J. 1991); GMAC v. Ryan, 183 B.R. 288 (M.D. Fla. 1995); In re Knaus, 889 F.2d 773, 774-75 (8th Cir. 1989) ("the duty [to turnover property repossessed before the filing of a bankruptcy petition] arises upon the filing of a bankruptcy petition. The failure to fulfill this duty, regardless of whether the original seizure was lawful, constitutes a prohibited attempt to exercise control over the property of the estate' in violation of the automatic stay."). A creditor rejecting the debtor's tender of protection as inadequate may not retain the property, but must turn over the property to the debtor and turn to the bankruptcy court for relief. Id.

There is an emerging minority view that a creditor need not turn over collateral seized prepetition until adequate protection has been provided. See In re Spears, 223 B.R. 159, 166-67 (N.D. Ill. 1998); In re Fitch, 217 B.R. 286, 291 (S.D. Cal.

1998); In re Young, 193 B.R. 620 (D.D.C. 1996) (rejecting *In re Knaus* and finding that creditor that seized collateral before bankruptcy petition filed was entitled to demand adequate protection before turning over collateral); In re Richardson, 135 B.R. 256 (finding that the automatic stay is designed to preserve the status quo at the time of bankruptcy petition's filing and that refusal to return automobile seized before petition filed is consistent with maintaining the status quo and not a violation of the automatic stay). These cases hold that the creditor is entitled to retain possession of the collateral until the adequate protection question has been resolved. In re Spears, 223 B.R. at 166. The creditor may hold the collateral until the bankruptcy court determines that the debtor or bankruptcy trustee has met its burden of proving adequate protection under 11 U.S.C. §363(o)(1). See In re Young, 193 B.R. at 625.

The record shows that Mitchell provided BankIllinois proof of insurance on the vehicle in her initial March 12, 2002 letter demanding that BankIllinois return the vehicle. BankIllinois refused to return the vehicle after Mitchell demanded its return and provided proof of insurance. "Adequate protection" is meant only to assure that a secured creditor does not suffer a decline in the value of its interest in the estate's property, rather than to compensate the creditor for the bankruptcy-imposed delay in enforcing its rights in that property. In re Addison Properties, Ltd. P'ship., 185 B.R. 766, 769 (N.D. Ill. 1995). Courts consider proof of insurance adequate protection for a creditor's interest in a debtor's automobile. See In re Fitch, 217 B.R. at 291 ("Demanding proof of insurance is a valid request for assurance [that prepetition position will be protected]."); Carr, 130 B.R. at 436 (creditor obligated to turn over automobile after filing of bankruptcy petition and verification of insurance); In re Matthews, 118 B.R. 398 (D.S.C. 1989) (ordering turn over of automobile upon debtor's providing proof of insurance). Mitchell's vehicle was insured, protecting BankIllinois's interest.

The record shows that BankIllinois waited a substantial amount of time before asserting its right to adequate protection. Mitchell demanded that BankIllinois turn over the vehicle on March 12, 2002 and provided proof of insurance. Mitchell repeated her demand on March 19, 2002. (Debtor's Ex. 8.) Mitchell filed her Complaint for Turnover and Damages on March 21, 2002. BankIllinois waited until March 27, 2002, more than two weeks after Mitchell demanded the vehicle's return and provided proof of insurance, to move for relief from the section 362 automatic stay and to assert its right to adequate protection.

A creditor has immediate access to the courts to obtain assurance adequate protection of the collateral under 11 U.S.C. §362(e)-(f). Under section 362(e), the court may condition or prohibit the debtor's use of collateral as necessary to provide adequate protection of the creditor's interest. In re Zaber, 223 B.R. 102, 104 (N.D. Tex. 1998). A creditor can seek such relief on an emergency basis under section 362(f), if the creditor's rights are threatened with irreparable harm. "The creditor with a secured interest in property included in the estate must look to [section 362(e)] for protection, rather than the nonbankruptcy remedy of possession." Whiting Pools, 462 U.S. at 204. "While the creditor may suggest terms of adequate protection, it may not unilaterally condition the return of the property on its own determination of adequate protection. . . . Any prerequisite to turnover is determined by the bankruptcy court, not by the creditor." In re Sharon, 234 B.R. at 686 (quoting In re Colortran, Inc., 210 B.R. 823, 827-28 (9th Cir. 1997), reversed in part on other grounds, 165 F.3d 35 (9th Cir. 1998)); see also In re Jackson, 251 B.R. 597, 600-01 (D. Utah 2000).

If BankIllinois considered the proof of insurance inadequate to protect its interest in the vehicle, it could have filed a motion under section 362(e), on an emergency basis if necessary under section 362(f). Instead, BankIllinois waited until after Mitchell twice demanded the return of the vehicle and filed her turnover complaint. It is true that BankIllinois offered to have "some serious Code Section 362 discussions" before Mitchell filed her turnover complaint. BankIllinois contends that these discussions would encompass the question of adequate protection. Once Mitchell provided proof of insurance on the automobile, however, BankIllinois could not retain the automobile based on its unilateral determination that the insurance was not adequate protection. The record and applicable law support the bankruptcy court's determination that BankIllinois's refusal to return the vehicle violated the section 362 automatic stay.

C. Damages

The bankruptcy court awarded Mitchell $8,520.97 in actual damages, declining to award punitive damages under section 362(h). BankIllinois challenges the actual damages award as unreasonable.

Section 362(h) provides that "an individual injured by any willful violation of a stay provided by [section 362] shall recover actual damages, including costs and attorneys' fees, and, in appropriate circumstances, may recover punitive damages." A willful violation of the automatic stay occurs when the creditor acts deliberately with knowledge of the bankruptcy petition. In re Sharon, 234 B.R. at 687. A belief that withholding possession would not violate a stay does not preclude a finding of willful violation of section 362(h). In re Sharon, 234 B.R., at 687-88; In re San Angelo Pro Hockey Club, Inc., 292 B.R. 118, 125 (N.D. Tex. 2003).

Mitchell informed BankIllinois of her bankruptcy petition and provided proof of insurance on March 12, 2002. BankIllinois independently verified that the bankruptcy petition had been filed. BankIllinois continued to withhold possession of the vehicle deliberately and with knowledge of the bankruptcy petition. Even BankIllinois's asserted belief that it was entitled to retain possession of the automobile until Mitchell provided adequate protection for the bank's interest does not remove the willful nature of its actions. BankIllinois had ample opportunity to raise the adequate protection issue in the bankruptcy court before taking the actions that violated the automatic stay. In re Diviney, 225 B.R. at 774. Instead, BankIllinois waited for more than two weeks before raising the question of inadequate protection in the bankruptcy court, in response to Mitchell's turnover motion. BankIllinois willfully violated the section 362 stay and is liable for Mitchell's actual damages under section 362(h).

BankIllinois contends that Mitchell's legal fees are unreasonable. BankIllinois notes that Mitchell's initial complaint incorrectly alleged that the vehicle was repossessed after the bankruptcy petition was filed and the automatic stay went into effect. BankIllinois contends that Mitchell's counsel did not cooperate with its efforts to settle the case, delaying a resolution and increasing the attorney fees both parties incurred.

The bankruptcy court's award of attorney's fees is reviewed for abuse of discretion, as are determinations regarding rates and hours. . . .

The bankruptcy court noted the fact that much of the litigation in the adversary proceeding related to the issue of whether BankIllinois was liable for repossessing the vehicle postpetition, which resulted from the inaccurate allegation in Mitchell's complaint. The bankruptcy court also reviewed Mitchell's counsel's billing records as a whole and determined that some of the fees were charged for work unrelated to this case. The bankruptcy court reduced Mitchell's attorney fee recovery by $2,000 to account for these expenditures.

. . .

BankIllinois argues that Mitchell rejected its offers to negotiate a settlement, prolonging the action and unnecessarily increasing the attorney fees incurred. BankIllinois contends that "the bargaining leverage was all on the debtor's side" because BankIllinois, an out-of-town bank, was forced to defend a suit over a car with a value of only $7,650.

The record reveals that the bank's conduct contributed to the delays. Mitchell waited over a week before receiving a response to her demand. Mitchell made a second demand that BankIllinois return her car, threatening to begin a turnover proceeding, before BankIllinois responded to her request. BankIllinois's contention that Mitchell held "all the bargaining leverage" is inconsistent with the fact that BankIllinois retained possession of the vehicle even after Mitchell provided proof of insurance. The record shows that Mitchell lost wages and incurred rental car charges during the period BankIllinois refused to return the car. BankIllinois's decisions to retain the vehicle after demand and to delay any challenge to the adequacy of the insurance as protection for its interest violated the section 362 automatic stay. These decisions delayed the resolution of the action and caused Mitchell to bring this adversary action.

The fact that Mitchell's actual damages and attorney fees are roughly equal to the value of the vehicle does not make the award unreasonable. BankIllinois's failure to return the vehicle required Mitchell to file the turnover action. Disproportion alone does not make an award of attorney fees excessive. See Northwinds Abatement, Inc. v. Employers Ins. of Wausau, 258 F.3d 345, 354-55 (5th Cir. 2001) (award of attorney fees that was three times the size of trebled damages award not unreasonable solely on that ground). Mitchell prevailed on all her claims. An award of attorney fees roughly equal to the damages she suffered is not so disproportionate as to make the attorney fee award excessive. . . .

IV. CONCLUSION

The bankruptcy court's ruling is affirmed. Mitchell is entitled to receive $8,520.97 in actual damages, plus attorney fees and costs incurred in defending this appeal. Mitchell must submit documentation of the fees incurred in defending this appeal within ten days from the date this Memorandum and Order are filed.

———

As the bankruptcy case progresses, debtors enjoy the other benefits of bankruptcy: retention of property and a discharge of all or most of their debts. There are specific exemptions that either replace or supplement the state exemptions for bankruptcy debtors. 11 U.S.C. §522. Discharge in bankruptcy is a permanent injunction against taking any action to collect debts. Certain debts, such as domestic support obligations (known as spousal or child support outside the bankruptcy context), are not dischargeable. Other debts, such as taxes and student loans, are dischargeable only if certain conditions are satisfied. 11 U.S.C. §§523, 727. Note that the discharge does *not* prohibit the enforcement of a security interest or mortgage (a major difference between it and the automatic stay). If a debtor wants to retain collateral after the bankruptcy ends, she will need to be current on payments and otherwise not in default.

In chapter 7 bankruptcy, discharge usually occurs about four to six months after filing the case. In chapter 13 bankruptcy, discharge usually requires completion of the three to five year repayment plan. Nearly all debtors qualify for a discharge, with two notable exceptions. *Pro se* debtors often get tripped up by the paperwork requirements of bankruptcy and have cases dismissed for non-compliance. Repeat filers also are limited in how often they may receive a discharge, with at least four years and often as many as eight years, needing to elapse to renew eligibility. That said, only about 30-40 percent of those who file chapter 13 complete the promised repayment and receive a discharge. In chapter 7, the discharge rate is above 95 percent.

Problem Set 22

22.1. Household Helpers has store-front operations in low-income areas. It sells new and used household items and provides financing for purchases that exceed $100 in total. It also cashes paychecks and provides short-term emergency loans to its customers. Do the following transactions by Household Helpers violate the FTC Credit Practices Rule? 16 C.F.R. §§444.1-444.5.

a. Jacob Abiola would like to buy a washer/dryer set from Household Helpers. It has agreed to lend him 80 percent of the $1,000 purchase price. The contract requires that Jacob have the loan payments of $45 deducted from each of his paychecks. It also states that Jacob gives Household Helpers a security interest in the washer and dryer. State law specifies that such property is exempt.

b. Solomon Willig purchased a new Blu-Ray DVD player and video gaming system from Household Helpers. He borrowed $200 at the time of the transaction, offering the DVD player and gaming system as collateral. He made all the payments as they came due and paid off the loan in six months, at a total cost of $250. He would now like to buy a used personal computer from Household Helpers. It is willing to lend him $400 for the computer purchase, provided that Solomon gives Household Helpers a security interest in the Blu-Ray DVD player and video gaming system.

c. On January 3, Abby Hoffman borrowed $400 from Household Helpers to pay her overdue heating bill. The interest rate was eye-popping but Household Helpers required no collateral, which was a relief to Abby, who didn't want to put any of her property at risk. The loan payments began two weeks later. Abby made the first payment of $75 in full and on time on January 17. She paid her second $75 payment, due one week later on January 24, two days late, on January 26. Household Helpers sent her a letter stating that she owed them a $20 late fee and to send them $95 by February 9. Abby only had $75, however, but she mailed in that amount on time by February 9. Household Helpers applied $20 of the $75 payment to the late fee, leaving her short on making the regular payment of $75. It then assessed her account another $20 late fee for failing to pay the $95 by February 9.

22.2. Dean Peters is employed as a free-lance graphic designer by an advertising agency and his expected calendar year earnings are $52,000. Finance Co. recently obtained a $10,000 judgment against Dean Peters. If Peters' weekly "disposable earnings" are $800, how long will it take Finance Co. to satisfy its judgment by garnishing his wages? Can you take any additional steps to collect the judgment if (a) Peters deposits his earnings in a checking account at First Bank and (b) the checking account currently has a balance of $12,000? Assume that only federal law is applicable. See 15 U.S.C. §§1672 and 1673.

22.3. Masu Haque has come to see you about her serious debt problems. She makes about $28,000 a year as a teacher's aide in a preschool but was out of work last year for three months after a back injury. Her current wages are reduced by $100 per week because a credit card company obtained a garnishment order. She owes about $13,700 in unsecured debt, including medical bills, an unsecured loan from her credit union, and store credit cards. She also owes $7,500 on her car loan and another $400 to an auto repair garage. Her ex-husband is owed $400 in overdue alimony; while Masu has limited money, he is unemployed and desperately needs her to pay him so he has some funds. Masu is worn down with the collection calls and worries that her chiropractor is going to refuse to see her for ongoing treatment unless she pays him off. She is twelve days behind on her rent, and she fears her landlord will act quickly to evict her. She hastens to add that even if she stays in her apartment, she is just waiting for the lights to go out, as she is three months behind on her electrical bill. She wants to know if she files chapter 7 bankruptcy whether that will solve her immediate problems with paying her bills. What do you tell her? See 11 U.S.C. §362(a) and (b).

Assignment 23.   Debt Collection Abuses

Debt collection is a fairly common experience. In 2014, the Urban Institute found that 35 percent of Americans have at least one debt in collection. While some of these creditors have given up, debt collectors are a part of many Americans' lives. Estimates are that about one in seven households has contact with a debt collector in a year. In part, the incidence of debt collection reflects default rates, but it is also shaped by greater use of technology such as remote call centers and consumer information databases. It is easier and cheaper to email someone than chase a debtor physically across the West to Texas, a refuge in America's early years for debtors. *See* Bruce Mann, *Republic of Debtors: Bankruptcy in the Age of American Independence* (2002).

Many Americans find their interactions with debt collectors to be unsatisfying, to understate the situation. In each of the last several years, the most complained about industry to the Federal Trade Commission was debt collection. In 2014, debt collection was the subject of more than one-third of complaints to the Consumer Financial Protection Bureau. *Consumer Response Annual Report* (2014), http://files.consumerfinance.gov/f/201503_cfpb_consumer-response-annual-report-2014.pdf.

The federal statute, the Fair Debt Collection Practices Act (FDCPA), is the foundational law. It is fairly well settled, in part because for a number of years there was little public enforcement. Between 2005 and 2010, the FTC brought an average of just two actions per year against collectors. Jessica Silver-Greenberg, *Consumers Cry Foul Over Debt Collectors*, WALL St. J. C1 (Dec. 15, 2011). That seems poised to change. In late 2015, the state attorneys general, the CFPB, and the FTC announced a collaborative initiative to enforce the laws applicable to debt collectors. Yuka Hayashi, *Regulators Ramp-up Debt Collection Crackdown*, WALL St. J. (Nov. 4, 2015). Late 2015 saw over 30 enforcement actions, multiples of prior years. Some companies were shut down, while others faced multi-million dollar fines. Debt collection law is entering a regulatory renaissance, much to the chagrin of the industry and cheers from consumers.

A.   Prohibited Acts

The basic approach of the FDCPA is to ban certain kinds of practices, and then provide a non-exclusive list of specific acts that fit into those categories. The trio of prohibited practices are those that are "harassment or abuse," §1692(d), "false or misleading representations," §1692e, and "unfair practices," §1692(f). Although the case below is an oldie, the tactics of debt collectors have changed little in subsequent decades. The kinds of tactics that motivate debtors to pay have remained unchanged. This case provides a detailed description of the pattern of conduct often involved in the collection process.

––––––––––

Bingham v. Collection Bureau, Inc.

505 F. Supp. 864 (D.N.D. 1981)

Van Sickle, District Judge.

This is an action by consumers, Michael and Peggy Bingham, against two related collection agencies, Collection Bureau, Inc. (CBInc), and Collection Bureau of North Dakota, Ltd. (CBLtd) for violations of the Fair Debt Collection Practices Act, 15 U.S.C. §1692 et seq.

Plaintiffs allege that the defendant CBInc violated the act in the following particulars:

a. Failure to give the written notice required by 15 U.S.C. §1692g.
b. The making of an unconscionable interest claim in violation of 15 U.S.C. §1692f(1).
c. Harassment by annoying telephone calls in violation of 15 U.S.C. §1692d(5).
d. Extortion by threat of imprisonment in violation of 15 U.S.C. §1692e(4).
e. Harassment by false threats of intent to take legal action in violation of 15 U.S.C. §1692e(5).
f. Slanderous representations that debtors were committing a crime in violation of 15 U.S.C. §1692e(7).
g. Falsely threatening nonjudicial attachment and garnishment in violation of 15 U.S.C. §1692f(6).
h. False and deceptive means to collect a debt by using two corporations with deceptively similar names in violation of 15 U.S.C. §1692e(10). . . .

The defendants generally deny all allegations of wrongdoing . . . and allege conscientious efforts to obey the spirit and language of 15 U.S.C. §1692, et seq. (Fair Debt Collection Practices Act), while still performing their economic obligation of liquidating bad debts.

FACTS

. . .

Michael and Peggy Bingham are a young married couple who must rely on the unskilled labor market for their livelihood. They have two children, Rebecca, born in 1977, and Robert, born in 1978. Peggy Bingham, who claims substantial damages to her personality by virtue of the conduct of the collectors, is 22 years old, obese, doll like, described by a psychologist witness as unsophisticated, immature, with limited ability to act without a leader, having an inadequate dependent personality. In 1977 they were living in Brinsmade, North Dakota. Rebecca was born in Mercy Hospital, Devils Lake. The Binghams had made several payments on current services but the 1977 bill and several subsequent accounts had been written off by the creditor hospital, and set over for collection.

March 23, 1979, Mercy Hospital sent to CBLtd a list of accounts for collection. The accounts, due by the Binghams, as transferred showed a balance of $958.65 due, included no loading for interest, and were computed from the hospital records by the hospital finance officer, Mr. Lindell. . . . Both parties have agreed that the first notice of a five notice system was sent and received sometime between March 23, 1979 and April 24, 1979.

First was the "Urgent" notice.

April 24, 1979 the "Past Due" notice was sent.

April 24, 1979 the "Please Take Notice" notice was sent.

(Why they were sent out the same day was never satisfactorily explained except for the suggestion this occurred during the changeover from manual to computer record keeping.)

May 5, 1979 the "Avoid Further Action" notice was sent.

May 14, 1979 the "Notice of Further Action" notice was sent.

These five notices had in common:

a. They showed CBLtd as mailer.
b. They directed payment to Mercy Hospital.
c. They showed the balance due as $958.65.

CBLtd sent these notices out for a fee of $4.95. They were sent with an understanding between the hospital and the collector that upon completion of the five notice series, the hospital, if it assigned the account for more aggressive collection, would assign it only to CBInc. CBInc took such assignment on a fee schedule which was computed at one-third for collection prior to authorization to sue, and 50% if the creditor did in fact authorize suit.

The five notices elicited no response from either plaintiff. Mr. Bingham explained that:

"I had heard from other guys it was hard to talk to the management at Devils Lake so I didn't try."

Mrs. Bingham asserted that she had no recollection of receiving the first notice. She received the second and third cards at the same time. And from the language of the fourth card she perceived a threat to put her in jail. She interpreted the fifth notice as a threat to bring a civil action to collect, carrying it to judgment if necessary. The first payment made in 1979 was made on June 1, 1979. It was received by the hospital and credited to a more recent account which had not been written off as a bad debt and set over for collection.

At the conclusion of the five notice program, CBLtd, then . . . [went] forward with the next collection stage, that is, the telephone collector stage.

This stage called for skip tracing the debtor to determine whether telephone contacts were possible, and to gather information which would assist in a recommendation to sue or not to sue out the account, while exerting telephonic pressure to effect collection. This stage and the litigation stage were both handled under the name of CBInc. . . . Vickie Eichbaum, a skip tracer, traced the Binghams to Maddock, North Dakota. Michael Bingham answered the call to the Maddock number.

In keeping with well established policy the skip tracer, immediately upon learning that she was talking to the debtor, transferred the call to Jerry Huseby whose telephone alias was "Mr. Mattson." The call should normally have gone to Clyde Hardesty whose telephone alias was "Mr. Hager," because Mr. Hardesty was handling the debtors' names from A to F.

Mrs. Bingham testified precisely and consistently as to the time, circumstance, and language of each telephone call. In fact, on cross examination she was unable to discuss the calls except in the order of her recital, thus communicating the suggestion of rote, rather than recollection testimony. Mrs. Bingham testified:

That all calls except the call-back of June 19, made at 10:30 to 11:00 P.M., were made at 10:30 to 11:00 A.M., and she knew this because they all came while she was preparing potatoes for lunch. That the caller always gave his name (alias), the name of his employer (CBInc.), and the name of the account (Mercy Hospital).

She testified to a total of 14 calls as follows:

1. June 11, 1979, Monday. First call, a woman may have asked her to hold. Then Mr. Mattson stated he was calling for Mr. Hager. Stated it was about the hospital bill, amount $958.65, inquired about deposits, land, stock, inheritance, jewelry, "do you have a wedding ring?" Told her unless she paid her bills she could go to jail. Asked to have her husband call back.

2. June 18, 1979, Monday. Mr. Hager called. Inquired where Michael worked, she told him but told him not to call the place of work. How much he made. She told him $120.00 a week. Asked for one whole check. She said she could not. Asked for $70.00 from each check. She offered $10.00 per week. He stated that was not enough.

3. June 19, 1979, Tuesday. Mr. Hager called. Said $10.00 was not enough. Said she shouldn't have children if she couldn't afford them. She told him that she, a Catholic, couldn't break her marriage vows.

4. June 20, 1979, Wednesday. Mr. Hager called. Wanted them to borrow the money.

5. June 21, 1979, Thursday. Mr. Hager called. Wanted to be paid right now.

6. June 25, 1979, Monday. Mr. Hager called. Told her to borrow from her parents. Unless paid he would garnish their wages and would have papers served on them.

7. June 26, 1979, Tuesday. Mr. Hager called. Urged them to borrow. Threatened garnishment.

8. June 27, 1979, Wednesday. Mr. Hager called. Said pay by July or else we will serve papers and garnish.

9. June 28, 1979, Thursday. Mr. Hager called and asked if she had the money. She said no.

10. June 29, 1979, Friday. Mr. Hager called.

11. June 29, 1979, Friday. Mr. Hager called in the evening.

12 & 13. July 6, 1979, Friday (long 4th of July weekend). Mr. Hager called. Michael Bingham answered. Hung up. Hager called back in a few minutes. Peggy's mother answered. Told Hager she was paying the phone bill and he was not to call on her phone again.

14. July 11, 1979, Wednesday. Mr. Hager called. She told him "anything further, call my lawyer."

Jerry Huseby (Mattson) testified that he spoke to Peggy on June 11. That despite the policy to record all debtor contacts, he did not record on either the account card, or the computer, this call. He denied he has ever threatened any debtor, including Peggy, with "going to jail." He denied any reference to a wedding ring. . . . Clyde Hardesty (Hager) stated that he was on vacation June 2 through 18, 1979. That he knew he was subject to telephone monitoring; that he called at the most on any account every other day. That he realized the danger of a claim of harassment, and as a business man he knew that given the work load of a collector, in excess of 100 calls a day, even an account this size could not be worked more often than every second or third day. He recalled two contacts on the 28th of June, and two contacts on the 11th of July. One was the call-back when he talked to Peggy's mother and one was a late call as authorized by Peggy. He did not always record no-answer calls. He denied using profanity. He denied calling to harass. . . .

He denied making any call on June 19, 1979. He claimed he never has and never would have told a woman she should not have children unless she could afford them. He denies he called on June 20, 1979. He would tell a debtor that legal action to enforce a claim was a possibility and such an action could result in judgment and garnishment in aid of execution. He does ask if a young debtor can get help from parents. He did not and would not tell a debtor that it was illegal to refuse to pay a debt and he or she could go to jail.

On July 2, 1979 he recommended an assignment of the Bingham account and when it was returned to him, in the usual manner referred the claim to the legal department for suit. Return of the assignment began the third stage, reduction of the claim to judgment. In the course of this stage, Binghams received a notice of referral for action. . . .

The following payments were made in the course of the collection efforts:

June 20, 1979, $10.00 paid to hospital; June 26, 1979, $10.00 paid to hospital; July 03, 1979, $10.00 paid to hospital; July 19, 1979, $10.00 paid to hospital; July 25, 1979, $10.00 paid to hospital.

This extended recital of the facts is made because of the numerous issues raised as to the application of a statute that has heretofore received little judicial interpretation.

GENERAL PRINCIPLES

In 1977 a new title was added to the Consumer Credit Protection Act. It was the Fair Debt Collection Practices Act, 15 U.S.C. §1692, which is in the tradition of "social legislation" so dear to the heart of William O. Douglas. His attitudes have been reflected in the approach and policies of the Federal Trade Commission since the days when he headed it in the early 1930's.

It was in keeping with this tradition that the statute was drafted for administration by the Federal Trade Commission. It is clearly addressed to protecting the weak and unsophistical debtor from abusive, dishonest and sharp collection practices. The initial paragraph of the statute reads:

15 U.S.C. §1692(a). "There is abundant evidence of the use of abusive, deceptive and unfair debt collection practices by many debt collectors. Abusive debt collection practices contribute to the number of personal bankruptcies, to marital instability, to the loss of jobs, and to invasions of individual privacy."

. . .

However the framers of the statute recognized that the vast majority of the collectors are ethical persons and a purpose of the act was not to impose unnecessary restrictions on ethical debt collectors. U.S. Code Cong. & Admin. News, 1977, Vol. 2, pp. 1695, 1696.

The drafters recognized that:

"Unlike creditors, who generally are restrained by the desire to protect their good will when collecting past due accounts, independent collectors are likely to have no future contact with the consumer and often are unconcerned with the consumer's opinion of them." U.S. Code Cong. & Admin. News, supra, p. 1696.

But, nevertheless, the abrasive persuasive collector is the adverse side of the coin of the unctuous persuasive credit extender, and the statute must be considered with that fact in mind.

. . .

FINDINGS AND CONCLUSIONS

. . .

Before evaluating the lawfulness of the telephone contact program, a few general observations are in order:

The telephone collectors who testified had certain characteristics in common. They were all young, competent verbalizers, with resonate voices and an authoritative manner of speech. They had better than average intelligence and had a touch of arrogance and of ruthlessness.

Telephone contacts as distinguished from personal contacts, while more efficient in terms of number of contacts made, and increased gross collections, are less efficient in terms of excellence of each contact, and extent to which an accurate evaluation of the debtor's situation, capacity, state of mind, etc., can be made.

Statements made and language used in a telephone contact can be and often are more oppressive than the same communication made in a face to face situation.

Plaintiffs claimed a total of fourteen calls. Defendant stated that the policy, subject to judgment decisions of the collector, was to average not more than one call every other day. "Hager" also claimed that aside from the opening call taken by "Mattson" he was on vacation and unable to make that many calls. "Mattson" took the call of June 11. "Hager" was absent until June 18. "Hager" stated he must have been absent until June 24 because he bought gas in North Sioux City, South Dakota, on June 22, and in Fargo on June 23. But the calls were logged on June 21 and June 25. "Hager" could easily have driven to North Sioux City, South Dakota, on the week end of June 21, leaving after work on Thursday. The Binghams made their first remittance generated by the collection effort on June 20. This payment was more likely caused by calls on June 18 and June 19, than the week old call of June 11. And while all telephone contacts are supposed to be logged, admittedly the call records on the computer printouts are not accurate.

Finally, fourteen calls between June 18 and July 11 is about one call every other day. So I conclude that it is more likely so than not so that the schedule of calls reported by Peggy is accurate.

Plaintiffs claim harassment was evidenced by the number of calls and the time of day of the calls. 15 U.S.C. §1692d(5) describes the violation of:

> "Causing a telephone to ring or engaging any person in telephone conversation repeatedly or continuously with intent to annoy, abuse, or harass any person at the called number."

The calls came in a pattern of four days of calls, then four days of no calls. The calls produced results in terms of payments, and neither Peggy nor Michael told the caller to stop calling until July 11, when he did stop.

So I find no harassment in the number of calls.

As to the time of day of the calls, 15 U.S.C. §1692c(a)(1) provides that generally a debt collector may not communicate with the debtor:

> "at any unusual time or place or a time or place known or which should be known to be inconvenient to the consumer. In the absence of knowledge of circumstances to the contrary, a debt collector shall assume that the convenient time for communicating with a consumer is after 8 o'clock antimeridian and before 9 o'clock post-meridian, local time at the consumer's location."

I interpret this statute to apply to telephonic communications.

The June 29 evening call was at the suggestion of Peggy. It was not harassment. It was not at an unreasonable time.

The July 6 call was terminated when Michael hung up after both parties were identified to each other. The recall came immediately. That was harassment.

As to the contents of the calls: My conclusion that the calls were made does not include a finding as to the contents of the calls.

As to the call of June 11, and the reference to the wedding ring. Inquiry as to the assets of the debtor is a necessary step for a collector to take. Inquiry as to jewelry, including rings, is not surprising in light of the current news coverage of the liquidation of jewelry because of the inflationary price of gold. I conclude that an inquiry as to assets including jewelry, for example, wedding rings, was made. But the inquiry was not interpreted as the inquirer intended. This is an example of the risk of telephonic communications with the less sophisticated. The applicable statute to this situation is the general prohibition against harassment, 15 U.S.C. §1692d.

I conclude that a telephonic inquiry by the collector about personal jewelry, which includes references to highly personal items like wedding rings, does have a natural consequence to harass, and therefore find it was harassment.

As to the threat of "going to jail." Peggy first claimed the threat was embodied in Form No. 4, then she found it again in the call of June 11. I conclude that her testimony as to this threat is not reliable.

As to the call of June 19, and the claimed statement by "Hager" that Peggy should not have children if she could not afford them. This call was one covered by Peggy's testimony from notes. This remark is not the kind which would have been pulled out of thin air by the witness. Her claimed response that she protested she could not violate her marriage vows shows she may be coloring the original remark by her recollection of the response. I conclude that some remark to that sense was made. I also conclude that any remark of that tenor in a telephonic collection contact is egregious and that the remark was harassment.

As to the claim of repeated threats of garnishment not in aid of execution. Peggy admitted she kept no notes of what was said after the first few calls, and her recollections ran together. Cross examination of the collectors demonstrated that they were sensitive to the risk of oppression by inaccurate and repeated threats of judgment, garnishment, attachment, etc., all of which can only follow a decision to sue, a successful suit, and proper procedures in aid of execution of a judgment.

But a discussion of the ramifications of suit does have its place in collection dialogues. I conclude that the plaintiffs have failed to establish that they suffered harassment and abuse because of improper discussions by the collector, of the possibility, and foreseeable consequences of civil action to collect.

. . .

B. Scope of FDCPA

Although the FDCPA could sweep in a large number of practices, its reach is sharply limited because it does not apply to all entities. The FDCPA only applies to "debt collectors," defined as "any person who uses any instrumentality of interstate commerce or the mails in any business the principal purpose of which is the collection of any debts, or who regularly collects or attempts to collect, directly or indirectly, debts owed or due or asserted to be owed or due another." 15 U.S.C. §1692a(6). The key exclusion is also made explicit. A debt collector is not "any officer or employee of a creditor, while in the name of the creditor, collecting debts for such creditor." The FDPCA only applies to third-party debt collectors, not those working on behalf of themselves. The effect is to prohibit certain behavior by certain people, not to prohibit the behavior regardless of the actor.

There are several explanations for the limited scope of the FDCPA. At the time of its enactment, the worst abuses may have been committed by third-party debt collectors. Without evidence of problematic actions by creditors, perhaps Congress simply wrote a narrow statute. The counterpoint is that if creditors were already following the law, then what is the harm in extending its reach to apply to them? And any suggestion that creditors and debt collectors use different debt collection practices begs the question why creditors might be more restrained. One answer is reputation. Debt collectors may benefit from being known as ruthless or tough. Who would you pay first, "Brass Knuckles Collection" or "Fluffy Kitten Collection"? If a consumer is scared or upset, that just makes for easier work the next time the debt collector calls them. Original creditors, on the other hand, deal primarily with consumers as purchasers of goods or as borrowers who do repay their obligations. These customers might go elsewhere if a store's or business's reputation was unsavory. Another explanation is that debt collectors might be difficult to sue because they have few assets and simply close down if sued and reopen as new legal entities. This may well be true but it suggests a different enforcement mechanism for debt collectors, not different substantive liability. The most cynical explanation is that debt collectors do not have the lobbying power of original creditors, which include large retailers who sell on installment credit, and so Congress "solved" the problem of debt collection by imposing restrictions only on a small segment of those engaged in collection.

But not all those who fancy themselves as having political clout escaped the FDCPA's scope. You, dear future lawyer, need to read on.

Dickman v. Kimball, Tirey & St. John, LLP

982 F. Supp. 2d 1157 (S.D. Cal. 2013)

MILLER, District Judge.

ORDER DENYING DEFENDANT's MOTION TO DISMISS

On August 27, 2013, Plaintiff filed a complaint alleging Defendant violated the Federal Fair Debt Collection Practices Act ("FDCPA"). . . .

BACKGROUND

On June 15, 2012, Plaintiff entered into a residential lease agreement for property located in Escondido, California ("the Escondido Property"). Plaintiff signed the lease on June 27, 2012, for a one-year term starting on July 1, 2012, and ending on June 30, 2013; however, Plaintiff alleges the lease contains a typographical error stating that it terminated on June 30, 2012. Plaintiff entered into the lease agreement with ENL Investments, LLC and Ed Forrester. Ed Forrester is the owner of ENL Investments, LLC, and he was Plaintiff's point of contact regarding the lease agreement. Plaintiff began residing at the Escondido Property on July 1, 2012.

The lease agreement required Plaintiff to make monthly rental payments of $1,900.00 by electronic deposit into ENL Investments, LLC's bank account. Plaintiff alleges that it was her regular practice to timely make these deposits at the beginning of each month. Plaintiff's payments were processed online by her bank and cleared her account on the next business day.

Unbeknownst to Plaintiff, a notice of default and notice of trustee's sale had been recorded against the property prior to the date that she signed the lease agreement and took possession of the property. On July 5, 2012, Mr. Forrester filed for bankruptcy relief under Chapter 7 of the bankruptcy code. As a result, a pending foreclosure sale on the Escondido Property was rescheduled for August 23, 2012. Mr. Forrester filed papers with the bankruptcy court claiming to be an owner of the Escondido Property pursuant to an unrecorded quit claim deed prepared prior to the date that he filed for bankruptcy relief. Plaintiff alleges she was unaware of the scheduled foreclosure sale of the Escondido Property.

On August 23, 2012, U.S. Financial, LP ("U.S. Financial") bought the Escondido Property at the trustee's sale without Plaintiff's knowledge. A trustee's deed was delivered to the County recorder's office for recording on August 31, 2012. As a result of the standard procedures used by the San Diego County Recorder's Office, the transfer deed did not become visible in the public record until two business days later on September 5, 2012. Plaintiff received no notice of the recorded deed prior to its public filing.

During the foreclosure process, Plaintiff initiated the electronic funds transfer on Saturday, September 1, 2012, to pay rent to ENL Investments, LLC for the month of September. As the payment was made on a three-day weekend, the payment did not clear Plaintiff's bank account until September 4, 2012. Plaintiff alleges that she did not have actual or constructive notice of the transfer of the Escondido Property to U.S. Financial at the time she made the September rent payment.

On about September 9, 2013, Don Rady, the owner of U.S. Financial, left a business card for Plaintiff at the Escondido Property. The back side of the business card had a handwritten note stating that "we are the new owners of this house, please call us." This card was the first actual notice Plaintiff received that ownership of the Escondido Property had changed hands. On September 13, 2012, Defendant, acting as legal counsel for U.S. Financial, drafted, signed, and directed that a three-day Notice to Pay Rent or Quit ("Notice") be served on Plaintiff. Plaintiff received service of the Notice on September 13, 2012.

The Notice demanded payment of $1,900.00 for September rent "WITHIN THREE DAYS" or legal proceedings would be instituted to recover possession of the subject premises, court costs, attorney's fees, and statutory damages up to $600.00. The Notice further informed Plaintiff that if she failed to pay the requested $1,900.00 within three days, the owner of the subject premises would elect to declare Plaintiff's rental agreement for the Escondido Property forfeit. This suggested to Plaintiff that her rental agreement was still in effect.

At the same time that Defendant served the Notice on Plaintiff, Defendant also sent a letter to Plaintiff stating: "If we receive a judgment against you, the Sheriff will remove you from the premises. Our client could also garnish your wages, levy on your bank accounts, and/or attach your non-exempt personal property for judicial sale in order to collect all monies due." This letter further stated: "This debt will be assumed to be valid unless you notify us within 30 days of receipt of this letter that you dispute all or part of the debt. If you notify us in writing within this same 30-day period, we will send you verification of this debt. Upon written request within the thirty-day period, we will provide you with the name and address of the original creditor, if different from the current creditor."

On about September 17, 2012, after expiration of the three-day Notice, U.S. Financial sent a letter acknowledging that Plaintiff had paid the rent to the prior owner, and claiming that Plaintiff "failed to acknowledge [U.S. Financial] as the owner of the Property, [Plaintiff] completely disregarded the tenant questionnaire and [Plaintiff] improperly paid rent to the prior owner of the Property." However, Plaintiff had received no notice regarding where to send rent to the new owner until she received the September 13, 2012 three-day Notice to pay or quit.

Despite knowing that Plaintiff had already paid rent to the prior landlord, Plaintiff alleges that Defendant filed an unlawful detainer action against Plaintiff on October 3, 2012. The complaint claimed that Plaintiff owed rent in the amount of $1,900.00 for the month of September 2012 and referenced the three-day Notice to pay rent or quit that Defendant served on Plaintiff. On November 20, 2012, after a civil trial, the court dismissed Defendant's unlawful detainer action against Plaintiff because the required 60- and 90-day notice under California and Federal law had not been given and because the elements of an unlawful detainer had not been met.

Based upon these factual allegations, Plaintiff alleges Defendant violated the FDCPA. According to the complaint, Defendant's violations of the FDCPA include, but are not limited to the following:

a. 15 U.S.C. §1692e(2)(A) by making a false representation of the character, amount, or legal status of the alleged debt;
b. 15 U.S.C. §1692e(5) by threatening to take an action that cannot legally be taken or that is not intended to be taken;
c. 15 U.S.C. §1692e(10) by making use of a false representation or deceptive means to collect or attempt to collect a debt;
d. 15 U.S.C. §1692f(1) by attempting to collect an amount not permitted by law;
e. 15 U.S.C. §1692f generally by using an unfair or unconscionable means of collecting a debt in contravention of federal and state laws protecting tenants at foreclosure.

As a proximate result of the alleged FDCPA violations, Plaintiff seeks actual damages pursuant to 15 U.S.C. §1692k(a)(1), statutory damages in an amount up to $1,000.00 pursuant to 15 U.S.C. §1692k(a)(2)(A), and reasonable attorney's fees and costs pursuant to 15 U.S.C. §1692k(a)(3). For actual damages, Plaintiff claims emotional distress in the amount of at least $15,000.00.

. . .

DISCUSSION

The sole cause of action raised by Plaintiff's complaint is Defendant's alleged violation of the FDCPA. The FDCPA was passed to prevent abusive debt collection practices, including the use of "false, deceptive, or misleading representation or means in connection with the collection of any debt." 15 U.S.C. §1692e. Under the FDCPA, debt collectors are prohibited from engaging in certain inappropriate communications with consumers, harassing or abusing consumers, or engaging in other unfair practices, such as collecting fees not specified in the agreement creating the debt. See 15 U.S.C. §§1692c, 1692d, and 1692f. The FDCPA defines debt collectors as those who collect or attempt to collect a debt owed to another entity, although the definition carves out several exceptions to the definition. See 15

U.S.C. §1692a. However, the Supreme Court in *Heintz v. Jenkins* held that the FDCPA "applies to attorneys who regularly engage in consumer-debt-collection activity, even when that activity consists of litigation." Heintz v. Jenkins, 514 U.S. 291, 299 (1995).

CALIFORNIA LITIGATION PRIVILEGE IN CALIFORNIA CIVIL CODE SECTION 47(b)

First, Defendant argues that its actions are protected by the litigation privilege. Specifically, Defendant argues the litigation privilege set forth in California Civil Code Section 47(b) protects any publication or broadcast made in any judicial proceeding. Defendant argues the alleged violations of the FDCPA in the complaint, i.e. filing and litigating a lawsuit as well as serving a three-day Notice and sending a letter regarding said litigation, are all actions properly protected from attack by the litigation privilege.

In response, Plaintiff contends the United States Supreme Court ruled in *Heintz v. Jenkins* that the FDCPA covered litigation activities. 514 U.S. 291, 295 (1995). As a result, Plaintiff argues it has been nationally recognized since 1995 that the litigation privilege does not apply to claims under the FDCPA. Indeed, the California district court in *Oei v. North Star Capital Acquisitions, LLC* indicated that "[i]t is well settled that the Supremacy Clause of the United States Constitution grants Congress the power to preempt state and local laws . . . As a result, it is equally well settled that California's litigation privilege does not apply to federal causes of action, including FDCPA claims." Oei v. North Star Capital Acquisitions, LLC, 486 F. Supp. 2d 1089, 1098 (C.D. Cal. 2006). . . .

Having reviewed the cases relied upon by the parties, the court finds the California litigation privilege does not bar Plaintiff's FDCPA claim. See Holmes v. Electronic Document Processing, Inc., 966 F. Supp. 2d 925, (N.D. Cal. Aug. 15, 2013) (noting it is well established that the California litigation privilege does not apply to FDCPA claims); see also Heintz, 514 U.S. at 298 (concluding the FDCPA "applies to attorneys who 'regularly' engage in consumer-debt-collection activity, even when that activity consists of litigation"). Notably, Defendants have not cited any legal authority for the proposition that the litigation activities alleged by Plaintiff are privileged from liability under the FDCPA. Accordingly, Defendant's motion to dismiss Plaintiff's FDCPA claim on the basis of the California litigation privilege is denied.

. . .

UNDERLYING LITIGATION AS A DEBT COLLECTION

Defendant argues the unlawful detainer action was not a debt collection under the FDCPA. As alleged in the complaint, Defendant served Plaintiff with a three-day Notice to pay rent or quit the Escondido Property and subsequently filed an unlawful detainer action. Defendant contends both of these actions primarily seek possession of the property rather than debt collection. Defendant contends a debt collector's actions to evidence a debt rather than collect a debt are not actionable, i.e. a trustee's deed upon sale evidences a sale, rather than collection of a debt, and therefore is not subject to the FDCPA.[1] For these reasons, Defendant contends it is not liable for the conduct alleged within the complaint, and the motion to dismiss should be granted accordingly.

Plaintiff contends Defendant's actions constitute debt collection as defined by the FDCPA. The FDCPA applies to debt collection of consumer debts with "debt" broadly defined as follows:

> any obligation or alleged obligation of a consumer to pay money arising out of a transaction in which the money, property, insurance, or services which are the subject of the transaction are primarily for personal, family, or household purposes, whether or not such obligation has been reduced to judgment.

15 USC §1692a(5). As support for her argument, Plaintiff relies upon decisions from other courts that have found that rent owed pursuant to a lease is an obligation within the scope of the FDCPA's definition of "debt." See Romea v. Heiberger & Assocs., 163 F.3d 111, 114-15 (2d Cir. 1998); Leasure v. Willmark Communities, Inc., 2011 U.S. Dist. LEXIS 60986, 2011 WL 2267598, at *2 (S.D. Cal. June 7, 2011) (finding persuasive the Second Circuit's holding in *Romea* that, in light of the language of the FDCPA, there was no reason why residential rent incurred by a consumer should not constitute a debt). Here, Plaintiff alleges Defendant's actions were designed to coerce Plaintiff into paying rent for September, which she had already paid to the prior landlord and did not owe to the new owner, and threatened Plaintiff with removal from her home in doing so. Plaintiff contends these actions constitute debt collection, and they are therefore covered by the FDCPA.

. . .

Having found back rent constitutes a debt under the FDCPA, the Second Circuit then concluded that delivery of a three-day rent demand notice, as required by New York law as condition precedent to summary eviction proceeding, was a "communication" to collect a debt, within the meaning of the FDCPA, and the attorneys were acting as "debt collectors" for FDCPA purposes. Romea at 116-18.

Once again, Defendant has not provided the court with any authority suggesting that its alleged conduct does not constitute debt collection under the FDCPA. Under the circumstances, the court finds the analysis in *Romea* provides a reasonable basis for finding Plaintiff has sufficiently alleged Defendant engaged in debt collection under the FDCPA. Accordingly, Defendant's motion to dismiss Plaintiff's FDCPA claim for failing to allege debt collection activities covered by the statute is denied.

. . .

---

1. As support for this proposition, Defendant cites Wade v. Reg'l Credit Ass'n, 87 F.3d 1098, 1099 (9th Cir. 1996). In *Wade*, the Ninth Circuit determined that a debt collector's innocuous debt collection attempts did not violate the FDCPA, despite being in violation of state law requiring debt collectors to obtain state debt collection licenses. Id. After reviewing this case, the court is unclear how this case pertains to Defendant's argument as it does not relate to a trustee's deed of sale or the distinction between debt collection and attempts to evidence a sale.

CONCLUSION

Based on the foregoing, Defendant's motion to dismiss is denied. Defendant is ordered to file its answer within 20 days of the filing of this order.

C. State Debt Collection Laws

All but seven states have laws that deal with abuses in debt collection. The state debt collection statutes, in an analogy to UDAP, should not be thought of as "mini" FDCPAs because they often have broader reach and greater remedies. Specifically, they frequently apply to creditors, not just to third-party debt collectors, and they often have statutes of limitation that are longer than the one-year period in the FDCPA. The statutes sometimes go beyond prohibiting acts and practices to take preventative approaches such as requiring the licensing or bonding of debt collectors.

The statutes are part of a cumulative approach used by plaintiffs whereby a violation of federal law triggers a violation of a particular state law, which may also trigger a violation of a more general state UDAP law. This case illustrates that approach, and also provides a look at some of the threshold legal issues presented in an FDCPA case.

Finley v. Dynamic Recovery Solutions LLC

2015 WL 3750140 (N.D. Cal. June 15, 2015)

HENDERSON, U.S. District Judge

BACKGROUND

In June of 2001, banks and debt collectors started contacting Plaintiff Nancy Finley ("Plaintiff") regarding a debt she owed of approximately $18,000. California's four-year statute of limitations for Plaintiff's debt appears to have run sometime in 2004 or 2005. Nonetheless, debt collection agencies continued to contact Plaintiff, off and on, for almost ten years after the statute of limitations expired.

On January 15, 2010, Defendant Accelerated Financial Solutions ("Accelerated") purchased Plaintiff's debt. Also, sometime in April of 2010, Plaintiff received a letter from Defendant Consumer Recovery Associates ("Consumer"), requesting repayment of the debt. Plaintiff's counsel sent a letter to Consumer on April 29, 2010, notifying Consumer that Plaintiff was represented by counsel and making other demands.

Sometime between January 27 and February 4, 2014, Accelerated opened an account with Defendant Dynamic Recovery Solutions ("Dynamic") for the purposes of collecting Plaintiff's debt. On May 7, 2014, Dynamic sent a debt collection letter to Plaintiff, requesting payment of $39,969.99. The collection letter offered to "settle [Plaintiff's] account" under various payment plan arrangements.

Plaintiff also alleges that Dynamic called her approximately nine times between March 8, 2014, and June 7, 2014.

Plaintiff brought suit in August of 2014 against Defendants Accelerated, Dynamic, and Consumer, alleging violations of the federal Fair Debt Collection Practices Act, the California Rosenthal Act, . . . and the California Unfair Competition Law. Defendants Accelerated and Dynamic now move for summary judgment on all of Plaintiff's claims against them.

. . .

I. Plaintiff's Fair Debt Collection Practices Act Claims

a. Both Defendants Are Debt Collectors and Are Subject to the Act

The federal Fair Debt Collection Practices Act, Title 15, United States Code, section 1692 et seq., prohibits debt collectors from taking certain actions in the course of collecting a debt. The statute distinguishes between "debt collectors," to whom these prohibitions apply, and "creditors," to whom they do not; "these two categories—debt collectors and creditors—are mutually exclusive." Schlosser v. Fairbanks Capital Corp., 323 F.3d 534, 536 (7th Cir. 2003).

A "debt collector" is defined as "any person who uses any instrumentality of interstate commerce or the mails in any business the principal purpose of which is the collection of any debts, or who regularly collects or attempts to collect, directly or indirectly, debts owed or due or asserted to be owed or due another." 15 U.S.C. §1692a(6). A "creditor," on the other hand, is defined as "any person . . . to whom a debt is owed, but such term does not include any person to the extent that he receives an assignment or transfer of a debt in default solely for the purpose of facilitating collection of such debt for another." 15 U.S.C. §1692a(4).

Because of the latter clause in the "creditor" definition, courts around the country have found that businesses are debt collectors, and subject to the requirements of the Fair Debt Collection Practices Act, where they purchased a debt that was already in default for the purpose of debt collection. E.g., Ruth v. Triumph Partnerships, 577 F.3d 790, 796-97 (7th Cir. 2009) ("Where, as here, the party seeking to collect a debt did not originate it but instead acquired it from another party, we have held that the party's status under the FDCPA turns on whether the debt was in default at the time it was acquired."); see also Guerrero v. RJM Acquisitions LLC, 499 F.3d 926, 931 (9th Cir. 2007) (explaining that a party that purchases a debt can still be subject to the Act).

Courts in this district have relied on *Ruth* and *Guerrero,* and looked to whether a debt was in default at the time of its purchase to determine whether the purchaser is a creditor or a debt collector. E.g., McQueen v. Am. Exp. Centurion Bank, 2012 WL 5301075, at *2-3 (N.D. Cal. Oct. 25, 2012).

Here, it is clear that Defendant Dynamic is a debt collector within the meaning of the Fair Debt Collection Practices Act. The collection letter that Dynamic sent to Plaintiff stated "This is an attempt to collect a debt by a debt collector. . . ." Dynamic does not argue otherwise.

Accelerated is also a debt collector covered by the statute, under the reasoning of *Ruth, McQueen,* and *Suellen.* Accelerated purchased Plaintiff's debt while it was in default: Plaintiff started receiving collection letters as early as 2001, and Accelerated purchased the debt on January 15, 2010. Accelerated is therefore subject to the requirements of the Fair Debt Collection Practices Act, discussed below.

b. Plaintiff Shall Conduct More Discovery to Determine Whether Defendants Knew Plaintiff Was Represented

Among other requirements and prohibitions, the Fair Debt Collection Practices Act prohibits a debt collector from communicating directly with a consumer "if the debt collector knows the consumer is represented by an attorney. . . ." 15 U.S.C. §1692c(a)(2).

Courts considering allegations that a debt collector communicated directly with a represented consumer under section 1692c require that the consumer show the debt collector had "actual knowledge" that the consumer was represented. Randolph v. IMBS, Inc., 368 F.3d 726, 729 (7th Cir. 2004); Offril v. J.C. Penny Co., Inc., No. C 08–5050 PJH, 2009 WL 69344, at *3 (N.D. Cal. Jan. 9, 2009). This is because, unlike the other provisions of the Act, section 1692c makes it a violation to communicate directly to a consumer "if the debt collector *knows* the consumer is represented by an attorney." 15 U.S.C. §1692c(2).

The Act also has an affirmative "bona fide error" defense, whereby a debt collector will not be held liable if it shows "by a preponderance of evidence that the violation was not intentional and resulted from a bona fide error notwithstanding the maintenance of procedures reasonably adapted to avoid any such error." 15 U.S.C. §1692k(c). Some courts, considering allegations under other provisions of the Fair Debt Collection Practices Act, have held that it is a "strict liability offense," subject to the affirmative bona fide error defense described above. E.g., Reichert v. National Credit Sys., Inc., 531 F.3d 1002, 1005 (9th Cir. 2008) (considering alleged violation of section 1692f); Clark v. Capital Credit & Collection Servs., Inc., 460 F.3d 1162, 1176 (9th Cir. 2006) (considering alleged violation of section 1692e). However, the Court is not aware of any case holding that the "actual knowledge" requirement of section 1692c is also subject to the reasonable procedures required in the bona fide error defense.

Here, the evidence suggests that neither Defendant had actual knowledge that Plaintiff was represented by an attorney when Dynamic sent its letter and called her. Accelerated's CEO testified in a declaration that the company "did not know Plaintiff was represented by counsel when it sent the account to Dynamic. . . ." Dynamic's CFO similarly testified that the company "did not have notice of any prior letters from Plaintiff and/or her counsel prior to sending its letter," and it "did not know Plaintiff was represented by counsel in connection with the subject debt."

However, Plaintiff submitted evidence that Plaintiff told another Defendant, Consumer, that she was represented and was disputing the debt, and that Consumer subsequently placed a "cease and desist" label on her account to stop collection. Ex. B to King Decl. Plaintiff is already conducting discovery on the question of what information Consumer communicated to Accelerated in the process of attempting to collect Plaintiff's debt. May 7, 2015 Order at 2.

Plaintiff shall be allowed to conduct additional discovery regarding what, if anything, Consumer told Accelerated and/or Dynamic regarding Plaintiff being represented by an attorney. . . .

c. Defendants May Have Made Misleading Statements Regarding the Debt

The Fair Debt Collection Practices Act also prohibits debt collectors from using "any false, deceptive, or misleading representation or means in connection with the collection of any debt," including "the false representation of . . . the character, amount, or legal status of any debt;" "the threat to take any action that cannot legally be taken;" and "[c]ommunicating . . . to any person credit information which is known or which should be known to be false, including the failure to communicate that a disputed debt is disputed." 15 U.S.C. §1692e & (2)(A), (5), (8).

"Whether conduct violates §1692e requires an objective analysis that takes into account whether the least sophisticated debtor would likely be misled by a communication." Gonzales v. Arrow Fin. Servs., LLC, 660 F.3d 1055, 1061 (9th Cir. 2011) (alteration and quotation omitted). "The 'least sophisticated debtor' standard is lower than simply examining whether particular language would deceive or mislead a reasonable debtor." Id. (quotation omitted).

Federal courts disagree about whether a debt collector can be liable under the Fair Debt Collection Practices Act for sending a collection letter to a consumer for an unenforceable debt, such as where the statute of limitations has expired. Alborzian v. JPMorgan Chase Bank, N. Am., 235 Cal. App. 4th 29, 36–37 (Cal. Ct. App. 2015) (collecting cases). In the Sixth and Seventh Circuits, a debt collector may be liable if the collection letter would mislead the least sophisticated debtor about the enforceability of the debt. Buchanan v. Northland Group, Inc., 776 F.3d 393, 399 (6th Cir. 2015); McMahon v. LVNV Funding, LLC, 744 F.3d 1010, 1020 (7th Cir. 2014) ("The proposition that a debt collector violates the FDCPA when it misleads an unsophisticated consumer to believe a time-barred debt is legally enforceable, regardless of whether litigation is threatened, is straightforward under the statute."). In the Third and Eighth Circuits, however, such a collection letter is only actionable if it is accompanied by a threat of litigation. Huertas v. Galaxy Asset Mgmt., 641 F.3d 28, 32–33 (3d Cir. 2011); Freyermuth v. Credit Bureau Servs., Inc., 248 F.3d 767, 771 (8th Cir. 2001) ("[I]n the absence of a threat of litigation or actual litigation, no violation of the FDCPA has occurred when a debt collector attempts to collect on a potentially time-barred debt that is otherwise valid.").

The Ninth Circuit has not yet determined whether a threat of litigation is required for such a debt collection letter to be actionable. Two cases in this district, both decided prior to the Seventh Circuit decision of McMahon, have followed the approach of the Eighth Circuit and required a threat of litigation in a debt collection letter. Abels v. JBC Legal Grp., P.C., 428 F. Supp. 2d 1023, 1027 (N.D. Cal. 2005); Perretta v. Capital Acquisitions & Mgmt. Co., No. C–02–05561 RMW, 2003 WL 21383757, at *4 (N.D. Cal. May 5, 2003). In Perretta, Judge Whyte applied the "least sophisticated debtor" standard to the potential threat of litigation, and found that a letter threatening "further steps would be taken" could be threatening to the least sophisticated debtor. 2003 WL 21383757, at *4.

Here, Defendants have neither shown the absence of dispute as to any material fact, nor that they are entitled to judgment as a matter of law. It should be noted, first, that Defendants only raised arguments under this section in their replies. Second, it is undisputed that Dynamic did not tell Plaintiff that the statute of limitations had expired on her debt when it communicated with her. Third, Dynamic's letter to Plaintiff offered to "settle her account." *Id.* It is plausible that the least sophisticated consumer could view an offer to settle as a veiled threat of litigation, or, at the least, as a misrepresentation that a debt is still enforceable. McMahon, 744 F.3d at 1020.

Moreover, Defendants did not discuss Plaintiff's claim that they failed to communicate the legal status of her debt *to each other* whatsoever in their briefing. Yet, under section 1692e(8), quoted above, there is a possible cause of action if any Defendant failed to communicate to another that Plaintiff was disputing the status of her debt. Because this cause of action potentially exists, and Defendants did not argue the issue at all, they are not entitled to summary judgment on this claim.

Accordingly, Defendants' motions for summary judgment on Plaintiff's claims under section 1692e of the Fair Debt Collection Practices Act are DENIED.

II. Plaintiff's Rosenthal Act Claims

Plaintiff also brought claims under California's Rosenthal Fair Debt Collection Practices Act, California Civil Code §1788 et seq. The Rosenthal Act explicitly incorporates the federal Fair Debt Collection Practices Act by reference, except for its definitions section. Cal. Civ. Code §1788.17; Alborzian, 235 Cal. App. 4th at 36. Defendants are entitled to summary judgment on the Rosenthal Act claims only to the extent that they are entitled to summary judgment on the federal claims. See Diaz v. Kubler Corp., 785 F.3d 1326 (9th Cir. May 12, 2015) ("The Rosenthal Act mimics or incorporates by reference the FDCPA's requirements. . . . The parties do not dispute that the Rosenthal Act claims at issue in this appeal rise or fall with the FDCPA claims.").

Just as Defendants have not shown that they did not violate sections 1692c and 1692e of the federal statute, they also have not shown that they did not violate the Rosenthal Act. Defendants' motions for summary judgment on Plaintiff's Rosenthal Act claims are denied.

. . .

IV. Plaintiff's Unfair Competition Law Claim

Plaintiff also brings a claim under California's Unfair Competition Law ("UCL"), Business and Professions Code §17200 et seq. "The UCL borrows violations of other laws and treats them as unlawful practices that the unfair competition law makes independently actionable. Further, the UCL creates three varieties of unfair competition — acts or practices which are unlawful, or unfair, or fraudulent." Wilson v. Hewlett-Packard Co., 668 F.3d 1136, 1140 (9th Cir. 2012) (quotation omitted). Individuals suing under the UCL cannot recover damages; rather, they are limited to restitution and injunctive relief. Korea Supply Co. v. Lockheed Martin Corp., 29 Cal. 4th 1134, 1150 (Cal. 2003).

Defendants argue that Plaintiff's UCL claims must fail to the extent that they are based on any of the statutory claims discussed above. However, as discussed above, Defendants have not shown that they are entitled to summary judgment on Plaintiff's Fair Debt Collection Practices Act and Rosenthal Act claims. As a result, Plaintiff may still maintain claims under the "unlawful" prong of the UCL.

Moreover, Defendants made no argument regarding the "unfair" and "fraudulent" prongs of the UCL. They therefore have not shown that they are entitled to summary judgment on these separate causes of action under the UCL, and Defendants motions regarding Plaintiff's UCL claims are denied.

CONCLUSION

For the reasons set forth above, the Court grants in party and denies in part Defendants' motions for summary judgment. Defendants' motions regarding Plaintiff's Fair Debt Buying Practices Act claims are granted. Their motions regarding Plaintiff's Fair Debt Collection Practices Act section 1692e claims, and related Rosenthal Act and UCL claims, are denied. The Court reserves judgment on Defendant's motions regarding Plaintiff's section 1692c claims until Plaintiff has conducted additional discovery.

IT IS SO ORDERED.

D.   Debt Buyers

While a consumer continues to be bound to pay a debt, the lender may exit the deal. The originator may sell the debt to another entity. Sometimes this is part of a "high finance" deal such as a securitization of debt and other times it is a "spoiled fruit" deal whereby the company just wants to get difficult to collect accounts off its books.

Consumer debts are normally transferred in bulk pursuant to a purchase and sale agreement. Portfolios are made up of debts that share common attributes such as the type of credit issued, the elapsed time since the consumer accounts went into default, and the number of third party debt collection firms with which creditors placed the accounts prior the creditors offering them for sale. The price of the debt is negotiated and reflects not only the amounts owed, but also the credit risk of the portfolio. Upon consummation of the sale, the debt buyer has the right to receive the consumer's payments on the debts and inherits other rights, including standing to sue to collect the debt, if defaulted under the terms of the loan. The consumer is not a party to the purchase and sale debt contract and typically will not receive any notice that a sale has occurred. Delinquent debts are more likely to be sold, and the older and less collectible the debt is, the more brisk the market of companies willing to try to recover by dunning, having paid only pennies per dollar owed.

As part of the sale, debt buyers are given some information about the consumer debtor and the nature of the debt. Often, particularly in some industries such as credit card or medical debt, the information received is inaccurate or incomplete. Debt sellers are under no obligation to release additional information to either debt buyers or consumers once the debt has been sold.

When debt buyers file suits for judgment in state courts, most consumers do not respond. Estimates are that as many as 90 percent of debt collections from debt buyers are achieved through defaults in the court system. Legal requirements for default are easy to meet because the lawsuit is usually filed as an "account stated" or "open account." Bare information identifying the debtor and the amount due is generally all that is contained in the complaint. Those minimal requirements facilitate debt buying because they lower the amount of information that must be retained and transferred between creditors. But for consumers, the complaints are often a source of confusion and frustration. Consumers cannot figure out how they came to owe a particular company, which they never borrowed from.

Debt buying is not for the faint of heart. Jake Halpern's book, *Bad Paper* (2014), is a highly readable look at the dealings of debt buyers with consumers and with each other.

> One of Brandon's first jobs in collections was at a law firm in Boston that had two divisions, one composed of collectors stationed at phone banks and the other manned by lawyers who sued debtors in court. Brandon was appalled by how the office worked. "There was a lot of crooked stuff going on," he told me. "I noticed it right away and I put a stop to it." . . .
>
> It wasn't long before Brandon's abilities as a collector, combined with his efforts to clean up the office, caught the attention of one of the firm's owners, a well-regarded lawyer named Jeff Schreiber. On their first encounter, Brandon introduced himself . . . by explaining that he was a former armed robber who did "ten years in the can." Jeff was not impressed. "He made me cringe when he told me about going to prison [and that] he's a convicted felon," Jeff told me. "I thought, *Oh great, this is what I have on my payroll.*" And yet that didn't stop Jeff from soon promoting Brandon to become a manager. . . .
>
> In addition to collecting on debt, Brandon began buying and selling it as well. He talked to everyone, did his research, and found opportunities that no one else could—like a portfolio of paper that no one had touched for five years, other than an incompetent call center based in Brazil. "I am a bottom feeder," Brandon told me. "I specialize in finding paper that everyone else thinks is worthless." As far as Brandon was concerned, the older and more beaten-up that debt *appeared* to be, the better. People falsely assumed that it was very difficult to collect on old debt, but it all depended on the history of the portfolio—who exactly had tried to collect on it, how long they had been trying, and how successful they had been. Brandon's specialty became finding old debt that paid. "I buy old crap," Brandon told me. "I'm the King of Crap."

Id. at 41-42, 44-45.

Just as debt collectors were singled out in the 1970s by the FDCPA from creditors collecting their own debts, debt buyers are being identified as a major reason for the complaints about debt collection. About a dozen states have passed legislation to impose additional duties on debt buyers. California's law, the Fair Debt Buying Practices Act, intervenes to limit when a debt buyer may make any written statement to a consumer or when a default judgment may enter in favor of a debt buyer. Cal. Civ. Code §§1788.50-1788.64 (2013). Under the statute, a debt buyer means a person who regularly purchased consumer debt that has been charged off, defined as being removed from the creditor's books as an asset and treated as a loss or expense. Debt buyers must provide key pieces of information about a debt, including the amount, nature, and reason for all post-charge-off interest and fees, the dates of default and last payments, and the identity of the charge-off creditor and all entities that purchased the debt after charge-off. The law also prohibits a debt buyer from filing suit or initiating an arbitration if the statute of limitations for the debt has expired. Cal. Civ. Code §1788.56. This transforms the common law rule that a statute of limitations is an affirmative defense that must be pled when answering a complaint.

As evidence of the political and normative complexities of regulating debt collection, note that a few states have gone the opposite direction. In the last few years, Arizona, Tennessee, and Arkansas have all made it easier to obtain a default judgment on a debt collection suit.

E.   Debt Settlement or Consolidation

Consumers often are eager for a way out of the sweat box of dunning or collection. Companies are all too willing to promise to handle a consumer's debts—for a fee. While there are non-profit credit counseling agencies that receive funding from major philanthropic organizations, many companies promise to consolidate or settle debts without delivering on their promises. In a typical set-up, the consumer is asked to give permission for the company to pull a credit report and required to provide all mailings from creditors. The company then contacts the creditors and asks if they will agree to a reduced payment, either in lump sum or over time. The consumer meanwhile is depositing money each week or month in an account with the company. The idea is that the consumer's savings will be doled out to the creditors, eliminating debt entirely for less than half of what is owed.

There is nothing wrong with this arrangement in and of itself. Indeed, it is trying to solve the very real problem of each creditor wanting all the debtor's scare money for itself and the debtor being overwhelmed by the collective dunning effort. The problem is with the fees.

The FTC's Telemarketing Sales Practice Rule prohibits charging upfront fees for debt settlement. 16 C.F.R. §310. The CFPB has joint authority to enforce this rule. Often, the situation is pretty straightforward as a legal matter. The company took a fee and then did nothing. In addition to violating the FTC Telemarketing Sales Practice Rule, this is clearly an unfair and deceptive practice. Indeed, it comes close to conversion or theft. The trickier situation is when the debt settlement company does perform services, but at a very steep price, such as several hundred dollars to eliminate only a few thousand dollars of debt.

Problem Set 23

23.1. Teddy Moore loves his neighborhood bar. Built in the 1940s, it features an old-fashioned atmosphere, complete with record jukebox and photos of patrons hanging everywhere, all shot by bar owner, Pauline Jones, an amateur portrait photographer. The bar also has antiquated payment policies. Patrons can either pay cash or run up a monthly tab: no credit or debit cards are accepted. For over a year, Teddy has enjoyed good times that worked out to about a $75 tab. He has always paid it up when reminded, but this month simply doesn't have the cash. He explained his situation to Pauline, but she turned hostile on Teddy snatching back the draft that she had just poured him. Teddy has ventured in the bar one time since but was shocked to discover that the portrait that Pauline had taken of him now featured a big hot pink post-it note with the word "deadbeat" written on it over his face. Teddy fled the bar before Pauline or anyone else saw him, but several of his friends have since kidded him about the situation. He wants to know if Pauline's actions have violated the federal FDCPA or the California Rosenthal Fair Debt Collection Act. *See* 15 U.S.C. §§1692a; 1692c; 1692d; Cal. Civ. Code §§1788.2; 1788.12.

23.2. To finance his undergraduate studies at Humongous University, Alan Parker obtained a $15,000 student loan from Students First Bank. Parker discontinued his studies at Humongous University in 2013 and has been living with his parents ever since. On December 25, 2015, Parker received a telephone call from Martha Raven, an account manager employed by the Business Collection Bureau. Raven told Parker that Business Collection Bureau had been engaged to collect the loan extended by the Students First Bank. She had begun to outline various repayment plan possibilities when Parker interrupted her to say that he had no intention of repaying a single cent of his student loan and that he would appreciate it if she would refrain from calling him again about the matter. On February 1, 2016, Raven again called Parker at his parents' home. Parker responded to her proposal of an extended repayment plan by reiterating his unwillingness to repay any part of his student loan. Has Raven violated any provisions of the Fair Debt Collection Practices Act? *See* 15 U.S.C. §§1692c; 1692g.

23.3. Julia King is the billings manager for a pediatric practice group, Lil' Health Hugs, that serves a low- to moderate-income community. The sign above the reception desk states that "payment is due at time of service" but as a matter of practice, very little money is collected. Most patients are harried, dealing with sick kids, and are not sure how much of the visit will be covered by insurance. The Lil' Health Hugs' doctors grew frustrated with the 90-120 day delay in payment by most patients and told Julia to speed up collection.

Julia has hired an "early action" firm, Wickets & Wappers LLP, to contact patients as soon as the pediatrics practice has submitted its claim to insurance, usually one week after the patient visit. The firm is run by two local lawyers. They supervise a large staff that calls patients and reviews the explanation of insurance benefits over the phone, and asks for a payment of the amount of patient responsibility. If the money is not paid, Wickets & Wappers LLP then sends a letter, "on behalf of Lil' Health Hugs," stating that payment of the patient responsibility amount of $X is due immediately." Two follow-up phone calls are made, a week apart. If 75 days from the patient visit and 70 days from submission to insurance, the patient responsibility amount is not paid, Wickets & Wappers returns the debt to Lil' Health Hugs. At that point, Julia sells the debts to a debt buyer that specializes in filing small claims actions to recover.

You provide general legal advice on matters such as employment, insurance liability, and partnership law to Lil' Health Hugs. Julia has asked you to "take a quick look" at the new debt collection scheme and make sure it checks out, including whether Wickets & Wappers are bar members in good standing. Having validated the latter, is Lil' Health Hugs in violation of the FDCPA? 15 U.S.C. §1692a(6).

23.4. As deputy chief of staff for the state's attorney general, you got to a lot of community meetings on her behalf. Per instructions, you take notes, nod to show that you are listening, and exuberantly thank people for their thoughts and comments. You recently went to the Consumer Coalition meeting, which consists of practicing attorneys from several legal aid organizations and a couple of not-for-profits that do policy work. When you arrived ready to listen, you were met with a visual assault. The entire room was decorated with gigantic posters that reproduced debt collection letters that clients of the organizations had received. Big red arrows labeled areas of the letters that threatened to file lawsuits, "Shame on You," or "Bad Bad."

The meeting went downhill immediately, with the advocates pressing on a very specific issue: Will the attorney general sue debt collectors who send dunning letters when the applicable statute of limitations for the debt has expired? You stuck to your small guns, repeating over and over again, "I'll look into that and get back to you." Having escaped back to the office, what is your conclusion on the legality of the practice? You need to brief the mayor and the head of Consumer Affairs and provide a legal analysis and a range of options for their consideration. So far, you have figured out that in your state any violation of the federal Fair Debt Collection Practices Act is a *per se* violation of the state unfair and deceptive acts and practices law. *See* 15 U.S.C. §1692e.

Assignment 24. Public Enforcement

Consider a business that is sued for an unfair practice and offers two settlement options: 1) payment of $10,000 to the aggrieved party plus that party's attorneys' fees and litigation costs, or 2) a settlement that promises to stop the unfair practice and provides an education campaign to improve consumers' abilities to protect themselves in similar situations that might arise. A private litigant is powerfully motivated to take the money and recover costs. A public litigant may prefer to end the unfair practice; it remedies the problem going forward even if it provides no restitution to the aggrieved party.

The barriers to private litigation are substantial. The legal process may be too complex or expensive for private parties to use or a law may not give any remedy to private parties. Because private parties file suit to vindicate their own rights and obtain relief for personal wrongs, they may lack a broad perspective on the issue or a desire to reshape the marketplace. Attorneys general are insulated from restrictions on class actions that let them pursue aggregate litigation when private litigants cannot. Myriam Gilles & Gary Friedman, *After Class: Aggregation Litigation in the Wake of AT&T Mobility v. Concepcion*, 79 Univ. of Chi. L. Rev. 623 (2012). For these reasons, public enforcement is a cornerstone of consumer protection activity. It occurs at the federal, state, and even local levels, with these agencies having overlapping authority that sometimes raises preemption issues or policy tensions about the best actor to enforce a law.

Notwithstanding its power, public enforcement can be curbed. Agencies face resource constraints from taxpayer funding and competing priorities. Political pressure may influence elected officials to forsake or abandon enforcement. The private interests of regulated groups may drive policy decisions to the point where agencies are "captured" and no longer acting in the public interest. Last, but not least, public enforcement may not identify or focus on the issues that are salient to consumers in the real world. Rights may be vindicated in a way that does not provide redress to harmed consumers, such as when agencies obtain an injunction to change future conduct but no restitution damages. Public aggregate litigation may not be bound by sufficient procedures to ensure due process or adequate representation of potential private claimants. Margaret H. Lemos, *Aggregate Litigation Goes Public: Representative Suits by State Attorneys General*, 126 Harv. L. Rev. 486 (2012).

A. Federal Actors: CFPB and FTC

The Dodd-Frank Act greatly reduced the number of federal actors with enforcement responsibilities for consumer law. Instead of responsibility for even a single given law scattered among several regulators, the Consumer Financial Protection Bureau (CFPB) and the Federal Trade Commission (FTC) are now the only major players at the federal level. Their authority is divided in two ways: the laws for which they are responsible and the market actors over whom they have jurisdiction.

The CFPB enforces "federal consumer law," a term defined to include the consumer protection aspects of seventeen different statutes.[1] The CFPB also has the power to take enforcement action against unfair, deceptive, and abusive acts and practices. 12 US.C. §5531. The FTC has enforcement powers under the Unfair and Deceptive Practices Act, 15 U.S.C. §45.

On some basic level, the CFPB has authority over financial services companies as to federal consumer law. Technically, it much more complicated. There are several relevant definitional terms. 12 U.S.C. §5481. The CFPB has authority over "covered persons" and "service providers" who offer or provide a "consumer financial product or service." The latter term incorporates a complex definition of "financial product or service. 12 U.S.C. §5481(15). Additionally, the CFPB can reach "related persons," who include, *inter alia*, directors, officers, employees, shareholders who have managerial responsibility or materially participate in the conduct of covered persons.

Consumer Financial Protection Bureau v. ITT Educational Services, Inc.

___ 123 F. Supp. 3d ___, 2015 WL 1013508 (S.D. Ind. Mar. 6, 2015)

BARKER, District Judge.

. . .

FACTUAL AND PROCEDURAL BACKGROUND

Plaintiff Consumer Financial Protection Bureau ("the Bureau"), a United States federal agency, has brought this suit against Defendant, alleging violations of provisions of the Consumer Financial Protection Act ("CFPA"), 12 U.S.C. §§5531(a), 5536(a), 5564(a), & 5565, the Truth in Lending Act ("TILA"), 15 U.S.C. §§1601 et seq., and regulations thereunder. Because this cause is before us on a motion to dismiss, we consider the facts as presented by the Bureau's Complaint.

---

1. The enumerated statutes are the Alternative Mortgage Transaction Parity Act, Consumer Leasing Act, Electronic Fund Transfer Act, Equal Credit Opportunity Act, Fair Credit Billing Act, Fair Credit Reporting Act, Homeowner's Protection Act, Fair Debt Collection Practices Act, Federal Deposit Insurance Act, Gramm-Leach-Bliley Act, Home Mortgage Disclosure Act, Home Ownership and Equity Protection Act, Real Estate Settlement Procedures Act, S.A.F.E. Mortgage Licensing, Truth in Lending Act, Truth in Savings Act, and the Interstate Land Sales Full Disclosure Act.

Defendant ITT Educational Services, Inc. ("ITT") is a publicly-traded, for-profit company offering post-secondary courses and degrees to students at more than 100 locations nationwide. Many of ITT's students and prospective students have limited financial means, and ITT therefore derives much of its revenue from federal aid, including loans, secured by the students. Some 80% of ITT's revenue, in fact, comes from aid granted under Title IV of the Higher Education Act of 1965, 20 U.S.C. §§1070 et seq. ("Title IV Aid"). However, a large number of students are still unable to afford full tuition to enroll at ITT even with federal assistance. To enable students to close this "tuition gap," ITT extended to many of them short-term, no-interest loans called "Temporary Credit." The Temporary Credit packages were offered to students at the beginning of an academic year, and payment was due nine months later, at the close of the school year.

ITT's Aggressive Tactics

The Bureau alleges that ITT employed the Temporary Credit loans as an "entry point" for "pushing" students into taking out private loans when the Temporary Credit came due and students were again unable fully to afford tuition for coming school terms. According to the Bureau, ITT misled students about the balance of costs and benefits associated with ITT enrollment—thus guiding them into an unmanageable financial predicament—in a number of ways.

In the first place, ITT represented to students through oral representations and advertisements that its programs greatly advanced an enrollee's career prospects and job placement rates; the Bureau alleges that these representations were exaggerated and were based on incomplete information. The Bureau utilized "mystery shoppers"—young men or women presenting themselves as prospective students—who reported that ITT staff made exaggerated claims about student success, such as that graduates with associates' degrees "usually make six figures." In contrast to these claims, ITT's annual disclosures in 2012 indicated that "reported annualized salaries initially following graduation averaged approximately $32,061 for the Employable Graduates in 2011."

The Bureau alleges that ITT also misleadingly represented to prospective students that its "national accreditation" placed it on par with other major educational institutions. In fact, while a "national" accreditation sounds authoritative, most non-profit colleges and universities are "regionally" accredited; such institutions accept transfer credits from for-profit schools like ITT only on a case-by-case basis. According to the Bureau, ITT not only created an inaccurate overall impression in this respect, but also misled some prospective students in a more specific way: one recruiter claimed that ITT had the same accreditation as "all other schools"; another falsely claimed that "ITT Tech is accredited by the Department of Defense."

Having given prospective students an inflated notion of the standing of the school and the career benefits derived from the degrees it bestowed, the Bureau alleges that ITT's recruiting staff engaged in heavy-handed methods to convince students to enroll. These methods included frequent phone calls and in-person multimedia presentations that mystery shoppers described as overwhelming in nature. Prospective students were encouraged to take an admission test that, in fact, was "virtually impossible to fail," but was used to give them the impression that the school had rigorous admissions standards and that their passing the test augured well for their prospects. Despite the volubility of the overall sales pitch, the Bureau maintains that ITT recruiters were instructed to be vague and evasive on the question of costs; they responded to applicants' questions by stating, "I cannot tell you what your exact cost will be," or by asking, "Do you want a discount education, or a valuable one that will give you a return in the future?"

Once students agreed to enroll, the Bureau alleges that ITT then switched gears, hurrying them through the enrollment and financial aid processes — so quickly that "many consumers did not know or did not understand what they signed up for." Specifically, ITT required enrollees to sign an Enrollment Agreement before they could receive any information about their financial aid options or meet with financial aid staff. Mystery shoppers reported being rushed through e-signatures of documents, including authorizations to request transcripts and credit check approvals without understanding the nature of the forms they were signing. . . .

Once students had completed an academic term at ITT, the time came for them to "repackage" their financial aid and loans for the next year. The Bureau alleges that ITT's financial aid staff employed aggressive tactics in seeking to repackage students, including tracking them down on campus, barring or pulling them from class, and enlisting the aid of other ITT staff such as professors. An ITT executive conceded that the school also used the threat of withholding course materials and transcripts as "leverage" to ensure that students would repackage. At both the initial and repackaging stages, ITT staff encouraged students to rely on school representatives in seeing them through the process, including the use of forms that automatically populated and required only the students' signatures at the conclusion of the process. An executive stated that ITT was "essentially holding [the students'] hands"; one mystery shopper stated that a financial aid coordinator told him that he would "get more free money that I don't have to pay back if I let them take care of my paperwork."

THE "PRIVATE LOANS"

The Bureau's claims against ITT focus on its assertion that, having knowingly cajoled and guided students into a financial predicament in which they were already heavily invested in an ITT degree yet lacked the financial resources to complete it — with the Temporary Credit expiring and financial aid insufficient to fully cover the "tuition gap" — ITT then persuaded continuing students to take out financially irresponsible "private loans" from third-party lenders. In the Bureau's words:

> ITT Financial Aid staff coerced students into taking out loans that they did not want, did not understand, or did not even realize they were getting. . . . ITT sought to have its students pay for the tuition gap with ostensible third-party loans because outside sources of payment could be booked as income to the company, improving its free cash flow and the appearance of its financial statements, and because outside sources of revenue helped ITT meet a requirement by the Department of Education that at least 10% of its revenue be derived from sources outside Title IV loans and grants.

One of the sources of the students' predicament was ITT's alleged failure to adequately disclose the nature of the nine-month Temporary Credit to new students. Students who received the Temporary Credit signed a "Cost Summary Payment

Addendum" (CSPA), which stated that the loan was to last for the length of an academic year and carry no interest. According to the Bureau, however, the CSPA's references to "new temporary credit" and "renewal of carryforward temporary credit" could mislead students into believing that renewal of the no-interest loan for future academic years was available. Some students believed that the Temporary Credit would be available until they graduated and a mystery shopper reported that she had been led to believe that future years' costs would be "covered under a new temporary credit and that I would owe no money out of pocket." One director of finance at an ITT location instructed staff to describe the Temporary Credit as "funding" rather than as a loan that would have to be repaid. ITT was aware that many or most students lacked the ability to repay the Temporary Credit, and it characterized them as "doubtful accounts" on its balance sheets.

The Bureau alleges that, beginning in 2008, ITT constructed [a] "private loan" program as a vehicle for students to discharge the Temporary Credit: continuing students would use the cash they received from the new loans to pay off their debt to ITT and thus remove the "doubtful accounts" from ITT's balance sheets. . . . The Complaint asserts that ITT was heavily involved in the creation of the SCUC program: developing its underwriting criteria, providing a credit facility, paying the credit union membership fees in the lead credit union on behalf of the students taking out the SCUC loans, and providing the SCUC loan originators with a stop-loss guarantee that it would make them whole for losses if defaults on the loans exceeded 35%. ITT was the "sole intermediary" between SCUC and its students; funds were disbursed through ITT to the student, and could be used only to pay ITT for tuition and not for any other purpose. Additionally, eligibility criteria for the loans were tailored such that, if students had received Temporary Credit, they were automatically eligible for an ITT private loan.

The loans granted under the SCUC program carried a 10-year term. For students with credit scores below 600, the interest rate after April 2011 was 13% plus prime — or 16.25% — in addition to a 10% origination fee. Nearly half of the students taking SCUC loans fell into this low-credit-score cohort. These rates are drastically higher than those available under federal Stafford loans, whose rates since 2009 have ranged from 3.4% for subsidized borrowers to 6.8% for unsubsidized borrowers. Despite their exacting terms, some 79% of the SCUC loans issued went to continuing ITT students who had previously received Temporary Credit in their first year at ITT. As of May 2011, ITT's consultant for loan default analysis projected a gross default rate of 61.3% for the existing SCUC loans.

Crucially, the Bureau alleges that these "private" loans, though nominally originated by third-party lenders, were the brainchild of ITT and that ITT consciously steered economically distressed students, faced with indebtedness upon the expiration of the Temporary Credit, into the SCUC loans. ITT executives, in quarterly earnings calls with investors and analysts, stated that the ITT private loan program was a vehicle for taking the Temporary Credit off of ITT's balance sheets. . . .

According to the Bureau, many students did not migrate from the Temporary Credit to the "private loans" with eyes fully open: some accepted the new loans in reliance upon ITT's acting in their interests, while others did not realize they had incurred a new type of debt because of the "rushed and automated manner" in which ITT financial staff processed the students' paperwork.

For those students who had Temporary Credit debt at the close of their first year at ITT but who did not take out "private loans," ITT offered them an incentive to pay off the debt in a lump sum upon graduation — in the form of a 25% discount. For those students who were unable to pay off the Temporary Credit debt in a lump sum, ITT offered a "temporary credit installment plan" involving monthly payments that ranged, depending on the total amount owed, from six months to more than six years. According to the Bureau, the paperwork students were given upon enrolling in the installment plan did not disclose this forgone 25% discount as constituting a "finance charge."

· · ·

DISCUSSION

This suit arises primarily under the Consumer Financial Protection Act (CFPA), the Bureau's organic statute. Congress enacted the CFPA as Title X of the "Dodd–Frank Act" of 2010, with the stated purpose of "ensuring that the federal consumer financial laws are enforced consistently so that consumers may access markets for financial products, and so that these markets are fair, transparent, and competitive." 12 U.S.C. §5511(a). Counts One through Three of the Complaint allege that ITT engaged in "unfair" and "abusive" acts or practices, in violation of the CFPA's operative provisions, 12 U.S.C. §§5531(c)(1), 5531(d)(2)(B) & 5531(d)(2)(C). The Bureau further alleges in Count Four that ITT's nondisclosure of a finance charge violated the Truth in Lending Act (TILA), 15 U.S.C. §§1601 et seq., and its implementing Regulation Z, 12 C.F.R. §1026.17.

ITT seeks dismissal on three broad grounds. First, it contends that the Bureau lacks standing to bring this suit because it is an unconstitutional entity and the CFPA's prohibitions violate the due process clause. Second, ITT urges that the complaint fails to state a claim because ITT is not a covered entity subject to its provisions. Lastly, ITT argues that all four counts fail on their merits. We address these bases of ITT's motion in turn.

I. Constitutionality of the CFPA

A. Removal Power and the "Take Care" Clause

ITT argues that the CFPA violates the constitutional separation of powers by unduly restricting the President's authority to remove the Bureau's Director if he "loses confidence in the intelligence, ability, judgment, or loyalty" of that officer. Because the Bureau is an unconstitutional entity and thus lacks standing, ITT urges that the suit must be dismissed in its entirety for the absence of a judiciable case or controversy. To explain ITT's misreading of the constitutional protections afforded the President's power to remove officials like the Director of the Bureau, it is necessary to review the evolution of the doctrine.

· · ·

ITT first argues that, because "the limitations on removal here are far more restrictive than a 'good cause' provision," the CFPA runs afoul of *Free Enterprise*

Fund's dictum that "the President cannot 'take care that the Laws be faithfully executed' if he cannot oversee the faithfulness of the officers who execute them." Free Enter. Fund, 561 U.S. at 484. In fact, however, the CFPA specifies precisely the same grounds for removal as the archetypal "for cause" provision approved by the Court in *Humphrey's Executor*: the President may remove the Bureau's director only for "inefficiency, neglect of duty, or malfeasance in office." 12 U.S.C. §5491(c)(3). Compare with 15 U.S.C. §41 ("Any Commissioner may be removed by the President for inefficiency, neglect of duty, or malfeasance in office.").

ITT's notion that the degree of insulation from executive oversight afforded the Bureau's Director is explicitly proscribed by precedent therefore lacks merit. The Director is responsible directly to the President, without the additional layer of screening the Court found problematic in the structure of the Public Company Accounting Oversight Board. Cf. Free Enterprise Fund, 561 U.S. at 507 (distinguishing circumstances where "the President has . . . authority to initiate a Board member's removal for cause"). The CFPA's structure is thus unconstitutional only if the authority wielded by the Bureau exceeds the bounds recognized by *Humphrey's Executor* and *Morrison*.

Here, there is no doubt that the Bureau partakes of some of the quasi-legislative and quasi-judicial functions that characterize an independent regulatory agency. It is invested with the authority to engage in rulemaking to further implement Congress's enactments on the subject of consumer financial protection, and its regulatory powers include administrative adjudication. 12 U.S.C. §§5511, 5562–5565. Cf. Humphrey's Executor, 295 U.S. at 628 (noting that the FTC "is an administrative body created by Congress to carry into effect legislative policies embodied in the statute"); Buckley v. Valeo, 424 U.S. 1, 140-141 (1976) (noting that the "administrative" functions performed by the Federal Election Commission are "of kinds usually performed by independent regulatory agencies"). The Bureau also undoubtedly wields paradigmatic "executive" powers—notably the authority to bring suit on behalf of the United States—but we find no basis for concluding that the Director's powers are so great that the inability to remove him or her at whim fatally undermines the President's constitutional prerogatives.

While it is true that the Bureau does not operate only for a fixed time like a Department of Justice independent counsel, cf. Morrison, 487 U.S. at 672 ("[T]he office of the independent counsel is 'temporary' in the sense that an independent counsel is appointed essentially to accomplish a single task . . ."), its enforcement powers are constrained within the subject-matter of its organic statute. ITT objects specifically to CFPA's grant of litigating authority, arguing that the Bureau has "broad jurisdiction and significant power over numerous industries," and that "without meaningful Presidential control over the Director, the Director could initiate suits advancing his—and not the President's—views on the proper construction of federal laws." But courts have long and consistently upheld the endowment of regulatory agencies with law enforcement powers against constitutional challenge. See Bowsher v. Synar, 478 U.S. 714 (1986) (implicitly affirming the proposition that "officers of the United States" other than the President and Attorney General, such as FTC commissioners, may engage in the enforcement of federal law). This is true of the Securities and Exchange Commission, whose commissioners are subject to removal only for cause and which enjoys broad enforcement powers over publicly traded companies.

See SEC v. Blinder, Robinson, & Co., Inc., 855 F.2d 677, 682 (10th Cir. 1988) (upholding the SEC's constitutionality). . . .

We therefore reject ITT's argument that the Supreme Court's established removal power jurisprudence forecloses the for-cause removal protections of the Bureau's Director.

3. ITT's Alternate Grounds of Unconstitutionality

In its reply brief, ITT shifts gears. Rather than contending that the Bureau runs afoul of any particular precedent, it asserts that no federal entity has heretofore "combine[d] the Bureau's panoply of problematic features" — including the length of the Director's tenure, 12 U.S.C. §5491(c)(3); for-cause removal of the Director, id. at §5491(c)(3); the fact that the Bureau's authority is concentrated in a single director rather than a multi-member commission, id. at §5491(b)(1); its "unconstitutionally appointed" Deputy Director, id. at §5491(b)(5); its "immunity from the congressional appropriations process," id. at §5497(a)(2)(C); and its "unprecedented restrictions on judicial review," id. at §§5512(b)(4)(B), 5513(a), 5513(c)(3)(B)(ii), & 5513(c)(8); among other ostensibly problematic features.

There are at least two problems with ITT's "mosaic" theory of the Bureau's unconstitutionality. First, ITT never offers a convincing basis for the conclusion that many of these features of the CFPA contribute, even in a piecemeal sense, to the Bureau's unconstitutionality. Second, its generalized assault on the "unprecedented" nature of the Bureau proceeds from the mistaken premise that that which is not specifically approved by precedent is forbidden.

ITT notes, for instance, that the CFPA empowers the Director to delegate any or all of his powers to any "duly authorized employee, representative, or agent." 12 U.S.C. §5492(b). . . . We have difficulty extracting from this language any notion that the Constitution is offended by allowing a presidential appointee to delegate some of her own authority to her subordinates; such delegation is a commonplace and unavoidable feature of any large institution. See, e.g., 21 U.S.C. §871(a) (permitting the Attorney General to "delegate any of his functions [under the Controlled Substances Act] to any officer or employee of the Department of Justice"). . . .

Turning to the Bureau's funding, ITT complains that the "Director may unilaterally claim up to 12% of the Federal Reserve's budget . . . without Congress's approval." 12 U.S.C. §5497(a). According to ITT, this "immunity from the Congressional appropriations process" further contributes to the Bureau's unconstitutionality. ITT overstates the degree of the Bureau's insulation from congressional control; more to the point, it neglects to explain how the Bureau's source of funding implicates constitutional concerns. The CFPA does indeed restrict the House and Senate Appropriations Committees from reviewing the Bureau's primary funding source, see 12 U.S.C. §5497(a)(2)(C), but it does not strip Congress as a whole of its power to modify appropriations as it sees fit. As the Bureau has pointed out, the Constitution does not prohibit Congress from enacting funding structures for agencies that differ from the procedures prescribed by the ordinary appropriations process. . . . ITT's conclusory assertion that the CFPA's funding structure violates the Origination Clause, U.S. Const. Art. I, §7, cl. 1, is therefore without merit.

Lastly, ITT argues, in a footnote, that the "CFPA . . . limits judicial oversight in ways that are relevant to separation of powers analysis." ITT cites three statutory provisions in support of this point. Two of them, 12 U.S.C. §5513(a) and 12 U.S.C. §5513(c)(3)(B)(ii), have nothing to do with judicial review. The third cited provision does concern judicial review, stating that "the deference that a court affords the Bureau with respect to a determination by the Bureau regarding the meaning of interpretation of any provision of a Federal consumer law shall be applied as if the Bureau were the only agency authorized to apply, enforce, interpret, or administer the provisions of such Federal consumer financial law." 12 U.S.C. §5512(b)(4)(B). This merely prescribes that the Bureau's constructions of organic law in its subject area are to be given deference, in accordance with the well-established principles first enunciated in *Chevron U.S.A., Inc. v. Natural Resources Defense Council, Inc.*, 467 U.S. 837 (1984). ITT has not succeeded in identifying anything remotely problematic about the CFPA's provision for judicial review of the Bureau's decisions.

Regardless of the groundlessness of its individualized objections to the Bureau's statutory features, ITT's argument in reply proceeds from a flawed premise. The CFPA is undoubtedly new — and its combination of features thus, in some sense, "unprecedented." Its constitutionality has not yet been subject to authoritative review by the Supreme Court or by any of the Courts of Appeals. . . .

Apart from two law review articles and an opinion piece in the *Wall Street Journal*, ITT cites no authority for its theory that the Bureau's amalgamated features render it unconstitutional. Rather, it appears to argue that, because precedent does not explicitly sanction the Bureau's structure and range of powers — which ITT asserts constitute "a gross departure from longstanding practice" — the CFPA exceeds constitutional bounds. This inverts the premise from which we must start in exercising judicial review over Congress: the presumption of constitutionality. Morrison, 529 U.S. at 607. . . . ITT thus bears a considerable burden in arguing that, though none of the CFPA's features is itself expressly unconstitutional, the statute as a whole nonetheless runs afoul of the separation of powers. . . . As we have already noted, we believe that the structure and powers of the Bureau are sufficiently analogous to those of the FTC, SEC, and other regulatory agencies that the question of the constitutionality of the CFPA's removal provision is settled. . . .

II. Whether ITT Is a "Covered Entity"

ITT argues that Counts One, Two, and Three of the Complaint fail to state a claim because ITT is not a covered entity subject to suit under the CFPA. We conclude that, taking the Bureau's factual allegations as true, the pleadings place ITT within the statute's purview.

The operative provisions under which the Bureau has sued ITT apply only to a "covered person" or "service provider." 12 U.S.C. §5536(a)(1). The Act defines a "covered person," in turn, as "any person that engages in offering or providing a consumer financial product or service." 12 U.S.C. §5481(6)(A). A "product or service," as the phrase implies, is more than simply the direct extension of a loan to a consumer: it may include "brokering" or servicing loans, 12 U.S.C. §5481(15)(A)(i), as well as "providing financial advisory services . . . to consumers on individual financial matters." Id. at §5481(15)(A)(viii). The CFPA defines a "service provider," on the other hand, as one who "provides a material service to a covered person in connection with" the covered person's offering of a "consumer financial product." Id. at §5481(26)(A). Such material service may include participating in "designing, operating, or maintaining the consumer financial product or service," or processing "transactions relating to the consumer financial product or service." Id.

. . .

The Bureau has, however, sufficiently stated a claim that ITT engaged in conduct qualifying as the provision of "financial advisory services." The Act specifies that such advisory services include, without limitation, "providing credit counseling to any consumer" and "providing services to assist a consumer with debt management or debt settlement, modifying the terms of any extension of credit, or avoiding foreclosure." 12 U.S.C. §5481(15)(A)(viii). The Complaint includes allegations that ITT advised students on how to manage their debt to the school after having taken out Temporary Credit; this advice often channeled the students into the private loan programs. According to the Bureau, ITT completed nearly every step in the process of acquiring CUSO loans on the students' behalf, including filling out the requisite forms (save signatures) and forwarding them to the lending credit union. At a minimum, we conclude that such conduct, if proven, would fall within the realm of "credit counseling" and "assist[ing] a consumer with debt management."

. . .

ITT offers another, related argument against interpreting the CFPA's "financial advisory services" to include its interactions with its students. "Congress," it reminds us, does not "hide elephants in mouseholes." Whitman v. Am. Trucking Ass'ns, 531 U.S. 457, 468 (2001). Including an educational institution like ITT within the ambit of entities liable under the statute for providing financial advisory services is such a significant step, ITT insists, that Congress could hardly have taken it without more explicitly saying so. In American Bar Association v. F.T.C., 430 F.3d 457 (D.C. Cir. 2005), which ITT cites in support of its argument, the D.C. Circuit rejected the FTC's attempt to regulate a law firm as a "financial institution." There, the FTC had supported its expansive reading by pointing to the statute's broad definition of a financial institution as "any institution the business of which is engaging in financial activities," and by noting the same lengthy list of permissible non-banking activities for "financial institutions" that we have already discussed above. 430 F.3d at 467. The court ruled that the statutory framework governing financial institutions, including Congress's definition of the term, contained insufficient ambiguity to warrant deference to the agency's attempt to cram a "rather large elephant in a rather obscure mousehole." Id. at 469.

While we do not question the wisdom of the D.C. Circuit's decision in American Bar Association, we find it distinguishable. The Consumer Financial Protection Act is aptly named: Congress stated that its purpose is to ensure "that markets for consumer financial products and services are fair, transparent, and competitive." 12 U.S.C. §5511. As we have already discussed, the statute does not restrict its regulatory reach to "financial institutions." See 12 U.S.C. §§5536, 5481. In the absence of any indication that holding educational institutions — or law firms, for that matter — liable for unfairness to consumers is contrary to the statute's goals, we see no reason to circumscribe what Congress has spoken broadly. While it may be an unacceptably dramatic conceptual leap to label a law firm as a "financial institution," it is hardly a leap at all to say that a school offers "financial advisory services" to its students — particularly on the facts alleged here.

ITT also qualifies as a "service provider" under the CFPA. As we have previously noted, the statute extends its reach to any entity that "provides a material service to a covered person in connection with" the covered person's offering of a "consumer financial product." A "material service" may include participating in the "designing, operating, or maintaining" of the consumer financial product or service in question. See 12 U.S.C. §5481(26)(A)(i).

ITT does not dispute that the third-party originators of the SCUC "private loans" were "covered persons" based on the Bureau's allegations. See 12 U.S.C. §§5481(5), 5481(6). . . . The Complaint alleges that ITT used Temporary Credit as a tool to pre-qualify students for the private loans, that ITT developed the loans' underwriting criteria, that it paid the credit union membership fees in the lead credit union on behalf of the students who took out the loans, and that it provided a stop-loss guarantee to the programs' lenders — covering any losses from defaults exceeding 35% of participating students. These allegations are more than "unsupported generalities" — as ITT calls them — and they suffice to meet the Bureau's burden at this stage of the litigation. Cf. Ashcroft v. Iqbal, 556 U.S. 662, 678 (2009).

· · ·

IV. Count Four: Violation of the Truth in Lending Act

"Regulation Z," promulgated by the Federal Reserve Board in implementation of the Truth in Lending Act, 15 U.S.C. §1601 et seq., requires the disclosure of certain "finance charges," as defined by the Act, in writing before the consummation of the transaction giving rise to the charges. 12 C.F.R. §§1026.17, 18(d). See also 15 U.S.C. §1605(a) (defining "finance charge"). The Bureau alleges that the discount ITT offered students who paid off their Temporary Credit balances in a lump sum constituted a finance charge, and that ITT's failure to disclose the charge violated TILA and Regulation Z. We do not reach the merits of the claim, because we agree with ITT that Count Four is barred by the applicable statute of limitations.

ITT contends that this claim is governed by the section of TILA governing "civil liability," which provides that "any action under this section may be brought in any United States district court, or in any other court of competent jurisdiction, within one year from the date of the occurrence of the violation." 15 U.S.C. §1640(e). Because the Complaint was filed on February 26, 2014 — well more than one year after the conduct described in the allegations occurred — ITT asserts that this action lies outside the limitations period.

The Bureau counters that its claim in Count Four is governed not by TILA's civil liability provision, but by 15 U.S.C. §1607, the section of the statute which grants the Bureau — together with several other federal agencies — power to "enforce[e] compliance with any requirement imposed" by the Act. 15 U.S.C. §1607(a)(6). Enforcement actions brought under 15 U.S.C. §1607 are not subject to the one-year statute of limitations imposed by Section 1640. See Fed. Reserve Bd. Consumer Compliance Handbook, Regulation Z, at 57. See also Household Credit Servs., Inc. v. Pfennig, 541 U.S. 232, 238 (2004) (noting that the Federal Reserve Board and its staff have been designated by Congress as the primary source for interpretation and application of TILA).

We disagree with the Bureau's interpretation of the distinction between the two statutory provisions. First, we see no persuasive evidence that 15 U.S.C. §1640 governs only private civil actions. The provision itself does not exclude actions in which a government agency is the plaintiff, and in fact it explicitly recognizes the possibility of intervention by federal agencies in civil suits initiated by private parties. 15 U.S.C. §1640(e)(1). Second, agency interpretations support the conclusion that the agency enforcement powers contemplated by Section 1607 are administrative in nature, and are separate from any authorization to file civil suits. . . . [T]he Federal Reserve's interpretive manual for Regulation Z states that "regulatory administrative enforcement actions . . . are not subject to the one-year statute of limitations." Fed. Reserve Board Consumer Compliance Handbook, Regulation Z at 57 (Nov. 2013). . . .

Here, Congress demonstrated its "concern that a creditor not face limitless liability in terms of time" by setting a one-year statute of limitations for the filing of civil suits under TILA. Consol. Bank, N.A., Hialeah, Fla. v. U.S. Dep't of Treasury, Office of Comptroller of Currency, 118 F.3d 1461, 1467 (11th Cir. 1997). When the government chooses to enforce the Act by filing a civil suit rather than resorting to the administrative actions under its power, we see no reason why the same congressional concerns should not apply — indeed, they may apply with still greater force. . . . [W]e decline to read an exception for agency plaintiffs into the one-year statute of limitations imposed by TILA's civil liability provision. We therefore dismiss Count Four as time-barred. . . .

The FTC regulates a much broader swath of businesses, including those selling non-financial products and services. Remember, for example, that the FTC brought an action against Kraft for false advertising of its cheese slices. The FTC also has authority over auto-dealers, carved out from the reach of the CFPB. An example may help illustrate the division of labor, and potential overlap, between the CFPB and the FTC. If a company advertises and sells identity-theft monitoring, they are within the purview of the FTC because they are engaged in interstate commerce. The CFPB would not have jurisdiction because the identity theft company is not selling a consumer financial product or service. If the identity theft monitoring company also offered credit report error correction, however, then it would be a "covered person" or a "service provider" subject to the CFPB's enforcement process. Many mobile payments companies, which think of themselves as Silicon Valley tech startups, were surprised to learn that the CFPB had jurisdiction over them under laws such as the Electronic Funds Transfer Act. Because these companies are not financial institutions, they were not subject to examination and supervision by prudential regulators such as the Federal Reserve, FDIC, or state banking authorities. The FTC and the CFPB are required to coordinate enforcement, including providing notice before action is taken. 12 U.S.C. §5514(c)(3).

The CFPB has authority to use a wide variety of public enforcement tools. It may seek any appropriate legal or equitable relief, including:

(A)   rescission or reformation of contracts;
(B)   refund of moneys or return of real property;
(C)   restitution;
(D)   disgorgement or compensation for unjust enrichment;

(E)   payment of damages or other monetary relief;

(F)   public notification regarding the violation, including the costs of notification;

(G)   limits on the activities or functions of the person; and

(H)   civil money penalties, as set forth more fully in subsection (c).

12 U.S.C. §5565(a)(2). The CFPB cannot, however, pursue exemplary or punitive damages. 12 U.S.C. §5565(a)(3). The civil penalties for violating a law, rule, or final order or condition imposed in writing by the CFPB may not exceed $5,000 for each day during which such violation or failure to pay continues but can go as high as $25,000 for reckless acts and, $1,000,000 for knowing acts. The CFPB can file suit in federal court but it also has the authority to set up an administrative tribunal and to bring cases before its own administrative law judge.

In its first years, the CFPB has brought dozens of actions, including against some of the largest players in the financial service industry. It also has sued smaller companies such as debt settlement organization or debt collectors. While it initially relied on unfair or deceptive authority, the CFPB now alleges abusive conduct in its complaints. It has focused heavily on fines and restitution in its complaints, giving companies a fresh taste of what Senator Magnuson (yes, the namesake of the Magnuson-Moss Warranty Act) called the "Robin Hood method: a combination penalty-restitution — taking the profits away from the swindlers and returning them to the cheated consumers." Warren Magnuson, *The Dark Side of the Marketplace* 71-72 (1968).

Because it is a Commission, the FTC requires consensus before it can take an enforcement action. The FTC is required to consider the public interest in deciding whether to challenge a practice as unfair or deceptive. 15 U.S.C. §45(5)(b); see also 15 U.S.C. §45(n) (allowing the FTC to consider "established public policies as evidence," but not as its primary basis for a determination) that a practice is unfair. The FTC can issue cease and desist orders, which if violated, can allow it to file a civil suit to recover penalties of $10,000 per violation. 15 U.S.C. §45(m)(1).

For decades, there has been a vigorous debate about whether regulators are engaged in over- or under-enforcement of consumer law. One study created a "Shadow FTC" of those with prior employment experience at the FTC or as commissioners and asked it to evaluate cases brought under the state consumer protection acts by either states attorneys general or private litigants. The Shadow FTC believed that only 22 percent of the case scenarios described illegal practices, although litigation was brought in all the case scenarios. This suggests that the FTC may hold itself to a very high standard in deciding to bring an enforcement action as compared to states attorneys general or private litigants. Henry N. Butler & Joshua D. Wright, *Are State Consumer Protection Acts Really Little-FTC Acts?* 63 Fla. L. Rev. 163 (2011). The critiques of the study were fierce, however, noting that there was little transparency in the methodology. *See, e.g.,* Dee Pridgen, *Wrecking Ball Disguised as Law Reform: ALEC's Model Act on Private Enforcement of Consumer Protection Statutes*, 39 N.Y.U. Rev. of Law & Soc. Change 279, 292-293 (2015). States also may be more responsive to local or regional concerns and be more nimble; the FTC's national focus and commission structure may hamper it.

Both the CFPB and the FTC share enforcement authority over their rules with state attorneys general. The CAN-SPAM Act, which sets rules for email that advertises or promotes commercial products or services is illustrative of overlapping enforcement authority. It provides that compliance shall be enforced by a laundry list of regulators, including the Office of the Comptroller of the Currency for national banks, the Federal Reserve for member banks (other than national banks), the FDIC for banks insured by it (other than banks that are members of the Federal Reserve System), the Securities and Exchange Commission with respect to any broker or dealer, state insurance authorities, the Secretary of Transportation for air carriers, and the Federal Communication Commission for anyone under its authority. 15 U.S.C. §7706(b). It also authorizes an attorney general, or an official or agency of a state, that has "reason to believe that an interest of the residents of that State has been or is threatened or adversely affected" by a violation to bring a civil action on behalf of residents of the state in U.S. district court. 15 U.S.C. §7706(f). The benefit of this kind of approach is that there are many "cops on the beat" with regard to the law. One drawback, however, is that the agencies may defer to each other or fail to communicate. Another problem is that it is difficult for any agency to develop expertise in a law — and produce coherent policy — when authority is scattered.

B. State Attorneys General

The roots of the office of state attorney general run deep in American jurisprudence. All thirteen American colonies had an attorney general and today all fifty states have an office of state attorney general. Although each state has its own constitution and statutes, laws and traditions bring remarkable similarity to the roles of state attorneys general. Unlike private and other government lawyers, who work in areas of narrow jurisdiction subject to ethical rules that defer decision making to clients, state attorneys general have significant discretion in their advice and litigation decisions. They possess extraordinarily broad jurisdiction. Precisely because of their broad legal powers, state attorneys general operate within shifting budgetary, political, and ethical parameters. Within those parameters, state attorneys general have considerable autonomy to choose which issues to pursue in the name of the public's interest.

The doctrine of "parens patriae" underlies much of the jurisdiction and culture of state attorneys general. This doctrine originated in English common law to permit the king to protect and act for minors or incompetents — those who could not protect themselves. Attorneys general have the duty to represent all the citizens of a state and not just the interests of a client. But "[i]t is a short step from the state's assertion of its own damages to assertion of claims on behalf of its citizens for damages arising from the same torts." Jack Ratliff, *Parens Patriae: An Overview*, 74 TULANE L. REV. 1847 (2000). Parens patriae is often specifically alleged in consumer protection litigation, and in a broad sense it describes the "fix it" culture that pervades attorneys general practice.

Most state UDAP statutes give the attorney general broad remedial authority to protect the public against deceptive or unfair conduct. An attorney general may seek injunctive relief, which can be useful even if the defendant has gone out of business or changed its business because it serves as a warning to other entities with similar business models. In most states, the attorney general also can seek civil penalties and the recovery of the costs of its investigation. Increasingly, attorneys general seek restitution for injured consumers, rather than the more traditional public relief discussed above.

The largest consumer protection action by state attorneys general is the $25 billion national mortgage settlement, which was signed in February 2012 by 49 state attorneys general and the five largest mortgage servicers. The relief included hundreds of specific practices to be reformed or adopted, promises to provide loan modifications to homeowners facing foreclosure that equaled billions of dollars, and cash payments of civil fines to each state. The settlement was controversial for its size, for its imposition of an "independent" monitor (paid for by the settling banks, however), and for its implementation. This headline reveals one critique. Shaila Dewan, *Needy States Use Housing Aid Cash to Plug Budget,* N.Y. TIMES (May 15, 2012) (noting that only half of states devoted all their funds to housing programs and that some states sent millions straight to their general funds). The settlement also raised the issue of the degree to which it is appropriate to use litigation to prospectively change conduct. "While there are no neat dividing lines dictating or allocating permissible regulatory and enforcement powers between government branches," regulating prospectively through large monetary settlements may "circumvent traditional law making through the legislature and often fail to satisfy basic due process concerns such as notice, participation, and adequate representation." Elizabeth Chamblee Burch, *Revisiting the Government as Plaintiff,* 5 J. OF TORT L. 227, 228 (2014).

In obtaining such broad relief, attorneys general may deliver "corrective justice" to harmed consumers. While that may sound like a nice thing, scholars have noted that the theory of corrective justice is "inherently retrospective, intrapersonal and incremental." Adam Zimmerman, *The Corrective Justice State,* 5 J. OF TORT L. 189 (2014). Public law, by contrast, is supposed to promote the public interest in a prospective, general, and comprehensive way. As attorneys general have pursued broader remedies, some have complained that these suits lack procedural protections. *See, e.g.,* Margaret Lemos, *Aggregate Litigation Goes Public: Representative Suits by State Attorneys General,* 126 Harv. L. Rev. 486 (2012).

West Virginia v. CVS Pharmacy, Inc.

646 F.3d 169 (4th Cir. 2011)

NIEMEYER, Circuit Judge.

The State of West Virginia, by its Attorney General, commenced this action in state court against CVS Pharmacy, Inc., and five other pharmacies (collectively, the "Pharmacies"), alleging that the Pharmacies sold generic drugs to West Virginia consumers without passing along to the consumers the cost savings of generic drugs over brand name equivalents, in violation of West Virginia Code §30-5-12b(g), regulating the practice of pharmacy, and the West Virginia Consumer Credit Protection Act, prohibiting "unfair or deceptive acts or practices in the conduct of any trade or commerce," West Virginia Code §46A-6-104, and "excess charges," id. §46A-7-111. The State, claiming to act in its "sovereign and quasi-sovereign capacity," seeks injunctive relief, restitution and disgorgement of "overcharges," recovery on behalf of the consumers of "excess charges," civil penalties, interest, costs, and attorneys' fees.

The Pharmacies removed the action from state court to the district court under the Class Action Fairness Act of 2005 ("CAFA"), Pub. L. No. 109-2, 119 Stat. 4 (2005), arguing that the action is a "disguised class action" and therefore was subject to removal under CAFA.

On the State's motion, the district court ordered that the action be remanded to state court, holding that the action was not a "class action" under CAFA, but rather a "classic parens patriae action" intended to vindicate the State's quasi-sovereign interests and the individual interests of its citizens.

. . .

Attorney General Darrell McGraw commenced this action in the Circuit Court of Boone County, West Virginia, naming as defendants CVS Pharmacy, Inc., Kmart Holding Corporation, the Kroger Company, Wal-Mart Stores Inc., Walgreen Co., and Target Stores, Inc., and alleging that in filling drug prescriptions, these Pharmacies overcharged West Virginia citizens, in violation of two laws, West Virginia Code §30-5-12b (the "Pharmacy Act") and West Virginia Code §§46A-6-104 and 46A-7-111 (the West Virginia Consumer Credit Protection Act or "WVCCPA"), and thereby obtained unjust profits.

The Pharmacy Act requires pharmacists to fill prescriptions with generic drugs, when appropriate, and to pass on to the consumer the savings in the cost of the generic drugs. Thus, when a pharmacy acquires a brand name drug at $30 and a generic equivalent at $10, the pharmacy must pass on at least the $20 difference to the consumer. See W. Va. Code §30-5-12b(g). But it must also pass on any other savings, such as the savings represented by the difference in the retail prices. See id. The Attorney General contends that violations of the Pharmacy Act also constitute violations of the WVCCPA, which prohibits "unfair or deceptive" trade practices and the collection of "excess charges." See W. Va. Code §§46A-6-104, 46A-7-111.

As authorized by these Acts, the West Virginia Attorney General is, in this action, seeking a temporary and permanent injunction against further violations of the Acts; "[e]quitable relief, including but not limited to restitution and disgorgement of monies obtained as a result of the overcharges"; repayment of the "excess charges" to affected consumers; civil penalties of up to $5,000 for each willful violation of the WVCCPA; pre-judgment and post-judgment interest; and costs including legal fees. The State alleges that it is pursuing these remedies "in its sovereign and quasi-sovereign capacity."

The Pharmacies removed the action to federal court, relying on several distinct grounds for doing so, including CAFA. To justify removal under CAFA, the Pharmacies asserted that because the "complaint [was] a disguised class action" designed "to recover funds on behalf of those consumers who have allegedly paid overcharges," it was a removable class action. In particular, they pointed to Count III, which is dedicated to the remedy of collecting, on behalf of consumers, excess charges under West Virginia Code §46A-7-111(1). That section provides that if "an excess charge has been made, the court shall order the [defendant] to refund to the consumer the amount of the excess charge." Id. Noting the large number of consumers in West Virginia and prescriptions filled for them, the Pharmacies argued that Count III met CAFA's numerosity and amount-in-controversy requirements. Because the Pharmacies are not West Virginia citizens, they also argued that minimal diversity was satisfied. Finally, because the Attorney General was seeking refunds on behalf of each affected West Virginia purchaser of generic drugs, the Pharmacies contended that the action was a representational proceeding, qualifying as a "class action" under CAFA.

The district court granted the State's motion to remand, rejecting each of the various grounds relied on for removal. With respect to the CAFA ground, which is the only issue on appeal, the court concluded that this action was "a classic parens patriae action that is neither a class action nor a mass action contemplated by CAFA." West Virginia ex rel. McGraw v. CVS Pharmacy, Inc., 748 F. Supp. 2d 580 (S.D. W. Va. Sept. 21, 2010). In concluding that this action was a parens patriae action, the district court noted that the WVCCPA authorized the Attorney General to act "as an administrator of the law," independently of individual consumer complaints. Id. at *36-37 (quoting Manchin v. Browning, 296 S.E.2d 909, 919 (W. Va. 1982)); see also id. at *42 (observing that the Attorney General is charged with "a freestanding consumer-protection duty"). The district court also noted that the State's action was "imbued with a 'disgorgement' purpose," "separate and apart from the interests of particular consumers in obtaining recompense." Id. at *38-39. In this sense, the court explained, "the Attorney General's paramount goal [was] to extract from the alleged wrongdoers every penny associated with the excess charges, along with civil penalties flowing to the State alone," thereby "warning . . . future violators that they [would] not long profit from consumer fraud." Id. at *39-40. . . .

In arguing that the district court erred in concluding that this action was not removable as a class action under CAFA, the Pharmacies acknowledge that the Attorney General did not purport to bring his action as a class action but rather relied on his authority under the Pharmacy Act and the WVCCPA. But the Pharmacies argue:

> It is well-settled that "in determining whether there is jurisdiction, federal courts look to the substance of the action and not only at the labels that the parties may attach."
>
> . . .
>
> Thus, the AG may not plead around federal jurisdiction merely by labeling his claims as brought in the state's sovereign or quasi-sovereign capacity.
>
> . . .
>
> Instead, this Court must consider whether, in substance, the Amended Complaint satisfies CAFA's requirements for a "class action." That analysis makes clear this case is properly removed as a CAFA class action, and that the district court erred by remanding it.

(Quoting Louisiana ex rel. Caldwell v. Allstate Ins. Co., 536 F.3d 418, 424 (5th Cir. 2008)). After asserting that the requirements for minimal diversity, the jurisdictional amount, and numerosity were in fact satisfied, the Pharmacies assert, as they must, that the state statutes on which the Attorney General relied were "similar" to

Federal Rule of Civil Procedure 23. They explain that the statutes are "similar" because, in particular, the WVCCPA allows the Attorney General "to represent in a single action thousands of consumers who all suffer a similar injury—excess charges." "That similarity alone," they argue, "is enough to satisfy federal removal jurisdiction.

To determine whether the Pharmacies' position is sustainable requires a straightforward statutory analysis of CAFA.

CAFA authorizes the removal of any civil action which is a class action in which (1) "the matter in controversy exceeds the sum or value of $5,000,000, exclusive of interest and costs," 28 U.S.C. §1332(d)(2); (2) "any member of a class of plaintiffs is a citizen of a State different from any defendant," id. §1332(d)(2)(A); and (3) there are 100 or more plaintiff class members, id. §1332(d)(5)(B). And it defines "class action" to mean "any civil action filed under rule 23 of the Federal Rules of Civil Procedure or similar State statute or rule of judicial procedure authorizing an action to be brought by 1 or more representative persons as a class action." Id. §1332(d)(1)(B).

Inasmuch as West Virginia's action was commenced in state court, it was obviously not commenced under Federal Rule of Civil Procedure 23. Thus, it would be removable only if it were filed under a "*similar* State statute or rule of judicial procedure authorizing an action to be brought by 1 or more representative persons as a class action." 28 U.S.C. §1332(d)(1)(B) (emphasis added).

A state statute or rule is "similar" to Federal Rule of Civil Procedure 23 if it closely resembles Rule 23 or is like Rule 23 in substance or in essentials. See Merriam-Webster's Collegiate Dictionary, 1161 (11th ed. 2007). Moreover, as CAFA requires, the state statute or rule must resemble or be like Rule 23 by "authorizing an action to be brought by 1 or more representative persons *as a class action.*" 28 U.S.C. §1332(d)(1)(B) (emphasis added). While the statutory definition is, to some degree, circular, Congress undoubtedly intended to define "class action" in terms of its similarity and close resemblance to Rule 23.

At its essence, Rule 23 provides that "one or more members of a class may sue or be sued as representative parties on behalf of all members only if" the criteria for numerosity, commonality, typicality, and adequacy of representation are satisfied. Fed. R. Civ. P. 23(a) (emphasis added). Without this representative nature of the plaintiffs' action and the action's satisfaction of the four criteria stated in Rule 23(a), the action is not a class action. It is not fortuitous that CAFA parroted Rule 23 language when it required that a "similar" state statute or rule "authoriz[e] an action to be brought by 1 or more representative persons as a class action." 28 U.S.C. §1332(d)(1)(B). Thus, while a "similar" state statute or rule need not contain all of the other conditions and administrative aspects of Rule 23, it must, at a minimum, provide a procedure by which a member of a class whose claim is typical of all members of the class can bring an action not only on his own behalf but also on behalf of all others in the class, such that it would not be unfair to bind all class members to the judgment entered for or against the representative party. West Virginia Civil Rule of Procedure 23 would satisfy the "similarity" requirement, but it was not invoked here.

Instead, the Attorney General filed a statutorily authorized action on the State's behalf, asserting claims arising exclusively under state consumer protection statutes. Count I alleges that the Pharmacies violated state law regulating the practice of pharmacy in West Virginia, particularly West Virginia Code, §30-5-12b(g).

Counts II and III allege that the Pharmacies violated portions of the WVCCPA, a wide ranging statute designed "to protect consumers from unfair, illegal, and deceptive acts or practices," as prescribed in West Virginia Code, §46A-6-101 et seq. West Virginia ex rel. McGraw v. Scott Runyan Pontiac-Buick, Inc., 194 W. Va. 770 (W. Va. 1995). For its enforcement the WVCCPA grants the Attorney General "broad powers to supervise, investigate and prosecute violations." Id. at 525 (quoting Harless v. First National Bank, 162 W. Va. 116 (W. Va. 1978)). Although the Attorney General may "[r]eceive and act on complaints," the WVCCPA also empowers him to "commence proceedings on his own initiative." W. Va. Code §46A-7-102(1)(a).

Section 46A-7-111, on which Count III is based, authorizes the Attorney General to pursue refunds on behalf of consumers affected by "excess charges" and to seek civil penalties where the excess charges were repeatedly and willfully collected by a defendant. W. Va. Code §46A-7-111(1)-(2). Here, the Attorney General has exercised both of these powers, as this action seeks repayment to consumers under §46A-7-111(1) and penalties inuring to the State of "up to $5,000 for each repeated and willful violation" under §46A-7-111(2).

These West Virginia statutes, on which the Attorney General relies for his claims, contain virtually none of the essential requirements for a Rule 23 class action. To begin with, the Attorney General is not designated as a member of the class whose claim would be typical of the claims of class members. Rather, he is authorized to file suit independently of any consumer complaints, as a parens patriae, that is, as the legal representative of the State to vindicate the State's sovereign and quasi-sovereign interests, as well as the individual interests of the State's citizens. Indeed, the fact that the Attorney General is acting to obtain disgorgement of ill-gotten gains, "separate and apart from the interests of particular consumers in obtaining recompense," CVS Pharmacy, Inc., 748 F. Supp. 2d 580, validates this action as a parens patriae action. See In re Edmond, 934 F.2d 1304, 1310 (4th Cir. 1991).

Moreover, neither the Pharmacy Act nor the WVCCPA contains any numerosity, commonality, or typicality requirements, all of which are essential to a class action.

Finally, these Acts authorize the Attorney General to proceed without providing notice to overcharged consumers, which would also be essential in a Rule 23 class action seeking monetary damages. See Phillips Petroleum Co. v. Shutts, 472 U.S. 797, 812 (1985).

The Pharmacies argue that the suit is nonetheless a "disguised class action" because Count III is a representative action in which the Attorney General acts on behalf of the citizens, each of whom allegedly suffered a common injury. See Louisiana ex rel. Caldwell v. Allstate Ins. Co., 536 F.3d 418 (5th Cir. 2008). But that type of representation is not the type that would make the State's action a class action. A class action is an action filed by an individual as a member of a class and whose claim is typical of the class members' claims. Thus, for a representative suit to be a class action, the representative party "must be part of the class and 'possess the same interest and suffer the same injury' as the class members." Gen. Tel. Co. v. Falcon, 457 U.S. 147, 156 (1982). The Attorney General's claim on behalf of the State, however, does not require the State to be a member of the class, to suffer the same injury as class members, or to have a claim typical of each class member's claim. Rather, in representing the citizens, the State acts more in the capacity of trustee representing beneficiaries or a lawyer representing clients, neither of which is the type of representation essential to the representational aspect of a class action.

Indeed, the West Virginia Attorney General's role here is more analogous to the role of the EEOC or other regulator when it brings an action on behalf of a large group of employees or a segment of the public. Yet, the Supreme Court has concluded that such a regulator's action is not a class action of the kind defined in Rule 23. For example, in *General Telephone Co. v. EEOC*, 446 U.S. 318, 334 (1980), the Supreme Court held that a sex-discrimination suit brought by the EEOC under Title VII was "not properly characterized as a 'class action' subject to the procedural requirements of Rule 23." The Court reached that conclusion despite the fact that the suit sought back pay and other relief on behalf of all of the employer's adversely affected employees in California, Idaho, Montana, and Oregon. Id. at 321, 324. Likewise, in *Edmond*, we held that a bankruptcy claim brought by the Maryland Attorney General's Office "on behalf of itself and all [affected Maryland] consumers" did not need to comply with Rule 23, even though one of the claim's primary purposes was to provide individual citizens with refunds pursuant Maryland's Consumer Protection Act. See 934 F.2d at 1306; see also id. at 1310-13.

Much like the statutes at issue in *General Telephone* and *Edmond*, the WVCCPA authorizes the Attorney General to bring enforcement actions against violators and, in so doing, to pursue relief on behalf of aggrieved individuals. See Scott Runyan, 461 S.E.2d at 523-24. Yet that type of representation by the State is no more characteristic of the representational nature of a class action than were the claims in *General Telephone* and *Edmond*. Neither the State nor the Attorney General is a member of the class purportedly represented, and neither suffered the same injury as the citizens in that class.

The Pharmacies nonetheless argue that CAFA's legislative history supports their position. . . . Moreover, while some floor statements cited by the Pharmacies are favorable to their arguments, others cited by the Attorney General, from the same Senator and the same page of the Congressional Record, point in the opposite direction. Compare 151 Cong. Rec. S1163 (daily ed. Feb. 9, 2005) (statement of Sen. Charles Grassley that a subsequently defeated amendment intended to exempt suits brought by state attorneys general would have "create[d] a very serious loophole"), with id. (statement of Sen. Charles Grassley that "the amendment [was] not necessary" because "cases brought by State attorneys general will not be affected by this bill"). This legislative history is hardly probative.

In sum, we conclude that because the action before us was not brought under Federal Rule of Civil Procedure 23 or a "similar State statute or rule of judicial procedure authorizing an action to be brought by 1 or more representative persons as a class action," 28 U.S.C. §1332(d)(1)(B), the district court did not err in remanding this case to the Circuit Court for Boone County.

The West Virginia Attorney General initially filed this action in a West Virginia state court to enforce, on behalf of West Virginia and its citizens, state consumer protection laws applicable only in West Virginia. Were we now to mandate that the State was not entitled to pursue its action in its own courts, we would risk trampling on the sovereign dignity of the State and inappropriately transforming what is essentially a West Virginia matter into a federal case. The Pharmacies nonetheless rationalize such a transformation on the basis that the Attorney General somehow mispleaded his case, disguising what would otherwise be a CAFA class action.

The Pharmacies' approach, however, would have to ignore the Attorney General's stated basis for his action of seeking to vindicate West Virginia's interests in how pharmacies may charge West Virginia consumers in filling prescriptions. If we accept the Attorney General's good faith in pleading his claims — and we are given no reason not to — the Pharmacies have no basis, real or postured, to assert that this is an "interstate case of national importance," the defining federal interest animating CAFA's removal provisions. See CAFA, Pub. L. No. 109-2 §2(b)(2). . . . In this case, where West Virginia has raised no federal question and where all persons on whose behalf West Virginia has filed this action are West Virginia citizens, the "claim of sovereign protection from removal [arises] in its most powerful form." In re Katrina Canal Litig. Breaches, 524 F.3d 700, 706 (5th Cir. 2008). . . .

We conclude, in the circumstances presented here, that CAFA does not clearly demand that West Virginia's action, which is essentially a parens patriae type of action for enforcement of its own laws on behalf of itself and its citizens, be removed to federal court, even though the Pharmacies are citizens of States different from West Virginia. The Pharmacies are summoned to West Virginia courts only because they do business in West Virginia and, while there, allegedly violated its laws. . . .

Accordingly, the district court's order remanding this matter to the Circuit Court for Boone County is affirmed.

GILMAN, Senior Circuit Judge, dissenting:

The majority has concluded that the Class Action Fairness Act (CAFA) does not provide federal jurisdiction over the West Virginia Attorney General's lawsuit because this case is a parens patriae action and not a "class action" as defined by CAFA. For the reasons set forth below, I respectfully disagree.

The primary difficulty in this case, as I see it, is that CAFA does not actually define a class action. As the majority notes, CAFA's definition of a class action is essentially circular: "the term 'class action' means any civil action filed under rule 23 of the Federal Rules of Civil Procedure or similar State statute or rule of judicial procedure authorizing an action to be brought by 1 or more representative persons as a class action." 28 U.S.C. §1332(d)(1)(B). And CAFA gives no guidance as to what type of state statute or rule of judicial procedure should be considered "similar" for purposes of conferring federal jurisdiction.

In my view, the essence of a class action is set forth in the first sentence of the term's definition in Black's Law Dictionary: "A lawsuit in which the court authorizes a single person or a small group of people to represent the interests of a larger group. . . ." Black's Law Dictionary 284 (9th ed. 2009). I believe that the present suit brought by the Attorney General squarely fits within that authoritative definition of a class action.

. . .

The Attorney General brings this suit in what he alleges is West Virginia's parens patriae capacity. "In order to maintain such an action, the State must articulate an interest apart from the interests of particular private parties," also known as a "quasi-sovereign interest." Alfred L. Snapp & Son, Inc. v. Puerto Rico ex rel. Barez, 458 U.S. 592, 607 (1982). The Supreme Court has stated that there are two general categories of quasi-sovereign interests: (1) a state's interest in the physical and economic well-being of its citizens in general, and (2) a state's interest in "not being discriminatorily denied its rightful status within the federal system." Id.

[E]xamples of successful parens patriae actions include cases where a state has sought to enjoin a public nuisance or ensure the economic well-being of its citizenry generally. See, e.g., Missouri v. Illinois, 180 U.S. 208, 248 (1901) (holding that Missouri could pursue an injunction to prevent the defendants from discharging sewage in such a way that polluted the Mississippi River in Missouri); Pennsylvania v. West Virginia, 262 U.S. 553, 592 (1923) (recognizing Pennsylvania and Ohio as the proper parties to represent the interests of their citizens in maintaining access to natural gas produced in West Virginia). . . .

Here, the Attorney General asserts that the defendants (the Pharmacies) violated West Virginia's Pharmacy Act and the WVCCPA, and he seeks damages payable directly to the allegedly aggrieved West Virginia purchasers of generic drugs under WVCCPA §46A-7-111(1), civil penalties under WVCCPA §46A-7-111(2), injunctive relief, and other appropriate remedies. Utilizing a claim-by-claim framework, I believe that the primary thrust of this case is the excess-charges claim (Count III) for which the Attorney General seeks reimbursement payable directly to the affected consumers under WVCCPA §46A-7-111(1).

I reach this conclusion for two reasons: (1) the WVCCPA provides that a ruling that the consumers have been overcharged will result in those overcharges being remitted directly to the consumers, and (2) injunctive relief and any civil penalties are discretionary with the court and require more stringent proof on the part of the Attorney General. Compare West Va. Code §46A-7-111(2) (requiring proof of repeated and willful violations of the WVCCPA before civil penalties may be awarded) with West Va. Code §46A-7-111(1) (allowing the Attorney General to bring an action against a creditor for charging consumers in excess of what the law permits, regardless of the creditor's state of mind).

The West Virginia Attorney General here does not have a quasi-sovereign interest in the refunds that the Pharmacies will be required to pay directly to the affected consumers if they are found to have violated the WVCCPA. Admittedly, the Attorney General is also seeking civil penalties and injunctive relief, these being the type of claims clearly within the state's parens patriae authority. But for the reasons stated above, I do not believe that these claims are the primary focus of this case, and are instead subsidiary claims that will be considered by the trial court only if the primary claim of reimbursement to the allegedly overcharged consumers is successful.

I believe that my analysis is strengthened by the fact that some of the same private attorneys representing the Attorney General here are simultaneously representing individuals who have filed essentially identical claims against the same defendants in Michigan and Minnesota. No one questions that those cases are class actions; in fact, they were filed as class actions. See Graphic Comms. Local 1B Health & Welfare Fund "A" v. CVS Caremark Corp., 725 F. Supp. 2d 849 (D. Minn. 2010). If one were to close one's eyes as to who the named plaintiff is in the three lawsuits, there is no way to detect a material difference between the Attorney General's request for repayment to overcharged consumers under WVCCPA §46A-7-111(1) in the present case and the same claims that are pending in Michigan and Minnesota.

CAFA's legislative history, which is admittedly limited, also supports my conclusion that this case is simply not a parens patriae action. During the debate in the U.S. Senate over CAFA, Senator Pryor proposed an amendment that would have exempted all class actions filed by state attorneys general from removal under

CAFA. See 151 Cong. Rec. S1157 (daily ed. Feb. 9, 2005). Both Senators Grassley (a cosponsor of CAFA) and Hatch (the former chair of the Senate Judiciary Committee) opposed the Pryor Amendment because, among other things, the Amendment risked "creating a situation where State attorneys general can be used as pawns so that crafty class action lawyers can avoid the jurisdictional provisions of [CAFA]" by "simply includ[ing] in their complaint a State attorney general's name as a purported class member." Id. at 1163-64.

The concern that Senators Grassley and Hatch expressed in opposing the ultimately defeated Pryor Amendment is exactly what has come to fruition here. I believe that the West Virginia Attorney General has been "used as a pawn" so that the private class-action lawyers can remain in state court and avoid the impact of CAFA, despite the fact that the real parties in interest are the allegedly aggrieved West Virginia consumers and not the state.

Having concluded that the affected West Virginia consumers are the real parties in interest, I find that this action should be removable under CAFA because the essential requirements of a class action are met given the factual circumstances of this case. . . .

[T]he allegedly overcharged consumer, like any putative class member considering whether to join a class action, has the ultimate say as to whether to be bound by the Attorney General's lawsuit. WVCCPA §46A-7-111(1) provides in pertinent part that

> [i]f a consumer brings an action against a creditor to recover an excess charge or civil penalty, an action by the attorney general to recover for the same excess charge shall be stayed while the consumer's action is pending and shall be dismissed if the consumer's action is dismissed with prejudice or results in a final judgment granting or denying the consumer's claim.

The Attorney General's power over a particular generic-drug purchaser's claim is thus ultimately controlled by the consumer. I therefore believe that WVCCPA §46A-7-111 is sufficiently similar to Rule 23 of the Federal Rules of Civil Procedure to meet CAFA's requirements for class actions. And because this is (1) a civil action (2) in which the amount in controversy exceeds the sum or value of $5,000,000 and (3) involves a plaintiff class exceeding 100 persons whose West Virginia citizenship is different from any defendant, none of whom are considered citizens of West Virginia, I would hold that CAFA's jurisdictional requirements are met. See 28 U.S.C. §1332(d). . . .

In sum, there is a saying that if something looks like a duck, walks like a duck, and quacks like a duck, it is probably a duck. To my mind this case "quacks" much more like a CAFA class action than a parens patriae case. I would therefore reverse the judgment of the district court and allow this case to proceed in federal court.

Consumer protection scholars have generally lined up opposite the civil procedure folks to make the case for wide-ranging public enforcement. One key point that they raise is that public suits do not foreclose private actions. This was true of the national mortgage settlement, although consumers had limited success in individual actions and virtually no success (at least yet) in class actions, despite the talents of some of the nation's best class action attorneys at work. Another defense of public enforcement is to note that it has substantial efficiency benefits. It is cheaper and quicker. As one scholar quipped, "Why pay for a 'private attorney general' when there is a public attorney general who works for free?" Jack Ratliff, *Parens Patriae: An Overview*, 74 TULANE L. REV. 1847, 1849 (2000). Others have noted that the calculation of public compensation is often based on restitution and recovery of illegal gain, rather than damages and loss. Given that, there should be less concern about the reduced procedural protections for consumers as compared to a private class action. *See* Prentiss Cox, *Public Enforcement Compensation and Private Rights*, __ MINN. L. REV. __ (2015).

An empirical study of actions by state attorneys general concluded that there was a "measured use" of enforcement powers and "robust cooperation between federal and state authorities" when there was express statutory authority for the states to litigate (as opposed to solely relying on parens patriae). Amy Widman & Prentiss Cox, *State Attorneys General's Use of Concurrent Public Enforcement Authority in Federal Consumer Protection Laws*, 33 CARDOZO L. REV. 53 (2011). And perhaps given Dodd-Frank's explicit adjustment of consumer law in favor of more limited federal preemption and authorization of state enforcement, these concerns will abate.

Because every state's unfair and deceptive statute includes a private enforcement mechanism, the state attorneys general are partners in enforcement with the private bar. By contrast, in the federal regime, the FTC or the CFPB have exclusive enforcement responsibility. While a private litigant may file suit under a specific statute, such as the Truth in Lending Act, individual or class actions cannot allege a violation of the federal unfair or deceptive (or abusive) statutes.

More than half of the state attorneys general have the authority to interpret state consumer protection statutes by way of rulemaking. The requirements for rulemaking generally follow the dictates of each state's administrative procedures act. Some state statutes provide that the attorney general's regulations have the force of law. In other states a violation of a regulation is prima facie evidence of a violation of the consumer protection statute.

Problem Set 24

24.1. Last year, the Rose State Attorney General filed suit against Active Arbitration (AA), a private dispute resolution company that operated nationwide. AA's headquarters were about 2,000 miles from Rose State and AA had no employees or operation in Rose State, except for when a consumer demanded an in person hearing after losing an arbitration based on paper filings. The Attorney General alleged that AA misled consumers with representations of neutral arbitration practices when in fact AA had financial ties to the credit card companies whose contracts required arbitration with AA. Just three days after filing suit, AA agreed to a consent judgment to stop arbitrating such complaints entirely. The attorney general crowed to you, his political advisor for his reelection campaign this fall, about this success, sending you multiple copies of the press releases on the suit. He suggests that you nickname him the

"Big Dog" and bragged that he singlehandedly stopped credit card arbitrations on a national basis.

You have recently caught wind that the opposing candidate for the attorney general's job has a different take on the AA litigation. He is developing a series of attack ads, asserting that the attorney general needs to avoid pursuing and creating national remedies because it is a waste of the taxpayers of Roses' dollars and that it reflects a sense of knowing what is best for everyone rather than doing the job at hand. Are these criticisms valid? In the upcoming debate, what arguments do you expect the opponent to flush out in support of his positions? How will you advise the incumbent attorney general to respond?

24.2. You work in the government services division of a major consulting firm, having left behind the world of law after a few years as an associate. The attorney general for the state of Union has hired your firm to evaluate its consumer complaint process. She believes the legislature might dramatically reduce funding for the attorney general due to budget constraints, and she has wondered if closing the consumer complaint division would be an effective cost-cutting measure. She provides you with the following information about Union's process. Consumers can submit complaints either by calling a 1-800 hotline or filing a complaint online. After making the initial complaint, the consumer has to mail in copies of any relevant documents that support a complaint, such as loan disclosures, leases, etc. After receiving the complaint, the Consumer Protection Division writes to the business to initiate a mediation with the business. If the business declines to respond, the Consumer Protection Division provides the consumer with a packet of information on how to file a dispute in small claims court.

Last year, the Division received 4,000 complaints. In 3,000 instances, the business did not respond to the mediation request. In 1,000 cases, the dispute was mediated to the satisfaction of the parties. Among the 4,000 complaints, the attorney general initiated an investigation in three cases and filed a lawsuit in two of those cases. One lawsuit resulted in injunctive relief; the other resulted in injunctive relief and a $500,000 restitution award. The attorney general filed 15 consumer protection lawsuits in total for the year; the other practices or businesses at issue in the other 13 actions were identified through the attorney general's staff conducting investigations at its own behest.

As part of your analysis, identify the purpose of a consumer complaint program. Who does it serve? Is it consistent with the public enforcement duties of an attorney general and the parens patriae theory? What problems or value do you see to the approach used by this attorney general and what suggestions might you make for improvement?

24.3. Henrietta just got a call from her law school classmate, Alberto, asking if she would represent him as he is being "sued by the CFPB." Henrietta, who specializes in professional misconduct cases, was surprised. First, she's never heard of the CFPB and has no idea why Alberto would call her when he well knows that she mostly represents attorneys in bar discipline cases. Second, she is surprised because Alberto was an upstanding person in law school and she knows he has built a successful firm that represents financial start-up companies.

Alberto says that he is so distraught that he cannot even read the complaint with any care but that he'll email it to Henrietta. Alberto says that as far as he can calm himself to scan the complaint, it seems to allege that he engaged in "unlawful conduct" in breach of his professional duties as a lawyer. He explains that his firm has filed more than a dozen cases last year challenging the constitutionality of the CFPB. While those claims have all been dismissed, he believes his strategy has slowed down litigation and helped clients negotiate settlements with the CFPB. On what basis could the CFPB have jurisdiction over Alberto? What might Henrietta argue in trying to have the complaint dismissed? *See* 12 U.S.C. §5481(25); 12 U.S.C. §5531; Fed. R. Civ. P. 11.

Assignment 25. Private Enforcement

In addition to public enforcement, most consumer law statutes allow individuals to bring claims, in addition to providing for public enforcement. To some extent, public and private enforcement can substitute for each other, but not wholly so. Public enforcement may be too slow, may not address the consumer's particular issue, or simply may not occur at all because government does not wish to take up the consumer's situation. Private enforcement has different purposes, including primarily redress for the individual consumer.

Even when consumers can file a lawsuit, however, they often do not. Most statutes are infrequently used, and may produce only modest success for consumers. Underenforcement via private lawsuit is perhaps the most vexing problem in consumer law. Its causes are multiple. Most importantly, law is not free. Consumer remedies are often difficult to use, and consumer lawyers are hard to identify and afford. Some statutes provide for no remedy other than restitution, which may be insufficient to justify filing suit, while others provide for only actual damages, which can be difficult to quantify or prove. Some laws try to remedy these problems with statutory or punitive damages or to permit class actions. These mechanisms appear to be only partially successful and work better for some kinds of wrongs than others.

Underenforcement raises both practical and theoretical concerns. For lawyers, inadequate remedies can make practice unprofitable or risky. For consumers, it can cause disillusionment with the legal system, larded on top of the actual harms suffered by the businesses' wrongdoing. For advocates, underenforcement makes it difficult to know whether the costs of obtaining new substantive protections are worthwhile, given the risk of non- or under-enforcement of those rights. How just is a system of consumer law that cannot produce a remedy for the aggrieved consumers? Different ideas of justice, such as deterrence or restorative justice, translate into different approaches to enforcement. Private remedies, as much as the substantive rights themselves, raise normative questions about the purpose and utility of consumer law.

A. Litigation Remedies

Little attention was given to remedies in much of this book. The focus was on the law itself and whether a legal violation occurred in particular circumstances—not on what an aggrieved party could (or would likely) do about it. Often in law school, the issue of remedies is ignored entirely. Many new lawyers dutifully explain a large body of legal rules to their clients, only to face pointed questions about just what the client can do or get.

One reason to cover remedies as a collective topic (rather than law by law) is that many consumer statutes share the same private enforcement scheme. The best example of this is the repetitive enforcement pattern in many subparts of the umbrella Consumer Credit Protection Act, which includes TILA, ECOA, FDCPA, FCRA, etc. While there are variations that justify examining each liability provision with care in practice, at a general level these laws offer three kinds of remedies to consumers: actual damages, statutory damages of a limited amount, and an award of attorneys' fees and costs of the action, if the consumer is successful. These remedies are discussed in order in this Assignment. The remaining sections consider some of the most contested issues in private enforcement: litigation costs and class actions.

As a reminder, a few of the exceptional remedies that apply to particularized products have previously been discussed. The most important of these are rescission for foreclosure, statutory discharge for student loans, and lawsuits under Magnuson-Moss for breach of U.C.C. warranties.

1. Actual Damages

When a statute provides any remedy, it usually permits "actual damages." This functions as kind of a minimum remedy. Indeed, if a consumer did not suffer any harm, the statute would likely not provide a private right of action at all. That said, it is extraordinarily difficult to establish actual damages for many consumer law protections. Several statutes illustrate the point.

The Truth in Lending Act makes a creditor who fails to comply with any requirement "liable to such person in an amount equal to the sum of . . . any actual damage sustained by such person as a result of the failure." 15 U.S.C. §1640(a). But what is the actual harm to a consumer who did not receive an appropriate disclosure? In most instances, consumers cannot show any monetary harm. The rate and other terms of the loan were not affected by the legal violation. Consumers could argue that they were harmed because they relied on the inaccurate disclosure and failed to shop for cheaper products. But remember that the Truth in Lending Act punishes both overdisclosure and underdisclosure of the finance charge, the APR, and the amount financed. And most consumers cannot show that they read, much less understood, the Truth in Lending Act disclosure at the time of the transaction or that they did shop or would have shopped for a better loan. Frequently, the violations raised are "technical," in the sense that the law was not followed but that fact did not change the outcome of the transaction. The consumer would have borrowed the money at the same rate from the same lender with or without an accurate disclosure. Courts are hard pressed to find actual damages in such situations.

To take another example, the Fair Debt Collection Practices Act also provides for actual damages. 15 U.S.C. §1692k. Consider a creditor who calls before 9:00 A.M., violating §1692c(a)(1), or who uses obscene or profane language, violating §1692d(2). These acts are annoying and may offend a consumer's sensibilities. They are also patently illegal. But is there an actual harm to being called a name or being awoken by the telephone? If so, what is the appropriate measure of monetary damages?

McGrady v. Nissan Motor Acceptance Corp.
40 F. Supp. 2d 1323 (M.D. Ala. 1998)

De Ment, District Judge.

. . .

FACTUAL BACKGROUND

On October 7, 1995, Plaintiff purchased a 1990 Nissan automobile from Dyas Nissan, Inc. The vehicle was financed with Defendant Nissan. Plaintiff entered into a Retail Installment Contract ("Contract") with Nissan whereby Plaintiff agreed to pay monthly installments. When Plaintiff signed the contract with Nissan, she understood that there would be a late charge if payments were not paid in a timely manner. Plaintiff also understood that the car would be repossessed if payments were not made. Plaintiff did not understand that the car could be sold upon repossession.

Over the course of the ensuing year, Plaintiff made payments to Nissan, but she was delinquent in making some of these payments. Throughout the year, Nissan employees called Plaintiff to inquire about delinquent payments.

On or about October 10 or 11, 1996, an employee from Nissan, ("Ed") called Plaintiff regarding her delinquent payment. Plaintiff and Ed reached an agreement whereby Plaintiff would pay Nissan one hundred thirty-two dollars ($132.00). Plaintiff and Ed did not discuss repossession of the car or whether the account would be considered current. Plaintiff sent a check for $132.00 to the Nissan employee on October 12, 1996.

On or about October 23, 1996, the vehicle was repossessed by Joiner's Recovery Service ("Joiner's"). Joiner's was hired by Defendant Nissan to repossess the vehicle. At the time of the repossession, Plaintiff did not know the identity of the men who came to repossess the vehicle. One of the men informed Plaintiff that he was acting for Nissan. Plaintiff was approximately one month behind in payment to Nissan. The men repossessed the vehicle from the parking lot of Plaintiff's place of employment. Plaintiff was employed by Trinity United Methodist Church in Opelika, Alabama, as the office manager. The repossession occurred while Plaintiff was at work, and Plaintiff was left with no means of transportation.

At the time of the repossession, Plaintiff by telephone spoke with a Nissan employee and explained to the employee the arrangement she had made with the Nissan employee Ed on October 10, 1997. The Nissan employee denied that there was any such arrangement. The Nissan employee told Plaintiff that "there was nothing that [Plaintiff] could do, just hand over the keys, and the account was now closed, it was over."

When the car was repossessed, Plaintiff had personal property in the car. Plaintiff attempted to retrieve her personal property at the time of repossession, but she was unable to recover all of it. Among the items remaining in the vehicle were tapes, personal papers, toys, movies, a children's coat, and a blanket. While Plaintiff retrieved the personal property she was able to, the Joiner's employee hooked up the car to be towed. The Joiner's employee informed Plaintiff that she could retrieve the remainder of her personal belongings upon paying $45.00 to Joiner's.

The repossession upset and embarrassed Plaintiff. While the vehicle was repossessed, members of the church walked by and watched. Plaintiff cried to one of the associate pastors as the vehicle was taken away.

Plaintiff did not know where the Joiner's employee worked or where he was taking the car. The Joiner's employee told Plaintiff he would contact her with information regarding where she could retrieve her personal belongings. The man never contacted Plaintiff.

On the morning of October 24, 1996, Plaintiff called and spoke with the Nissan employee Ed. She asked Ed why the vehicle had been repossessed subsequent to their agreement. Ed told Plaintiff he could not speak with her, and he informed her that she would have to pay $6,700.00. Plaintiff's understanding was that upon repossession of the vehicle, the account was satisfied.

Subsequent to the repossession, Plaintiff claims she received neither proper notice of her right to redeem the vehicle nor proper notice of the disposal of the vehicle. Thus, Plaintiff never knew where the vehicle was held or from where she could redeem it.

Unbeknownst to Plaintiff, Defendant Nissan sold the vehicle and received $3,200.00 from the sale. Plaintiff asserts that the sale occurred only two days after the repossession. Defendant Nissan claimed it was still owed a remainder of $3,824.68. Defendant Nissan contacted Defendant Nationwide Credit, Inc. ("Nationwide") and hired them to collect Plaintiff's account.

Plaintiff received three collection letters from Defendant Nationwide, dated March 4, 1997, March 27, 1997, and April 24, 1997. Each letter contained the address P.O. Box 740639, Atlanta, GA XXXXX-XXXX, near the bottom of the letter, and the second letter designated Pamela Rushforth as the contact person.

On March 7, 1997, a Nationwide employee called Plaintiff at Plaintiff's place of employment and identified herself as Pamela Rushforth, saying that she was from Nationwide Credit and that Plaintiff owed a debt to Nissan. Plaintiff explained that she did not believe she owed Nissan anything because the vehicle had been repossessed. Ms. Rushforth informed Plaintiff that the car had been sold and that Plaintiff still owed approximately thirty-seven hundred dollars. Plaintiff said she knew nothing about the car being sold. Further, Plaintiff informed Ms. Rushforth that she would be unable to pay that debt.

Ms. Rushforth called Plaintiff a second time on March 14, 1997. Ms. Rushforth demanded that Plaintiff send seven hundred and fifty dollars ($750.00) overnight through the mail. When Plaintiff said that she did not have the money, Ms. Rushforth said that Plaintiff could postdate the check to the end of the month. Plaintiff refused to send a postdated check, and Ms. Rushforth said that if Plaintiff did not pay, legal action would be taken. Ms. Rushforth used a rude tone of voice.

On March 17, 1997, Ms. Rushforth called Plaintiff at Plaintiff's place of employment numerous times and was rude to the receptionist when informed that Plaintiff was not available. Ms. Rushforth left messages that "Pam" called. Ms. Rushforth asked to speak to someone who could verify Plaintiff's employment, and the financial secretary spoke with her. Ms. Rushforth inquired about Plaintiff's length of employment and salary. The financial secretary refused to answer these questions. Ms. Rushforth also called Plaintiff's home numerous times that day and left messages that "Pam" called.

On March 17, 1997, Plaintiff sent Nationwide a letter in which she requested that Nationwide not call her at work and also informed Nationwide that she did not owe

Nissan any money because of the repossession. In the letter Plaintiff also requested that all future contact be restricted to the mail. Nationwide continued to call Plaintiff, her parents, and her employer.

On March 19, 1997, another Nationwide employee called Plaintiff at work several times and was told Plaintiff could not speak with him. On March 21, 1997, a third Nationwide employee called Plaintiff at work, and Plaintiff told her not to call her at work.

During the last week of March, Ms. Rushforth called Plaintiff at home and spoke with Plaintiff's mother. Plaintiff's mother told her not to call again. Ms. Rushforth yelled at Plaintiff's mother. Nationwide employees continued to call Plaintiff throughout April and May of 1997.

Plaintiff filed her complaint on September 5, 1997, in the Circuit Court of Lee County, Alabama, claiming that Defendant Nissan converted her personal property during the repossession; Defendant Nissan violated [Alabama's enactment of U.C.C. §9-501]; and Defendants Nissan and Nationwide violated the Fair Debt Collection Practices Act ("FDCPA"), 15 U.S.C. §1692, et seq. Defendants Nissan and Nationwide removed the action to this court on October 8, 1997. Defendants Nissan and Nationwide separately moved for summary judgment on July 31, 1998 and September 29, 1998, respectively.

. . .

IV. Defendant Nationwide's Liability for Mental Anguish Damages Pursuant to the FDCPA Is Not Limited to $1000

Defendant Nationwide moves the court for summary judgment on the issue of damages. The FDCPA provides in pertinent part:

> [A]ny debt collector who fails to comply with any provision of this subchapter with respect to any person is liable to such person in an amount equal to the sum of (1) any actual damage sustained by such person as a result of such failure; (2)(A) in the case of any action by an individual, such additional damages as the court may allow, but not exceeding $1,000.

15 U.S.C. §1692k. Defendant Nationwide asserts that Plaintiff does not claim any actual damages and, therefore, Plaintiff's potential recovery from Defendant Nationwide should be limited to a maximum of $1,000.00.

Although Plaintiff does not claim any physical injury or out-of-pocket loss caused by Defendant Nationwide's alleged violations of the FDCPA, Plaintiff claims that she "suffered mental anguish and has been upset and has been treated rudely." The court notes that the issue of whether mental anguish constitutes actual damages pursuant to the FDCPA is a matter of first impression in this Circuit. Thus, the court looks to other jurisdictions for guidance.

In *Carrigan v. Central Adjustment Bureau, Inc.,* the District Court for the Northern District of Georgia determined that damages for mental anguish constitute actual damages within the purview of 15 U.S.C. §1692k(a)(1). 502 F. Supp. 468 (N.D. Ga. 1980). In making this determination, the court decided that "[s]ince the particular section of the Act which has been violated is designed to stop harassment of debtors through repeated contact by the creditor, the Court holds that Plaintiff's entitlement to damages here should turn on whether or not he would be entitled to collect damages, were this a cause of action for the intentional infliction of mental distress." Id. at 470. Georgia law permits recovery of damages for mental suffering and emotional anguish "where there is intentional infliction of mental distress, without a showing of contemporaneous physical harm." Id. Thus, the court determined such damages to be recoverable as actual damages pursuant to 15 U.S.C. §1692k(a)(1). Id.

The District Court of Delaware employed different reasoning to reach the same conclusion. In *Smith v. Law Offices of Mitchell N. Kay,* the court found to be proper a jury instruction stating that "[a]ctual damages not only include any out of pocket expenses, but also damages for personal humiliation, embarrassment, mental anguish or emotional distress." 124 B.R. 182, 185 (D. Del. 1991). Rather than compare the FDCPA with a state law claim, the court reached this conclusion by comparing the FDCPA with the Fair Credit Reporting Act ("FCRA"):

> Under the FCRA, a statutory scheme very similar to the FDCPA, a plaintiff who proves a violation of the act is entitled to actual damages for emotional distress arising from the violation, without first having to prove a right of action under state law. This Court similarly holds that, when a violation of the FDCPA has been established, actual damages for emotional distress can be proved independently of state law requirements.

Id. at 188.

In the instant case, the court finds that damages for mental anguish are recoverable pursuant to 15 U.S.C. §1692k(a)(1). First, the court agrees with the *Smith* court's analysis analogizing the FDCPA to the FCRA. Further, under the methodology employed by the *Carrigan* court, damages for mental anguish are recoverable under 15 U.S.C. §1692k(a)(1) because Alabama law provides that such damages are recoverable pursuant to a cause of action for intentional infliction of mental distress. See Continental Cas. Ins. Co. v. McDonald, 567 So. 2d 1208, 1211 (Ala. 1990).

The court also notes that under Alabama law, the common law claim of invasion of privacy provides for recovery of unlimited mental anguish damages. See, e.g., Norris v. Moskin Stores, Inc., 272 Ala. 174, 177 (1961) (holding that a debtor has a cause of action sounding in invasion of privacy "for injurious conduct on the part of the creditor which exceeds the bounds of reasonableness"). As damages for mental anguish could be unlimited pursuant to an invasion of privacy claim, the court finds that damages for mental anguish should also be potentially unlimited pursuant to the FDCPA.

Finally, the court finds that common sense dictates finding that mental anguish damages falls within the purview of 15 U.S.C. §1692k(a)(1). Absent such a finding, a debtor suffering mental anguish without pecuniary or physical damages would be limited to recovering a maximum amount of $1,000 pursuant to the FDCPA. The court finds this to be an entirely unsatisfactory result as the harassment suffered by a debtor at the hands of a debt collector could well cause more than $1,000 in mental anguish damages. Just as Alabama law permits unlimited recovery for mental anguish damages in claims brought for intentional infliction of emotional distress and invasion of privacy, the court interprets the term "actual damages" in 15 U.S.C. §1692k(a)(1) as encompassing mental anguish damages and thus allowing unlimited recovery in this context. The court therefore finds that summary judgment is due to be denied on this point.

McGrady was lenient in allowing the plaintiff to go forward and try to prove mental anguish. You may have noticed that it cited "common sense" as its authority and wondered if other courts found more august authority. Indeed, there are opinions to the contrary. In *Branco v. Credit Collection*, 2011 U.S. Dist. LEXIS 94077, 2011 WL 3684503 (E.D. Ca. Aug. 23, 2011), the court noted a split of authority and were persuaded that the better approach was to require a plaintiff asserting intentional infliction of emotional distress as part of an actual damages claim to satisfy the requirements of state tort law for emotional distress. *See also Burns v. Anderson*, 2008 U.S. Dist. LEXIS 123632, 2008 WL 8834614 (D. Colo. Aug. 15, 2008).

A remedy for small actual damages is used in some state unfair and deceptive practices statutes. A plaintiff who proves a violation can receive double or treble actual damages as relief. *See, e.g.,* Mass. Genl. Laws §93A. This is a type of hybrid between actual damages and statutory damages.

2.   *Statutory Damages*

Statutory damages can be analogized to criminal or civil fines, whereby a legislatively-determined range of damages is added to the statute. "Statutory damages are explicitly a bonus for the plaintiff, designed to encourage private enforcement . . . ," *Williams v. Countrywide Home Loans, Inc.*, 504 F. Supp. 2d 176, 186 & n.3 (S.D. Tex. 2007). A more meaningful threat of enforcement, in turn, is designed to deter future misconduct. While statutory damages may seem like a boon to plaintiffs who in retrospect suffered little or no actual damages, their function might actually be to shape the behavior of defendants prospectively. In class actions, statutory damages can be costly for defendants.

Most liability provisions in the Consumer Credit Protection Act provide statutory damages of not less than $100 and not more than $1,000. *See, e.g.,* 15 U.S.C. §1693(m) (Electronic Funds Transfer Act). Some statutes, such as the FDCPA, do not have the $100 minimum, 15 U.S.C. §1692k, but have only a maximum. In some cases, that has led to statutory damages awards of $1, surely a disincentive to bringing suit. *Lester E. Cox Med. Ctr., Springfield, Mo. v. Huntsman,* 408 F.3d 989 (8th Cir. 2005).

Other statutes, presumably where the stakes are perceived to be higher, allow higher damages. For closed-end, mortgage credit violations, TILA allows quadruple the normal amount (minimum $400 and maximum of $4,000). 15 U.S.C. §1640(a)(2)(A)(iv). For open-end, non-mortgage consumer credit, TILA provides a minimum of $500 and a maximum of $5,000. 15 U.S.C. §1640(a)(2)(A)(iii). Notice that there are two remaining categories of cases: i) closed-end, non-mortgage credit (e.g., car loan), and ii) open-end mortgage credit (e.g., home equity loan). The statute is not well-drafted, having been the subject of several amendments and a Supreme Court case that resulted in five opinions on how to interpret its language, *Koons Buick Pontiac GMC v. Nigh*, 543 U.S. 50 (2004). It appears that the initial clause that liability shall be "twice the amount of any finance charge in connection with the transaction" 15 U.S.C. §1640(a)(2)(A)(i), is then capped for the two categories above at a minimum of $200 and a maximum of $2,000, despite there being language in clause (ii) that seems to concern only consumer leases. 15 U.S.C.

§1640(a)(2)(A)(ii). Even if the finance charge is less than the minimum, or there is no finance charge in the transaction, the consumer recovers the statutory minimum if there is a violation. *See Brown v. CitiMortgage*, 817 F. Supp. 2d 1328 (S.D. Ala. 2011).

3. Other Relief

In addition to actual and statutory damages, a few statutes offer other penalties. Depending on your client, the best and worst of these are punitive damages. Some statutes are generous. For example, an entity that violates the Credit Repair Organizations Act, 15 U.S.C. §1679 et seq., may be liable for punitive damages in "such additional amount as the court may allow." 15 U.S.C. §1679g. This puts the limit at due process. *BMW of North America, Inc. v. Gore*, 517 U.S. 559 (1996). Other statutes are much more restrained with regard to punitive damages. Civil liability for punitive damages for ECOA is capped at $10,000 in an individual lawsuit, and the lesser of $500,000 or 1 percent of the net worth of the creditor in a class action. 15 U.S.C. §1691e. And many statutes do not permit punitive damages at all.

Usury is an example of a consumer law statute that can result in criminal liability. There are others. Something as seemingly banal as the Electronic Funds Transfer Act can result in a year of imprisonment—but only if the violation was knowing and willful. 15 U.S.C. §1693n.

B. Litigation Barriers

Stronger enforcement is not merely about higher damages. It is also about expanding access to remedies for consumers, particularly disadvantaged ones. That goal, in turn, implicates the roles of lawyers and other intermediaries. A seminal study of private enforcement of consumer law illustrates the difficulties. In the wake of the widely heralded consumer victory of the passage of the Magnuson-Moss Warranty Act, most lawyers "knew next to nothing" about the law, and "many had never heard of it." Stewart Macaulay, *Lawyers and Consumer Protection Laws*, 14 Law & Society Review 115, 118 (1979). He concluded that without better understanding of the practice of consumer law, "reformers are likely to go on creating individual rights which have little chance of being vindicated, and, as a result, they may fail to achieve their ends repeatedly." *Id*. at 161.

Some would argue that is exactly what has happened in most areas of consumer law, and that the barriers to private litigation have grown more acute in the last two decades. Individual lawsuits are relatively rare when compared to the number of complaints or reported violations. The CFPB found that consumers filed only 1,200 federal lawsuits, on average, each year in six markets, including credit cards, payday loans, and checking accounts. Only two cases in the CFPB's sample went to trial. CFPB Press Release, *Study Finds that Arbitration Agreements Limit Relief for Consumers* (March 10, 2015). The proffered solutions range from the simplification of the law, *see, e.g.,* Melissa B. Jacoby, *Making Debtor Remedies More Effective,* http://ssrn.com/abstract=1550964, to encouraging "low bono" law practice that charges clients reduced fees to reflect the financial constraints of most consumers, *see, e.g.,* Luz Herrera, *Encouraging the Development of "Low Bono" Law Practices,* 14 U. MD. L.J. RACE RELIG. GENDER & CLASS 1 (2014).

Some types of litigation have blossomed in recent years, particularly state UDAP class actions. Businesses have raised concerns about excessive litigation and the costs of compliance, including the deterrence of valuable economic activity. Defense lawyers argue that UDAP statutes are being commandeered by plaintiffs' lawyers "who seek to circumvent traditional, rational requirements of the common law." Victor E. Schwartz & Cary Silverman, *Common-Sense Construction of Consumer Protection Acts,* 54 U. KAN. L. REV. 1,3 (2005). Because UDAP laws are statutes, it is not clear why common law requirements would be a valid concern, but nonetheless critics argue that elements such as reasonable reliance, willful or knowing intent, or injury in fact should be required for a plaintiff to bring a case. Consumer advocates have complained that the intent is to cripple consumer protection under the guise of reform. Dee Pridgen, *Wrecking Ball Disguised as Law Refom: ALEC's Model Act on Private Enforcement of Consumer Protection Statutes,* 39 N.Y.U. REV. OF LAW & SOC. CHANGE 279 (2015).

Nearly all states' consumer fraud statutes permit plaintiffs to recover attorneys' fees. Most federal consumer laws, such as the Truth in Lending Act, also do so. But these litigation incentives have run headlong into courts' unwillingness to apply such rules generously. *See* Margaret H. Lemos, *Special Incentives to Sue,* 95 MINN. L. REV. 782 (2011) (arguing that judges adopt procedural rules that counteract the effects of fee shifts). Sometimes the problems are compounded by the statutes themselves, which may leave attorneys' fees entirely in the discretion of the court. The more protective statutes require an award of "reasonable" attorneys' fees to prevailing plaintiffs, but even that term has raised consternation from courts. While the Supreme Court has affirmed that a fee award is not excessive merely because it exceeds the amount of damages, *Riverside v. Rivera,* 477 U.S. 561 (1986) (civil rights act case), courts consider several factors in determining the amount of attorney's fees to award a plaintiff's lawyer.

Sheffer v. Experian Information Solutions, Inc.

290 F. Supp. 2d 538 (E.D. Pa. 2003)

SCHILLER, District Judge.

This case reveals the potential problems that accompany the generally salutary effects of fee-shifting statutes. While fee-shifting provisions are intended to facilitate the pursuit of claims that vindicate both individual rights and the larger public interest, they can be misused when they become a mechanism for obtaining large attorney's fee awards in cases with de minimis returns for the client and society in general. Furthermore, the prospect of a fee award can skew attorneys' incentives when confronted with settlement offers that would more than compensate their clients, but that fall short of the large fees already incurred. These concerns are most prevalent in cases such as this, where recovery of private damages, rather than the vindication of constitutional rights, is the primary purpose. While it is Congress' duty to re-shape fee-shifting provisions to alleviate these concerns, it is this Court's duty to determine a reasonable fee in light of the de minimis victory achieved in this case. See Hensley v. Eckerhart, 461 U.S. 424, 436 (1983) (holding that "the most critical factor" in the analysis of a reasonable fee is "the degree of success obtained").

I. BACKGROUND

After a jury trial before this Court in the above-captioned matter, judgment was entered against Defendant Sears & Roebuck, Inc. ("Sears") in favor of Plaintiff's claims under the Fair Credit Reporting Act ("FCRA"). The jury awarded Plaintiff Richard Sheffer $1,000.00 in actual damages, but declined to award punitive damages. Now before the Court is Plaintiff's motion for attorneys' fees and costs pursuant to the fee-shifting provision of the FCRA, 15 U.S.C. §1681o(a)(2), and Federal Rules of Civil Procedure 54(d)(1) and 54(d)(2)(B). For the reasons that follow, I grant in part and deny in part Plaintiff's motion for attorneys' fees.

II. DISCUSSION

Plaintiff seeks an award of $126,543.33 in fees and $14,010.75 in costs, representing the work of the following three firms: Francis & Mailman, P.C., Thomas Lyons & Associates, P.A., and the Consumer Justice Center, P.A. Defendant Sears contests $54,024.47 of Plaintiff's fee request and $8,495.21 of Plaintiff's cost request. Defendant also broadly challenges the reasonableness of Plaintiff's attorneys' hourly rates and requests an overall two-thirds reduction due to Plaintiff's limited success.

The FCRA provides explicit statutory authority to award costs and counsel fees to a prevailing party "in the case of any successful action to enforce any liability under this section." 15 U.S.C. §1681o(a)(2) (2003). Plaintiff, as the prevailing party in this litigation, bears the burden of demonstrating that the fee request is reasonable. See Rode v. Dellarciprete, 892 F.2d 1177, 1183 (3d Cir. 1990). Courts assess the reasonableness of a claimed fee using the "lodestar" formula, which entails multiplying the number of hours reasonably expended by the appropriate hourly rate. See Hensley, 461 U.S. at 433; Maldonado v. Houstoun, 256 F.3d 181, 184 (3d Cir. 2001). Although the lodestar is presumed to yield a reasonable fee, a district court has considerable discretion to adjust the lodestar upward or downward after the opposing party objects to the fee request. See Rode, 892 F.2d at 1183 (citing Bell v. United Princeton Props., 884 F.2d 713, 721 (3d Cir. 1989)).

A. Plaintiff's Request for Attorneys' Fees

1. Reasonableness of the Hourly Rate

A court determines a reasonable hourly rate by assessing the prevailing party's attorneys' experience and skill compared to the market rates in the relevant community for lawyers of reasonably comparable skill, experience, and reputation. See Maldonado, 256 F.3d at 184. . . .

The Third Circuit has held that the attorney's fee schedule composed by Community Legal Services ("CLS") is "a fair reflection of market rates in Philadelphia." Maldonado, 256 F.3d at 187. Defendant contests the hourly rates of four of Plaintiff's attorneys because they exceed the prevailing market rates as set by the CLS schedule. The CLS schedule suggests that attorneys with six to ten years of experience should charge hourly rates between $190.00 and $240.00. . . . Given their relative experience, the guidelines set in the CLS fee schedule and the rates approved in comparable cases in this district, I find that Mr. Mailman, Mr. Francis and Mr. Lyons Jr. should reasonably receive $235.00 per hour. The $235.00 hourly figure is near the top of the guideline range and represents a slight increase above the hourly rates approved for these attorneys in the two recent cases cited above. I find that Mr. Soumalis should receive $160.00 per hour based on his experience and skill and because he performed the tasks of a junior associate in this litigation. Adjusted accordingly, Plaintiff's fee petition totals $106,569.38. This figure is the starting point for the further reductions enumerated below.

2. Reasonableness of Hours Expended

A prevailing party may request fees for work that is "useful and the type ordinarily necessary to secure the final result obtained." Commonwealth of Pennsylvania v. Del. Valley Citizens' Council, 478 U.S. 546, 560-61 (1986). The fee petition must be sufficiently specific to allow the court to determine if the hours claimed are unreasonable for the work performed. See Washington, 89 F.3d at 1037. A court has "the affirmative function" to "review the time charged, decide whether the hours set out were reasonably expended for each of the particular purposes described and then exclude those that are 'excessive, redundant, or otherwise unnecessary.'" Maldonado, 256 F.3d at 184. A court, however, cannot generally reduce hours *sua sponte,* rather, objections must be specific for a court to reduce the amount of fees requested. See United States v. Eleven Vehicles, 200 F.3d 203, 211-12 (3d Cir. 2000). . . .

Defendant Sears contests the reasonableness of Plaintiff's counsel's specific time entries on numerous grounds. To facilitate the Court's evaluation of each contested time entry, Defendants have submitted a chart that groups Plaintiff's contemporaneous time entries into various categories and includes a column detailing Sears' specific dispute with each entry. Although mindful of the Supreme Court's admonition that "this process should not result in a second major litigation," this Court has endeavored to address each of Defendant's numerous disputes. Hensley, 461 U.S. at 437.

. . .

b. Overstaffing and Excessive Fees

Defendants contend that Plaintiff's attorneys' hours should be reduced due to three instances of purported overstaffing. First, Defendant asserts that it was unnecessary for both Mr. Mailman and Mr. Francis to accrue hours responding to Sears' motion to dismiss and that the total hours expended on this task were excessive. Sears' motion to dismiss argued that Sears could not be sued under the FCRA as a furnisher of information, an issue that had not previously been addressed in the Third Circuit. Although other circuits had addressed the issue, it required considerable research by Plaintiff. In light of the nature and complexity of the arguments raised in Sears' motion to dismiss, I find that these hours were neither excessive nor duplicative. See Rodriguez-Hernandez v. Miranda-Velez, 132 F.3d 848, 860 (1st Cir. 1998) ("Time spent by two attorneys on the same general task is not, however, per se duplicative . . . preparation often requires collaboration and rehearsal.").

Second, Defendants claim that it was unreasonable for both Mr. Francis and Mr. Soumalis to attend the deposition of Equifax's representative, Alicia Fluellen, which they assert could have been handled by Mr. Soumalis alone. Since Mr. Francis and Mr. Soumalis's combined hours represent an unnecessary duplication of responsibilities, the Court will disallow the fees associated with Mr. Soumalis' mere attendance at the deposition. Finally, Defendants contest as duplicative time entries of Mr. Francis and Mr. Soumalis that refer to, *inter alia,* preparation of the proposed points for charge and verdict form, among other things. The Court finds that these hours reflect a reasonable time expenditure for the tasks described and a permissible degree of collaboration between the senior attorney working on this case and the junior associate.

In addition, Defendants contest four entries solely on the ground that the time expended was excessive in light of the work performed. After review of the entries, I disagree and find that these entries also reflect a reasonable time expenditure for the tasks described.

c. Trial Preparation and Attendance

Defendants ask the Court to decline to award fees related to trial preparation by Mr. Mailman and Mr. Lyons, Jr. because they did not attend trial and it is unclear from their time entries what type of trial preparation they performed. . . .

This Court acknowledges that reasonable trial preparation entails collaboration and rehearsal among attorneys. Rodriguez-Hernandez, 132 F.3d at 860. However, hours attributed to trial preparation and collaboration by Mr. Lyons, Jr. and Mr. Mailman are excessive and duplicative, especially given the fact that neither appeared at trial and the two highly experienced attorneys who served as lead trial counsel had ample access to each other for collaboration. Furthermore, many of the entries, tersely describing the activity as "trial prep," are not sufficiently specific to allow the Court to determine if the hours claimed are reasonable for the work performed. See Rode, 892 F.2d at 1190 (citing Pawlak v. Greenawalt, 713 F.2d 972, 978 (3d Cir. 1983)). This Court finds that the trial preparation hours billed by Mr. Lyons, Mr. Francis and Mr. Soumalis, together totaling 117.36 hours, were more than sufficient preparation for a trial that did not even last a full three days. Therefore, the 6.1 hours billed by Mr. Mailman and the 18 hours billed by

Mr. Lyons, Jr.—only four hours shy of the total trial preparation billed by lead counsel Mr. Francis—will be deducted.

Furthermore, Defendants object to expenses related to Mr. Soumalis's trial attendance. Plaintiff's counsel's table was amply staffed by Mr. Lyons and Mr. Francis. Mr. Soumalis was not the trial attorney; he did not participate in the examination of any witnesses and did not sit at counsel's table. Rather, Mr. Soumalis served as an actor, reading the deposition testimony of two third-party witnesses who did not attend trial. Therefore, Sears should not be charged for Mr. Soumalis's trial attendance and Mr. Soumalis's acting skills should be compensated at $50.00 per hour, rather than his associate rate of $160.00 per hour.

· · ·

e. Allocation of Responsibilities Among Partners and Junior Associates

Sears objects to several of Plaintiff's fees on the ground that certain tasks could have been accomplished more cost effectively by a junior associate. Although a court must exclude hours that reflect "the wasteful use of highly skilled and highly priced talent for matters *easily* delegable to non-professionals or less experienced associates," delegation is neither always possible in a small firm nor always desirable. Ursic v. Bethlehem Mines, 719 F.2d 670, 677 (3d Cir. 1983) (emphasis added). First, a duty to delegate presupposes that the attorneys charging maximum rates readily have junior associates and supporting paralegals at their disposal. See Poston v. Fox, 577 F. Supp. 915, 919-20 (D.N.J. 1984) (finding that it is not always possible to delegate in small office). Although Plaintiff was represented by attorneys from three different law firms, attorneys in small firms often have limited access to junior associates. Given the number of junior attorneys available to work on this litigation, this Court does not find Plaintiff's attorneys' non-delegation of responsibilities unreasonable. Furthermore, it is reasonable for lead trial counsel to desire to expend his or her own time on some activities that, although within the competency of less highly paid associates, are better performed by the lead counsel to ensure the smooth functioning at trial. Thus, Mr. Francis's assistance in preparing the trial binder and other trial preparations are reasonable given his position as trial counsel. Regardless, these alleged instances of non-delegation are not frequent enough to mandate reducing the number of hours that will be computed in the lodestar. See Poston, 577 F. Supp. at 920.

f. Clerical Work

Defendant objects to the clerical nature of certain tasks performed by paralegals Sue Wolsfeld, Patti Sullivan, and Dania Richardson, all of which were billed at a $95.00 hourly rate. Clerical tasks should not be billed at senior associate or paralegal rates. See Missouri v. Jenkins, 491 U.S. 274, 285-88 (1989) (holding that "purely clerical or secretarial tasks should not be billed at a paralegal rate, regardless of who performs them"). Plaintiffs offer no explanation for why Sears should pay these fees and do not suggest that they constitute paralegal work. Since the costs of clerical work, such as filing and copying, are ordinarily considered to be part of an attorney's rate as office overhead, they will not be compensated.

g. Tasks Described Without Required Specificity

Defendant contests Mr. Goolsby's August 28, 2003 entry for "research" as insufficiently specific. See Washington, 89 F.3d at 1037 (stating that fee petition must be sufficiently specific to allow court to determine if hours claimed are unreasonable for work performed). In response, Plaintiffs supplement Mr. Goolsby's entry, claiming that the ten hours were spent researching the fee petition. The Court finds that this is a reasonable amount of time and that the Plaintiff is entitled to recover for time spent preparing a fee application. See Hernandez v. Kalinowski, 146 F.3d 196, 199 (3d Cir. 1998) ("[C]ourts consistently have interpreted fee shifting statutes . . . to provide for reasonable fees . . . related to the preparation and litigation of motions for attorney's fees.").

. . .

[Ed. Note — The court also reduced fees in response to defendant's objection for overbilling for deposition work and adjusted fees based on apportionment of the work billed to Sears, one of four defendants in the initial case.]

The reductions in attorneys' fees enumerated above reduce the lodestar amount to $78,749.97.

B. Reduction for Lack of Success

After determining the lodestar, a court's duty in determining a reasonable fee award is not completed. The Supreme Court has cautioned that if "a plaintiff has achieved only partial or limited success, the product of hours reasonably expended on the litigation as a whole times a reasonable hourly rate may be an excessive amount." Hensley, 461 U.S. at 436. In measuring the level of success a plaintiff has achieved, the district court may consider the amount of damages awarded compared to the amount of damages requested. Farrar v. Hobby, 506 U.S. 103, 114 (1992) (quoting Riverside v. Rivera, 477 U.S. 561 (1986) (Powell, J., concurring in judgment) ("Where recovery of private damages is the purpose of . . . civil rights litigation, a district court, in fixing fees, is obligated to give primary consideration to the amount of damages awarded as compared to the amount sought.")); see also, Hensley, 461 U.S. at 436 (stating that "the most critical factor" in determining reasonableness of fee award "is the degree of success obtained"). It should be noted that this assessment is distinct from a proportionality analysis between the amount of damages awarded and the amount of counsel fees requested, which is an impermissible basis upon which to reduce a fee award. See Washington, 89 F.3d at 1042 ("[T]he reason why the damage amount is relevant is not because of some ratio that the court ought to maintain between damages and counsel fees. Rather, the reason has to do with the settled principle . . . that counsel fees should only be awarded to the extent that the litigant was successful.").

In making a downward adjustment for partial success, "the district court may attempt to identify specific hours that should be eliminated, or it may simply reduce the award to account for the limited success." Hensley, 461 U.S. at 436–37. The Supreme Court has rejected "a mathematical approach comparing the total number of issues in the case with those actually prevailed upon." Id. at 435 n. 11. Courts in this circuit have taken a wide array of approaches to the reduction of attorneys' fees for lack of success. See, e.g., Washington, 89 F.3d at 1043 (finding that reduction of attorney's fees by fifty percent was appropriate where plaintiff requested more than $750,000.00 in damages and the jury awarded "nominal victory of $25,000.00"); Hall v. Am. Honda Motor Co., Civ. A. No. 96-8103, 1997 WL 732458, at *4, 1997 U.S. Dist. LEXIS 18544, at *11 (E.D. Pa. Nov.24, 1997) (reducing award by ten percent where plaintiff sought damages in excess of $50,000.00 and received final judgment of $4,000.00); Hilferty v. Chevrolet Motor Div. of Gen. Motors Corp., Civ. A. No. 95-5324, 1996 WL 287276, at *6-7, 1996 U.S. Dist. LEXIS 7388, at *24-25 (E.D. Pa. May 30, 1996) (reducing fee award by approximately two-thirds where plaintiff recovered only eight percent of damages sought.)

In the instant case, Plaintiff sought $300,000.00 in damages, comprised of a $50,000.00 claim for actual damages, arising out of purported credit denials and emotional distress, and $250,000.00 for statutory and punitive damages. Despite Plaintiff's request, the jury awarded the nominal amount of $1,000.00. Although this Court cannot be certain of the basis for the $1,000.00 award, the only testimony at trial specifically assigning a monetary value to any of Mr. Sheffer's purported damages consisted of testimony regarding a $1,000.00 retainer that Mr. Sheffer paid to Mr. Lyons' law firm. Thus, it appears that the award, rather than indicating the jury's valuation of Mr. Sheffer's compensatory damages, was in fact designed to reimburse Mr. Sheffer for his out-of-pocket expenses associated with this lawsuit. Furthermore, the $1,000.00 judgment Mr. Sheffer derived from this lawsuit is significantly less than the $30,000.00 amount Sears' offered in settlement. It would be inappropriate and unreasonable to award Plaintiff for such a modest result by granting the fees Plaintiff seeks. See Farrar, 506 U.S. at 115 (stating that fee shifting statutes were never intended to "produce windfalls to attorneys") (quoting Riverside v. Rivera, 477 U.S. 561, 580). Given Plaintiff's limited success in this lawsuit, this Court finds that $25,000.00 is reasonable compensation.

. . .

III. CONCLUSION

In sum, the revised hourly rate reduced Plaintiff's lodestar to $106,569.38 and the subsequent reductions detailed in Part II.A.2 resulted in an adjusted lodestar amount of $78,749.97. This amount was further reduced to $25,000.00 to account for the de minimis level of success achieved by Plaintiff's attorneys. Therefore, I conclude that Plaintiff, as the prevailing party, is entitled to attorneys' fees in the amount of $25,000.00. . . .

———————

As the case illustrates, attorneys face some risks in recovering fees, even if their client prevails. While many plaintiffs' attorneys recover all or nearly all of their fees, there is a chilling effect from the scrutiny and uncertainty. One study found that when state UDAP law had a discretionary rather than mandatory attorney's fee provision, that most consumers and attorneys were statistically less willing to bring both a "strong meritorious" case and a "good faith extension of the law" case. Debra Pogrund Stark & Jessica M.

Choplin, *Does Fraud Pay? An Empirical Analysis of Attorney's Fees Provisions in Consumer Fraud Statutes*, 56 Cleveland St. L. Rev. 483, 514-515 (2008). This research echoes the observation of Professor Macaulay, quoted above, that it is necessary to understand how attorneys and potential clients make decisions to design consumer remedies.

Pure economic reasoning would suggest that a consumer would never bring a claim for $1,000, if she would forego dozens of hours of lost leisure or work time in serving as plaintiff. In fact, some of the most well-publicized consumer law disputes have been raised by professors. *See, e.g., Gray v. American Express Co.*, 743 F.2d 10 (D.C. Cir. 1984) (law professor specializing in fraud brought Fair Credit Billing Dispute case); *Ben Edelman, Harvard Business School Professor Goes to War Over $4 in Chinese Food*, Boston.com (Dec. 19, 2014) (alleging that business charging prices that were higher than its online website was a violation of the Massachusetts UDAP statute). Professor Rick Hasen, a remedies expert, recently put his professional knowledge to personal use.

> I just bought a ticket for a work trip to Japan, and it turns out that Expedia failed to disclose that this a special fare that does not allow seat selection until 72 hours before flight time, and Expedia misrepresented the ticket could be changed (such as to a higher class of service, so I could do seat selection) with a change fee. It is totally non-changeable. I've now started action against Expedia in small claims court. . . . No doubt this is a first-world problem, and there are many more pressing things in the world. But it is one of the many examples of large corporations counting on individuals to not have the time or means or experience to file one of these lawsuits. . . .
>
> Most people, I know, give up and don't bother filing an actual small claims lawsuit against a big company. It's a lot of paperwork and it can be confusing. But as a professor teaching Contracts, Remedies, and Torts for over 20 years (Google me), I think I can handle the paperwork.

Rick Hasen, *Beware Buying Overseas Airline Tickets @Expedia: No Seat Selection or Changes — And No Disclosure!* Election Law Blog (Nov. 22, 2015). Ideal plaintiffs have substantive expertise, a normative commitment to the rule of law, and flexible work schedules. Consider the life realities of a low-wage shift worker, or a working parent of young children, or an elderly person in a rural area without Internet access and whether they would be able to find a lawyer, file a small claims action by themselves, or even know which regulator might hear their complaint. These obstacles to enforcement are difficult to overcome.

While lawmakers have tried to increase private litigation through rules that shift attorneys' fees for prevailing plaintiffs, countervailing measures have been stronger. Some statutes now even go the other direction, upsetting the American Rule that each party pays its own costs in favor of the business. If a consumer brings and does not win a lawsuit, he or she may be liable to the defense for its costs and attorney's fees. *See, e.g.,* Cal. Civ. Code §1780(e) (permitting the court to award "reasonable attorney's fees to a prevailing defendant upon a finding that the plaintiff's prosecution of the action was not in good faith.") Such liability is usually limited to situations of groundless, spurious, or harassing litigation, but still may chill private enforcement. Consumer advocates criticize these defendant fee-shifting statutes on the ground that baseless litigation is already barred by the professional rules of conduct, such as Federal Rule of Civil Procedure 11.

C.   Class Actions

Class actions can help enable the vindication of rights that would not be litigated in an individual case. Class actions can also broaden the dissemination of relief to consumers who did not know their rights or would not have served as a plaintiff. Individual class members do not have to appear in court but their interests are represented by one or more class representatives, who are the named plaintiffs. In a world of mass production, global media, and large corporations, thousands or hundreds of thousands of consumers may have suffered nearly identical harms. It is more efficient to litigate these common legal and factual issues one time in one court. It also ensures parity of remedy to all similarly affected consumers, rather than allowing for a large judgment for the first plaintiff, with dwindling resources for each subsequent plaintiff.

Procedurally, class actions are governed by Federal Rule of Civil Procedure 23 or its state law equivalents. There are four initial criteria that must be met for class certification. First, the class must be so numerous that joinder of all members is impracticable. This typically means dozens, if not hundreds of plaintiffs. Second, there must be common questions of law or fact. Third, the claims or defenses of the class representative must be typical of those of class members. Fourth, the representatives must be able to fairly and adequately protect the interests of the class. The shorthand, which you may remember from Civil Procedure, is numerosity, commonality, typicality, and adequacy of representation. Most consumer class actions are brought on the grounds that a class action is "superior to other available methods for fairly and efficiently adjudicating the controversy." Fed. R. Civ. P. 23(b)(3). In making that determination a court will consider the "manageability" of the class litigation. If these requirements are satisfied, the court will certify the class. For many consumer actions, this is a critical moment. Without certification, plaintiffs may have no remedy. With certification, a business may be cowed into settling by the size of its risk, despite a meritorious defense.

If a class action settles, the court must review and approve the settlement. It will require notice through publication or other means to try to advise class members of the settlement and provide an opportunity to opt-out of the proposed relief. The court will hold a fairness hearing after the notice period expires. Along with the plaintiffs' relief, the court also will scrutinize the arrangements to pay plaintiffs' counsel.

A developing area of class action law is the requirement of "ascertainability" of class members. While this requirement is not explicit in Rule 23, courts have become increasingly stringent in scrutinizing whether plaintiffs—at the outset—can identify class members with certainty. In *Carrera v. Bayer Corp.*, 727 F.3d 300 (3d Cir. 2013), the Third Circuit denied certification because it found that the plaintiff's proposed methods of identifying purchasers of a nutritional supplement using store brand loyalty cards and consumer affidavits attesting to purchase were insufficient to determine whether some-one is in the class. The court identified three justifications for a "rigorous approach at the outset" to ascertainability: 1) that a clearly identifiable class was necessary to allow potential class members to opt out; 2) that a defendant's rights are protected by the class mechanism; and 3) that class members can be identified in a manner consistent with the efficiencies of a class action. *Id.* at 307. The contrary view of ascertainability is that it is an administrative issue to be addressed at the time of dissemination of relief to avoid a windfall to those seeking the class benefits who cannot show eligibility. The Seventh Circuit refused to impose "a new requirement that plaintiffs prove at the certification stage that there is a 'reliable and administratively feasible' to identify class members." *Mullins v. Direct Digital LLC,* 795 F.3d 654 (7th Cir. 2015). It ruled that such an approach is inappropriate because it moves "beyond examining the adequacy of the class definition itself to examine the potential difficulty of identifying particular members of the class and evaluating the validity of claims they might eventually submit." *Id.* at 657.

Class actions increasingly turn on statistical social science methods. A company might present a survey of customers or a plaintiffs' firm might pro-pose to use data mining to identify likely purchasers. Courts are sometimes uncomfortable with such methods or require more detail than plaintiffs have provided to prove their validity. In another Third Circuit case hostile to class certification, the court was skeptical that purchasers of Skinnygirl Margaritas could find receipts or recall details about the date or place of purchase. It also rejected "sophisticated and state-of-the-art data matching techniques" to identify duplicative claims. *Stewart v. Beam Global Spirits & Wine, Inc.,* 2015 WL 3613723 (D.N.J. June 9, 2015). The court rejected plaintiffs' efforts to rely on defendants' sales data to determine damages, seemingly requiring consumers to have proof of purchase. The next time someone asks why your wallet is overflowing with paper receipts, you can respond that you want to do your part to shape class action law.

D. Non-Enforcement

Problems with private enforcement mean that many, and perhaps most, con-sumers do not sue or even consult an attorney. The person may experience the situation as a grievance but not act to obtain a remedy. This do-nothing strat-egy has a name in the academic literature: "lumping it." Marc Galanter, *Reading the Landscape of Disputes: What We Know and Don't Know (and Think We Know) About Our Allegedly Contentious and Litigious Society,* 31 UCLA L. Rev. 4, 14 (1983) ("Even when injuries are perceived, a common response is resignation, that is 'lumping it.'").

Consumers may choose to lump it for a variety of reasons. As an initial issue, consumers may not know that their grievance actually is a legal violation. As you have seen this semester, consumer law is complex and public awareness of such laws is often very limited. This is a problem that can be tackled to some degree by education and public awareness campaigns, both for consumers and for lawyers.

Consumers may lump it because they wish to avoid a conflict. The consumer with an FDCPA violation claim against a debt collector may not want to engage someone who has treated them poorly (even in litigation, armed with an attorney) or the consumer may feel that they share some of the blame for the situation because they did not pay the debt. *See* Ronald J. Mann & Katherine Porter, *Saving Up for Bankruptcy*, 98 Geo. L.J. 298, 334-335 (2010). Lumping it can also result from economic pressures. Consumers may recognize that they have been wronged and be willing to fight to have it remedied, but lack the resources in the form of time, money, or expertise to pursue a claim.

Ultimately, enforcement of consumer law depends not just on the substantive remedies but on recognizing that those remedies are imbedded in a system of actors, including consumers, lawyers, and judges. Changing the level of protection requires thinking about consumers' awareness of legal rights and their incentives to vindicate wrongs of those rights, courts' behavior in "judging" in consumer disputes, and lawyers' motivations to settle or litigate cases.

Problem Set 25

25.1. Albert Hamm bought an entertainment system for $1,500 on credit from Constant Co., but defaulted on his payments when the system broke down and Constant refused to repair it. Constant filed a lawsuit to recover the unpaid balance on the loan of $1,150. Hamm hired May Marion to represent him in the lawsuit because he feared damage to his credit report and a garnishment action. She reviewed the loan disclosures and identified several TILA violations. She counseled Hamm that they would counterclaim under TILA, likely receive statutory damages, and that Constant would be required to pay Marion's fee. Hamm was delighted at the news that he could obtain representation without having to pay Marion.

After Marion filed the answer with the counterclaims, she received a call from Constant Co.'s attorney, suggesting a "wash" — a settlement in which Constant would drop the debt collection suit for $1,150 in return for Hamm releasing Constant from the TILA claims. Marion advised Hamm not to take this deal, but when she recounted the story to you over dinner the following night, you suggested that she immediately stop talking. You, by the way, are ethics counsel for the state bar. Was Marion correct in advising Hamm to continue the suit? Is Marion an ethical attorney? 15 U.S.C. §1640.

25.2. You represent a cosmetic company that marketed and sold 'Round the Clock Rouge. The advertisements and packaging said the product would "stay bright as long as you stay awake." A class action complaint alleging false advertising seeks restitution for all monies paid for the rouge, which totaled $180 million in sales since the product went on the market three years ago. The class representatives are three women who said that they chose 'Round the Clock Rouge specifically because they worked 24-hour shifts in a hospital and that the makeup did not last anywhere near 12 hours, much less 24 hours.

You've been in touch with the manufacturers, and they have offered up the following items for you to consider in crafting a response to the motion for class certification:

- A market study showing that 'Round the Clock Rouge is priced exactly at the average cost for similar make-up;
- Customer care data showing that approximately 2,700 consumers contacted the company about 'Round the Clock Rouge and 500 of these complaints were about the product's staying power or performance. Each of these 500 consumers were issued a refund check for the purchase price;
- A survey of past purchasers, conducted by a marketing expert after the litigation was threatened, that found that less than 10 percent of purchasers expected the product to last 12-24 hours; and
- Analysis of data from the largest retailer selling 'Round the Clock Rouge showing that 50 percent of people purchased the product more than one time in its three years of existence.

What legal and factual arguments will you make in your motion based on these documents? Fed. R. Civ. P. 23.

25.3. U.S. Senator Tuz is deeply committed to libertarianism. He believes most government intervention is suspect and is particularly frustrated by what he sees as "anti-democratic" institutions such as federal judges imposing "the equivalent of taxes" on businesses. He is supporting legislation that would amend about three dozen federal consumer protection statutes to require that an individual plaintiff or a representative class plaintiff show actual harm to bring suit. He wants to put an end to "no injury" cases and has asked you to identify legal and policy arguments that he can offer in support of his legislation.

Assignment 26. Alternative Dispute Resolution

Alternative dispute resolution (ADR) refers to processes for parties with a disagreement to come to a solution outside of litigation. Sometimes ADR can be incorporated into litigation, such as a settlement conference facilitated by a judge other than the person assigned to the case, but the major focus is on the system that exists outside of the courts. ADR is touted for many benefits, including being cheaper and faster than litigation. It may produce a more satisfactory outcome for all parties through negotiation and compromise, rather than a winner-take-all outcome that can follow from litigation.

ADR is an umbrella term that encompasses a wide variety of processes. In the United States, the most common forms of ADR are negotiation, mediation, and arbitration. Negotiation refers to voluntary efforts to reach a compromise, usually without third-party intervention. Mediation usually means the use of a third party to guide the parties in their discussions and sometimes to suggest a resolution, which the parties can accept or not. In consumer law, mediation is often offered as a precursor to full litigation. For example, in Problem 24.2, the state Attorney General was trying to facilitate a mediation process between disgruntled consumers who called registered complaints and the businesses of concern.

Given the problems with public and private enforcement discussed in the preceding assignments, one might expect consumers to be eager for alternatives and flock to ADR processes. Businesses, however, have been the driving force behind the expansion of ADR into consumer law. Most ADR in consumer law is not the result of parties suggesting a voluntary alternative to litigation after the dispute arises, but rather a predetermined decision that was built into the boilerplate of the contract. Limits of the right to access to courts is disfavored by consumer advocates, but that perspective is countered by the general attitude in most fields that ADR should be promoted and favored by the law.

A. Arbitration and Its Premises

Arbitration in the consumer context nearly always means predispute mandatory arbitration imposed by contract. The consumer becomes bound to arbitrate at the time of the agreement, not at the time of the dispute. The key feature of this kind of arbitration is that a private third-party will impose a resolution on the parties. The contractual agreement to arbitrate prevents the parties from choosing to pursue their rights in courts and will often specify the name of the arbitration association or the rules of the arbitration, or give one party (usually the business) the right to determine those things. The determination of the third party is not "law" in the sense that it is not prece-dential and is not a result of a public process. But between the parties, it is law. It is a final decision that resolves all issues. Federal law sharply curbs the right to appeal from an arbitration decision, making arbitration into a one-proce-dure resolution.

There are a few leading arbitration organizations in the United States that seem to garner the bulk of the work for nationwide businesses that put arbi-tration clauses in their consumer contracts. It is not simple to determine how frequently such businesses use arbitration clauses. First, these are private con-tracts, so it requires work to collect them from various businesses. Second, there seems to be a size effect. One study of credit card contracts, for which the conventional wisdom was that predispute mandatory arbitration clauses were nearly universal, found that while 95.1 percent of outstanding loans have credit card agreements, 82.9 percent of issuers do not put them in agreements. The study found that card issuers were more likely to require arbitration if they specialized in credit card loans, had larger credit card portfolios, and made riskier loans. *See* Christopher R. Drazhol & Peter B. Rutledge, *Arbitration Clauses in Credit Card Agreements: An Empirical Study*, 9 J. EMPIRICAL LEGAL STUD. 536 (2012). Third, it is not clear whether the appropriate analysis of the effects of arbitration can be globalized to all "consumer contracts" or if such clauses should be examined in a context-specific setting, for example, by looking at their use and function with various consumer products such as tangible goods, services, mortgages, car loans, deposit accounts.

B.   Invalidating or Limiting Arbitration in Consumer Contracts

1.   Unconscionability and State Law

Concern about the harms of predispute mandatory arbitration clauses to con-sumers' ability to vindicate the substantive rights of consumer law has produced numerous court challenges to ADR. Several of these have found their way to the Supreme Court, which has also ruled on several ADR issues in the context of commercial contracts. The two most recent decisions both limit the authority of courts to deny or limit the enforcement of arbitra-tion clauses.

In *Rent-A-Center v. Jackson*, 561 U.S. 63 (2010), an employee challenged the enforceability of an arbitration agreement that he had signed in his employ-ment contract on the grounds that requiring him to pursue arbitration was unconscionable. The Court's opinion defined when and how unconscionabil-ity may be used to challenge an arbitration provision. The Court treated as distinct two provisions in the parties' arbitration agreement: (1) the basic provision calling for arbitration of "'past, present or future disputes arising out of [the employment contract]," and (2) the provision delegating "gateway" issues to the arbitrator ("[t]he Arbitrator . . . shall have exclusive authority to resolve any dispute relating to the . . . enforceability . . . of this Agreement"). Justice Scalia treated the clauses as severable and held that when a contract "clearly and unmistakably" delegates gateway questions to arbitrators, unconscionability challenges brought in courts must be focused on the delegation provision alone. He concluded that such a delegation clause was enforceable under Section 2 of the Federal Arbitration Act and that the arbiter's decision that that the contract was not unconscionable must not be disturbed. If the contract is written to give the arbiter the power to determine the enforceability of the arbitration clause, courts should heed to the delegation of that power to the arbiter and not impose independent judgment. The effect of the case is to close the court house doors so that individuals cannot even get the issue of unconscionability of arbitration to a judge.

In the case below, the Court revisits the intersection of the federal and state law, this time in the context of class action waivers that are routinely used in tandem with predispute arbitration.

AT&T Mobility LLC v. Concepcion

131 S. Ct. 1740 (2011)

Scalia, Justice.

Section 2 of the Federal Arbitration Act (FAA) makes agreements to arbitrate "valid, irrevocable, and enforceable, save upon such grounds as exist at law or in equity for the revocation of any contract." 9 U.S.C. §2. We consider whether the FAA prohibits States from conditioning the enforceability of certain arbitration agreements on the availability of classwide arbitration procedures.

I.

In February 2002, Vincent and Liza Concepcion entered into an agreement for the sale and servicing of cellular telephones with AT&T Mobility LCC (AT&T). The contract provided for arbitration of all disputes between the parties, but required that claims be brought in the parties' "individual capacity, and not as a plaintiff or class member in any purported class or representative proceeding." The agreement authorized AT&T to make unilateral amendments, which it did to the arbitration provision on several occasions. The version at issue in this case reflects revisions made in December 2006, which the parties agree are controlling.

The revised agreement provides that customers may initiate dispute proceedings by completing a one-page Notice of Dispute form available on AT&T's Web site. AT&T may then offer to settle the claim; if it does not, or if the dispute is not resolved within 30 days, the customer may invoke arbitration by filing a separate Demand for Arbitration, also available on AT&T's Web site. In the event the parties proceed to arbitration, the agreement specifies that AT&T must pay all costs for nonfrivolous claims; that arbitration must take place in the county in which the customer is billed; that, for claims of $10,000 or less, the customer may choose whether the arbitration proceeds in person, by telephone, or based only on submissions; that either party may bring a claim in small claims court in lieu of arbitration; and that the arbitrator may award any form of individual relief, including injunctions and presumably punitive damages. The agreement, moreover, denies AT&T any ability to seek reimbursement of its attorney's fees, and, in the event that a customer receives an arbitration award greater than AT&T's last written settlement offer, requires AT&T to pay a $7,500 minimum recovery and twice the amount of the claimant's attorney's fees.[1]

The Concepcions purchased AT&T service, which was advertised as including the provision of free phones; they were not charged for the phones, but they were charged $30.22 in sales tax based on the phones' retail value. In March 2006, the Concepcions filed a complaint against AT&T in the United States District Court for the Southern District of California. The complaint was later consolidated with a putative class action alleging, among other things, that AT&T had engaged in false advertising and fraud by charging sales tax on phones it advertised as free.

In March 2008, AT&T moved to compel arbitration under the terms of its contract with the Concepcions. The Concepcions opposed the motion, contending that the arbitration agreement was unconscionable and unlawfully exculpatory under California law because it disallowed classwide procedures. The District Court denied AT&T's motion. It described AT&T's arbitration agreement favorably, noting, for example, that the informal dispute-resolution process was "quick, easy to use" and likely to "promp[t] full or . . . even excess payment to the customer *without* the need to arbitrate or litigate"; that the $7,500 premium functioned as "a substantial inducement for the consumer to pursue the claim in arbitration" if a dispute was not resolved informally; and that consumers who were members of a class would likely be worse off. Laster v. T-Mobile USA, Inc., 2008 U.S. Dist. LEXIS 103712, *34, 2008 WL 5216255, *11-*12 (S.D. Cal., Aug. 11, 2008). Nevertheless, relying on the California Supreme Court's decision in Discover Bank v. Superior Court, 36 Cal. 4th 148 (2005), the court found that the arbitration provision was unconscionable because AT&T had not shown that bilateral arbitration adequately substituted for the deterrent effects of class actions. Laster, 2008 U.S. Dist. LEXIS 103712, 2008 WL 5216255, *14.

The Ninth Circuit affirmed, also finding the provision unconscionable under California law as announced in *Discover Bank*. Laster v. AT&T Mobility LLC, 584 F.3d 849, 855 (2009). It also held that the *Discover Bank* rule was not preempted by the FAA because that rule was simply "a refinement of the unconscionability analysis applicable to contracts generally in California." 584 F.3d, at 857. In response to AT&T's argument that the Concepcions' interpretation of California law discriminated against arbitration, the Ninth Circuit rejected the contention that "'class proceedings will reduce the efficiency and expeditiousness of arbitration'" and noted that "'*Discover Bank* placed arbitration agreements with class action waivers on the *exact same footing* as contracts that bar class action litigation outside the context of arbitration.'" Id., at 858 (quoting Shroyer v. New Cingular Wireless Services, Inc., 498 F.3d 976, 990 (9th Cir. 2007)).

We granted certiorari, 560 U.S. 923 (2010).

---

1. The guaranteed minimum recovery was increased in 2009 to $10,000.

II.

The FAA was enacted in 1925 in response to widespread judicial hostility to arbitration agreements. See Hall Street Associates, LLC v. Mattel, Inc., 552 U.S. 576, 581 (2008). Section 2, the "primary substantive provision of the Act," Moses H. Cone Memorial Hospital v. Mercury Constr. Corp., 460 U.S. 1, 24 (1983), provides, in relevant part, as follows:

> "A written provision in any maritime transaction or a contract evidencing a transaction involving commerce to settle by arbitration a controversy thereafter arising out of such contract or transaction . . . shall be valid, irrevocable, and enforceable, save upon such grounds as exist at law or in equity for the revocation of any contract."

9 U.S.C. §2. We have described this provision as reflecting both a "liberal federal policy favoring arbitration," Moses H. Cone, supra, at 24, and the "fundamental principle that arbitration is a matter of contract," Rent-A-Center, West, Inc. v. Jackson, 561 U.S. 63, 67 (2010). In line with these principles, courts must place arbitration agreements on an equal footing with other contracts, Buckeye Check Cashing, Inc. v. Cardegna, 546 U.S. 440, 443 (2006), and enforce them according to their terms, Volt Information Sciences, Inc. v. Board of Trustees of Leland Stanford Junior Univ., 489 U.S. 468, 478 (1989).

The final phrase of §2, however, permits arbitration agreements to be declared unenforceable "upon such grounds as exist at law or in equity for the revocation of any contract." This saving clause permits agreements to arbitrate to be invalidated by "generally applicable contract defenses, such as fraud, duress, or unconscionability," but not by defenses that apply only to arbitration or that derive their meaning from the fact that an agreement to arbitrate is at issue. Doctor's Associates, Inc. v. Casarotto, 517 U.S. 681, 687 (1996); see also Perry v. Thomas, 482 U.S. 483, 492-493, n. 9 (1987). The question in this case is whether §2 preempts California's rule classifying most collective-arbitration waivers in consumer contracts as unconscionable. We refer to this rule as the *Discover Bank* rule.

Under California law, courts may refuse to enforce any contract found "to have been unconscionable at the time it was made," or may "limit the application of any unconscionable clause." Cal. Civ. Code Ann. §1670.5(a). A finding of unconscionability requires "a 'procedural' and a 'substantive' element, the former focusing on 'oppression' or 'surprise' due to unequal bargaining power, the latter on 'overly harsh' or 'one-sided' results." Armendariz v. Foundation Health Psychcare Servs., 24 Cal. 4th 83, 114 (2000); accord, Discover Bank, 36 Cal. 4th, at 159-161.

In *Discover Bank*, the California Supreme Court applied this framework to class-action waivers in arbitration agreements and held as follows:

> [W]hen the waiver is found in a consumer contract of adhesion in a setting in which disputes between the contracting parties predictably involve small amounts of damages, and when it is alleged that the party with the superior bargaining power has carried out a scheme to deliberately cheat large numbers of consumers out of individually small sums of money, then . . . the waiver becomes in practice the exemption of the party 'from responsibility for [its] own fraud, or willful injury to the

person or property of another.' Under these circumstances, such waivers are unconscionable under California law and should not be enforced.

Id., at 162 (quoting Cal. Civ. Code Ann. §1668). California courts have frequently applied this rule to find arbitration agreements unconscionable. See, e.g., Cohen v. DirecTV, Inc., 142 Cal. App. 4th 1442, 1451-1453 (2006); Klussman v. Cross Country Bank, 134 Cal. App. 4th 1283, 1297 (2005); Aral v. EarthLink, Inc., 134 Cal. App. 4th 544, 556-557 (2005).

III.

A.

The Concepcions argue that the *Discover Bank* rule, given its origins in California's unconscionability doctrine and California's policy against exculpation, is a ground that "exist[s] at law or in equity for the revocation of any contract" under FAA §2. Moreover, they argue that even if we construe the *Discover Bank* rule as a prohibition on collective-action waivers rather than simply an application of unconscionability, the rule would still be applicable to all dispute-resolution contracts, since California prohibits waivers of class litigation as well. See America Online, Inc. v. Superior Ct., 90 Cal. App. 4th 1, 17-18 (2001).

When state law prohibits outright the arbitration of a particular type of claim, the analysis is straightforward: The conflicting rule is displaced by the FAA. Preston v. Ferrer, 552 U.S. 346, 353 (2008). But the inquiry becomes more complex when a doctrine normally thought to be generally applicable, such as duress or, as relevant here, unconscionability, is alleged to have been applied in a fashion that disfavors arbitration. In Perry v. Thomas, 482 U.S. 483 (1987), for example, we noted that the FAA's preemptive effect might extend even to grounds traditionally thought to exist "'at law or in equity for the revocation of any contract.' Id., at 492, n. 9. We said that a court may not "rely on the uniqueness of an agreement to arbitrate as a basis for a state-law holding that enforcement would be unconscionable, for this would enable the court to effect what . . . the state legislature cannot." Id., at 493, n. 9.

An obvious illustration of this point would be a case finding unconscionable or unenforceable as against public policy consumer arbitration agreements that fail to provide for judicially monitored discovery. The rationalizations for such a holding are neither difficult to imagine nor different in kind from those articulated in *Discover Bank*. A court might reason that no consumer would knowingly waive his right to full discovery, as this would enable companies to hide their wrongdoing. Or the court might simply say that such agreements are exculpatory — restricting discovery would be of greater benefit to the company than the consumer, since the former is more likely to be sued than to sue. See Discover Bank, supra, at 161 (arguing that class waivers are similarly one-sided). And, the reasoning would continue, because such a rule applies the general principle of unconscionability or public-policy disapproval of exculpatory agreements, it is applicable to "any" contract and thus preserved by §2 of the FAA. In practice, of course, the rule would have a disproportionate impact on arbitration agreements; but it would presumably apply to contracts purporting to restrict discovery in litigation as well.

Other examples are easy to imagine. The same argument might apply to a rule classifying as unconscionable arbitration agreements that fail to abide by the Federal Rules of Evidence, or that disallow an ultimate disposition by a jury (perhaps termed "a panel of twelve lay arbitrators" to help avoid preemption). Such examples are not fanciful, since the judicial hostility towards arbitration that prompted the FAA had manifested itself in "a great variety" of "devices and formulas" declaring arbitration against public policy. Robert Lawrence Co. v. Devonshire Fabrics, Inc., 271 F.2d 402, 406 (2d Cir. 1959). And although these statistics are not definitive, it is worth noting that California's courts have been more likely to hold contracts to arbitrate unconscionable than other contracts. Broome, An Unconscionable Applicable of the Unconscionability Doctrine: How the California Courts are Circumventing the Federal Arbitration Act, 3 Hastings Bus. L.J. 39, 54, 66 (2006); Randall, Judicial Attitudes Toward Arbitration and the Resurgence of Unconscionability, 52 Buffalo L. Rev. 185, 186-187 (2004).

The Concepcions suggest that all this is just a parade of horribles, and no genuine worry. "Rules aimed at destroying arbitration" or "demanding procedures incompatible with arbitration," they concede, "would be preempted by the FAA because they cannot sensibly be reconciled with Section 2." Brief for Respondents 32. The "grounds" available under §2's saving clause, they admit, "should not be construed to include a State's mere preference for procedures that are incompatible with arbitration and 'would wholly eviscerate arbitration agreements.'" Id., at 33.[2]

We largely agree. Although §2's saving clause preserves generally applicable contract defenses, nothing in it suggests an intent to preserve state-law rules that stand as an obstacle to the accomplishment of the FAA's objectives. Cf. Geier v. American Honda Motor Co., 529 U.S. 861, 872 (2000); As we have said, a federal statute's saving clause "'cannot in reason be construed as [allowing] a common law right, the continued existence of which would be absolutely inconsistent with the provisions of the act. In other words, the act cannot be held to destroy itself.'" American Telephone & Telegraph Co. v. Central Office Telephone, Inc., 524 U.S. 214, 227-228 (1998).

We differ with the Concepcions only in the application of this analysis to the matter before us. We do not agree that rules requiring judicially monitored discovery or adherence to the Federal Rules of Evidence are "a far cry from this case." The overarching purpose of the FAA, evident in the text of §§2, 3, and 4, is to ensure the enforcement of arbitration agreements according to their terms so as to facilitate streamlined proceedings. Requiring the availability of classwide arbitration interferes with fundamental attributes of arbitration and thus creates a scheme inconsistent with the FAA.

---

2. The dissent seeks to fight off even this eminently reasonable concession. It says that to its knowledge "we have not . . . applied the Act to strike down a state statute that treats arbitrations on par with judicial and administrative proceedings," post, at 366, 179 L. Ed. 2d, at 767 (opinion of Breyer, J.), and that "we should think more than twice before invalidating a state law that . . . puts agreements to arbitrate and agreements to litigate 'upon the same footing'" post, at 361, 179 L. Ed. 2d, at 763-764.

B.

The "principal purpose" of the FAA is to "ensur[e] that private arbitration agreements are enforced according to their terms." Volt, 489 U.S., at 478. This purpose is readily apparent from the FAA's text. Section 2 makes arbitration agreements "valid, irrevocable, and enforceable" as written (subject, of course, to the saving clause); §3 requires courts to stay litigation of arbitral claims pending arbitration of those claims "in accordance with the terms of the agreement"; and §4 requires courts to compel arbitration "in accordance with the terms of the agreement" upon the motion of either party to the agreement (assuming that the "making of the arbitration agreement or the failure . . . to perform the same" is not at issue). In light of these provisions, we have held that parties may agree to limit the issues subject to arbitration, Mitsubishi Motors Corp. v. Soler Chrysler-Plymouth, Inc., 473 U.S. 614, 628 (1985), to arbitrate according to specific rules, Volt, supra, at 479, and to limit *with whom* a party will arbitrate its disputes, Stolt-Nielsen, supra.

The point of affording parties discretion in designing arbitration processes is to allow for efficient, streamlined procedures tailored to the type of dispute. It can be specified, for example, that the decision maker be a specialist in the relevant field, or that proceedings be kept confidential to protect trade secrets. And the informality of arbitral proceedings is itself desirable, reducing the cost and increasing the speed of dispute resolution. 14 Penn Plaza LLC v. Pyett, 556 U.S. 247, 269, (2009); Mitsubishi Motors Corp., supra, at 628.

The dissent quotes Dean Witter Reynolds Inc. v. Byrd, 470 U.S. 213, 219 (1985), as "'reject[ing] the suggestion that the overriding goal of the Arbitration Act was to promote the expeditious resolution of claims.'" Post, at ___ (opinion of Breyer, J.). That is greatly misleading. After saying (accurately enough) that "the overriding goal of the Arbitration Act was [not] to promote the expeditious resolution of claims," but to "ensure judicial enforcement of privately made agreements to arbitrate," 470 U.S., at 219, *Dean Witter* went on to explain: "This is not to say that Congress was blind to the potential benefit of the legislation for expedited resolution of disputes. Far from it. . . ." Id., at 220. It then quotes a House Report saying that "the costliness and delays of litigation . . . can be largely eliminated by agreements for arbitration." Ibid. (quoting H. R. Rep. No. 96, 68th Cong., 1st Sess., 2 (1924)). The concluding paragraph of this part of its discussion begins as follows:

> We therefore are not persuaded by the argument that the conflict between two goals of the Arbitration Act—enforcement of private agreements and encouragement of efficient and speedy dispute resolution—must be resolved in favor of the latter in order to realize the intent of the drafters.

470 U.S., at 221. In the present case, of course, those "two goals" do not conflict—and it is the dissent's view that would frustrate *both* of them.

Contrary to the dissent's view, our cases place it beyond dispute that the FAA was designed to promote arbitration. They have repeatedly described the Act as "embod[ying] [a] national policy favoring arbitration," Buckeye Check Cashing, 546 U.S., at 443, and "a liberal federal policy favoring arbitration agreements, notwithstanding any state substantive or procedural policies to the contrary," Moses H. Cone, 460 U.S., at 24. Thus, in Preston v. Ferrer, holding preempted a state-law rule requiring exhaustion of administrative remedies before arbitration, we said: "A prime objective of an agreement to arbitrate is to achieve 'streamlined proceedings and expeditious results,'" which objective would be "frustrated" by requiring a dispute to be heard by an agency first. 552 U.S., at 357-358. That rule, we said, would "at the least, hinder speedy resolution of the controversy." Id., at 358.[3]

California's *Discover Bank* rule similarly interferes with arbitration. Although the rule does not *require* classwide arbitration, it allows any party to a consumer contract to demand it *ex post*. The rule is limited to adhesion contracts, Discover Bank, 36 Cal. 4th, at 162-163, but the times in which consumer contracts were anything other than adhesive are long past.[4] Carbajal v. H&R Block Tax Servs., Inc., 372 F.3d 903, 906 (7th Cir. 2004); see also Hill v. Gateway 2000, Inc., 105 F.3d 1147, 1149 (7th Cir. 1997). The rule also requires that damages be predictably small, and that the consumer allege a scheme to cheat consumers. Discover Bank, supra, at 162-163. The former requirement, however, is toothless and malleable (the Ninth Circuit has held that damages of $4,000 are sufficiently small, see Oestreicher v. Alienware Corp., 322 Fed. Appx. 489, 492 (2009) (unpublished)), and the latter has no limiting effect, as all that is required is an allegation. Consumers remain free to bring and resolve their disputes on a bilateral basis under *Discover Bank*, and some may well do so; but there is little incentive for lawyers to arbitrate on behalf of individuals when they may do so for a class and reap far higher fees in the process. And faced with inevitable class arbitration, companies would have less incentive to continue resolving potentially duplicative claims on an individual basis.

Although we have had little occasion to examine classwide arbitration, our decision in *Stolt-Nielsen* is instructive. In that case we held that an arbitration panel exceeded its power under §10(a)(4) of the FAA by imposing class procedures based on policy judgments rather than the arbitration agreement itself or some background principle of contract law that would affect its interpretation. 559 U.S., at 684-687. We then held that the agreement at issue, which was silent on the question of class procedures, could not be interpreted to allow them because the "changes brought about by the shift from bilateral arbitration to class-action arbitration" are "fundamental." Id., at 686. This is obvious as a structural matter: Classwide arbitration includes absent parties, necessitating additional and different procedures and involving higher stakes. Confidentiality becomes more difficult.

---

3. Relying upon nothing more indicative of congressional understanding than statements of witnesses in committee hearings and a press release of Secretary of Commerce Herbert Hoover, the dissent suggests that Congress "thought that arbitration would be used primarily where merchants sought to resolve disputes of fact . . . [and] possessed roughly equivalent bargaining power." Post, at ___, 179 L. Ed. 2d, at 765. Such a limitation appears nowhere in the text of the FAA and has been explicitly rejected by our cases. "Relationships between securities dealers and investors, for example, may involve unequal bargaining power, but we [have] nevertheless held . . . that agreements to arbitrate in that context are enforceable." Gilmer v. Interstate/Johnson Lane Corp., 500 U.S. 20, 33 (1991); see also id., at 32-33 (allowing arbitration of claims arising under the Age Discrimination in Employment Act of 1967 despite allegations of unequal bargaining power between employers and employees). Of course the dissent's disquisition on legislative history fails to note that it contains nothing—not even the testimony of a stray witness in committee hearings—that contemplates the existence of class arbitration.

4. Of course States remain free to take steps addressing the concerns that attend contracts of adhesion—for example, requiring class-action-waiver provisions in adhesive arbitration agreements to be highlighted. Such steps cannot, however, conflict with the FAA or frustrate its purpose to ensure that private arbitration agreements are enforced according to their terms.

And while it is theoretically possible to select an arbitrator with some expertise relevant to the class-certification question, arbitrators are not generally knowledgeable in the often-dominant procedural aspects of certification, such as the protection of absent parties. The conclusion follows that class arbitration, to the extent it is manufactured by *Discover Bank* rather than consensual, is inconsistent with the FAA.

First, the switch from bilateral to class arbitration sacrifices the principal advantage of arbitration — its informality — and makes the process slower, more costly, and more likely to generate procedural morass than final judgment. "In bilateral arbitration, parties forgo the procedural rigor and appellate review of the courts in order to realize the benefits of private dispute resolution: lower costs, greater efficiency and speed, and the ability to choose expert adjudicators to resolve specialized disputes." 559 U.S., at 685. But before an arbitrator may decide the merits of a claim in classwide procedures, he must first decide, for example, whether the class itself may be certified, whether the named parties are sufficiently representative and typical, and how discovery for the class should be conducted. A cursory comparison of bilateral and class arbitration illustrates the difference. According to the American Arbitration Association (AAA), the average consumer arbitration between January and August 2007 resulted in a disposition on the merits in six months, four months if the arbitration was conducted by documents only. AAA, Analysis of the AAA's Consumer Arbitration Caseload, online at http://www.adr.org/si.asp?id=5027. As of September 2009, the AAA had opened 283 class arbitrations. Of those, 121 remained active, and 162 had been settled, withdrawn, or dismissed. Not a single one, however, had resulted in a final award on the merits. Brief for AAA as Amicus Curiae in Stolt-Nielsen, O.T. 2009, No. 08-1198, pp. 22-24. For those cases that were no longer active, the median time from filing to settlement, withdrawal, or dismissal — not judgment on the merits — was 583 days, and the mean was 630 days. Id., at 24.[5]

Second, class arbitration *requires* procedural formality. The AAA's rules governing class arbitrations mimic the Federal Rules of Civil Procedure for class litigation. Compare AAA, Supplementary Rules for Class Arbitrations (effective Oct. 8, 2003), online at http://www.adr.org/sp.asp?id=21936, with Fed. Rule Civ. Proc. 23. And while parties can alter those procedures by contract, an alternative is not obvious. If procedures are too informal, absent class members would not be bound by the arbitration. For a class-action money judgment to bind absentees in litigation, class representatives must at all times adequately represent absent class members, and absent members must be afforded notice, an opportunity to be heard, and a right to opt out of the class. Phillips Petroleum Co. v. Shutts, 472 U.S. 797, 811-812 (1985). At least this amount of process would presumably be required for absent parties to be bound by the results of arbitration.

We find it unlikely that in passing the FAA Congress meant to leave the disposition of these procedural requirements to an arbitrator. Indeed, class arbitration was not even envisioned by Congress when it passed the FAA in 1925; as the

---

5. The dissent claims that class arbitration should be compared to class litigation, not bilateral arbitration. Post, at ___ - ___, 179 L. Ed. 2d, at 765-766. Whether arbitrating a class is more desirable than litigating one, however, is not relevant. A State cannot defend a rule requiring arbitration-by-jury by saying that parties will still prefer it to trial-by-jury.

California Supreme Court admitted in *Discover Bank*, class arbitration is a "relatively recent development." 36 Cal. 4th, at 163. And it is at the very least odd to think that an arbitrator would be entrusted with ensuring that third parties' due process rights are satisfied.

Third, class arbitration greatly increases risks to defendants. Informal procedures do of course have a cost: The absence of multilayered review makes it more likely that errors will go uncorrected. Defendants are willing to accept the costs of these errors in arbitration, since their impact is limited to the size of individual disputes, and presumably outweighed by savings from avoiding the courts. But when damages allegedly owed to tens of thousands of potential claimants are aggregated and decided at once, the risk of an error will often become unacceptable. Faced with even a small chance of a devastating loss, defendants will be pressured into settling questionable claims. Other courts have noted the risk of "in terrorem" settlements that class actions entail, see, e.g., Kohen v. Pac. Inv. Mgmt. Co. LLC & PIMCO Funds, 571 F.3d 672, 677-678 (7th Cir. 2009), and class arbitration would be no different.

Arbitration is poorly suited to the higher stakes of class litigation. In litigation, a defendant may appeal a certification decision on an interlocutory basis and, if unsuccessful, may appeal from a final judgment as well. Questions of law are reviewed *de novo* and questions of fact for clear error. In contrast, 9 U.S.C. §10 allows a court to vacate an arbitral award *only* where the award "was procured by corruption, fraud, or undue means"; "there was evident partiality or corruption in the arbitrators"; "the arbitrators were guilty of misconduct in refusing to postpone the hearing . . . or in refusing to hear evidence pertinent and material to the controversy[,] or of any other misbehavior by which the rights of any party have been prejudiced"; or if the "arbitrators exceeded their powers, or so imperfectly executed them that a mutual, final, and definite award . . . was not made." The AAA rules do authorize judicial review of certification decisions, but this review is unlikely to have much effect given these limitations; review under §10 focuses on misconduct rather than mistake. And parties may not contractually expand the grounds or nature of judicial review. Hall Street Assocs., 552 U.S., at 578. We find it hard to believe that defendants would bet the company with no effective means of review, and even harder to believe that Congress would have intended to allow state courts to force such a decision.[6]

The Concepcions contend that because parties may and sometimes do agree to aggregation, class procedures are not necessarily incompatible with arbitration. But the same could be said about procedures that the Concepcions admit States may not superimpose on arbitration: Parties *could* agree to arbitrate pursuant to the Federal Rules of Civil Procedure, or pursuant to a discovery process rivaling that in litigation. Arbitration is a matter of contract, and the FAA requires courts to

---

6. The dissent cites three large arbitration awards (none of which stems from classwide arbitration) as evidence that parties are willing to submit large claims before an arbitrator. Post, at ___ - ___, 179 L. Ed. 2d, at 766. Those examples might be in point if it could be established that the size of the arbitral dispute was predictable when the arbitration agreement was entered. Otherwise, all the cases prove is that arbitrators can give huge awards — which we have never doubted. The point is that in class-action arbitration huge awards (with limited judicial review) will be entirely predictable, thus rendering arbitration unattractive. It is not reasonably deniable that requiring consumer disputes to be arbitrated on a classwide basis will have a substantial deterrent effect on incentives to arbitrate.

honor parties' expectations. Rent-A-Center, West, 561 U.S., at 67-69. But what the parties in the aforementioned examples would have agreed to is not arbitration as envisioned by the FAA, lacks its benefits, and therefore may not be required by state law.

The dissent claims that class proceedings are necessary to prosecute small-dollar claims that might otherwise slip through the legal system. See post, at __. But States cannot require a procedure that is inconsistent with the FAA, even if it is desirable for unrelated reasons. Moreover, the claim here was most unlikely to go unresolved. As noted earlier, the arbitration agreement provides that AT&T will pay claimants a minimum of $7,500 and twice their attorney's fees if they obtain an arbitration award greater than AT&T's last settlement offer. The District Court found this scheme sufficient to provide incentive for the individual prosecution of meritorious claims that are not immediately settled, and the Ninth Circuit admitted that aggrieved customers who filed claims would be "essentially guarantee[d]" to be made whole, 584 F.3d, at 856, n. 9. Indeed, the District Court concluded that the Concepcions were *better off* under their arbitration agreement with AT&T than they would have been as participants in a class action, which "could take months, if not years, and which may merely yield an opportunity to submit a claim for recovery of a small percentage of a few dollars." Laster, 2008 U.S. Dist. LEXIS 103712, [WL] at *12.

Because it "stands as an obstacle to the accomplishment and execution of the full purposes and objectives of Congress," Hines v. Davidowitz, 312 U.S. 52, 67 (1941), California's *Discover Bank* rule is preempted by the FAA. The judgment of the Ninth Circuit is reversed, and the case is remanded for further proceedings consistent with this opinion.

It is so ordered.

[ED. NOTE: The concurring opinion of Justice Thomas is omitted.]

Justice BREYER, with whom Justice GINSBURG, Justice SOTOMAYOR, and Justice KAGAN join, dissenting.

The Federal Arbitration Act says that an arbitration agreement "shall be valid, irrevocable, and enforceable, *save upon such grounds as exist at law or in equity for the revocation of any contract*." 9 U.S.C. §2 (emphasis added). California law sets forth certain circumstances in which "class action waivers" in *any* contract are unenforceable. In my view, this rule of state law is consistent with the federal Act's language and primary objective. It does not "stan[d] as an obstacle" to the Act's "accomplishment and execution." Hines v. Davidowitz, 312 U.S. 52, 67 (1941). And the Court is wrong to hold that the federal Act pre-empts the rule of state law.

I.

The California law in question consists of an authoritative state-court interpretation of two provisions of the California Civil Code. The first provision makes unlawful all contracts "which have for their object, directly or in-directly, to exempt anyone from responsibility for his own . . . violation of law." Cal. Civ. Code Ann. §1668. The second provision authorizes courts to "limit the application of any unconscionable clause" in a contract so "as to avoid any unconscionable result." §1670.5(a).

The specific rule of state law in question consists of the California Supreme Court's application of these principles to hold that "some" (but not "all") "class action waivers" in consumer contracts are exculpatory and unconscionable under California "law." Discover Bank v. Superior Ct., 36 Cal. 4th 148, 160, 162 (2005). In particular, in *Discover Bank* the California Supreme Court stated that, when a class-action waiver

> is found in a consumer contract of adhesion in a setting in which disputes between the contracting parties predictably involve small amounts of damages, and when it is alleged that the party with the superior bargaining power has carried out a scheme to deliberately cheat large numbers of consumers out of individually small sums of money, then . . . the waiver becomes in practice the exemption of the party 'from responsibility for [its] own fraud, or willful injury to the person or property of another.'

Id., at 162-163. In such a circumstance, the "waivers are unconscionable under California law and should not be enforced." Id., at 163.

The *Discover Bank* rule does not create a "blanket policy in California against class action waivers in the consumer context." Provencher v. Dell, Inc., 409 F. Supp. 2d 1196, 1201 (C.D. Cal. 2006). Instead, it represents the "application of a more general [unconscionability] principle." Gentry v. Superior Ct., 42 Cal. 4th 443, 457 (2007). Courts applying California law have enforced class-action waivers where they satisfy general unconscionability standards. See, e.g., Walnut Producers of Cal. v. Diamond Foods, Inc., 187 Cal. App. 4th 634, 647-650 (2010); Arguelles-Romero v. Superior Ct., 184 Cal. App. 4th 825, 843-845 (2010). And even when they fail, the parties remain free to devise other dispute mechanisms, including informal mechanisms, that, in context, will not prove unconscionable. See Volt Information Sciences, Inc. v. Board of Trustees of Leland Stanford Junior Univ., 489 U.S. 468, 479 (1989).

II.

A.

The *Discover Bank* rule is consistent with the federal Act's language. It "applies equally to class action litigation waivers in contracts without arbitration agreements as it does to class arbitration waivers in contracts with such agreements." 36 Cal. 4th, at 165-166. Linguistically speaking, it falls directly within the scope of the Act's exception permitting courts to refuse to enforce arbitration agreements on grounds that exist "for the revocation of *any* contract." 9 U.S.C. §2 (emphasis added). The majority agrees. Ante, at ___, 179 L. Ed. 2d, at 753.

B.

The *Discover Bank* rule is also consistent with the basic "purpose behind" the Act. Dean Witter Reynolds Inc. v. Byrd, 470 U.S. 213, 219 (1985). We have described that purpose as one of "ensur[ing] judicial enforcement" of arbitration agreements.

Ibid.; see also Marine Transit Corp. v. Dreyfus, 284 U.S. 263, 274, n. 2 (1932) ("'The purpose of this bill is to make *valid and enforcible* agreements for arbitration'" (quoting H. R. Rep. No. 96, 68th Cong., 1st Sess., 1 (1924); emphasis added)); 65 Cong. Rec. 1931 (1924) ("It creates no new legislation, grants no new rights, except a remedy to enforce an agreement in commercial contracts and in admiralty contracts"). As is well known, prior to the federal Act, many courts expressed hostility to arbitration, for example by refusing to order specific performance of agreements to arbitrate. See S. Rep. No. 536, 68th Cong., 1st Sess., 2 (1924). The Act sought to eliminate that hostility by placing agreements to arbitrate "'*upon the same footing as other contracts.*'" Scherk v. Alberto-Culver Co., 417 U.S. 506, 511 (1974) (quoting H. R. Rep. No. 96, at 2; emphasis added).

Congress was fully aware that arbitration could provide procedural and cost advantages. The House Report emphasized the "appropriate[ness]" of making arbitration agreements enforceable "at this time when there is so much agitation against the costliness and delays of litigation." Id., at 2. And this Court has acknowledged that parties may enter into arbitration agreements in order to expedite the resolution of disputes. See Preston v. Ferrer, 552 U.S. 346, 357 (2008) (discussing "prime objective of an agreement to arbitrate").

But we have also cautioned against thinking that Congress' primary objective was to guarantee these particular procedural advantages. Rather, that primary objective was to secure the "enforcement" of agreements to arbitrate. Dean Witter, 470 U.S., at 221. See also id., at 219 (we "reject the suggestion that the overriding goal of the Arbitration Act was to promote the expeditious resolution of claims"); id., at 219, 217-218 ("[T]he intent of Congress" requires us to apply the terms of the Act without regard to whether the result would be "possibly inefficient"); cf. id., at 220, (acknowledging that "expedited resolution of disputes" might lead parties to prefer arbitration). The relevant Senate Report points to the Act's basic purpose when it says that "[t]he purpose of the [Act] is *clearly set forth in section 2,*" S. Rep. No. 536, at 2 (emphasis added), namely, the section that says that an arbitration agreement "shall be valid, irrevocable, and enforceable, save upon such grounds as exist at law or in equity for the revocation of any contract," 9 U.S.C. §2.

Thus, insofar as we seek to implement Congress' intent, we should think more than twice before invalidating a state law that does just what §2 requires, namely, puts agreements to arbitrate and agreements to litigate "upon the same footing."

III.

The majority's contrary view (that *Discover Bank* stands as an "obstacle" to the accomplishment of the federal law's objective, ante, at __ - __, 179 L. Ed. 2d, at 754–759) rests primarily upon its claims that the *Discover Bank* rule increases the complexity of arbitration procedures, thereby discouraging parties from entering into arbitration agreements, and to that extent discriminating in practice against arbitration. These claims are not well founded.

For one thing, a state rule of law that would sometimes set aside as unconscionable a contract term that forbids class arbitration is not (as the majority claims) like a rule that would require "ultimate disposition by a jury" or "judicially monitored discovery" or use of "the Federal Rules of Evidence." Ante, at __, __, 179 L. Ed. 2d, at 752, 753. Unlike the majority's examples, class arbitration is consistent with the use of arbitration. It is a form of arbitration that is well known in California and followed elsewhere. See, e.g., Keating v. Superior Ct., 109 Cal. App. 3d 784 (App. 1980) (officially depublished); American Arbitration Association (AAA), Supplementary Rules for Class Arbitrations (2003), http://www.adr.org/sp.asp?id= 21936; JAMS, The Resolution Experts, Class Action Procedures (2009). Indeed, the AAA has told us that it has found class arbitration to be "a fair, balanced, and efficient means of resolving class disputes." Brief for AAA as Amicus Curiae in Stolt-Nielsen S. A. v. AnimalFeeds Int'l Corp., O. T. 2009, No. 08-1198, p. 25 (hereinafter AAA Amicus Brief). And unlike the majority's examples, the *Discover Bank* rule imposes equivalent limitations on litigation; hence it cannot fairly be characterized as a targeted attack on arbitration.

Where does the majority get its contrary idea — that individual, rather than class, arbitration is a "fundamental attribut[e]" of arbitration? Ante, at ___, 178 L. Ed. 2d, at 753. The majority does not explain. And it is unlikely to be able to trace its present view to the history of the arbitration statute itself.

When Congress enacted the Act, arbitration procedures had not yet been fully developed. Insofar as Congress considered detailed forms of arbitration at all, it may well have thought that arbitration would be used primarily where merchants sought to resolve disputes of fact, not law, under the customs of their industries, where the parties possessed roughly equivalent bargaining power. See Mitsubishi Motors, supra, at 646 (Stevens, J., dissenting). This last mentioned feature of the history — roughly equivalent bargaining power — suggests, if anything, that California's statute is consistent with, and indeed may help to further, the objectives that Congress had in mind.

Regardless, if neither the history nor present practice suggests that class arbitration is fundamentally incompatible with arbitration itself, then on what basis can the majority hold California's law pre-empted?

For another thing, the majority's argument that the *Discover Bank* rule will discourage arbitration rests critically upon the wrong comparison. The majority compares the complexity of class arbitration with that of bilateral arbitration. See ante, at ___, 179 L. Ed. 2d, at 756. And it finds the former more complex. See ibid. But, if incentives are at issue, the *relevant* comparison is not "arbitration with arbitration" but a comparison between class arbitration and judicial class actions. After all, in respect to the relevant set of contracts, the *Discover Bank* rule similarly and equally sets aside clauses that forbid class procedures — whether arbitration procedures or ordinary judicial procedures are at issue.

Why would a typical defendant (say, a business) prefer a judicial class action to class arbitration? AAA statistics "suggest that class arbitration proceedings take more time than the average commercial arbitration, but may take *less time* than the average class action in court." AAA Amicus Brief 24 (emphasis added). Data from California courts confirm that class arbitrations can take considerably less time than in-court proceedings in which class certification is sought. Compare ante, at ___, 179 L. Ed. 2d, at 756 (providing statistics for class arbitration), with Judicial Council of California, Administrative Office of the Courts, Class Certification in California: Second Interim Report from the Study of California Class Action Litigation 18 (2010) (providing statistics for class-action litigation in California courts). And a single class proceeding is surely more efficient than thousands of separate proceedings for identical claims. Thus, if speedy resolution of disputes were all that mattered, then the *Discover Bank* rule would reinforce, not obstruct, that objective of the Act.

The majority's related claim that the *Discover Bank* rule will discourage the use of arbitration because "[a]rbitration is poorly suited to . . . higher stakes" lacks empirical support. Ante, at ___, 179 L. Ed. 2d, at 757. Indeed, the majority provides no convincing reason to believe that parties are unwilling to submit high-stake disputes to arbitration. And there are numerous counterexamples. Loftus, Rivals Resolve Dispute Over Drug, Wall Street Journal, Apr. 16, 2011, p. B2 (discussing $500 million settlement in dispute submitted to arbitration); Ziobro, Kraft Seeks Arbitration In Fight With Starbucks Over Distribution, Wall Street Journal, Nov. 30, 2010, p. B10 (describing initiation of an arbitration in which the payout "could be higher" than $1.5 billion); Markoff, Software Arbitration Ruling Gives I.B.M. $833 Million From Fujitsu, N.Y. Times, Nov. 30, 1988, p. A1 (describing both companies as "pleased with the ruling" resolving a licensing dispute).

Further, even though contract defenses, *e.g.*, duress and unconscionability, slow down the dispute resolution process, federal arbitration law normally leaves such matters to the States. Rent-A-Center, West, Inc. v. Jackson, 561 U.S. 63, 68 (2010) (arbitration agreements "may be invalidated by 'generally applicable contract defenses'"). A provision in a contract of adhesion (for example, requiring a consumer to decide very quickly whether to pursue a claim) might increase the speed and efficiency of arbitrating a dispute, but the State can forbid it. See, e.g., Hayes v. Oakridge Home, 122 Ohio St. 3d 63, 67 ("Unconscionability is a ground for revocation of an arbitration agreement"); In re Poly-America, L. P., 262 S.W.3d 337, 348 (Tex. 2008) ("Unconscionable contracts, however — whether relating to arbitration or not — are unenforceable under Texas law"). The *Discover Bank* rule amounts to a variation on this theme. California is free to define unconscionability as it sees fit, and its common law is of no federal concern so long as the State does not adopt a special rule that disfavors arbitration

Because California applies the same legal principles to address the unconscionability of class arbitration waivers as it does to address the unconscionability of any other contractual provision, the merits of class proceedings should not factor into our decision. If California had applied its law of duress to void an arbitration agreement, would it matter if the procedures in the coerced agreement were efficient? . . .

What rational lawyer would have signed on to represent the Concepcions in litigation for the possibility of fees stemming from a $30.22 claim? See, e.g., Carnegie v. Household Int'l, Inc., 376 F.3d 656, 661 (7th Cir. 2004) ("The *realistic* alternative to a class action is not 17 million individual suits, but zero individual suits, as only a lunatic or a fanatic sues for $30"). In California's perfectly rational view, nonclass arbitration over such sums will also sometimes have the effect of depriving claimants of their claims (say, for example, where claiming the $30.22 were to involve filling out many forms that require technical legal knowledge or waiting at great length while a call is placed on hold). *Discover Bank* sets forth circumstances in which the California courts believe that the terms of consumer contracts can be manipulated to insulate an agreement's author from liability for its own frauds by "deliberately cheat[ing] large numbers of consumers out of individually small sums of money." 36 Cal. 4th, at 162-163. Why is this kind of decision —

weighing the pros and cons of all class proceedings alike — not California's to make?

Finally, the majority can find no meaningful support for its views in this Court's precedent. The federal Act has been in force for nearly a century. We have decided dozens of cases about its requirements. We have reached results that authorize complex arbitration procedures. E.g., Mitsubishi Motors, 473 U.S., at 629 (antitrust claims arising in international transaction are arbitrable). We have upheld nondiscriminatory state laws that slow down arbitration proceedings. E.g., Volt Information Sciences, 489 U.S., at 477-479 (California law staying arbitration proceedings until completion of related litigation is not pre-empted). But we have not, to my knowledge, applied the Act to strike down a state statute that treats arbitrations on par with judicial and administrative proceedings. . . .

These cases do not concern the merits and demerits of class actions; they concern equal treatment of arbitration contracts and other contracts. Since it is the latter question that is at issue here, I am not surprised that the majority can find no meaningful precedent supporting its decision.

IV

By using the words "save upon such grounds as exist at law or in equity for the revocation of any contract," Congress retained for the States an important role incident to agreements to arbitrate. 9 U.S.C. §2. Through those words Congress reiterated a basic federal idea that has long informed the nature of this Nation's laws. We have often expressed this idea in opinions that set forth presumptions. See, e.g., Medtronic, Inc. v. Lohr, 518 U.S. 470, 485 (1996) ("[B]ecause the States are independent sovereigns in our federal system, we have long presumed that Congress does not cavalierly pre-empt state-law causes of action"). But federalism is as much a question of deeds as words. It often takes the form of a concrete decision by this Court that respects the legitimacy of a State's action in an individual case. Here, recognition of that federalist ideal, embodied in specific language in this particular statute, should lead us to uphold California's law, not to strike it down. We do not honor federalist principles in their breach.

With respect, I dissent.

Taken together with *Rent-A-Center*, the *Concepcion* decision seems to sharply limit the utility of further court challenges to predispute mandatory arbitration. Consumer advocates may increasingly focus their efforts on state legislatures or Congress, where they have had recent success in limiting arbitration agreements.

2. Statutory or Other Prohibitions

Congress has enacted legislation to restrict the use of arbitration clauses in certain consumer contracts. For example, the Dodd-Frank Act gives the Securities and Exchange Commission the power to limit or prohibit agreements requiring customers of any broker or dealer to arbitrate future disputes under federal securities laws. No such rule has been forthcoming. With regard to mortgage loans, Congress took more definitive action. The Dodd-Frank Act prohibits arbitration clauses in residential mortgage loans. It amended the Truth in Lending Act to prohibit a mortgage loan or home equity line of credit from requiring arbitration or any other nonjudicial procedure as the method for resolving any controversy or settling any claims arising out of the transaction. 15 U.S.C. §1639c(e)(1). The statute's effect is likely to be moderate, however, given that in 2004, both Fannie Mae and Freddie Mac informed lenders that they would not purchase or guarantee any mortgages that contained mandatory arbitration language. As these two entities have been involved in the large majority of home mortgages since 2008, the Dodd-Frank statute may be mostly useful to prevent the reintroduction of arbitration clauses in non-government supported mortgages, if and when that private market is resurrected. The move by Fannie and Freddie to ban arbitration clauses in mortgages is an important example, however, of how limits on arbitration can arise without congressional action.

More broadly, Dodd-Frank gives the Consumer Financial Protection Bureau (CFPB) the authority to prohibit or impose conditions on mandatory arbitration that involves "consumer financial products or services." 12 U.S.C. §5518. As a precursor to doing so, the CFPB was to conduct a study of such issues and report its findings to Congress and decide whether the "prohibition or imposition of conditions or limitation is in the public interest and for the protection of consumers." Id. Any such rules to be enacted can only apply to new contracts entered into 180 days after the rule.

In March 2015, the CFPB issued a report on arbitration. CFPB, *Arbitration Study: Report to Congress, Pursuant to Dodd-Frank Wall Street Reform and Consumer Protection Act §1028(a)* (March 2015). Its 728 pages are great reading, if you have several months on your hands. The punchline is that the CFPB has . . . drumroll . . . not decided yet whether to regulate arbitration in consumer financial contracts.

C. Evaluating Arbitration

1. Arguments for Arbitration

The arbitration clause at issue in the *Concepcion* case contained many consumer-friendly aspects, such as the requirement that AT&T would pay all costs of arbitration for non-frivolous claims and that if the consumer received an award that was larger than the company's prior settlement offer, that AT&T would pay a minimum recovery to the consumer and twice the consumer's attorney's fees. You might have wondered as you read this, exactly why a company would agree to such provisions? Wouldn't they be better off with the litigation system, where they would not normally be liable for such things? Put another way, "well-informed people do not ordinarily pay thousands of dollars to get what they can get elsewhere for free." Christopher R. Drahozal &

Stephen J. Ware, *Why Businesses Use (or Not Use) Arbitration Clauses?*, 25 OHIO ST. J. ON DISP. RESOL. 443 (2010). The authors go on to ask why sophisticated parties choose arbitration over litigation and conclude that all the possible reasons fall into two categories: process and outcomes. The authors then list the particular reasons why parties might agree to arbitrate:

- arbitration may be faster and cheaper than litigation, at least for some types of disputes;
- arbitration may lessen the risk of punitive damages awards or aberrational jury verdicts;
- arbitration may decrease exposure to class actions or other forms of aggregate litigation;
- arbitration may result in more accurate outcomes because of arbitrator expertise and incentives;
- arbitration may better protect confidential information from disclosure;
- arbitration may enhance the ability of parties to have their disputes resolved using trade rules; and
- arbitration may enable the parties to better preserve their relationship.

Id. at 451-452.

Of course some of these features benefit only businesses. Consumers, as plaintiffs, do not benefit from eliminating punitive damages. But many of the benefits, such as faster resolution and simplified procedures are responsive to the exact problems that have been identified with private rights of action for consumers. Taking the list as a whole, it is not clear whether public policy should favor arbitration. Many of the identified benefits of arbitration, including more accurate outcomes and more efficient process, can be articulated as "system improvements" over litigation. Dispute resolution scholars have been good at pressing these points, building up an entire legal field devoted to studying and promoting the benefits of ADR.

As further evidence that alternative dispute resolution is not itself the problem—at least at a theoretical level—consider that in Europe, there are many ADR entities that are publicly funded with an explicit mission of providing a venue for consumers to raise issues with businesses. For an overview of the European Union's ADR Directive (2013/11 EU), see Pablo Cortes, *A New Regulatory Framework for Extra-Judicial Consumer Redress*. 35 LEGAL STUDIES 114 (2015).

2. Arguments Against Arbitration

One of the principal objections to predispute mandatory arbitration is simply that it results from a term in a contract of adhesion. Because consumers do not have bargaining power and such contracts are not the result of a negotiation, such contracts should be disfavored, including by law limiting the terms that may be included therein. The lack of real choice in adhesion contracts is counter to a basic principle of ADR, which is a process that is more beneficial to both sides.

Another objection to arbitration is that it worsens the "repeat player" disparity between businesses and consumers. Because businesses will arbitrate thousands of disputes a year, and consumers will perhaps be involved in one such case in a lifetime, businesses have much stronger incentives to learn the rules, develop relationships with arbitration organizations and the arbiters themselves, and generally steer the procedural rules of the process in their favor. Of course, the rules for litigation may also favor those with expert knowledge (such as lawyers and not *pro se* consumers) but there is at least a public and transparent process for making such rules and a recourse to democratic institutions, like legislatures, if the system becomes seriously broken.

As *Concepcion* highlights, mandatory arbitration is an individual process. While one could use a variety of ADR techniques to resolve a dispute with many consumers, the outcome of mandatory predispute arbitration has typically been to prohibit the right of a consumer to join a class action. While that form of litigation is itself controversial, one of its purported benefits is that it is more likely to produce sweeping law reform because the higher stakes motivate businesses to agree to comprehensive relief, including changes in future practices. In the arbitration or single-plaintiff litigation context, the relief is more likely to be remedial instead of prospective.

3. Barriers to Effective Evaluation

The biggest disagreements between advocates and critics of ADR center on two questions: Does ADR produce different outcomes than litigation? And is ADR faster, less expensive, and more efficient? In other words, does ADR reach the "right" result, as compared to litigation, and does it do so via sleeker processes. The problem is that answers to either of these questions have proved elusive.

The data are thin and mixed on whether arbitration is less expensive or more rapid than litigation. Theorists suggest that it must be so, or businesses would not prefer it. But court processes vary, based on aspects of court design such as the level of procedural protections, judicial workload, and the like. Arbitration may better protect businesses from the worst-case scenario of a major court loss and punitive damages award, even if it costs them additional money in routine cases.

A 2007 study of credit card arbitrations found that the National Arbitration Forum arbitrators made awards in favor of creditors and debt buyers in more than 96 percent of the cases. Simone Baribeau, *Consumer Advocates Slam Credit Card Arbitration*, CHRISTIAN SCIENCE MONITOR (July 16, 2007). This is obviously an excellent success rate for business and an epic fair for consumers. The study does not, however, offer up any comparable outcomes. If one were to examine credit card collection actions filed in state courts of general jurisdiction or small claims courts, how frequently would businesses win? Would the rate of default judgments be different? The lack of data on outcomes from consumer litigation makes it difficult to know if ADR is skewing the results or if there are more widespread problems in consumer-business dispute resolution. The fundamental fact may be just that consumers infrequently have any defense to credit card collections—regardless of the method or focus of dispute resolution.

The *Christian Science Monitor* piece exposed an additional issue with law of NAF arbitrated credit card contracts. The choice of arbiter mattered dramatically, and not in a way that merely reflects diversity of opinion, as we might expect with random assignment of a judge. The ten most frequently used arbitrators—who decided almost 60 percent of the cases heard—decided in favor of the consumer only 1.6 percent of the time, while arbitrators who decided three or fewer cases decided for the consumer 38 percent of the time. Because the NAF controlled assignment of the arbiter to the case, the dispute resolution provider could stack the odds against consumers. If a provider showed a consumer bias, the solution was to assign fewer, or even no, further cases to that arbitrator. Because businesses chose the dispute resolution company, keeping them satisfied with their success rate may drive outcomes in an unfair way. The fallout from the article and related investigations was an investigation by a state attorney general (remarkably, and not coincidentally similar to that described in problem 24.1) and the subsequent decision of NAF to withdraw entirely from arbitrating any consumer disputes. *See* Robert Berner, *Big Arbitration Firm Pulls Out of Credit Card Business*, BUSINESSWEEK (July 19, 2009).

The CFPB's 2015 report on arbitration is the most wide-ranging empirical analysis available. While tens of millions of consumers are covered by arbitration clauses, the CFPB estimates only 600 arbitrations annually are filed by consumers. And only about one-third of those cases result in a decision by an arbitrator within two years. Among a sample of 1,060 decided arbitrations filed in 2010 and 2011, consumers received a combined amount of $400,000; businesses were awarded $2.8 million, predominantly for disputed debts. Most ambitiously, the CFPB analyzed whether arbitration clauses reduced prices for consumers. In the market for credit cards—the only one in which the necessary data was available (and then only because a group of card issuers agreed to eliminate arbitration clauses for a few years in a settlement)—the CFPB found no statistically significant evidence that companies changed prices in either direction relative to the use or disuse of arbitration clauses.

The hidden nature of alternative dispute resolution makes effective evaluation difficult, leaving the parties to make naked assertions and policymakers to retreat to normative perspectives or lobbying dollars to guide legislation. The resulting "policy polemic" has led to competing efforts to ban all arbitration agreements and to further entrench them in business practice. An intermediate approach would focus on procedural fairness in arbitration. For a description of the harms of "all or nothing" and the conflict between Congress' anti-arbitration leanings and the Supreme Court's pro-arbitration decisions, see Amy Schmitz, *Arbitration Ambush in a Policy Polemic*, 3 PENN STATE YEARBOOK ON ARBITRATION AND MEDIATION 52 (2011).

Problem Set 26

26.1. You have a nationally-regarded practice representing consumers in cutting-edge cases. A few years ago, before the passage of the Credit CARD Act that reined in card fees, you undertook the representation of a group of consumers who had taken out so-called subprime "fee harvester" cards. The cards charged consumers high fees and offered low amounts of credit, which reduced the issuers' risk, but also made the products very expensive for consumers. You struggled to find anything illegal with the issuers' practices under existing law, although you certainly found it morally despicable. Driving home from work one day after working on the case, you saw a billboard for such a card that heralded that opening an account would help consumers "improve their credit rating" and "rebuild their credit." You had an epiphany. You would allege that such cards violated the Credit Repair Organizations Act, which applies to any person who sells services for money that have an "express or implied purpose of—(i) improving any consumer's credit record, credit history, or credit rating; or (ii) providing advice or assistance to any consumer with regard to any activity or service described in clause (i)." 15 U.S.C. §1679a(3). The statute requires credit repair organizations to include a number of mandatory disclosures in contracts with consumers, none of which, of course the issuers had included. You filed a class action and started counting up your fees.

Three years later, the case is a mess. The card issuers had their own clever argument, which was that the mandatory predispute arbitration clauses in their contracts with issuers preclude the class action, and indeed, any redress from litigation. You have fought this issue before but the Supreme Court precedent is mounting against you. You plan to argue that the Credit Repair Organizations Act guarantees a right to access the courts. You plan to rely on the mandatory disclosure required by the Act: "You have a right to sue a credit repair organization that violates the Credit Repair Organizations Act." Will this argument prevail? What will the issuers rely on to support their argument that the predispute mandatory arbitration clause eliminates litigation as a consumer remedy? 15 U.S.C. §§1679c, 1679h; 9 U.S.C. §2.

26.2. Senators Heft and Ho have introduced a bill that would amend the Federal Arbitration Act to invalidate all arbitration clauses in consumer contracts. Senator Floof is a newly elected Senator who managed to secure election without once fielding a question about alternate dispute resolution. She knows nothing about the issues and has asked you to prepare a list of issues for her consideration. She specifically wants a list of at least five intelligent questions that she should ask at the upcoming committee hearing on the bill. She wants the questions to show that she is smart and thoughtful; she is naïve enough to want to genuinely educate herself on the issues before deciding on a policy position. Make a list of five questions for her to ask the witnesses, who include: two consumers who had negative experiences with arbitration (one with a cellular telephone contract and one with a computer purchase); the president of a leading arbitration provider; the general counsel of a financial services company; and the chair of a state bar's litigation section.

26.3. You have been hired as outside counsel to Fruity Fresh to clean up what the CEO colorfully called "a big heap." Fruity Fresh sells a wide variety of food products through grocery stores, online shopping sites, and drug stores, including its signature applesauce. The General Counsel (on her way to being former GC) told the CEO that the best way to reduce legal costs was to begin imposing binding arbitration on all claims with consumers. To effectuate the change, the GC had the Director of Digital Strategy to add a header to the top of Fruity Fresh's website: "Attention: We have new Legal Terms that require all disputes related to the purchase or use of any Fruity Fresh product or service to be resolved through binding arbitration." In the New Legal Terms, which could be viewed by hovering over the term or by download, consumers were bound by the terms (whether they knew it or not) "by using our websites, joining our sites as a member, joining our online community, subscribing to our email newsletters, downloading or printing a digital coupon, entering a sweepstakes or contest, redeeming a promotional offer, or otherwise participating in any other Fruity Fresh offering."

Some reporter's kid loves Fruity Fresh and when he went to the site to order a promotional stuffed Fruit toy, available for $9.99 and a dozen proofs of purchase of Fruity Fresh products, he noticed the Legal Terms. A very unfavorable news article and a bunch of negative social media followed. The Director of Digital Strategy, on orders from the CEO, then reversed the policy, and removed the website header and reverted to the prior Legal Terms. She then put out the following press release:

> A few weeks ago, we changed our Legal Terms. Those terms — and our intentions — were widely misread, causing concern among consumers.
>
> So we've listened — and we're changing them back to what they were before.
>
> We rarely have disputes with consumers — and arbitration would have simply streamlined how complaints are handled. Many companies do the same, and we felt it would be helpful.
>
> But consumers didn't like it.
>
> So we've reverted back to our prior terms. There's no mention of arbitration, and the arbitration provisions we had posted were never enforced. Nor will they be. We stipulate for all purposes that our recent Legal Terms have been terminated, that the arbitration provisions are void, and that they are not, and never have been, of any legal effect.
>
> That last bit is from our lawyers.
>
> We'll just add that we never imagined this reaction. Similar terms are common in all sorts of consumer contracts, and arbitration clauses don't cause anyone to waive a valid legal claim. They only specify a cost-effective means of resolving such matters. At no time was anyone ever precluded from suing us by purchasing one of our products at a store or liking one of our Facebook pages. That was either a mischaracterization — or just very misunderstood.
>
> Not that any of that matters now.
>
> On behalf of our company and our brands, we would also like to apologize. We're sorry we even started down this path. We also hope that you'll continue to download product coupons, talk to us on social media, or look for recipes on our websites.

Unfortunately for Fruity Fresh, some enterprising law professor was not content with the apology. In fact, she has filed a suit against Fruity Fresh alleging that the press release is deceptive because it misleads consumers about the nature of the Legal Terms. The complaint seeks $2 million in damages, noting that this is 5 percent of Fruity Fresh's gross revenue last year.

As outside counsel, your job is to determine the merits of this deception suit and provide advice to the CEO — litigate or settle? Additionally, you received a voicemail from an arbitrator stating that the professor has filed an arbitration notice and the hearing can begin in one week on the professor's claim that the Fruity Fresh toy was not delivered as promised.

Part Five.   Consumer Law Policymaking

Assignment 27.   The Future of Consumer Law

Two major forces have disrupted consumer law in the last decade. The first is the creation of the Consumer Financial Protection Bureau. Its role as a regulator is evolving. In its early years, the CFPB focused on rulemakings that were required by the Dodd-Frank Act, and its touch in some markets remains light. In the coming years, subsequent directors will provide new priorities and leadership. Its partnerships with other federal and state agencies will mature, as efforts to join forces prove fruitful or strained. The existence of the CFPB also will change the agenda of other federal and state regulators. The "law" aspect of consumer law is in motion as at no other time since the 1970s.

The other major force reshaping consumer law is operating on the "consumer" aspect of the deal. Technology is the main driver, as platforms and applications increasingly blur the lines between commercial and consumer activity. Connectivity, data, and analytics are uniting people who want to engage in for-profit transactions with each other. Recall that in the first assignment of this book, a core definition of "consumer law" was the existence of a transaction in which a business was one party and a consumer was the other party. The swell of consumer-to-consumer transactions makes it an exciting time to study, and practice, consumer law.

This Assignment looks at three emerging topics in consumer law. Whether these trends endure or fade, the fundamental challenges of consumer law are likely to remain:

- What does the good or service do and why does it appeal to consumers?
- How do consumers engage or act if they purchase the good or service?
- What is the existing law that applies? Is it adequate and how would one measure that?
- What are the unsolved problems for consumers with the good or service?
- Is the law an appropriate vehicle to address these problems? Or should they be left to the market?
- If law is the solution, how should the substantive law and enforcement mechanisms be crafted so as to be effective?

The topics below give a chance to think about these issues, but this assignment is as much about trying your hand at asking these questions in the context of nascent markets, as it is about reasoning to any firm conclusions.

A.   Future Money

Technology is driving changes in payments and banking as discussed in Assignment 19, but even more fundamentally, it may transform the nature of money itself. In some ways, this is a return to the past (or a leap to a different culture) where money was something other than government-backed paper currency or coinage. "Money" eludes easy definition. Perhaps its most common use is as a means of exchange. It solves the problem of barter when one party wants to buy something, but the counterparty does not want the "thing" that the buying party is offering. Money's value is not intrinsic. It comes from institutions, often but not necessarily, including legal institutions. As money has adapted to the digital world, innovations have created products that are outside the bounds of consumer protection law. That is unlikely to remain the situation, however, if digital currency becomes more widespread.

1.   Bitcoin

Bitcoin is a private digital currency. It is "mined" by individuals who allocate their computer resources to solving complex algorithms. The resulting product is a "cryptocurrency" that has no physical presence. The open source algorithm permits the creation of new bitcoins at an ever-decreasing rate, with an estimated upper limit of 21 million bitcoin. It is similar to gold in the sense that the amount of currency is finite. As it has grown in popularity, exchanges for trading bitcoin have developed, including those that allow for currency swaps between U.S. dollars and bitcoin.

To spend a bitcoin, one must authenticate it using a virtual "key," which is essentially a very large number. The ledger of bitcoin transactions is public, although users retain a high degree of anonymity. Because everyone has a copy of all transactions in a shared database, and all transactions are continuously verified, there is little risk of duplication—essentially counterfeit bitcoin. This digital trail is called the "blockchain." Another prominent feature of bitcoin is the lack of government involvement. Bitcoins have no inherent value and no central entity that manipulates their price. Supply and demand entirely determines the worth of bitcoin. In these regards, bitcoin is not unlike ancient currencies. *See* Bill Maurer, *How Would You Like to Pay? How Technology Is Changing the Future of Money*, Tbl 2.1 (2015) (analyzing common features of Bitcoin and Mesopotamian Contracts as forms of money).

Bitcoin does not fit easily into commercial law's definition of money. *See, e.g.*, U.C.C. §1-201(a)(24) (defining money as a medium of exchange current authorized or adopted by a domestic or foreign government). Bitcoin also does not meet the legal definition of negotiability under the Uniform Commercial Code, meaning that the rules of loss and risk that govern the presentment and honoring of checks and other negotiable instruments do not apply. *See* Jeanne L. Schroeder, *Bitcoin and the Uniform Commercial Code* (Cardozo Leg. Stud. Research Paper No. 458, 2015), http://papers.ssrn.com/sol3/papers.cfm?abstract_id=2649441.

2. Digital Fiat

Bitcoin is not fiat money, which is made legal tender through an act of government. Neither its manufacture nor its distribution is a public function. In the future, governments may move to digital currency that is "coined" via code created by a central bank. Because the government would control the software that minted the digital money, it could control the amount of currency released in accordance with its monetary policy. A major benefit of such a move is cost. Estimates are that digital money would equal only 10 percent of the costs of minting paper bills. Ryan Tracy, *Central Bankers Explore Response to Bitcoin: Their Own Digital Cash*, WALL ST. J. (Dec. 9, 2015). A start-up, eCurrency Mint, has proposed a currency product that would centralize the creation and management with government but maintain anonymity of users. Its digital "cryptocomplex" would move via existing money delivery systems and be loaded by commercial banks and financial products into their networks. Penny Cronman, *A Digital Currency a Banker Could Love*, AMERICAN BANKER (Dec. 15, 2015). As of 2015, Ecuador and Canada have experimented with government-issued digital currency, but no country has adopted it as a full-fledged companion to, or replacement for, tangible currency.

In lieu of outright digital fiat money, the government may take on only certain functions of digital currency. One commentator has suggested that government should avoid involvement in systemic operation of digital currency, but could usefully enact and enforce laws that protect end-users. *See* Mark Edwin Burge, *Apply Pay, Bitcoin, and Consumers: The ABCs of Future Public Payments Law*, 67 HASTINGS L.J. __ (2016). An analogous approach is the way in which the FDIC does not dictate bank operations but does provide insurance on deposits.

3. Consumer Protection Issues

Lawmakers' initial engagement with digital currency stemmed from its anonymity. That feature made it useful for criminal enterprises, and drew interest from the FBI and other law enforcement agencies. The Financial Crimes Enforcement Network, an arm of the U.S. Treasury, has issued guidance on virtual currency and the U.S. Department of Justice has brought enforcement actions, such as efforts to subject bitcoins to criminal forfeiture.

Obviously most consumers are not criminals, so the more pertinent worries for a typical consumer who adopted a digital currency would be fraud and loss. These problems are compounded by limited regulatory oversight and uncertainty about which laws apply. Some of the problems are uniquely digital, such as the funds being rendered worthless by a virus. Other potential sources of loss have equivalents to paper money. If you delete your bitcoin, it is like cash in an envelope that is accidentally tossed out with the trash. Similarly, if you do not keep your private key to the currency confidential, it is analogous to someone taking cash out of an unguarded wallet. In fact, one can probably think about hacking bitcoin as a less physically dangerous, but no less costly, version of being mugged for one's wallet.

The companies that create and manage digital wallets also pose risks. These companies could fail, making it difficult to access digital funds. In 2015, the

New York Superintendent of Financial Services issued the first license to a company that plans to offer a bitcoin-based mobile payment system. The FTC encourages consumers to file complaints about bitcoin if they encounter problems, and the CFPB has issued four (admittedly vague) principles for digital currency: 1) control, 2) privacy, 3) fraud protection, and 4) transparency. Consumer Financial Protection Bureau, *Consumer Protection Principles: CFPB's Vision of Consumer Protection in New Faster Payment Systems* (July 9, 2015) http://tinyurl.com/j4t4jll. These principles are the likely pillars of any consumer protection regime that may develop.

Existing laws may sweep in digital currency but many unknowns exist. Conventional money transmitter statutes, which exist in nearly all states, do likely apply. The Uniform Money Services Act, section 102(14), defines a "money transmission" to include "receiving money or monetary value for transmission." These typically require licensing of the business and reporting suspected criminal activity, but provide little else in the way of consumer protections. The applicability of the Electronic Funds Transfer Act (EFTA) to digital money is much less certain. The definition of "account," 15 U.S.C. §1693a(2), does not seem to include something like bitcoin, for which the digital code is itself the repository of value. Advocates for bitcoin have argued that specialized regulation for digital currency would violate the idea of "technological neutrality," (not that this idea has ever particularly applied to payments in the United States as checks, electronic transfers, and credit cards have long had specific rules). Jim Harper, *Consumer Protection in the Bitcoin Era*, AMERICAN BANKER (May 14, 2014). Industry preference seems to be that existing legal and regulatory regimes adapt to digital currency. The Bitcoin Foundation actually has pointed to two facets of private digital currency that improve consumers' ability to oversee currency: 1) the cryptographic proof of reserves in a public ledger permits an audit by any interested party; and 2) "multisignature" transactions can allow consumers to require more layers and parties to assent to control their funds. *Id.*

If you could not follow these two purported consumer protections, consider how a typical, non-law-educated person will fare in a world of digital currency. Innovation has a dark side in the consumer world, which is the capacity for scammers to exploit consumer confusion. Already, the FTC has gone after an unscrupulous bitcoin operation. The company, Butterfly Labs, marketed "BitForce" mining computers powerful enough to quickly manufacture bitcoin, selling them for prices ranging from $149 to $29,889 based on purported computing power. In fact, the company failed to deliver many computers or delayed in delivery so long as to render the computers nearly obsolete for bitcoin generation due to improvements in processing speeds. FTC Press Release, *At FTC's Request, Court Halts Bogus Bitcoin Mining Operation* (Sept. 23, 2014).

B.   Digital Media: Video Games

Just as books and music are increasingly purchased solely in digital format, video games are moving in that direction too. The digitalization of any media can be potentially disruptive to settled law, but because video gaming itself is a far newer creation than books or music, the issues are less resolved. The lack of legal clarity also could stem from the fact that video game purchasers may not be litigious types, or more likely because few judges are big "gamers" (in the sense of video games; this assignment excludes gambling from the concept of gaming).

Gaming is big business to the companies involved and to its billions of users. In 2005, the U.S. video game industry surpassed the U.S. movie industry for total revenue, and in 2007, it passed the music industry as well. Valuations of the global video gaming market put it between $45 and $50 billion, with rapid growth forecast to continue. The rise of the nerds has begun.

1. Intangible Digital "Goods"

Digital video games illustrate the multiple areas of law involved in consumer conflicts with businesses. As is often true, contract law is foundational, but digital game purchases twine together contract and property, specifically licenses and intellectual property. Digital purchases challenge conventional ideas of rights and ownership. With a tangible object that contains intellectual property content, such as a novel, the author retains the copyright, and the purchaser has the good. For example, when a consumer goes to a big box retailer and purchases a physical copy of a game, that purchaser owns the right to play the game at any time at will, to resell the game, or to lend it to a friend.

Compare that to when a consumer visits a game studio's website, pays online to purchase the game, and downloads the content from one of the game studio's digital distribution channels. Video games may be single-player or multi-player. If the latter, the consumer needs to connect with other users and would expect to either need to be physically connected to friends (local multiplayer) or need an Internet connection (online multiplayer). Many single-player games have identical Internet connectivity requirements, however, which can be a surprise to those who downloaded the game without reading the clickwrap contract. In such a situation, the consumer cannot access the game without online access. There is no option to convert the game to a tangible form or play it without online personal validation. Without these abilities, the consumer also cannot resell or gift the game. The digital game is inextricably tied to the consumer's account, verified and validated solely through online means. In this sense, many digital game purchases are more akin to a non-transferrable license such as with software, than a full-fledged purchase as with tangible medium games.

At the heart of the problem with digital video games is that first word: digital. Aside from reaching out and touching the screen, the consumer does not have something that is tangible. Instead the digital nature of the purchase takes it outside the definition of goods and into the realm of an intangible. The Uniform Commercial Code defines "general intangibles" as any personal property, including software. U.C.C. §9-102(a)(42). Software "means a computer program and any supporting information provided in connection with a transaction relating to the program. The term does not include a computer program that is included in the definition of goods." U.C.C. §9-102(a)(76). Does a digital mode of purchase change the law's treatment of a consumer's rights? Christine Jackson, *Consumer Rights Act—How Will It Affect Developers and Their Gamers?* (June 2015), https://www.wrighthassall .co.uk/knowledge/legal-articles/2015/06/19/consumer-rights-act-developers. ("The key concern . . . [is] whether 'digital content', e.g. mobile phone apps and virtual in-app purchases, fell within, or outside of, consumer law.")

To see the issues in more detail, consider the following scenario. In March 2014, Blizzard Entertainment launched an online collectible card game called Hearthstone, modeled after physical trading card games such as Magic the Gathering and Yu-Gi-Oh. In July 2014, Blizzard released an expansion to the base game called "Curse of Naxxramas," which players could purchase for $20. For some, the purchase of the expansion was uneventful. For others, however, the transaction "bugged up," and although the consumers had already paid $20 for the expansion, the entire game told them that it was locked, unplayable, and unpurchaseable. Mark Judge, *Hearthstone Players Experiencing "Purchase Failed" Error in Curse of Naxxramas,* LoadtheGame.com (Jul. 30, 2014), http://tinyurl.com/hkuvznq. If the game had been a physical deck of cards with an expansion pack, the consumer could have continued to enjoy the initially purchased cards and returned the defective expansion pack (say, with half the cards printed blank) to the store. Under the U.C.C., the consumer would have been entitled to an immediate refund, backed by the warranty of merchantability that accompanies goods.

With digital game purchases, the consumer may need to rely on the means of payment for a remedy. As discussed in Assignment 15, the Truth in Lending Act gives consumers the right to withhold payment to a card issuer based on a dispute with a merchant. *See* 15 U.S.C. §1666i; 12 C.F.R. §1026.12(c). The exercise of this "chargeback" right, however, can create more problems than it solves for a consumer. Gaming companies typically suspend an entire account or ban a person from being a player in any game when a consumer initiates a chargeback. To illustrate the breadth of this remedy, imagine a consumer who complained to a store retailer about a defective disc of a movie produced by Studio X, and in response, upon learning of the complaint, Studio X seized all discs owned by the consumer that contained Studio X content. Further, Studio X would have a mechanism to prevent the consumer from purchasing more discs until the dispute was resolved.

From a consumer perspective, the above example is horrifying. The offense may be particularly deep if the consumer actually contributed content to the game, such as by designing a character or virtual world, or had some type of game "currency" earned but not redeemed. From the business perspective of a game developer, however, the policies around digital game purchases are in place to protect the business *from* consumers. Piracy and fraud are serious risks of loss. An unscrupulous individual may purchase a digital product and file a chargeback, asserting that the product was defective but actually have tried the game and not liked it—or worse, somehow copied it. Initially, the rationale for requiring online access even to play an offline, single-player game was to permit video game developers to authenticate legitimate purchases. The point was to eliminate the opportunity to torrent (illegally copy or download) a game and use it without the company's knowledge.

2. Legal Framework

The United States has not yet adopted legislation on digital media and digital transactions. The most recent venture to create consumer law protections for digital media is a decade old. This effort at "modernization" of the law was the debate over the Digital Media Consumers' Rights Act. H.R. 107, 108th Cong. (2003). The legislation focused on copyright protections and deceptive labeling practices for CDs and did not address online digital transactions. Ultimately, the bill died but portions touching upon copyright were enacted in broader intellectual property reforms. In terms of the issues discussed above, the bill largely was a misnomer.

In 2011, the European Council of Ministers adopted the EU Consumer Rights Directive. Aimed at a broad swath of online markets, not solely digital video game, the Directive created new obligations for "traders" that included online sellers. *See generally* European Union Council Directive 2011/83/EU, available at http://eur-lex.europa.eu/legal-content/EN/TXT/PDF/?uri=CELEX: 32011L0083&rid=1. This was a crucial step towards subjecting the online economy to existing consumer law. In October 2015, the UK Consumer Rights Act provided even greater clarity and rights (albeit only for residents of the United Kingdom). "The Act applies to business-consumer transactions where a digital game is bought from a store (Steam, etc.), in-game purchases within Free-to-Play games, and even digital 'Early Access' games." Peter Parrish, *UK Consumer Rights Act 2015: What It Means for Digital Game Purchases* (Oct. 1, 2015), http://www.pcinvasion.com/uk-consumer-rights-act-2015-what-it-means-for-digital-game-purchases. Digital content must be of satisfactory quality, fit for a particular purpose, and as described in any marketing material. Thomas Coe, *Summary Guide to the Consumer Rights Act 2015*, WrightHassal.co.uk, (Oct. 1, 2015), http://tinyurl.com/zg9xd3a. The Act provides remedies for defective digital content, including repair or replacement, price reduction, a claim for damages, or a full refund. The law purports to apply whenever a customer is located in the UK, regardless of where the seller is located, although its reach is uncertain. The EU Consumer Rights Directive and the UK Consumer Rights Act should encourage game developers to move towards consistent global standards on how they distribute games and handle disputes. Gaming is a global enterprise, with players connecting online from around the world to play with each other. The community is international, even if the law is not yet there. Cutting against global standards, however, is the relatively small size of the EU markets (and within that, the even smaller UK market). In 2015, China topped the game market with $22.23 billion in revenue. *Leading Game Countries Worldwide by Revenue 2015*, Statista. com, http://tinyurl.com/hzmjszb. The U.S. came in second with $21.96 billion; the UK was 6th, bringing in only $3.53 billion. To the extent that consumers in the U.S. and China generate gaming revenues that dwarf other countries, gaming companies are likely to focus their compliance on U.S.

and Chinese law. Neither country provides significant rights to consumers who make digital game purchases.

3. *Consumer Protection Issues*

As technology advances, the legal issues related to digital gaming also advance. Even the U.K.'s 2015 law fails to tackle the newest problems and allegations of consumer exploitation. The gaming companies in the U.S. seem to be floating along on a sea of misunderstanding and apathy from lawmakers about the nature of gaming.

With any game release, a consumer takes a gamble on the game's quality. The EU Directive and the UK Consumer Rights Act of 2015 give the consumer remedies if the game is defective or the quality is poor. Built into the regulations is the pervasive consumer expectation that every game will have "bugs"—glitches in the game. Some bugs do not noticeably detract from game play and therefore are not deemed significant. Other bugs "break the game" in the gaming lingo. The player is either unable to play the game at all, or unable to play it properly. "Patches" or updates are often released with online digital games to address bugs. Other games run on annual release dates, with minor bugs addressed in the new release. These fixes are not free for consumers, however, as the new content is considered an expansion that is a new product bearing a new purchase price. Under the EU and UK regulations, a consumer who buys a defective or poor quality game has a solution. The law gives the right to a refund or a repair of a "buggy" game.

When consumers could use some assistance—and when there has yet to be any intervention from regulators—is in the above-mentioned scenario about lock-outs from content based on a single game issue. A consumer whose entire account with a developer is suspended has no clear rights and no clear remedy. Indeed, it is not even clear to what regulator a consumer should turn to complain (the FTC? the state attorney general?). It is similarly unclear which policymakers should be evaluating whether legal rights are needed. The intellectual property community does have advocates for end users, but that frame for thinking about protection may differ from those who work on defective products or financial transactions as matters of consumer protection. As of 2015, purchases of digital content occur in the Wild West for consumers, who remain at the mercy of developers until either U.S. regulators catch up with digital developments or the marketplace evolves to provide contractual rights as a matter of competition.

Game developers are likely to push back against consumer protection regulation on the grounds that licensing law is adequate to cover disputes. From this perspective, a digital game purchase is a consumer paying for a license to use software. As with word processing programs or operating systems, there are updates to the software available to the licensee, and eventually the developer may stop releasing updates for old 'software' because a newer version has been released and the older one is no longer kept up. The available remedies come from terms of the licensing agreement, but when one studies that fine print, there are in fact few to no consumer protections. The added complication for games is the degree to which players themselves create content. Gamers' play of the game contributes to the product in a way that is more creative and additive than a computer user typing up a private document in Microsoft Word.

Another area of concern for consumers is new pricing models. Increasingly, the gaming industry makes a profit by initially giving the game away for free and then later profiting handsomely when consumers charge "in-game" fees. These purchases are known as microtransactions because they may cost only a dollar or two, but the overall cost can aggregate quickly. As discussed in Assignment 20, several lawsuits have been filed against mobile app developers for the ease of making microtransactions in mobile apps, particularly for not policing purchases by children. Video game developers are hearing a similar buzz of feedback from consumers regarding microtransactions that are embedded in personal computer or console games (not just mobile games). Electronic Arts was criticized in 2015 "for removing content form the original [Star Wars: Battlefront] game only to sell it back later as downloadable content you have to pay for." Dave Smith, *I Miss the Days When I Only Had to Pay Once for a Video Game*, BUSINESS INSIDER, (Apr. 22, 2015), http://tinyurl.com/z3ugtu7. The game developers are trying to hit the maximum ceiling price that a consumer is willing to pay for a game, without making that final cost obvious to consumers. Consumers that would balk at a $60 boxed console game may quickly exceed that in six months of playing a $19.99 game that required many microtransactions to unlock features.

The stakes are high in getting the pricing correct. Game development costs have soared with game sophistication and consumer expectation. As an illustration, Rockstar Games, the developer of Grand Theft Auto V, spent $265 million to create and market the game, but brought in $800 million in the first 24 hours of its release for sale. *Id.*, http://tinyurl.com/z3ugtu7; *see also* Patrick Dane, *'Grand Theft Auto V' Makes $800 Million in Its First 24 Hours*, Gamerant.com, http://gamerant.com/grand-theft-auto-5-sales-first-day (last visited Jan. 14, 2015). Not all games do so well, however, and then developers may face fierce consumer pressure to remedy problems. Final Fantasy XIV, a "massively" multiplayer online roleplaying game, was heavily criticized by consumers for poor quality upon its initial release. The developer's response was to completely overhaul the game, even working the "redo" into the plot of the rereleased game. Like any market, the gaming industry has some incentive for self-regulation from consumer behavior. Word of mouth and large participant bases are important. Unlike a novel that may only have one appreciative reader, most games require mass participation for any player to benefit. If consumers lose trust or the company's reputation plunges, consumers will move on to another developer or game series.

C. Socialization of Finance

Consumers can prevent scams, frauds, mistakes, or imprudent decisions by communicating with other consumers about their experiences with a particular business. The word-of-mouth tradition of consumer protection is old. It gave rise to much of the common law of slander and libel, which can give a merchant a way to silence or punish a consumer that wrongfully attacked a reputation. In a small village, bad actors were quickly ferreted out through word of mouth. As the geography and economy of the United States expanded, consumers had a harder time keeping up with businesses and communicating with each other across the expanded market. Government also had trouble keeping tabs products and transactions, especially as westward settlement — and commerce — outpaced government and law enforcement.

Internet technology is reconnecting consumers, providing avenues for consumer-generated feedback about dealings with businesses. In fact, the top consumer watchdog in the U.S. is probably either Yelp or Google, not the CFPB or the FTC. While this idea may seem strange from a legal perspective, the reality is that only a pittance of society engages with government for consumer advice, compared to millions a day who search online or leave feedback. Innovations in technology are driving a new era of socialization.

In consumer finance, social connectivity is creating opportunities for consumers to engage in borrowing, lending, and investing that required a business as intermediary in the 20th century. Technology can increase transparency for regulators and consumers alike, and allow consumers to join forces to move markets in ways favorable to them. The outcomes could be democratic and empowering for consumers, but also could go the other direction. Greater socialization of finance creates risks for consumers. They can more easily enter into transactions but may be unable to assess its potential downsides or protect against harms. The ease of interface, driven by technology, can mask risks and prompt consumers to feel safe even in unfamiliar transactions.

1. Crowdfunding

This book has distinguished an individual's identity as an investor from that of identity as a consumer. Crowdfunding, in which consumers make contributions outside traditional investment platforms, blurs the investor versus consumer distinction. The idea of crowdfunding is that people contribute financial support for a project. If this sounds like what happens when a pension fund buys corporate bonds to lend a corporation cash to expand, there are certainly similarities. But bond offerings and pension funds are highly regulated; they reside squarely in the world of high finance. Those who participate in crowdfunding are termed "supporters" and what they earn are called "rewards." Contrast this to "investors" who earn "profits" when they contribute capital to a business venture. In Silicon Valley lingo, crowdfunding enables creators to disrupt finance channels through social networks. At the core, the difference may be primarily one of scale. Most platforms for crowdfunding have dollar caps, partly to avoid more stringent regulation. The aggregate dollars are significant, however, with an estimated $10 billion in contributions in 2014.

Crowdfunding can operate using two types of business models. In the first, the support is functionally a charitable contribution or a donation to personal fundraising. The proponent may offer a reward, such as a DVD of a film after it is produced or recognition as a contributor at an art showing. Kickstarter and

Gofundme are large players as of 2016. The other model is closer to traditional equity investing, in the sense that the reward is a partial ownership interest in the company. Prominent companies are AngelList, Fundable, and Crowdfunder. In either model, social networks are crucial. An entrepreneur will start a campaign, choosing a site that permits the kind of project that is contemplated (for example, Kickstarter only allows projects related to arts and technology, such as game design, music, or publishing). Once consumers discover the campaign and donate, they can use social networking tools to publicize their contributions. If a friend of a supporter also makes a donation, and in turn spreads the word, additional traffic is driven to the crowdfunding campaign. The more visitors, the more contributions, and as the site's reputation grows for successfully funding, more entrepreneurs list their projects and more supporters visit. These strong network effects permit rapid, viral growth as compared to in-person, targeted pitches for funding.

Crowdfunding sites typically generate income through a fee that corresponds to a percentage of the transactions. This revenue stream provides a consistent incentive to exaggerate the investment opportunities and downplay the risks. The platforms disclaim responsibility for the information presented by fundseekers and typically exercise only minimal controls over listings. By comparison, for public equities investments traded on the New York Stock Exchange, the exchange itself has minimum requirements designed to limit participation to higher-quality investments (on top of SEC-required disclosures for public securities.) To date, the platforms have succeeded in eliminating liability for the actions of fundseekers. Additionally, the platforms must mitigate any insolvency risk by only serving as an intermediary — not a holder — of funds and must safeguard consumer financial data collected via the site.

2. Peer to Peer Lending

Peer to peer lending is ancient, and it has never disappeared from U.S. society. Particularly for borrowers outside a bank's comfort zone, such as students or undocumented individuals, family and friends are valuable lenders. Peer to peer lending is different, however, because it uses technology and big data to create "peer" relationships outside real-world social networks. That is, instead of asking your rich uncle Jimmy for a loan, you can ask your classmate's rich aunt Joan in a network of connections.

In its truest form, peer to peer lending occurs across a platform that connects willing individual lenders with needy individual borrowers. The platform's role is to facilitate — not fund — the transaction. It provides technology that may verify a borrower's information such as name and social security number, standardize loan requests such calculating an accurate APR, and gathering or analyzing data on repayment risk. Online-only data such as IP addresses and web browsing patterns feed new analytical models for assessing risk, and social media platforms can provide real time monitoring of borrowers. A prospective lender may see photographs of borrowers and be able to read narratives about the reasons that loans are desired. Examples of borrower activity that may raise red flags are posting to Facebook about a car breakdown, using all capital letters in a loan request, or jumping quickly when browsing the platform to high-dollar loans. Elizabeth Dwoskin, *'Big Data' Doesn't Yield Better Loans: Consumer Group Says Crunching Such Numbers Doesn't Make a Big Difference; Lenders Disagree*, WALL ST. J., Mar. 17, 2014. Peer to peer lending generally ignores or relies much less heavily on traditional credit reports than bank or finance company lending.

These consumer (borrower) to consumer (lender) transactions are different than broader "marketplace" lending, which usually denotes a non-bank, technology-driven lender that offers up its own capital or draws funding in from relativelysophisticated, larger-scale private investments. Both Prosper and Lending Club started as peer to peer but now attract investments from hedge funds and use a bank intermediary to process loans. They are still available to individual investors who do not qualify as institutional or accredited investors, designations requiring that a showing of entity formation or significant assets as proxies for financial sophistication.

Peer to peer platforms earn money in ways similar to crowdfunding sites. They usually charge an origination fee of 1 percent to 2 percent of the loan amount and a servicing fee, typically 1 percent of the outstanding balance, for the duration of the loan. Peer lenders have no physical branches, which lowers costs, but they also enjoy significant operational savings from not having to hold capital as a bank does when a loan is on its books. In the peer to peer context, the company is an intermediary.

SoFi is an exemplar of the evolution of peer to peer lenders. It began with student loans, targeting those who attended Ivy League schools and earned degrees in typically high-paying fields, such as MBAs. Its initial funding came from graduates of the schools for which SoFi was willing to facilitate refinancing of student loans. SoFi even matched students with potential lenders based on shared interests, such as major. The alumni also were asked to act as informal mentors to borrowing and to help them locate job opportunities. SoFi now offers higher education loans for students, parents, and alumni, as well as personal loans. In 2015, it became the first U.S. peer to peer lender to offer mortgages. It is a nonbank, advertising "[t]his is the beginning of a bankless world." However, it must hold one or more state licenses in each place where its borrowers reside.

In the future, peer to peer financial services may extend beyond loans. Companies have launched applications that permit peer to peer ATM transactions. A consumer with some cash to spare can direct an ATM to permit a withdrawal for a selected peer. Philip Ryan, *Peer-to-Peer Lending Gets Real With a P2P ATM*, BANK INNOVATION (Jan. 14, 2014), http://tinyurl.com/jjk93vg. The transaction may be validated via an authorization code or QR code on the consumer's mobile phone. Peer to peer lenders have even cropped up to make loans in bitcoins. Combining two innovative finance industries together may be genius — or just double the risks to all involved.

3. Consumer Protection Issues

The legal issues in crowdfunding and peer lending are similar but not identical. The commonality is that from a consumer protection standpoint, it is not clear which consumer needs protecting. Is it the quasi-investor/ loan funder? Or the fundseeker/borrower? On both ends of these transactions are consumers, in the sense of individuals acting on their sole behalf. Admittedly, one consumer has funds to spare and the other consumer needs money. Both sides, however, lack the legal protections of entity status and the experience that comes with a larger-scale business. Socialized finance shakes up the core ideas of consumer law discussed in Assignment 1, What Is Consumer Law and Assignment 2, Who Is a Consumer?

From a legal standpoint, crowdfunding and peer lending sites/applications repeatedly and loudly have proclaimed that they are mere "platforms." They argue that all transactions are solely between the creator/borrower and backer/lender, and that they bear no liability for losses by either party to any transaction. Kickstarter, for example, has disavowed any role akin to a securities broker. Peer lenders have taken care to avoid becoming banks, avoiding holding deposits or loans on their books, even if they need to partner with a bank to avoid doing so.

Traditional contract law clearly applies that apply to social finance transactions. Even then, however, the platform is arguably not a party to a contract. In the strongest form of the argument, these companies are just digital equivalents of the landlord that provides offices for loan officers at a bank, the printing company that produces loan application forms, or the manufacturer of secure collection boxes for charitable donations. The reality is more complicated, however, as intermediaries in financial transactions often are subject to regulations that would not exist outside in non-financial contexts.

Peer lenders and crowdfunders reside presently in a kind of regulatory purgatory. On the one hand, agencies have made noises that they could assert authority over social finance companies. On the other hand, they have been slow to actually do so. There are very few promulgating regulations that address the particulars of consumer-to-consumer funding via a platform model. Congress added a provision to a financial stimulus law in 2012 that exempted crowdfunded projects under $1 million from most securities laws, including registration. Peer to peer lenders arguably are covered by this law's definition of crowdfunding. Lending platforms usually take responsibility for producing disclosures and advertisements, have systems to protect data, and some controls to guard against money laundering. Compliance in areas such as credit discrimination, debt collection, and underwriting is much less certain. While some of these laws may apply only to those engaging in a certain volume of business, other laws such as usury statutes and unfair or deceptive acts and practices may apply to anyone making a profit, including the platform and consumer on the funding side of the transactions.

In 2015, regulators started to bring suit against crowdfunders. The Washington Attorney General obtained a default judgment against an individual who failed to deliver his crowdfunding project. The "consumer" raised $25,000 on Kickstarter to create a card game and then disappeared without delivering refunds. The lawsuit raised eyebrows because of the actual damages to Washington residents: $664 in contributions from 31 backers. The judgment was for $50,000, however, with $1,000 in statutory damages for 31 harmed consumers under the state's UDAP law and attorneys' fees. The Washington Attorney General characterized the defendant's actions as "crowdfunding theft" and was explicit that the lawsuit was designed to send a message to people seeking consumer's money in what he called a "new frontier." Taylor Soper, *Kickstarter Fraud: Washington Files First Consumer Protection Lawsuit Involving Crowdfunding*, GEEKWIRE.COM (May 1, 2014), http://tinyurl.com/lyzcfm9. The FTC also acted in 2015 against a person who raised crowdfunds to create a board game but abandoned the project. It sued under its unfair or deceptive acts or practices authority and obtained a settlement that included a monetary judgment of over $110,000.

The SEC could act to monitor potential risks to consumers who contribute by treating these people as investors, but it seems that "borrower" protections in crowdfunding would remain under the jurisdiction of state regulators. Similarly, the CFPB could declare that crowdfunding projects and peer loans are "consumer financial products." Even then, the CFPB may be more likely to focus on examination and supervision of the platform business, leaving most of the work of stopping scams and seeking restitution for consumers to state attorneys general or the SEC.

With an undefined legal framework, consumers on both sides of social finance are largely required to rely on their own judgment about who to trust. It is precisely the social nature of these transactions, however, that facilitates such a willingness to trust. The additional information and real time feedback from technology-driven social networks is substituting for reliance on legal systems and regulatory actors to vet and police.

A final note: Social networks are themselves dependent on the law. While the U.S. Constitution may have seemed distant from the financial and commercial transactions studied in this book, free speech is a powerful form of consumer protection. In countries in which speech is curbed, consumers lack an important way to protect each other from scams and frauds. Vibrant speech, stemming in part from comparatively weak laws on libel and slander, allow U.S. consumers to sound off about their consumer rights in ways that are unthinkable (due to the threat of prison, for example) in some countries. Consumer protection in buying and borrowing may depend on political freedoms as well as economic ones.

D.   Conclusion

It is incorrect to conclude that the new forms of money, digital gaming, and social or peer lending are "outside the law." Principles of consumer law run deep in tort and contract doctrines, and by their nature as part of the common law, such laws can be applied to any dispute brought to a court. The more pressing question is when regulation is appropriate. In the United States, the approach usually is to wait until a product or transaction establishes a firm place in the market, and then have the federal or state legislature act to create statutes that provide product-specific boundaries. The drawback to this after-the-fact approach is that the common law may leave consumers with no rights or remedies in the intervening period. That fact may, in turn, influence how the product or transaction develops. Without strong and widely accepted consumer protection norms at the outset, the law is positioned to be reactive to unchecked market behavior that initially favors businesses. Perhaps this is inherent in the nature of capitalism and is an acceptable cost to bear for the prosperity and opportunity created in a free market system. The scammed consumers may see it differently, however, and depend on government to curb market forces.

Economic and social forces will continue to push consumer law in new directions, as the three topics in this assignment illustrate. Yet, recall the common lesson of *Carbolic Smoke Ball* and *Airborne*. As long as there are gaps in experience, knowledge, technology, and the like between buyers and sellers (or between lenders and borrowers), there will be consumers who feel cheated. The question for consumer policymaking is whether the consumer should be given a right and corresponding remedy, or be left with only regret. Lessons learned the hard way may stick with us in a way that no legal effort — even a textbook on consumer law — ever can.

Problem Set 27

27.1. Think about yourself, friends, and family members as consumers. Now think about consumers that you may infrequently observe: those purchasing a Bugati car, those who pawn goods one month only to redeem them in the next month, those who carry a $13,000 balance on their credit cards but never seem to make a dent in it, those young veterans trying to buy a first home. Are the topics discussed in this final assignment important to your network? Are they important to these "other" consumers? Which issues and in what ways? Do you think consumer law in the future will be more focused on higher-income, sophisticated consumers or lower-income, less-experienced consumers? Assuming that equal attention cannot be paid to all consumers, which group do you think is the harbinger? In selecting a group of consumers, think beyond income to other characteristics. Articulate an argument to your class about which consumers should be the focus of the next wave of consumer protection and why.

27.2. You were excited about the final assignment for Consumer Law, and not just because a TV binge or a night out drinking was your planned reward for wrapping up classes. Instead, you put faith in the author that the last assignment would cover the topics that you had been waiting to learn about all semester. To your chagrin, the topics seemed so "yesterday." And all that, despite an Assignment title of "The Future of Consumer Law." In response to your dissatisfaction, your professor suggested that you take up your rights as a consumer. (No, there are no refunds for purchasing this book.) The professor noted that the author invited your feedback as a reader. Outline the content for a topic that you think should be included in this Assignment on future consumer law. For your topic, address briefly the following: What is the consumer need that this product or business fulfills? What are analogous goods, services, or market leaders being displaced? What applicable law exists? (Name some specific statutes or common law doctrines.) What are the key consumer protection issues that any new law for this topic should address?

27.3. Once upon a time, your law school offered a Consumer Law course. You remember it fondly, especially now that the studying and exam are years behind you. In your decade of general litigation practice at a mid-sized firm, you have handled some consumer matters over the years, including cases alleging breach of warranty, unfair and deceptive practices, false advertising, and disclosure violations. You've learned from interviewing students at the local law school for summer jobs that a consumer law course never has been offered (or at least not in the memory of the octogenarian registrar). You think this is a shame, but upon raising this with the dean at a cocktail mixer are told that the best solution is for you to propose teaching a Consumer Law course as an adjunct instructor. Prepare a one-paragraph course description that describes the two or three main themes of the course and lists at least a half-dozen specific topics to be covered. You can rethink the course that you took, or engage in a *Back to the Future* exercise and guess what will be the most salient topics in twenty years. Be prepared to read your description in class.

Table of Cases

Principal cases are in italics.

Index